About the Author

Janine Harrington is Secretary of the worldwide RAF 100 Group Association, and Editor of their quarterly magazine. Her mother's wartime fiancé Vic Vinnell with Canadian pilot Jack Fisher served in 192 Squadron at Foulsham, Norfolk, under RAF 100 Group. Their disappearance in November 1944 remains a mystery today.

RAF 100 GROUP
Kindred Spirits

Voices of RAF & USAAF
on secret Norfolk airfields
during World War Two

by Janine Harrington
Secretary, RAF 100 Group Association

With author Stephen Hutton's chapter on
The Mighty 8th's Squadron of Deception

Foreword by Wing Commander Weeks-Dix
OBE, AFC, QCVSA

AUSTIN MACAULEY
PUBLISHERS LTD.

ISBN 978-1-78612-396-1 (paperback)
ISBN 978-1-78612-397-8 (hardback)

www.austinmacauley.com

First Published (2015)

Austin Macauley Publishers Ltd.
25 Canada Square
Canary Wharf
London
E14 5LQ

Printed and bound in the British Isles.

Dedicated to all who served in:

RAF No. 100 (Bomber Support) Group
&
USAAF's 803rd & 36th Bomb Squadron Radar Countermeasure Units

ACKNOWLEDGEMENTS

This book would not have been possible without so many wonderful people who supported me in its creation, sharing wartime experiences, secrets finally told. It is impossible to include everyone, but please know that each and every one of you is valued. I remain indebted to:
- Stephen Hutton – a valued friend;
- Wing Commander Weeks-Dix OBE, AFC, QCVSA – for endorsing the book;
- Evelyn Bartram – hoping I have done justice to Len's life & work;
- Eric Dickens – for visiting the National Archives in search of present-day 'Truths'.

I remain passionate about preserving stories of veterans who served under Bomber Command in the secret RAF No. 100 (Bomber Support) Group or flew in partnership with them. It remains my privilege and honour to serve and work alongside veterans as Secretary of RAF 100 Group Association. Over the past twenty years, I have received hundreds of writings, poems and photographs from around the world, each a treasure from a time out of Time.

One veteran's words sums up those of many:

We became forgotten heroes, with no medals to honour everything we gave ... we weren't in it for the glory, but I lost so many dear friends. I'm the last man standing out of a crew who remain forever young ... yet people don't remember us because they didn't even know we were there or what we were doing ... it was all so hush-hush ...

So many secrets over too many years. Still today all truths are not known and cannot be told.

In giving this book life, my hope is that it becomes a Memorial dedicated to all who served under RAF No. 100 (BS) Group and US 36th Bomb Squadron who worked in partnership on so many operations, to whom we owe so much.

My heartfelt thanks to my publishers for believing in me enough to publish this book, bringing these stories into the light where readers can spend many hours touched by its magic and memories.

I also wish to acknowledge the Defence Intellectual Property Rights (MOD) who granted permission for use of all RAF No. 100 (BS) Group Squadron crests.

CONTENTS

FOREWORD

As a ten-year-old schoolboy in 1940, I was walking through Bournemouth pleasure gardens when I stumbled across a very long strip of metallised material approximately two feet long, half an inch wide; rather like Baco-Foil today. At one end was a long length of nylon material resembling a petticoat shoulder strap attached to a heavy piece of lead. Little did I know that I had made my acquaintance with an invention named ... 'WINDOW' ... Radar reflections from these falling strips gave a false impression of range and number of aircraft to the primitive radar of the day. The length of these strips was governed by half wave-length multiples of the defending radar.

Neither did I know that a device called 'Chain Home' radar research was being carried out near Swanage on the nearby Dorset coast.

As with many electronic deception devices, specially modified aircraft and their specialist aircrews would be required to fly secret missions in order to decoy and disguise the true presence of allied aircraft flying the main Bomber Command Squadron against their German targets.

Again, little did I realise that ten years later, I would be flying Lincoln aircraft on No. 101 Squadron, now in No. 1 Group; where during World War Two these special aircraft flew in No. 100 Group. Later, I joined No. 192 Squadron with much more sophisticated radar countermeasures and specialist recording capabilities.

This Foreword for the No. 100 Group book introduces the roles of No. 100 Group in much more detail and gives long overdue credit to the aircrews that flew these dangerous missions in top secret, never allowed to reveal the nature of their work even to wives and families.

It is my great pleasure to recommend this book to readers, especially in memory of the men who flew these sorties and often died in their execution.

Wing Commander Kenneth John Weeks-Dix
O.B.E, AFC, QCVSA, RAF (Ret'd)

Wing Commander Kenneth John Weeks-Dix
OBE, AFC, QCVSA, RAF (Ret'd)

INTRODUCTION
On a Wing, In a Prayer

Love is eternal![1]

The inspiration for this book reaches back seventy years, to a young airman and his fiancée, a WAAF, stationed at RAF Wheaton Aston, Staffordshire.

As we step through the portal of time to join them, it is spring 1944. War is ravaging Britain. The world is in crisis. The roar of Merlin engines fills the skies. Yet the couple can look down in wonder at buds of new growth breaking through the earth. The air is sweet with birdsong. Trees burst with colour, flakes of blossom falling like confetti to create a carpet of tenderness and beauty. Just the other day, this couple ran across fields, vibrant and free, unleashed from the shackles of duty, filled with joy and excitement. Here in the countryside, it was easy to pretend war could not reach them. The remains of their picnic eaten an hour or so ago is tucked inside a bag as they cycle side by side down narrow lanes bordered with high hedges. They appear oblivious to the world around them, captivated in their love for one another, laughing with gay abandon, happy to have these precious moments to share.

We follow in their footsteps awhile.

Day darkens, drawing into night. It is almost nine o'clock. In a few short minutes the clock in the church tower at Blymhill will send chimes ringing out across the sleepy village – nine deep booming notes to mark a trysting hour. The wooden gate creaks as a boy in Air Force blue opens it for the girl who steps through dressed in the uniform of a WAAF. Together they walk the path to the church door, stopping to admire fresh daffodils on a silent grave. They shiver as a sudden shadow passes over them, moving quickly on into the porch to stand for moments, breathing in the cool night air. He takes off his cap. The dying rays of the sun alight on his bared head, turning crisp curls to threads of gold, illuminating his face with a soft warm glow.

Something stirs deep within them as they take one another's hand and gently push the heavy oak door to enter.

Inside, all is dark and still. Slowly, they tiptoe past the stone statue to their low wooden pew at the back of the church. The last rays of daylight slant across deserted pews towards the shining cross on the altar still visible in the gathering gloom. Almost shyly they smile, feeling a strange quickening of heart, the pulsing warmth flowing between them ... connecting. His clasp of her hand tightens. Both are aware of a Presence as they bow their heads in prayer. The boom of the chimes marks off the minutes while they pray that soon there may be no more partings, no more 'Goodnights'. Soon, ('*please God!*') may they be with one another for all time, living their dream in a home filled with happiness and love.

Solemn now, with the opening bars of Felix Mendelssohn's: '*Wedding March*' whispering in their ears, they open a Prayer Book to read aloud the words. Gazing deep into one another's eyes, each whispers in turn: '*I will*', before moving on in hushed tones to promise to '*love, honour and obey, to cherish one other in sickness and in health until the Dark Angel spreads his wings*'. The clock chimes one final time. As the echoes die, tears roll down the cheeks of the WAAF. He kisses them away. Then taking hold her hand, they leave the church, joined as man and wife in their hearts and in God's eyes. They are inseparable, two people living, thinking, acting, breathing and loving as one.

Nina's birthday: 9 April 1944. She is twenty-six years old and passionately in love. Born in Cheshire in 1918, her father William, with a rocklike faith, died when she was six years old leaving her to take responsibility for two young brothers and Emily, her mother in poor health. Nina and her father shared a close bond. His death affected her deeply. For a year and more she effectively had a breakdown and was taken out of school. Known as her '*Desert Experience*', she sought God as a solace and strength. Her mother's response to her beloved husband's passing was to shield her children, putting out his possessions, resuming the life they shared. In 1939/40 Nina's two brothers went away to war. Their home was bombed. Living in rented accommodation, her mother's health deteriorated, nerves shredded by endless bombing and sirens. All she wanted was her family safe. Nina became her sole carer until, in late 1940, she joined the WAAFs to become an LACW (Leading Aircraft Woman) Clerk GD, posted away to RAF Wheaton Aston where she met Vic in December 1943.

Henry Victor Alexander Vinnell was a Flight Lieutenant in the Royal Air Force Volunteer Reserves. Vic, as he became known, was born an only child on 21 September 1922. His mother spent most of her married years in a mental hospital, while Vic was brought up by an aunt. Home was London, while his father maintained his distance. An Assistant Salesman at a wholesale grocers, from a young age Vic nurtured the dream of becoming a writer. But as war broke out, in December 1940, against his father's wishes he joined the Royal Air Force Volunteer Reserve (RAFVR), training in Winnipeg, Canada, and returning to Britain with Flying Wings awarded in 1942. He served with the RCAF, 418 Squadron, on Night Intruding Operations. After completing thirteen sorties, he spent time at No. 1 Radio School, Cranwell, re-mustering from NAV/B to NAV.B/W for which he qualified in September 1943. He arrived at RAF Wheaton Aston in October that year, pending a further posting.

When Vic met Nina at a Christmas Eve dance, it became a forbidden love. Officers didn't fraternise with Clerks. But Vic was smitten. With so little love in his life, Nina became his world. With her he discovered an all-encompassing love, embracing her not only as sweetheart and soulmate, but as mother, sister, confidante, best friend. The only blot on their perfect landscape was war, otherwise he would go to the ends of the earth to make her happy, wishing only they might start to live their dream. After they became engaged, Vic spent all Leaves in Cheshire, his adopted home. Her mother already accepted him like a son, and by the spring of 1944, their wedding day was being prepared.

Less than a month on from that April evening, Vic was summoned to London for an interview with the Air Ministry regarding Special Signal Duties. Days later, he was posted to the lead 192 Squadron of the newly-formed RAF No. 100 (Bomber Support) Group, based at Foulsham, Norfolk. It must have been strange not to see one another during their daily duties, share cycle rides, walk and dream away the hours. However, their hearts remained as one, yearning for the day war was done and they could share the rest of their lives. Hundreds of letters were penned and passed between them, sharing affairs of the heart. But as well as distance separating them, the nature of Vic's work meant he was constrained by the Official Secrets Act. He could no longer talk about his days, with times he couldn't communicate at all.

As a Flight Lieutenant in 192 Squadron, he flew with his Canadian friend and pilot Jack Fisher all hours of the day and night as Navigator/Special Duties Operator. Their Mosquito DK292 was named: 'N for Nina'.

Jack Glen Millan Fisher was born in 1923. He grew up in Saskatchewan, Canada, with six sisters. His parents, John and Sarah, shared a close family. He went on to serve with the Royal Canadian Air Force (RCAF).

I remain in contact with Jack's family today. His mother would visit when I was a child, although I had no idea then of the remarkable story behind these meetings. When she died, it was his sister Audrey who continued writing. It's been lovely through the years to learn more and more about Jack, and as I write this book, I have received a letter from another sister, Gloria:

> ... you must know I still miss my dear brother. I was fifteen when we heard the bad news. He was full of fun, loved to tease Mom and us six girls. We lived twenty miles from High School and farming wasn't great, but he was determined to go to school so able to work for room and board, helping out in the Nursing Home where he was born and other odd jobs. It left a hole in our hearts when the war was over and he didn't return ... [2]

War tore him from home and all he knew and loved as it did so many young people. Vic and Jack became close friends, allies flying across skies over Germany, completing vital and very secret operations. Serving under 192 Squadron meant they were amongst a group of airmen flying in all weathers day and night. Information they brought back was classified, but crucial in determining what other Squadrons became a part. It was a huge responsibility placed on such young shoulders. There were times Vic was in Sick Bay with exhaustion. Nina noted dark black circles under his eyes during fleeting times they met, with an often jaded absentminded manner, as if he carried the shadows of war in his head. War dictated he perform hazardous duties of which he couldn't speak. Everyone depended on his Group bringing this war to a successful conclusion. Meanwhile, Nina took cold comfort from the growing sense of unease and fear that radiated around his untold activities.

Operations flown under RAF No. 100 Group were so secret that even today many remain under a 100 Year Rule. Not even airmen flying at the time understood what they were doing and why. Certainly the main RAF knew nothing of their existence.

It was the night of 26/27 November 1944, a few days before Nina and Vic were to marry and make their home with her mother in Cheshire. Vic and Jack were sent on a secret operation from which they never returned. The fate of Mosquito DK292 remains unknown. Vic and Jack to this day have no known grave. Their names appear at Runneymede, their only remembrance.

A part of Nina, my mother, died with him that night. She was never the same woman again. Until the end of her days, in 1996 when she died from cancer, she never gave up hope that one day he might find her, one day he might return to that home within her heart. At her funeral, it was her cousin, Mary, who shared with me how it had been for her as a teenager when Nina was dating Vic.

> **As he came through the door he lit up the room, and yet only had eyes for his Nina. He had a vibrancy, an aura, their love was so real you could almost reach out and touch it. But then, suddenly he was gone, and the sun no longer shined. I had no idea how she could go on living without him.** [3]

'Love is eternal' – words used so often between them. Yet, when finally she learned that Vic and Jack were 'Missing believed killed' my mother's unswerving faith inherited from her father, crumpled, withered, died, as she fell apart inside.

News didn't reach her immediately. She had put in for a posting to Foulsham to be close to Vic. Instead, she was posted to 14 Base, RAF Ludford Magna, Lincolnshire. It was a part of Bomber Command, as was Vic's Squadron; otherwise they were poles apart! Her mother was in hospital when telegrams concerning his plight slipped through the letterbox of a still and empty house in Cheshire. Each night, Nina walked the few miles to a telephone box, increasingly puzzled, confused, concerned, frustrated at not being connected with her fiancé. Given the secrecy surrounding the Squadron, no-one was telling her anything. Only on her mother's return from hospital were telegrams forwarded and her world fell apart. In a state of collapse, she was granted the afternoon off and advised: 'Go and get stinking drunk!' Instead, she walked the countryside, bright moonlight spilling shadows across hedge-lined lanes, until hours later, she knocked on the door of a farmhouse to be given a cup of tea as she poured out her heart.

Days later, she wrote one final long letter, smearing the paper with tears, feeling as if somehow, lifting her pen from the page might break the fragile connection between them:

… Vic, my dearest one, please come to me soon. This horrible agony of suspense, of not knowing where you are or what has happened is more than I can bear. Remember Vic, we promised we would always be together – the undivided front? It is my business to find the place where you have gone so that I can follow … I will not give up hope. You told me once not to worry if you were ever reported missing. You would always find your way back to me again … there is nothing left in this world for me without you. I have walked a long long way tonight, further than I thought, until I came to turn back. There was a moon, pale and clear and just past the full. It looked painfully beautiful. I watched it rise. As it climbed slowly into the sky, it seemed to tear something from out of myself. Our Star was there too, Vic darling. I wonder if you can see this same Moon, this same Star … [4]

In the weeks that followed, she neither wrote nor completed diary entries, fulfilling WAAF duties on auto-pilot before resolutely returning to the telephone box, making calls to RAF Foulsham, fervently hoping to hear, suddenly, the voice of the man she loved.

She kept trying to imagine herself in 'N for Nina', desperate for answers, following the sequence of events from facts gleaned from spurious sources to the time the aircraft touched Mother Earth. *Trouble with their oxygen supply? How did they come to be flying so low? They flew at 33,000 feet out of reach of German AA guns, didn't they? Engine failure? Did they crash-land or bale out? Were they safe in some far and distant land?*

No-one had facts she could work with. Questions were left unanswered. Layers of secrets covered what they had been doing that night. Their work was classified. Secrecy must be maintained! Then somehow, through a fog of uncertainty and fear, she heard the whispered words of a Map Clerk:

Mossies missing a week last Monday (26/27 November 1944), two over Germany, one over France, on Special Signals raid. [5]

Her world went black.

The following year she was granted Compassionate Leave one month at a time, then posted to RAF West Kirby before leaving the Service.

On 27 November 1945, one year on, she won a prize for an article entitled: '*My Dream Home*' about her RAF fiancé who did not return from war. The winning entry was published in *The Daily Express*. She received hundreds of letters from readers identifying with her experience, and for years they kept in touch. Then, in 1949, a stranger wrote, hearing about her from his friend '*Dewie*', an ex-PoW of the Japanese, who had gained valuable support in writing to her. The stranger was RAF Flight Sergeant John Harrington. In September 1950, they married. I was their firstborn.

I was just three years old when my mother took me to Runneymede in London, to introduce me to Vic. Kneeling beside the cold hard stone, her fingers running over the imprint of his name, she talked about me to him, sharing as if they were still a young couple, moments stilled in Time. Today, their writings are amongst my most treasured possessions, together with the few photographs of Vic, a pair of inner silk flying gloves, and a long rusty nail taken as a memento of their nine o'clock tryst at Blymhill Church when they shared their wedding vows.

Mum received nothing of Vic's as his possessions passed directly to his father, despite the fact he had disowned him when he joined the Services. Even their bespoke wedding rings were gone. She had no claim as a fiancé. It's the reason their letters became all the more precious.

Vic and Jack received no medals, nothing in recognition of the very secret work in which they were involved, even though it helped bring the war to an early conclusion. However, a few years ago, Canada honoured its war heroes by naming previously un-named creeks after them, hence there exists '*Fisher Creek*'.

2014 marked the 70th Anniversary of the death of Vic and Jack.

I remain passionate that such courage and commitment and love deserves our respect and remembrance. Their names, their story, must live on ... together with all who served alongside them in Squadrons under RAF No. 100 (Bomber Support) Group.

Vic and Nina's story is one among many, and this book ultimately brings together voices of those who feel the time is right to share secrets rather than take them to the grave. It provides a collection of personal writings and photographs, shared experiences and poems of those who, like Vic and Jack, served under Bomber Command during World War Two in 100 Group, illustrating the very human face of war.

INTRODUCTION

I grew up with my mother's unworn wedding dress at the back of her wardrobe, the hundreds of letters tied with red ribbon lovingly kept in a shoebox. At nine o'clock throughout the rest of her days, she'd gaze at the clock on the mantle remembering their trysting hour; grieving that part of her which died with her wartime fiancé Vic on that night of 26/27 November 1944. *Was it mere coincidence that my father, John Harrington, died on 27 November 2006?*

Norfolk remains home to 100 Group in a very real way today because of the RAF 100 Group Association borne just over twenty years ago. One long May weekend each year it is an absolute joy to return with veterans, their family and friends from around the world to remember those of 100 Group who did not return. We lay wreaths at airfields where Squadrons of the Group served. Norfolk once more comes alive with the chatter and laughter of airmen as we share stories from the past.

As I cross the border into Norfolk it is for me like entering a portal.

Time stands still.

Merlin engines roar overhead. People working in fields stand, heads raised, watching and listening as machines darken the skies, blocking the sun, turning the air bitter. As I draw close to Foulsham, the spirits of Jack Fisher, Vic Vinnell and a girl named Nina reach out to draw me in. Voices whisper on a gentle summer breeze. Goose-bumps appear on my arms coupled with that familiar tingly feeling at the nape of my neck. I know from those moments until the point when I leave that Jack, Vic and Nina will be right there with me just as surely as if they were alive today. It's wonderful to have members share experiences of their Squadron, aircraft they flew, aching to be back up there amongst the clouds.

Kindred Spirits one and all!

It is the spirit of understanding, friendship, comradeship, compassion and love that lies at the heart of our Association, bringing veterans and their loved ones back year after year to Norfolk, a place they once called Home.

No matter who we are or how far distant we live from one another, we remain part of a wider Family in the truest sense of the word. Each and every member of our Association is loved and valued. It is important to know and to remember that. We send cards and gifts on birthdays and at Christmas, share day-to-day experiences. We have our own Family Tree reaching back through Time, connecting past with present and with one another, linked by those who did not return.

This year, 2015, we collectively remember the 70th Anniversary of the end of the Second World War, and the many lives sacrificed for the freedom we have today.

My hope is that this book will highlight the work of a Group still not recognised for its wartime achievements and the many under Bomber Command who received no medal, no award. Those who survived take their secrets to the grave, leaving loved ones ignorant of the vital role they played in bringing an early end to war, saving so many thousands of lives.

Seventy years on it is vital to keep these memories alive, to honour those who did not return. For those who came back, it becomes equally important to come together as a collective, one unified voice, to tell what they know that we may learn from their experiences for the future. Veterans are at the heart of the story of World War Two. It is vital their voices be heard ... that their experiences live on and be told and shared with future generations. Only through them can we ever really know the meaning of what was lost and what was won.

This then is the people's story of RAF No. 100 (Bomber Support) Group.

Kindred spirits - ordinary people living extraordinary lives.

We *will* remember them!

GLOSSARY

Codewords and abbreviations used during the Second World War in connection with operations carried out by the Royal Air Force and USAAF:

- **RAF** – Royal Air Force
- **USAAF** – US Army Air Force
- **HDUs** – Home Defence Units set up in small coastal stations, working with the Admiralty as an anti-invasion measure
- **GAF** – German Air Force
- **PATHFINDERS** – specialised target-finding force
- **TARGET INDICATORS** – large coloured flares used as markers
- **RCM** – radio countermeasures
- **R/T** – Radio Transmission
- **SPOOF** raids – drawing enemy fire away from the main force
- **BSDU** – Bomber Support Development Unit
- **PRG** – Photo Reconnaissance Group
- **RWE** – Radio Warfare Establishment (Watton)
- **CSE** – Central Signals Establishment (Watton
- **ECM** (Electronic Counter-Measures)

Codenames:

RAF:

- **WINDOW** – Metallic-backed paper strips which, when thrown from a flying aircraft, confused enemy radar with false signals, indicating far more aircraft than there were ... and in different positions
- **Mandrel, Carpet, Shiver** – airborne radio transmitters to jam and swamp German ground radar such as Freya and Wurzburg.
- **Boozer** – on-board equipment warning bomber crews when they were tracked by German radar.
- **Monica and Fishpond** – fitted to bombers to give warning of approaching German fighters.

- **Tinsel and Jostle** – radio transmissions from bombers to drown out radio communications between German fighters and their Controllers.
- **Cigar and Corona** – German-speaking RAF operators assigned to transmit false and confusing directions to German fighters.
- **Serrate** – airborne radar fitted to RAF night-fighters on intruder operations, enabling them to track and attack German night-fighters.

German:

- **Freya** – ground based long-range radar.
- **Wurzburg** – ground based shorter range radar giving information on approaching bombers to searchlights, flak and fighters.
- **Naxos and Flensburg** – fitted to German fighters to home onto radio transmissions from bombers (e.g. onto bombers' H2S transmissions)
- **Leichenstein** – airborne radar fitted to fighters to detect bombers.

Codewords:

- **Angels** – height in thousands of feet
- **Bandit** – identified enemy aircraft
- **Bogey** – unidentified (possibly unfriendly) aircraft
- **Channel Stop** – Air operations intended to stop enemy shipping passing through the Straits of Dover
- **Circus** – bomber attacks with fighter escorts in day time. Attacks were against short range targets intent on occupying enemy fighters, keeping their fighter units in the area concerned
- **Flower** – patrols in the area of enemy airfields, preventing aircraft taking off while attacking aircraft that succeeded
- **Gardening** – mine-laying operations
- **Instep** – missions to restrict attacks on Coastal Command aircraft by maintaining a presence over Western Approaches
- **Intruder** – offensive patrols usually at night, intended to destroy enemy aircraft over their own territory
- **Jim Crow** – coastal patrols to intercept enemy aircraft crossing the British coastline, originally used in 1940 to warn of invasion
- **Kipper** – patrols to protect fishing boats in the North Sea against attack from the air

GLOSSARY

- **Mahmoud** – sorties flown by de Havilland Mosquitoes equipped with backward radar – when enemy aircraft were detected, a 180° turn enabled an attack
- **Mandolin** – attacks on enemy railway transport
- **Ramrod** – short range bomber attacks to destroy ground targets, similar to Circus attacks
- **Ranger** – freelance flights over enemy territory by units of any size, to occupy and tire enemy fighters
- **Rhubarb** – operations when sections of fighters or fighter-bombers, taking full advantage of low cloud and poor visibility, crossed the English Channel before dropping below cloud level, searching for opportunity targets such as railway locomotives and rolling stock, aircraft on the ground, enemy troops and vehicles on roads
- **Roadstead** – dive bombing and low level attacks on enemy ships at sea or in harbour
- **Rodeo** – fighter sweeps over enemy territory
- **Rover** – armed reconnaissance flights with attacks on opportunity targets

CHAPTER I
RAF No. 100 (BS) Group

'Confound & Destroy'
Reproduced with permission of the MOD

Origins & Effects

By the end of World War One, bombing beyond the front battle-lines was commonplace. In 1915, the Germans launched Zeppelin airship bombing raids over London. In the summer of 1917, they hit London with heavy bomber aircraft. It brought an end to *'Rules of Engagement'*. Britain, determined to show Germany there would be consequences to their actions, prepared to bomb German industrial cities. War ended before the newly-formed RAF could carry out attacks against the enemy.

People settled to a new kind of peace, burying loved ones, struggling to create a better and brighter future to pass on to their children with the belief this was the end of war for all time. Naïve? No. Simply put, the war years brought too much hardship, too many deaths, too much pain. No-one believed another war possible.

But the threat hadn't gone away. Behind closed doors, plans were forging ahead.

Endings and Beginnings

In 1936, the RAF was divided into four separate Commands:
- Fighter Command,
- Bomber Command,
- Coastal Command
- Training Command.

Officialdom at least felt the likelihood of war increasing. *Another war?* It hardly seemed credible. But there were rumblings and rumours. They needed to be ready, determined not to be caught off-guard. New aircraft with trainee aircrews were already in place. There was no shortage of volunteers from within Britain, nor within the Commonwealth or even the USA. Flying was seen as something exciting and glamorous, adventurous and brave.

Only those who lived through the First World War knew different.

****

It is at this point there is one thing readers need to bear in mind. Everyone has their own agenda. You wouldn't believe, or then again perhaps you might; the number of times I have read about the same battle, the same incident or experience, each very different. Like witnesses of a car accident or crime, it is possible to discover a totally different scenario when compared with others. Likewise with history, and not just because of which side you are on, or what you believe. You don't even have to have been there. There are truths, there are half-truths, there are lies, and there is concealment in not discussing a particular issue, or failing to ask the right questions.

In wartime, truth is so precious that she should always be attended by a bodyguard of lies. [6]

This comment was made by Winston Churchill to Joseph Stalin at the Tehran Conference in 1943. The word *'bodyguard'* was deliberately used, the name for an operation aimed at misleading the German High Command about the time and place of the invasion of north-west Europe – part of the build-up to the invasion of Normandy. It was a feint, meant to confuse the truth with lies.

****

With the division of the RAF into four separate Commands, it is Bomber Command which concerns us here. It was under Bomber Command that RAF No. 100 (Bomber Support) Group was born. To fully appreciate wartime experiences of veterans, it is necessary to understand the background of Bomber Command and how 100 Group came into being.

BOMBER COMMAND

'Strike Hard, Strike Sure'
Reproduced with permission of the MOD

World War Two began in September 1939 despite the determined belief there would never be another war. From the outset, Bomber Command faced four immediate problems:-

- **Lack of size**. Bomber Command wasn't large enough to effectively attack the enemy as a stand-alone strategic force,
- **Rules of engagement**. At the start of the war, targets given to Bomber Command were not wide enough in scope,
- **The Command's lack of technology**, specifically radio or radar-derived navigational aids to allow accurate target location at night or through cloud,
- **Limited accuracy of bombing**, especially from high level, even when the target could be clearly located by the Bomb Aimer.

They faced one further crucial problem – a lack of good aircraft. Their main aircraft comprised of:

- Vickers Wellington,
- Armstrong Whitworth Whitley,
- Handley Page Hampden/Hereford

All were designed as tactical-support medium bombers, with neither the range or ordnance capacity to provide anything other than a limited strategic offensive.

Bomber Command also became smaller after the declaration of war. Squadrons of Fairey Battles left for France to form the Advanced Air Striking Force, operating against German targets which they lacked the range to do from British airfields. This left Bomber Command with a small number of slow aircraft carrying primitive navigation equipment, including sextants. Not wanting to provoke the Germans, RAF bombers dropped only propaganda leaflets by night. At the time, it was the most they could do. German fighters were faster. When the RAF did attempt daylight raids on enemy shipping and occupied airfields, bombers were shot down and heavy losses incurred.

On 1 September 1939, Franklin Roosevelt, President of the then neutral United States, issued an appeal to confine air raids to military targets only. The French and British agreed, provided 'that these same rules of warfare would be scrupulously observed by all opponents'. This policy changed dramatically and decisively on 15 May 1940 when the German Luftwaffe bombed Rotterdam. As a result, Bomber Command came under orders to immediately bomb Germany despite Roosevelt's appeal and their small under-equipped ineffectual force, desperately ill-equipped for the job.

The British Army had been evacuated from Dunkirk back to Britain. The Royal Navy was protecting vital supply convoys from Canada and the USA. There was only Bomber Command to do what was needed in the light of Germany's Army and Air Force controlling Europe from Northern Norway to France's border with Spain.

The following month, Winston Churchill wrote privately to Lord Beaverbrook:

When I look round to see how we can win this war there is only one sure path ... an absolutely devastating, exterminating attack by very heavy bombers from this country upon the Nazi homeland. [7]

Invasion

Germany was preparing to invade Britain, moving forward with immense force towards its goal. Enemy bombing of Belgium, Holland, France and all neighbouring countries became relentless. Hundreds of barges gathered in French and Dutch coastal ports, including Calais, Rotterdam, Le Havre and Antwerp. Germany had taken and now occupied the whole of North West Europe, clearing a path towards Britain believing nothing could stand in its way.

Operation 'SEALION' had begun.

Bomber Command consistently attacked invasion barges, enemy air bases, fuel supply depots, aircraft factories, to undermine and out-manoeuvre the Luftwaffe, forcing Germany to postpone their invasion – but at a devastating price.

More RAF bomber crews than fighter pilots were killed during the Battle of Britain, while Germany began a night-time 'Blitz' on London and other British cities – Coventry, Glasgow, Plymouth, Bristol and Birmingham. Enemy U-boat (submarine) attacks on vital supply routes from America of food, fuel and military equipment caused terrible losses to merchant shipping, threatening to cut off the British Isles completely, forcing it to stand alone.

Bomber Command became Britain's most potent offensive weapon, despite bombers being equipped with totally inadequate navigation aids, forced to fly at night to avoid enemy fighter attacks and anti-aircraft fire.

Churchill was worried. He knew the truth of the situation.

In March 1941, he ordered Bomber Command to attack German submarine bases, factories, and shipping, working in partnership with Coastal Command. Battle-cruisers *Scharnhorst* and *Gneisenau* were bombed in Brest preventing them joining the *Bismarck*. This severely hampered Germany's Navy attacks on British shipping. Meanwhile, mines were laid at sea by low-flying bombers, successful in sinking German ships.

It wasn't enough.

Primitive navigation aids remained a major issue, ill-equipped for flying in darkness and bad weather. Bombing was ineffective. Churchill remained frustrated with the heavy responsibility imposed by his position to maintain Britain's safety and the lives of people depending on him to do the right thing.

New Hope

The turning point came in 1942 when new four-engine bombers such as Lancasters arrived with advanced navigation aids. Bomber Command also acquired a new Commander – Air Marshall Arthur Harris. His reputation as blunt and unapproachable actually belies his true character.

Born in 1892 at Cheltenham, England, his father was a member of the elite Indian Civil Service. Early education was at Allhallows School, Dorset. In 1908, he elected to go to Rhodesia where he had reasonable success as a farmer, shunning his parents' choices of either the Army or travelling to one of the British colonies. When war broke out in 1914, he enlisted with the 1st Rhodesian Regiment and saw limited action in South Africa and German South-West Africa before returning to England in 1915.

However, he had developed a love for flying. After earning his Wings with the newly-formed Royal Air Force, he moved to France in 1917, his ability as a pilot recognised as he flew Strutters and Sopwith Camels. He ended the war an Ace Pilot with five kills of German aircraft and was awarded the Air Force Cross.

Between the wars, he took assignments in India, Mesopotamia and Persia, studying the tactics of strategic bombardment, convinced future victory lay in this field and with 'Total War' – mass scale bombing of civilian targets and cities.

On his return to England, in 1929 he took command of the RAF's first dedicated heavy bomber Squadron as Senior Air Officer in the Middle East Command. In 1939, recalled back to England, he was given command of No. 5 Group.

It is worth noting at this point that Churchill's approval of so-called 'carpet bombing' of German cities was to become relevant as war moved on.

As Harris took up his new position as Commander of Bomber Command he realised the bombing campaign was in crisis, and from experience, understood the crucial reasons why. Poor navigational aids on which aircrews were reliant made precision bombing impossible as one in every ten bombs fell within five miles of their German target. He commented: 'the average crew in average weather could not find their way to the target'.

An area bombing policy was formally published in February 1942 prior to Harris' arrival. As Air Marshall and now Commander of Bomber Command, Harris submitted a Paper on 'Carpet Bombing' to Winston Churchill for consideration, receiving support from Professor Frederick Lindemann, close confidante of the Prime Minister. An official directive followed, endorsed by Churchill, strongly supported by his scientific advisor Lord Cherwell; ordering specific targeting of fifty-eight major German industrial cities. Officially, reasons were described as: 'the morale of the enemy civil population and in particular, of industrial workers'. Cherwell called the policy 'de-housing', arguing that houses of German war factory workers were a legitimate target: 'If they had nowhere to live, they couldn't work!'

Harris Bomber Offensive

On 30/31 May 1942 'Operation Millennium' began in earnest. Harris scraped together every available aircraft, including those training, to send 1,000 bombers on a huge night raid to Cologne, endless waves of bombers reaching across the skies. The German night fighter defence was finally overwhelmed. Severe damage was caused to the city. The first 1,000 Bomber Raid was a success. Aircrew's morale lifted. Confidence in Bomber Command soared. A further two 1,000 Bomber Raids quickly followed.

The advent of bigger and better bombers like the Lancaster and Halifax allowed Harris as Head of Bomber Command to execute further raids on German cities. In conjunction with the US Army Air Force (USAAF) 'Operation Gomorrah' was launched against Hamburg. Ten square miles of the city was levelled.

From August 1942, the specialist Pathfinders target-finding force began operating. They flew ahead of bombers, located the target, marking it with large coloured flares (Target Indicators) for the main force to aim at. Throughout the raid, an experienced Commander, known as '*Master Bomber*', circled the target, sending instructions to an incoming stream of bombers, ensuring accuracy was maintained.

Bomber Command's nightly pounding of Germany became relentless, including 800 and more aircraft against a major industrial centre. If weather conditions precluded a heavy raid, fast Mosquitoes flew over Berlin or the Ruhr industrial area to maintain the ongoing wail of air raid sirens, keeping German war workers from their beds.

In November 1943, Harris planned a similar blanket raid on Berlin, known as the '*Battle of Berlin*'. Raids however, were a failure with the loss of over 1,000 aircraft.

In 1944, after a brief lull during the Allied landing in Normandy, Bomber Command under Harris recommenced area bombing of Germany well into 1945. These were to become controversial attacks as Germany was already defeated.

The bombing of Dresden came on the night of 13/14 February 1945, resulting in tens of thousands of civilian deaths.

Sir Arthur Harris, Commander-in-Chief of Bomber Command has been criticised ever since -for the area bombing campaign, but more particularly the bombing of Dresden so near the end of the war. It has been cited as the reason why Harris, together with Bomber Command and those who served under it, were denied recognition or reward, including RAF No. 100 Group. Others argue the RAF's campaign against German cities was a mistake.

Yet it was the Germans who introduced mass bombing. The flattening of Coventry is just one example with huge psychological effects, together with devastation and cost to human life. The *Baedeker* raids, where Germans bombed towns and cities without obvious reason also contributed to a willingness to take war to German civilians - where better than Berlin and Dresden, Germany's biggest cities.

Arguments and discussion rage on today. However, it cannot be denied that Harris was a strong leader, respected by his men, with a deep under-standing born of research and experience of bomber aircraft and difficulties his aircrews endured.

It should also be noted that the decision to area bomb was first taken by the Air Ministry in 1941, long before Harris became Commander of Bomber Command. The decision was supported by Churchill. Churchill ordered

Dresden to be bombed. Harris was acting on orders. Yet he remains a much maligned character, despite fierce loyalty shared by his men today.

Secret Warfare

During World War Two, there were two faces of war. The physical war raged on the ground, on the seas, in the skies. But there was the secret side to this war in which RAF No. 100 (Bomber Support) Group were involved, confusing the enemy where it couldn't be seen, and ultimately where it could do most damage.

From the start of the war, both Britain and Germany were using ground-based radar to detect approaching aircraft. The Germans developed 'Freya', a long-range radar detecting aircraft 100 miles away. They also installed a chain of 'Wurzburg' radars stretching down the whole of western Germany to control an integrated defensive system of searchlights, flak and night-fighters.

Meanwhile, some British bombers were fitted with a device called 'Mandrel', jamming the enemy's 'Freya' radar, rendering it useless. British scientists also came up with 'Tinsel' – a microphone placed in a bomber's engine bay recording the deafening engine roar. When the Wireless Operator transmitted this blast of noise on German ground-to-air radio frequencies it was impossible for night-fighters to speak to their Controllers. German-speaking RAF personnel also tuned in to Luftwaffe night-fighters' radio frequencies giving false and misleading instructions.

British scientists then came up with a simple device which proved spectacular in the number of lives it saved.

'WINDOW' was the code name given to small metallised strips, like tin foil, designed to be dropped in bundles from RAF bombers. The resulting cloud of metallic strips let loose in the air completely confused German signals on radar screens, concealing the position and number of actual bombers.

Use of this top secret 'WINDOW' was delayed in case Germans found the metallised strips on the ground and used the same idea against Britain, disabling vital early warning radar that proved so crucial in winning the Battle of Britain. It wasn't known then, but Germans already had the 'WINDOW' effect, not using it for the same reason!

Meanwhile, Bomber Command's losses became unbearable. Air Marshall Arthur Harris insisted the RAF be allowed to use 'WINDOW' to save aircrew lives. With the required authorisation, 'WINDOW' was first used during a series of night attacks on Hamburg - on 24/25 July 1943, followed in quick succession on 27/28 and 29/30 July. A fourth raid on 2 August failed due to a massive thunderstorm over the target.

Strips of silver foil 30 cm. long and 1.5 cm. wide were dropped at a rate of a bundle a minute. 200 strips would sound to German *Wurzburg* operators like the echo of a heavy bomber. The effect that first night was dramatic. The entire German radar system was disrupted. Searchlights waved aimlessly. Anti-aircraft fire was hesitant and inaccurate, giving way to barrage fire. German fighter pilots became frustrated and the intercepted radio traffic showed enemy ground controllers hopelessly confused.

700 - 800 RAF aircraft dropping 'WINDOW' created on German radar screens the suggestion of 11,000 bombers about to attack. The results spoke for themselves.

Only twelve aircraft were lost on that first Hamburg raid. Hamburg's defences were crippled, much of the city destroyed. On the second and third raids, losses rose to seventeen and twenty-seven aircraft - but remained below previous loss rates.

'WINDOW' became routine on every flight until the end of the war, manufactured in varying dimensions to match different frequencies.

American Involvement

An American component under RAF 100 Group involving the USAAF is best explained through this de-classified correspondence:

SECRET

SUBJECT: 803rd Squadron, 100th Group
To: Director of Operations
From: Signal Communications Officer
Date: 27 June 1944

1. In accordance with your verbal request, I am submitting the following review for the reasons of establishing the American component of RAF 100 Group, based on studies of our files covering this subject;

a. In order to effectively prosecute the RCM (Radio Countermeasures) Program, it was felt desirable to set up an American component of 100 Group. This USAAF Squadron would be able to secure additional intelligence information which, combined with British intelligence, would enable us to plan effective countermeasures, and predict future trends of the enemy's electronic aids.

b. A Squadron of this type would also be available for a number of RCM problems requiring prompt action on a relatively small scale, such as countermeasures against radio-controlled missiles and special search missions.

c. It was also felt that a separate American RCM Squadron was needed to aid in the search program to be conducted in both operational groups and in single aircraft.

d. This American Squadron would be available for testing new installations and developing new methods of radio countermeasures.

e. ABL-15 felt that an RCM organisation was needed for prototyping installations and employment of search equipment in experimental aircraft, in coordination with their laboratory at Great Malvern.

2. The following additional uses of the American component (803rd Squadron) of 100 Group have been developed since the original concept of this organisation:

a. The Squadron is available for special RCM missions, such as the 'Jostle' project in support of the Eighth and Ninth Air Forces and Ground Troops.

b. Also provides training facilities and instruction for crew members on special RCM equipment, such as training of spot-jamming operators for the 2nd Division of Eighth Air Force.

c. Another function of the 803rd Squadron can be the searching and jamming of frequencies used for radio-controlled missiles.

3. It is our understanding that the American component (803rd Squadron) of 100 Group is under the direct control of Eighth Air Force Headquarters. Necessary liaison is maintained between

the RCM Squadron, Headquarters, USSTAF and Headquarters ASC-USSTAF, by our representatives of the Signal Section.

Signed

George Dixon
Colonel Air Corps
Signal Communications Officer [8]

This was one of a series of TOP SECRET communiques passed between the USAAF and the RAF. Radio countermeasures were instigated as early as Autumn/Winter 1942 when the two parties came together to discuss details about joining forces in this area. Influenced by success of the British and equipment being developed and used, the United States Strategic Air Force were keen to become involved.

A Collective of Radio Counter-Measures (RCM)

By 1943-1944, the air battle over Germany was intense and complex.

The most important decision was to bring under one Command all units engaged in radio countermeasures and bomber support operations, to establish a specialist RAF Unit responsible for the operational development, application and co-ordination of all RCM programmes – from the air and from the ground.

New Squadrons would be formed, more brought in from other Groups. The best in men and materials were made available. The USAAF were involved from the outset, with a high level of secrecy surrounding this Group from the start.

On 8 November 1943, authorisation to form No. 100 (Bomber Support) Group was issued. Its staff assembled at Radlett, Headquarters of No. 80 Signals Wing. Air Vice-Marshal Edward B. Addison CB, CBE, OBE, MA, CENG, FIEE as he became in later years; a specialist in electrical engineering, was ideally suited to head Bomber Command's new Group. He remained 100 Group's only Commander during its short two year wartime existence, until it disbanded on 17 December 1945. However, even when Addison retired from the RAF in 1955, he maintained a close involvement with the electronics field. On his retirement in 1975, he was Director of Intercontinental Technical Services.

The Group's Senior Air Staff Officer was Wing Commander (later Air Commodore) R. Chisholm CBE, DSO, DFC – experienced Mosquito Night Fighter Pilot.

Group Captain S. Goodman CBE was appointed Chief Signals Officer.

Other senior Officers included Wing Commander N. C. Cordingly OBE, previously Directorate of Radar at the Air Ministry; Wing Commander W. McMenemy, Wing Commander Dunning-White and Wing Commander Well.

A civilian scientist on the staff was Dr Leonard Lamerton, an expert in x-rays.

An American 8th Air Force Liaison Officer was attached to the staff.

After forming at Radlett, their Group Headquarters moved to West Raynham airfield where the Group's first Squadron, No. 141, was almost ready for action.

RAF No. 100 (Bomber Support) Group

'Confound & Destroy'
Reproduced with permission of the MOD

From its beginnings it was designed to confuse the enemy, both with its number: '100', and the number of Squadrons involved. Rather than using sequential numbers, Squadron numbers were chosen at random. They were based at RAF stations in East Anglia, mainly Norfolk; where even the creation of the airfields was secret, using about 100 aircraft for bomber support.

B-17 (Flying Fortresses) and B-24 (Liberators) carried jamming equipment and flew with the bomber stream. Halifaxes and Stirlings flew separate operations, producing false radar echoes of spoof and decoy raids by creating *'ghost'* Squadrons using 'WINDOW' and other devices to confuse the enemy. They also flew Beaufighters and Mosquito Night Fighters, carrying airborne radar for tracking and destroying enemy Night Fighters.

B-17 Fortresses had the ability to fly particularly high. Their radio transmitters jammed German early warning radar and fighter control communications. A German-speaking crew member operated jamming equipment, giving false instructions to Luftwaffe Night Fighter pilots. B-17s flew 5,000 feet above the main bomber stream, throwing out a protective electronic *'cloak'* to conceal attacks. Similar work was carried out by B-24 Liberator bombers.

Main flying crews of the RAF had no idea about 100 Group *'Guardian Angels'* in the skies during harrowing attacks on the enemy. It was secret even within the RAF itself.

Under complete secrecy, RAF No. 100 (BS) Group became operational in December 1943.

192 Squadron commenced radio search operations for the Group on 2 December 1943. While the first Bomber Support Operation was flown on 16 December by 141 Squadron when two Beaufighters and two Mosquitoes supported the main force.

By the end of the year, the Group had expanded with new airfields and Squadrons, while Group H.Q. moved to its permanent home at Bylaugh Hall, near Swanton Morley, Norfolk.

Airfields, Squadrons and Units taken over by the Group

1943	
November 8	RAF No. 100 Group officially authorised
December 3	West Raynham
December 3	Great Massingham
December 3	141 Squadron
December 7	Foulsham
December 7	Oulton
December 7	North Creake
December 7	Swannington
December 7	169 Squadron
December 7	192 Squadron
December 7	1473 Flight
December 7	1692 Flight
December 9	239 Squadron
December 15	515 Squadron
1944	
January	Sculthorpe
January	214 Squadron
March	803 Squadron USAAF
April 1	85 Squadron
April 10	BSDU
April	1694 Flight
May 1	199 Squadron
May	23 Squadron
May	157 Squadron
June	1699 Flight
August 13	103rd Bomb Squadron reconstituted as 36th Bomb Squadron Radar Counter Measure Unit RCM
August 23	223 Squadron
August 28	7th Photographic Reconnaissance Group USAAF Detachment
September 7	171 Squadron

December 22	462 Squadron RAAF
1945	
February	'WINDOW' Research Flight

Duties were complicated and diverse:

- Provide direct support to RAF bombers, using RCM, 'WINDOW' and Night Intruder Operations with Mosquitoes,
- Exploit enemy air and ground RCM,
- Investigate development of enemy radar and radio equipment by airborne signals intercept, undertaken by 192 Squadron, the lead Squadron,
- Build a body of knowledge as a basis for planning future operations,
- Make use of immediate information about enemy fighter movements.

As far as 100 Group were concerned, it was a continuous game of cat and mouse. As fast as enemy systems were found and jammed, new and more complicated systems appeared. Some operated only seconds per transmission, whereas others played music as coded messages.

Who Was Involved?

RAF Bomber Command

The most controversial aspect of Bomber Command during World War Two remained the area bombing of cities. All large German cities contained important industrial districts, considered legitimate targets by the Allies. New methods of finding these were to create *'firestorms'*.

The legality became the subject of an article in the International Review of the Red Cross, which stated:

In examining these events (aerial area bombardment) in the light of international humanitarian law, it should be borne in mind that, during the Second World War there was no agreement, treaty, convention or any other instrument governing the protection of the civilian population or civilian property, as the conventions then in force dealt only with the protection of the wounded and the sick on the battlefield and in naval warfare, hospital ships, the laws and customs of war and the protection of prisoners of war.[9]

Bomber Command crews suffered extremely high casualties:

- 55,573 killed out of a total of 125,000 aircrew.
- A further 8,403 wounded in action.
- 9,838 became PoWs.

This covered all Bomber Command Operations, including tactical support for ground operations and mining of sea lanes. A Bomber Command crew member had a worse chance of survival than an infantry officer in World War One. In comparison, the US 8th Air Force, which flew daylight raids over Europe, had 350,000 aircrew during the war:

- 26,000 killed
- 23,000 became PoWs.

RAF Bomber Command personnel killed during the war included:

- 72% British,
- 18% Canadian,
- 7% Australian,
- 3% New Zealanders.

The greatest contribution to winning the war made by Bomber Command was in the huge diversion of German resources in defending the homeland.

Working alongside RAF 100 Group were:

- **RAF Y-Service** – the progressive analysis and interpretation of German Air Force radio traffic.

- **Bletchley Park Air Section** – widely known as the place where the Enigma was broken and the most important source of intelligence in World War Two. The Intelligence output from the Air Section at Bletchley Park supplied Bomber Command with knowledge of enemy night fighter intentions and their execution.

- **German Air Defence System** – the night-fighter control system became known and much of its method of operational working was deduced from the Y-Service intercepts and other signals intelligence.

Working together, sharing information, including the production of Enigma; was the key to success to bring the war to an early conclusion. The Y-Service and those in partnership created an authoritative source of intelligence without which the war might not have been won.

What Did RAF No. 100 (BS) Group Achieve?

100 Group totalled 16,740 operational sorties.

At the end of the war, Bomber Command held the view that 100 Group Operations together with the innovative work and success of British scientists in the *'electronic war'*, saved approximately 1,000 bomber aircraft and up to 7,000 aircrew.

The combination of scientific and military skill was even recognised by the Germans. The Luftwaffe's leading fighter ace, General Galland, commented:

> The combination of the Pathfinders' Operations, the activities of No. 100 Group, the British advantage in radar, jamming and WINDOW techniques combined with intelligent attacking tactics, as well as the discipline and bravery of RAF crews, have been remarkable. We had severe problems in trying to defend Germany in the air. [10]

100 Group aircraft were equipped with jamming signals intercept equipment. They were tasked to find, fix, jam and deceive enemy radio, radar, navigation and control systems, using special equipment against German equipment – Lichtenstein, Freya and Wurzburg radars – including:

- **AIRBORNE CIGAR (ABC)** – jammer,
- **JOSTLE** – jammer,
- **MANDREL** jammers, creating an electronic screen to hide approaching RAF bombers from the enemy long-range FREYA radars,
- **AIRBORNE GROCER** – jammer,
- **PERFECTOS** – homer,
- **SERRATE** – homer,
- **CORONA** – spoofer,
- **LUCERO** – homer,
- **CARPET** Transmitter/Receivers to detect and jam WURZBURG Anti-Aircraft Gun Laying and night fighter GCI radars,
- **WINDOW** (aluminium strips) disrupting enemy radars. A few 100 Group aircraft could simulate a major raid to 'spoof' enemy air defences,
- **TINSEL and JOSTLE** to jam enemy radio systems,
- **PIPERACK** transmitters to jam enemy night fighter Air Interception radars.

100 Group Squadrons were based at RAF stations in East Anglia, chiefly Norfolk:

Squadron	Aircraft	1st 100 Group Operation	Base
192 USAAF 7th PRG	Mosquito II, BIV, BXVI Wellington B.III, Halifax IV Lightnings P-38	Dec 1943 Aug 44 – Mar 45	RAF Foulsham various
141	Beaufighter VI, Mosquito II, VI, XXX	December 1943	RAF West Raynham
219/239	Mosquito II, VI, XXX	20 January 1944	RAF West Raynham
515	Mosquito II, VI	3 March 1944	RAF Little Snoring

169	Mosquito II, VI, XIX	20 January 1944	RAF Little Snoring RAF Great Massingham
214	Fortress II, III	20/21 April 1944	RAF Sculthorpe RAF Oulton
199	Stirling III, Halifax III	1 May 1944	RAF North Creake
157	Mosquito XIX, XXX	May 1944	RAF Swannington
85	Mosquito XII, XVII	5/6 June 1944	RAF Swannington
23	Mosquito VI	5/6 July 1944	RAF Little Snoring
223	Liberator VI, Fortress II, III	September 1944	RAF Oulton
171	Stirling II, Halifax III	15 September 1944	RAF North Creake
462 (RAAF)	Halifax III	1 January 1945	RAF Foulsham
36 & 803 BS	Boeing B-17F P38	January 1944	Sculthorpe Oulton
857 & 858 BS	Consolidated B-24G	January 1944	Oulton

Other Units and Stations:

- No. 1692 Flight RAF at RAF Little Snoring
- No. 1699 Flight RAF at RAF Oulton to train Boeing Fortress crews for 214 Squadron
- No. 100 Group Communications Flight at RAF West Raynham, later RAF Swanton Morley
- No. 80 (Signals) Wing from November 1943 based at RAF Radlett, controlled

Meacon beacons and other radio counter-measures and intelligence work.

Communication aircraft were based mainly at Swanton Morley, not far from Group H.Q. A few small light aircraft operated from a tiny airstrip in Bylaugh Park close to H.Q at the Hall.

Today, the name of RAF No. 100 (Bomber Support) Group is generally not known and rarely mentioned except amongst its own. Veterans do not share openly. Following their deaths, it is only in dusty cupboards and attics when family sort belongings that hidden treasures come to light: Log Books, documents, diaries, writings and photographs, leaving unanswered questions for those they knew and loved.

Officially, there are secrets of the Group that remain under a 100 Year Rule. It means the planning and more importantly reasons behind operations will not be known during their lifetime.

Given that they were formed under Bomber Command, the only real tribute to their commitment and courage is the Bomber Command Memorial dedicated on 28 June 2012 in Green Park, London ... and more recently a Bomber Command Clasp which attaches to the 1939-1945 Star for which anyone who flew at least one operational sortie qualifies. It took many years of campaigning by veterans to gain this small token of gratitude that still does not equal the medal they are long overdue. It is also difficult for many to obtain the Clasp, with strict conditions surrounding it.

Is this Bomber Command Clasp enough when almost a quarter of a million veterans and their families have waited tens of years to have the recognition they deserve?

Veterans Minister Mark Francois stated in 2012:

All who served our country in Bomber Command ... deserve nothing but the utmost respect and admiration from us. [11]

Veteran Air Gunner, Norman Storey, tells of a limited edition Bomber Command medal privately manufactured in the 1980s to honour those who fought under Bomber Command, including 100 Group. It begs the question: *how many veterans were aware of this medal and how many actually applied for and received it, given it wasn't an official medal presented in the usual way?*

Norman died just after Christmas 2014. He chose not to apply for the limited edition Bomber Command medal. To him, it wasn't a *'proper medal'*, not presented by the Forces or Royalty:

During the war, the men of Bomber Command were heroes. The day war ended, they were mass murderers, and murderers don't get medals! Top politicians who fully supported Arthur Harris during the war wanted to disown any connection with the bombing of Germany. Did they want to appease those nice Germans who bombed London, Coventry and Plymouth? Bomber Command was never

represented in the Victory Parade. Their attitude – 'let Harris carry the can'. Members of Bomber Command and most of the general public considered this an insult, especially as Bomber Command did more than any to bring about the defeat of Germany. However, a small consolation was the decision of The Coin and Medal News magazine to arrange for the issue of a Bomber Command Medal. The cost of the Medal was £15.95. This could not be worn with official medals, but underneath them. As President of the Air Gunners' Association, I annually laid a wreath on behalf of the Association at the annual Memorial Service at Runnymede. After the issue of the Medal I saw ex-Bomber Command veterans wear the Medal with pride, and rightly so. I could never bring myself to wear a Medal I could buy, but I fully support those who did. However, on receiving an application for the Medal, I was surprised and proud that the illustration of a crew on the front of the application was the photograph taken by the Lincolnshire newspaper after our ten Ops on Berlin with 103 Squadron ... [12]

The brochure advertising the medal shows Geoffrey H Richmond, Co-ordinator of Adult Studies at Scarborough Technical College, as designer of the only Bomber Command Medal. During the Second World War he served in the RAF as a Wireless Operator in Iraq, Egypt, Malta, France and Germany. A member of the Orders and Medals Research Society and interested in Bomber Command, he felt that its aircrews' special service was under-valued at the end of the war due to political factors prevalent at the time.

The medal was chosen by a panel of experts from a large number of entries submitted in May 1984 to a 'Design a Medal for Bomber Command' competition, the brainchild of regular RAF columnist Alan Cooper believing members of Bomber Command received inadequate award for their courage and skill during the Second World War.

In response to an overwhelming number of requests from veterans of Bomber Command, a limited number of medals were struck, intended as a tribute to the bravery of those who flew and to the dedication of the skilled Ground Crew whose contribution was so essential. For each medal purchased, a donation of one pound was made to the newly-formed Bomber Command Association which lives on today.

The late Sir Arthur Harris, Bt GCB OBE AFC LLD, Commander in Chief of Bomber Command during the war, gave his blessing to the competition shortly before his death in 1984. He accepted one of the medals on behalf of Bomber Command. A special striking of the medal in sterling silver was presented to the Bomber Command Museum at Hendon for permanent display. The ribbon colours are blue grey, midnight blue, flame (signifying the North Sea, night over enemy territory, target, return trip). The Laurel wreathed brevet letters of the aircrew supporting that of their pilot on one side signifies courage, team spirit and leadership. On the reverse is a Lancaster, Sir Arthur Harris's 'Shining Sword'. The epitome of night bomber development ... symbolising the supreme technical achievement of industry and ground staff, on which the aircrew's lives depended.

Amongst veterans, however, there remains the feeling that RAF No. 100 Group under Bomber Command have been ignored compared to colleagues in Fighter Command. While Fighter Command, made up of Spitfires and Hurricanes, did invaluable work protecting skies over Britain, Bomber Command attacked enemy sites abroad, flying dangerous sorties against munitions, factories, ships, troops and air bases.

Those who survived operations under RAF No. 100 (BS) Group during the war remember, holding the secret of their stories of courage with a degree of humble pride. It is on their behalf I remain passionate about giving them a voice, including as many of their writings and memories as possible within these pages in tribute. Their names should never be forgotten, their deeds recognised and remembered. The name of RAF No. 100 (Bomber Support) Group should be spoken, that we remember our debt to those who paid the ultimate price for the freedom we enjoy today.

On 3 November 1943, the same month and year RAF 100 Group was formed, Air Marshall Arthur Harris wrote to Churchill giving a brief summary of Bomber Command's great achievements over that year, listing targets still to be destroyed. At the head of his list was the Reich Capital:

> I await promised USAAF help in this, the greatest of air battles. But I would not propose to wait forever, or for long if opportunity serves. We can wreck Berlin from end to end, if the USA will come in on it. It will cost us between 400 and 500 aircraft. It will cost Germany the war. [13]

On the night Harris dispatched his letter to Churchill, he staged a new demonstration of Bomber Command's might with an operation of 589 aircraft to Dusseldorf, at the same time as fifty-two Lancasters and ten Mosquitoes carried out a diversionary raid on Cologne.

It is in tribute to all who served, both under RAF No. 100 (Bomber Support) Group and the USAAF that this book is written.

CHAPTER 2
The Mighty Eighth Air Force's Squadron of Deception
The 36th Bomb Squadron Radar Counter Measure (RCM) Unit in World War Two
by

Stephen Hutton, son of 36th Bomb Squadron S/Sgt Iredell Hutton:
Aerial Tail Gunner B24 Liberator nicknamed 'The JIGS UP'

RAFU 36th Bomb Squadron crest
(courtesy Stephen Hutton)

They flew in four engine heavy bombers, but never dropped a single bomb. They were an American Eighth Air Force (8AF) Squadron, but flew their first missions with the British Royal Air Force (RAF). Initially, they flew night missions with the Royal Air Force and later daylight missions with the Mighty Eighth. On all these missions their aircraft preceded the Allied bombers to the target. They flew at times when the RAF and the 8AF had no operations, and they flew on days when the 8AF stood down because of weather. They were a unique and secret Squadron that saved many Allied lives during World War Two. They were the 36th Bomb Squadron Radar

Counter Measure (RCM) Unit, the only electronic warfare Squadron of the 8AF. Their nickname was 'The Gremlins'.

The 36th Bomb Squadron (36BS) as a radar countermeasure unit did not drop bombs and was not involved in typical 8AF missions as other Bomb Squadrons in Europe. Its only comparison with other Bomb Squadrons was the fact that B17 Flying Fortress and B24 Liberator heavy bombers were used. The Bomb Squadron name was designed to mislead the enemy and Allied personnel with no 'need to know' into believing this was just another American Bomber Squadron. For the most part, the bombers looked alike, but instead of bombs loaded in the bomb bays, radar countermeasure aircraft carried high voltage jammers. This Squadron functioned as a special Bomber Support Unit to protect Allied bombers and also to conduct experimentation of new electronic warfare equipment.

Electronic warfare was in its infancy and the United States were following on the coat-tails of Great Britain. The ingenious British had learned that RCM (radio countermeasures) had reduced bomber losses by an astounding fifty percent. The 36BS performed radar countermeasures by jamming German radar, giving them early raid warnings and also controlled enemy fighters, flak batteries or anti-aircraft guns and searchlights. Using RCM operational tactics, missions of the 36th also created spoofs and diversions causing confusion to German defenders. Successful RCM missions left Germans guessing the size of invading forces, where to direct critical defences and whether a threatened mission was real or just a 'spoof'. By spring 1944, the Germans could ill afford to waste its resources of pilots, fuel and aircraft. Through deception then this special bomber support function, part of a larger electronic warfare effort, would save many Allied lives.

The 36th was born out of the 803rd Bomb Squadron (Provisional). The 803rd was not yet fully organized. Initially, it began work with the RAF No. 100 (Bomber Support) Group at RAF Sculthorpe, England in March 1944. Air Vice Marshal E. B. Addison led the RAF Group whose motto was 'Confound and Destroy'. Captain George E. Paris was chosen to command the 8AF's fledgling 803rd. Captain Paris and this first attachment of airmen had already completed an operational tour flying the required twenty-five missions. The radar countermeasure effort came under RAF Bomber Command and performed a variety of special operational activities. Secret missions used exotic hardware, the simplest nicknamed *CHAFF* or *WINDOW* as the British called it – aluminum strips, not unlike tinsel, dropped from aircraft to obscure the enemy's radar screen with 'snow'. On a side note, it was discovered that in dropping tinsel over the continent, in addition to fouling enemy radar, cows were eating it and dying of indigestion. So, it had a bad side effect for cows as well as the enemy!

As previously stated, Captain Paris had already completed an operational tour having earlier served as Assistant Operations Officer for the 368th Bomb Squadron, 306th Bomb Group (Heavy) where he had flown B17 Flying Fortresses. By that time he had already distinguished himself in combat, sometimes as lead pilot, and been awarded the Silver Star, Distinguished Flying Cross, Air Medal with 3 Oak Leaf Clusters, plus other medals. Captain Paris recalled:

> I finished my missions in December 1943 and was invited to go down to 1st Division Headquarters and interview. They had a certain number of jobs available. Subsequently, they needed people to do other things like this 803rd. I was assigned and took the detachment there [to Sculthorpe]. We were the first contingent of the 803rd to go to the base. [Later on at Oulton] the British Commander, Group Captain Dickens, had an assortment of crew members from all over. They had Icelanders, Indians, Canadians, all the Allied forces, Pilots and other grades, Navigators and radio people. I liked the British and Canadians very much. We got along splendidly. Also, it was a chance to continue flying. We knew we were going to win over there, we just didn't know when, so all of us wanted to stay.
>
> We had some technical people that knew aspects of radar countermeasures. They had experience in this and worked with the British. The base was kind of low key. They had training in the morning and some flying in the afternoon. Our job was to check out the guys in the B17 which could fly higher than their ships. The end objective was to use the B17 flown by British flyers to do diversionary tactical flights; to try and divert German fighters from the place that they [the British] were actually going to bomb. The ships that would drop chaff, the tin foil; would go up to the North Sea on a diversionary tactic. Then, of course, the bombers would go in lower south of there to another target and bomb it. Supposedly they [the Germans] would have less prior notice of incoming bombers, and therefore [the bombers] might run into less flak and certainly less fighters. At that time German forces were becoming limited as far

as fuel goes and also aircraft and crew members too. We had at that time very good support in P51s with extended range tanks on them and also P47s. It was getting to be there was hardly any opposition.

Other special equipment utilized in *The Gremlins'* bag-of-tricks were powerful electronic jammers. These devices had unusual nicknames like *MANDREL, DINA, JACKAL, JOSTLE*, plus others. *MANDREL*, for example was an airborne transmitter tuned to radiate noise over enemy radar frequencies. This disturbance tended to obscure the size of Allied attacking forces on the enemy's radar screens and also caused the enemy to conclude an attack was imminent when one was not. Another airborne electronic jammer, nicknamed *JACKAL* was used to jam German tank communications during the Battle of the Bulge in the winter of 1944 – 45. Many of the aircraft jamming systems were developed and tested by Allied scientists associated with the American-British Laboratory Division 15, or ABL-15 as it was called. They were part of the British Telecommunications Research Establishment, or TRE, located at Great Malvern.

George Klemm, who would later head Division 15's Antennae Group in England remembered the beginnings of this elite group of scientists and researchers:

I was donated by a general radio company in Cambridge. I was doing my co-op work from Northeastern [University] at that time and was about ready to graduate. They hired me in the spring of 1942. Well, [Dr. Fred] Terman assembled this group and our assignment was to investigate radar, what the enemy had, and what could be done about it. We were to design investigative equipment. We made all kinds of receivers, some of them you just twiddled the dial, others were automatic you could put aboard planes. These flew over enemy territory and we searched out the location of various enemy radar. With that information, we knew where to go and use our countermeasure equipment. ABL was set up in Great Britain in order to introduce American forces to radar countermeasures. Since it was too late to get radar countermeasures in the table of organization of the Army and Navy, we as civilians worked with all Services in applying the various pieces of equipment which had been designed back here in the United States.

In April 1944, Lt Col Clayton A. Scott replaced Captain Paris and assumed command of the 803rd. At this time the secret Squadron included nine crew and six B17 aircraft. The next month the Squadron moved from Sculthorpe to RAF Oulton airfield and commenced night-time RCM operations supporting the RAF as they pounded the Nazis relentlessly. For the new 803rd and for the Allies the most important electronic warfare mission of World War Two was soon to take place.

The first operational mission for the 803rd was on D-Day. This historic mission used four 803rd B17 aircraft on the night of 5/6 June along with aircraft from RAF 100 Group's 101 and 214 Squadrons. Its purpose was to mask the Allied invasion fleet and support airborne operations on the Normandy beachhead. The aircraft with their bulky *MANDREL* jamming boxes bolted onto metal-framed shelves in the bomb bays were in their assigned orbit positions over the English Channel from 2235 hours on 5 June to 0450 hours on 6 June. The official Squadron history record stated: '*This mission proved very effective in countering the enemy warning system and contributed materially to the success of the landings on the beachhead.*' With this first mission the 803rd flew into RCM history most honorably.

One Squadron Adjutant expressed his strong sentiments about this truly historic day:

Invasion Day – from the dark, chilled, early hours of the morning, well into the night, all officers and enlisted men were at their post of duty, eager to perform any order of the day with complete disregard for the size of the task. Every job was important. Every man was important. No man shirked his duty. No man allowed fatigue to overcome the complete performance of his duty. This was the long awaited day. We were making our first thrust across the English Channel, to free an enslaved country, France, from the fiendish rule of a ruthless group and their fanatical followers, whose beliefs in every phase and form of life are completely opposite to all that we, Americans, hold close to our hearts. France was the pathway to the destruction of Hitler and Company. Nothing must stop us. Nothing will stop us.

Sgt Charles Sanders, an 803BS B17 Mechanic recalled D-Day preparations:

They had told us for some time that the first maximum effort we would have would be the invasion of Europe. We had gotten a new B17 and supplies to equip for night flying. Captain Preuss [Engineering Officer] told us that the Colonel said many lives depended on us getting these planes in the air as soon as we can. That night we did almost the impossible. We put the flame suppressors on all four engines in about three hours. We had four planes that took off. We all figured this was the big night. I can assure you it was a long night.

Our planes were flying an assigned area. If a German fighter should see them, they would be a sure target. This was the first time I had sweated out the planes since leaving the 92nd Bomb Group. It was that suspense of hoping everybody would get back with no enemy contact.

June 6 1944, was the big day. I don't think I have ever heard as many planes as I did that night. They just kept on coming over. We did not know when to look for our planes back. Sometime early morning we had four planes come in pretty close together. I had been up about twenty-six hours.

On June 7, the Colonel told us the 803rd and RAF Squadrons had saved hundreds of lives. He said we would never know just how many. He also told us that the top Army men had expected about a forty percent loss in paratroopers and airborne troops. Due to the radar screen, they had less than a two percent loss. He said surprise made the difference. The MANDREL would stop German radar from picking up activities in England. They told us it was like having a solid fence between us and the Germans.

D-Day B17 Pilot Captain Robert Stutzman, who served as the Squadron Operations Officer for the 803BS and later as the same in the 36th Bomb Squadron RCM, said:

Late in the afternoon or early evening of June 5 our Squadron was alerted that the long awaited invasion was on. I received a copy of General Eisenhower's letter to the troops thanking them for the noble adventure they were about to undertake. I recall getting the flight crews together and briefing them for the mission laid on by RAF 100 Group. We did jamming and led groups of paratroopers and gliders that were flying. We were ahead of them, jamming. We saw gliders being towed by C47 aircraft, many flights of C47s with para-troopers. We did jamming so that the C47s carrying paratroopers and gliders wouldn't be sitting ducks. While we were in our orbiting position we could see flashes of guns from the naval bombardment. We could see the firing, the softening up of the beaches there. We hoped our jamming would conceal the presence of airborne troops from the Germans.

Lt. Wade Birmingham, Navigator for Captain Stutzman, wrote this detailed account of the events on 6th June:

For the last eight or ten days our Squadron has been alerted – an air of mystery was hovering over our entire base. We knew deep down that the mighty invasion was just a matter of days off; and when the time came the 803rd Squadron was to play an important role. In fact the importance of our work gave us all quite a start. We could hardly believe at last, our four months of waiting was to bring a rich reward. We had all been waiting for this moment and now we were to be back in operations we all felt 100% better. Morale was at its highest peak.

Early in the afternoon, 5 June, our C.O. alerted four of our trained crews; myself having the privilege of being on one of these choice few. Of course, we did not know that this, at long last, was the real thing. We had an idea it was just another night practice flight; perhaps a *Bullseye*, practice for searchlights. The Navigators were called imme-diately after supper and, with an air of question surrounding our being, we entered the British Intelligence briefing room. There on the map we found the answer to our questions – we were to cover the airborne and seaborne invasion with special MANDREL equip-ment. Our ships were equipped to put out a screen, a screen that rendered the Jerry's radar-receiving equipment useless. They could not tell what was going on behind the screen, nor could they use radar for aiming their coastal installation guns. In other words, our 'sets' would play havoc with the entire radar system and communi-cation system of our enemy.

To make our job a success, we, the Navigators were entirely indis-pensable. Our duty was to patrol within five miles of a certain point near mid-channel and this five miles had to be stayed within. Each aircraft had an individual point and the points were so set that the screens would blend together without an opening. Our take-off was set for 10:05 and landing the morning of the 6th was supposed to be near 6:30 – eight hours of flying in a small area, in the dark – quite a job. However, we knew we must make good.

The success or failure of the invasion, the amount of losses, both naval and aircraft; these were all piled upon the shoulders of the 803rd. [After] take off we proceeded to Portland Bill, and made good our time – now to Point 11 and on went our sets at 11:35 – that time had to be made to the minute and luckily our GEE set was working fine; no jamming interference, therefore my navigation was very precision-like. We began our orbiting eight minutes one leg, two and a half the other. We had one helluva wind blowing from the northwest and a velocity of near eighty mph. In other words if we weren't careful, we would be blown too far to the south and over enemy territory. Also our screen would be broken, our whole task a failure. I began to sweat. *Are we right? Did I judge this wind correctly? Will they send night fighters after us? Will our engines hold out?* Two were running rough now. *Would our oxygen hold out? Our gasoline?* Hundreds of petty thoughts ran through my mind as we continued circling at Point 11.

At about 12:00 we watched the fireworks begin. As we were over an overcast, we couldn't see what was going on beneath the clouds. However, we could see huge flashes under the stuff. This no doubt was the fleet's pounding of the coast, the prelude to the airborne fleet. All during the night these flashes kept going at a mighty pace; I felt a surge of pride within me – this is truly it and my part is being carried out! About 01:30 we could see the marker flares of RAF ships. These boys were now doing their part – precision bombing at night. We watched great flashes as bombs found their targets. This is where the invasion took its first step. The remainder of the night was a repetition of this – flashes, gunfire we could see but not hear. Flak bursts at night are horrible sights. I was thankful I was sitting up here at 20,000 feet away from enemy fire.

As time passed we all began to tire, Gunners began to see planes that did not exist; stars looked like lights of planes. I had taken so many GEE fixes I could do it without thinking, almost with my eyes closed. About four o'clock, daylight began to come into being – and what a spectacle it brought! We watched fighters and bombers going over to take part, hundreds of planes, all kinds. How we wished the cloud cover was gone so we could see the sea power at work – the 4,000 landing craft and ships that took part. All were beneath us, but not one could we see.

At 4:50 we cut off our sets and started for the base. 6:15 our wheels set down and ten very tired young men went into interrogation. Tonite we were told that our part was played to perfection, the screening was perfect. Also we were told our job had caused slight losses of the first blow – fifteen transport planes and just three ships. We felt wonderful! We had a job to do and we had done it.

In the 8 June message of congratulations from T. C. Dickens, Group Captain Commanding RAF Station Oulton to Officers Commanding RAF 101 and 214 Squadrons and the 803rd Dickens said:

The results achieved on the night preceding invasion day were highly successful. This has already been established. It may be found that your achievement was of even greater importance than can be known at present. I appreciate that the culmination of your effort can only have been achieved by careful training and attention to detail. This is reflected by the results of the crews concerned. Great appreciation has been expressed by Naval Commanders of the support from the Squadrons and it can now be disclosed that the work of 101, 214, and 803 Squadrons succeeded most effectually in confusing the enemy as to the point of landing, thus permitting the tactical surprise which we gained.

Like many thousands of young American GIs entering the British Isles daily, S/Sgt Iredell Hutton (father of author: Stephen Hutton) from North Carolina; sailed from America on the ocean liner *Queen Elizabeth*. Assigned to the 803rd as Tail Gunner in Lt William 'Mac' McCrory's crew, he arrived on 5 June, just before D-Day, with heightened excitement and anticipation. He began a personal diary in spite of Army Air Corp regulations strictly forbidding diaries in fear they might fall into enemy hands.

At last from the deck of the *Queen*, Hutton's eyes grew wide as he first sighted land: the high mountains in Ireland. As waves swept by, the ship continued and sailed on, finally docking at Greenock, Scotland. Here, he wrote about beginning his new adventure in a new land:

> It was about 2 pm when we pulled in. Never in my life have I seen such beautiful country. It looked so peaceful and one would never know that they were at war if there hadn't been so many battleships around. After a short while we began to move towards shore. When we docked we were near the railroad station. We saw some pretty girls in a tower who were sending messages to battleships and flat-tops stationed all around the Queen Elizabeth.

Later, traveling on the train to his assigned station, Hutton elaborated about what he saw:

> When we had pulled out of the station, we headed for England. As we rode, people were standing along the railroad, houses and gardens, waving 'V' for victory at us. They were happy because the invasion which they had waited for so long had just come off. The country was a lot different from that which we have back in the States. Each hill where the water ran down was all covered with grass. We didn't see any soil erosion. From the window we could see castles way up on distant hills. All of the hills were barren of trees. All that was growing on it was grass and a few crops. The soil was too rocky for much farming. Each farm was separated by high rock walls. It took years and years to build these walls.
>
> Around 10:45 pm when we pulled into the station, we put on our musette [canvas] bags and gas masks and proceeded to get off the train. The officers were first marched away and then we were loaded into trucks.

In August 1944, personnel from the 803rd merged with select men of the 856th Bomb Squadron and 858th Bomb Squadron of the 492nd Bomb Group to form the new 36th Bomb Squadron (Heavy) RCM Unit. A Squadron insignia was designed for this new special outfit. The 36th insignia depicted a winged radar gremlin whose body and nose consisted of radio tubes and from whose fingertips emitted the radio transmissions which fouled enemy radar devices. Placed between the wings above the '*Gremlin*' was the term RAFU, meaning Radar All Fouled Up. This term was related in a way similar to the term 'SNAFU' – Situation Normal – All Fouled Up!

At this time, the Squadron packed up and moved from Oulton to Army Air Field Station 113 Cheddington, thirty miles northwest of London. (Cheddington later became famous as the place of the Great Train Robbery.) At Cheddington, Major Robert F. Hambaugh assumed command of the Squadron and continued in that capacity until war's end.

After assuming his new command Major Hambaugh, wrote to his folks in Birmingham Alabama:

> **Dearest Folks, I am getting along fine, plenty to eat and its good food and a nice place for my Quarters. I have a good Squadron and good boys. We do special work, that's all I can say.**

Squadron photographer Frank Trovato fondly remembered Robert Hambaugh:

> **Major Hambaugh [later Lt Col] was well known to me and a swell guy. Everybody liked him. I think he was kind and considerate. I remember taking pictures of him, one a nice close-up portrait; also others of him as he was making medal presentations to crew members.**

Hambaugh was also popular with his pilots, Lt Joe Brookshire for one:

> **Hambaugh and I got along real good. He was a good guy. He used to let me get away with what I thought was murder. My brother was stationed not too far from Bristol. He came over to the field and the Colonel let me have an old B24 to take him up and give him the thrill of his lifetime – flying in a '24. I got him up in the air and I let my brother fly.**
>
> **When we would come home from missions I'd make fighter approaches to landing, where you get a B24 up at some altitude and cut off all four engines and do a hundred and eighty and come in on your final approach that way. He [Lt Col Hambaugh] let me do it. I did it two or three times which is a good way to get killed. That '24 flew like a rock.**

During August 1944 half of the sixteen operational missions were flown from RAF Oulton with the remaining half from Cheddington. In addition to MANDREL patrol missions, the Squadron flew four frequency search missions at the request of ABL-15. These data-gathering missions contributed to RCM research being carried out by ABL-15 scientists and technicians. Naturally the Squadron had to know what radio and radar frequencies to jam because the enemy's frequencies changed on a regular basis.

Squadron Navigator Lt Joseph Thome recalled serving at Cheddington as well as working with ABL-15:

> Some work we were doing there was pretty highly classified. We worked real close with the ABL – the American British Laboratory. They were providing the Americans [8AF] with their electronic knowledge. They were quite a bit ahead of us. We worked together. That's the reason of course we were there. We loaned them the airplanes to put their equipment aboard. And when we weren't flying combat missions, we were flying for ABL. We were trying to prove over England what we were going to perhaps do later over on the continent. They [ABL-15] were very successful in what they were doing. They were so far ahead of us it was terrible. They came out with some pretty good inventions. We just tried to keep everything way above board. We didn't ask questions. We just went out there, turned certain switches on and turned them off as they programmed us to do.

Soon it was found that the B24 Liberator was better suited to delivering a more ample power supply to high voltage jammers than the B17. By September, with great diligence, the Squadron completed the changeover to an all B24 Liberator fleet. Iredell Hutton and the McCrory crew named the B24 Liberator they flew *The JIGS UP*. However, for seven of the eleven war-weary Fortresses the 803rd had flown, their duty was not yet over. These aircraft were later used to serve in *Project Aphrodite*, the ambitious program to destroy Adolph Hitler's V1, V2 Vengeance weapon sites and submarine pens. It was this secret project that took the life of Lt Joseph P. Kennedy Jr., the brother of President John F. Kennedy.

Another most effective jamming mission for the new Squadron using its new aircraft took place on the evening of 15/16 September when seven Squadron B24s successfully completed a moving MANDREL patrol, jamming from 2215 hours to 0235 hours. Over 600 RAF aircraft were dispatched with seven failing to return for a loss rate of 1.1%. The main target for the attack was Kiel. The Raid Analysis Report stated in part:

> To cover the attack on Kiel, the MANDREL screen moved up at 2300 hours from a patrol line extending from coordinates 5345N – 0320E to 5033N – 0250E to fresh positions from 5505N – 0635E to 5318N – 0325E. The enemy was thus deprived of early warning, and it may well be that he again anticipated nothing more than a spoof attack with the result that fighter action was not initiated until after bombers had crossed the coast.

The 36th Gremlins were effective again!

During October 1944, RCM night missions continued in support of RAF Bomber Command whose targets included Bremen, Cologne, Essen, Frankfurt, plus others. Successful *spoof* jamming missions also commenced when Bomber Command had no operations. Deceived by the *spoof*, believing a RAF bombing raid was approaching enemy territory; enemy controllers at radar stations would initiate fighter action, thereby wasting manpower and fuel. Reduced bomber losses over the continent were being attributed to the screening efforts.

A classic electronic warfare mission occurred on the evening of 6/7 October. This mission produced significant results as the jamming *Gremlins* worked their special magic. A flight of seven Liberators was dispatched and success- fully completed their mission without incident, jamming from 1815 hours to 2145 hours. The screen was in support of RAF Bomber Command attacks on Dortmund and Bremen. Like the night before, it was a moving MANDREL screen. The RAF had 484 aircraft attack Dortmund with a loss of five aircraft, or 1%. The attack on Bremen had 246 aircraft, incurring a loss of five aircraft or 2%. An Interception Tactics Report stated that the operations were highly successful:

To have succeeded in penetrating 120 miles beyond the battle-line to the Ruhr and in carrying out a major attack on Bremen, for the loss of five aircraft on each, was an extraordinary encouraging outcome. Tactical surprise was evidently achieved in the north by use of a MANDREL screen, a low level approach as far as was possible towards the mouth of the Weser, an unusual approach route and restrictions on signals with the result that fighters were able to get to the target only after the bombing had been in progress for about ten minutes. The raid in the north and its protective screen were intended to lessen fighter opposition further south, but it appears that even without this there was sufficient confusion in the enemy's control over southwest Germany to prevent any well organized interceptors from coming up.

Dr. Reginald V. Jones, Great Britain's foremost electronic warfare wizard, Assistant Director of Scientific Intelligence, and Prime Minister Churchill's advisor in the countermeasures program wrote in his book *Most Secret War*:

One of the examples we enjoyed most occurred on 6 October, when we obtained General 'Beppo' Schmid's [Commander of the German night fighter organization] personal reaction to the fact that our losses were only thirteen out of 949 aircraft. The night's major operations were twin attacks on Dortmund and Bremen. In the latter, our bombers made a low approach under radio silence, while the German early warning radar was jammed by a screen of 100 Group aircraft operating MANDREL jammers; as a result the night fighters were only able to attack after our bombers had been over the target for ten minutes. Similarly, the Dortmund force flew low over France and turned north and climbed towards the Ruhr again screened by MANDREL aircraft, while a spoof force of Mosquitoes went on to threaten Mannheim. The result was confusion to the defenses, and General Schmid reacted with a castigatory diatribe to the whole German night fighter organization: 'I am astonished that in spite of pains, admonitions, and orders throughout the whole year, I have not succeeded in bringing the Jagd Divisionen [fighter divisions] at least to the point of being able to distinguish in what strength and in what direction the enemy is approaching. In my view, there is no excuse whatsoever for this failure.' [14]

The next evening, the night of 7/8 October, the Squadron succeeded in another electronic warfare jamming spoof, one truly for the record books. There was no offensive by Bomber Command this night, however, six B24s of the 36th were successfully dispatched and completed their mission without incident. The jamming was between 1845 hours and 2200 hours. The Raid Analysis Report described the operations:

> Taking advantage of the fact that there was to be no bomber night offensive on this night of 7/8 October, a spoof attack by the MANDREL screen and special WINDOW dropping aircraft, supported by high and low Intruders [RAF Mosquitoes attacking enemy airfields] was planned against Bremen. Following the attack on that city the previous night, when practically no enemy activity was recorded, it was anticipated a threat to the same would serve a number of useful purposes. All evidence so far received shows that the whole operation went according to plan and was an unqualified success. Enemy radar stations plotted the formation, as it was anticipated they would; and enemy controllers, deceived by the spoof, initiated fighter action in accordance with our purpose.

The Gremlins fooled the Germans once more!

The mission of 30/31 October had seven 36BS Liberators dispatched. All completed their mission, jamming from 2005 hours to 2205 hours. Aircraft in three northern positions on return faced possible collision because they were at conflicting altitude with the returning RAF Bomber stream at 5030N – 0400E. The screen was over the continent in support of Bomber Command's attack on Cologne.

Pilot Captain Dick Sackett remembered such hazardous incidents – near misses when flying his Liberator nicknamed *Ramp Rooster*:

> This operation ahead of the RAF was with no lights whatever. Nobody used any navigation lights of any kind. Of course, you were always ahead of the RAF bomber stream. You always started the return about the time they were nearing the target, which meant you would have to turn around and head back westward toward the base and all these aircraft are coming from all over England at various altitudes from 5000 anywhere up to 15,000 or 18,000, all

headed in the opposite direction. With no lights it furnished a lot of thrills, scary thrills many many times. Coming back west there always seemed to be a light side to the sky and you would see shapes, movement in front of you, and you had to take evasive action quite a few times. It generated what the pilots and the airmen called a 'pucker party'. It was pretty scary. Also at night you kept advising or reminding all your crew members to keep their eyes open for aircraft because it would be a shadowy apparition appearing in front of you. Many times you'd be flying along smoothly, climbing or flying level when all of a sudden the airplane would just bounce and you knew you had just run through somebody's propwash and nobody had called the sighting of an aircraft because it was so dark, so pitch black all the time. It was pretty hairy a lot of times.

In his diary, Iredell Hutton, Tail Gunner in *The JIGS UP* also wrote of the same hazard and his good luck on this mission:

Tonight we had another mission. This time it was along the battle-line in France. The moon was really beautiful. It was so peaceful riding up there among the clouds. The RAF tonight struck at Cologne and Berlin. Can't see how in the heck there is anything left of Cologne. On our way back some RAF planes came flying in at our altitude. We had to dodge to keep from hitting several of them. One came so close that Mac [pilot] told us to shoot them. Not one of us fired a shot.

The Squadron achieved great acclaim for a successful *spoof* mission the following month.

On the night of 9/10 November the Squadron had seven B24s dispatched, all completing their assigned mission. The RAF main attack included a small number of RAF Mosquito aircraft on miscellaneous targets in Germany. The results indicated the enemy reacted in considerable strength to the *spoof* WINDOW force that was put up along with the screen. No Bomber Command aircraft were reported missing. Sadly though, the 36th experienced its first loss of airmen and aircraft when Lt Joseph Hornsby's crew in their B24 #42-51226, R4-L were hit by flak while returning to base. Lt. Hornsby ordered his crew to jump, but for unknown reason three airmen failed to parachute and were killed when their bomber plowed into a field in Boucly, France.

Radio operator for the crew, Sgt Joe Danahy, spoke about the crash of his B24 nicknamed: *I Walk Alone*:

Lord God in the mountains, well the thing, it was a miserable airplane. This plane, it was a real loser. We took off about two-thirty in the morning. The plane caught fire, number three engine probably, and we of course had no extinguishers or anything like that. He [Hornsby] tried a shallow dive ... tried to blow it out. That didn't do any good. He told me to send an SOS. They had this big liaison transmitter, it was under the table in my little compartment – a big transmitter. I reached down and turned the switch on the light over the table – kind of a spotlight to see by. It just went dim and went out.

The propeller governors were electric on those planes as opposed to hydraulic on a B17. So the electric system failed for some reason and the other engines ran away. They had no control over them. They were just roaring out of control. I remember seeing the two of them [Hornsby, the pilot and Robert Casper, co-pilot] on the controls. They were wrestling that plane around trying to keep it flying. He [Hornsby] sent me back to the Waist. Ray Mears was back there. He was a Waist Gunner, my assistant radio man. I remember checking him out to make sure his leg straps were alright. I got the trap door open back in the Waist. I went out the trap door. He should have come right along too, but he never did. We assumed he went forward because his buddy [Frank] Bartho, was up in the nose with Fred Grey, the Navigator. He evidently wanted to see if his buddy was alright or something, (a real fatal mistake to do that). Hornsby hung on to the controls. Casper went out. When Hornsby thought and hoped everybody was out of there, he let go of things, headed for the bomb bay and jumped out. His chute opened and hit him on the chin. It kind of knocked him out for a minute. He landed alright. There were still three fellows on the plane. I think they were all up in the nose by that time. Mears, no doubt about it, he went up front to see what was what with his pal Bartho.

I tried to get back in the plane. You were supposed to squat down and kind of roll out if you were going to jump. So I just sat on the edge and dangled my legs and [I] went out and hung by my hands and changed my mind. I couldn't chin myself back in, so I had to let go! The real hero, the real heroic type action. Oh Jesus, it was a bad time.

Later, however, for this mission special commendations were received from General Jimmy Doolittle and Air Vice Marshal Addison for the activities this night. Gen. Doolittle's commendation letter read:

> Jamming, screening and diversionary efforts of the 36th Bomb Squadron have contributed greatly to the effect of RAF bombing efforts. [The] Mission of 9/10 November was one of the most effective in confusing the German Air Force and causing them to assemble in great haste to intercept the bomber stream which was not there, and reflects great credit to the Command and the individuals concerned.

The special congratulation to the Squadron from the Air Officer Commanding RAF 100 Group, Air Vice Marshal Addison stated:

> The results of last night's *spoof* operation were most gratifying. Our aim was amply achieved in that the enemy was induced to react in a very big way indeed; first in the *spoofed* – the threatened area, until he eventually became aware he was being *spoofed* after the WINDOWers returned, and then in the Ruhr area when he believed a real raid was to follow the *spoof*. I know how difficult were the conditions last night, and how these were aggravated by last minute changes in the program. The latter, however, were made to take advantage of the best possible weather conditions on a bad night as revealed by weather reports. I congratulate all crews who took part in this difficult operation. Their determination enabled the group to score a very distinct success. Well done.

Dr. R. V. Jones book '*Most Secret War*' adds:

> Besides providing diversions, *spoof* raids could be used to get German night fighters up, and so tire them on nights when we were making no major raids. On 9/10 November, although the Germans had originally thought that bad weather would prevent us operating,

they were deceived into treating a *spoof* raid on Mannheim as a major one, and when they had unraveled the deception, they further deceived themselves by concluding that it must be a prelude to a major raid. As a result, aircraft of six Gruppen were airborne for two and a half hours.

Five nights later tragedy again struck the Squadron when two airmen of Lt Norman Landberg's crew were killed. Their B24 Liberator #42-51219, R4-L suffered instrument failure and crashed in dense fog on take-off from Cheddington. The crash killed Lt Walter S. Lamson, the Navigator and Pfc. Leonard L. Smith, a Gunner. Another Gunner for the crew, Sgt Lester Jones suffered a fractured leg. All other crew members survived. Pilot Landberg remembered the crash very distinctly:

Oh, I can picture it very clearly. The plane had been redlined that afternoon, had flown on a mission and the crew chief told me they had repaired the vacuum system on number two engine. That was the inboard engine next to the pilot. The units were operated either on number two engine or number three, but number two was considered primary. The vacuum system operated all the flight instruments, the artificial horizon, the needle and other pieces of equipment. I took off about three to four minutes before midnight. We took off in absolutely zero-zero [ceiling zero, visibility zero or worst weather] conditions.

Landberg continued:

The plane had been cleared to fly a second mission the same day and I was flying that second mission. I just started to get airborne, my crew chief used to squat between myself and Lloyd Sanderlin, the co-pilot. He used to be on one knee, and on take-off, especially on instrument take-off; with a flashlight in the event we lost our instrument lights, because in the B24 at that point in time they were not backlit lights, they were reflective lights. We had little spotlights that would hit the radium dials, so in the event that the little spotlights went out he would have the flashlight and we would be able to see the instruments. I became airborne and my instruments tumbled, which means the vacuum system became defective again. At the same time, all the lights went out and I had no contact, no vision at all of the instrument panel. The crew chief in his zeal to see that I could see the instruments hit me right in the eyes with the beam of the flashlight and I was completely blinded, and at that time my left wing caught [the ground effects] and we started to tumble. How anybody ever walked out of that I'll never know. I literally unsnapped my safety belt and stepped out on the ground. There was no aircraft left around me. I had a bruised knee but lost my Navigator, Walter Lamson and [Gunner] Leonard Smith. I lost those two men. Sanderlin, I was able to drag him out. The aircraft never burst into flames even though gasoline was spewing out all over the place.

Beginning on 25 November 1944, night operations with the Royal Air Force were scaled back, with RAF 100 Group's 199 and 171 Squadrons taking their place. Greater support was now given to the 8th Air Force each morning on daylight penetration raids. The 36th was now charged to provide a VHF radio screen. This screen was different to the RAF screen in that it attempted to deny the enemy the ability to listen in on 8AF radio communications during the assembly of the bomb divisions. It had been learned from captured enemy signal documents that the Germans had secured a great amount of valuable information from monitoring VHF radio transmissions of 8AF aircraft while they were assembling. MANDREL equipment was used for this VHF screen along with a new jammer named DINA.

The 36BS employed a new *spoof* at this time. Special operations, using a prepared dialogue to simulate bomb division assembly, were employed on days when there were no bombing operations. This *spoof* had airmen of the 36th read from a prepared script over the VHF radio channels to simulate Bomb Group assembly. More operations of this type were later used in December on missions during the time of the Battle of the Bulge and on days when the rest of the 8AF did not fly. The intent of these efforts was to further extend and waste the enemy's valuable resources.

Sadly, the aftermath of the VHF screening mission of 19 December proved fatal for eight of ten men in Lt. Harold Boehm's crew. For the mission, seven Squadron Liberators provided a VHF screen in support of 8AF bombing operations. After completing the mission, foul weather at Cheddington prevented the B24s from landing at home base, so all seven aircraft were diverted to Manston airfield on the south-east coast of England. Safe at Manston, the seven crews and their aircraft had a three-day layover waiting for the weather at Cheddington to improve. On the afternoon of 22 December the crews were given the 'all clear' to return. However, the weather at home base closed in for a second time and the seven B24s were diverted again, this time to Atcham airfield 100 miles northwest of Cheddington. There, four of the Liberators were able to land before that field also closed in. One of the lucky B24s that landed included the McCrory crew and Iredell Hutton. As fate would have it, on this occasion they were fortunately not in their regular B24 – *The JIGS UP*.

The three remaining Squadron B24s were diverted once more, this time ninety miles further northwest to Valley airfield in Wales. At Valley it was now dark. The three remaining Squadron Liberators found their fuel tanks dangerously low and the Valley weather deteriorating. Lt Harold Boehm and crew were not in their regular ship nicknamed *Beast of Bourbon* but in *The JIGS UP* and when over Atcham *The JIGS UP* had lost its GEE box – its primary navigation equipment. This left Lt Boehm's crew unsure of their exact position. Adding to his troubles, Lt Boehm found he could no longer communicate with Valley Control Tower, so messages were relayed through another Squadron aircraft. Soon *The JIGS UP* ran out of gas in two engines. Lt Boehm instructed his crew to get ready to parachute. Unknown to the pilot was that part of his holding pattern was over the Irish Sea, and when the men jumped they did so without lifejackets and rafts. Only Lt Boehm and his co-pilot Lt Donald Burch parachuted to safety, landing on the shore. The other eight men of Lt Boehm's crew fell to the frigid Irish Sea and were never found. The plane crashed and exploded on Mt Holyhead, not far from the water's edge.

Lt Ralph Angstadt, the pilot who was there in the B24, #42-50844, R4-I nicknamed, *Miss-B-Haven*, painfully remembered that fateful night:

The GEE box got us to Valley. This was after flying a mission, being diverted from our own field; taking off again to come back to our field, being diverted again, being sent up to Valley. Valley did have the low frequency navigational aid, but they wouldn't give us the frequency. So we couldn't orient ourselves. It was a foggy night. I think the ceiling level was somewhere around 900 feet. The hills up there, some of them are higher. I remember flying around that after-noon, we almost landed up on a hill, trying to keep contact with the ground and trying to find ourselves. We were at the end of our gas tank. They [Valley Flight Control] wouldn't give us the [airfield

landing beacon] frequency. They wouldn't broadcast it in the clear. No German aircraft had been over the place in a year or so, nevertheless they wouldn't give the information out in the clear. So, we had to do it. They fired flares up from the field. We could actually see, clouds lighted up where the flares were. We circled the flares losing altitude. We were told that we could come on in and land as soon as we saw the field and were in contact. I can still remember. It was a very emotional time.

Angstadt continued:

As we broke out of the overcast we were headed in almost the exact opposite of the landing direction and at the bottom of the clouds. The runway was practically beneath us. We had to make really more than a one-eighty. We had to turn to the right a little bit in order to make the one-eighty back onto the field. We made a very tight turn. We both knew we were sucking fumes. There was no second shot at a landing. As we got off to the right a little bit, we of course lost sight of the runway. But then, as we turned back to the left, we could see the runway again. We were losing altitude. We really wrestled that airplane around. I can remember, in order to line up the airplane, we both got on the rudder and just kind of bowed the airplane around.

When we landed I don't think we had enough gas in the airplane to taxi us. When we got into the operations office we found out that Boehm had crashed. We were told that he bailed out his crew, so spent most of the night looking for them. What we were further told was that the way they had tracked the aircraft was such that he was mostly over water when the crew was bailing out. When the last two or three crew members bailed out, they were actually coming over a neck of land before it went into water again. I think the airplane was finally found in water. Two of the crew members managed to parachute onto land. I think they were both picked up.

One of the two *Jigs Up* survivors, Lt Donald Burch, co-pilot for the Lt Boehm crew, would forever remember this tragic event:

We had been on a flight which went over the Continent to a town in the southern part of Germany. We were ahead of the bombing formation. That was the furthest we ever flew over the Continent, the deepest. We went in, came around and came back according to the Flight Plan. It was the first time we ever ran into any flak. It wasn't too bad really. We came back and our field was socked in. We had to land at a field [Manston] on the southern coast of England. We were socked in to that field. We were lucky to get into it. Finally, the home base called and told us we could take off and come on up and land.

So we took off and on the way up to our base it socked in again. We couldn't land and they told us to keep on going. We had to go up to Wales. We couldn't get in there and that was mountainous country. On the way up we lost an engine. We started to run out of gas. We ended up losing two engines and we lost our radar and radio on the way up.

Our Navigator [Lt William Lehner] did a fantastic job. He brought us in over the base. He said: '*Fly two minutes in this direction and make a hundred and eighty degree turn and come around and you'll be right over the base*', and I think we were. He told us just by wind information he accumulated on the way up there, wind speed, direction and all. We could see once in a while a break in the clouds and mountains and some of the planes were lucky to get in there. I remember breaking through clouds and seeing the base for just a few seconds. Then we were in the soup again. The planes were having a hell of a time getting in there. I don't know how they did it, but they did. We never made it. We lost a second engine and the pilot gave the warning signal to get ready to bail out. Then he gave the final signal to bail out. I looked back in through the Waist and the rest of the crew apparently didn't wait. They bailed out, I think, on the first signal because everybody was gone when I looked back. Then I went. As I broke through the clouds I could see the ocean on the one side of me, but I was over land ... barely. I landed in a farmer's field. The other guys must have gone into the water and they never found them. My pilot was the last one to leave. We were the only ones to survive that thing.

December and into the new year, January 1945, brought continued VHF jamming screens for the 8AF as operations in support of the RAF ended on 3 January. Another new and special jamming operation began during this time. These operations involved an electronic jammer nicknamed JACKAL. JACKAL jammers were designed for disrupting German tank communications. These operations commenced during the time of the Battle of the Bulge. An example of the JACKAL mission from the Squadron File stated:

> On the 2nd, 5th and 7th of January, JACKAL or tank-jamming missions, were flown over the enemy salient in the Ardennes area in Belgium. Two or three aircraft equipped with JACKAL equipment and one equipped with Ferret or search receiver equipment with a German speaking operator was dispatched on these dates. On one occasion, on 7 January mission, a considerable amount of enemy radio traffic was monitored. A study of the Special Operator's Log indicates the jamming equipment disrupted the enemy's tank communication system to a considerable degree.

Once more, the Gremlins succeeded!

During the third week of January, S/Sgt Herman J. Wolters, a Radio Operator working on a special project on detached service from the Squadron, died as a result of electrical shock. This terrible loss of life occurred when the airman was performing his duties at Namur, Belgium on 19 January. No other details about his death are known.

In February, the 36BS continued to provide its VHF screen for 8AF heavy bombardment operations. This was the only type of operation the Squadron employed during the month. Then on 5 February the Squadron suffered its greatest single loss when Lt John H. McKibben and his entire crew of ten failed to return from their assigned mission. Lt McKibben and crew were flying in B24 aircraft #42-51239 R4-C, nicknamed *The Uninvited*. When nothing was heard from the aircraft it was presumed to have crashed in the North Sea due to icing conditions with all crew members lost.

Pilot Lt Royce Kittle especially remembered the loss of Lt. McKibben's crew and for good reason:

> Gaylord Moulton [Lt. McKibben's co-pilot] told me one day that he wanted me to trade co-pilots. He and I were very good friends and he wanted to co-pilot my plane instead. I said: "*Well, you've put me on the spot. I don't feel like I can do that.*" We dropped it there. They [Lt. McKibben's crew] didn't come back and that bothered me ever

since. If I had traded co-pilots, my co-pilot would have been the one killed.

Two weeks later tragedy again struck the Squadron. On 19 February, B24 Liberator #42-50485, R4-H, nicknamed *Beast of Bourbon* piloted by Lt Louis McCarthy and crew crashed on take-off from Cheddington. At the time, Lt McCarthy was giving Lt Victor E. Pregeant III, a new pilot to the Squadron; a check-ride for an operational mission. The crash was attributed to instrument failure. Of the ten crew members aboard, three were killed, two were moderately injured, and five slightly injured. The aircraft with its flamboyant nose art was a total loss.

Lt Louis McCarthy, the senior pilot giving Lt Victor Pregeant the check-ride, spoke of the crash of the *Beast*:

It was a terrible morning. Everything happened so fast. The fog was right down to the tops of the grass. They lined us up on the runway with flashlights. We should never have been allowed to take off. They pushed it and why they did I don't know. The plane just gave out on take-off. There was no power on any of the engines for some reason and that's when we hit. It was a terrible foggy morning. The thing caught fire. I don't know whether gasoline spilled on the hot engines or what. We had to duck because all the ammunition started going off. We got everybody out, including the ones who got killed. I remember looking out through the top of the thing and counting the yellow May Wests, counting numbers to make sure everybody was out. We should never have been sent out that morning, it was so bad.

On 1 February, S/Sgt Hutton having finally completed all of his missions – fifty-four in all, wrote in his diary:

Since writing last, we have completed our tour of duty. I'm glad in some ways that I didn't keep a diary from day to day after we started flying with the 8th Air Force, because there are a lot of things I don't wish to recall. I've seen ships going down in flames, blow up right beside us with none of the crews coming out. Several friends of mine I made over here have gone down. Some have come back, others haven't. Our plane, *The Jigs Up* went down. The reason being there wasn't enough gas to get it to another base. It couldn't return to ours because it was closed in, as it has been ever since we moved here.

On 27 and 28 February the Squadron loaded up their aircraft along with eighty trucks from the 2nd Strategic Air Depot and moved from Cheddington to AAF Station 102 at Alconbury. It has been noted that the air base at Cheddington was attacked by German aircraft during the time of the Squadron move. Station Headquarters Adjutant, Sergeant-Major Henry Woolf wrote of this time:

> Early in 1945, no German planes having been in the area for a good while, our Flight Control men put the airfield lights on one night as our planes were returning from the Continent. There was a sudden burst of gunfire from German planes trailing the bombers home; but there were no casualties. We all gave the Flight Control men a good ribbing.

Missions in March continued to provide radio and radar countermeasures for 8AF bombardment operations. Squadron operations were increased during the month as compared with February. The VHF screen was put up on twenty-seven days out of thirty-one. On the date of the 12th Army Group's crossing of the Rhine, 24 March, the screen was flown for both a morning and an afternoon bombing attack. On this screening mission, 36BS aircraft orbited over fixed coordinates over the North Sea. The B24s were equipped with the special ORVIL VHF jammers. From data obtained by search operators on the B24 search missions, coverage of the screen appeared to be good.

Frequency search operations were also conducted from specially equipped P-38 aircraft on six days during March. The modified P-38 Lightnings or F5s called 'Droop Snoots' were placed on detached service from Lt Col Elliott Roosevelt's 7th Photo Reconnaissance Group. Now aiding the 36BS, they flew a number of frequency search missions against the enemy early warning radar system by patrolling the coast from Dunkirk to Denmark and into the Ruhr Valley. The purpose of these searches was to investigate German radar in Holland and also along the Front battle lines.

On 20 March B24 Liberator #42-50844, R4-I nicknamed *Miss-B-Haven*, with Lt William Sweeney as pilot crashed on take-off for an operational mission. All crew members escaped serious injury, although the aircraft was a total loss. Sgt Francis Preimesberger, Flight Engineer and Gunner for the crew, spoke of the crash:

> We crashed on take-off on one of our missions. The airplane just seemed to mush in. We couldn't kick extra power to it. She just wouldn't get off the runway very far. There was a fire in the engine, but they claim that was from dragging along the ground – a friction fire. I think the engine itself must have been defective and not producing enough power. That might be one reason it crashed rather than a friction fire from running down the runway because, if there was a fire in the engine while taking off, well, it would lose power and naturally couldn't get off. We all got out all right. We washed it out. It never flew again.

It could be said that Sgt Preimesberger was a hero that day. Radio Operator Sgt Dick Mulligan saw his buddy Preimesberger come to the rescue of the men up front. He spoke of what he saw:

> We cracked up and it did catch on fire. Preimesberger was the guy who was the first one out. He stood on that wing and got us all out of there or we would have been gone. The rest of the plane was really a total loss. The guys came out of the back. They got out pretty good. But in the front which was the pilot, the co-pilot, the navigator, and me, all of us had to get out. We had all of our gear on, our flight jackets and everything. He was the guy that stood up there and got us all out of there. Otherwise, we wouldn't have been able to get out.

All Squadron operations ceased by April 30, 1945 – the day Adolph Hitler committed suicide. All totaled, there were 1166 effective sorties flown on 220 missions during the life of this very unique outfit. The 36th Bomb Squadron lost twenty-seven airmen and six B24 Liberators in service with the RAF and the Mighty Eighth.

After VE-Day, on 5 June 1945, a Commendation to the Squadron came down from Headquarters' 8th Air Force. It read in part:

> The advance of the Allied Ground Forces has exposed the effectiveness of air bombardment activities in the destruction of the fighting

potentialities of our enemy. The special activities conducted by the 36th Bombardment Squadron (RCM) cannot be over-emphasized in the contribution of the unit to the striking power of this Air Force.

Yours was the assignment of catching the enemy at his own game, and in effectively accomplishing this task, the whole nature and tactics of your missions changed as enemy scientists devised methods of overcoming our countermeasures. The complexity of your work included jamming of enemy radar, screening of our bomber VHF channels while bombers were assembling, carrying out spoof raids, jamming enemy tank communications, and performing special electronic search missions as directed by this Headquarters. The material advantage of these operations may never be adequately assessed and it is impossible to fully evaluate the number of aircrews, as well as bomber and fighter aircraft, saved when enemy fighters discovered too late the essential interception data.

After VE-Day how did the men of the 36th feel about the part they played in the air war over Europe?

With most mission results unknown to the men it's impossible to know for sure. The Squadron did suffer losses. However, one airman, Nose Gunner S/Sgt Richard Catt, in considering the real costs, the American sacrifices, looked at it this way:

It's a thing that you just took it like they say – you took it one day at a time. It's one of those things, you go up there and you sweat it out and hope that the next one doesn't get you, but it got a lot of guys you know. There were a lot of losses. It was very depressing at the time because of so many. It seemed like we had an endless supply of people and they just kept putting planes up.

For scientists and engineers of ABL Division 15, what were their sentiments at this time?

George Klemm, Head of the Antennae Group for ABL-15 summed it up this way:

They [the Germans] sat on the Continent side and we [ABL-15] sat on the island side and tried to figure out what the other was doing. How closely we were followed or we were leading the Germans in the development of radar and radar countermeasures during World War Two, was a hairbreadth difference most of the time. It was rather interesting. We came up with some funny ideas at times. You know, this war was won not by us who were tearing our hair out ... but by the fellows who fought it.

So what was the significance of these efforts?

It is difficult to calculate. However, the renowned electronic warfare historian Dr Alfred Price, author of 'The History of U.S. Electronic Warfare' has written:

Taking conservative estimates, radio countermeasures probably saved about 600 Air Force heavy bombers during operations over Europe.

That amounts to about 6,000 airmen lives, as there were generally about ten men in each heavy bomber aircraft.

No other Squadron in the 8th Air Force carried such a variety of electronic warfare equipment or flew such special operations. Yes, this Squadron was most extraordinary. Its men performed their duties most admirably and were truly pioneers in electronic warfare. Because of its significant value, similar support functions continue in the United States Air Force today as the 36th Electronic Warfare Squadron. No, the 36th Bomb Squadron was not really a Bomb Squadron; however, by deception they did save many Allied lives.

For further reading and information about World War Two's 36th Bomb Squadron Gremlins see the book 'Squadron of Deception' by Stephen Hutton, website (www.36rcm.com).

CHAPTER 3
Another Trip to 'Flak Alley'

by

Jack Hope: Tail Gunner
Lt Brookshire's Crew, USAAF

Stephen Hutton is a remarkable man in having the ability to research U.S Air Force records of the 803rd and 36th Bomb Squadron after the secrecy was lifted following World War Two. I was honored to know his father, a Tail Gunner on our B24s in my Squadron. In fact, we returned to the USA together on Dutch ship 'New Amsterdam' following our duty with the 36th Bomb Squadron. I am honored to have my 'Flak Alley' account following Stephen Hutton's chapter.

I called the area along the Rhine River in Western Germany 'Flak Alley'. I suppose other air crew members, flying at different times during the war gave that same name to other areas.

Certainly there were specific places where heavy concentrations of German anti-aircraft artillery fire could always be expected. Another area that I also thought was of special intensity was the Zuider Zee and the West Frisian Islands of The Netherlands. It seemed that every time we were there on either night or day missions, we were greeted with intense fire.

One special day, our crew was chosen for a special mission in the 'Alley'.

Early one morning, we were called to a Briefing. At the very outset, it was obvious we were in for something different. In the first place, the fog was so thick it was not easy to find our way to the chow hall where we enjoyed a breakfast of fried cold storage eggs, a treat even though they had a special taste not known to fresh ones. We wondered why we were the only crew present.

From there we made our way to the Briefing room. As we entered, we thought we must be early because there were so few people around. When we noticed our Squadron Commander, Lt Col Robert F. Hambaugh accompanied by a full Colonel, we began to get the idea we were in for something special. As Briefing got under way, we were told we would be flying a specific course along 'Flak Alley' in the southern part of Germany.

The Operations Officer, Captain R. G. Stutzman, told us we would be making an instrument take-off under zero-zero (no ceiling – no forward visibility) conditions. However, in order to provide our pilots with a reference point, a very high intensity flare would be positioned part way down the runway as a reference point to stay aligned with the runway. I believe that if we had been given a choice at that point, I would have opted out of making the trip. No such offer was made.

To make it more uninviting, the Intelligence Officer told us that each one of us would be issued an 'Escape and Evasion Kit'. He explained we had about a fifty-fifty chance of returning from this mission in our airplane. That is, we would be susceptible to being shot down, but these marvelous kits would provide us with equipment needed to evade the German Army, Heinrich Himmler's SS Troops, local cops, and German citizens in case we hadn't yet got the full picture. Even before further explanation, I had my doubts. However, I was quite impressed with the kits! They had a lot of good stuff packed into a small space. As I recall they had tricky little things like:

a) An official looking German National Identification Card, with our photograph in civilian clothes.

b) Maps of possible escape routes made of rice paper so we could eat them in case we were caught.

c) A 'sewing kit' that included a common looking sewing needle that was magnetized and coated, so when carefully placed in a cup of water it would float and the point of the needle would swing to the North. This would turn that innocent looking item into an important tool that could help us avoid Berlin when we were hoping for Madrid.

d) Some common looking shirt buttons with rounded surfaces on the inside position. One had a very small dot in the edge of the outer surface. When one was placed face down and the other balanced on it face up, the little dot would swing to the North. Another shot at Madrid or Geneva!

e) Some of the current version of German food ration stamps.

f) Some German folding money.

g) Some high energy pills that could give new strength when it was thought to be all gone.

One thing that I thought lacking was our inability to speak the German language. About the only words I knew were '*Guten Morgen*', '*verboten*', and '*Heil Hitler*'. Somehow I thought this would not be enough if I happened to need to cross a canal bridge guarded by a German soldier. As a personal back up, I usually wore a thin handle and long bladed very sharp knife strapped to the calf of my right leg and a small roll of wire in my back pocket. These were to be used as weapons in case I could wait until dark and have the chance to sneak up on a guard from the rear and put him out of commission. The wire could be used to pull around the neck tightly and giving a couple of twists, let it do its job. While all of these things were welcome, I was holding on to the thought that perhaps, instead of bailing out, we could limp across the line into Switzerland, a neutral country where we would be safe.

Then, during Briefing, the strangest fact of all was revealed. We were introduced to Colonel A. F. Sullivan, Director of Communications of the 8th Air Force with the news that he would ride along with us on the trip.

After briefing, the fog was so thick we had difficulty finding our way to our airplane. After we went through our habit of thoroughly checking out the airplane to make sure everything was in place and ready for service, our pilots and engineer started the unbelievable task of taxiing the airplane to the take-off position on the runway.

Our ground crew members, both walking and in a Jeep, used flashlights to follow closely the center line of the taxiways all the way to the take-off position. Our pilots and engineer had the difficult task of following the Jeep with the airplane going under its own power. At times people on the ground would need to stop us to be sure that they were on the right path.

After arriving at the runway, the next requirement was to be sure the airplane was in the very center, nose pointed exactly down the center line of the runway. Runways had small blue lights along each side, placed precisely parallel to each other approximately ten to twenty feet apart. Sergeant Hulne would look out of a hatch in the ceiling of the flight deck and direct the pilot to maneuver the airplane so that the wing tip on each side of the airplane would align with the corresponding blue light. If this was done *perfectly*, the airplane would be pointing exactly down the runway. Also the pilot set his directional gyroscope instrument in the compass direction of the runway.

This is a reasonable portrayal of the take-off *but is from memory after many years after the fact*. Since Lt Brookshire was the person most responsible for this outstanding feat of flying, I insert his remembrance of the event:

One day the Colonel in charge of Communications for the Eighth Air Force showed up at our field. He apparently had a very important mission. As usual my CO asked me to fly it. Our field was absolutely socked in when it came time to take off. The fog was so thick they had to light a brilliant flare a short way down the runway in order for me to get lined up for an instrument take-off. The flare burned out and we couldn't see it! About that time my CO 'jeeped' out to my plane, climbing aboard to tell me he would never ask a man to take off in such conditions. Instrument take-offs were rarely done in those days and only on solo missions by experienced pilots. To do it, the plane had to be lined up with the runway at the start because once the plane started moving, the pilot couldn't see out his windshield. The fog became as dense as a white sheet. Instead of calling it off, I said that if the Colonel still wanted to go, I would take him. I was mad at him for not calling off the mission before this. He must not have had much flight experience, because he wanted the mission to continue.

Since the flare had not been enough, I tried to imagine where the runway was by positioning the plane midway between a blue runway light under my right wing and one under my left wing. I was close to being right. I tried a short field take-off and, just as we got up to 100 mph, I felt my left wheel leave the asphalt. It was too slow to take off and too fast to stop. I knew one of the high railroad embankments common in England was looming ahead. I hit the lever to raise my wheels and knocked the safety stops off the superchargers in order to get an emergency surge of power to the engines, gently milking the plane into the air. But it wasn't enough. I saw the mailman on the sidewalk turning into the walk to my mother's house in Joplin. He rang the doorbell and gave her a letter when she opened the screen door. Looking over her shoulder, I could read the words, 'We regret to inform you ....' That vision covered at least a minute, but took only a second of real time! At that moment I felt a little bump. Men on the ground watching us later told me that when we came down, we hit on a narrow taxi strip leading to the runway. My wheels had unlocked but not started to retract and we got enough bounce to make it into the air again. There would not have been any bounce had we hit the muddy field instead of the asphalt strip. The timing was too exquisite for human capabilities. Somehow we cleared the railroad embankment and when we got to 300 feet altitude, my legs started shaking so hard I couldn't push the rudder bars. My co-pilot, good ole loyal Bob, had sat there through it all, with nothing he could do and not really knowing how close we had come. I told him: 'You've got it!' He flew the ship until I got myself together. Later, I received a letter of commendation, a yellow sheet of paper, from Headquarters, Eighth Air Force, for this mission. As far as I know the Colonel never got off the bench behind my seat. I heard that he received the Distinguished Flying Cross. [15]

It is obvious from his remarks here and at other times that Lt Brookshire did not think much of Colonel Sullivan. I remember the Colonel flying with us on at least two more missions, all considered special activities for our Squadron. On each, our crew was selected to be the only one to fly. On all these missions, I was told that Colonel Sullivan lay on a couch that was a part of the flight deck of our airplane. Our flight deck crew said that on each of these trips, as soon as we reached altitude and leveled out, Colonel Sullivan would stretch out on the couch and read comic books. Only on occasion, especially when the flak was intense, would he raise up and peer out of a small window above the couch.

On return from one such mission I got up enough nerve to question the Colonel on his actions. I said something like: 'Colonel, please do not be offended, but I am curious as to why you come to Cheddington to fly these missions that seem to be so life threatening, but you seem to have no part of crew participation or responsibilities.' He replied that it was his difficult duty to order these missions. He said in his entire career he vowed he would not order anyone to do something he would not do himself. He considered these missions to be very important to the war effort. Our crew had the reputation within our Squadron to be the best qualified to carry them out. The only way he could prove to himself he was willing to take the risk along with us was to come down and go along. I told him that I deeply appreciated his leadership and bravery. I said that since knowing his feelings, I would be honored to fly with him anytime.

The following is a copy of Colonel Sullivan's farewell letter to the 36th Bomb Squadron:

HEADQUARTERS EIGHTH AIR FORCE

Office of the Director of Communications
APO 634

31 December 1944
SUBJECT: New Year Greetings.
TO : Commanding Officer, 36th Bomb Squadron (RCM),
AAF 113, APO637

I wish to extend to the Officers and Enlisted Men of the 36th Bomb Squadron my heartiest greetings for the New Year, and my sincere thanks for the excellent and efficient manner in which they have carried out their various duties during the old year.

It is with deep regret that I leave the Eighth Air Force, and it is with deeper regret still, that I am forced by turn of war to separate from the 36th Bomb Squadron.

During the past year, we have seen a great Air Force become greater and each and every member of the 36th Bomb Squadron has contributed his part to that enviable achievement.

I am proud of you and now on taking leave of you, I wish to express my heartfelt gratefulness to you all for the part you have so gallantly and unselfishly played in this world struggle for righteousness and justice.

(Signed)
A. F. SULLIVAN
Colonel, Signal Corps
Director of Communications [16]

I am extremely proud of the role of Lieutenants Brookshire and Young in demonstrating the character, skill, stamina, brilliance, and determination to do their parts in bringing an end to the war.

It has been estimated that the activities of the 36th Bomb Squadron saved the lives of 6,000 Allied airmen. For me, that is a great reward for the inconveniences I endured. However, the *rewards* for our efforts were even higher. There is no way to clearly estimate the number of allied *ground troop* lives saved by our actions against the German Army. During the closing days of the war, we flew many missions screening our bombers from German resistance against the 8th and 9th Air Forces bombing of highways, railroads, canals and bridges to hinder the flow of German soldiers and equipment into the Battle of the Bulge and the general progress of Allied Armies in the occupation of German territory.

I had the greatest respect and confidence in both our pilots. I was honored and blessed to have such men as our leaders. They were unusually well qualified and successful in their duties. They were legends in our Squadron. I once received an email from one of the original enlisted men assigned to the 803rd Bomb Squadron (Provisional), the 'Mother' unit of the 36th Bomb Squadron. He wrote: *'I know that the Brookshire crew was held in high esteem by the Squadron.'*

Being a member of the crew paid off for me one time. The winter that we were there was proclaimed *'the worst in thirty-five years'*. Our huts were heated by coke burning stoves, but we were rationed – the coke to be burned, but not enough to keep the hut warm. I often slept in my sheepskin high-altitude flying clothing to keep warm. One day I became upset by being cold all the time, so I went to the Orderly Room to complain. I walked in and confronted our First Sergeant. I am sure my irritation showed through in my choice and manner of words. Suddenly our Squadron Adjutant came out of a back room and said to the First Sergeant: *'Take that man's Liberty Pass!'* Then he looked up at me and said: *'I am not doing this because you are complaining about the coke. I am doing it because you are wearing a hat in the Orderly Room'*. It is true that I was wearing a heavy wool stocking cap. I apologized and removed it. I said I wore it all the time in my hut as well as outside because it was always cold in the hut as it was outside, so had forgotten it was on my head. He then asked me: *'Whose crew are you on?'* I answered: *'I am Lt Brookshire's Tail Gunner, Sir.'* He turned to the First Sergeant and said: *'Give him back his card'* and turned and disappeared through a door.

I believe that Lt Brookshire had considerable experience in flying B-24 Liberators prior to joining us at Pueblo, Colorado and becoming our combat crew pilot. He told me that, after completion of flying school and check out in B-24s, he was retained for a considerable period of time to help teach other B-24 pilots the techniques of instrument flying. I know from experience he was a master at flying the airplane under extreme instrument conditions. There were times when we would return from a mission where two to six more of our airplanes were dispatched. If on returning from these missions the weather was very low and landing at our base was difficult, our aircraft controller would instruct all but our crew to form a holding pattern above our base. Lt Brookshire would be cleared to land. If he succeeded on the first pass, the other airplanes were also cleared to attempt landing.

Lt Young was a fully qualified pilot, authorized to be the command pilot of a B-24 crew. However, he did not want the *primary* responsibility for a crew and asked to be assigned as a co-pilot. This certainly was a bonus for the rest of the crew. Lt Brookshire said that much of our success and reputation was because of the expertise of Lt Young. I am sure many of the successes in recovering from close calls we had in fighting the weather and other difficulties would not have been possible without the superb qualifications of this young officer. When things got rough, he remained cool and concentrated totally on recovery from the difficulty. Although I had very deep respect and approval of Lt Brookshire as an Air Force Officer, I also had the feeling that he was 'marking time' in his military uniform, awaiting the day when he could trade it for a swank business suit and executive position to match. He was a college law student at the time of his entry into the Army. I believe he passed the Bar after return to civilian life, and reached the goals he sought. In his notes he reminisced:

> During my tour, I never got the idea that we were doing anything important for the war effort. At our debriefings, we didn't have much to say. I cannot remember ever being told that our efforts had been effective. Everyone around me was doing the same thing so there wasn't any reason to think we were something special. This was my feeling then and for more than fifty years, when, out of the blue, I was contacted by a man who was engaged in writing a history of our Squadron. His research and observations gave me, for the first time, some sense that what we did saved many English and American airmen and contributed to their successful missions. I am grateful for his input. Otherwise there would be little to show for my years in the Military. If a purpose of autobiography is to see where one has been, the war years for me were not noteworthy. A war that destroyed millions of men, women, and children, destroyed a portion of my life. These years put me on hold.

A book has been written about my 36th Bomb Squadron: '*Squadron of Deception*' by Stephen Hutton. It is described as:

> the exciting story of the Eighth Air Force's only Radar Countermeasure Squadron that flew from England ... of the men of the elite Squadron and the special operations they flew in modified B-24s to jam German radar which controlled the fighter and flak batteries.

It describes night missions with the RAF and daylight missions with the Eighth. The first jamming mission on the morning of D-day:

> ... contributed materially to the success of the landings. Later missions during the Battle of the Bulge involved trickery, ingenious deception, spoofs, and tank communications jamming.'
>
> This Squadron saved many Allied lives during World War Two. Reviewing this book confirms my memory that I lived in a small circle, spending my time with men of my crew, generally ignoring most of my fellow officers and their crews. Perhaps I didn't want to get to know them because they probably wouldn't be around long. There was not the interdependence among our crews that existed with ground troops for instance where each life depended on the others, but there was a strong bond within each crew. [17]

His words come across as being rather sorrowful to me – sorry he was forced to be involved in the Great War. He wanted to be a lawyer, not a Pilot. He wanted to help people, not kill them.

I understood that. It ought to be the dream of every young person to line out a plan to be an honest worker toward the attainment of the most good and success. He or she ought to be able to pursue that course with a dogged determination. It would be great if all could have that goal and 'run the race', to gain the prize. However, starting with the first family near the beginning of humanity, there have been those who rise up and pursue the goal of inflicting evil, greed, and dominion into the lives of others. Always there has been the insertion of the wicked and destructive desires of a Hitler, a Himmler, a Mussolini, or a Tojo to reach for the attainment of their desires, no matter how many millions must suffer and die for their dementia. But, the attempt must be made to stop them! That is where the Brookshires, the Youngs, and the Hulnes, were asked to set aside personal pursuits and reach for the universal good.

They did and they won!

CHAPTER 4
Len Bartram: 'Just a Norfolk Boy'

Len Bartram was ten years old when war broke out, born into a family living in a little village called Hindolveston in the Norfolk countryside. The village has an entry in the Domesday Book of 1085, recorded by the name *Hidolfestuna*. It is said to have been in the ownership of Bishop William, with a church, twenty cattle, two beehives and forty goats. The name derives from the Anglo-Saxon language *Hildwulfes tun*, meaning *'farmstead belonging to a man called Sword-wolf'*. Even as a young boy, Len, was already part of history and the land, interested in the changing seasons around him, curious about the way things worked. But then, at ten years old, his ordinary life was to become extraordinary, and not at all in the way expected.

He attended the village school. However, his mind was not on his lessons, but rather caught in a place not far across the fields where, from his chosen window seat, he wondered at the strange secret happenings going on. Adults didn't answer his questions. Why were adults so concerned? He loved puzzles, enthralled by secrets and mysteries. Like any child, he was curious ... curious enough to want to find out more.

At first, fields became surrounded by barbed wire and fencing. Then men and women in uniforms began appearing. The veil of secrecy deepened. But he wasn't going to be so easily shut out!

As war picked up apace, bombers could be seen taking off and landing at the newly created airfields. Len's attention focused more on what was happening outside the walls of his school than within and he was moved to the centre of the classroom; meant as a deterrent and bring his mind crashing back to earth to the lessons in hand. Instead, it only made him more determined. At the end of a long day anxiously awaiting the bell to bring an end the school day, young Len was first out the door, bouncing onto his waiting bicycle, pedalling like fury to visit local airfields within range. Pencil and paper in hand, he would jot down incoming and outgoing aircraft, talk to airmen, collect things he spied on the ground, always on the look-out for where an aircraft had crashed or clipped a wing. He stored these treasures of war in the garden shed. However, afraid of them blowing up, his mother had other ideas. It was his much prized ammunition collection one day she threw down the garden well! There would be no more ... but then young determined curious Len had other ideas.

A German bomber deposited incendiary bombs on a local farm. Len and his brother were immediately there, digging them up, adding them to their increasing collection, oblivious to the dangers, hiding them away from prying eyes of parents eager to scupper their 'finds'. Then unexpectedly, his father became Night Watchman at an airfield. He was right there beside him, eager to talk and share with people in uniform, finding out as much as he was able about what they were doing, why new airfields in that part of the world, how was it helping the war? What would happen for the future? His eagerness could not be equalled, and he became a friend to all, well known for his accumulative knowledge in the area.

Post-War, Len completed three years National Service in the RAF as an Airframe Fitter, becoming Leading Aircraftsman Len Bartram and met his future wife, Evelyn. They married at nearby St Peter-in-Park Church, Melton Constable.

He became a Queen's scholar, studying forestry in Sweden, receiving a Gold Medal from Queen Elizabeth, the Queen Mother. He went on to hold the record for the greatest number of trees planted in one day. However, if this subject was ever mentioned in his presence, a shy smile would be followed by 'It was sandy soil'.

Fifty years on, his early enthusiasm still very much to the fore; once again Len put pencil to paper, this time in a shed at the bottom of his own garden. Adding to information he'd collected as a boy, he contacted ex-servicemen and researched various Squadron histories, building up a thorough and most impressive reference library.

Now a consummate expert on local airfields, especially those to come under No. 100 (Bomber Support) Group, he gave talks across the county. Finally, after fifteen years of research, he produced seven home-spun informative booklets on Norfolk airfields encouraged and supported by his wife, bringing together the maps, drawings, notes and information he had gathered as a boy.

One day, a brother and sister came calling. Evelyn remembers that day:

Len and I first met Eileen and Martin one Thursday evening early September when they had just started to think about a Memorial for Oulton. I was at the kitchen sink washing up, it was about 7.30; a knock at the door and Martin and Eileen asked if Len Bartram lived here. They said someone from Sussex had told them the chap you want to see and talk to is Len B. Anyway, they said they wouldn't stay long, but we all got on so well they stayed until 11.15pm. We really liked them, friends from the start. Two weeks later, they came again with two of their friends. Once again, a short visit, they said. After endless cups of tea and home-made scones, it was 11.45pm before they left. We had so many happy times.

When they were not in Norfolk, they would telephone sometimes three times a week. The talk was about Oulton and a few other RAF Stations came into the conversation. They could talk for an hour on the phone. They were really lovely people and I do miss them very much. After Len died, Martin still telephoned me every week like many people. I miss that. But it was an honour to have known them and they have many who they made happy by starting the RAF 100 Group Association. We all made many friends. [18]

Eileen Boorman's husband was Stafford Sinclair of 214 Squadron, RAF 100 Group, based at Oulton. He was killed in the war. Her brother Martin Staunton was supporting her in creating a Memorial at Oulton in his memory and to all others lost in the war. However, on meeting Len Bartram, they were inspired by the thought of bringing together people Len had written about as a boy. It was to be the start of a lifelong friendship, and the beginning of something remarkable.

Eileen met her husband, Flying Officer Stafford Sinclair DFM, when he was on his first tour of Operations over Germany. In December 1944 they were married. He became a Pilot Officer. But just three short months later, on 21 March 1945, while flying from RAF Oulton over Hamburg, his aircraft was shot down. His death affected her so badly it cast a shadow over the rest of her life.

In 1991, Eileen with her brother Martin, visited Norfolk to revisit the site of the airfield from which her husband had flown. Only derelict buildings remained. It was such a sad sight. But what they saw, and talking with Len and Evelyn, inspired them to erect a Memorial at the site of Oulton airfield as well as placing a Book of Remembrance in the local church. The dedication of that Memorial in 1994 was attended by representatives of all the Commonwealth Air Forces and the American Air Force who sent a Colour Party and Escort.

This was not just a personal achievement on the part of a brother and his sister. Details of tasks carried out to protect the main RAF Main Force bomber crews remained secret until 1976. There is still much that remains secret today, locked under a 100 Year Rule. Those of RAF 100 Group who lost so many friends and comrades, as they came together for the first time since the war, expressed the view that their work and sacrifice had never been acknowledged.

So what had it all been for?

There were many disappointments and setbacks for Eileen and Martin in identifying a place willing to display wartime memorabilia in Norfolk. However, this task was finally completed in September 1997 when the City of Norwich Aviation Museum at Horsham St Faith agreed to open a room specifically for RAF 100 (BS) Group. And the pleasure and satisfaction on Eileen's face on seeing for the first time her husband's uniform in a showcase is clearly visible in a video made of the Opening.

Len's knowledge of civil and military aviation in Norfolk was encyclo-paedic. It was he and his wife Evelyn, together with Eileen and Martin; who formed what is known today as the RAF 100 Group Association, welcom-ing not only veterans who served on airfields around Norfolk, but also their families and friends, and anyone wishing to know and to understand more. It remains a thriving worldwide Association taking on more and more members, meeting at Reunions every year in Norfolk.

(Details of how to become a member can be found at the back of this book.)

It was my privilege to update Len's booklets and publish them in 2014 as a favour to his widow Evelyn, each focused on a separate airfield under RAF 100 Group in Norfolk. As a set of twelve, they include new material and photographs, their readership reaching around the world, carrying a picture of what it meant to live and work in Norfolk during the war, sharing the story of how the airfields were created. In reading them, you can almost hear Len's voice whispering beyond the horizon of this world, still no doubt keeping a watchful eye over the goings-on in his old hunting ground: Norfolk.

Len passed away in 2002. He lived and worked in Melton Constable for the Forestry Commission for fifty years, planting trees on the now redundant airfields where, years before, he'd watched bombers come and go, so many never to return. Yet his memory lives on:

Len was a much loved husband, father, grandfather and brother, a wonderful work colleague and friend, this quite remarkable man had a full rich life. Born in Gunthorpe, Len was firstly a paper boy, later a gardener and Park Keeper for the Festival of Britain, then becoming a nursery man. Len is perhaps best known as forester and planter of a quarter of a million trees, and I misquote: 'If you seek his monument, go into the Stody Estate and look around you'. He is the recipient of the Winston Churchill Memorial Trust Medal, presented to Len by the Queen Mother following his forestry journey around Sweden as a Churchill Travelling Scholar. A very knowledgeable and careful researcher with a keen eye for detail, this clever man was a keen photographer, our villages' historian, a self-taught computer-literate, introducing the villagers' Millennium video; an RAF historian; he took seven years to organise the RAF Foulsham Reunion for those scattered worldwide ... [19]

In one of Len Bartram's original booklets, he offers a special tribute to the Special Wireless Operators (S/Os) of 100 Group. The overall success of many wartime operations depended on them.

Their skill and efficiency in operating new unknown and often unreliable equipment in the confined space of an aircraft often for many hours at a time was paramount to the success of the Group. Most of these men were specially picked for the job. Some had already completed an operational tour, while others were taken straight from training schools. The need for utmost secrecy of their role was stressed to them. Extra training was given at the T.R.E or by a two or three week's course on their Squadron.

With high secrecy surrounding the Group and its activities, I often wondered why the number 100 was chosen for the Group which, in itself, seems to signify something special and out of the ordinary. The carrying of Squadron codes on aircraft was another give-away which any schoolboy would have known!

The highest number of 100 Group sorties flown on one night was carried out on 4/5 April 1945 when 136 aircraft supported the main force Operations to Harburg, Leuna and Lutzkendorf.

On 25 April 1945, special permission was given for a single 100 Group 192 Squadron Halifax to carry a full bomb load and join 359 Lancasters in a pin-point attack on Hitler's chalet and the SS Barracks at The Eagles Nest Berchtesgaden. S/Ldr D. Donaldson DFC, DSO, the 192 Squadron Commander, was the Pilot. [20]

It is Len's unique scribbled notes and drawings gathered as a curious school-boy that provide a thread throughout the pages of this book, binding airfields and Squadrons which flew from them together under RAF No. 100 (Bomber Support) Group to which they belonged.

CHAPTER 5
Bylaugh Hall
RAF No. 100 (BS) Group Headquarters

A Brief History

Bylaugh Hall (*pronounced bee-la*) built in the 15th century, has a chequered and deeply unhappy past. From the back, the eye is drawn to the distinctive Saxon round-towered church nestling by the river Wensum which flows into Norwich.

The Hall is part of an Estate originally acquired in 1789 for the Lombe (later Evans-Lombe) family by Sir John Lombe, a Derbyshire silk miller. The exact manner in which the Estate was acquired is steeped in legend. Some say he won it from Richard Lloyd in a game of cards; some say the Lloyds' butler drugged his wine. The Hall was also reputedly cursed, presumably by the heirs of the losers of the original card game, and history determines the curse at least to be true. Further secrets exist surrounding the circumstances of what happened next. Did Sir John simply die in 1817 and as a result the Estate passed on? Or was the Estate exchanged for land owned by Sir John Lombe in the middle of the Holkham Estate?

What is certain is that, with no children to inherit, the Estate passed to Sir John's brother Edward, with the proviso that, before the full monies be divided, £100,000 be spent on building a stately home on the highest part of the Estate, the position the Hall stands today. This was a dream of Sir John Lombe's, a dream he was determined would be achieved ... but a dream almost destroyed ... and then again, a dream regained, given the curse that hung over it.

The dream remained dormant for years despite the terms of the Will, and might have remained so had it not been for the intervention of the Court of Chancery, who instructed that monies in the Trust be used for the purpose intended.

Sir Charles Barry, and later his son Charles Barry Junior, together with Richardson Banks, both from the firm who designed the Houses of Parliament; were commissioned to design a suitable house. William Andrews Nesfield advised on its exact position, and became responsible for laying out the grounds and gardens – a most important job given that this needed to commence well in advance of the actual building, and took several years in the making.

The house was eventually started in 1850 and completed in 1851. Together with the Victoria Tower of the Houses of Parliament, they were the first buildings to employ steel in their supporting structure. The exterior stone-work, the balustrades and terrace walling were of magnesium limestone from Ansen near Northampton, known as Ansen stone, used also in the building of the Houses of Parliament – the only difference being that Bylaugh retained its original stone where it was not damaged or removed, whereas the Houses of Parliament has had its stone replaced several times through the years.

Bylaugh Estate, when complete, was the third largest in Norfolk with over 19,000 acres.

On its completion, the new owner, Charles Lombe, requested that the Trustees release all remaining monies. They refused, demanding that the substantial allocated balance be spent on enhancing the house and its grounds. Stables, clock tower, eight-miles of Estate walls, and three lodges – Elsing, Swanton Morley and Bawdeswell – were constructed as a result.

The Evans-Lombe family continued living in the Hall until the 1880s when the house and grounds were leased to Sir William Knox D'Arcy, the founder of what is now BP. Then unexpectedly came the First World War, which led to the Evans-Lombe family selling the House and Park, including its many tenanted farms and smallholdings by auction in 1917.

The House was acquired by the Marsh family from America and was last occupied by Mrs Marsh (nee Wilkinson) until 1935. However, not everything was sold at this auction and it appears that Harrods eventually sold the house a few years on. Other unsold lots were then sold by Case and Dewing of Dereham. The Marsh family used the House and grounds mainly for hunting and shooting. It is said that King Edward VII as well as the Prince of Wales, later King Edward VIII; stayed at the Hall. These social gatherings continued until the House was requisitioned by the RAF at the beginning of the Second World War.

At first it was occupied by WRENS. But then Bomber Command 20 (Bomber Support) began using it as a Command Centre, and from late 1943, it became HQ to RAF No.100 (BS) Group. It was from here the now famous Dam Busters raid was planned, and even more secretly, radar jamming. The Commanding Officer was Air Chief Marshall Sir Basil Embury, and amongst people who visited during the war was 'Ike', later President Eisenhower.

After the RAF left in 1945, it was de-commissioned and bought by a local builder with the express purpose of demolition. In 1950, while Ancient Monuments were trying to list the property, it was stripped of its lead roof, all interior fittings and walls and effectively abandoned to the weather. However, before anything further was settled about its buildings and grounds, almost one hundred years to the day after the alleged curse by the loser at a game of cards, in 1952 the Hall mysteriously burned down. Its remains were then sold to a local farmer who kept pigs for fifty years.

It wasn't until the year 2000 that the Vince family purchased Bylaugh. It became their dream to restore the Hall and grounds to their former glory, for use as a Country House Hotel, Conference Centre and Wedding venue. Its opulent surroundings boasted one hundred en-suite bedrooms, five large magnificent function rooms, and a host of smaller rooms, with two major kitchens to serve the needs of those who, like the RAF 100 Group Association during one particular visit, shared a wonderful two-course lunch of roast beef and yorkshires followed by a scrumptious crumble and tasters.

For Stephen and Muffy Vince, Bylaugh Hall became home.

The re-making of Bylaugh Hall and its grounds was an ongoing work of love for the owners, together with a dedicated team of Norfolk craftsmen and builders who helped save this remarkable building, with a dream derived from Cockerell's original 1832 design, drawn by the great Victorian classical architect William Wilkins.

Sadly today, renovation work has ground to a halt, while the dream project remains in administration, its future unknown.

****

The War Years, 1943–1945

Bases & Units

FOULSHAM
192 Squadron - Wellington, Mosquito, Halifax
462 Squadron (RAAF) - Halifax
1473 Flight - Wellington
BSDU - Mosquito,
USAAF 7PR Group - Lightning

GREAT MASSINGHAM
169 Squadron - Mosquito
1692 Flight, 1694 Flight

LITTLE SNORING
23 Squadron + 515 Squadron - Mosquito
169 Squadron - Mosquito
1692 Flight, USAAF Intruder Detection
1473 Flight

NORTH CREAKE
171 Squadron - Stirling, Halifax
199 Squadron - Stirling, Halifax

OULTON
214 Squadron - Fortress
223 Squadron - Fortress, Liberator
803 BS (USAAF) - Liberator
1699 Flight - Fortress, Liberator

SCULTHORPE
214 Squadron - Fortress
803 BS (USAAF) - Fortress
1699 Flight - Fortress

SWANNINGTON
85 Squadron & 157 Squadron - Mosquito

SWANTON MORLEY

BSDU, 100 Group Communications Flight
'WINDOW' Research Unit

WEST RAYNHAM

141 Squadron – Mosquito
239 Squadron – Mosquito

During the war years, Bylaugh Hall was situated in a large park with adjoining woodland about two miles from what was then RAF Swanton Morley (now Robertson Barracks). It was first used as accommodation for Officers from the Station, including American aircrew who flew the first USAAF bombing operation from this country.

In May 1943, the Headquarters of No. 2 Group moved from Huntingdon to the Hall to be near its medium Bomber Bases. Air Chief Marshall Sir Basil Embery, GCB, KBE, DSO (3 Bars) was appointed Air Officer Commanding on his return from France.

No. 2 Group left Bomber Command to join the new 2nd Tactical Air Force (TAF) in readiness for the invasion of Europe. But until the 2nd TAF was formed, the Group operated for a while under the control of Fighter Command.

During January 1944, Group H.Q moved down to Berkshire to be with its Squadrons nearer the south coast. Immediately 2 Group vacated the building, staff for 100 Group H.Q started to arrive. Other buildings were erected in the Park and Woodland, including billets for WAAF MT drivers who drove H.Q staff cars and vans. The General Office was in the stables. They used to drive through the archway to the Smithy and Brewery to pick up Officers.

100 Group H.Q remained at Bylaugh Hall until the Group disbanded in December 1945.

There are many veterans who carry strong memories of their HQ, Bylaugh Hall, during the war years.

Sergeant Air Gunner Edward Gill from 226 Squadron came to Bylaugh in 1941 until 1944. His Squadron was based at Swanton Morley and they shared meals in the Mess at the Station, while sleeping in Bylaugh Hall. Richard Murdoch was an Intelligence Officer at Swanton Morley but lived at Bylaugh all the time.

Dominic Parslow's great uncle, Peter Scott, was Wing Commander and part of the Dambuster's Planning Team based at Bylaugh.

Corporal Fred Holland of Dereham was stationed at the Hall. He was a driver and it was his duty to deliver the next day's plans to surrounding Norfolk airfields, travelling via the pubs! The Orangery, a beautiful period conservatory set on one side of Bylaugh Hall, was used for social evenings. It was during one such occasion, Corporal Fred Holland won the knobbly knees competition! Later, he was to be Court Marshalled for being AWOL in Dereham whilst visiting his mother at Christmas.

Bob Moorby, a Wireless Operator with 214 Squadron at Oulton, visited Bylaugh Hall as a Warrant Officer when it was HQ of 100 Group. He was interviewed in September 1944 by Air Vice Marshall Addison when he received his Commission.

Clare Pollard never knew his father. He was killed before he was born. Serving in 214 Squadron, his father took off from Oulton on 6 November 1944 to provide electronic counter-measures to a main force raid of Lancasters. His aircraft failed to return. The ten crew members are buried at Reichwald War Cemetery.

Gerhard Heilig came to England in 1938 as a refugee from Austria and went to school in Yorkshire. He joined the RAF as a Wireless Operator in March 1944 and was posted direct to 214 Squadron at RAF Oulton, then stationed at Sculthorpe where he converted to B17 Flying Fortress. He flew on its first mission in its new role on 20 April 1944, Hitler's birthday: *'It was a pleasure to help deliver my worst regards!'*

Len Vowler was an Air Gunner with 223 Squadron also based at Oulton, from September 1944 to 21 March 1945. He was shot down and killed on a diversion raid dropping 'WINDOW'.

Roger Jones was thirteen years old when he first heard by telegram that his brother Bob was missing on 22 March 1945. His was the last Fortress lost over Germany. He would have been twenty-one years old on 22 April.

Alan Mercer was a Navigator in 214 Squadron based at Oulton during the last months of the war until the Squadron disbanded in July 1945. Alan attended 100 Group Association Reunions every year and was greatly appreciative of the support of local people keeping memories alive of missing comrades.

Sidney Pike first came to Bylaugh in January 1945 for an interview for a Commission after his first tour at Oulton.

Margaret Taverham is daughter of Flt Lt Leonard Dellow. Her father was in 88 Squadron. Whilst stationed at Swanton Morley, he received his Commission at Bylaugh Hall.

Peter Witts was a legend during his lifetime, well-known and well loved by all members of the RAF 100 Group Association. During the war, he was promoted first as a Sergeant and later a Flight Sergeant Air Gunner. He flew on 223 Squadron at RAF Oulton in Flight Lieutenant Woodward's crew and then transferred to 214 Squadron to fly as Mid-Upper Gunner on B17s in Flight Lieutenant Allies' crew. At his request, he was posted to RAF Foulsham where he flew Halifax Bombers as Rear Gunner with the Royal Australian Air Force: Squadron 462, in Flight Lieutenant Bruce Drinkwater's crew till war ended. He was the only person to serve in three RAF 100 Group Squadrons.

WAAF Dorothy Hudson (nee Howard) was Met Girl for RAF Swannington:

> I have no real memories of Bylaugh Hall. We were directly under the command of the Met Office. All I can remember of HQ was that the 'Head Sarang' of the Met office was a Mr FROST!

WAAFs were stationed in huts at the beginning of the long driveway leading up to the Hall and there were so many more women than men with two huts only set aside for the men!

Nancy Hewitt (nee Marshall) met her husband at Bylaugh where he was a Meteorologist. She worked as a Clerical Officer at Bylaugh Hall in 1944 for Wing Commander Dunning-White. Nancy still has fond memories of her time shared with other girls at the Hall:

> In the old days, we would take a bus to Norwich from Bawdeswell and on our return, we walked about two miles through a wooded area back to the Hall. My friend Peggy tried to 'hitch' back once when we missed the bus and ended up walking twenty-six miles – but that's another story! We spent many pleasant evenings roasting potatoes and listening to the 'Ink Spots' on the wind-up gramophone which we somehow acquired. I am still in touch with Joan and Peggy, but wonder where the others are now.

PERSONAL EXPERIENCES

LACW Peggy Pollard
Life at Bylaugh Hall

Group Captain Porte was a tall, austere, impeccably uniformed officer, strictly correct in his attitude and conscious of his position as Commanding Officer of the HQ Unit. The only time I knew him to show any feeling for me as a person was when a bird flew in through the open windows of the large room which was his office on the top floor of Bylaugh Hall, overlooking the beautiful countryside sloping down to the river winding its way through the Estate. He was on the phone at the time while I sat, notebook on lap, and he remarked to his caller '*My typist seems rather alarmed!*' as the poor bird swooped round and round.

It was not unusual to hear the occasional shot ring out as Wing Commander Dunning-White took a pot shot at a pheasant from his office window on the floor below.

My office was just round the corner from the Group Captain's and he would press a loud buzzer when he wanted to dictate. One had to drop everything and hurry in. A corridor ran round the building on all floors (seventy-eight stairs from top to bottom), and use of the Officers' loo on the second floor was strictly forbidden to Other Ranks. I shared a tin room (must have been a servant's bedroom originally) with another WAAF typist and it was nothing to open our desk drawers and find our typing paper chewed to shreds overnight by mice when we arrived for work in the morning.

Surrounded as we were by American Air Bases, a number of WAAFs had USAAF aircrew boyfriends. We would watch the B-17s and B-24s forming up high in the skies early in the morning before flying off on daylight bombing operations over Germany. On one occasion, a returning USAAF Bomber Squadron buzzed Bylaugh Hall, flying extremely low over the building and straight down the drive. I was taking dictation at the time and Group Captain Porte got through immediately to the American Air Force authorities to make a complaint. Needless to say, it was our habit to count the number of U.S bombers returning, mission completed later in the day, to see if any of the Squadron's aircraft were missing.

The small church on the Estate had fallen into disuse, but Group Captain Porte had the interior cleaned up and arranged for the Padre from RAF Swanton Morley nearby to take a regular Sunday morning 11 am service. He also formed a small choir (myself an enthusiastic member) and we had regular practices. He would play the organ at these services and I clearly remember one occasion being most impressed by his Voluntary – Bach's 'Jesu Joy of Man's Desiring'. In January the churchyard would be a mass of snowdrops, and the winding path to the church flanked by celandines in Spring.

I was with 100 Group from its formation, having been posted on my own from No.1 Signals Depot, West Drayton. A group of us met up at East Rudham railway station – each of us from a different Unit in the UK. We were greeted by trucks and taken to RAF West Raynham where 100 Group took shape before moving to Bylaugh Hall a few weeks later.

I well remember that day.

We arrived at the Hall in trucks in very cold weather and a penetrating drizzle. The WAAF site was a group of Nissen huts set under tall fir trees (the cones from which would drop with a 'ping' on the roof during the night); half a mile away from the Hall. We lined up at the Stores and were issued with bedding blankets. I still recall that long walk through the drizzle carrying my unprotected bedding, being directed to Hut 5. 2nd TAF had been the previous occupiers and the mattress 'biscuits' left on the beds. How cold and damp everything was. We set to, gathered what twigs we could find, collected fuel from the Compound on our site and eventually managed to get the stove in the middle of the hut going. Our damp 'biscuits' sent up clouds of steam as we attempted to air them round the stove. We all felt we were in the middle of nowhere.

We had two severe winters there – snow for six weeks one winter. The hut toilets and water in the Wash House froze up and a third pair of shoes had to be issued to us as our two issue pairs, ruined by snow, were being repaired at RAF Foulsham, there being no servicing facilities on the Camp.

However, the summers were glorious. We sent home for our bikes – Dad sent mine by rail which I collected from East Dereham Railway Station – and became a great cyclist, transport being scarce. If you were lucky you might get a lift on the Post Office van which made a daily run to Dereham, our main destination. The little country town would be full of servicemen and women, British, Commonwealth and American from surrounding Bases. The Corn Exchange showed the latest films and in the evenings pubs would be full to overflowing – thick with cigarette smoke. Many is the night that I cycled back along dark country roads with my bicycle dynamo (half blacked out) showing me the way.

Bylaugh Hall was very isolated, the little village of Bawdeswell providing the nearest pub and village shop. A local farmer would lead his bull by a rope tied to a ring through its nose at lunchtime and terrify all the poor WAAFs if we ventured to the shop on our bikes. One or two women in the village would take in Officers' washing. Cycling to Bawdeswell involved a hair-raising ride through the wood, which in Spring was a mass of rhododendron blooms.

A regular Liberty Run was set up – a truck – between the Camp and Norwich, sixteen miles away. It left Bylaugh early evening and returned from Norwich Cattle Market at 10.30 pm. As there was no other form of public transport, you were in dire straits if you missed it!

There was little formal discipline – no parades – and no fenced-off boundaries, so those erring souls who did not wish to tie themselves down to the official booking-in time could avoid booking-out in the Guard Room by using one of many unofficial exits into the 'back line'.

A Convenient farm kept our hut supplied with milk, one of our number had a regular liaison with a local farmer so we always had eggs. On Sunday mornings we would give the Cookhouse breakfast a miss, boil eggs, make toast and tea using the boiler-room furnace on the WAAF site. I discovered a gravel pit for swimming a bike ride away, and sometimes fitted in a swim during lunch hour. It was a beautiful spot to be stationed when the weather was fine.

During the summer of 1944, Group Captain Porte had a request from local farmers asking help with the pea harvest – farm labourers having been called up. Volunteers were called to go pea-picking. It was during a heat-wave and airmen worked in the fields stripped to the waist. Several reported sick with severe sunburn and Group Captain Porte warned that any man who allowed himself to get sunburned would be put on a Charge.

This is not to say that we didn't work extremely hard and very long hours, especially during the six months leading up to 'D' Day. One duty we WAAF clerks dreaded was our turn to be Duty Clerk. This meant, following our normal day's work, we would report to the Operations Officer and all night had to pass teleprinter signals from Signals Room to Duty Ops Room Officer. We were also called on for any typing that might be needed. On a quiet night we might snatch an hour's sleep on the camp bed in the office. We could go over to the Cook House for a supper and be relieved next morning by day staff coming on duty. At first, after a Cookhouse breakfast, we were expected to do our normal day's work without a break. Eventually we were allowed the morning off before going back to work.

Every Tuesday night all WAAFs were confined to camp, it being designated 'Domestic Night'. We were meant to spend the evening giving our hut a special clean, mend clothing, etc. It was a restriction much resented by us girls, especially as no such ruling applied to airmen. Whether he realised this I don't know, but Group Captain

Porte decided to organise an entertainment on Tuesday nights at 8 pm, with a small band playing 'Lyons Corner-House' type music. The band came over from RAF Swanton Morley run by Sgt Ray Ellington, who had been Harry Roy's drummer. I had last seen him performing at the Croydon Empire in 1939. Given the opportunity, the band would revert to jazz and had a wonderful *boogie-woogie* pianist. We would also have Spelling Bees, and I remember playing the part of Maria Martin in a scratch performance of 'Maria of the Red Barn'. The only comment I received from the Group Captain next morning was 'I didn't know you had it in you!'

There are many other recollections such as the 'odd character' airman who trapped rabbits in the woods and made a business of selling them to villagers; the airwoman messenger who left some Top Secret files on the incinerator in 'The Rattery' (the haunt of the ACH G/Ds); the WAAF who feigned madness in order to obtain her discharge; and one of the inmates of our Hut who went AWOL with an American airman, never to be seen again, etc.

****

Sgt Ron Pollard (Peggy's Husband)

I only arrived at Bylaugh Hall just after Christmas 1944, so my stay was pretty short.

When I received my posting notice to 100 Group, HQ Bylaugh Hall, I thought it sounded as though it would be reasonably civilised.

However, after two years at an S.F.T.S in Canada with centrally-heated barrack blocks and all mod cons and plenty of good food, I found the Nissen Huts primitive, to say the least! Walking through the snow from the sleeping hut to the wash hut where we washed and shaved from tin bowls (I'm not sure whether the water was cold or not, probably cold) was not exactly the epitome of gracious living. The food in the Sergeant's Mess was actually quite good, in spite of the habit of one Sergeant ringing up his WAAF girlfriend, a waitress in the Swanton Morley Officers Mess; to ask what was on that day, then making his choice.

However, as the weather got warmer and the rhododendrons on the approach to the Hall came into glorious bloom, together with the meadow at the back leading to the River Wensum, it all became very acceptable, although very isolated.

Regarding Air Commodore Chisholm, his office was one floor above mine, and I saw very little of him. The main contact was by telephone. It would ring and a conversation on the following lines would take place:

Me: 'Air Staff Clerks.'

SASO: 'Sergeant, where is my Secretary?' (WAAF Corporal named Willans)

Me: 'I'm sorry, Sir, she is not here and I really do not know where she is.'

SASO: 'Find her!'

Me: 'But she may be in the toilet, Sir.'

SASO: 'I said '**Find her**'!'

End of conversation. Fortunately, I had four WAAF Clerks in my office who immediately knew what was happening, and one of them would go and look for Corporal Willans.

I found Air Commodore Chisholm very austere and cold, and frankly I was dead scared of him. Actually, Peggy's description of Group Captain Porte could easily fit Air Commodore Chisholm!

On the whole, I found my time at Bylaugh (January 1945 – October 1945) very enjoyable, and certainly with the Signals for the Ops Room coming through my office I felt just a bit nearer the sharper end of things than I did in Canada.

*****

UPDATE

During annual RAF 100 Group Association May Reunions over the past twenty years, it became part of our programme to visit Bylaugh Hall for Friday lunch at the start of our weekend. The Vince family were attempting to restore the building to its former glory. As Headquarters of 100 Group during World War Two, veterans decided it was the place for an unveiling of a Plaque commemorating the many lives lost. On the day of the

Commemoration, we were treated to a superb two-course lunch before the Plaque was unveiled and blessed by Rev. Beane, then Vicar at Horsham St Faith. His Blessing and Dedication were notable:

Thank you for your generous invitation to be with you this morning here at Bylaugh Hall, your HQ during those war years. It is a remarkable honour for a young man like me to stand surrounded by true heroes. The Second World War to me is history. I can't experience it and I can't remember it. For me it is my grandparents' generation who have memories and stories to share. I can see only through the window of your personal experiences and memories; through books, film and museums. But today it is as if a window into the past is being opened linking past, present and future. We stand here and remember, knowing that the veil between earth and heaven, between past and present is thin ...

Having read a little about the work of 100 Group one thing stands out for me. You were ordinary guys, using ordinary equipment, ordinary aircraft; but your skills, wisdom, and intelligence turned what was ordinary into something extra-ordinary.

St Paul once wrote about how we were like earthenware jars that hold treasure. These jars were used to hold ordinary and everyday items like water, flour and oil. We might be ordinary and everyday on the outside, but inside these ordinary exteriors you were heroes ... you are the treasure in clay jars.

Today we unveil and dedicate this plaque to the memory of lost friends; to the dedication and sacrifice of all members of the RAF 100 Group; to the peace younger generations have known thanks to the heroes of the past; to the ordinary and everyday people who acted in extraordinary ways and to the glory of God who knows, loves and keeps each of us in the palm of His Hand.[21]

The Plaque bearing the RAF 100 Group crest, reads:

This tablet commemorates the men and women who served in the RAF's 100 (Bomber Support) Group during the Second World War.

Formed in November 1943 within Bomber Command the Group set up its permanent Headquarters at Bylaugh Hall in January 1944 where it remained until it was disbanded in December 1945.

Under the command of Air Vice-Marshal E. B. Addison CB CBE the Group was established to carry out airborne Radio Counter Measures in support of Bomber Command night bombing operations. This role included high and low level night fighter intruder sorties; signals intelligence gathering; jamming and disruption of German air defence ground and airborne radars; and the jamming and disruption of Luftwaffe night fighter control and direction communication systems. To undertake this commitment the Group employed twelve RAF Squadrons, one RAAF Squadron; Bomber Support Development Unit together with six specialist flights. A Squadron of the USAAF also operated under the Group's control for a period during 1944.

The Group's flying and ground based units carried out this role from its nearby Norfolk airfields.

CONFOUND AND DESTROY

Given the demise of Bylaugh Hall today, the Plaque is now displayed during each of our annual May Reunion weekends as a reminder to families and friends of veterans what it means and why it remains so special to share these special moments together.

A local newspaper attending its initial unveiling ceremony, later released information about 100 Group which many would hear for the first time:

They saved at least 1,000 bomber aircraft and helped destroy German battleships during the Second World War, but due to the covert nature of their work their efforts have remained largely unknown. Now the RAF's Norfolk-based 100 (Bomber Support) Group has been given a lasting Memorial to mark their efforts to *confound and destroy* the enemy, as their motto reads.

Former members of the 100 Group who worked from its Bylaugh Hall Headquarters, near Dereham, and airstrips around the area are holding a Reunion this weekend visiting their old haunts. Yesterday they unveiled a plaque recording their work at the Hall where only a few derelict Nissan huts hint at the past.

Phil James MBE, from Port Talbot, Wales, (now Lifetime President of RAF 100 Group Association) was a Flight Engineer with a Canadian crew flying Halifaxes:

'There is very little known about the 100 Group. The records about what we did have not been released, so if you mention the 100 Group, people have never heard of it. During the war it was all secret. Our mail used to be censored.'

The main objective of the Group, set up in 1943, was radio counter-measures, or RCM. Among their duties was flying alongside bombers in planes kitted out with radio and electronic equipment so they could interfere with transmissions between German ground and aircrew. They also flew spoof missions to confuse the enemy and investigated enemy radar and radio equipment. And they had their successes. One was finding the *Tirpitz*, a German battleship hiding in a Norwegian fjord, posing a great threat to the allies. Thanks to a sortie more than nine hours long, 100 Group was able to find her location and enable a bomber Squadron to destroy her.

Stanley Forsyth of Southport, a Radar Support Operator, was awarded a DFC (Distinguished Flying Cross) for his role in the mission. He ended up working on Control at Bylaugh Hall Headquarters: *'We went out with the bombers on raids,'* he said, *'trying to find the enemy frequencies. It was very early days for that sort of technology.'*

Peter Witts went on to be Headteacher at Beachamwell Primary School, but was a Gunner in a Liberator, also flying Fortresses and Halifaxes. He was among the raids on Dresden: *'They used to try to shoot us down. They gave us a very hot welcome, then tried to get rid of us.'* [22]

****

CHAPTER 6
RAF Foulsham: 1942–1954
Birth of an Airfield

It was Foulsham that Len Bartram, the curious schoolboy, could see from his classroom window, and pedalled furiously at the end of each school day to try to uncover the mystery of what was happening there. It was intriguing. He wanted to be a part of this history in the making. As the airfield began to re-define the fields he knew so well, with aircraft of all shapes and sizes arriving, an air of mystery and excitement caught hold:

My father worked as a Night Watchman during the building of Foulsham airfield. He had his own small hut on one of the Guestwick sites. His duty was to patrol various sites and keep watch on the contractors' machines and materials, also to apprehend any intruders. To obtain any assistance, he had to telephone the RAF Guard Room at West Raynham. I sometimes stayed the night in his hut during school holidays and weekends.

When the first RAF personnel arrived, RAF police took over all security duties. Father was then employed by the Air Ministry Works Dept AMWD on general maintenance work. There was a gang of about six men and a tipper lorry. Their depot was on the main Tech Site, just past the MT section. I sometimes went and lit the fire in their hut. I also did a few days cleaning walls inside the Airmen's Mess ready for painting during August 1943 after the Mitchell Squadrons left. This was for T. Gill Contractors from Norwich.

During the early stages of construction, with other local lads on Sunday afternoons we would cycle along the runways to see how work was progressing. When the Mitchell Squadrons arrived, security was still quite low key and we could cycle in past the Guardroom unchallenged. Later, during the time of 100 Group, there were barbed wire fences and armed guards, but even then we often climbed over fences to look inside Fortresses parked near the road.

We also visited the rubbish dump to look for bullets and pieces of aircraft.

From the WINDOW compound, we collected damaged packets of the material which we took home for making Christmas decorations. I had a collection of about six different types varying between boxes of tiny confetti-like strips to packets of long pieces six feet long. We collected live and spent ammunition. I had Mortar bombs, smoke grenades and live incendiaries which we dug up out of cornfields at Blue Tile Farm, Hindol. Eventually Mother found my collection and dropped it down the village drinking water well ... [23]

Construction commenced during 1941. The major firm employed was *Kirk & Kirk* working alongside local labour. The land was mainly wet meadows and small arable fields with high hedges and old trees. Extensive drainage and pipe-laying was carried out during early stages of development and a minor public road to Wood Norton closed as two or three buildings were demolished. Numerous tipper lorries of dripping wet sand and gravel created a continuous daily convoy passing through Foulsham village. A check-in hut at the Brick Yard crossroads counted in each load, cement arriving in hundreds of bags carted from Hindolveston railway station. Steel girders for hangars and giant underground fuel storage tanks were brought on long lorries from Melton Constable railway station, with other materials arriving at stations at Guestwick and Foulsham. Guestwick was the nearest railway station to the airfield and well used by personnel, especially for journeys to Norwich. During summer 1942, people worked seven days from early morning until dusk.

Two T2 hangars were built, later to accommodate 100 Group aircraft and gliders, with hangars increasing to nine T2s and one B1 type, more than other airfields built at this time. An RAF policeman stopped traffic while aircraft were towed across two designated crossing places. Len watched impressive American Lightning aircraft cross to a hangar, where they remained at all times except when flying. He nicknamed them 'spy planes' with hardly any markings visible.

RAF personnel arrived during May 1942, and the airfield opened on 5 June 1942. An Official Opening was planned for 26 June, but didn't happen, while personnel included nine Officers, four W/Ops, six F/Sgts, twenty-seven Cpls and 153 Airmen. On 30 July, the AOC of No. 2 Group, accompanied by the Earl of Brandon and Group Captain Mills (West Raynham) visited the airfield to see how work was progressing – it was on schedule, but far from ready to receive aircraft.

On 3 August 1942, a single German Dornier Do.217, believed to be on a reconnaissance mission, circled the airfield at about 100 feet. Despite a veil of secrecy, the enemy was keeping a keen eye on activities in Norfolk. Its burst of machine-gun fire fell like rain ... hitting the airmen's toilets where airmen donned metal wash basins on their heads as make-shift helmets.

During September, a number of HE bombs dropped on the airfield during a night raid. Later, two other separate machine-gun attacks were made by lone Do.217s. When the airfield was in regular use, several anti-personnel (*Butterfly*) bombs were dropped. Len recalled incendiary bombs, and a giant land mine failing to explode, dropped in the Foulsham area. The large red parachute from the land mine was put on display in the local Hall.

First personnel to arrive came from nearby West Raynham - Police, Fire, Medical, Cooks, Transport and Office Staff. The firemen were nearly all Jamaicans and for many villagers these were the first black people ever seen! Looked on with deep suspicion, their kind and friendly manner soon made them friends. First airmen to arrive likened the place to a vast muddy builder's yard!

The first Station Commander was Group Captain M. P. Dalrymple RAFVR arriving on 1 June 1942. He served in the First World War flying as an Observer in RE.8s on the Western Front, and was with the Forestry Service in India when recalled at the start of the Second World War to serve at Fighter Command HQ. He was Adjutant to Wing Commander Sir Hughie Edwards VC prior to coming to Foulsham. While at Foulsham he lived with his wife in rooms at Foulsham Rectory. Mrs Dalrymple retained fond memories of beautiful flowers and lovely trees, recalling visits by Wing Commander Hodder and Lower, also Bill Edrich, the Norwich cricketer – Flight Commander at Foulsham. Officers posted during June/July 1942 included Squadron Leader R. F. Stubbs from West Raynham as Medical Officer, P/O J. L. Adams from Polebrook as M/T Officer, P/O L. S. Edwards from Benson as Engineering Officer, F/Lt B. R. Milton from Swanton Morley as Station Adjutant and Rev S/Ldr J. H. Fisher as Chaplain.

In August 1944, 2,000 RAF and 300 WAAF personnel were based at the airfield, equal to the population of a small Norfolk town, increasing when the Australian Squadron arrived during December.

All Officers, NCOs and Airmen were issued with official service bicycles to reach their place of work two or three miles from their billets. They was also useful for sorties to local pubs, dance halls, chip shops and girlfriends. Foulsham pubs were well patronised, each Squadron using a particular House as its local. A dance hall in Reepham also had regular visits. In Norwich, pubs, dance halls, girls young and not so young were virtually taken over by the American 8th Air Force. Lower-paid RAF didn't stand much chance! Entertainment on camp included the cinema with a good selection of newly-released films. There were regular live shows in the gymnasium given by ENSA and visiting concert parties. Celebrities such as 'Jane' from the Daily Mirror were entertained in the Officers' Mess.

First Squadrons

No. 98 Squadron
No. 180 Squadron
No. 12 GMS Glider Maintenance Squadron
Foulsham Station Flight
No. 320 Royal Netherlands Naval Air Services –
Squadron: B-25c Mitchell B2
No. 514 Squadron
No. 1678 HCF Heavy Conversion Flight

No. 98 Squadron:

'Never Failing'
Reproduced with permission of the MOD

Squadron badge featured a Cerberus (three-headed watchdog) relating to the way the Squadron barred the German retreat front and rear, in 1918. The motto commemorates a message of congratulations from the General Officer Commanding.

From a Reconnaissance and Day Bomber Unit, it reformed with Hawker Hind light bombers during 1936, serving in France during 1940, operating as a Training and Reserve Unit. Its return to England that year sadly resulted in the loss of many personnel when the ship SS *'Lancastria'* carrying them was sunk on 17 June. Squadron remnants reformed in July as the first ever RAF Squadron to serve in Iceland for one year. It again reformed on 12 September 1942 as the first RAF Mitchell Squadron at Foulsham under the command of W/Cdr L. E. G. Lewer.

No. 180 Squadron:

'Agreeable in Manner. Forcible in Act'
Reproduced with permission of the MOD

Squadron badge depicts a velvet glove in front of two upward-pointing crossed swords.

A brand new Unit not having seen service, became the second RAF Mitchell Squadron at Foulsham formed on 13 September 1942.

First aircraft arrived on 27 September 1942 with more following. The Squadron Commander, W/Cdr C. C. Hodder AFC, joined the RAF in 1933, serving in India with 27 Squadron. Foulsham became his first wartime operational post. One of the Flight Commanders was S/Ldr Bill Edrich DFC, Norfolk county and England cricketer, having completed a tour on Blenheims.

Both above Squadrons settled at Foulsham, with daily training commencing at a hectic pace preparing for the *Eindhoven Raid* on 6 December 1942.

First Operation

On 22 January 1943, twelve Mitchells, six from each Squadron, took off for the first RAF Mitchell raid of the war, and first bombing raid from Foulsham airfield. The target was an oil refinery and storage facilities along the Terneuzen canal near Gwent in Belgium.

W/Cdr Lewer led 98 Squadron with S/Ldr Slocombe, S/Ldr Pitcairn, P/O McDonald, P/O Woods and F/Sgt Calder. W/Cdr Hodder led 180 Squadron with P/O Cappleman, P/O Dawes, Sgt Martin, Sgt Fooks and Sgt Roe.

The attack was made at 1,500 feet with low level in and out from the target. Heavy AA fire was encountered, with P/O Woods shot down. On leaving the area, the Mitchells were attacked by Fw190s. P/O Cappleman was shot down. W/C Hodder's aircraft was seen to be hit and badly damaged, failing to return. Sgt Martin was repeatedly attacked, but managed to get away. Three were lost including a CO, a bad start for Mitchell operations - a tragic day for RAF Foulsham.

W/Cdr G. R. *Digger* Magill DFC from 226 Squadron took command of 180 Squadron, with Gr/Cap L. W (*Bull*) Canon appointed as new Station Commander.

Future Mitchell operations would take place at higher altitudes, above the range of light AA guns. Training continued until May 1943 when operations commenced. These continued from Foulsham until 18 August 1943 when both Squadrons moved to Dunsfold.

No. 12 GMS Glider Maintenance Squadron

Forty Airspeed Horsa Gliders arrived at Foulsham during April 1943, towed by Albermarles and Whitleys tug aircraft, and parked in open storage around the airfield perimeter. A hangar was used for repair and maintenance of the gliders, often damaged by high winds. All were moved to bases in the south west and took part in the D-Day Landings.

Foulsham Station Flight

The Flight used various aircraft - Tiger Moths, Leopard Moth, DH Moth Minor, Oxford, Anson, Argus, etc. A captured Ju88 and He111 visited in April 1943, and a Ju88G during Sept/Oct 1945.

No. 320 Royal Netherlands Naval Air Services

Squadron: B-25c Mitchell B2:

'We are guided by the mind of Liberty'
Reproduced with permission of the MOD

Squadron badge depicted a fractured and eradicated orange tree in front of a fountain. The orange tree referred to its link with the Netherlands, and the fountain to operations over the sea.

Squadron Codes used:

SP	Allocated Apr – Sep 1939
TD	Jun 1940 – Oct 1940
NO	Oct 1940 – Aug 1945

In 1940, Germans closed in on Royal Netherlands Naval Air Service bases. Eight Fokker T.VIIIW twin-engined patrol seaplanes escaped successfully to England and Pembroke Dock.

The Dutch Naval personnel formed No. 320 Squadron, part of Coastal Command, on 1 June that year, flying anti-submarine patrols in Fokkers until aircraft became unserviceable due to lack of spares. The men were re-equipped with Ansons in August, supplemented in October with Hudsons.

Low on numbers with insufficient personnel, on 18 January 1941 the Squadron was absorbed into No. 321 (Netherlands) Squadron, and on 1 October, re-equipped with Hudson IIIs, moved to RAF Leuchars to continue flying patrols and anti-shipping attacks in the North Sea.

Detachments were located at RAF Silloth and RAF Carew Cheriton, until 24 April 1942 when the Squadron moved to RAF Bircham Newton.

At the end of March 1943, the Squadron moved again, this time to Attlebridge where it changed both as a Group, and in role and equipment, joining No. 2 Group under Bomber Command. Attlebridge was a satellite to Foulsham from where Mitchells often flew, especially after July when re-construction work commenced at Attlebridge in preparation for the arrival of USAAF Liberators.

On 17 August 1943, the first 320 Squadron Mitchell bombing operation was carried out, flown from Foulsham by six aircraft led by Pier Van Waart in FR141 NO/B. The target was the rail yards at Calais. Heavy flak was encountered with all aircraft suffering damage. On 19 August twelve Mitchells left Foulsham to bomb Poix airfield, each aircraft carrying eight 500-lb bombs.

Their final Foulsham operation next day included twelve Mitchells bombing the Dornier factory at Flushing. Heavy flak was encountered. FR143 NO/A Pilot Sillevis was damaged. FR147 NO/C Pilot Neinhous was hit in the port engine which stopped, with the aircraft ditching in the North Sea, its crew picked up from their dinghy by an ASR Walrus and taken to Coltishall.

A final Parade took place on 31 August, 64th birthday of Queen Wilhelmenia, before the Squadron moved to Lasham, Hampshire to join other ex-Foulsham Mitchell Squadrons at Dunsfold to form 139 Wing 2nd Tactical Air Force (TAF) ready for the invasion of Europe.

In the final week of war it was based on German soil, and on 2 August 1945, transferred to the Royal Netherlands Navy where it was disbanded as an RAF Unit.

Tribute should be paid to pilots who escaped in Fokkers as Germans closed in on Royal Netherlands Naval Air Service bases and went on to fly from Foulsham:

- Van Amsterdam
- J. G. Roosenburg
- A. de Liefde
- W. M. A Van Rossum
- K. J. Meester
- N. J. Van Lessen
- E. O. Loeff
- P. Van Waart
- J. C. Sillevis

No. 3 Group RAF Bomber Command

On 1 September 1943, Foulsham airfield was placed under the control of RAF No. 3 Group Heavy Night Bombers. Lighting systems were quickly installed on approaches to all runways, while on 8 September a new Station Commander, Group Captain E. P. MacKay arrived.

No. 514 Squadron:

'Nothing Can Withdraw'
Reproduced with permission of the MOD

This new Squadron formed at Foulsham on 1 September 1943. Its badge presented later depicted: '*A sword piercing a cloud formation*', illustrating the Squadron's role of blind *Gee* bombing through cloud.

Its aircraft were a new version of the Lancaster Mk II bombers, powered by four Bristol Hercules radial engines instead of the well-known Merlin, like other Lancs. The Commanding Officer was Wing Commander A.V. Sampson DFC. Training commenced and continued around the clock.

Their first operation was flown on the night of 3 November 1943. Two Lancasters joined the main force to bomb Dusseldorf, while four others went mine-laying. Operations continued until 23 November 1943 when the Squadron was suddenly told they were moving within forty-eight hours to Waterbeach, Cambridgeshire, UK. Some aircraft on ops that night returned direct to their new base while one 514 Lancaster failed to return. Local people were told runways were unsafe, but this was not true. The base had been taken over by the new secret No. 100 Group.

In June 1944, the Squadron was re-equipped with Lancaster Mk I and Mk III bombers, and on 22 August 1945, finally disbanded. The Squadron completed 3,675 operational sorties, losing sixty-six aircraft. Its members were awarded one DSO, eighty-four DFCs; one Bar to the DFC and twenty-six DFMs.

No. 1678 HCF Heavy Conversion Flight

Formed at East Wretham during March 1943, it later moved to Little Snoring and onto Foulsham on 16 September 1943. Like 514 Squadron, it was equipped with Lancaster Mk 2s, its duty being to convert and train crews for Squadrons operating this type of Lancaster. Some crews were fresh from O.T.U, others had served on Stirling Squadrons.The Flight was commanded by S/Ldr P. L Chilton AFC, DFC. Crews who completed the course with the Flight at Foulsham went on to 514 Squadron.

F.I.D.O – Fog Investigation and Dispersal Op

Foulsham was one of the few airfields to be fitted with FIDO in 1944, a system used to disperse fog enabling aircraft to land safely. The device was developed at the department of chemical engineering at the Birmingham University, UK, during World War Two. Formerly attributed to Dr John David Main-Smith, ex-Birmingham resident and Principal Scientific Officer of the Chemistry Department of the Royal Aircraft Establishment at Farnborough, Hampshire; as a courtesy, the joint-patent (595,907) held by the Ministry of Supply was shared by Department Head, Dr Ramsbottom.

The first use of FIDO was reported on 21 September 1944.

Three large petrol storage tanks were situated in the north-west corner of the airfield. The pump house and control point were nearby. Pipes and burners were placed each side of the main long runway. The system was ignited during severe fog conditions; with the burn rate approximately 1,000 gallons a minute. The tanks held about 480,000 gallons pumped in via an underground pipeline from Foulsham Railway Station. The system proved effective and many aircraft from Foulsham and other fog-bound bases made safe landings with visibility down to less than 100 yards.

No. 192 Squadron:

'Dare to Discover'
Reproduced with permission of the MOD

192 Squadron's badge depicts an owl's head over a lightning flash.

Squadron code – DT

192 Squadron was based at Foulsham from 25 November 1943 – 22 August 1945. However, its early history is complicated.

On 4 July 1942, 'A' Flight 109 Squadron became 1473 Flight at Upper Heyford, while on the 10th, 'B' Flight 109 Squadron became 1474 Flight at Gransden Lodge, before becoming 192 Squadron on 4 January 1943. Both Flights were engaged in Signals investigation duties which 192 now took over.

On 5 April, 192 Squadron moved from Gransden to Feltwell and on to Foulsham on 25 November 1943 where it came under the command of 100 Group. 1473 Flight also came to Foulsham via Feltwell and Little Snoring. By 1 February 1944, most of the Flight was absorbed into 192 Squadron.

At Foulsham, 192 Squadron was made up of three Flights:
- 'A' Wellingtons, and Halifaxes by 1944 end,
- 'B' Halifax B3s,
- 'C' Mosquitoes.

192 Squadron took the lead role, with work carried out by other Squadrons relying on information obtained direct from 192. The Squadron's aircraft carried special extra radio equipment, devised by scientists at the *'Tele-communications Research Establishment'* at Malvern. With it, all kinds of enemy signals traffic and transmissions were investigated and frequency of German radio and radar signals recorded, some on paper-tape machines, others onto cathode-ray tubes where images were photographed by German-made

cameras. Code-names identified different equipment, with special incendiary devices carried to destroy this equipment in the event of aircraft coming down in enemy territory. 100 Group Squadrons had the ability using this equipment to jam or mislead enemy transmissions. A small number of 192 Halifaxes carried a second extra man, an Air Gunner, to operate a ventral position machine gun.

Special attention was given to identify signals connected to V-1s and V-2s, with U-Boat and fighter R/T transmissions being checked. Jamming was also carried out by 192 Mosquitoes. *Window* was also carried and dropped.

192 detachments operated from Blida in North Africa and Lossiemouth in Scotland, investigating the German Battleship *Tirpitz* moored in a Norwegian fjord. 192 Wellingtons and Halifaxes carried extra fuel tanks in their bomb bays; with Halifaxes carrying bombs in their wing bays if required.

Post-war, 192 Squadron reformed at Watton, Norfolk on 15 July 1951 as part of the Central Signals Establishment to continue its wartime task, but with a new enemy to watch. On 1 August 1958, the number '51' was given to the Squadron.

No. 192 Squadron: A Clearer Picture

Courtesy: Len Bartram

Len Bartram in adulthood updated his writings, never forgetting his schoolboy thrill, watching in excitement the airfield taking shape, strange aircraft shadowing the skies:

No. 192 Squadron was part of the secret 'Y' Service, its primary role – a full and detailed analysis from the air of enemy signals services.

This was first done by the RAF when The Blind Approach Training Development Unit (BATDU), in addition to normal work, flew Anson aircraft investigating German *Ruffian* and *Knickebein* ('knock-knee' or '*crooked leg*') radio beams transmitted over Britain. Crashed enemy bombers, on examination, showed that their Blind Approach equipment was adapted to use these beams for accurate pin-point bombing of targets on British towns and cities. In the blitz of London, for example, the Luftwaffe used the *Knickebein* system – bombers followed one radio beam broadcast from ground stations on the Continent until that beam was intersected by another at a point over the target.

Special Duties of BATDU were later taken over by a new Unit: The Wireless Investigation Development Unit (WIDU), leaving BATDU to carry on its normal tasks. Based at RAF Boscombe Down, the WIDU also used Anson aircraft and later Wellingtons. The scope of work by the Unit increased daily and on 10 December 1940 the Unit was re-designated No. 109 Squadron. A month later, the Squadron divided into three separate Flights, each with its own particular task.

Our concern is 'B' Flight of 109 Squadron, carrying out signal investigations over enemy territory with Wellingtons.

On 10 July 1942, this 'B' Flight became No. 1474 Flight, based at Gransden Lodge. No. 1474 Flight was re-designated No. 192 Squadron on 4 January 1943 with eleven Wellingtons, two Halifaxes and three Mosquitoes.

On 5 April, 192 Squadron moved from Gransden to Feltwell in Norfolk and on to Foulsham on 25 November 1943 where it remained until after the end of the war.

Meanwhile 'A' Flight, 109 Squadron, became No. 1473 Flight based at Finmere, Feltwell, Little Snoring, arriving at Foulsham where, on 1 February 1944, it merged with 192 Squadron.[24]

Base: RAF Foulsham – November 1943 to August 1945
                             with a detachment to Ford, Sussex

Disbanded: 22 August 1945

Aircraft: de Havilland Mosquito Mk IVs
                       Vickers Wellington Mk Xs
                       Handley Page Halifax Mk IIIs
                       Lockheed P.39L Lightnings

Officers Commanding:	Sqdn/Leader, Wing Commander & Air Commodore Vic Willis DFC, DSO; Wing Commander E. P. M. Fernbank DFC from 12 March 1944. Wing Commander D. W. Donaldson DFC DSO: 13 June 1944 – 22 August 1945

PERSONAL EXPERIENCES
192 Squadron
Canadian Pilot: Jack Fisher
Navigator/Spec Op: Henry Victor Alexander Vinnell

On 3 May 1944, Nina (my mother) met Vic, her fiancé, off a London train. The previous month, on her birthday, they had shared vows in Blymhill Church, close to their base at RAF Wheaton Aston, cycling through darkened lanes, praying for a ray of hope to lighten their path through those shadowed times. Vic had presented his fiancée with a brown lizard-skin powder compact, a note within:

> To my Sweetheart
> May your future be full of happiness, Nina,
> And may I have the honour of sharing that happiness with you?
> Your Lover for all time
> Vic xxxxxxxxxxxxxxxxxx

Now, she waited eagerly at Stafford railway station as Vic attended an interview with the Air Ministry regarding Special Signal Duties. They dined at the Station Hotel. However, words passed during the interview were cloaked in secrecy. He could tell her nothing, other than he was being posted ... and soon. It was very hush-hush, frustrating for them both!

One week on, Vic was posted to Foulsham. Distance was to remain an urgent issue when arranging any rendez-vous for the future. Through ensuing months, hundreds of letters passed between RAF Wheaton Aston, Staffs, and RAF Foulsham, Norfolk, often two and three times a day. They were making plans for the future. The path of love filled them with hope, longing, and a promise kept.

Suddenly, from the night of 26/27 November 1944, letters from RAF Foulsham ceased. They came no more.

Len Bartram was first to make contact with me fifty years on. Mum and I had responded to his advertisement in *'You Magazine'* promoting a new RAF No.100 Group Association bringing veterans together, but also to answer questions from family members about secrets surrounding 100 Group. Len was Committee Historian:

> ... there was a cover-up of most 100 Group operations up to the 1970s, even now all will never be revealed. In particular, 192 Squadron operations were classified, very top secret. Flight Lieutenant Vinnell operated special equipment which could identify and jam enemy radio/radar wave-lengths, confusing transmissions. They would operate in support of the RAF main bomber force, often carrying extra fuel tanks for long operations, flying with the bombers then as a decoy to another target, then to German night-fighter assemble areas, then back to and from the bomber stream. Great skill was required by these Navigators/Special Operators of the aircraft. 192 aircrew were specially picked to serve in that role ... in great danger of being found by night-fighters because their equipment gave off signals the enemy could home in on. But overall, 100 Group losses were below average, much less than expected ... [25]

Len, his wife Evelyn and I became firm friends. I shall never forget the look on my mother's face as, for the first time in over fifty years; she was able to talk to people who had known Vic and worked alongside him.

Ted Gomersall, Acting CO of the so-called *'Communications Flight'* on 192 Squadron, explained how it had happened at the time:

> Vic and I were close. Shortly before he and Jack went missing the night of 26/27 November 1944, we'd been to London together. Flying was off for some reason. He introduced me to the *Wings Club* in Grosvenor Square, and we gate-crashed some posh parties in Belgravia! *'Bud'* George, known universally as George the Automatic

Pilot; and Jack Fisher were close friends – they came to the UK together after training in Canada. George was my pilot. I too was a Special Operator/Navigator in 192, using equipment to identify enemy radio/radar wavelengths, confusing and jamming transmissions. I would say that Vic was occupied in some such activities on the night of 26/27 November 1944 – hardly an 'intruder mission', although it could conceivably have been in support of Qud. I see from my Log Book I wasn't flying that night, but on ops to Neuss the following night, the 27th.

My wife and I were married in 1937, and during my time in the RAF, we wrote to each other every day – a bit of a struggle at times! However, Hilda kept all my letters and I can best help by giving you relevant extracts:-

Sunday 26.11.44 ... In the evening, Vic and I went to the flicks, and saw '*Lifeboat*' ...

Monday 27.11.44 ... Jack Fisher and Vic failed to return last night, we have no news of them yet. There is a slight possibility they managed to get down in Belgium or France. I hope so. It's times like this one realises the futility of war ... they're probably ok at some airfield across the Channel.

Tuesday 28.11.44 ... Still no news of Jack and Vic. Today they are officially posted as '*Missing*'. Vic was to be married on his next Leave. His girl in the WAAF, was trying to get posted to Foulsham. He was half-expecting her coming this week ... there is still hope they put down at some obscure airfield in France. If it was a larger airfield we would have heard. They might have baled out over France or Germany. George, my pilot, is very shaken up about Jack ... they were close friends ... rather naturally, I suppose, being the only Canadians in the Flight at the moment ...

Wednesday 29.11.44 ... No news of Jack and Vic. Their names have been rubbed off the crew bit ...

Thursday 30.11.44 ... still no news. It begins to look as if they bought it, reluctantly as one is to come to that conclusion.

Sunday 3.12.44 ... Our worst fears are confirmed. Jack's cap and a sock with Vic's name on were washed up on the south coast yesterday. It's almost certain they came down in the drink, and yet there remain certain mysteries which I believe will never be cleared up ... Vic was actually talking about Nina, his fiancée and his plans just prior to the night of the 26/27th when he disappeared with Jack, his pilot.

The operation on 27.11.44 from which their Mosquito DK292 (code DTJ) failed to return was a Bomber Support Radar/Radio ELINT (Electronic Radio Countermeasure operation in the Neuss area of Germany on the edge of the Rhur) ...

It was the only 'ending' Mum was ever likely to get. In 1996, as she prepared to meet veterans Vic had known, she died of cancer. It was one of the first Reunions of its kind. But at least these wonderful people through their writings brought comfort and relief, a chance to understand the secret work in which he was involved.

Flight Lieutenant R. W. Dobson
by son Roger Dobson
(Chairman: RAF 100 Group Association)

Richard William Dobson was born in Patricroft, Eccles, in March 1916. His father was a time-served engineer at Locomotive manufacturers Naismith & Wilson, his mother a seamstress at Nassau Mill. Academically very bright, he had to leave school at sixteen when his father became redundant in the great Depression. Apprenticed to a local Pharmacy, he studied at Night School, qualifying as a Pharmacist at Manchester University in July 1938. He volunteered for the RAF soon after war broke out, but was not allowed to enlist until 1941.

My father's Observer and Air Gunner's Flying Log Book records that he flew from Wrexham to Foulsham on 15 May 1944 to take up a posting with 192 Squadron. During June he flew on what look like training flights, five times in Wellingtons and once in a Halifax. In four of the Wellington flights he was designated Special Operator. There was also a flight with Lt. Richards USAAF in a P38 Lightning. He first flew with F/Lt Gordon (*Nobby*) Clark in a Mosquito on 14 June 1944 when they flew to Peterborough, Chipping Norton, Barmouth, Fishguard, Camarthen, Tewkesbury, Bury St Edmunds before returning to Foulsham two hours, thirty-six minutes later. All his forty-six flights in Mosquitoes were with F/Lt Clark. Of these, twenty were operations, all but one at night, ranging from V1 targets in the Calais area to St Quentin, Paris, Lille, Koln Stuttgart, Dijon, Brunswick, Stendal, Kiel and Bremen. Their final five patrols (3 – 20 September 1944) are all described as '*Patrol Holland*' where I believe they were monitoring V2 activity at Peenemunde. Of the little my father said about his war service he did describe crossing the North Sea at very low level and that they flew alongside the Zuider Zee Dam below the level of the dam!

I also have a copy of his Service Record as made by him. It is interesting to note that he was in training for three years prior to being posted to an operational Squadron:

Flight Lieutenant Richard William Dobson Service Record as recorded by RWD

05.04.1941	Volunteered	Air Crew
25.06.1941	Cardington	Attested
23.02,1942	ACRC (Air Crew Reception Centre)	St John's Wood Flight 32/35A A Squadron
19.03.1942	No 11 I.T.W. (Initial Training Wing)	Scarborough?
01.07.1942	No 6 E.F.T.S.(Elementary Flying Training School)	Sywell, Northampton
05.08.1942	Manchester	(Heaton Park Aircrew Despatch centre?)
09.09.1942	Cranwell	RAF College, Sleaford, Lincolnshire
03.02.1943	Bridgnorth No1 Air navigation School	

04.04.1943	No 5 A.O.S.(Air Observers	RAF-Jurby, Isle of Man
20.09.1943	School)	
03.10.1943	Shawbury 11(P)AFU (Pilot)	Shawbury is six miles NNW
04.10.1943	(Advanced Flying Unit)	of Shrewsbury
05.10.1943	Condover 11 (P)AFU Condover,	A satellite of RAF Shawbury
06.10.1943	Shropshire	specialising in navigation training
07.10.1943	South Cerney 3 (P)AFU 4 miles	
23.10.1943	SE Cirencester, Gloucestershire	
24.10.1943	Shawbury 11(P)AFU	
25.10.1943		
26.10.1943	Condover 11 (P)AFU	
26.01.1944		
27.01.1944	Wrexham 11 (P)AFU	
15.05.1944		
16.05.1944	Foulsham 192 Squadron	
04.11.1945		
23.09.1944	Crashed Briston North Norfolk. Admitted Norfolk & Norwich Hospital	
02.01.1945	Transferred to RAF Hospital Ely	
30.06.1946	Posted No. 1 PMU* Gloucester	
13.07.1946	Started leave notice	
01.10.1946	Invalided from RAF	

* Possibly Patient Monitoring Unit or Physiological Monitoring Unit

On 20 September 1944, Nobby Clark and my father borrowed Wing Commander Donaldson's Tiger Moth T6906 for twenty-four hours Leave in Cambridge. Apparently in poor visibility they landed at an RAF airfield en-route to check their location. My father asked directions at the Control Tower and was told to go out of the gate, turn right at the main road, and follow it to Cambridge. This they did, reportedly at ten feet. On return to Foulsham they were put on a charge for low flying!

The following Saturday, 23 September, they took off in Mosquito 'J' DZ535 from Foulsham at 1100 for a fighter affiliation exercise, rendez-vousing with a Halifax over the North Sea. On completion of the exercise, with time to spare, for fun they practiced aerobatics for ten minutes. They then set course due south for home. According to my father, the feathering mechanism (this adjusts the pitch of the propeller) on one propeller failed at about 5000 feet and they began to lose height.

Parachuting into the cold North Sea was not appealing. By the time they were over land they were too low to jump. They tried to make it back to Foulsham, tracked by radar and in radio contact with their Control. With six miles to go they were faced with the prospect of landing in trees if they didn't make it. They identified an attractive field on the edge of the village of Briston and decided to make a belly-landing. The field is immediately behind the *Plough Inn* at a small hamlet, Craymere Beck. They came in very low over a farm-yard and made a belly- landing in one field, then careered through a hedge into a second field close to the *Plough* and two small rows of cottages. They were both injured and rescued from the wreckage by some very courageous locals who included two sisters and another woman, Ellen Hall. The time was exactly midday.

By great good fortune driving through Briston at the time of the crash was an Army ambulance complete with a doctor. The immediate medical aid may well have saved my father's life. Although severely injured, he was conscious and greatly concerned his rescuers did not light any cigarettes! His pharmacy training came into action and he instructed the doctor to write down drugs he administered on a card and tie it to his neck.

They were transported to hospital in Norwich where my father remained for four months before being transferred to the RAF Hospital at Ely. His injuries were severe: the left leg was amputated below the knee and his right ankle had to be rebuilt. He lost two or three inches in height. In all, he was in hospital for almost two years before returning to civilian life. After a short period working as a sales representative for May & Baker he returned to the pharmacy in Eccles and built a very successful business from which he retired fifty years after he first joined.

Nobby Clark, who became my sister's godfather, returned to flying duties and stayed on in the RAF after the war. The last letter I can find from him was probably written in December 1949:

At present I am stationed at Farnborough having finished the Empire Test pilots course; but in January I'm due to go to Boscombe Down for a couple of years. The work is most interesting as we see all of the new types of aircraft as they come out; and fly them before going to service with the RAF. There's plenty of variety and always the chance of a trip...

We now know that Nobby was awarded the DFC in December 1944 and, as Squadron Leader, was awarded a Queen's commendation for his work at Boscombe Down. Tragically he was killed when his De Havilland Venom collided with a Valetta transport on 25 November 1952.

DZ535 was a MKIVB Mosquito and had an interesting history. It was acquired by Vickers probably for experimental work on High Ball, the naval version of the Barnes Wallis bouncing bomb; and then transferred to 618 Squadron, formed to attack German naval targets with this new weapon. A lack of targets caused 618 to be disbanded and DZ535 was transferred to 192 Squadron.[26]

AUTHOR NOTE: 'Dobbie', as Roger's father was known during his RAF years, is mentioned in Vic's letters to Nina, my mother, and became a firm friend. His son Roger made contact with me after unexpectedly finding my book: 'Nina & Vic – A WWII Love Story' published in 2004 to commemorate the 60th Anniversary of the death of Vic and Jack. He saw references made to 'Dobbie' his father and with his sister Susan became members of RAF 100 Group Association of which, in 2014, Roger became Chairman.

Air Commodore Vic Willis
Commanding Officer: RAF Foulsham

Air Commodore Vic Willis was twice decorated for gallantry for his operational flying in the top secret world of signals intelligence, radio countermeasures and electronic warfare.

In late October 1941, he was the pilot of one of six specially equipped Wellington bombers sent to the Middle East to provide electronic counter-measures in support of an expected offensive in the Libyan Desert. The objective was to jam communications on the 28-34 mega-cycles waveband used between enemy-armoured columns. Operating from an advanced landing ground, the first sortie over the Sidi Omar area on 20 November satisfactorily caused a breakdown of tank-to-tank communications.

The following day, two Wellingtons took off for the Fort Capuzzo area. Vic Willis was pilot of one; the other, with the Army's top specialist in radio countermeasures on board, was lost. Fifteen minutes after starting the jamming operation, three Italian fighters pounced on Vic's lone aircraft. One of the fighters was shot down, but the Wellington was severely damaged with its rear gun turret put out of action and members of the crew wounded. Vic managed to escape into a patch of cloud and eventually limp back to base where it was discovered that his aircraft was damaged beyond repair.

A few days later, again flying alone deep over enemy occupied territory, his aircraft was attacked by a German fighter. His gunners damaged the enemy and drove it off. Vic completed his task of jamming enemy communications despite damage to his aircraft. Shortly afterwards it was announced that he had been awarded an immediate DFC.

Son of the regimental Sergeant Major of the Duke of Cornwall's Light Infantry, Charles Victor Douglas Willis, was born on 11 November 1916, at Calbourne, on the Isle of Wight and educated at Bodmin County School in Cornwall. In September 1933, he joined the RAF as an apprentice Engine Fitter at Halton where he excelled, finishing third in the order of merit and top in educational studies. As a result, he was awarded a cadetship to RAF College Cranwell where he was presented the Kings Medal for passing out first in the order of merit. He was assessed as the best pilot in his entry, and given the JA Chance Memorial Prize. He also excelled at sport, gaining his colours at hockey and soccer.

Vic initially flew London and Sunderland flying boats with No. 201 Squadron, also fulfilling the duties of Squadron Adjutant. At the outbreak of war, the Squadron was based at Shetland, flying patrols over the North Sea and to the Norwegian coast searching for surface raiders. In July 1940, he joined the recently formed Blind Approach and Training Development Unit at Boscombe Down, to become the source of some amusement for other pilots speculating how long it would be before the former flying boat pilot committed the unforgivable and land with his wheels retracted – he never did.

Vic was one of the initial group of pilots who investigated invisible beams guiding German bombers to their targets in the summer of 1940. These flights had to be undertaken during periods of enemy activity, often under hazardous flying conditions, in order to gather essential data for scientific analysis of the *Knickebein* beam. Data Vic and his colleagues gathered formed the principle for the development of Blind Landing Techniques based on the German Lorenz beam. This in turn became the basis of the ground-controlled blind-bombing system called *Oboe*.

After the experimental unit was re-designated 109 Squadron, Vic was made Flight Commander with particular responsibility in the early development of *Oboe*. Such a revolutionary device inevitably suffered setbacks. But, in due course, it became the primary blind-bombing aid used by Bomber Command's Pathfinder Force to pinpoint targets and achieve previously unattainable bombing accuracies.

After his encounter with fighters over the desert, Vic remained in the Middle East and joined the newly-formed 162 (Special Signals) Squadron at Kabrit in Egypt. Flying Wellingtons, the Squadron investigated and jammed enemy radio signals. Vic flew sorties over Greece and Crete to determine the nature of the defences, before another series of sorties to jam radios of enemy tanks in the Western Desert. As the campaign in Greece finished, Vic and his crews transferred their attention to the location and jamming of radar installations at Benghazi and Derna.

In June 1942, Vic re-joined No. 109 just as the Squadron started to train for *Oboe* operations with the Mosquito. By the end of the year he was promoted to Wing Commander and ordered to form a new Squadron, No. 192 – its role to conduct exploratory flights over enemy territory to identify radars and the operating wavelengths used.

Flying just off the coast, data was gathered, enabling counter-measures to be developed. Vic flew many sorties over the North Sea and the Bay of Biscay, but by early 1944 his Halifax and Wellington aircraft flew in support of bomber streams, gathering signals information and jamming enemy night-fighter frequencies. During the night of the Normandy invasion, Vic and his crews flew along the English Channel gathering signals information. After eighteen months in command, and on continuous operations, he was awarded the DSO, described as a fine leader, whose example of courage and devotion to duty had been worthy of the greatest praise.

Promoted to Group Captain in November 1944, Vic assumed command of RAF Foulsham, home to 192 Squadron and other specialist radio counter-measure Squadrons. In addition to his decorations, he was twice mentioned in dispatches (1941 and 1945). After the war, he continued to work in the secret world of signals and spent two years commanding flying operations of the Central Signals Establishment. In December 1948, he joined the RAF Mission in Greece where he spent the next two years at a particularly diffi-cult time in Greek politics. He was appointed an OBE.

After a period of instructing at the RAF Staff College, Bracknell, and on the Air Staff at Headquarters Bomber Command, Vic Willis was appointed Senior Air Staff Officer at the Central Reconnaissance Establishment. He then commanded RAF Luqa, the large airfield in Malta – home to two reconnaissance Squadrons monitoring movements in the Mediterranean of the Soviet Black Sea Fleet. On promotion to Air Commodore in September 1962, he was appointed Commandant of the RAF Staff College at Andover before retiring in March 1965[27]

Flight Lieutenant Vic Parker, RAFVR

In 1945, I served as a Mosquito Pilot in C Flight of 192 Squadron under Air Commodore Vic Willis when he was Group Captain of RAF Foulsham. Although I was a *'johnny-cum-lately'* to the clandestine and *'confounding'* operations of the Squadron, I became aware of the activities in RCM of F/Lt Vic Willis in 1942. The following account explains how this came about.

During 1941 and 1942, I was flying Wellingtons with 70 Squadron, based at Kabrit in the Suez Canal Zone. On the night of 2 January 1942, flying Wellington K8884, we were returning from an operation on Ras Lenuf in the Gulf of Serti (Tripoli) when, due to a navigational error caused by a failure to read a flashing light beacon correctly, we became unsure of our position and, being low on fuel, I decided to make a precautionary landing on the beach at Buq. However, due to the soft sand and steeply sloping beach, the aircraft swung violently into the sea. Luckily, all of us were able to evacuate the aircraft and wade ashore.

Having collected ourselves together and decided on our next course of action, we set off walking south in anticipation of being able to intercept the coastal road. By good fortune, as we finally reached the road, an Army lorry, laden with cans of petrol, happened to come along and stopped when the driver saw us with our hands above our heads! We identified ourselves to the driver's satisfaction and boarded his lorry, driving south into the desert to a South African Infantry Brigade H.Q. to which the petrol was being delivered. The Brigade had been involved over the previous few days in pushing elements of the Africa Korps out of Egypt.

From this H.Q we were then driven to a Hurricane Squadron, No. 30, based at Sidi Barrani by the shore and left there temporarily in the care of the Medical Officer. Whilst with him, he received a message that his services might be required as a motor launch had been seen drifting onto the shore. We joined the M.O in his ambulance and witnessed a dozen or so Germans and Italians, carrying little attaché cases, stepping ashore and looking so disconsolate as they were taken prisoner. They had put out from the port of Badia ahead of the advancing Eighth Army, hoping to escape capture, but run out of fuel! Such are the fortunes of war!

As we were not exactly welcome guests of 30 Squadron, they drove us south into the desert to a Forward Landing Ground, No. 09, from where it was known Wellington aircraft had been operating. On arrival, most of my crew, except my Rear Gunner and myself, were soon able to hitch a lift in an aircraft returning to Shalufa in the Canal Zone. Whilst waiting in the hope of soon getting a lift, I discovered a Wellington damaged by enemy action needing an engine change, was awaiting the availability of a pilot qualified to fly it out to Shalufa. It turned out to be Vic Wills' aircraft: Z9017 – but he had already departed, leaving behind his co-pilot, Sgt Humphries and W/Op Appleby to take care of the aircraft. Sgt Humphries had not been checked out as a first pilot, hence not qualified to act as pilot-in-command of the Wellington aircraft. In the circumstances, I persuaded the officer-in-charge of the FLG that I should take over with Sgt E Humphries as co-pilot. Together, we returned the aircraft safely to Shalufa on 6 January.

By coincidence, Vic Willis' W/Op. Sgt Appleby, came from my parents' home town, Boston, Lincolnshire, and his and my letters to our respective parents reporting our meeting led to perhaps an even greater coincidence. Sometime later, my mother was shopping in Boston when she overheard one woman saying to another that her son had met me in the Western Desert!

I heard later that Sgt Appleby was drowned when a York aircraft, carrying members of the Prime Minister's staff to the Yalta Conference, crashed into the sea off Malta. I never heard whether Sgt Humphries re-joined Vic Willis' crew or continued to be engaged in 100 Group RCM operations. [28]

Wing Commander Donaldson, DSO and Bar, DFC

Wing Commander Donaldson took over command of 192 Squadron from Wing Commander E. P. M Fernbank DFC on 13 June 1944. He was a man well respected by people who served under him.

David Donaldson was born in 1915 at Southampton, son of the Managing Director of the Thornycroft shipyard. He was educated at Charterhouse and Trinity College, Cambridge, where he was a keen rower. Taking a boat over to Germany with the First Trinity Boat Club in the mid-1930s, he enjoyed the hospitality of boat clubs in the Rhineland – at the same time sharply aware of the culture of aggression taking over the German psyche with the advent of Hitler.

In 1934, he joined the RAF Volunteer Reserve as a weekend pilot, and did much of his flying training at Hamble. After graduating at Cambridge and joining a firm of London solicitors, his Articles were interrupted in September 1939 when he was called up.

After basic training he did operational training on Wellington bombers and on 20 September was sent to 149 (Wellington) Squadron at Mildenhall, Suffolk. No. 149 had already been involved in desperate missions – the attack on German shipping at Wilhelmshaven on 18 December 1939, the attempt to stem the German advance in the Low Countries in May 1940, and the brave but futile transalpine lunge at Genoa in June after Italy entered the war on the German side. Now it was ordered to attack the invasion barges collecting in Channel ports, and Donaldson's first sortie was a daytime raid on Calais harbour.

With the end of the Battle of Britain, No. 149 was redirected to strategic bombing. This was soon revealed as far too dangerous against flak and fighter defences by day, and therefore reverted to night, when (frequent) bad weather made locating targets extremely difficult in the state of development of navigational aids at that time.

During the winter of 1940 – 41, the main effort was against targets in the relatively close Ruhr, but then in October, a much longer sortie to Berlin, in vile weather. This ended with Donaldson's Wellington becoming lost on the return trip. With fuel perilously low, he achieved a casualty-free forced landing at St Osyth, near Clacton.

There were further attacks on northern Italian industrial cities, one of which, an attack on the Fiat works at Turin, Donaldson was asked by the BBC to describe in a radio broadcast in December 1940. Instead of dwelling on the difficulties of such a mission, he eloquently described the majesty of the snow-covered Alps!

Donaldson won his DFC for a highly successful raid on Merignac aerodrome near Bordeaux, which he bombed from a height of 1500 feet, destroying its large hangers. Further publicity for these early efforts by Bomber Command came from featuring in a series of propaganda photographs taken by Cecil Beaton, entitled: 'A Day in the Life of a Bomber Pilot'. One of these, featuring the aircrew of a 149 Squadron Wellington at Mildenhall, adorns the cover of a recently published video of the 1941 propaganda film: 'Target for Tonight'.

Donaldson was 'rested' after completion of this tour in March 1941, but seconded to the Air Ministry to help buy aircraft in the U.S. This turned out to involve hazardous ferrying across the Atlantic of American aircraft that had been purchased, notably the invaluable Hudson long-range patrol bomber for Coastal Command.

In September, Donaldson returned to operations with 57 Squadron, another Wellington Unit. In a raid over Dusseldorf in October, Donaldson's aircraft was badly shot up, limping home without hydraulics. The undercarriage could not be lowered and the sortie ended with a crash- landing at Marham. After several more raids, Donaldson succumbed to the strain and at the end of the year was admitted to hospital.

After a period of sick leave he was posted as Group Tactical Officer to 3 Group, but in July 1942, posted on to No. 15 Operational Training Unit for six months as a Flight Commander. Though this was not a front line unit, he did get in one operational trip to Dusseldorf during this period.

In January 1943, he was appointed Flight Commander to 156 Squadron, an original Pathfinder Force unit. The four-engined Lancaster was now the mainstay of Bomber Command and with No. 156, Donaldson carried out twenty-three raids, awarded the DSO and promoted to Wing Commander at the end of his tour. Rested again in June 1943, Donaldson commanded a conversion unit and then went as Staff Officer to No. 100 (Special Duties) Group.

Just after D-Day, Donaldson was back in the air in command of 192 (SD) Squadron. Leading the Squadron in a Halifax III, Donaldson flew twenty-five more sorties, some in daytime. On one daylight operation he was attacked by two Me109s. Rather than trying to shoot it out with the cannon-armed fighters using the Halifax's 303 machine guns, Donaldson chose to elude the foe by violent and skilful evasive action, bringing his aircraft and crew safely home. He was awarded his second DSO in July 1945.

Donaldson had no ambition to further his career in the RAF and on demobilisation he resumed his law Articles to qualify as a solicitor. After four years in the City firm Parker Garrett, he joined National Employers Mutual Insurance, where he became Company Secretary and later a Director. He left NEM to become Chairman of an industrial tribunal, which he greatly enjoyed, presiding over some notable cases. He finally retired in 1987. [29]

Navigator/Special Operator Eric Clarkson
Night Sortie

Most of my flying in Mosquitoes was done at night, so I will start in the morning of a typical day.

My pilot's name was F/O Joe Reay. If we were required to undertake a sortie that night we'd be told where our destination was to be and I would be given flight directions and went to plan the route. I would also be given details of special operations I was to carry out.

Later in the day we attended the Briefing, held in the Briefing Room behind closed doors for obvious reasons of security. If other crews were involved, they also would attend. The Squadron Commanders would be present as would W/Cdr Donaldson.

Briefing covered such things as where the German flak belts were, warning to Air Gunners by the Air Gunners Leader to maintain alertness at all times. The colours of the day usually were given, a combination of three colours red, white or green. The weather forecast was made by the Met Officer with warnings about possible fog conditions on return and diversion aerodromes stated. Cloud conditions were of obvious concern to Bomb Aimers. Radio silence would be observed by Wireless Operators except in an emergency. Navigators were given various courses to fly by the Nav Leader, although these would have been given at a previous Briefing, attended by me.

As a Mosquito crew, we usually had a much more detailed Briefing as we had a particular job to do over the target area using *Piperack* jammers. We would be told when to switch these on to make it almost impossible for those on the ground to communicate with their nightfighters. Often we orbited the target area for up to forty minutes at a height of between 25,000 and 28,000 feet, generally out of range of the anti-aircraft guns.

All crews would have had their pre-op meal and then all went to the locker room to pick up parachutes and other items of flying clothing, including a jacket to which the parachute would be attached if we needed to bale out. As Mosquito crews were not required straight away with a much shorter flying time, take-off times could vary by as much as half an hour or more to the main force.

At RAF Foulsham there was a sort of ritual which included singing popular songs of the time. It lightened what otherwise would have been a pretty serious matter seeing that many of those who sang it might in the immediate future or at some more distant time, not survive.

My first trip in a Mosquito was a '*Big Ben*' operation. This meant we were on a Special Duty Patrol, searching over Belgium and Holland to see if there were any radio signals emanating from that region which might have significance in regard to the V2s.

Our aircraft was a Mosquito Mk IV numbered W4071 and lettered DT/K. It may be of interest to know that this aircraft was among the first batch of Mosquitoes ever built in 1941, still flying in February 1945!

This aircraft had seen better days and one of its problems was that it could not reach an altitude much above 22,000 feet, unlike the Mk XIVs which we got towards the end of the war in April 1945, and which were pressurised, and had a very good heating system to the extent that we only needed our ordinary uniform plus flying boots and a helmet with an oxygen mask. We were completely unarmed.

To return to the basic script, we were fed and watered. We were also required to empty our pockets of anything of interest to the Germans if captured. Even a bus ticket, or an address would have been of interest to them and such was the fear of giving some-thing which might indicate where we were stationed, we religiously observed the need to make sure we gave them nothing. After visiting the crew room to pick up parachutes etc. we went to our dispersal which was next to Flying Control building.

Seating in a Mosquito is a tandem arrangement, with the Pilot sitting on the left with his instruments in front of him, such as the control column, and pedals under his feet which help steer the plane on the ground and also act as brakes. The throttle controls are to his right as are the controls for changing pitch, and a lever which controls the flaps. He has a compass in front plus all the other dials which show engine temperature, petrol gauges, altimeter, rate of climb, and turn and bank indicators. He is in touch with me via his intercom.

My 'office' is slightly behind and to his right. In front of me is the principal navigation display called 'GEE'. Behind me are the radios and a wire recorder, with switches to control 'Piperack' operated as and when needed. The 'Piperack' is actually in the bomb bay, but we will not be using it on this occasion.

I will have already given Joe Reay the Flight Plan from which he can see what course to steer, the time he is to turn on to the next course(s) to fly, and at what height and speed he should maintain.

It is the pilot's responsibility to sign 'Form 700' before climbing on board. This shows an acceptance that all parts and controls that need to be checked are OK. This Form 700 was always signed and it may well be the procedure still, and will be examined should there be a fault or the aircraft does not return.

The Pilot gets in first with his parachute just as I get out first at the end of the trip. There is precious little room in a Mosquito. We buckle our seat belts and plug in the intercom. Once ground crew has closed the doors, the Pilot is ready to start the engines. He always begins with the port (right), then the starboard (left) motor. Once the engines are running properly, all that needs to be done is to get permission from the Control Tower so we can move off. We taxi to the end of the runway and await a green light from the Ground Controller. The reason for this procedure is that we have to be reasonably assured that there are no other aircraft either coming in or already on the runway.

Off we go into the wide blue yonder and tell the Control Tower we are airborne. The Pilot climbs on to the course I have given and he switches off our navigation lights and switches on the IFF (Identification Friend or Foe) which gives out a signal to friendly AA gunners and fighters as soon as we judge we have reached the English Coast. This IFF had a drawback because it could be detected by the enemy, so needed to be switched off as soon as the enemy coastline came into view. We also have a rear-facing radar aerial called 'Boozer'. Here again it had to be used with care because of the ability of German night fighters to home on to it. Often we would either not use it at all or only do so over the target area.

As soon as we reach 8000 feet the pilot tells me to switch on the oxygen. The Pilot might need to alter course fairly soon and by following the Flight Plan we are on our way. On this occasion we knew we were unlikely to see the ground as we had been told to expect 10/10ths cloud all the way there and back. (I found out recently we were the only aircraft sent out on 12 February 1945!)

However, our troubles were only just beginning. After half an hour or more, the GEE equipment failed. It meant we were left to fly on Flight Plan, unable to see the ground at all. We'd been told prior to take-off that we only needed to do one leg and return of the Antwerp plot and then turn for home. At the time I was not unduly worried as I thought the Met forecast could not be too far adrift. How wrong I was!

Having not seen hide nor hair of any V2s despite regular searching on frequencies I'd been given to scan, we turned for home. We didn't make any calls by radio for at least twenty minutes. Radio silence was a must. I could judge by then we might at least be over the coast of England, but through a brief break in the clouds I could see we were still over unfamiliar land. We didn't know where we were. We were lost!

Nav to Pilot – *'I think we may be lost, but I'll try my GEE box again to see if it's working.'*

Nav to Pilot – *'No joy from GEE. You have some frequencies you can try.'*

Pilot to Nav – *'Okay, I'll do that.'* (Pilot tries the frequencies.)

My Pilot had a number of frequencies he could call up, some of them on the Continent, but none answered.

Pilot to Nav – *'No response from anyone. Got any other frequencies?'*

Nav to Pilot – *'I'll have a look on the map to see if there are any other 'dromes in France where we can get in touch. We could try Juvincourt?'*

Pilot tries the frequency. Still no answer. Was the R/T working?

All this takes a long time while we continue to maintain the Flight Plan Course.

Nav to Pilot: *'Any joy?'*

Pilot to Nav: *'Not a sausage!'*

Nav to Pilot: *'You could try calling 'Cartwright'.'*

Pilot to Nav: *'No reply from Base. I'll give it another go.'*

Pilot to Nav: *'Still no response, do you think a 'Mayday' might do the trick? I'll give it a go.'*

Pilot to Nav: *'There's a faint call from 'Kingsley'. Can you hear it?'*

(Later we were to find this was Tangmere.)

Nav to Pilot: *'Ask them to give you a QDM for Foulsham.'*

Pilot to Nav: *'The course they have given means we're way off our Flight Plan. I'm turning onto that course now.'*

After some time ...

Nav to Pilot: 'Try 'Cartwright'. They must be within calling distance by now.'

'Sturgeon 10 from 'Cartwright'. Steer 045 Magnetic.'

Imagine our surprise and puzzlement as we needed to make a full ninety degrees to get on the bearing of the course given!

Our call sign was 'Sturgeon 10'. The Foulsham call sign was 'Cartright'. We had the best part of 200 – 250 miles to go! Fortunately we had an adequate amount of fuel and barring any further mishaps, would arrive in about an hour. Which we did!

After we were both debriefed, we deposited parachutes etc. and reported the failure of the *GEE* equipment. We went back in a van to our meal of egg and chips in the Mess and so to bed. Neither my Pilot nor I were in the same Nissen Hut, so we could only discuss the matter the following morning.

When we calculated the back-plot next day, we reckoned we'd been at least 100 miles further south than we should have been. We were in the Rouen area. What happened was that, unbeknown to us, there was an intense area of low pressure in the area we were flying. At the height we were flying, wind speeds are very strong, up to 80–100 mph. The wind forecast meant to be in a *southerly* direction turned out to be in a more *northerly* direction and we had, in fact, on our Flight Plan been adding some sixty miles each way because of the incorrect forecast. It's no wonder we didn't pick up any transmissions – we were over friendly territory!

By the way, there weren't any transmissions to be recorded in any case since V2s were not guided missiles, but we didn't know that at the time. [30]

F/Lt Henry Bradfield (*Hank*) Cooper, DSO DFC

Flight Lieutenant Hank Cooper played an important role in the secret radio war waged over German skies; for this he received a DSO, a rare award for a Wireless Operator/Air Gunner.

Hank had completed more than thirty bombing operations when he joined No. 192 Squadron at Foulsham, Norfolk, in November 1943. The

Squadron had only recently been formed to provide radio countermeasures to confound the German night fighter and air defence system, and reduce the RAF's heavy bomber losses.

Flying in specially equipped Wellingtons and Halifaxes amongst the main bomber attack force, Hank had the task of gathering signals intelligence on German radar and radio transmissions.

After ten operations collecting data on frequencies used by early warning radar sites positioned along the coast of the North Sea and the Bay of Biscay, he started flying over Germany in a two-seat Mosquito. Undeterred by the fact he hadn't trained as a Navigator, he went on to complete many long-range operations over Germany.

He completed a further thirty operations and was awarded a DFC for bringing back exceptionally valuable 'Y' information (signals intelligence). His Commanding Officer commented that he had *'never seen Hank ruffled on returning from any operation'*.

The son of a builder, Henry Bradfield Cooper, always known as Hank, was born on 4 May 1919 at Chevington, near Bury St Edmunds. After attending West Suffolk County School, and excelling at sport, he joined the Post Office as Apprentice Engineer in 1936. At the outbreak of war, he was working on secret transmission systems at RAF Mildenhall. Within a few weeks he was called up by the RAF.

Hank trained as a Wireless Operator and Air Gunner before joining No. 149 Squadron based at Mildenhall, operating the twin-engine Wellington bomber. He flew his first operation against Gelsenkirchen in January 1941. Over the next six months he completed thirty-two raids on Germany, attacking Berlin, Hamburg and Cologne. He described this period as his most *'frightening and hair-raising'*. By the end of the war, he and one other were the only survivors from his crew of six.

At the end of his Tour, he was mentioned in dispatches and commissioned to Pilot Officer. For his Rest Tour, he instructed at an Operation Training Unit at Wellesbourne, near Warwick.

On the night of 30 May 1942, Hank attacked Cologne during the first of Air Marshal Sir Arthur 'Bomber' Harris's 1,000-bomber raids, *'Operation Millennium'*. To achieve this, Harris employed almost 400 aircraft from bomber training units, manned by Instructors. Two nights later, they flew a second 1,000-bomber raid to attack Essen.

After completing his Tour on No. 192 Squadron, Cooper spent time working in the Air Intelligence Branch at the Air Ministry. '*I didn't like this inactive work*', he recalled; '*so strove hard to get back on operations.*' In November 1944, he volunteered to return to No. 192 and, over the next four months, flew a further thirty-five Operations over Germany. As war drew to a close, jamming and diversionary operations became the primary role for No. 192.

Hank's last flight, on 24 April 1945, was when he accompanied the bomber force to Munich. It was his 100th operation over Germany, a unique record recognised by Geoffrey de Havilland, and workers at his Mosquito factory, who presented him with a painting of his aircraft. Shortly afterwards, it was announced he had been awarded a DSO. Hank's Squadron Commander commented:

> ... his keenness for operational flying is quite exceptional. His great technical ability, cool skill and strong sense of duty have caused him to be chosen for the most difficult tasks. His devotion to duty has been exemplary. [31]

When war ended, Hank was sent to the Radio Warfare Establishment, where he continued to work in the secret world of radio and radar surveillance. Always a modest man, all he would say of this was: '*... we investigated various radars*'. Some of these included captured German systems.

In autumn 1948, he returned to the GPO. In the course of the next 32 years there, he received regular promotions, culminating in his appointment in 1976 as Deputy Telephone Manager for the City of London. During his GPS service, he was awarded their silver medal for his Paper on '*The Gas Pressurisation of Cables*'.

Hank retired to Suffolk in 1980, moving to Cornwall three years later. A first-rate squash player, he represented the RAF in 1948 and in the 1950s was twice champion of Suffolk. He also won the Civil Service championship and represented Cambridgeshire until 1962. At the age of 50, he regained his Club Championship. In 1970, he joined the British champion, Jonah Barrington, to make a series of squash tutorial programmes for Anglia Television.

Hank also enjoyed shooting and fishing, and remained a strong supporter of the Cromer tennis and squash club. He always had a strong sense of humour. [32]

Special Operator Stan '*Ginger*' Forsyth, DFC
The Long and Winding Road

As a family we all knew that Dad, now 93, had been in the wartime RAF and awarded the DFC. He didn't speak about his war experience or what happened to him, but he was always talking of wanting to return to Norfolk to see if he could find old air bases where he had been stationed. A few years ago we took Dad back to Norfolk. It was on that trip we discovered and joined the RAF 100 Group Association which he's been involved with ever since. It's a long journey by car from Norwich to Liverpool and it was on the journey home after attending our first 100 Group Reunion weekend that he started to share his war experiences with us. It was clear Dad didn't feel his story was special enough to put to paper – he was '*just doing his job*' like all those other young men in Bomber Command. Meeting other veterans at that first 100 Group Reunion and listening to their stories, had a profound effect on all my family. It made us realise how lucky we were that our Dad had made it through the war and appreciate what sacrifices so many young men of Dad's generation made. After much persuasion Dad agreed to let us record his memories of that time so that the efforts of the men of 100 Group will never be forgotten and in tribute to those '*who never made it home*':

This is Dad's story:

When war was declared I was eighteen and working as a postal telegraphist in Liverpool Head Post Office. Like many working-class lads from the area I was keen to volunteer for service. After gaining my employer's permission to sign up, and completing necessary paperwork, I applied to join the RAF – choosing this over other Services with the idea of flying, something I'd never done; an exciting prospect. My dad served with the Cold Stream Guards in the First World War. He'd told me of his awful experiences in the trenches and I didn't much fancy that for myself!

On joining in January 1941 I was posted to RAF West Kirby and then on to RAF Skegness to complete basic training. I remember that time with feelings of excitement mixed with homesickness at being away from my family for the first time. Like many others, I wondered where I would be sent next. This was soon decided when one of my superiors discovered I'd been a telegraphist before joining and told me this *'made me a natural for wireless training'*. I was duly posted to Blackpool for initial Wireless Operator training and later to Wiltshire for advanced wireless training.

Once qualified as a fully-fledged Wireless Operator, I completed a flying course at RAF Mallom in Cumberland and a gunnery course at Stormeydown, South Wales, at the end of which I was promoted to Sergeant and given my 'wings'. I was granted a week's leave prior to reporting to RAF Cottesmore for bomber training and I remember how proud I was returning home to see my family and fiancé with my 'wings' proudly on show.

The Liverpool I returned to however, was greatly changed from when I left, having suffered severe damage from the blitz bombing. My family lived near the city centre and bomb damage in my neigh-bourhood was a stark reminder of what war could do. It made me feel I'd been protected from the realities of war while away train-ing and began to realise just what I was getting involved in. During that leave I remember taking my fiancé Gertie to the cinema and, because of a heavy bombing raid, ended up getting stuck overnight in the cinema, unable to get home until the following day. Being young and in love we made the most of our time together, but when we emerged from the cinema next day it seemed half the city had been destroyed. I'll always remember the walk home, being met by both my mother and future mother-in law who had worried all night for our safety. They met us with tears of relief, mixed with anger at our stupidity for going to the 'pictures' on the night of one of the worst bombing raids that Liverpool endured.

During that week's leave I received a telegram cancelling my planned posting for bomber training, telling me instead to report to RAF Penrhos, Wales, to commence as a Flying Instructor. I was there from December 1942 until January 1944 during which time I was promoted to Flight Sergeant. It seemed my skills at wireless ops had also been noted during my training hence my posting as an Instructor. I was initially disappointed not being able to complete bomber train-ing because, like most of my colleagues, I wanted a more 'active' role in the war. But I understood the RAF knew what was needed to win the war and we all had to accept orders and the role we would play.

I made the best of the time in Wales with a great bunch of lads, enjoying the benefits of the hospitality of farmers in the area and local produce. I even indulged my love of singing by joining with two other lads posted there to form our own acapella 'Group', performing at camp concert nights. Such was our success that our reputation spread and we were even asked to perform at concert nights at the local Army bases!

I remember one particular training flight in an Avro Anson whilst at Penrhos which turned out to be very eventful. On our return flight we encountered severe fog and equipment failure which meant we had no idea where we were. Flying as low as we safely could, our plan was to find a landmark to establish our location. After what seemed an age we finally found something – a tower looming out of the fog so close we nearly demolished it – Blackpool Tower! Using this landmark we followed the coastline down to Penrhos where I experienced my first crash landing, overshooting the runway directly adjacent to the sea. Thankfully the pilot did a great job of putting us down safe on the beach and we climbed out of the plane to walk across the beach towards camp. As we neared the fence, we were met with lots of staff waving madly at us – we thought they were just glad to see us, but then realised they were trying to tell us we were walking through a live minefield! We all reached camp safely and I remember feeling I must have had a guardian angel looking out for me – a feeling that stayed with me for the rest of the war.

In January 1944 I was called for an interview at the Air Ministry in London for 'Special Duties'. I remember feeling excited as I had never been to our capital city and had no idea what 'Special Duty' had in store for me. After a successful interview, I was posted to 192 Squadron at RAF Foulsham under Bomber Command.

I didn't see much of Norfolk for the first three months as I was put immediately onto an intensive course of training with new radar equipment, essential in my future role as a 'Special Operator'. Along with other lads we commenced training, which I was told would normally take a year but we only had three months to complete! We worked day and night, breaking off only for meals and a few hours' sleep each night. But we didn't mind as we knew we had an important role in helping win the war. As part of the training we were sent to various Radar Stations along the Kent coast to observe operations. It was here I experienced the awful shelling from Germans across the Channel. This served to reinforce my view that I was glad I joined the RAF. It gave me even more respect for those lads in the Army who faced that kind of ordeal all the time.

Upon completion of my special training, I then had three air experience trips where I put into practice new techniques learned, before finally joining up with my crew. I was attached to an established crew at Foulsham consisting of F/O Ken Macdonald, a Canadian pilot, F/S Stan C. Crane, Canadian Navigator, and fellow Canadian Bomb-Aimer F/S Barney E. Vanden (later nicknamed 'Vital' as we never actually carried bombs on operations, but he made himself invaluable in many other ways!). The British part of my crew comprised: F/S Don Maskell, Mid-Upper Gunner, Sgt Paddy Nevin, Rear-Gunner, Flt/S Geordie W. McCann as Wireless Operator, and Sgt Les Coggins our Flight Engineer.

Joining an established crew was a daunting prospect for us all. Aircrews bonded just like a family unit with established ties and rituals. But I couldn't have wished for a better bunch of lads who accepted me into the fold very quickly. I was soon given the nickname 'Ginger' by being the only redhead in the crew. We lived, worked and slept together and established friendships like no other I have made since. I was to complete all but two operations of my first tour with this crew and grateful to do so as we were lucky to come home unscathed from most of our flights.

To maintain our good luck we had our own special rituals, including everyone urinating on the rear wheel before take-off – probably as much from nerves and a desire to avoid having to use the bucket on-board reserved for anyone caught short! Our pilot Ken had a little old doll he would not fly without and I remember our driver being sent back to the locker room on more than one occasion when he forgot to bring it with him – we never flew without it and she certainly was our lucky mascot. Ken was a man short in stature but large in character and he almost had to stand up to reach the pedals when landing the plane. He was affectionately nicknamed 'Gill' – Canadian lads called him 'half-pint', but us British lads soon changed that to '*Gill*' being a smaller measure because he was too short to be a '*half-pint*'!

My own lucky charm was an English pound note that I carried on every operation. Before each flight we were issued with a sealed pouch containing foreign currency so that, if we had to bale out, we had local money to assist our plight. I also believed that an English pound note would help if I needed to prove I was British, so I hid it in my flying gear for each trip. Thankfully I never needed it, but to this day, more than seventy years on, I still carry that same note in my wallet as my own lucky charm.

Despite our lucky charms we did have hairy moments during our tour. I remember an encounter with a German FW190 over France which our Rear Gunner spotted attacking us from the rear. Whilst firing at the attacker, he ordered the skipper to corkscrew to starboard and continued firing as the fighter closed to within 200 yards. The German FW then dived away deeply to port and exploded on the ground, later claimed as '*probably destroyed*'.

As Special Operator, my location within the Halifax was such that I couldn't see much of what was happening both within and outside the aircraft during flights. This is highlighted in my memory of one of only two operations I carried out flying with a different crew.

I was already anxious because I wasn't flying with my own, when I discovered I was to take part in a daylight raid to Essen with Squadron C/O: W/C Donaldson as pilot. During the raid, we were flying above the mainstream when one of our Lancasters a hundred yards below, took a main hit from German A/A guns and exploded mid-air. All I remember from my location on the aircraft was the noise and smell of the explosion. The Flight Engineer scrambled round the plane checking we were all okay and told me what happened – we were lucky and made it home, unlike the crew of the Lancaster who were all killed. When we left the craft that day and I saw how much damage we sustained I thanked God for our safe return and for once was glad that, as a Special Operator, I didn't have a window to look out from!

The equipment and Special Duties part of my role was regarded by Air Ministry to be of such importance I was not even allowed to let the rest of my crew know what I was doing. This resulted in much leg-pulling by the crew about my *'activities'*, especially when it resulted in me being left on the plane under special guard. If we made any unexpected landings at other RAF bases because of weather problems or refuelling needs, I had to stay on the plane with my 'special equipment' whilst they were off for refreshments etc. After any operation, the first port of call for any Special Operator was to take all information gathered during the flight to our superiors for debriefing purposes. At the time we didn't realise just how important that information was or how it was used. Only many years later did it become evident that Special Duties performed by RAF 100 Group actually served to alter the course of the war. Using information we retrieved, others working behind the scenes at places such as Bletchley Park, came up with targets and plans that would ultimately defeat the enemy.

One such target was to prove my most memorable operation involving a trip to the Arctic Circle.

On 31 August 1944 my crew and four other Halifaxes were dispatched to RAF Lossiemouth in Scotland where we were instructed that we had to perform a *'signal search'* of the Norwegian Fjords. Each Halifax had to investigate specific wireless frequencies and each was allocated its own individual waveband to search and monitor. We soon realised this operation was to be a *'big one'* as each craft was fitted with three additional fuel tanks in the bomb-bays to enable larger distances to be covered.

In my Log Book I recorded our take-off at 22.21 hours and our return as 07.17 hours the next day. I remember clearly the freezing conditions as the coldest we ever experienced. With very low cloud most of the way up to Norway it was necessary to fly below cloud level to avoid the wing flaps icing up. For much of the flight, visibility over the water was so limited the Rear Gunner had to drop smoke bombs regularly to determine the wind drift. Whilst the rest of the crew were working to get us safely to our target, my job was to keep my eyes glued to my radar screens and equipment, logging every signal I detected. I remember feeling so cold it was difficult to concentrate on the screens for over nine hours!

I was fortunate to pick up the hoped-for signal both on our outward and return flight over the target and duly recorded the location in my Logs. We made it back safely to Lossiemouth with the information, not realising until much later that the location I found was a gap in the enemies' defence radar. This information later led to successful sorties against enemy ships, the most important of which turned out to be the famous *Tirpitz*.

I was later to be awarded the DFC for my part in this operation – an achievement of which I was very proud and I will always be grateful to the rest of my crew, who I believe deserved to share it with me.

It was the skill and spirit of this crew that only a month or so earlier, on 12 July 1944, had kept us all alive when forced to crash-land on return from an operation to Revigny in France. The port engine of the Halifax failed and we limped back to Foulsham to discover our braking system had also suffered damage. Our pilot '*Gill*' managed to get us down and we ended up off the end of the runway in the adjacent field, with the undercarriage wrenched free and the aircraft practically on its side. Fearing a fire, we evacuated through the roof of the craft and scrambled to safety via the upturned wing, not realising we then had a twenty-foot leap to the ground. Needless to say, we never let '*Gill*' forget that landing and many a pint was sank to celebrate our safe return in local Foulsham pubs.

At the end of my tour of operations at Foulsham I was sad to be separated from my crew as I was chosen to be posted to RAF 100 Group HQ at Bylaugh Hall in Norfolk as Assistant Controller in the Operations Room, having by now been commissioned as a Pilot Officer. My role was to co-ordinate information and orders between various Bases comprising 100 Group and Bomber Command and to prepare daily Reports on activities for the AOC at Bylaugh. I adapted to my new role and enjoyed the more luxurious surroundings of this lovely Estate. I even took up 'hunting' as the AOC had a habit of supplementing our diet with fresh rabbit and pheasants he shot on the Estate. I was taken along on these trips to carry the 'spoils of the hunt' back to the kitchen – needless to say for a lad from Liverpool these were not the usual dishes on my menu!

In order to maintain our skills and the additional pay we received for 'flying duties', staff at Bylaugh were encouraged to keep up their flying hours by using a few Tiger Moths kept at nearby RAF Swanton Morley. Naturally we all availed ourselves, flying to Bases up north, using it as an opportunity to have a quick unofficial visit home to loved ones. Whilst at Bylaugh I had the opportunity to meet a number of my war heroes including W/C 'Tirpitz' Tait who completed the task I started when locating the *Tirpitz*. The most amusing hero I met was Squadron Leader Micky Martin of the Dambusters who used one of the Tiger Moths from Swanton to perform the best low flying aerobatics display I have ever seen over Bylaugh Hall, much to the AOC's dismay. I was ordered to find out *'who that bloody fool was and tell him to report to the AOC on landing'*. At the time I didn't know who the culprit was, but when I found out I made sure his identity was never revealed. Both W/C Tait and S/L Martin went on to become regular staff at Bylaugh Operation Command.

At the end of the war in Europe I was posted to RAF Watton and resumed flying duties as a Special Operator. The war in Japan was still ongoing and we were preparing to move the unit and operations to Ceylon when the Atom bomb was dropped in Japan and all postings to the Far East were postponed.

In 1946 I was finally demobbed as a Flying Officer and married my fiancé Gertie that year, returning to work for the Post Office.

In 1951, I was approached by the Army Postal Services and offered a Commission in the Army which I accepted and served for over seven years, enjoying the opportunity to travel and see the world. My family joined me for some postings and I earned the General Services Medal for my time in Malaya. Although I was to wear the uniform of an Army Officer and enjoyed my time in this Service, I always remained a *'Fly-Boy'* at heart, much to the chagrin of my Army colleagues. I eventually left the Army in 1958 and again returned to the Head Post office in Liverpool where I remained until I retired in 1981 as Assistant Head Post Master.

I was happy to have further involvement with the RAF when my son persuaded me to join his local ATC Squadron in Liverpool and I was re-commissioned as Flying Officer for a six-year period from

1965. It was a great time helping these young people to experience the activities and benefits the RAF offered and made me value even more the friendships made as a result of my involvement with the RAF over the years. [33]

Joe Sayers, Leading Aircraftsman (LAC)

Most airmen are, as one would expect; Radio Fitters or Mechanics and worked in the Nissen hut. Some are Carpenters and one is a Blacksmith who worked in the Station Workshop together with a Sheet Metal Worker. Jim Everton and I first worked from the Mod (Modification) Section which was mostly concerned with Bomber Command Modifications which had to be done to all aircraft from time to time. It will be recalled that 192 Squadron had three types of aircraft – Wellington, Halifax and Mosquito. Later, Jim Everton and I with Gordon Ashton worked from a Nissen hut near the Special Signals Section, but across the road which, to the left, went past the church down to Foulsham village. Jim, Gordon and I were by trade Fitter II A's (Airframe Fitters) where we worked solely for the main section.

The carpenters were involved in the manufacture and fitting of tables for the various electronic boxes in Wellington and Halifax aircraft. They also had certain work to do on Mosquitoes. The Blacksmith and Sheet Metal worker would do specialist work that airframe fitters required from time to time.

By the nature of work carried out by the Squadron, aircraft needed extra aerials fitted and this was done by the three airframe fitters. Most aerials were common to all Wellington and Halifax aircraft and assembled from manufactured parts, although we did make the elements ourselves in such a way that they could be changed when necessary. Some aerials were completely made in the Section and covered by a Perspex blister. Sometimes we were required to fit a special aerial on particular aircraft.

I was the airframe fitter that was sent to RAF Deptford, referred to on page 47 in the book by William & John Rees: 'Espionage in the Ether'. I actually made and fitted a waveguide to an H2S scanner. I also fitted the aerial in the nose of a Mosquito referred to on page 55 and later removed.

Sergeant R. B. Hales
Taking no Prisoners!
by David Hales (nephew)

Sergeant R. B. Hales, a Flight Engineer, aged twenty years old; was posted to 192 Squadron on 23 October 1944. He was my uncle. The rest of his crew were:

W/O B. H. Harrison (Pilot, aged 29)
Sgt R. P. Clancy (Mid-Upper Gunner, aged 21)
Sgt T. D. McGill (Rear-Gunner, aged 20)
Sgt A. P. Bloomfield (Bomb-Aimer, aged 20)
F/Sgt J. G. Smith (Wireless Operator)
Sgt S. Wharton (Navigator)

They flew only four operational flights (one aborted shortly after take-off). Their final flight was in Halifax MZ806 DT-R, taking off from Foulsham at 16.00 hours on 21 November 1944, to accompany a raid on railway yards in Aschaffenburg. Their task was to investigate transmissions from rotating *Freyas* and the Special Operator on board was W/O J. R. Sutton, aged 24 years old. While over the target area they were attacked by a night-fighter which resulted in their aircraft crashing at a place called Langenbromach, near the town of Koenig (now Bad Konig).

Sadly Harrison, Clancy, McGill and Sutton perished in the aircraft. However, my uncle, Sergeant Hales, together with Bloomfield, Smith and Wharton, baled out and landed safely, although Sgt Wharton suffered injuries which were treated by local people before he became a PoW the next day. F/Sgt J. G. Smith (RAAF) laid low until he was apprehended and he also became a PoW.

My uncle and Alec Bloomfield landed near to a village, Nieder Kinzig, and treated civilly by the local community before being taken under escort to Koenig where they were to be held overnight.

Unfortunately, in the nearby town of Erbach, a number of local Party members, together with a Wehrmacht Officer, heard of the crash and set off to track down any parachutists they could find. They eventually caught up with them in Koenig and took my uncle and Alec Bloomfield into their custody. Under the surveillance of Horn, Mayer, Haigis, and Geisler they were marched back towards Erbach. Maurer and Jaeger followed in their car. But then Maurer and Jaeger overtook the group near the southern city limit and stopped. Maurer remained in the car, while Jaeger stepped into the November night. He ordered the prisoner group to turn from the road onto a foot-path. Shortly after, several shots were heard. Alec Bloomfield was killed instantly. My uncle disappeared into the darkness, to be found next day one hundred yards away in a field with a chest shot.

Three weeks following the shooting, two of those involved, Jaeger and Sauer, were killed in a car accident. Another named Giesler was never tracked down, and it is suspected he fled to the Russian zone. Those who died in the aircraft were initially buried in a cemetery at Kirchbrombach (close to Langenbrombach) and my uncle and Alec Bloomfield were buried in the cemetery at Koenig. The remains of all those who perished that night were subsequently moved to their final resting place at the CVGC cemetery at Durnbach, south of Munich, which is approximately 275 miles from the aircraft's crash site.

After the war, their murder was investigated and some of the perpe-trators tried in Hamburg and found guilty of committing a war crime, receiving various prison sentences. However, the main criminals died before being brought to justice. With Horn committing suicide by hanging himself in his cell ten days before the start of proceedings against them, only Schwinn, Maurer, Mayer and Haigis were put on trial. In court, Mayer said that it was Haigis, Jaeger and Horn who delivered the fatal shots. All four were found guilty and sentenced: Maurer to fifteen years in prison, Schwinn to twelve years, Mayer to seven years, and Haigis to five years. It should be noted, however, that the twelve-year sentence imposed on Schwinn was not upheld as it was deemed unsafe.

In June 2010, I undertook a lone pilgrimage by car to visit the area around Bad Konig to find the site of the crash and scene of the murders. With local assistance I discovered the crash site, but from files held in the local Government Offices it was established that any remains of the aircraft had been destroyed years earlier and there was nothing more to be seen. In these files there was also a record made of a visit by Stan Wharton in October 1985 (his first since the crash). I did however find the path outside Bad Konig where my uncle and Alec Bloomfield were murdered. I laid a wreath, which was quite emotional. I also continued on to visit the cemetery at Durnbach to pay my respects to all those who perished, promising to return.

It was to coincide with the anniversary of the loss of this aircraft and those murdered including my uncle, that I visited Germany 18 – 24 November 2011, including a visit to the CWGC in Durnbach, where those who were killed are buried. My personal interest lies with 192 Squadron. But I have also identified crews from two other aircraft buried there (Halifax NA241 DT-O and Halifax MZ449 DT-Y).

I am aware the entire crew of a 214 Squadron Fortress are there also (HB785 BU-A). My aim was therefore, during my visit to my uncle's final resting place, to specifically pay my respects on behalf of the RAF 100 Group Association, to all these crews.

This was to be my third trip, all by car, and I can only wonder at the ease of driving that distance, putting blind faith in satellite navigation. My schedule took me to Bad Konig (in Odenwald), arriving 18 November and staying two nights. This allowed me to again visit the *'scene of the crime'* where my uncle Sergeant. R. B. Hales, and Flight Sergeant A. P. Bloomfield met their untimely end on the night of 21 November 1944. I left two poppy-crosses in remembrance.

I left Bad Konig early on 20 November heading for my next hotel in Miesbach (south of Munich), where I'd stayed previously when visiting Durnbach CWGC. En-route, I decided to stop at the Dachau Concentration Camp Memorial Grounds which, as expected, was a sombre and thought-provoking experience and one which I probably will not repeat.

On 21 November, I spent all day at Durnbach CWGC. I was the only visitor. However, although alone, I did not feel so. Firstly I paid my respects at the grave of my uncle and others of the crew of Halifax MZ806 lost on 21 November 1944. I then moved on to the crews of three other RAF 100 Group aircraft I was aware also lay in that cemetery. These aircraft and those who perished are as follows:-

192 Squadron Halifax MZ806 DT-R in support of Main Force operation against Aschaffenburg railway yards – shot down by night-fighter, 21 November 1944:

    Warrant Officer B. H. Harrison RAFVR (Pilot)
    Sergeant R. P. Clancy RAFVR (Air-Gunner)
    Sergeant R. B. Hales RAFVR (Flight Engineer)
    Sergeant T. D. McGill RAFVR (Air-Gunner)
    Flight Sergeant A. P. Bloomfield RAFVR (Air-Bomber)
    W/Officer J. R. Sutton RAFVR (Spec/Op/Air-Gunner)

192 Squadron Halifax NA241 DT-O In support of Main Force operation against Pforzheim – cause of loss not established, 23 February 1945:

    Flight Lieutenant W. H. P. Mitchell RAAF (Pilot)
    Sergeant R. N. Seager RAFVR (Air-Gunner)
    Sergeant F. Parkins RAFVR (Flight Engineer)
    F/S J. L. Kerr RAFVR (Wireless Operator/Air-Gunner)
    Sergeant A. K. Goodall RAFVR (Navigator)
    Flying Officer A. W. Clark RAFVR (Air-Bomber)
    Flight Sergeant T. G. Campbell RCAF (Air Gunner)

192 Squadron Halifax MZ449 DT-Y. In support of Main Force operation against Pforzheim – shot down by night-fighter, 23 February 1945:

    Flight Sergeant G. A. C. Morgan RAFVR (Pilot)
    Flight Sergeant D. J. Paterson RAAF (?)
    Sergeant E. Spencer RAFVR (Flight Engineer)
    Sergeant W. M. Wilkinson RAFVR (Air-Gunner)
    Flight Sergeant A. M. Brunton RAFVR (Navigator)
    Flight Sergeant J. F. Carvell RAFVR (Air-Bomber)

214 Squadron Fortress HB785 BU-A in support of Bohlen operation. Lost 20/21 March 1945

Flying Officer R. V. Kingdon RCAF (Pilot)
Flying Officer D. N. Nugent RCAF (Air-Bomber)**
Sergeant W. D. Dale RAFVR (Flight Engineer)
Pilot Officer H. M. Carter RCAF (Air-Gunner)
Pilot Officer W. A. Routley RCAF (Navigator)
Sergeant W. Perkins RAFVR (Air-Gunner)
W/O Class II R. G. Wilson RCAF (Air-Gunner)
F/S D. F. Miller RAFVR (Wireless Operator/Air-Gunner)
P/Officer J. W. Pellant RCAF (Air-Bomber)
Sergeant D. Parker RAFVR (Air-Gunner)

** F/O Nugent, although serving with RCAF, he was an American from Indianapolis, U.S.A.

I now understand that on the night of 15 March 1945 nine crew members of 214 Squadron Fortress HB779 BU-L baled out over enemy territory, and five were subsequently executed (murdered) on 17 March 1945. The following now also rest at Durnbach:

F/Officer J. W. Vinall RAFVR (Flight Engineer)
Flight Lieutenant S. C. Matthews RAFVR (Air-Gunner)
Flying Officer G. A. Hall RAFVR (Air-Gunner)
Flight Sergeant E. A. Percival RAFVR (Air-Gunner)
Flying Officer H. Frost RAFVR (Air-Gunner)

Although Remembrance Day had already passed I took a poppy wreath with me to Durnbach and, during the day, laid it at the cemetery on behalf of RAF 100 Group Association.

I returned to the cemetery on 22 November where I spent the morning (again alone) paying my final respects before returning to Bad Konig. On earlier trips in 2009 I had made a number of friends in Bad Konig and used Wednesday 23 November to visit and catch up with them.[34]

Flight Sergeant John '*Shorty*' Eggert
That Was a Long Time Ago

Some years ago, with my family, I was on a motoring holiday in Norfolk. Acting on impulse, I deviated from the intended route to pull up outside a farmhouse on the outskirts of Great Ryburgh. I rang the doorbell and, when the lady of the house opened the door, introduced myself. The response was a blank look. I continued:

'*When you last saw me I was running down the hill at the rear of your house.*'

'*Were you in the Halifax bomber that crash landed on our land?*'

Yes, I certainly was. I was the Flight Engineer. The other crew members were Australian. Suddenly the years rolled back and it was all happening again.

We were normally engaged on night operations from our base at Foulsham, but this trip was different – a daylight raid, our first and, for me, the last. The target was Munster. Take-off was scheduled for 1400 hours on 18 November 1944. It was a beautiful day, but started badly. Our usual aircraft (U for Uncle) proved unserviceable, so we transferred to another Halifax (V for Victor). This was usually flown by our Squadron Leader who happened to be on Leave at the time. It was rather unusual, rigged up with special equipment that jammed the wavelengths Buzz-Bombs operated on, causing them to crash into the sea.

We commenced take-off at the planned time, the Bomb-Aimer acting as Co-Pilot. He had two prime duties during take-off. His left hand was placed behind the throttle levers and, as the Pilot opened them up, his hand followed behind until take-off speed was reached. The Pilot then removed his hand, leaving the Co-Pilot to push the throttle levers fully forward to obtain maximum power. His other job was to watch the four engine rev counters for a tell-tale flick of a temporary drop in revs. This would signify a sudden failure of power on an engine. After a failure, the engine revs would pick up to the original speed as the propeller '*windmilled*'. It was important to spot this flick so the correct engine could be '*feathered*' (stopped).

This had to be done without delay otherwise a tremendous drag effect would be caused.

Sure enough, we had an engine failure on the starboard side, just as take-off speed was reached. The Pilot knew on which side the failure was, but not which engine. Unfortunately the Co-Pilot had not been watching as closely as he should and, as the Pilot shouted: *'Engine failure on starboard side, which one?'* he noticed the Starboard Inner engine was not giving the normal full power take-off revs of 2800. Usually this was nothing to worry about. *'Starboard Inner'* he reported incorrectly, and shut it down. So there we were, about twenty feet off the ground, with one engine *'feathered'* (stopped) and the other, on the same side; not giving any power at all, but wind-milling and causing drag. The skipper realised he couldn't gain height, nor dare he attempt to turn the aircraft to land, as it would have spun into the ground. Just to cheer us up, I realised that, as well as full fuel tanks in the wings, we also had three long-range tanks in the bomb-bay just under my feet. The order came over the intercom *'Crash – Crash – Crash'*. This was the order we dreaded, and the signal for all except the Pilot to leave their normal positions and proceed without delay to Crash Positions in the strongest part of the aircraft, rear of the rear spar. The escape hatches opened. We took up our positions on the floor of the aircraft and awaited results.

We travelled about six miles in a straight line, and lobbed into the first open space that turned up – a field planted with turnips. Our Pilot's name was Field, so you can guess what his nickname was from then on! The aircraft roared up a hill, over the top, and stopped halfway down the other slope. As we slowed to a stop the starboard wing broke off and caught fire. For some never explained reason the bomb-doors had been ripped open, the long-range tanks torn out, and the bomb-doors closed again. The rear entrance/escape hatch burst open and the bottom edge acted as a scythe. As the aircraft slewed round, it chopped up about half a ton of turnips. They piled up in the rear of the plane, about two feet deep. Needless to say we all shot out of the top escape hatches without delay. We ran down-hill to the farm where the skipper telephoned our base. Fire engines arrived and the fire extinguished. This was not accomplished without humour as three thousand gallons of hundred-octane fuel ran down the hill, setting fire to the firemen's hoses with which they were attempting to put out the fire!

Later in the day it occurred to me how very lucky I had been. Many, many times we had practiced the crash landing procedure in an aircraft on the ground. My position was rear of the rear spar, hard up against the starboard side of the aircraft. However, when I arrived at my position on this particular day I found the Mid-Upper Gunner occupying it. I didn't argue, but sat next to him. When the wing broke off, the rear of it lanced through the fuselage just below the Gunner's feet. As he was considerably less than my six feet three inches, his act probably saved my feet being chopped off. He had never sat in my place before, and still cannot think why he did on this occasion.

This was the farmhouse my family and I called at – I remembered it so well! [35]

No. 462 (Royal Australian Air Force) Squadron
(*No Badge Authorised*)

No. 462 Squadron is a Royal Australian Air Force (RAAF) Squadron, forming part of the Information Warfare Wing in the RAAF's Aerospace Operational Support Group. It came under RAF 100 Group in 1944, based at Foulsham alongside 192 Squadron.

462 Squadron was formed as a Heavy Bomber Unit at Fayid in the Suez Canal Zone of Egypt on 7 September 1942. It came together through the amalgamation of Nos 10/227 and 76/462 Bomber Squadrons as the first Middle East Halifax Squadron. Tobruk was its first target on 8/9 September. Thereafter, its operational area was steadily widened to include, in addition to much of North Africa; Italy, Greece, Crete, the Dodecanese islands and Sicily.

Disbanded in March 1944, it reformed in the United Kingdom on 12 August that same year at Driffield, Yorkshire as No. 462 RAAF Squadron. A Heavy Bomber Squadron in No. 4 Group, it was made up mainly of Australian crews and aircraft from 466 Squadron, although some Flight Engineers and Air Gunners were British as also were many Ground Staff. Equipped with Halifax B.III aircraft it operated in the Main Force with No. 466 RAAF Squadron, its sister unit at Driffield, on both day and night ops. The number 462 was taken from another Australian Halifax Squadron serving in the Middle East. This Squadron was hence remembered by No. 614 Squadron.

On 22 December 1944, it was screened from operations pending a move to Foulsham in No. 100 (BS) Group, and at the end of that month, as 462 RAAF Squadron, it moved to Foulsham for bomber support duties.

The Commanding Officer of 462 Squadron was Wing Commander D. E. S. Shannon DFC. The Wing Commander had previously served as a Flight Commander with 466 Squadron. Earlier he served with Nos 99, 109 and 152 RAF Squadrons. The transfer of the Squadron to Foulsham was under the command of Squadron Leader P. M. Paull DFC who then assumed command of the Squadron. A parade of aircrew was held at Foulsham on 11 January 1945 to wish farewell to Wing Commander Shannon returning to Australia to join Quantas Airways. Shannon was from Geelong, Victoria.

Aircraft of 462 Squadron carried distinctive tail markings of yellow vertical stripes. These had been applied to aid Squadron recognition during daylight raids with 4 Group. The Squadron's aircraft code letters carried by all Halifaxes was Z5.

About twenty-four aircraft moved with the Squadron to Foulsham, with two or three on arrival being transferred to 192 Squadron. The original intention had been to make No. 462 a Radio Counter Measures Unit with aircraft fitted with the latest W/T, R/T and radio equipment, the most important items of which being ABC (*Airborne Cigar*) and W/T jammer known as *Carpet*. Used for jamming purposes, these aircraft had two extra tall aerials mounted on top of the fuselage. An extra letter /G was also added to the normal aircraft serial number. This signified that secret equipment was on board and the aircraft should be guarded at all times. There were eleven such aircraft in the Squadron, with an extra crew member, the Special Operator, to operate it. The first operational use was on the night of 13/14 March 1945. Thereafter, ABC Halifaxes operated in small numbers continuously and the re-equipment of aircraft progressed steadily until the end of hostilities in Europe.

Other aircraft also carried an extra crew member, sometimes an Air Gunner, to dispense WINDOW to confuse enemy radar.

However, when the Squadron first arrived at Foulsham, some crew members were not happy at being taken off bombing just to drop what they considered to be strips of silver paper let loose in the skies. The reason for doing this was highly classified. Not even those carrying out the task knew or understood its importance. From their point of view, it seemed a ridiculous idea, having no knowledge whatever of the confusion it caused to enemy radar. As a pacifier, it was decided that a number of bombs should also be carried with them on operations to be dropped in feint attacks. Later, TIs (Target Indicators) were also dropped to mark target areas by blind bombing methods.

The first WINDOW spoof Operation was flown from Foulsham on the night of 1 January 1945. Operations were flown regularly almost every night thereafter until the end of the war.

PERSONAL EXPERIENCES

Les Pedley, Navigator/Bomb Aimer
462 Squadron

I was a member of 462 Squadron, stationed at Driffield, also home to another Australian Squadron, 466. Our crew were not posted with the rest of the Squadron to Foulsham.

At the time the proposed transfer was scheduled to take place, the Squadron had, naturally, to remain operational, so on 6 October 1944, we embarked on a daylight raid to Sterkrade in the Ruhr. We met extremely heavy flak and suffered heavy damage, during which our Rear Gunner was killed. We returned to Driffield and subsequently took Jimmy's body to his home at Glasgow where he was buried with his family and our crew in attendance. Also with our party was Bill Glennister, Rear Gunner from another crew, Jimmy's friend from training days.

On returning to Driffield, we were told Bill's crew had been on an operation with a spare Gunner and been lost over Germany. Our crew was given a few days Leave and on return found 462 Squadron had gone to Foulsham.

The outcome was that we were a crew with no Rear Gunner and Bill Glennister a Rear Gunner with no crew. Obvious solution ... Bill became our Rear Gunner and our crew were signed over to 466 Squadron. We remained at Driffield, finally completing thirty-eight Operations on Halifax Mk IIIBs.

Incidentally, although it has never been disproved, I think I have the dubious honour of being, at five feet and one half inch, the shortest Navigator/Bomb Aimer in the Commonwealth Air Forces! [36]

Arthur Newstead, Flight Engineer

My skipper was F/O H. R. Anderson, DFC, RAAF, of 462 RAAF Squadron. Andy was only twenty years old when we commenced operations, flying Halifax IIIs at Driffield before moving to Foulsham in December 1944 to continue operations there until the end of the war. The Squadron actually ceased operations from Driffield (4 Group) on 22 December and transferred to Foulsham on 27 December 1944.

On 1 January 1945, the Squadron sent four aircraft on a *spoof* WINDOW operation to the Bremen area, all aircraft returning safely. The following night, the Squadron sent eight aircraft on a *spoof* raid to the Hannau area.

Our first operation from Foulsham as a crew was on 6 January 1945, a 'spoof' raid to release WINDOW in the target area of Heligoland and on the following night the Squadron were again operational, losing our first (100 Group) aircraft and seven crew members on a 'spoof' raid in the Hamm/Munster area.

I think March was the date of commencement of ABC sorties, the first of which I am reasonably sure took place on 13 March 1945 against Frankfurt in which we took part. An ABC sortie was primarily to jam the enemy fighter controller's instructions. Originally this was done by a German-speaking Special Operator countermanding these instructions to, hopefully, utterly confuse enemy pilots. Later, Special Operators simply jammed transmissions. In an ABC Halifax, jamming equipment occupied the whole of the port side of the rest position and in addition to the Special Operator usually, but not always, carried a spare bod who threw out WINDOW. The spare bod was a member of another crew.[37]

Sgt Kenneth Spriggs
Warrant Officer 1st Class, Air Gunner
by Richard Forder (co-author: *Special Op Liberators*)

The Service Number of 1869863 issued to Kenneth Spriggs was an early one from a batch allocated in May 1943 to No. 2 Recruit Centre at RAF Cardington in Bedfordshire. It is therefore likely he joined the RAF during that month.

Following Air Gunnery training, he would have been posted to a Wellington Operational Training Unit (OTU) where he would have helped form the nucleus of a heavy bomber crew comprising Pilot, Navigator, WOP, and two Air Gunners.

Following successful completion of the OTU course, the group of five would have moved on to a Halifax Heavy Conversion Unit either at 1658 at RAF Riccall or 1663 at RAF Rufforth that trained crews for 4 Group, Bomber Command. Here, the crew would be joined by an Air Bomber (B/A) and a Flight Engineer to form a complete heavy bomber crew. Apart from converting to the Halifax, the crew's training would prepare them for bomber operations with long navigational exercises, bomb dropping on the bombing range, fighter affiliation to exercise the crew, especially the Pilot and Air Gunners in evasion manoeuvres.

This would have been the early RAF career of Sergeant Spriggs.

It is worth noting that any reader wanting to know the RAF career path of a family member should apply for their RAF Record of Service from the MOD (*full details are at the back of this book*). This would need their written permission if they are still living. However, the majority of information can be supplied, including the important list of all movements within the RAF and relevant dates; by simply writing to the MOD. The only missing information would be a few personal details.

Sgt Spriggs and his crew were posted to 462 (RAAF) Squadron at RAF Driffield in early November 1944. The Squadron was equipped with Handley Page Halifax III aircraft and reformed at Driffield under Wing Commander D. E. S. Shannon RAAF in August that year after service in the Middle East. Although 462 was an Australian Squadron and largely manned by Australians, Kenneth Spriggs' crew were all RAF. The crew listed below would stay together through the Squadron's time with both 4 Group and 100 Group. There were four occasions however, when replacements flew with the crew, possibly due to sickness or other unspecified reasons. It is interesting to note that Ken Spriggs was an ever-present member of the crew on all their ops with both 4 and 100 Groups:

P/O J. N. Boyd (Pilot/Captain)
Sgt K. E. Hamilton (Bomb Aimer)
Sgt J. Mortimer (Navigator)
Sgt W. Evans (Wireless Operator)
Sgt B. Compton (Rear Gunner)
Sgt K. Spriggs (Mid-Upper Gunner)
Sgt P. C. Taylor (Flight Engineer)

Pilot Officer Boyd and crew were soon in action on 6 November when they participated in an attack on Gelsenkirchen. They would carry out a further eight operations from Driffield before the Squadron moved to RAF Foulsham in Norfolk to join 100 Group.

The Squadron moved to RAF Foulsham with effect from 29 December 1944 under the command of Wing Commander P. M. Paull DFC who had taken over from Wing Commander Shannon. It was intended that the Squadron would join other heavy Units of the Group in protecting Bomber Command's Main Force bombing operations by jamming the radio transmission (R/T) control system of the German night-fighter defence system, their radar controlled anti-aircraft and searchlights; and the night-fighters' airborne inter-ceptor (AI) radars. The aircraft also dropped quantities of WINDOW (strips of aluminium foil) to simulate a large bomber stream, using this deception to mount *spoof* raids to confuse the German defences and draw their night-fighters away from the real Main Force bomber stream and targets.

The plan for 462 Squadron was that their Halifaxes would be equipped with Airborne Cigar jammers (ABC) to jam the night-fighter R/T control system; *Piperack* to jam the night-fighter AI radars and *Carpet* jammers to jam the *Wurzburg* gun-laying anti-aircraft radars. Unfortunately, there was a long delay in getting the agreed equipment fit and ready, and the Squadron were not able to commence their new role until March 1945. In the meantime they participated in the Window Force operations, but unlike other heavy Units, 462 would drop bombs and flares to add authenticity to the attacks on *spoof* diversionary targets. In their new role in 100 Group, the crew would be joined by a Special Operator, sometimes two, to operate the Special Equipment.

Commencing operations on the night of 21/22 January 1945 with a *Spoof* Raid to the Bonn area, Pilot Officer Boyd and his crew were to complete fourteen operations with 100 Group plus one early return when their Special Equipment failed. Their final operation was a *Spoof* raid on the Heligoland area on 23 April 1945. A very creditable performance, and one which Sgt Spriggs' family should be very proud of. [38]

Bomber Support Development Unit (BSDU)

This unit moved to Foulsham on 21 April 1944 and received its first Mosquito. Formed on 10 April 1944 at West Raynham under Wing Commander R. F. H. Clerke DFC, its aircraft was an Avro Anson. Once at Foulsham, experienced aircrew from 85 and 141 Squadrons came to join the Unit, and on 28 May, a Tiger Moth was acquired.

On 1 June, the AOC from 100 Group inspected the Unit. Three more Mosquitoes arrived. The first operational sortie was flown on 4 July when the CO with F/L Weldon as Navigator, investigated flying bomb activity. A few days later, W/O Preston with Sergeant Verity were active along flying bomb routes.

On 7 August, F/L H. White DFC together with F/L M. Allen DFC chased a flying bomb, and later that month, Bomber Support Operations commenced in earnest and was to become the main role of the Unit, trying out new equipment in high level escort work (Mk X A1 *Serrate*) and low level intruding (*Perfectos*). Other duties included development and installation of new radar/radio equipment and evaluation of new tactics for their use.

The Unit had its own special workshops section in large Nissen huts. The Signals Officer was F/O D. Jones from 515 Squadron. In charge of Ground Radar was P/O G. Malik from 223 Squadron, and in charge of flying was S/L

B. Gledhill. New aircrew continued to arrive from West Raynham and 169 Flight.

By November, the Unit strength was nine pilots, seven Navigators and 238 other ranks. Ten Mosquitoes are known to have served with the Unit, a mixture of variants – NF2, FB6, NF19 and NF30s. The aircraft include – HJ917, NT112/M, PZ231/N, MM638/G, MM684/H, MM797/K, 181, 619, 712, 337/F.

In addition to names listed, other aircrew included – S/L N. E. Reeves DSO, F/L Bear, F/L Howard, F/O Bellis, F/O Clay, F/L L. Cunningham, F/L J. Tweedle, F/L J. Wright, F/L H. Vine, P/O C. Hamilton, F/O A. O'Leary DFC, DFM; P/O R. Phillips, F/O T. Groves DFC, F/S R. Dockeray DFM and F/L Welfare DFC.

On 21 December 1944, the Unit moved from Foulsham to Swanton Morley, where it was linked to the WRS WINDOW Research Section of No. 100 Group. WRS was commanded by S/L C. J. Merryfull MBE, responsible for most of the research for the development of WINDOW dispensers for use in 100 Group aircraft. Sadly, the Squadron Leader was killed while performing aerobatics in a Mosquito PZ178, which broke up in flight over Docking airfield on 8 July 1945.

It is believed that the Ground Radar workshops of the BSDU at Foulsham were responsible for fitting special equipment into North Creake Stirlings, as well as development work on equipment for 100 Group Halifaxes. An aircraft used for trials was NA148/G.

American Involvement at Foulsham
13 Squadron 7th Photo Reconnaissance Group, USAAF

A detachment of four Lockheed P-38J Lightnings from the 7th PRG based at Mount Farm, Oxford, operated with 192 Squadron at Foulsham from August 1944 until March 1945. The Unit was commanded by Captain Kasch, an Intelligence Officer. The aircraft had been specially converted into two-seaters with a second crew member. Special radio equipment was carried in the extended nose of the aircraft. Pilots were from the 7th PRG. The Special

Operators were volunteers from 8th Air Force Bomber Groups. Their duties, while at Foulsham, included the investigation of possible radio control of the V-2 rocket.

Lightnings at Foulsham

On 18 August 1944, inter-ally cooperation became a tangible reality when five men dressed in the uniform of the United States Army Air Force reported to RAF Foulsham for duty with 192 Squadron.

During its short existence, 192 was undeniably the world's pre-eminent airborne signals investigation organisation, a discipline now referred to universally as electronic intelligence or ELINT and a key element in the prosecution of the radio war against Germany by 100 Group.

Four Special Wireless Operators – Lieutenants William B. Stallcup, William Zeidler, Francis I. Kunze and T. C. Holt, under the Command of Captain Howard Kasch – were the core of a small temporary addition to 192's strength that would have positive repercussions for the Americans right to the present day. These five men ultimately formed a substantial part of the foundation on which today's massive U.S airborne intelligence gathering capability is based.

It is generally written that the American unit originated with the 7th Photographic Reconnaissance Group, but this is untrue. It was a specialist Radio Warfare Unit and certainly Francis Kunze had no connection what-soever with the 7th PRG or the art of photographic reconnaissance. He enlisted in the USAAF in 1942 and, after basic training, was sent to the Radio Mechanics/Aircraft Radio Maintenance Technical School, Sioux Falls Army Air Base, South Dakota, where he was trained in the technical aspects of radio. Post-graduation, he attended a Radar Course (probably H2S/H2X, known to the Americans as 'Mickey') at Eglin Field, Florida, where he gained the coveted flying wings of a 'Radar Observer'. Francis was posted overseas to the 305th Bomb Group (H) 1st Air Division at Chelveston (US Station 105), England, during March 1944 and the next reference to him appears in the 364th Bomb Squadron Diary for 8 May when it is recorded: *'Lt Francis I. Kunze, previously assigned to 305th BG on 27 April, now assigned to 364th Squadron'.*

Further scrutiny of this document indicates that Francis was never assigned to a crew which may be because specialist training was often provided by the Squadron to other elements of the 8th Air Force - it operated H2X equipped B17G Fortresses in a Pathfinder role. Shortly thereafter, on 5 June, the Officer attended a week long course at No.7 Radio School (RAF), at the Science Museum, South Kensington, London, before being posted on DS (Detached Service) to RAF Foulsham, on 16 August. [39]

The pilots were just that, being highly experienced operators of the Lockheed F5 photographic reconnaissance version of the P38 Lightning with the 7th Photographic Reconnaissance Group. The 7th PRG was the natural choice for the provision of pilots and led to members of the 13th and 22nd Squadrons at Mount Farm being seconded for short periods to Foulsham. It was not a popular posting, although some of the most experienced and decorated PR Pilots took their turn in ferrying Special Wireless Operators wherever and whenever required on missions from Foulsham.

On 28 August 1944, four brand new Lockheed P38J-20-LO *Droopsnoot* aircraft were delivered to the Station for use by the embryonic Signals Investigation unit. The *Droopsnoot* was originally born of an idea raised in 1942 as an attempt to reduce the staggeringly high casualties being sustained by the 8th Air Force on daylight operations over Europe. The concept was to utilise the P38 fighter fleet as daylight level bombers, which isn't such a ridiculous idea as it may seem. This extremely powerful and rugged aircraft could lift a pair of 2000-lb bombs for a short distance or a single bomb and a large drop-tank for longer range missions, offering a very useful payload in both configurations. The forward section was lengthened, a plexi-glass nose fitted and a Norden bombsight installed for the Bomb Aimer. A single two-seat *Droopsnoot* acted as Master Bomber for a fleet of bomb-armed standard P38s that would simultaneously drop their loads when the Master Bomber was seen to drop his.

In practice, it worked remarkably well. The aircraft were all modified at the Lockheed Overseas Corporation facility at Langford Lodge, Northern Ireland, from standard P38J day fighters - total production being in the region of twenty-six plus one hundred *Droopsnoot* kits. Interestingly, the Foulsham aircraft are recorded in official U.S documents of the time as '*on loan to 192 Squadron, RAF*', further evidence that their connection with the 7th PRG was limited to Pilots and the provision of servicing and repair. Although described officially as being *on loan* to 192, the four aircraft, 43-28479, 44-23156, 44-23501 and 44-23515, retained their U.S markings and serial numbers so were never taken on charge by the RAF.

The American unit functioned under RAF control, locally under the direction of 192 Squadron and 100 Group at Bylaugh Hall. The Special Wireless Operators were soon involved in ground and airborne training provided by the Squadron's Special Signals Section in preparation for 'live' operations.

The special wireless equipment 'fit' in the P-38 was very limited because it was such a small aircraft. It could not accommodate the range of equipment considered 'normal' for a Wellington, Halifax or Mosquito of the host Squadron and therefore operated at reduced capability. Nevertheless, the Americans made best use of what they had and on 1 September, Lt Bill Zeidler and Lt W. F. Alley of the 7th PRG completed a sortie in 44-23156 south of the Zuider Zee to establish what might be reasonably expected of the Lightning Flight over coming months.

Concurrently, the V-2 ballistic missile offensive (code-name 'Big Ben') began to cause fear, trepidation and significant loss of life in attacks on the United Kingdom and elsewhere in liberated Europe. Werner von Braun's masterpiece weapon struck without warning at colossal speed and could not be intercepted en-route to its target. 192 Squadron was to expend considerable time and effort on 'Big Ben' as it sought to identify a guidance signal associated with the missile. Countless hours were spent patrolling the Dutch coast and it was in this particular task that the P38s would prove their value. The aircraft could top 30,000 feet and possessed a good turn of speed, ideal for daylight operations in areas where enemy opposition might be expected.

Intensive 'live' operations began 12 September with each of the SWOs completing a sortie over the next three days. All were 'Big Ben' related, completed in daylight at high altitude off the Dutch coast south of the Zuider Zee. By the end of the month, the Unit had completed no less than twenty-two sorties without incident.

Operations continued unabated well into October. Then, on 26 October, tragedy struck. At 12.34pm Captain Fred B. Brink Jr of 13th Photographic Squadron, 7th PRG and his Special Wireless Operator, Lt Francis I. Kunze took off from Foulsham in 44-23515 to carry out a 'Big Ben' patrol in the area of the Zuider Zee. They crossed the North Sea climbing to 30,000 feet, but at 1.21 pm, less than an hour into the sortie, a radio message was received at Foulsham indicating an engine had failed. The *Droopsnoot* lost altitude rapidly and at 1.23 pm, when the aircraft was at 22,000 feet, Fred Brink transmitted another message to Foulsham indicating the second engine had also failed, turning the P38 into an overweight glider with an appalling glide angle.

In a third transmission Brink is reported to have told Foulsham that: '*Both engines are gone, I'm going into the sea in one minute*'. From that short signal, the D/F station at Leiston obtained a fix on 44-23515, placing it approximately forty miles east of Lowestoft. Nothing more was heard. The RAF Air/Sea Rescue service was alerted and at Foulsham four aircraft were scrambled to search for the missing P38. The C/O of 192 Squadron, Wing Commander David Donaldson, took Captain Kasch as '*Tail End Charlie*' in Halifax DT-P (MZ706), together with:

- Flight Lieutenant Hazelhurst and crew in DT-R (MZ906),
- Flight Lieutenant Hicks and Warrant Officer Robinson in Mosquito DT-I (DZ590)
- Pilot Officer George and Flying Officer '*Ted*' Gomersall in Mosquito DT-J (DK292).

(*It was in this last aircraft DT-J (DK292) the following month that Canadian Pilot Jack Fisher with Navigator/Special Operator Vic Vinnell were to fly on a secret operation the following month, and never be heard of again.*)

The aircraft performed a square search in the vicinity of the last 'fix' obtained for Brink and Kunze. 'Ted' Gomersall was to record in his Flying Log Book: '*wreckage, consisting of empty black dinghy (U.S origin), an aircraft wheel and minor bits and pieces found*'; but nothing was ever seen of the American crew.

A British air/sea rescue launch eventually reached the scene to salvage the black dinghy, an aircraft wheel, a fuel tank, several pieces of radio equipment, a leather flying helmet and a flying Log Book in the name of Lieutenant T. C. Holt. The presence of Holt's Log Book caused American authorities some concern and confusion, requiring the exchange of several communications with 192 Squadron to establish that he was, in fact, safe. The most likely explanation is that he had left the document in the aircraft following his last sortie. We will never know what caused the catastrophic failure of the P38's engines but, with John and William Rees, his father (authors of '*Espionage in the Ether*') having spoken with several veteran engine mechanics; it seems likely the problem was petrol related. Neither Francis Kunze nor 44-23515 were replaced at Foulsham, subsequent operations being completed by the three remaining SWOs in two aircraft, 44-23156 and 44-23501.

Between 5 and 24 November, thirteen missions were completed in an extended area between Utrecht and Luxembourg and between 25 November and 5 December a further ten were completed in search of signals between

30 and 70 M/C (*Freya* early warning radar). No operations were undertaken between 6 December 1944 and 5 January 1945 so Christmas and New Year was a good period for the Unit as they enjoyed a period of respite from the war.

During the first quarter of 1945, the Lightning crews completed a raft of sorties investigating a much broader range of enemy equipment, including air and ground based radars. These flights took them far and wide over occupied Europe, some as far as the Swiss border.

The honour of the last American sortie from Foulsham fell to Lieutenants Burnell and Stallcup on 6 March 1945 when they completed a patrol off the Dutch coast investigating '*Chimney*' and '*Hoarding*' early warning radars.

The following day, the Unit quietly packed up and moved to Alconbury to join the 36th Bombardment Squadron (H), the USAAF's only RCM flying unit.

During their attachment to 192 Squadron, the total number of sorties attempted was ninety-nine, with ninety-four of these being successful. Five were aborted due to mechanical or special wireless failure.

Now under U.S control, the three remaining Lightnings went on to complete a limited number of signals investigation sorties in support of the 8th Air Force until all operations by the 36th BS finally ceased on 30 April 1945.

There is no doubt that this small group of Americans enjoyed a happy and productive association with 192 Squadron, 100 Group and the Royal Air Force in general, as they learned their trade in signals investigation.

Sadly, back in Oklahoma and Georgia, the Brink and Kunze families were left to mourn the loss of their young men in a far-off war in a far-off land. They have no known graves. Whenever a modern Boeing RC135 reconnaissance aircraft is seen, therefore, we should spare them a thought because they were the pioneers, operating as part of No. 100 (Bomber Support) Group, Royal Air Force.

The P38 Lightning aircraft were nicknamed '*Droop Snoots*' because of their extended nose. Their serial numbers were: 328479, 423156, 423501 and 423515.

328479 crashed at Alconbury on 26 January 1945 where they were based with 36 Squadron USAAF after leaving Foulsham.

Pilots at Foulsham included – Bruce Edwards, Mike Dembrowski, Lt Brunell, Lt Fish, Lt Vaughn, Lt W. Stallcup, Captain Quiggens and Captain H. Kasch.

Special Wireless Operators included – Lt T. Holt, and Lt W. Zeidler.

Lt William Stallcup, Pilot with 7th PRG said:

> I was ... asked if I would volunteer to participate in a secret project code named '*Big Ben*'. They told me nothing of the project; only that it would keep me busy. I agreed ... and was sent immediately on temporary duty to RAF 192 Squadron at Foulsham. There I joined three other RCM officers: Lt Thomas Holt, Francis Kunze, William Zeidler, and our Commanding Officer, Captain Howard Kasch ... [40]

R.W.E – Radio Warfare Establishment

This new Unit was formed at Foulsham during September 1945. Its role was to continue the duties of 100 Group, in particular that undertaken by 192 Squadron from Foulsham.

At first, aircraft and personnel were mainly from 100 Group Squadrons. They included Halifax Mk3s from Foulsham and North Creake and Fortresses from Oulton.

After forming, the Unit moved to RAF Watton. During 1946, the Flying Wing Section operated from Shepherds Grove. Later the Unit was to take the Squadron number 192 again. But eventually this was changed to No. 51.

Dummy Aerodrome

There was a Dummy (Decoy) aerodrome site, A-'K' later a 'Q' site at nearby Fulmodeston. Its position was the north side of Hindolveston road, not far from Raw Hall farmhouse.

It was constructed during 1940/1941 as a decoy for West Raynham when a number of wooden dummy Blenheim bombers were seen on the site. Later, it acted as a decoy for Foulsham and Little Snoring. Mock runway lights were then installed. These lights were operated by a two-man crew from a semi-underground bunker on the edge of the site. An air raid shelter was constructed by the RAF for the occupants of the farmhouse. A number of bombs were dropped close to the site.

Final Wartime Operation

The final Bomber Command operation of the war took place on the night of 2/3 May 1945 when aircraft from No. 8 and No. 100 Groups attacked German-occupied airfields and troops in the Kiel/Flensburg area. It was suspected that enemy forces were preparing to move to Norway to make a last ditch stand.

Every available aircraft at Foulsham took part and this time all carried a full bomb load. One 100 Group Mosquito from Great Massingham was shot down and two Halifaxes from North Creake collided over the target area – these being the last Bomber Command operational losses of the war.

V.E. Night

At Foulsham airfield on V.E Night there was a large bonfire and fireworks display to which local residents were also invited. There was free food and drink and good bangs all round. The curious schoolboy, Len Bartram, was later to quip: *'I never did understand why so many airmen and WAAFs were laying on the ground!'*

After V.E. Day

Soon after V.E Day, the Foulsham Halifaxes took most of the Ground Staff on *'Cooks Tours'* a round trip over German cities to see the bomb damage. They also took part in Exercise *'Post Mortem'* when mock air attacks were made on targets in North Germany and Denmark to evaluate enemy radar and control defences.

By the end of October 1945, all 100 Group flying had ceased at Foulsham and most personnel quickly departed.

On 10 November 1945, Maintenance Command took over. Surplus radio and other equipment were stored, sorted and public sales took place. Various small Maintenance Units served there until 1954 with No. 99 MU being the last. This was a Storage Unit for new RAF motor vehicles.

A USAF/Army Radar Unit connected with Sculthorpe was based there during the mid-1950s.

Soon after the RAF finally left Foulsham, the land was sold and returned to agricultural use, including pig and poultry units, with hangars used for grain storage. However, flying returned again later when Mr W. Cubitt operated a crop spraying and aircraft engineering business from part of the old airfield. Sadly, Mr Cubitt was killed in a flying accident in June 1993.

During 1943/44, many USAAF Fortresses returning damaged from raids on Germany landed at Foulsham often with dead, wounded and frost-bite victims on board. Two red flares would be fired from a stricken bomber as it landed to alert crash crews and ambulance. F/O C. Morgan, a Fortress co-pilot, was awarded the United States Medal of Honour for bringing his aircraft back to Foulsham after his pilot was seriously injured over Germany.

Foulsham Airfield Public Open Day
Saturday 15 September 1945

It was a day of celebration and remembrance, as well as a chance for villagers to take a peek at an airfield cloaked in secrecy right on their home doorsteps. A short flying display was given by a Stirling and Horsa glider, Halifax, Fortress, Mosquito and Anson, with an impressive number of Halifaxes from 462 Squadron and the RWE, together with Fortresses from RWE/223 Squadron parked on the airfield in awesome splendour. Ground displays were given by the Foulsham crash crew and a visiting ATC band played well-known music. The Control Tower was also open to the public. Suddenly the veil of mystery was lifted. Villagers looked on in wonder and excitement. There was also a crew bus service to the Communal Site where various buildings were open for inspection.

Curious schoolboy, Len Bartram, remembers the only thing to jar with an otherwise perfect day was the weather – dull and cold with low cloud and windy. However, he estimated that, despite the weather, approximately 3,000 people attended this spectacular day.

Foulsham Flowers and Fliers

> In late August, almost September
> For the people of Foulsham a day to remember

RAF FOULSHAM: 1942-1954

The church all a-glow
What a wonderful show!
It was the village Open Day
With flowers so bright, to match the sun's rays,
The ladies of charm, with tea at fifteen pence,
Stories of a boy who once looked through a fence.
Boys of the RAF Squadrons came to say 'Thanks',
Stories of Wimpys, Halliebags and Lancs.
For a while the air was alive,
Tales of Mossies and B-25s.

Foulsham had a place in Europe's turmoil,
The base had FIDO burning gallons of oil.
If you should pass this way from Jan to December
Please pause a while just to remember.

Amongst the acres of corn and beet
Warriors of the air and many a brave feat
Once the Merlins crackled over the dome,
Now birds and flowers can make a home.

The laughter of children
And the be-ribboned airmen
We prayed with the Bishop of Lynn
And a coach to go for a spin.
With a stone to unveil
We come to the end of our tale.
RAF Honington's band played for marching on
The village pub with locals looking on.

We came to the end of the day
And all had to go our separate ways.
So many thanks to give to our hosts
On Foulsham's now silent airfield are their ghosts.

By James Chainey, August 1989

This poem was written in memory of the Foulsham Festival weekend: 27 – 29 August 1989. Over 100 personnel who served at RAF Foulsham 1942-1947 made a return visit with relations and friends to join several hundred local people for the unveiling by Len Bartram (*the curious schoolboy*) of two commemorative plaques at the base of the village sign. A brass plaque was also hung in the village church. It reads:

IT WOULD BE A PITY WERE GENERATIONS TO GROW UP UNAWARE THAT HISTORY WAS ENACTED ON THEIR OWN DOORSTEPS

Foulsham Roll of Honour lists 186 names.
May we always remember them!

CHAPTER 7
RAF Little Snoring: 1942–1944

A Brief History

Through the eyes of a schoolboy, airfields and aircraft must have seemed like a kind of magic, filled with wonder and excitement. Len used to play in these fields when he was young. He knew the grassland around his home, took a keen interest in wildlife, and his love of nature remains tangible in the number of trees he planted in adult years, winning an award from the Queen Mother.

As war encroached on his once idyllic lifestyle, he pulsed with excitement as a whole new vista of opportunities emerged. This wasn't Toy Town, but something very real and vital, and it wasn't about to be cleared away any time soon with things returning to normal. He yearned to be a part of it, making copious notes as his father became Night Watchman, and a bicycle to travel independent of his family.

It is through his eyes, from his notes, we learn about the beginnings of each airfield – green fields becoming concrete bases housing weapons of war to defend our country against an enemy unseen. It gave a young boy plenty to think about, mapping each stage of development as a very real part of history in the making.

Work began on a new airfield at Little Snoring in September 1942. Land was cleared in preparation for building to commence with hedges removed, trees cut down, stumps dynamited out.

Taylor Woodrow constructed the airfield to 'Class A' standard with a suitable design for the take-off and maintenance of heavy bombers.

Three runways – 1,400 yards long, 2,000 yards long and 1,400 yards long, with thirty-six concrete hard standings around the runways and a perimeter track made best use of the gradient of the land at the north end of the airfield.

As the road to Thursford and Little Snoring crossed the site, it was closed as construction work began, with two huge T2 hangars placed between the main technical site on the south side of the airfield, and two T2 hangars built on the north side. One B1 hangar was located between the head of runways 01 and 25, just off the southeast perimeter.

Little Snoring airfield was to come into the sector of No. 2 Group, RAF Bomber Command.

The camp was dispersed around Little Snoring village. According to Air Ministry specifications, it consisted of eight Domestic, two Messes and one Communal Site for 1,807 men and 361 women. However, it wasn't until summer 1943 that RAF Little Snoring became available for use as the strategic placement of the RAF was changing. No. 2 Group, for whom the airfield had been intended, was moving its Units south. It was No. 3 Group which would now fill vacated airfields, including Little Snoring.

First to move in was 115 Squadron from No. 3 Group in August, flying Lancaster IIs. On 16 August 1943, the Group's Heavy Conversion Unit, No. 1678 Flight, joined them, supplying 'acclimatised' crews for the Lancaster II. Also in 1943, Bomber Command decided to reorganise its Groups, with No. 3 Group being centralised and No. 8 Group Pathfinders, moving inland.

RAF No. 100 (Bomber Support) Group was being formed. RAF Little Snoring was to come under this Group, tasked with taking on German Night Fighters to protect the main bomber streams. It meant 115 Squadron's stay at the airfield was unexpectedly short, its last sortie from Little Snoring flown on 26 November 1943.

As was common when moving from one base to another, the Squadron's aircraft took off from Little Snoring one night, knowing at the end of their operation they would land at their new Base of operations, Witchford. Their aircraft were heading to Berlin crammed with the Squadron's personal possessions - including on one aircraft seven bicycles.

Aircraft, DS680, was lost on this raid, shot down by a German Night Fighter near Hermee in Belgium. The wreckage must have been a strange sight for Germans, packed as it was with the aircrew's belongings!

115 Squadron lost eighteen Lancaster IIs on operations from little Snoring, plus one on a training flight. The Lancaster II was better in many respects than its predessesor, but without as long a range operationally as the Mark

I. These aircraft were issued to 115 Squadron. The visible difference was the radial Hercules engines instead of the normal 'Merlins'. However they were popular with the crews.

On 7 December 1943, the Station transferred to RAF 100 Group. This coincided with the arrival of 169 Squadron and Wing Commander E. J. Gracie with Beaufighter VIs for training. More Beaufighters followed, joined by 1692 Flight arriving from Drem the same month with several Defiant IIs. The arrival also of several Mosquito IIs allowed the Squadron to continue training crews on Mosquitoes and Radar to be deployed against the enemy.

On 15 December, 515 Squadron arrived from Hunsdon with Beaufighter IIs. However, it wasn't until February the following year that 515 was allocated and received Mosquito IIs. They would join 169 Squadron, who, on 20 January 1944, began offensive operations. High up in the bomber streams their task was to intercept and deal with German Night Fighters.

Gradually the Squadron stepped up their sortie rate, with twenty-eight operations carried out in February that year, followed by fifty-nine in March when an HE177 was downed by the Squadron's Wing Commander. 515 Squadron finally flew its first operations from Little Snoring in April 1944, with a detachment at Bradwell Bay, sharing 605 Squadron Mosquitoes.

On 20 April, German Intruders hit Little Snoring airfield, distributing anti-personnel bombs along one of their runways. Enemy aircraft had managed to remain undetected, hiding amongst the returning bombers, catching them by surprise.

June 1944 saw the arrival of 23 Squadron, and the departure of 169 Squadron and 1692 Flight to Great Massingham. 169 Squadron was to continue its ongoing campaign, while 1692 Flight provided crews to Intruder Squadrons whose campaigns in the air reached their zenith, within six months.

No. 23 Squadron

Semper Aggressus – 'Always on the Attack'
Reproduced with permission of the MOD

23 Squadron's badge depicted an eagle preying on a falcon, approved by HM King George VI in April 1937.

The Squadron's Battle Honours during its long and illustrious history include:

- Home Defence 1916
- Western Front 1916-1918
- Somme 1916
- Arras, Ypres 1917
- Somme 1918
- Channel and North Sea 1939-1940
- Fortress Europe 1940-1944
- North Africa 1943
- Sicily 1943
- Italy 1943-1944
- Anzio and Nettuno, France and Germany 1944-1945
- Ruhr 1944-1945
- Kosova, Iraq 2003

I reach back in time because there are little gems that would otherwise be missed which still have relevance today. One example is that, when the Squadron first formed at Fort Grange, Gosport, on 1 September 1915, it came under the command of one of the RAF's most experienced operational pilots: Captain Louis Strange.

The Squadron's Founder, Lt Colonel Louis Strange DSO OBE MC DFC, retired from Service through ill health in 1921, but subsequently enjoyed an eventful career in Civil Aviation, before returning to battle in 1940 as a fifty-year-old Pilot Officer in the Volunteer Reserve. During his 'third' career, he won a Bar to his DFC flying a Hurricane, pioneered the parachute training of Britain's airborne Forces, and established the Marine Ships Fighter Units for the catapult-launching of convoy defence Hurricanes. He continued to fly after the war and died in 1966 aged seventy-five years. It is in recognition of the high esteem in which he is held and his important contribution to Military Aviation, that the Squadron Briefing Room in the new No. 23 Squadron Headquarters building, officially opened by the AOC in C Strike Command on 2 April 1997; has been named 'The Strange Room'.

Douglas Bader was also a member of 23 Squadron when he crashed carrying out low-level aerobatics, losing both his legs in the process. He went on to become one of the highest scoring aces of the RAF in World War Two.

Before I move forwards into the Second World War, it is worth mentioning the detachment of Royal Aircraft Factory B.E.2cs (Bleriot Experimental) deployed to Sutton's Farm to act as Night Fighters, opposing raids by German Zeppelins over London, with no successful interceptions recorded. However, when the Squadron moved to France on 16 March 1916 it was flying FE2b two-seater Pusher Fighters. The Squadron used the FE2b on close escort duties and standing patrols to engage hostile aircraft wherever they were found, helping to establish air superiority in the build-up to the Battle of the Somme. A little gem of which I spoke, lying in the shadows of history, comes through the words of Sgt Leonard Herbert Emsden, DCM, an F.E.2d Observer and Gunner, demonstrating the use of the rear-firing Lewis gun which required him to actually stand on his seat while in the air, unheard of today!

When you stood up to shoot, all of you from the knees up became exposed to the elements. There was no belt to hold you. Only your grip on the gun and the sides of the nacelle stood between you and eternity. Toward the front of the nacelle was a hollow steel rod with a swivel mount to which the gun was anchored. This gun covered a huge field of fire forward. Between the Observer and Pilot a second gun was mounted for firing over the F.E.2d's upper wing to protect the aircraft from rear attack ... Adjusting and shooting this gun required that you stand right up out of the nacelle, with your feet on the nacelle combing. You had nothing to worry about except being blown out of the aircraft by a blast of air or tossed out bodily if the

Pilot made a wrong move. There were no parachutes and no belts. No wonder they needed Observers. [41]

Thankfully, by the end of the year, the F.E.2d, or *'Fee'* as it was known, was obsolete and the Squadron received SPAD S.VII single-seater fighters in February 1917, with its last F.E.2s in April that same year. 23 Squadron flew its SPADs both on offensive fighter patrols over the front and low-level strafing attacks against German troops.

In December 1917, the Squadron replaced its SPAD S.VII with the more powerful and heavier armed SPAD S.XIII before converting in April 1918 to Sopwith Dolphins.

23 Squadron disbanded on 31 December 1919.

On 1 July 1925, No. 23 Squadron was reformed at RAF Henlow with Sopwith Snipe aircraft, replaced shortly after with Gloster Gamecocks, then in 1931, was tasked with carrying out trials on the new Hawker Hart two-seaters, taking the production version, known as *Demons*, on strength in 1933.

In late 1938, 23 Squadron took on the role of a Night Fighter Squadron using Bristol Blenheims. Following the outbreak of the Second World War, in 1941, Blenheims were replaced by the Douglas Havoc, used with great success in the Intruder role, until, in turn, they were replaced by the de Havilland Mosquito in mid-1942.

Between 1942 and 1944, the Squadron was transferred to Malta to fly Intruder missions over Sicily, Italy and Tunisia. With Allied armies in Italy in December 1943, the Squadron moved to Sardinia, expanding its range of operations to include northern Italy and the south of France. This Public Relations Release document discusses the actions of 23 Squadron, based in Sardinia, North Africa, in the early part of 1944:

H-482   February 12 1944
ISSUED BY RAF PUBLIC RELATIONS

Lone night raiders of an RAF Mosquito Squadron now shooting up German transport in northern Italy made 68 attacks on road vehicles during the past month while 43 trains were bombed or shot up with cannon and machine guns. Not one aircraft was lost on these operations.

The main work of the Squadron, which belongs to the Mediterranean Allied Coastal Air Force, is to harry and destroy road and rail transport supplying the German battle lines in Italy.

Their sorties at night thus compliment the work of the strategic and tactical aircraft which bomb road and rail choke points, and of the Coastal Air Force B-25 Mitchells and Spitfires which bomb ship-ping, the only alternative means of supply, trying to creep along the coast from ports in the South of France across the Gulf of Genoa and down the west of Italy.

The outstanding example of a road convoy attack during the month was provided by a Flight Sergeant who blew up 20 vehicles near Rimini.

When the Squadron first started attacking road convoys in north-ern Italy they found columns of lorries going along the roads with their headlights blazing. The Mosquitoes took such good advantage of these easy targets that nowadays lights are doused and convoys pull into the side of the road when drivers hear the sound of aircraft engines approaching.

The Mosquitoes are thus delaying convoys over the whole of northern Italy, upsetting their schedules in addition to destroying vehicles.

'This somewhat accountable demonstration of nervousness on the part of drivers, coupled with the increasing irritability of the ground defences; suggests that the affection held by the R.A.F. for Mosquitoes, is not shared by the enemy', reported one pilot.

The operational area of the Mosquito Squadron stretches from the Bay of Biscay on the west coast of France, to the Gulf of Venice, north-east of Italy. In addition to attacking trains and transport, the Mosquitoes 'intrude' over airfields in the south of France, shooting down enemy bombers as they take off or return to base, and in many cases, keeping them grounded by their mere presence.

During the whole of last month, there were only six nights during which the Mosquitoes were not operating, a record which says much for the skill and daring of the pilots and observers in combat-ing adverse weather conditions and for the work of Ground Crews in maintaining a very high standard of serviceability.

Sorties during January numbered more than 200, all by lone aircraft.

It was members of this Squadron who, on the night of January 6/7, shot down three of the enemy over an airfield near Toulouse and caused the ground defences to shoot down one of their own aircraft in mistake for the intruder.

Flying from one of the most forward bases in Allied hands, they form the night spearhead of Air Vice Marshall Sir Hugh Lloyd's Mediterranean Allied Coastal Air Force in its harrying of enemy transport by land and sea.

RAF No. 100 Bomber Support Group

When 23 Squadron returned to England in June 1944, it was to serve in the newly-formed RAF No. 100 Group under Bomber Command. Based at Little Snoring, Norfolk, it became an Intruder Squadron, targeting German Night Fighters over Western Europe.

The Station had a new Commander, Wing Commander B. R. O. B. Hoare DSO and Bar, DFC and Bar. Little Snoring now took up the composition which remained unchanged until the end of the war, with two Squadrons: 515 and 23 together with permanent staff.

As with all Fighter Stations there were a permanent 'skeleton' staff which administered the site, manned the Control Tower and performed other functions the Squadrons did not provide, but had personnel to augment these operations for them.

The aircrew got used to hearing the last words spoken to them from the Control Tower upon returning from an operation unscathed. It was generally a '*Good night, old boy*' that signalled they were 'Home' and down safe. It became a feeling of safety treasured by all Intruder crews after yet another hellish operation. Not enough praise can be offered in their direction, but as in all these things, it was a team effort always.

Located on the lefthand side of the road past St Andrews church, away from the airfield, it was in accommodation areas that all Air and Ground crew were billeted. Officers and NCOs were segregated into their own huts, much the same as Mess arrangements, with an Officers and separate NCO Mess.

Huts had a concrete path segregating one from the other, while within, each was equipped with a potbellied stove. They were not popular! Cold, wet and windy days were worst. The weather made it impossible to keep warm. A constant supply of coal for the stove was essential during bleak and harsh winters. But this was wartime. They were surrounded by reminders of war, and at least huts were better than tents. Many in the Squadron still remembered being under canvas in Alghero, Sardinia earlier that year.

Ultimately, it was these basic huts that became a home from home, and when off duty men relaxed, sometimes including high jinks. On the airfield, 23 Squadron 'A' Flight Office was about 200 yards from 515 Squadron 'B' Flight Office. One set of high jinks came when Squadron Leader Paul Rabone playfully fired a .303 just above the head of Squadron Leader Henry Morley in 515 Squadron 'B' Flight Office. Tom Cushing, a schoolboy during the war; met Henry on several occasions who shared with him this episode, saying that afterwards he made certain his blinds were firmly closed! Christmas Eve 1944 was to see more high jinks in the huts, and inevitably many Squadron parties went off with a bang.

The Sergeants and enlisted men's huts were open plan. Officers' huts had 'cubicles', or partitions. It meant for the lucky few, a small modicum of privacy. Additionally Officers had a Batman assigned to their hut to look after them. Several had 'pets' or 'mascots' which stayed with them in their huts. However the Squadron mascot, Herbert the pig, was strictly confined to his hanger on the airfield.

The village of Little Snoring became effectively a satellite for the airfield. All living quarters were separate and accommodation sites were huge compared to the village outside. The road through the village of Little Snoring was called *The Street*. It is almost the same today, except there are no huts on the side of the road.

The Locals ... No, not the Pubs!

Surrounding families and households became used to 'Squadron visits' visiting in groups, pairs or singly. The provision of food by local farming families was gratefully received, with reciprocal 'booze' being brought to the table by aircrew. Two local farming families particularly well-known were the Joyces and the Whiteheads.

The Whiteheads had a daughter, Sheila, the same age as many younger pilots, and pretty too! Johnny Rivas and Frankie Thomas amongst others would see the Joyces on a regular basis.

Tom Cushing's family extended the same hospitality, often seeing F/L Dick Gunten, and those further afield such as George Mackie, a 214 Squadron pilot based at Oulton. Tom Cushing's father knew Group Captain Hoare and 'Sticky' Murphy – given the nickname because he could never let go of a problem until it was solved! The Cushings lived to the north of the airfield in Thursford, which forms a triangle between Great and Little Snoring.

Tom's father was a Haulage Contractor with lorries and steam rollers which helped build Little Snoring airfield. Tom as a young lad, went with him many times during its construction. He and his brother, both under ten, found the airfield and its Lancasters, then Mosquitoes irresistible, and like schoolboy Len Bartram, would spend time following progress, revelling in the delight of having real heroes round for Sunday lunch and dinner.

Tommy Cushing never forgot the sights and sounds of 1943, 1944 and 1945. His most formative years were spent watching heavily-armed Night Fighters training and then one by one taking off, like lone wolves into the night.

Many surrounding families who shared their homes, particularly with aircrew, did so knowing many would not return. They considered they were 'doing their bit', offering some semblance of comfort while away from home. In many cases, losses of the Squadrons would be felt just as keenly by these families as with aircrew themselves.

Although not part of the airfield, the local church, St Andrews, remains firmly linked with Squadrons both during the time they served, and today. With the Air Force, Church parades were held each Sunday with services daily. During time of war, congregations are always higher. The Church, certainly the tower, is pre-Norman, possibly Saxon, Len Bartram believed; and the building had stood for over a thousand years before the airfield, mentioned in the Doomsday Book.

There is a Memorial plaque inside St Andrews church dedicated to the Royal Air Force over the years they served at Little Snoring, 1944 and 1945. The church also became the place where Squadron 'Scoreboards' were kept – two boards listing 515 and 23 Squadron Honours, with two boards listing their kills respectively. They were all handpainted by Douglas Higgins, one of the Ground Crew, who, by all accounts, was an exceptional artist, responsible for many pieces of nose-art adorning Squadron Mosquitoes from the Mediterranean to Berlin.

No. 23 Squadron was disbanded, following the war's end, in September 1945.

PERSONAL EXPERIENCES

Group Captain 'Bertie' Rex O'Brien Hoare
DSO & Bar, DFC & Bar
Base Commander of Little Snoring Airfield

'*Sammy*' Hoare was one of the RAF's most famous wartime fighter Pilots and probably 100 Group's greatest characters. With his red hair and six-inch handlebar moustache he is acknowledged as one of the finest Mosquito Intruder Pilots. Remarking on his trademark moustache, he reckoned that if both ends couldn't be seen from behind it wasn't worth the name '*handlebar*'! Some of his successes can be seen on the 'Victory Board' on display in St Andrews church at Little Snoring.

'*Bertie*' was born on 6 June 1912 to Cyril Bertie Edward O'Bryan and Isabel Mary Hoare of Hove, Sussex. As many young gentlemen of the age, he was sent to a private school at Harrow. His education continued at Harrow & Wye Agricultural College, completing the skills that someone from the 'landed gentry' would require.

However, early in 1936, in a swift career move no doubt prompted by tensions in Germany and the threat of war, he joined the RAF, and on 18 May, took a short Service Commission with the RAF. As 'Acting Pilot Officer', on 2 June he was posted to the flying training school at Wittering.

On completion of his flying training, he was posted to 207 Squadron flying Fairey Battles, before being graded as a Pilot Officer on 23 March 1937. The London Gazette for 4 May that year confirmed his appointment. Bertie's home for the next two years was to be on A Flight, 207 Squadron, where he made many friends. He followed the Squadron to Worthy Down through to April 1938, and on to Cottesmore where he was promoted to Flying Officer. By August 1939, he was at Cranfield. It was here, sometime between July 1938 and the outbreak of war, that an incident occurred which gave birth to the legend leading Bertie to become known as 'Nelson of the RAF'.

He was flying a Battle from Cranfield with Douglas Wilson. During the flight, an engine cowling cover unexpectedly came loose, smashing through the cockpit, hitting Bertie full in the face, causing much damage and taking an eye out of its socket. Incredibly, Bertie managed to get the Battle back to Cranfield and unbelievably land, be it in a very hairy manner; whereupon he was rushed to hospital.

It should be said there are varying accounts to be found in books about Bertie's accident and the loss of his eye so early in his flying career. One account says he was injured in flight when 'a duck flew through his windscreen', and that afterwards he had a glass eye, '... one brown eye, one blue, so no-one seemed to know which one was false ...' [42]

Another account reads:

> **About the time that the war started in Europe, Bertie was piloting a Fairey Battle Mk. I from Cranfield. With him was Doug Wilson, an NCO. Wilson went on to become Group Douglas Captain Wilson. Bertie took a hit in the face from a loose engine cowling. The result-ant blow popped an eye out of its socket and he landed due to his great skill and a bit of luck. Bertie was hospitalised for a six month period ...** [43]

Speaking with 23 Squadron veterans who knew and worked alongside Bertie during his time with them, they confirm the second story. He spent several months in hospital when it was discovered remarkably that the damaged eye had unusually good night vision, hence the reason he ended up as a Night Fighter ... and one of, if not THE BEST! Something else which needs to be remembered is the companionship of his beloved Spaniel *Tadzee* who was to see the war through with him from start to finish.

The outbreak of war changed everything. All available Pilots were needed, even those with one eye! Bertie took to wearing what he termed his '*lucky hat*' which he once went back to another Station to retrieve rather than risk going on Ops without it!

In 1940, Acting Flight Lieutenant Bertie Hoare joined 23 Squadron. He was an early exponent of intruding, flying Blenheim Is on Intruder missions, aircraft which didn't prove that successful, tactics still having to be evolved and the shortcomings of the plane making it less than ideal. Switching to Havocs was a better move for the Squadron as a whole. As a result of the change, in 1941, on the nights of 3rd and 22nd April, Bertie was able to report one *'probably destroyed'* German aircraft, and one destroyed Focke Wolfe 200. This success continued into May where, on the night of the 3rd, he destroyed a Heinkel III and claimed a Junkers 88 as another *'probable'*. On the 11th, he would claim another *'unidentified'* as damaged.

On 30 May 1941, The London Gazette commended Bertie Hoare for his *'skilful, effective night missions and his bravery'*. And again in October 1942 when he *'completed numerous operational sorties over enemy occupied territory during which he destroyed six enemy aircraft'*.

As a result of his undoubted courage and bravery, with his one good daytime eye, and one good night-time eye; he was awarded his first Distinguished Flying Cross for his efforts in April and May 1941. His Citation reads:

> Since January 1941, this Officer has carried out many night operational missions. His bombing attacks have been delivered with great skill often in the face of severe opposition from ground defences, and, despite the hazardous nature of these sorties, he seldom returns without valuable information. Flight Lieutenant Hoare has destroyed at least two enemy aircraft and certainly damaged others. He has shown great enthusiasm and gallantry throughout.

In September, he claimed two HE IIIs on the night of the 13th – one damaged, one destroyed. Within one year, Bertie added a Bar to his DFC. He was then rested towards the end of the year, returning to 23 Squadron in April 1942 as Squadron Leader, this time flying Boston IIIs. His success rate continued, damaging two Dornier 217s on the night of the 2nd, within days of his return, followed by a non-identified *'probable'* on 28 May. The Citation for the Bar which followed was no less praising:

> Since being awarded the Distinguished Flying Cross in May 1941, this Officer has completed some 38 Intruder sorties during which he has destroyed at least three and damaged several more enemy aircraft. He has at all times set an inspiring example.

In July 1942, No. 23 became the first Squadron to convert to the Mosquito II, especially adapted for night fighting. It was no surprise to anybody that the Squadron's first 'kill' with this new aircraft was chalked up to Bertie on the night of 6 July – another DO 217 that succumbed to three bursts of cannon fire just east of Chatres. On the night of the 30th, he destroyed another unidentified German aircraft, while September saw the same result on the night of the 10th, before he was 'rested' from operations. His tally was 'six confirmed'.

In October, he was awarded the DSO for his efforts together with those of his Squadron. His DSO Citation read:

> This Officer has completed numerous operational sorties over enemy-occupied territory during which he has destroyed six enemy aircraft. Since Wing Commander Hoare assumed command, the Squadron has destroyed at least seven enemy aircraft and damaged others, a result reflecting the greatest credit on this Officer's excellent leadership. He has inspired confidence in those under his command.

He would write:

> Night fighter pilots chosen for Intruder work were generally of a different type to the ordinary fighter pilot. They must like night fighting to begin with, which is not everyone's meat. They must also have the technique for blind flying, and when it comes to fighting, must use their own initiative and judgement since they are cut off from all communication with their Base and are left as freelancers, acting entirely on their own resources.

It was at this point that Bertie left the Squadron to set up a special Night Fighter 'Intruder' Training School at Cranfield, home of 51 O.T.U. 23 Squadron, meanwhile, departed overseas in December to Malta for a continuation of their Intruder operations against the Axis Forces in the Mediterranean.

In 1943, Bertie, now Wing Commander, was more popularly known as 'Sammy' as he moved from 51 O.T.U. at Cranfield to form 60 O.T.U. at High Ercall. It was here he was re-acquainted with Phil Russell as an Instructor, and met for the first time one of his new Flight Commanders, Squadron

Leader Alan Michael 'Sticky' Murphy, and Flying Officer Duncan 'Buddy' Badley.

In September that year, he moved again, this time to No. 605 (County of Warwick) Squadron as their Commanding Officer.

Incredibly, on his first sortie for the Squadron, he, in now typical 'Sammy' style, scored a victory. More memorable was the fact that, on the night of 10 January 1944, he destroyed a Ju 88 near Chievres which marked the County of Warwick's Squadron 100th victory! A celebratory dinner was held in London at the Dorchester Hotel with Sammy as Guest of Honour. Twenty-six pre-war members of the Squadron were hosts to the thirty present members of the Squadron who were guests. Honorary Air Commodore Sir Lindsay Everard, MP, chairing the occasion, presented Squadron members with a silver Mosquito bearing the identification codes of Sammy's Mosquito. [44]

Sammy's time at 605 would also see the accolade of a BAR to his DSO, with the Citation reading:

This Officer has participated in more than 100 sorties, involving attacks on airfields in Germany, Belgium, Denmark, Holland and France, escort to bomber formations and a variety of other missions.

He is a magnificent leader whose personal example of courage and devotion to duty has inspired all.

In addition to his activities in the air, Wing Commander Hoare has devoted much of his energy and skill towards the training of other members of the Squadron with excellent results. This Officer, who has destroyed at least eight enemy aircraft, has rendered most valuable service.

Within six months, in April 1944, he moved again for the appointment he would most be remembered for, that of Station Commander at RAF Little Snoring.

It was no accident that, a little over two months on, 23 Squadron returned to the UK, posted to RAF Little Snoring under the Squadron's former Commander, Bertie Rex O'Brien Hoare DSO and Bar, DFC and Bar. All those who had served under him would remember him for many things, and one Briefing in particular when he said:

Gentlemen, tonight there will be flak. It will certainly be heavy flak. If you cannot go over it, go under it. If you cannot go under it, go

over it. Gentlemen, if you can do neither of these things, you will go through it.

Throughout his period as Station CO at Little Snoring, he continued to fly and score victories, remembered on the scoreboards preserved in St Andrews Church. However, it is the manner of his sudden and unexpected death which remains a mystery to this day.

On 22 December 1945, Sammy Hoare married Lucy Watson, daughter of Richard Nimmo Watson. Lucy had gained the rank of Senior Officer in the service of the Women's Auxiliary Air Force (WAAF). Post-war, Sammy opted to remain in the RAF, and in 1946, was posted to 84 Squadron.

In 1947, Sammy with Navigator, F/O W. Colvin, were on a delivery flight for the RNZAF, on detachment, completing the delivery of Mosquitoes from England to New Zealand via Singapore and Australia. Lucy, pregnant with their first child; was going to arrive in Sidney and fly on to meet him in New Zealand where they would 'tour' together.

Sammy and F/O Walter Colvin, took off at 09.08 hours in Mosquito TE746 on 26 March from Darwin in company with a second Mosquito: TE927. Both encountered the same tropical storms on route. Both aircraft were reported overdue in bad weather at 12.35. The two became separated in the storm, and radio requests for a report yielded nothing. However, TE927 touched down shortly after 13.00 at an emergency landing ground at Macrossan, some sixty miles south of Townsville. But there was no sign of its companion, nor any radio transmission. Extensive aerial searches over the next week failed to find the missing TE746. Both Lucy, now in Australia, and Sammy's mother at home in D'avigdor House in Hove, Sussex, were interviewed by the press about the missing airmen. Both women remained convinced the missing pair would turn up. After all, Sammy had survived operational flying since 1936.

On 3 April, the authorities received a radio transmission from a Mission Station on Mornington Island in the Gulf of Carpentaria. A native had reported finding the wreckage of a plane two days earlier, washed up some twenty miles away on the beach at Sydney Island. A launch was sent from Mornington Island, and on reaching Sydney Island, found a wrecked Mosquito lying in the shallows. It is thought that, due to a faulty radio set, they had been unable to establish a bearing, flying in a turbulent storm with poor visibility. This had caused them to drop to a very low altitude, sea level, to try and establish a bearing ... in this case, flying over the sea, to find a landmark. In the course of doing so, it was thought they had flown directly into the waters.

In the same storms, a Dutch Navy C-47 was forced down in the Northern Territory, performing a '*walk away*' belly-landing approximately fifty miles north-east of Katherine.

The day before, an RAAF Mosquito crashed on the approach to Townsville, flying into a mountain near Cromarty. Both crew were killed. It is believed Sammy and his Navigator suffered the same fate.

The Australian Air Force broke the sad news to Sammy's mother:

AIR MINISTRY
(Casualty Branch)
2 Saville St
Knightsbridge
London S.W.1

13 June 1947

Madam,

I was directed to refer to the Department's letter of 10 June 1947 regarding the death of your son, Wing Commander B. R. O'B. Hoare, DSO, DFC, Royal Air Force, sad to say that further information, of which you would no doubt wish to be advised, has now been received.

The Report from the RAF Mission to Australia states that, owing to the severity of the crash, it was not possible for the Medical Officer or the Coroner in Townsville to establish definitely the human remains recovered from the wrecked aircraft or, in the circumstances, to issue a certificate of death. This most unfortunate situation created a most unhappy difficulty in the matter of the burial arrangements and after consultation with the Royal Australian Air Force Headquarters, it was decided that, when the Court of Inquiry had reached a decision on the deaths of both members of the crew, the remains should be enclosed in a leaden casket, and dropped with due honours from an aircraft over the sea and that a Memorial Service should be held. This, it is understood, has now been done, and the Memorial Service was held at St Matthews Church, Townsville,

Queensland, on Sunday June 1st, the service being conducted by the Rev J. G. Johnstone, a former Padre of the Royal Australian Air Force.

The Department is advised that your daughter-in-law was interviewed by the Royal Australian Air Force representative in Sydney and informed of the reasons for the delay in the funeral arrangements, and she is presumably in possession of all the sad details. [45]

Official records state:

Mosquito FB.VI TE746 crashed into the Gulf of Carpentaria on March 26 1947 with the loss of both crew (W/C B. R. Hoare and F/O W. Colvin RAF)
W/Cdr (37853) Bertie Rex O'Brien Hoare (pilot) RAF – killed
P/O (194.363) Walter Colvin (nav.) RAFVR – killed

Colvin was not a New Zealander, but listed as a New Zealand casualty because he was lost in an RNZAF aircraft. He was attached from 84 Squadron RAF to the RNZAF Ferry Flight to undertake the delivery. He is mentioned in Don Neate's 84 Squadron History – 'The Scorpion's Sting' – as being 'an extremely popular Officer'.

There are various conflicting accounts of the death of Commander Hoare.

On 26 March 1947, Christopher Shores in 'Aces High' states that the Mosquito crash-landed on a remote island, the crew perishing of thirst before they could be found. Other sources state that the aircraft crashed into the sea. It is believed Sammy Hoare had a relative born in Christchurch, which may have attracted him to make the flight to New Zealand.

No-one knows the truth for certain. It remains another mystery of war, of which there were many. But it does seem unjust that Sammy lost his life postwar after surviving near misses during years engaged in aerial combat. He was just thirty-five years old when he died. His daughter, Rosemary Verity, was born seven months after his death, on 1 November 1947. His wife, Lucy never got over the untimely death of her beloved husband. When she died on 21 June 1970, she asked to be buried back at Little Snoring church where they had met. Sadly, she was buried in an unmarked grave at the top of the churchyard, in the farthest corner. However, a reunion of pilots in 1995 inaugurated the placing of a WAAF headstone including Sammy's details so that they might be remembered together. This was organised by Leslie Holland, formerly Warrant Officer at RAF Little Snoring Station; with the help of Tommy Cushing (one of two brothers who bought Little Snoring airfield following the war) with permission from the RAF. Lucy's husband also has a grave in Singapore, although it is unknown whether Bertie Hoare is actually buried in either grave, or just commemorated as '*Missing*'.

He is credited with nine victories on 23 and 605 Squadrons and decorated with the award of Companion, Distinguished Service Order DSO (1942) and Bar (1944). He gained the rank of Wing Commander in the service of the Royal Air Force. His details are officially listed:

HOARE, BERTIE REX O'BRIEN DSO & Bar, DFC & Bar
Wing Commander, 37853.
84 Squadron, Royal Air Force.
Died 26 March 1947. Aged 35.
Son of Bertie and Mary Hoare.
Husband of Lucy N. Hoare of Nairobi, Kenya.
Commemorated on the Singapore Memorial. Column 459.

The mystery remains, generating questions by all who read or hear the story of this remarkable man: *Did the plane crash into the sea, or did it make a success-ful landing on an isolated island? Were the bodies missing, or found 'lying under the wing of the aircraft'? Did they die of injuries, thirst and hunger, or even at the hands of natives who found them there? Was the wreckage discovered earlier than 3 April, but only reported at that time when both men were dead?*

We will never know.

As someone who has read this story many times, and admires the courage and fortitude of a man obviously admired, respected and loved by men he worked with and who served under him, together with his wife and family; one thing I do know for certain. Thinking back to my own mother's expe-rience of losing her wartime fiancé Vic Vinnell under similarly mysterious circumstances, she would say time and time again amidst a lake of tears: '*it is the **not knowing** that tears the heart*'. Whatever the truth, it is better **to know** in order to be able to understand what there is to deal with ... and move on.

W/Cdr Alan Michael Murphy DSO & Bar, DFC, Croix de Guerre

Alan Michael Murphy was born at Cockermouth in Cumberland on 26 September 1917. Soon after, his family moved to South Africa where he spent his early life. However, the ill-health of his father forced an early return to England for the family where Alan went to Seafield Preparatory School at Lytham on the north-west coast and became an accomplished sportsman by the time he left sometime in 1931.

In his mid to late teens he joined the RAF who were keen to use his athletic skills. His long jump, high jump and 440-yard dash were amongst the best and soon he was representing his Service, stealing the show in 1938 in an inter-Service challenge between Sandhurst, Woolwich and Cranwell, creating a long-standing record for the long-jump with a measurement of twenty-three feet and one-half inches.

This was a man who was a stickler for seeing something through, never letting go until the matter was resolved; job done. It earned him the nick-name 'Sticky'.

In July that year, he was commissioned as a Pilot Officer, training on Handley Page Hampdens of 185 Squadron, Cottesmore, and it is here he could have met Sammy Hoare flying Battles with 207 Squadron. He then spent time training others as Squadron Navigation Officer at 14 O.T.U which had absorbed 185 Squadron.

In March 1941, he joined 1419 Special Duty Flight at Stradishall, whose primary role was dispatching allied agents to aid the Resistance throughout occupied Europe. Later that year, he was one of the original founder Pilots of 138 (Special Duties) Squadron, which became one of the 'Moon' Squadrons, along with its later sister Squadron, 161; specialising in short take-off and landings in a Lysander on moonlit nights in occupied Europe. During the December moon period, No. 138 Squadron flew one pick-up mission which almost ended in disaster.

'Operation Stoat' began at 2210 hours on 8 December. Flt/Lt Murphy took off from Tangmere heading for a field near Neufchateau in Belgium. Once over the Channel, Murphy flew low to avoid German radar. As the coast of France loomed, he climbed swiftly to 3000 feet, a height good enough to pinpoint landmarks – too high for light flak, too low for heavy gunfire to reach them. Two hours later, he brought the Lysander down to 1000 feet, circling the snow-covered landing field, searching for the correct identity letter to be flashed by agent, Jean Cassart, a Captain in the Belgian Air Force. A light was flashing in an adjacent field. It wasn't the expected letter. It gave the impression the agent was in danger. He decided to land anyway, but without a flarepath. Switching on the landing light, he was about to touch down when he noticed what looked like a ditch in his path. Cursing the agent in charge of selecting the landing site, he over-shot and went round again, approaching the eastern side of the field instead, at the same time loosening his revolver in case of trouble. Something felt suspicious about this operation.

His landing was perfect. But as he rolled to a standstill, he was blinded by a searchlight shining directly at him. A shot rang out. The bullet hit him in the neck. Sticky went immediately into action mode, doing several things at once – dropping his revolver, he held one of his wife's stockings, always with him for good luck; to stem the flow of blood from his neck, while opening the throttle. The Lysander accelerated towards a line of trees at the end of the field. Hauling gently back on the stick with his free hand, he missed the treetops by inches, guiding the aircraft back into the skies, following the same journey in reverse back to Tangmere to discover on landing safely that the Lysander had taken thirty bullet-holes ... but with no passenger.

In the field behind, Cassart and his Wireless Operator Henri Verhaegen, had run into a German patrol, guided to the rendez-vous by information beaten out of a captured Resistance member. Jean was hit in the arm during the ensuing exchange of fire and Verhaegen was caught by one of the German soldiers, managing to shake free to make his escape. A party of more than twenty Jagdkommandos surrounded the field, some within thirty yards of Murphy's Lysander, with more than one hundred shots fired during the encounter. The wounded Cassart was captured a few days later and taken to Berlin by the Gestapo, but escaped to make his way back to England several months later. [46]

Jean Cassart was one of the French agents at Neufchateau in Belgium. He had run away, entering a graveyard to hide behind a headstone, only realising then he'd been shot in the arm during his dash for freedom. The Germans launched an immediate search of the area, and a young soldier found his hiding place. Cassart thought he'd be shot on the spot. But the young soldier looked at him ... and turned away without saying a word, or giving him away. There would therefore be at least two survivors to escape the Germans that night.

However, the resulting injury to Murphy's neck had cut many of the muscles, with the lasting effect of making it impossible to hold a beer glass traditionally, but rather to hold his drinking arm perpendicular to his body. Several fellow aircrew pointed out the immediate benefit it had of making it easy to spot him in a pub, or when drinking with his back turned towards them!

On 6 January, as Acting Squadron Leader, Murphy was awarded the DFC for his exploits to date. His Citation reads:

This Officer carried out a hazardous mission with complete success, despite navigational difficulties and adverse weather conditions. On a previous occasion, when returning from an operational mission, Squadron Leader Murphy passed over an enemy convoy at the low altitude of 100 feet. He noted its position, counted the ships and observed their course, and then reported the information to Base. The information proved of great value. This Officer has invariably displayed great courage and initiative.

In February 1942, No. 138 Squadron was expanded on the orders of the new Chief of SOE, Lord Selborne. At Newmarket, 161 (Special Duties) Squadron was formed. It contained a nucleus of 138 Squadron and the Kings Flight.

The Kings Flight had been formed in 1936 at Hendon and comprised of an Airspeed Envoy and a Lockheed Hudson. The first Captain of the Flight was Wing Commander 'Mouse' Fielden, and at the outbreak of war, they were officially allocated to No. 24 (Communications) Squadron. When 161 Squadron absorbed The Kings Flight, the Hudson was transferred to the new Unit, with Wing Commander *Mouse* Fielden its first Commanding Officer.

The new Squadron's A Flight was equipped with five Lysander IIIAs (SD), and B Flight was allocated seven Whitley Vs and two Wellington IIs. The Hudson became the Squadron bus.

On 22 February, the Squadron flew its first two covert missions.

'Operation Crème', was a standard Lysander pick-up flown by Flying Officer W. G. Lockhart, a former 138 Squadron pilot. Two agents were dropped off in a field near Villeneuve, north of Chateuroux, France.

'Operation Beryl III' was a first for the RAF and its pilot as a pick-up from France in a twin-engined aircraft – Avro Anson T.I.R3316. The navigation trainer from a local Bomber Command O.T.U. had been 'borrowed' and painted black for its forthcoming trip.

At 2100 hours, Pilot Squadron Leader Murphy with Navigator, Pilot Officer Henry 'Titch' Cossar, took off in an Anson christened 'Gormless Gertie', heading for one of their known landing fields at Segry. There were four passengers to be collected. The last pick-up had failed following a very eventful landing for Squadron Leader John 'Whippy' Nesbitt-Dufort on 28 January after 'icing-up'. He had been in hiding ever since with the two agents he was supposed to have picked up. They had been joined by a fourth passenger, Polish General Julius Kleeberg, code-named 'Tudor'.

The journey was made in driving rain and thick cloud. As a result, Murphy and 'Titch' were lost for more than an hour before finding their mark and landing at 0010 hours.

On landing, the four passengers fell into the back of the aircraft, and minutes later the Anson splashed determinedly across a very wet field to climb slowly towards Dieppe on the French Coast, then on to Tangmere. Whippy's quip on the reporting of his flight back to freedom summed up their journey: 'the skill of the Pilot and Navigator proved in this case exceptional, as we were only lost the majority of the way home!' Whippy had gained his nickname after previously losing several trainee pilots on a practice flight at an O.T.U who had unfortunately for him landed at Whipsnade Zoo!

Pilot Officer Henry Cossar was Navigator on the first twin pick-up to rescue Squadron Leader John Whippy Nesbitt-Dufort and his important passengers:

> Sticky came into the Mess 'looking' for a volunteer. There were five chaps in the Mess, all willing volunteers. Sticky picked me, 'Titch'. It was not apparent then why I was picked. But the penny started to drop once we were led outside to 'Gormless Gertie', the Anson. It was the most tired and sorry-looking example, one of the earlier models; with a wind-up undercarriage that I, of course, would be winding! Then it was obvious why I'd been chosen, with a twin-engine aircraft and the number of passengers to bring back (4), I'd been picked by Sticky due to my size and weight. The mission was of great importance, not just because of the passengers, but coming with them were top secret German plans – construction details on

the *Gneisenau* and *Scharnhorst*, Germany's latest two Battle cruisers that threatened to ravage the Atlantic. As it was, 'Gertie's' wheels sunk through the snow and ice into the field. To *'break the suction'*, Sticky made all of us, including our passengers, jump up and down in our seats, including the Polish General. [47]

In March, Sticky Murphy was officially promoted to Squadron Leader, taking command of A Flight. His natural flair for organising the Flight and his own, by now legendary daring and dauntless bravery; made him a natural choice. Leading 161 Squadron had also brought the award of the Distinguished Service Order (DSO) for the effort he had put in. His Citation read:

On five recent occasions, at night, this Officer has carried out operations demanding the highest qualities of skill and organisation. Squadron Leader Murphy has personally organised his Flight and trained his Pilots. He has displayed inspiring leadership.

June 1942 brought new surroundings. On the 20th, Murphy was posted to Whitehall for a rest, handing over command of 161 Squadron to Squadron Leader Guy Lockhart. He was attached to the Air Ministry, but still managed to fly whenever he had the chance. There were however, other benefits, such as enjoying married life in London. It was while in London that Murphy developed an unusual method of alleviating his boredom stuck in offices, away from flying which he loved. He had a miniature cannon – the perfect example of a 19th-century cannon, a fully working replica. Whether it was just a showpiece or a grand starting-pistol, its origins are unknown. However, it could apparently fire the contents of shotgun cartridges as well as paper. He took great delight blowing out office windows near or adjacent to his own, much to the annoyance of some more senior Officers. Perhaps then, it was these same Officers who were happy that he be posted as *'Active'* again, preferring to preserve buildings that otherwise lost windows on a daily basis the more Murphy's boredom grew. The Hun, after all, would make a far more suitable target for his talents!

Almost a year on from leaving 161 Squadron, on 20 June 1943, he arrived to take up his new posting at 60 O.T.U at High Ercall with a conversion to Mosquitoes and a crash course in the dark art of *'Intruding'* from mainland Britain into northern France and Germany. One notable moment that made a lasting impression on several pilots was the sight of their Flight

Commander caught on gun camera in his Mossie, doing a very slow roll for his audience!

On his 'Passing Out' from the Course, he was given a grading of 'Exceptional' in his Log Book by Wing Commander, 'Mouse' Fielden, his C.O on 161 Squadron in previous years.

Late September 1943 saw Murphy landing in Malta, joining the veteran 23 Squadron. His stay was spent getting acquainted with the Squadron and its blossoming social life, to which he took like a duck to water, and as one of the Squadron's most enthusiastic supporters of its history and 'esprit de corps'. He also became familiar with the 'Y-Service' on which 23 Squadron relied as a valuable source of information.

On 11 November, Murphy moved with B Flight to the forward area at Pomligiliano, Italy. A couple of nights later, he was chased by an ME210 on his way to his own strafing area. Jettisoning his 250-lb bombs to improve manoeuvrability and speed and, having slipped away from his attacker, Murphy discovered he had not selected properly and still had bombs on board. In typical style, he then dropped them on an enemy railway station, having already used most of his ammunition on their local train service.

At Pomigiliano, Murphy had a jeep, 'borrowed' from the Americans in Naples. In truth, it had been 'borrowed' for him by Navigator Norman Conquer and his Pilot Baron Goldie as an act of devotion for their Flight Commander! In turn, the Squadron also 'borrowed' it from Murphy, and in the Squadron's own affectionate way, because Murphy was an Irish-sounding name, painted 'THE DOITY TWENTY TWOID' across the bonnet.

While at Pomigiliano, the Squadron, such as it was, a single Flight and support staff, had a party. No different to any other night the Squadron had off … perhaps. Until Murphy leapt up in the midst of proceedings to declare:

'I'm going on an Op!'

'What? Where? Are you sure old boy? We've been partying for hours …'

A gentle chorus started:

'What's Sticky doing? What, going on an Op?'

'Well, we've all had a bit to drink … Steady on now, Sir!'

Sticky was not to be placated. As the seconds ticked by, his enthusiasm grew, until recklessly he bounded into action. He rushed into the Ops Room, actually a great wrecked Messerschmitt ME323 Gigant, prior to getting an

'*Ops Tent*'; where he proceeded to the Operations Board and map and, with great gusto, in one single motion, ripped off a large portion of map which accompanied him as he picked up a set of flying gear. Then he rushed off to an aircraft with Pat Rapson as his Navigator. Bud Badley recalled, as they climbed into the aircraft that it was possibly Norman Conquer who said:

'Hang on, Sticky, you've got nothing to drink!'

He handed a bottle of Chianti to him through the hatch, before the intrepid pair took off in a somewhat enthusiastic state and disappeared into the night ... actually to an Italian harbour where Murphy blasted away at everything before returning. It would be less than a year later when Pat Reid would remember this incident, and the fact that Sticky was gone for over three hours.

On 6 December, B Flight packed up to leave Pomligiliano to move to their new base at Alghero, Sardinia. W/C Burton-Giles, the Squadron C.O. was lost in an operation in the Genoa-Turin area just nights later. However, the first person already there, waiting to greet Squadron members was their new C.O., Sticky Murphy himself.

The end of the month, they had a visit by Air Vice Marshall Hugh P. Lloyd, Air Officer commanding the Mediterranean Air Force, and the Squadron. While there, he ventured the opinion that '*intruder work in the theatre was finished*'. His words were to come back to bite him in the not-too-distant future!

Murphy had already begun to look at other areas to operate, namely France. The 'Y-Service' at Bletchley Park, which kept the Squadron informed as to the disposition and movements of enemy war material, continued to forward information. His objective was to intercept reconnaissance aircraft from Montpelier and typically Istres, which were travelling along the African coast, gathering information on Allied movements. The information was used to provide strike targets for the German's latest development of a new radio-controlled bomb, forerunner to the '*Cruise Missile*'.

On 6 January, Murphy went hunting in France for the second time, destroying a Dornier 217 near Toulouse. Now, with Squadron strength in full complement, men and machines; he began to organise their most comprehensive month of the war since leaving Britain, culminating in 211 sorties.

Meanwhile, the rest of the Squadron were busy causing havoc in the Po Valley, following up Murphy's success at French airfields. In light of these recent events, Murphy communicated that in fact: *'intruding was not quite finished yet in the Mediterranean theatre'* to the same Air Officer Commanding: Air-Vice Marshall Hugh P. Lloyd, who had thought otherwise not so long ago!

In February, amidst much bad weather, Murphy organised a complete programme of destruction on the rail system in the Po Valley, much as the Squadron had done in January, while keeping up a programme of *'Intruding'*. Pilot Officer Rudd, as he was at this time, explains in his book: *'A History of 23 Squadron'*, that in this month the Squadron had a visit from four machines from No. 256 Squadron fitted with new AI Mk. 8 Radar. These four crews were then instructed in the dark art of intruding and a small gathering took place to make them feel at home. It justified one of Murphy's infamous parties, bringing two FANYs (First Aid Nursing Yeomanry) to the Squadron Bar with the words: *'I only brought them down for you chaps!'*

On 9 April, Murphy allowed a Day-Ranger to the French Riviera. He took Bud Badley as his No. 2, with Squadron Leader Phil Russell and Squadron Leader Smith forming another pair. Bud recalls:

Sticky was thoroughly enjoying himself, blasting away at everything, even at heavy equipment used in a quarry up in the hills. A large gasholder could not be missed, but did not produce a satisfactory explosion at all. Eventually, Sticky announced he was out of ammunication and was going home. I still had ammo. As no opposition was encountered, he didn't feel he needed to be No. 2, so gave permission to carry on by myself!

Sticky would continue to guide the Squadron's operations, creating further havoc in Po Valley, following up on initial success in France. However, on 5 May, Murphy broke the news to the Squadron they were to return to the UK leaving Sardinia for good. A mood of jubilation took over! And again, in recognition of the news, a huge farewell party was organised with Americans on the Base. The Squadron together with their charismatic Wing Commander achieved much success against the enemy, with a freedom of action that would never again go unregulated. *Sticky* as he was fondly known, had spent over six months with the Squadron as a Flight Commander and then Wing Commander, and was beloved by every man, from Aircrew down to Fitters. They all knew him as a man who would think nothing of letting them take a less rigorous mission, while he took the more difficult ones. This was not unknown for crews either inexperienced, or completing the end of their tours, often done in friendship rather than in the style of a command. *Sticky* gave aircrew the feeling that they '*belonged*', that he was looking after them and their interests. Flt/Lt Tommy Smith was to say on his arrival at RAF Little Snoring: '*It wasn't like joining a Squadron, Sticky welcomed you into a family!*'

On 2 December 1944, *Sticky* Murphy with Navigator Douglas Darbon were returning from a patrol at Gutersloh. They had strayed too far north, flying over marshalling yards near Zwolle, on the Dutch/German border where, each moonlit night, a Mosquito had been spotted strafing the yard. Germans were on the alert, flak guns placed strategically between two road bridges. They were after the rogue aircraft, but instead caught *Sticky*. Flak opened up while Buddy was talking to them on the radio, telling them to '*get out of it*'. Too late! The damage was done. The distinguished Wing Commander Alan Michael Murphy DSO & Bar, DFC, Croix de Guerre was no more.

George Stewart DFC recalls being sent to Guttersloh on his 49th trip, to see if he could sense anything that might have caused this one of two losses, but there was no activity, other than the usual scanning heard on their headsets. It was only later that facts emerged about the Mosquito for which Germans were waiting.

However, it is worth mentioning that, even seventy years on, new facts are emerging. Sticky Murphy's daughter Gail tells me that her father *Sticky* didn't actually have to go out on that final fateful mission, but elected to go anyway. He also wasn't flying with his regular Navigator, Jock Reid who, for whatever reason, wasn't able to join him. Douglas Darbon was therefore someone new and perhaps they weren't used to working together. A more interesting point is that *Sticky* for some reason shaved off his moustache before the operation, and remained quiet and pensive, quite unlike his usual self. *Did he have a premonition that something was going to happen and he might not return?* It wasn't uncommon.

Whatever the truths, the sudden and tragic loss of *Sticky* Murphy on 2 December 1944 would stay for the rest of their lives with aircrew and all those lives touched by this courageous man. Whenever they thought of friends who didn't return, *Sticky* was uppermost in their minds. It was agreed that a better friend and comrade no man could have.

It was '*Pic*' Pickard who commanded 161 Squadron after *Sticky*'s demise, well known as Squadron Leader Dickson, skipper of Wellington *F for Freddie*, in the popular Crown Film Unit 1941 production: '*Target for Tonight*'. He was also Commander of the legendary Amiens Prison Raid (*Operation Jericho*) when a British formation of fifteen Mosquito twin-engine bombers escorted by eight Typhoon fighters bombed the prison and Gestapo Headquarters at Amiens in Northern France. He was killed as he was departing, caught by two FW190s.

After the war, *Sticky* Murphy's widow Jean had to start life without him, somehow moving on with a small daughter to take care of alone. Whatever her thoughts, she would keep them to herself. *Sticky* was consigned to a place deep within her heart, locked tightly away. However, she did go on a cycling holiday to the Netherlands to find *Sticky*'s crash-site and was given the silver cigarette case bearing his name, the Dutch means of identification; and photographs of where his aircraft came down. The Hague Foundation paid for her daughter Gail, then aged ten or eleven; to visit *Sticky*'s grave. Gail's overriding memory is being made to wear a school hat which she didn't like when none of the other children had one! For them, the memory of the man they loved would never die as so many stories reached them of his love for his men and fearless acts of 'derring-do'.

It was to be years later when Jean began '*walking out*' with Squadron Leader Johnny Booth, another seasoned Pilot from RAF 100 Group.

Squadron Leader Johnny Booth, DFC and Bar: Night Fighter, '*Intruder*' and Test Pilot, was no less brave. He entered the RAF on a Short Service Commission in December 1938, serving in various Training Units until October 1939 when he went to France with No. 59 Army Co-operation Squadron as part of the British Expeditionary Force flying Blenheims. It was during that first tour of operations that Johnny earned his first DFC in the Battle for France. Wounded in May 1940, he was evacuated to England, staying at the Hatfield Military Hospital until August. On being discharged, he served as Flying Instructor in several Units until December. The following January, he was sent to Canada and served as a Flying Instructor, earning his qualification by the Central Flying School on 11 February 1942.

Just over a year later, in March 1943, Booth delivered a Boston bomber from Montreal to Prestwick, serving with the RAF Ferry Command at Dorval

City, with which he stayed through April. In May, he began his second tour of operations, serving successively with 51 O.T.U and 125, 151 and 239 Night Fighter Squadrons. During this period, Booth was awarded a Bar to his DFC after serving with Bomber Command on Night Intruder Operations until October 1944 with RAF 100 Group.

Booth's first experience of test flying was at Boscombe Down, where he served as a Test Pilot from October 1944 to March 1945. That month, he enrolled at the ETPS to complete No. 3 Course on 15 December 1945. In February 1946, Johnny became one of a group of Pilots who worked with Sir Frank Whittle at Power Jets (R&D) Ltd. He left that company in October and in November joined Short Brothers and Harland Ltd as a Test Pilot until January 1949. The following month, he started with Saunders-Roe as Deputy to their Chief Test Pilot, Geoffrey Tyson.

In February 1956, Johnny became their Chief Test Pilot and flew the famous SR.1A flying jet boat, taking part in tests of the Princess flying boat. He flew the prototype SR.53 on its initial flight at Boscombe Down on 16 May 1957, making a total of thirty-three flights on the SR.53. He had logged over 3500 hours on ninety different types of aircraft.

Sadly, after a distinguished career, Squadron Leader Johnny Booth DFC & Bar was killed on 5 June 1958 in the crash of the second SR.53 proto-type, number XD151, on take-off. The engine failed and he struck one of the aircraft landing-lights, rupturing the fuel tanks which burst into flames while coming off the runway. A few days later, he was posthumously awarded the Queen's Commendation for Valuable Service in the Air.

For the second time in her life, Jean was alone, consigning to her heart a man she had held dear while bringing up her teenage daughter Gail and half-sister Caroline Booth born in 1948 who both remain very close. However, she did marry again, finding happiness with her daughters with Dr Charles Bunting, a doctor whose feet were firm on the ground. The daily risk of death was remote, and as a family they enjoyed a relationship that lasted the rest of her life. However, Gail grew up with full knowledge of her father, the renowned *Sticky* Murphy who would never be forgotten.

On 31 May 2011, Gail and her husband Nic with their two sons, Sean and Marcus, made a pilgrimage from their home in South Africa to Oldebroek. A couple of days later, they were greeted by the Mayor and Town Council, and in the local Council Offices formal greetings were exchanged together with an expression of gratitude from the people of the Netherlands and Oldebroek for the sacrifice made by her father on 2 December 1944 ... giving his life while on operations over the Netherlands. The Council party, with Gail and her family and Pete Smith, son of Flt/Lt Tommy Smith also of 23 Squadron, 100 Group who arranged the visit; were then joined by Breedijks and Thibaut Westhof and taken to the town cemetery. The still quiet piece of land off the beaten track, tucked away behind the main streets overlooking green fields of Oldebroek, held souls now at rest. The entrance led down a long avenue of trees to where the graves of twenty-seven Allied Servicemen lay in a serene circle, all in stark contract to their final moments of life, forever representing all major nationalities of the Allied Front – Canada, Australia, New Zealand, South Africa, Great Britain, India and Poland. There was also the grave of an unknown airman. They followed the path beneath the trees to stand in resolute silence as the *Last Post* was played, flags at half-mast. There followed the sad sight of Gail, a loving daughter, laying flowers on the grave of a father she never knew, some sixty-five years after his death. *Sticky's* Navigator on that night, Douglas Darbon, lay there also, and was not forgotten by them.

As the party left the graveyard, they were shown the grave of Hendrik Krooneman who died on the day of liberation in the Netherlands, killed while playing with a hand grenade the day war ended. He was just ten years old. The party continued on to Wezep, in Oldebroek, behind the railway line into the woods which, in 1944, was heathland. The crash site was located by Dick Breedijk three days before they arrived. He was the same Dutchman to find the crash site of Flight Lieutenant Tommy Smith with Navigator A. C. Cockayne in Beckedorf, Germany, the previous year, as he had done on behalf of many hundreds of families of Allied airmen needing to know the final resting place of loved ones. The crash of Sticky Murphy's aircraft penetrated little more than several inches into the concrete-like soil which had once been covered with water. While no ashes remained, it was still possible to see grey deposits a couple of inches under the vegetation, making those moments all the more poignant.

On their way back, the crash site of another Mosquito crew was passed, not more than a mile away from that of *Sticky* Murphy and Douglas Darbon. The family gave the same consideration they had their own, not knowing them, but understanding what it meant to their loved ones.

The party moved from the Netherlands to Belgium for a celebration of his life at the scene of his greatest escape while flying a Westland Lysander in 161 Squadron for SOE in 1941-42. On their way, they made a small detour to Belgium, to the home of the Sabena 'Old-Timers' ('*Sabena*' was the original name of Brussels Airlines). The Club restores aircraft, with a view to keeping them flying as a part of living history. Incredibly, they were shown a Lysander painted in 161 Squadron colours, with the Squadron code of that which *Sticky* Murphy had flown. After much discussion on events that occurred at the landing site at Perchepet in the Municipality of Neufchateau, Gail was presented with two pictures of the Lysander flying where her father would have flown, piloted by Dany Stockmans of the Sabena Oldtimers. A fitting tribute!

Then it was onto Perchepet, the scene of a 161 Squadron 'routine' pick-up which had become a German ambush where Sticky was shot through the neck, surviving to fly the aircraft home. Thibaut Westhof attracted quite a crowd as he shared the story of what had happened, with surviving members of the Resistance coming to pay their respects, and local school children listening to history being passed down. As the party moved to the graveyard nearby where Cassert, shot and wounded, had hidden in fear of his life, it was time for Resistance fighters and family to join and offer a final thanks to the Allied fallen here.

At the Council offices of Neufchateau later, Gail and Peter (*son of Tommy Smith*) were presented with a medal for service given by their fathers during the war. [48]

It feels fitting that the final words of the shared wartime experiences of *Sticky* Murphy should go to his daughter Gail:

I feel a deep sense of pride in what was achieved by all the airmen of the time, those who died and in those who survived, but particularly, of course, in *Sticky,* my father. It was a wonderful experience meeting and talking to Resistance fighters who I was privileged to meet at Perchapet, and I felt inadequate and humbled almost to tears when they saluted me ... I was able to talk at length to a wonderful lady, also in the Resistance, whose husband was one of the Resistance fighters dropped in the area by *Sticky.* She was telling me that when she dies and goes to Heaven, she's looking forward to meeting up with *Sticky* and giving him hell for having dropped her husband several kilometres off target, resulting in a long walk at the dead of night through enemy territory while carrying heavy radio equipment!

I have a huge sense of gratitude to people of Belgium and Holland who keep history alive with such respect and honour in the way they lovingly maintain war cemeteries. My thanks to Dick and Dee

Breedijk who welcomed us with open arms into their lives and home, organising events in Holland. We are also grateful to Thibaut and his family in Belgium for our few days there, including the Perchepet ceremony, and in Brussels organising a face-to-face meeting with a lovingly restored Mosquito, not forgetting the up close and personal view of the Lysander – that still actually flies! The Lysander was one of the planes *Sticky* flew on his moonlight missions.

Lastly, I will be ever grateful to Pete Smith (son of Tom '*Tommy*' Anderson Smith, who also served in 23 Squadron) for being the catalyst and instigator-in-chief of the whole wonderful experience. [49]

The memory of *Sticky* Murphy lives on ... and will continue to do so in the hearts and minds of free people from five continents, nine countries and two small towns in Holland and Belgium, Oldebroek and Neufchateau, while Neufchateau wants to honour the events with a Monument for the future.

Canadian Pilot:
Flight Lieutenant George Stewart DFC

George Stewart and his wife Marion are firm and valued friends of the author, and George is a gifted writer. He is keen to help readers understand what it was like as a young man, leaving home in Canada for the first time, three months after turning nineteen years of age; arriving in a strange land with eyes wide open, soaking up the new experience.

It was the Lady Ryder Association which found homes for us to visit on Leave. I lucked in with the Colquhoun family at Whittington, near Litchfield, who took me in like a son. My real job, before enlisting, was a messenger on a bike for my father's shop where I earned $5 a week, paying $4 board. I wasn't much of a date as I didn't drink or smoke. You can imagine, arriving in England, and my astonishment as a Commissioned Officer, making **$7 a day** to fly the fastest aircraft in the world, my beloved de Havilland Mosquito, which went on to change my life forever! My peers, recognising my naivety, offered advice which I absorbed like a sponge (the most important Mosquito tip, from F/L Jaclie Curd: '*Get your power up on take-off as fast as you can! It will save your life some day!*') It did!! The charismatic Mosquito, to this day, has occupied a lot of my time, as interest in it never seems to flag.

But then, let me welcome you as a visitor to RAF Little Snoring where 23 Squadron are based. It is Saturday 4 November 1944, and we are living in a war...

Good afternoon. WOW, what a blustery day; and so cold; it seems to go right through you, doesn't it? Since you've recently landed in the UK, you've probably noticed differences from things back home. I remember when I first arrived it was quite a change from what I was used to. The '*Blackout*', for instance; I was amazed how people get around, and combined with thick English fog, it seemed impossible. And those '*Roundabouts*', I found them bewildering! However, with hooded headlights, driving slow, we manage quite well. Have you ever seen so many bikes? I'll explain everything during your visit today.

Welcome to RAF Station Little Snoring. This is home for our two 100 Group (BS) Squadrons (No! It means '*Bomber Support*'). 23 Squadron is led by W/C A. M. (*Sticky*) Murphy, DSO and Bar DFC and Bar, Croix de Guerre and Palm, and Chech Medal. 515 Squadron is headed up by Canadian W/C Freddy Lambert DSO, DFC. Our Station Commander is G/C Samuel (*Sammy*) Hoare, DSO and Bar, DFC and BAR, (nephew of Sir Samuel Hoare of The Home Office).

W/C Murphy is famous for dropping off, and picking up, agents (spies) from occupied Europe, in Westland Lysanders, landing at night in the dark, with only three flashlights, held by people on the ground, to form an 'L', to indicate the location of the landing strip. I picked him up one day from his Lysander base which he was visiting. He showed me around. I was impressed! There was nobody lower in rank than Flt/Sgt, a very special organisation.

G/C Hoare is recognised as one of the original '*Night Intruders*' in World War Two, and written up in the Rolls Royce Annals for his remarkable return, one night, from an Intruder operation over Germany. His Mosquito was hit by ground fire, damaging his oil lines; however, he was able to keep flying, alternating from one engine to the other. Just as one would overheat from lack of oil, he would feather its prop, and switch to the other, then back again. A truly remarkable feat of airmanship! I knew him when I was at High Ercall, the Night Intruder Mosquito Operational Training Unit. He was Commanding Officer.

My name is George Stewart. I fly with 23 Squadron, and presently, I'm the only Canadian pilot. I'll be acting as your host today. This is our Briefing Room, located behind Station Headquarters. It's the 'nerve-centre' of our base. The Intelligence Section, and its Library are next door. Crews flying on ops tonight are waiting there to be called in for Briefing which starts shortly.

As you can see, the Briefing Room is laid out like a classroom with long tables and chairs. Behind me, on the back wall, you'll notice a large map of Europe with ribbons taped to it. It's made with the identical maps our Navigators use when flying 'ops', so we plot our trips on the same scale. The ribbons show tracks the Main Force will follow to their 'Target for Tonight', and back home after dropping their bombs.

W/C Murphy, our CO, and S/L Charlie Price, our SIO (Senior Intelligence Officer) are going over details of tonight's operation before Briefing begins. I'm told Charlie went along on many heavy bomber raids as an Observer, to get the 'feel' of operations, thus making him a more informed Intelligence Officer. It took a lot of courage to do that, and we hold him in high regard! 515 Squadron, our 'Sister' Squadron has the night off. ('Stood Down').

The covered easel over to my right, holds our Crew-Allocation Board, where our individual patrol areas are listed; and of course, we are extremely anxious to see it, to know where the heck they're sending us tonight! Unfortunately, it won't be uncovered until after Charlie tells us about the overall operational picture, involving the Main Force, and supporting roles we'll be providing.

You've been given top security clearance, to be a 'fly on the wall' during our Briefing for tonight's operations. This is quite new to us! Please don't talk about it beyond this room. We don't want the enemy to know any surprises we have. You'll appreciate this even more after you've heard our Briefing which begins at 1400 hours. First, I'll freeze time to tell you about Little Snoring, our Squadron, our aircraft, and our role.

You must have been surprised on arrival at how suddenly you were at our main gate, having just turned the corner in the middle of our tiny village. Little Snoring is about three miles from Fakenham. (*Don't you just love those English 'place names*)? Was it a 'bedroom' community for Fakenham years ago? Like many wartime aerodromes, we are snuggled up against the north edge of town, and our main runways stretch about a mile over adjacent farmland. The two longer ones, (240 and 310) are angled to bracket the prevailing westerly winds. The short one (010) is seldom used, except for taxiing or emergency purposes. (I've never seen it used).

I found it strange when I first got here, to see aircraft so widely scattered around the outside edge of the airfield, unlike our neat arrangement back home, where trainers were neatly lined up along the tarmac in front of the row of hangars, a much more efficient layout, and 'user friendly' I'm sure you'll agree. This 'dispersing', as the scattering is called, is well planned, so our aircraft present less concentrated a grouping, therefore poorer targets when under attack from the air.

The station buildings also are located just outside the north part of town, positioned within a short walk of one another (Station Headquarters, Intelligence Section, various Messes, Sick Bay, Motor Pool, etc,). I'll tell you about our billets, in a bit. The CO's and Flight Offices, naturally, are located at the nearby edge of the airfield, as are our personal flying lockers. The few hangars situated on either side of the airfield, are also dispersed. You probably wondered why we have so few hangars. Well, this is because our aircraft stay out in the open, except when brought inside for inspections, or maintenance, (*that can't be done out at the dispersal positions*).

The runways must seem pretty messy to you, with all those wood chips strewn over their thresholds; but again there's a purpose. They ease the shock to our tyres as we touch down at about 120 mph, and in wartime we must save rubber! Also, you'll notice tyres are covered with tarps when aircraft are parked in their dispersals. This protects their natural rubber from harmful effects of engine, and hydraulic fluids dripping down on them from above.

That funny little van (*with the turret on the back*) sitting by the runway-in-use houses the ACP (Aerodrome Control Pilot), a very important job in our line of work. His job is to signal aircraft departing on operations – flashing a green light for permission to take off, or red, to hold, because we do so in radio silence, both day and night. All other flying is controlled by radio contact with the Control Tower.

Each Mosquito crew has an assigned parking spot for their aircraft out at the dispersals, and the aircraft sit on hard standings.

Our Crew Chief has a small office and servicing hut nearby where we go to sign our aircraft's L14, before and after we fly, noting anything that needs attention before the next flight. An Air Raid shelter trench near his hut is home to a stray rooster and our pet pig, (*which somebody won in a bond rally*). I certainly wouldn't want to jump in there, even if we were under attack! But I'll continue my story.

We are billeted in half-round corrugated-steel Nissen huts, grouped together in rows (*we call this area our 'Site'*), about a mile down the local country road. Each houses ten people (five crews), sharing a washroom hut with the one next door. We also have a '*Batman*', Charlie, who brings tea in the morning, tends our two tiny stoves, and generally keeps things neat. He has a small 'Scottie' dog called '*Angus*', who has adopted us all.

You can imagine the transportation problems this kind of Base layout presents, with everything so widely scattered. Well, a bicycle is the answer; so each of us is issued one (*and you thought we fought the war in aeroplanes!*) Remember bicycle clips? But our COs and Flight Commanders get an automobile. Bikes are great, except when it's pouring rain, or on a day like this, in a bitter, cold, strong wind. (*It makes you want to be a Flight Commander!*)

Squadron life is quite civilised. It hardly seems like there's a war on as we go about our daily life. We get four meals a day – breakfast served between 7:00 – 9:00 am, lunch 11:30 – 1:00, and we mustn't forget Tea Time: 4:00 – 5:00, with dinner 7:00 – 8:00 pm. It all appears so peaceful. We fly happily around during the morning, doing our NFTs, then relax in the Officers' Lounge, reading newspapers, '*Flight*', '*The Aeroplane*', or '*Tee Em*', visiting with Squadron mates, opening mail, or playing billiards, until lunch is served (*very gentile!*). However, all is not as it seems, as you will find out shortly.

Speaking of lunch, how did you enjoy that lovely RAF 'Cuisine'? Those steam tables! It's certainly nothing like Mother's cooking, but they do their best during wartime, with many shortages. HOWEVER, I swear; that if I survive the war, I WILL NEVER, EVER, EAT, ANOTHER BRUSSELS SPROUT!

It's spooky at night in the 'blackout', like a setting for Sherlock Holmes. They even drive on the wrong side of the road. Thank goodness their runways don't have two lanes. How about all those English expressions? They call their flashlights 'torches', gas: 'petrol', tires are 'tyres', batteries are 'accumulators', crashes 'prangs', 'Wizard', (Wizard Prang), pounds are 'Quids', halfpenny, a 'Haypenny bit', a quarter-penny, a Farthing, the threepenny coin: 'Threppence', the two-penny coin: 'Tuppence', 'Upon my Word', 'Jolly good Show', 'dear-dear-dear', 'my-my-my', 'Bad Form', 'What's the Form'? , 'Not Arf', ' Popsie', 'Bird', 'Goodness Me' 'goody-goody', 'I say old chap', 'knock her up', 'I'll knock you up at seven', 'everything's in a flap', 'Cheerio old boy', 'Chiddleeoo', a 'Cuppa', 'Struth' 'Spirits', a 'Pint" a 'Brew', 'Gin and It', 'Pim's Tin Cup' (with cucumber), 'Time Gentlemen, Please', 'Scrubbed', 'Went for the Chop', 'Bought It', 'Bought the Farm', 'Batting on a Sticky Wicket', 'Dicing' (Dicing with Death), 'Cream Teas', 'Lorry', 'Tram', Trailer (Caravan), 'what a clot', 'Ta Ta for now', the radio is the 'Wireless', The flying radio is the 'R/T', 'BBC English', 'King's English', 'Colonials', 'UK', 'Tea dances', the 'Hun', 'Boche', 'that's a bit Dod-gee', 'dim view of that', 'poor show', 'Guvner', 'Stand-up Fight', 'Wot Cheer Cock', (Wot Cheer me old 'Cock-Sparra'), the Cockney stairs are 'Apples and Pears' etc. You get used to it after a few weeks, but still, it all seems so … quaint?

We have a nice bar, with a fine selection of drinks. But they don't have the soft drinks we do back home. Did you see the little scrub brush hanging down from above the bar, with a single dice on the other end of the string? Well, when the scrub brush is lowered, it means that flying is cancelled and the bar is open. If, on the other hand, the dice is pulled down, the bar is closed, indicating that operations are being flown tonight, so, nobody drinks! (We are Dicing!)

23 Squadron dates back to World War One, and many famous pilots (such as Raymond Collishaw), served. Over the years, 23 has been equipped with various new types of aircraft, as technology

and tactics developed. We now operate the renowned de Havilland Mosquito MKVI Fighter Bomber, a truly remarkable aircraft. It's one of the best designs of World War Two, adapting to a multitude of roles: from high and low level, unarmed Photo Reconnaissance, and bombing activities, to rocket firing anti-shipping strikes, and torpedo attacks, and in our case, as a fighter bomber, carrying guns and bombs.

NOW ... how do you like our beautiful little aircraft? Aren't they awesome? It's hard to believe they're made of wood and about the fastest aircraft flying in the world. Not only that, they weigh over eleven tons. Not even a strong wind like we have today can force them to remain on the ground. Mind you, we have to lock our controls so they won't keep banging against their stops and cause them damage.

Our Mosquito has a deadly sting – four 20-mm cannons, four .303 machine-guns, and two 500-lb bombs, a formidable fighting machine, feared by the enemy. The machine guns are visible. You can see them sticking out of the nose; however, our cannons underneath them are hidden by fabric. This material covers the troughs in which their barrels are located, and it is replaced after each time the cannons are fired. Besides keeping foreign objects out of the cannon barrels, the fabric improves streamlining of the fuselage, and contributes to speed.

Our two 500-lb bombs are carried in the bomb-bay, under our cockpit, behind the cannons, with specially designed short fins to accommodate the cramped space available in its slender fuselage. The bomber version of the Mosquito is modified with a swollen belly, to make room for the 4000-lb bomb ('Cookie') it carries. Our exhaust stacks are shrouded to make us less visible at night. For those of you interested in aircraft, you'll likely be impressed by some of the technical facts about our lovely Mosquito.

With a fifty-four feet, two inch wingspan and weighing 22,600 lbs, it has a high wing loading of fifty pounds per square foot (*more than almost any other aircraft flying today, other than the Martin Marauder, which is sixty pounds*). ('One a day in Tampa Bay'.) The Mosquito stalls clean, (with undercarriage and flaps retracted) at 130 mph, and has a very high, single engine safety speed, of 170 mph, (or more, depending upon load). This means, if you're flying on one engine, the unbalanced thrust, of *'Climbing Power'* outruns your rudder control, unless you are going at least 170 mph.

At lower speeds, (if you apply climbing, or higher power), it will roll you right over on your back. This can be really nasty if you're low on final approach, on one engine, and for some reason you have to overshoot. Many lives have been lost this way! Our circuit is designed to improve our chances in cases like the above, and, because our undercarriage lowers at only half the speed than it does on both engines, we fly circuits at 1500 feet, instead of the traditional 1000 feet. This also gives a bit of height to dive, to get airspeed up to 170 mph, or more, if we are on one engine, (and, hopefully, time to raise our flaps and gear), and climb safely away.

There is, however, a point on final approach, where we have no option except to land. If we happen to be one engine, and don't have 1500 feet ceiling, we are permitted, (and advised), to do a wheels-up landing rather than try to land with wheels down.

The Mosquito can cruise at 200 mph on one engine, (trimmed *'hands-off'*). Its two Rolls-Royce Merlin engines each produce about 1700 hp, and with two-stage superchargers, they can operate at high altitudes. The internal fuel tanks hold 515 gallons of gas, and are supplemented with 50-, or 100-gallon-drop tanks, giving a possible 716 gallons, and long range. We use drop tanks, and outboard fuel tanks first; because, in case of engine failure, we can cross-feed only from our main, inboard tanks, to the live engine.

Our 20-mm cannon shells are mixed in a deadly assortment. The first round out the barrel is Ball, to create an opening through the fabric for the explosive shells that follow, (*an explosive shell leading the way, would likely blow off our nose!*). We carry a mixed load of cannon shells.

Ball rounds will penetrate 17 mm of armour plate at 1000 yards; and their muzzle velocity is 2860 feet per/sec. 'HE/AP' (high explosive armour-piercing) shells, will blow a 4 – 8 inch hole through 12 mm of armour plate at 1000 yards. 'SAP/IN' (semi-armour-piercing incendiary), will pierce 8 mm of armour plate, and shoot a seven-foot flame.

The above concentration of fire from the four cannons, together with the stream of bullets from our four machine-guns, does awesome damage to aircraft and other targets, such as trains. Imagine what it would do to your car!

We don't use tracers. They could give away our position during attacks.

Our eight guns are clustered in a small rectangle, four cannons, under four machine-guns, thereby requiring very little harmonising to converge at a point of greatest concentration. This arrangement provides a devastating group of damaging firepower.

The Mosquito is a wonderful, smooth gun platform, with its high weight and high speed.

Our two 500-lb bombs are fitted with an 11-sec. delay (after impact) to protect us from their blast and possible damage, since we drop them at fairly low levels. Our 'gun-sight', is projected onto the windscreen, in red, (to protect our night vision) and has adjustable wingspan bars. It is very comfortable to use. I also use it in dive-bombing.

(Of the many variants of the Mosquito, a bomber version (unarmed), can carry a 4000-lb bomb to targets like Berlin, the same load as the Flying Fortress, relying on its speed alone to get there and back safely). I think you'll find this interesting and I quote:

The Canadian staff of de Havilland worked out a figure of merit, military effectiveness per pound aeroplane produced. This was arrived at by multiplying the weight of bombs by the strike-range, and figuring, per man of crew per tare pound. The ratio was Fortress 24, Liberator 26, Halifax 62, Lancaster 68, and Mosquito 80.

Our major role, in flying bomber support, is Night-Intruding. We operate alone, usually deep inside enemy territory, patrolling German Night-Fighter bases, (for a period of one hour), making our presence known and generally, making things difficult for them. They don't like us very much. We've been told, that, if one of them manages to shoot us down, it counts double. This is very flattering, but also has its downside, because they would just love to 'get' us!

We've been told that often, upon their arriving home from harassing our bombers, low in fuel, out of ammunition, and finding us waiting for them, they may divert to another airfield, even at the risk of running out of fuel. So we also inflict psychological damage.

Group often finds other tasks for us under the general heading 'Bomber-Support'. We can operate as a *Spoof* force to draw German Night-Fighters away from our bombers, or provide daylight escort, or Ranger patrols, (day or night), to find targets of opportunity, (usually trains and planes). Our role is flexible. One particular example I would mention, was to have our two Squadrons fly a 'ground-strafing' 'Dawn-attack', on Leeuwarden aerodrome, an important German Night-Fighter base, the next day! We were briefed to do this, but at the last moment, thanks to a bit of thoughtful reconsideration, the operation was cancelled; the reason given that it would likely be too dangerous! We all agreed on this point, as we could have had many losses.

I was particularly relieved, because I was selected to be the last aircraft to attack!

We Canadian Airmen have a two-tour commitment; the first, (in night intruding) is thirty-five sorties, after which we are 'tour-expired' (screened), and have a rest tour for six months, instructing at an 'O.T.U', (Operational Training Unit), followed by a second tour of twenty-five trips; then, we could be sent home to instruct or be assigned other duties.

Our British counterparts, however, have no such luck. They just keep on going, operating then instructing, operating then instructing, until war ends or they are lost. We lost S/L Raybone on his sixth tour. He was noticeably tired from so many operations, with a nervous facial twitch. He should have been taken off operations a long time before that fateful trip. We all felt bad when he didn't get back. He was a great guy!

But let's get back to today, Saturday, November 4, 1944, from start to finish.

Charlie woke us this morning at 7:00 with the words: 'Good morning gentlemen, it's a cold windy day, and you'll need this hot cup of tea, believe me!' We jumped out of bed, and put on underwear and socks which we've had in bed all night with us, (to keep them warm and dry); then after a quick wash and shave, put on our 'Battle-Dress' and cycled to the Officers' Mess. (I'd hurried out on hearing my Flight Commander's car start up, asking to please put us on the 'Roster' for tonight's ops.) We fly operations two nights 'on', then one night 'off'; and this cycle repeats. This can change with weather, and operational requirements, which could interrupt the cycle, but it's the basic arrangement. We are also granted a week's Leave every six weeks, during operational service.

We see on the Bulletin Board, that Briefing has been called for 1400 hrs. Glancing briefly at 'DROs', (daily routine orders), we go in for breakfast. It is now 0800 hrs. There is a general hubbub of conversation, with usual questions about last night's operations. *Is anybody missing? If so, Who? How? Where? Were any enemy aircraft shot down? Was there any other action?* In a small group like ours, it's so much more personal to us, because we know one another, and some are close friends.

Our regular fare is on display on the steam table as we go along the cafeteria line: reconstituted scrambled eggs, fried 'spam' (*really delicious!*) sausages, toast, jam, tea and coffee. It's not the '*Ritz*', but there is choice, so we dive in!

0830. The CO, and Flight-Commanders stand up and leave for the Flight Offices. That's a signal for us to follow, to discover if we will be operating tonight. Off we go to cycle there. Sure enough, we see on the Status Board that seven crews are required for tonight. F/O Stewart and F/O Beaudet are assigned Mosquito YP-J (PZ448) our current aircraft. Mom's Nickname '*Toots*' is painted on the nose. The Flight Sheet is on the desk. I sign out for our 'NFT', (Night-Flying Test). Then we walk over to our lockers to pick up parachutes and helmets, standing by for a ride across the airfield to our dispersal point where our aircraft is parked, awaiting us.

A WAAF driver arrives with her 1500-wt truck. We hop in, and make around the airfield. *Golly! What a strong wind! And cold!* Once there, I put my stuff on the ground, and walk over to Chiefy's Office to sign the L14, and make sure our aircraft is serviceable; then back over to our aircraft, do a quick walk-around, which includes unscrewing the U/C locks, wrapping them up to stow in their leather pouches inside the wheel wells, and climbing onto the horizontal stabilizer, reach up to remove the Pitot-Head Cover from the top of the vertical fin. (*Usually our ground crew does this for us, especially at night.*) Meanwhile Paul settles himself on board. I climb up the tiny folding ladder, pushing my heavy parachute ahead of me, and strap in ready to start up.

After a short pre-start check: Gas On, Brakes On, Throttles Set, while George our ground crew, plugs in the battery cart, he primes the starboard engine, and stands by, waiting to give it more prime if needed. Meanwhile, I flip on the mag switches, then call out: 'Contact Starboard'. George replies: 'Contact Starboard'. I press the starter button and booster coil together, and the Merlin roars to life. The noise is deafening. After I catch the engine with throttle and settle it to idle smoothly at 1200 rpm, I'm ready to start the port engine, waiting for George to screw in and lock the primer pump, close and lock its little flap. Then he's underneath the fuselage to prime the port engine. He has to let me know he's ready for start, and because of the loud noise of the starboard engine, voice doesn't work. Instead, he raps on my side of the fuselage, a signal for me to start the other engine. *There it is*! I start up the port. Again George secures the primer. Then he unplugs the battery cart and comes round to the front left of the aircraft where I can see him, and waits for my signal to pull the chocks. By now, both engines are running smoothly. I turn on the generator switch and radio, and open my radiator flaps. I do my post-start check, and call the Tower:

'Hello Exking, this is Cricket 34, Radio check and taxi clearance for an NFT, please. Over'.

He replies: 'Roger 34 you are loud and clear, and clear to taxi to runway 24. Call us when you are ready for take-off. Over'.

'34 Wilco. Out'.

I signal George to remove the chocks, and he waves us out onto the perimeter track. I move slowly forward a few feet, stopping momentarily to check the brakes; then carry on around the perimeter track to runway 24, 'holding-short', to do our Pre-Take-Off ('Vital Actions') check, and Run Up.

Brakes – 200 lbs (Pneumatic Pressure)
Hydraulics – Bomb Doors – Closed, Gear – Selected Down
Hatches, Side windows – Closed and Locked
Harnesses – Locked for take-off
Trims – Elevator and Aileron Neutral, Rudder ½ division Right

Tit, De-Icing Tit – Neutral

Tighten – Throttle Quadrant, (as desired)

Temperatures, (minimum for take-off) – Oil, 15oC (Normal 60 to 90), Coolant – 60oC (Normal up to 105oC)

Mixture – (Automatic on our engines, but this is the standard place to mention Mixture)

Moderate – Superchargers Moderate

Pitch – Propellers – Full Fine

Pumps – Fuel Booster Pumps – On

Pressures – Fuel 4-6 lbs, Oil – 30 lbs (min)

Fuel – Contents – and Select – Outer Tanks

Flaps – Up (or as desired)

Gills – Radiator flaps – Open

Gyros – Artificial Horizon – Un-Caged, Directional Gyro – set to 240

Switches – Mags and Masters – On

I run up each Engine to zero boost, and check the Magnetos. We're set to go. I look around, and on the approach to see all is clear, and call the Tower.

'Hello Exking Cricket 34 is ready for take-off. Over.'
    'Roger 34, you are clear for take-off. Out.'

I taxi onto the runway, roll forward a few feet to straighten the tail-wheel, and gently squeeze the brakes until we stop. After re-setting the directional gyro to 240, and un-caging it, I move the throttles forward to zero boost; (balancing my power on both engines), then, in one smooth motion, releasing the brakes, I advance the throttles quickly to the 'gate', at the same time pushing the stick fully forward. Automatically, I apply the anticipated right rudder to counteract torque and any cross-wind. Our Mosquito moves quickly forward, rapidly gaining speed. The tail comes up at 70 mph, (*very soon in this wind*), and now with full rudder control, we keep accelerating down the centre-line of the runway. Then at about 120-125 mph, the aircraft starts to feel lighter, and I lift it gently a few feet into the air.

I keep it down to about fifty feet; give a short squeeze of brakes to stop the wheels turning, and select *'Undercarriage-Up'*. Meanwhile, the airspeed keeps building as we near the end of the runway. At 180 mph, I gently ease into a climb, and throttle back to climb-power (+6 lb boost and 2650 rpm). Then I do my post take-off check: Temps and Pressures, U/C – Up, turn off the fuel 'Booster-Pumps', and we climb away to about 1000 feet, close my rad flaps and turn away from the aerodrome. Now the thrill of flying begins, the Mosquito being the ultimate recreational vehicle!

The purpose of the 'NFT', is to make sure our aircraft will be serviceable for our operation tonight. This we do; but that doesn't stop us having fun. I often have mock dog-fights with other aircraft; or do some low flying; perform extreme 'wingovers', attack any aircraft we might find, as well as creeping into formation with other aircraft (like a Fortress). One time, after taking a pass at a Lancaster and rushing past, I saw the pilot had long red hair. It was a lady ATA pilot delivering it somewhere. Incidentally, that is how 23 Squadron received its first Mosquito, delivered by a lady ATA pilot. 'Good for you, Girls!'

Rejuvenated and happy, we return to Little Snoring, land, taxi back to our dispersal and shut down. When George signals the chocks are in place, and I feel the elevator and rudder external locks going in, I release the parking brakes and put on the internal control locks, to keep the ailerons still.

We know next time we climb in it will be dark. I leave all my parachute and Sutton harness straps 'just-so', ready for me to find them by 'feel'. I drape my helmet over the control column, and still leaving it plugged in, I set the trims for 'take-off', ensuring all switches are where they should be. The rudder pedals were adjusted when I first got in the aircraft. I climb out, and walk over to Chiefy's Office to sign the L14, and report any 'snags'. I see the NAAFI van is coming around the perimeter track to stop by 'Chiefy's' hut. Time for a welcome mug of hot tea, and also, I see our pig and rooster have come over for a treat! What 'Moochers!'

Later, we hitch a ride back to our Flight Office to sign in on the Flight Sheet and cycle back to the Mess. Meanwhile our aircraft will be refuelled and armed for us tonight.

Lunch is about to be served. We relax in the billiard room: read, visit, open mail, then head on in to the dining-room. We've plenty of time for a leisurely meal. With Briefing called for 1400 hrs, we know we'll have to leave here about 1330 hrs; ride over to Intelligence Section, and wait in the Library until called in.

1330. *'Okay Paul, let's go.'* We cycle over and assemble with other crews to wait and wonder what tonight will bring. We would choose some targets, over others! I will now unfreeze time, as I notice S/L Price is about to speak. A hush settles over the room.

'Orderly Officer, will you please ask the aircrews to join us.'
   'Yes Sir.'
He opens the door, and motions us enter, closing the door after. We all file in and sit down.
   'I will call the roll.'
He does this.
   'The roll call is complete. Briefing will now begin. Orderly Officer, please lock the door.'
   'Yes Sir.'

The Briefing begins: S/L Price giving an overview, and our role; then uncovers the *'Target Allocation Board'*, reading out each crew's target and patrol times, (*which they acknowledge in turn*). The Met Officer has his say, followed by Flying Control, the CO, and the Padre. Finally we synchronise watches. All this takes about an hour. When finished, each crew pairs off, and sits down to plan their trip.

My Navigator, Paul Beaudet, spreads his maps across the table, and we look at possible routes to Ardorf and return. That agreed, he then lays in the tracks and continues with his calculations. Meanwhile, I walk over to the Intelligence Section, and draw out *'Escape Kits'*, which contain enemy aircraft cockpit checks (*fat chance!*), maps, European Currency, concentrated food rations, first-aid supplies, Benzadrine tablets, water purifying tablets, our phony passport photos, small compasses, etc. I then draw out enemy *'Colours of the Period'* (ESNs), which we call *'Sisters'* – this information comes to us from the Underground by radio, just amazing! We don't know how they get it. All this stuff goes into Paul's Nav bag. I now wander over to the Intelligence Library where I pull out files on Ardorf, Marx and Varel. I want to know about aerodrome heights, obstructions, their

types of aircraft, and any other significant factors, like runway config-
uration, defences, station buildings, ammo dumps etc. which might
affect our visit tonight.

Paul by now has plotted all of his tracks to Ardorf, and marked
them and distances down in his Log, and, using the winds provided at
Briefing, worked out courses and ground speeds, so he knows how
long it will take to get there. By subtracting the total time to get to
Ardorf, from our time on target (2115 hrs) as briefed, he has found
that we will have to take off at 1900 hrs, leaving a few minutes to
spare just in case we need it. He also checks out Marx, and Varel, in
relation to Ardorf. Now we examine it, from start to finish, noting
'check points', and 'turning points'. At night, the only visible features we
can rely on are waterways, lakes, rivers, canals, etc. They are always
visible, no matter how dark it is, especially tonight with no moon and
the sky overcast.

Paul may have to make minor changes when he gets a wind update
just before we leave; but it likely won't make much difference to his
initial calculations, judging by the Met Briefing, and we are flying fairly
early. Everything now goes into his 'Nav' bag, which by now is quite
heavy, and he places it on a shelf in the Intelligence Section. With
all that done, we go back to relax in the Mess, knowing that 'Tea' is
about to be served, which for me is the best meal of the day.

We miss dinner because of early take-off, so we'll fill up at
'tea-time', and won't eat again until after we return from our trip.
(That is, we hope we return!) It is almost 1600 hrs. We have time to
think about the night ahead.

With mixed emotions, we contemplate the night before us. All
kinds of things go through our minds as we wait to fly. 'Death' is top
of the list, followed by 'Joy', 'Crashing', or 'Parachuting' into the black
windy night and evading capture; (it's so cold out there!), 'PoW', or, even
worse, just 'disappearing', our families never finding where or how
we died, never having 'closure'. Our 'job' is a pretty lonely one!

When you see us calmly sitting around like this, and later, with
our red goggles on, to protect our night vision, you couldn't imagine
these thoughts going through our minds. I must say that they're just
fleeting shivers which we don't share with anyone. It must be even
worse on a Bomber Base, with their high losses. Personally, I mentally
tuck my heart and soul into my bunk for the night, and send my body

off to do the trip, then join them back up when we return. It works for me.

1700. Feeling full from 'tea', we put on our red goggles; lean back and relax.

1745. Paul and I ride over to the Intelligence Section; put our personal valuables in a bag, (*sent home if we don't return*). He gets the latest winds, retrieves his Nav Bag, and we make our way to our lockers. He always complains about how heavy his load is, and I'm not too sympathetic (*usually joking about it*). I stop in at the Flight Office to sign out for our trip, and re-join him to put on Escape Boots, and 'Mae-Wests'. I loosen my tie and wrap my silken scarf around my neck to protect it from rubbing against my 'battle dress' tunic (*which is very rough*), as I constantly look around outside while we fly an 'Op'. Paul is quite lax about this. It's always a '*Bone of Contention*'.

We are then driven around the airfield to our aircraft in the 1500-wt, and I walk over, sign the L14, then it's back out to our aircraft where Paul stands shivering in the cold. We have only a few minutes until 1845 to climb aboard. It's not unusual to be cranky and short with one another. He's always reluctant to loosen his tie and this is my moment to remind him about the danger of strangulation if we end up in the drink. Our last ritual is to christen the tail-wheel before climbing in, ensuring we are upwind on a windy night like this! Our Mosquito has no bathroom facilities. (PRT)

1845. I climb aboard and do up straps in the dark, pulling on helmet as Paul follows and receives the folding ladder from ground crew. He stows it in its rack on the door (*after George closes and locks it*). The pre-start ritual is completed, battery cart plugged in, and George has primed the starboard engine and is waiting for my call to start.

1852. Eight minutes before take-off. I call out '*Contact Starboard*' and our Op begins. I follow the same starting routine as we did this morning, except for turning on U/V instrument lights, and '*Downward Recce Light*'. With both engines warming up and radio coming to life (*I can hear Paul breathing, and tell him to turn off his mike*), things immediately start to feel better. George waves us out to the perimeter track where I taxi to runway 240 following the dim blue taxi lights that guide us. After my checks and run-up are complete, I flash my downward light, *(leaving it off)*, to get an immediate Green from the ACP, for take-off.

1900. I taxi to position on the runway, roll forward a few feet to straighten my tail-wheel, and line up for take-off, rolling forward to begin our 38th operation. The aircraft seems heavy with a full fuel, and two 500-lb bombs. Night seems even blacker as we thunder down the runway ahead of us.

At last we lift off, climbing into the dark to 1000 feet to make a wide left climbing turn to set course over Base at about 5000 feet. Overhead, I signal 'V', with my navigation lights, leaving them on until we reach the coast. I'm indicating 240 mph, (260 mph 'true airspeed' at 5000 feet). However, with this strong tail wind, Paul tells me our groundspeed is 310 mph. We are going like a *'Ding-Bat'*. Our ETA at the coast is 1906. We steer 102o Magnetic.

1906. At the Haighsboro Light on the coast, Paul gives me a heading of 103oM for N. Egmond. ETA 1937. I switch off Nav Lights and dive to 500 feet over the water. At 500 feet we are under the German radar.

'*Wow Paul; look at that phosphorescence it's so bright!*'

We race on to Nord Egmond on the Dutch coast.

1933. I open up to *Climb-Power*, pulling up sharply to about 6000 feet. Then at 1935 hours we dive and weave as we cross the coast, to enter enemy territory to the tune of their scanning, which is an insect-like whine in our ear-pieces. Soon it stops, and we continue on inland.

'*Steer 085o George, and we'll be there in twenty-six minutes*' (the turning point on the Leda River).

We see a rotating beacon in the distance, as well as the odd searchlight. Over the Zuider Zee below we see the riding lights of small boats.

'*LOOK BACK PAUL!*' I say every few minutes as I pull up sharply.

He looks back for enemy aircraft (*we did see one once, right beside us ready to move behind, and shoot us down*). At the east coast of the Zuider Zee, a slight course correction to the Leda River, we fly on.

'*LOOK BACK PAUL!*'

'*There's Zuidlarder, George, we're right on track! Let me know when you see the Dortmund- Ems Canal.*'

I spot it. Then we arrive at our turning point on the Leda River.

2010. '*OK George turn left to 005, the Jade Canal is coming up in five minutes then Ardorf is four minutes at 299. You can drop down to 500 feet. now.*'

2015. Arriving at Ardorf we find their VL (*Visual Lorenz*) is lit. There is activity. A few minutes into our patrol: '*THERE'S ONE, PAUL!*'

I see an aircraft challenged by a searchlight, an answering flare in return. Quickly, I turn my gun switches to '*Fire*', and race around the circuit, catching up with him on final approach. I attack. He is silhouetted in his own landing lights. It's a JU88. I fire about a four-second burst, seeing strikes all over his nose and cockpit area.

Immediately, the aerodrome plunges into darkness as I pass over him, and race across at low level, turning sharp left, climbing to avoid possible return fire.

Pulling up into the darkness, I see a Heinkle III flying in the opposite direction, down-wind, and, amazed at a second sighting so soon, I zoom up behind his tail. In a sharp wingover to the left, I turn back towards him. (*My NFT hi-jinks are now paying off!*) As I curve in to attack, and come into range, I open fire, seeing strikes on the fuselage, bits falling off. Huge sparks trail behind him. Again all goes black. He is gone from view.

At this point we fly away a few miles to make them think we're departing. Returning about ten minutes later, we catch a glimpse of a III, but lose him in the dark. The VL is lit. We are challenged. We fire off a '*Sister*'. Searchlights go out. We continue to circle, just out of earshot. Meanwhile, there is a howling gale of about 60 mph going on down there, it's in our favour. We continue our patrol, check out Marx and Varel then return to Ardorf. Our hour is almost up. Having quietly climbed away a few miles, we return just as quietly, to dive in and drop our bombs on their nice runway at 2115 hrs.

Turning sharply away after releasing our bombs, we see an extra row of lights laid out beside the runway in use, suggesting the main runway is obstructed. There is also a confusion of lights and activity by the threshold where the JU88 must have crashed. Paul says:

'OK George, steer 293 for our spot over the North Sea, and we'll be there in twenty-two minutes, at 2137.'

I set course.

2135. At our invisible turning point, I alter course to 293 towards home. With this strong headwind, it will take sixty-one minutes to get there, our ground speed being only 200 mph.

'I'm tired Paul, how about holding on to this for a bit while I rest my eyes?'

It's so tiring, staring out into the dark as we do, over enemy territory. He reaches over, his left hand on the control column. I put my head back to relax for five minutes. (There were times when I wondered how I would be alert enough to land after getting home!) I take over again, and get ready to call Largetype.

Forty miles from the British coast, it's time to check in.

'Hello Largetype, this is Cricket 34 identifying, and my Cockrell is crowing (turned on) Over.'

This is our IFF, (Identification Friend or Foe, a small transmitter causing a distinctive blip to show up on their radar screen),

'Hello Cricket 34, we have you, please call as you pass overhead. Over.'
'Cricket 34, Wilco. Out.'

2245. 'Hello Largetype, Cricket 34, I'm drying my feet, and switching to Exking. Over.'

'Roger 34 Goodnight.' I change frequencies to Exking.

2250. 'Hello Exking, This is Cricket 34, overhead, please turn on the flare-path. Over.'

They go on instantly.

'Roger 34, you are clear to land on runway 240, and the wind is from 270. Over.'

'Thank you, Exking, 34 Out.'

I enter the circuit and land, aware of the crosswind from my right, then as I turn off at the end of the runway to taxi back to our dispersal, I say:

'*Cricket 34 is down and Turning Off, Goodnight 'Cobby'.*'

'*Roger 34, Goodnight 'old man'.*'

Arriving back at dispersal, we are guided to our parking spot by George. I shut down and, after he puts the chocks in place and the external control locks on the elevators and rudder, I put on the internals and release the brakes. He opens our door, reaching for the ladder from Paul. As we climb out, he asks: '*Any luck?*' I tease him saying: '*A bit*', then tell him about our trip. It's '*tail-wheel time*' again, (*after about four hours in the air, we need to!*) I walk over to sign the L14. I have a few words with Chiefy, about what we did with 'their' aircraft, (*they are just as pleased as we are when we've had 'Joy'*) and walk back to re-join Paul, waiting for the 1500-wt to come and pick us up. It sure is cold and blowing a gale (*almost 60 mph.*)

Our faithful WAAF '*Pip*' arrives to drive us back to our lockers, and with the sudden release of tension now we are safely home; we're in a lovely state of euphoria, laughing at anything and everything on the way around the airfield. There's another crew riding back with us. We're totally relaxed, but tired.

We put Parachutes, '*Mae-Wests*', '*Escape*' Boots, and Helmets in lockers. I sign in on the Flight Sheet, and we cycle back for de-briefing. Over a welcome cup of hot tea, the Duty Intelligence Officer takes down our report. We hand back Escape Kits, retrieve personal valuables, and ride over to the Sergeant's Mess for our post-op meal of eggs and chips. This is absolutely delicious! Nothing has ever tasted so good! It's one of the greatest rewards we look forward to after flying an operation.

Other crews are there. We swap stories about our trips for a while, then fatigue kicks in, and we ride down to our 'site' to crash into bed, exhausted but content. The time is 0010 hours. It feels so good!

More of the same tomorrow! We have just completed our 38th Op. We had requested and were granted an extension of fifteen trips over the 35 trips Tour requirement, so we have only twelve more to go, to become *'Tour Expired'*, (Screened). *What then?? Who knows?? We'll see!*

F/O Paul Beaudet
In Honour of a Valued Friend
'An Experience is never finished until it is written' [50]

My name is F/O George Stewart (J24403) from Hamilton, Ontario. I am the Pilot and my Navigator is F/O Paul Beaudet (J2477) from Montreal, Quebec. We love to fly, especially the de Havilland Mosquito named *'Toots'*, my mother's nickname. It is an awesome aircraft! I write this in honour of my friend.

Paul was a *'straight-shooter'*. A devout Roman Catholic, he was strong in faith and true to his beloved. He got married just before going overseas and was surplus from the previous Course of Pilots and Navigators who graduated at 60 Operational Training Unit, RAF High Ercall, near Wellington, Shropshire, England. This imbalance between Pilots and Navigators wasn't unusual when each Course finishes training, depending on how well the participants (Pilots in particular) cope during conversion to the Mosquito. A Pilot could be re-assigned to a different type of aircraft and job if converting to this aircraft was too much for him. Some Pilot candidates did not make the grade, and were washed out.

The Mosquito is quite a handful, with its high wing loading, stalling speed, power, and approach speed, and has some nasty little tricks to display during landing and take-off, particularly in a cross-wind (often the case). We trained on light, slower aircraft, and this was a broader jump than previously experienced. Navigators don't have many problems converting, except they occupy a small space, sitting on the main spar, slightly behind the Pilot, with no room for a plotting table on which to spread maps and Logs – like their counter-parts in the heavy bombers or other large aircraft. They have to make do with the dim light of a very small hand-held flashlight as they make their entries (on small 'Pilot-type' Log sheets), so as not to degrade their Pilot's night-vision. Along with the Pilot, over hostile countryside, most time is spent staring outside, looking out for enemy aircraft, as well as for land or water features, to keep out of harm's way and find the way in the black European night as they fly over enemy territory. They are constantly being hunted!

One morning –16 September to be exact – Paul came down to the flight-line and asked me if he could go for a ride in a Mossie. We were still at 60 Operational Training Unit, RAF High Ercall, training on the de Havilland Mosquito Night Fighter Bombers. He was hoping to team up with a Pilot and become 'crew'. I had by then a total of ten hours on type and only recently gone solo. I told him, but said he was welcome to come along. He said: 'No problem!'

At nineteen years of age, I was five years younger than Paul. But I was more like a naïve fourteen-year-old; I didn't drink or smoke and was very inexperienced about dating. Paul smoked but didn't drink much, so we spent a lot of time playing English billiards instead of going into the Bar. I envy my buddies, boasting about their conquests, and wonder how they go about it, but too shy to ask. Compared with me, they seem sophisticated, so worldly. But then, I can't help being terrified, should I ever get involved and the young lady becomes pregnant. *What would happen to her and our baby if I was shot down and killed? Or, even more frightening, should I survive, how could we exist in civilian life on my meagre earnings?* All my attention was taken up by the job at hand, flying the Mosquito. I didn't want distractions to complicate my life.

Learning to fly the Mosquito was a daunting task, for an impulsive nineteen-year-old, low-time (249 hours) Pilot like me. I found those early hours, in that eleven-ton, high-performance beauty, terrifying! It was one of, if not the fastest aircraft in the world at that time, and still on the 'Secret List'. I adored it!!

We flew, and that was our beginning. We became 'Crew', and continued to fly together from then on. The Pilot traditionally was Captain of the aircraft, but here, as a two-man 'Intruder Crew', we shared equal status. Crewing wasn't a casual choice. It was a very important relationship. Each had to rely totally on the other. It could mean the difference between life and death! We had to have confidence in one another's skills, agree equally, share difficult decisions, react instantly to threats over enemy territory, and be highly vigilant in our awareness of potential danger, as enemy Night Fighters could at any time be after us. We were a perfect fit!

Paul loved flying every bit as much as I. We worshipped the Mossie and took advantage of every possible opportunity to fly one, even to the point of volunteering to go to the Middle East because we'd likely get more 'Mosquito Time'. Did we ever! The Mossie was a real handful. One little move beyond its limit, and it'll bite you!

I flew the aeroplane, fired the guns, dropped the bombs and tried to avoid any visible threats. I was responsible for managing the fuel so as to have enough left to get us home after our patrol, or if in trouble deep inside Germany. Paul told me what pinpoints to look for as we flew each leg of our Op. He even anticipated my tendency to be to the left of our track, prepared to correct headings starboard as I wandered gently, moving up and down to present a difficult target for fighters to follow, while staring into the night sky. I operated the VHF radio.

Paul guided us along his planned tracks and others as needed. He operated the Gee Box over the UK and kept a sharp look-out with me en-route for 'hostiles'. He calculated new headings, telling me when to turn onto them. He always had an approximate heading home if suddenly it might be needed! Paul monitored fuel supply, changing tanks for me as I directed. We had to use it in its proper sequence, to have the mains available if we lost an engine. We used the outboard and drop tanks first, leaving the main tanks available to cross-feed to either engine. The outers could only feed the nearest engine. This was important!

Over the English Channel, on our way home, I would ask Paul to reach over and fly the aircraft with his left hand so I could lean my head back and rest my eyes for a few minutes. It felt SO GOOD! This was an enormous help ... I used to kid him about his poor instrument flying – a joke, of course!

His energies, like mine, were sharply focused on our job. We enjoyed every minute of it! Yes, there were nervous moments too. Meanwhile, at O.T.U he learned special intruder navigating and crewing techniques. We flew there as a crew during training, which included day and night cross-countries, practice intruder trips to Limavady and Long Kesh in Ireland using the Irish Sea as the English Channel. We took a Gunnery Course at Chedworth in Wales and did lots of low flying. Yet, with all that, he still had to keep up with navigation and make course adjustments on the go. *He was great!* In our operating period, we had no radar, relying on our night vision alone to spot the unlit enemy in the black sky around us. The last '*Cat's Eye*' Intruders! And wouldn't you know, they started fitting 23 with ASH after Paul and I became Tour-Ex! I flew some Navigators around in Ansons to practice ASH while waiting for our posting home.

To prepare our night vision for an Op, we wore red goggles for an hour in the Mess just before going to fly our trip. Once outside, we avoided, as much as possible, having it spoiled by white light. I recall often, telling the ground crew to turn off their 'torches' until we were in the aircraft! Then, just before climbing on board at fifteen minutes to take-off, we'd have a quick *'christening'* of the tail-wheel (downwind). Then, climbing into our Mossie in the dark, we'd strap in, put on our helmets, etc. As our instrument needs were lit, in a pale 'beige' shade by ultra violet light, my ring-sight was projected onto the windscreen in red to protect my night vision.

We kept ourselves fresh with our conservative lifestyle. It may have been a factor in our favour ... who knows? We survived! '*Hail Caesar! We who are about to die, salute you!*' shouted the Gladiators in ancient Rome. No thanks! We had no death wish. We had everything to live for. We were also very lucky. Paul and I would discuss our role at length, agreeing that surprise would be a big factor in our favour in attacking planes or trains. We decided together that, when attacking a target, I would make one really good firing pass, and never go back for a second run, thereby achieving total surprise. *Hit and run ... Gone!*

Bombing, however, was no surprise, as it happened at the end of our patrol. Sneaking away and climbing to about 7000 feet, then returning, and diving in quietly, worked for us. We learned since about one 23 Squadron Pilot who did go back in ... Tommy Smith with his Navigator '*Cocky*' Cockayne. On 15 January 1945 they were shot down on their second pass. Tommy Smith survived, but was horribly burned, and Cockayne died having jumped out too low for his parachute to open. They only had two more Ops to go! God only knows how many others were lost like that ... so sad!

Paul and I together tried to evaluate operational risks with their importance, and acted accordingly. Pressing on regardless to Guttersloh with a blown gasket on our 49th trip was one for us. Luckily we got away with it. Ken Eastwood and our C.O *Sticky* Murphy, with their Navigators didn't return. They died. We were sent to see if we could find out why. In our 50th Op Tour we never had one aborted trip … they called us '*Regardless*'!

The Amiens Prison attack and the Dam Busting were such cases where a '*Do or Die*' Op was considered worth the risk!

Our two Units at Little Snoring, 23 and 515 Squadrons, were briefed one afternoon to undertake a Dawn Attack and strafe Leeuwarden airfield in Northern Holland, an important German Night Fighter Base (*Lord knows who dreamed that one up!*). Up to thirty Mosquitoes were to be sent there. Paul and I were chosen to fly the last aircraft in to attack. Imagine how we felt knowing that the enemy gunners would have the most time to be ready for us, last one in! It was terrifying to contemplate. Saner minds prevailed (*lucky for us!*) as the whole insane operation was called off, having been considered much too dangerous. We slept soundly that night!

Crewing could have been a casual partnership based on the wrong parameters. I feel that in the case of Paul and I, we used wisdom beyond our years in deciding to fly together. For that fortunate choice, I am most thankful and proud to have shared those incredible times with him. He was outstanding!

> *Who is this man I'll never forget?*
> *He is my Navigator – Paul Beaudet!*
>
> *May he rest in peace!*

NOTE: George and Paul completed fifty sorties together: July – December 1944. Both attained Squadron Leader rank post-war. The words of George's poem are very telling:

I Asked God Why? Here's His Answer!

Sometimes I call to GOD above.
'Why'd you do this to one we love;
Who tried so hard here, to provide
A lifetime dream, you've now denied?'

GOD said: 'My son, let me explain;
Perhaps I can stop, or ease your pain.
What you know as 'Life' is short;
Up here in Heaven, is the Soul's resort!

I know it's sad to lose your friend,
He's up ahead, around the bend.
Life on Earth is just a whim,
Where he is now you'd envy him.

Do you think I waste my time on you?
I've got better things up here to do.
A Genius here, a Poet fair, they
Live forever, not just down there!

I have your friend safe in my care.
He's loved up here as he was down there.
Bless you for caring, and never fear
My line is open; I'm always here!

Go on with life; be what you can, and remember,
'FOREVER' is my 'PROMISED LAND'!
Thanks for your call.'

Warrant Officer Don Francis
From Bernelli to Blue Streak

The son of a Metropolitan Police Officer, Don's introduction to the world of Aviation came in 1935 when he became Junior Clerk in the Drawing Office of Handley Page. He recalls:

Even going to the toilet meant clocking on and off, with toilet paper rationed against wastage and 'no smoking' was a strictly enforced company rule.

The company were developing the Hampden and Harrow aircraft, the former being built to an Air Ministry specification which also saw Vickers competing with the Wellington. Despite the same specification, their appearance was totally different and, although the Hampden was some 30 mph faster than its competitor, it was the Wellington which eventually became the mainstay of Bomber Command during the early days of the war.

But Don was looking for further progression. He took the opportunity of joining Scottish Aircraft & Engineering as a Junior Draughtsman, purchasing his first motorcycle for forty shillings and the vendor threw in a gallon of petrol to get him to work – to Scottish Aircraft who commenced development of an unusual aircraft known as the *Bernelli*, designed as a twin-engine commercial aircraft capable of carrying fifteen passengers in an aerofoil-shaped cabin located between a twin-boom fuselage. In many respects, ahead of its time, the company ran into financial difficulties and although the unique design of the *Bernelli* was bought by the Cunliffe-Owen Company and eventually flew, it was not a commercial success.

For Don, it meant redundancy. But he soon found employment with a Swiss company, Scintilla, which developed and manufactured parts, including magnetos for the motor industry. However, a window of opportunity opened, allowing Don to return to Handley Page to work on the development of the Halifax bomber, where his principle role was weight control and calculations in respect of the aircraft's centre of gravity. Over this period, he decided to join the Royal Auxiliary Air Force and found himself mobilised during the 1938 crisis when he spent most of his time in North Weald ... painting fighter aircraft in camouflage!

War clouds were gathering.

Handley Page petitioned the Air Ministry to release employees who, in their eyes, would be more useful building aircraft than flying them. If war broke out, Don had said he didn't want to spend his time in a factory and on a subsequent business visit to London, in February 1939, his chance came. An RAF recruiting poster caught his eye. He was astonished to find that, within the space of a couple of hours, he was leaving the Recruiting Office having passed the Medical, the written exams, and been accepted as one of their own!

For the first two years of the war he served in his ground trade, but when, in 1942, with a shortage of aircrew, there was an opportunity to fly, he immediately volunteered and was accepted for training as a Navigator, following which he was posted to 23 Squadron, Little Snoring. The Squadron had recently been reformed, equipped now with the highly versatile Mosquito. Don was engaged on low-level *Special Duties*, flying deep into Germany to attack special targets such as enemy airfields and communication networks.

Don described their role as *'shooting anything we fancied and making ourselves a bloody nuisance!'* His wife-to-be wrote every single day (as did he), and they lived out unofficially when he was on ops.

When his first Tour of thirty-five ops was complete, he became an Instructor on *'Night Fighter Techniques'*, and as a Warrant Officer, when war came to an end, he was given the chance to re-enlist. Despite being offered a Commission he decided to return to Handley Page to resume his career in aeronautics where he was quickly promoted to head of a new section formed to deal with the logistics of converting the now redundant Halifax bombers into commercial aircraft.

Other aircraft projects followed, but these were constructed as commercial aircraft from the start, including the RAF's Hastings and its civil version, the Hermes, both capable of carrying over fifty people at speeds approaching 300 mph.

Another twist in his career came in 1947 when he saw an advertisement for De Havilland Propellers. Having had experience of variable pitch and constant speed varieties, he applied and was employed as their modification draughtsman at a greatly increased salary!

Technology was advancing rapidly in the world of aerospace. Guided missiles were being seen as an answer to manned aircraft. In 1951, Don was invited to join English Electric as their Assistant Chief Draughtsman engaged in missile design. By 1953, he had become Chief Draughtsman, and in 1954, there was a technical alliance between the UK and the USA.

Although some development had already taken place on the 'Black Knight' Project, in 1955 De Havilland Propellers were awarded a Government contract to develop an intercontinental ballistic missile (ICBM) known as the 'Blue Streak'.

Don was now their Chief Draughtsman with a prestigious office in London's West End and was asked to assemble a drawing office team of up to eighty members. De Havilland Aircraft, a separate company at that time, was to build the structure whilst Rolls Royce would be responsible for the propulsion motors. The enormity of the project was best illustrated by the fact that, by the time it ended, his team numbered 364 in the Drawing Office alone!

Woomera, in South Australia, was selected as the main Test Site. It was here in 1964 that 'Blue Streak' made its first launch. It was successful! Nine further launches were made during the 1960s. The missile was designed to carry a nuclear warhead and was nearly seventy feet in length with a diameter of ten feet. Its casing was made of mainly stainless steel approximately 4 mm thick whilst its fuel system, including 12,000 gallons of liquid oxygen, would be exhausted in a burn-time of only 155 seconds.

In 1972, the Launch Site moved from Australia to French Guiana in South America, and the following year the British pulled out of the project altogether, leaving it to the French. Don says there were a number of reasons for the decision – some Military, others political. On the Military side it was felt the fixed silos, although underground, could be vulnerable to a pre-emptive strike by an enemy and also the preparation time prior to launch was too long. Politically, there was a case for buying American weapons, in this instance, the newly developed Polaris missile.

Don has his own views, particularly as under the Exchange of Information pact much of their research had gone into the development of American missiles and also, on pulling out of Blue Streak and freely handing over all research to the French, we scored an own goal. The French used our technology to develop Arianne, which today is the most successful launcher of commercial satellites in the world.

On a personal note, Don said that the abandonment of Blue Streak meant he had to make 187 members of his staff redundant and he saw each one of them individually.

With the *Blue Streak* project abandoned, De Havilland now undertook research for other companies, including the European Space Agency and ELDO – the European Launch and Development Organisation. They also worked on projects such as the *Blue Steel* missile, capable of speeds up to more than three times the speed of sound. It was used operationally for six years, its design function being originally the protection of the RAF's V-bombers from enemy ground-to-air missile attack. Later, it was considered as a potential satellite launcher, although this aspect was not ultimately pursued.

Towards the end of his long career in the British aerospace industry, Don became De Havilland's Chief Procurement Engineer, responsible for the team writing specifications for, amongst other things, the RAF's Short Range Air-to-Air Missiles. He was also involved in the development of underwater launch missiles such as *Harpoon* and terrain-following weapons, although he was quick to concede that not all developments actually entered Military service. Invariably the research on one design helped that of another.

By the 1980s there was considerable consolidation in the aerospace industry as companies merged and British Aerospace emerged as the country's premier aerospace company. It was as a member of British Aerospace that Don finally retired from the industry in 1981.

In 2001, Don was presented the Aircrew Association's top award of a Presidential Commendation. Granted by its President, Air Chief Marshal Sir Andrew Wilson KCB AFC, the Citation reads:

As a mark of esteem and appreciation for the outstanding contribution made in promoting comradeship among military aircrew and the development of the Aircrew Association.

The award of a framed certificate was made by the Aircrew Association's National Chairman, Air Commodore Jack Broughton DL, during a visit to the West Country.

NOTE: One of Don's 23 Squadron Operations is described in full in Martin Bowman's book: 'The Men Who Flew the Mosquito', Chapter 11: *Night Intruders*; published by Pen & Sword.

Kindred Spirits
by Author, Janine Harrington

It is always a joy to be able to reunite veterans with someone who became very special to them in wartime. This was the case with George Stewart and his young MT Driver 'Pip' She would drive George and Navigator Paul Beaudet to their beloved Mosquito 'Toots', watching for their return to drive them back following an op. So little is said about MT drivers and indeed Ground Crew and the crucial role they played. We do have a few on the RAF 100 Group Association. It is always a pleasure to hear from them, to share their experiences.

Hi Janine,
Well what a time this is, first that very endearing letter from you, the DVD Gord, my son, put together for my 90th birthday about my past life which he sent you; and now, at 8 am, just as I was showering, a phone call from Pip. How amazing, that the power of friendship brings to life such vivid, high definition pictures of our past! The catalyst, of course is you, Janine, and on behalf of all whom you write, allow me to express very deeply, our gratitude in documenting that defining period in which we were actors and participants. My part, in comparison with my 23 Squadron aircrew members, was very small. We had a commitment, as Canadians, of only two tours of operations, whereas you 'Brits' had no end, but just kept banging away at 'Ops', until, either war ended, or tragically they did. Please, for my sake, record that in your book, because it made a huge difference in comparative risks we faced! They were in a much higher total exposure situation, and truly deserve to be shown as such, to say nothing of the fact that their families in Britain could also be in harm's way, whereas ours in Canada griped about gas and sugar rationing! Mind you, they could lose sons in the process ...
George

Hi Janine,
Dad is really enjoying talking to you and Pip. He loves to talk about his war years, and in particular anything Mosquito related. He adores flying and fortunate in flying as much as he has, his entire life. There was the war, and then years in China training pilots on the Mosquito.

Then he joined Hamilton 424 Reserve Squadron, and flew Mustangs at home in Canada. After that he flew all the war-birds at the Canadian Warplane Heritage (CWH) Museum collection until age sixty-five, when their insurance no longer covered him.

I am not sure if he talks about this period of his life with you, but he is very respected as one of the founding members of CWH, and was a key pilot trainer for all the aircraft collections – www. warplane.com

I have great memories flying Air Shows over North America as a child, in B-25s, Fireflys, Harvards, etc. Dad (George) kept his pilot's licence well into his 70s and often asked by friends who owned war-birds and hadn't flown in a while to check them out before they flew their aircraft.

At ninety, his medical has lapsed, but he still occasionally takes over the controls in my brother's float plane.

Gordon Lowe (George Stewart's son)

Dorothy *Pip* Wilkinson
MT Driver for 23 Squadron

I was born in Marlborough, Wiltshire in 1925. Stonehenge, Avebury, Bath, these were my childhood memories. One Sunday morning, I remember hearing on the radio Neville Chamberlain saying: '*We are at war with Germany!*' Posters appeared: '*Your Country Needs YOU!*' I enlisted – couldn't stand the thought of khaki, Wrens' hats, so unattractive, so it had to be … RAF! Thus my story begins.

I joined the WAAF – my first Posting was a Balloon Operator on the East Coast. Then from Balloons to Bombers, hence 23 Squadron, Little Snoring, Norfolk. I arrived at Little Snoring by train … sugar-beet land, totally alien country. I was issued with a bicycle and I certainly needed one, miles from my billet, to the Cook House, to M.T where I picked up my Buggy – a small vehicle with canvas on top and the front metal and two seats, mine at the front. As Mosquito crews were made up of a crew of two I suppose they thought a Buggy was large enough! Often I would drive round to Dispersal with cheery 23 Squadron bods sitting on the bonnet;

certainly over-loaded! There would be young Johnny Rivas, a very correct bod, ticking off another chap who might have used the word *'Damn!'* *'Steady on, old boy. Remember, we have a lady present!'* he'd say. Otherwise, it was back to a very cold Nissen hut with rows of beds, before back on duty driving crews to their kites – Mosquitoes – around a long perimeter. Very occasionally, I had to dive under my Buggy as a German fighter followed one of ours home, strafing the airfield with bullets!

My first great sadness came too soon.

Our C/O 23 Squadron was *Sticky* Murphy, who went missing and was later confirmed dead. It was the early days of the war. We'd been on duty all night. Crews were thinking he might have ditched, but then sadly ... no. It was the first time I was forced to take war and death seriously. As a very young driver, I realised that young crews were mostly in their late teens, early twenties. They were just so vulnerable. Yet always with such patriotic pride they continued flying night after night after night, on operations which seemed to last forever. *Sticky* Murphy's death was a great blow to us all.

Yet, despite that awful sense of loss, 23 Squadron, with its motto: *'Semper Aggressive'* continued on. The crews had a job to do ... they were determined to do it well.

December 1944 and January 1945 were freezing cold with snow. Sammy Hoare had crews sweeping snow from the runway. Group Captain Sam Hoare, one-eyed ex-Mosquito pilot with a moustache *'three inches wing tip to wing tip'* brought in an order that crews had to walk, **once** past the HQ on the way to de-briefing. I thought this was so unfair. I drove them to de-briefings and promptly so. It got me Jankers ... and then another Jankers, because I found wearing my cap a nuisance and left it off too often! Orders are orders ... and orders are to be obeyed!

1945 crews were fully operational over France, shooting up railways, Peenamunde, we lost quite a few crews and it was particularly hard for me, waiting as I did for them to return, collecting them from their aircraft at Dispersal. I remember to this day every single one!

For some inexplicable reason I was posted to 23 Squadron and not to the actual Station. Yes, 23 were at Little Snoring ... but it was a hundred men, and one girl. Me! Imagine how embarrassing that was when it came to Pay Parade, stepping forward, saluting and picking up my money in front of so many men!!

Other memories include Billy the pig. I have in my scrap album, I think it appeared in the Daily Sketch newspaper; how this pig was first in the queue when the NAAFI van arrived. I think Billy piglet was acquired by 23 Squadron. I remember going to the Cook House for swill to make sure he was well fed. I also cared for a small pup, Mozzie, I called him. When I was de-mobbed, I took it home to Marlborough and my Grandfather who needed a dog. Grampy had almost lost his sight. It became Mozzie who guided him around the country lanes until a very great age when both died.

My memories keep coming. They always will. I loved my time there with 23 Squadron. We were like Family. I remember to this day the names of the crews that never made it through. Always with a cheery smile, thanking me when, for me it was a privilege and I should be thanking them. We were all so young, so patriotic.

It was years later, staying with a friend on the Isle of Wight having been shown to our bedroom, there was a large photo of *Sticky* Murphy. Jean, his wife, a WAAF Officer he'd met when flying Lysanders dropping agents into occupied France … *Sticky* flying out from Newmarket racecourse … the Officers Mess in Bury Road … so many many memories rushing through my mind …

It reminds me of cycling to the '*Green Man*' on the way to Fakenham. I think lots of 23 Squadron bods were there, all singing the 23 song …

> '*We're a shower of Gremlins,*
> *Gremlins are we.*
> *We would rather drink*
> *Than fight for 23 …*'

I hope my memory serves me right! But then now I'm reminded of the cold 1944 and 1945. After dropping the crews I went back to my Nissen Hut for a hot bath. The bath and ablutions were several yards from the hut … very dark and very creepy, but lovely hot water … and so to bed on our three '*biscuits*' as we called our mattress.

Everything was 'Wacko! Bang on!' It was our slang, the words we used in every-day talk, language of the day.

Woodbridge was the first place I drove to collect crews. They had just made it. Now I live near RAF Mildenhall and Lakenheath. The U.S.A were stationed there. Never a day goes by when I don't hear present-day aircraft fly over. I look up and think about all those wonderful boys in No. 23 Squadron and my heart reaches out to them, all forever young in my mind's eye.

I just feel so so privileged to have been a part of 23 Squadron. Always, I will remember them!

GRACE

Her name was Grace, she was one of the best
But that was the night I gave her The Test.
I looked at her with joy and delight,
For she was mine, all mine for the night.

She looked so pretty, so sweet, so slim,
The night was dark, the light was dim;
I was so excited, my heart missed a beat
For she was nude – in for a special treat!

I'd seen her stripped, I'd seen her bare,
I'd felt around, I'd felt everywhere,
But that was the night I liked her best
If you listen, boys, I'll tell you the rest.

I slipped inside her, she screamed with joy,
For this was her first night with a boy.
I got up high as quick as I could,
I handled her good, for she was good.

I turned her over, then on her side,
Then on her back, that was all I tried.
I pushed it forward, I pulled it back,
I let it go till I thought she would crack.

She was one great thrill, she was grand,
My twin-engined Mosquito, the best in the land!

Ken Eastwood, 21 years old; 23 Squadron, Little Snoring, Norfolk

Like all pilots, Ken thought the Mosquito was the *bees' knees*, and lived to fly. As a young man, he typed the above lines on his love for his Mosquito the very first time he flew 'her'.

Post-War

23 Squadron's last official duty was to participate in the Battle of Britain Flypast on 15 September 1945 and then fly aircraft off to Maintenance Units, in this case mostly at Lichfield, completed by 20 September. There was nothing more for aircrews to do, apart from participate in Squadron parties.

It is said by villagers that it took two years to get used to the airfield being no longer active, Squadrons no longer there, the sound and sight of aircraft. However, the airfield, although much reduced, was called back into service in 1948, all of which is well documented elsewhere.

The airfield remained in the RAF until 1953, whereupon it was sold off and bought by Tom and Ross Cushing in 1963 who wished to preserve the airfield for future generations: although they could do little to stop the removal of dispersal areas and runways – a done deal on the sale of many airfields with outside contractors. However, *George Stewart Wood* remains, a reminder of one airman at least for whom Little Snoring became 'Home' in wartime, far away from his family in Canada.

Little Snoring continues to call her aircrew back, becoming a site of pilgrimage to veterans, their children, and their children's children for generations to come. Standing on the airfield out by the Control Tower after dusk, you might well hear on a cloudless night in the howl of the wind, the roar of twin Merlin engines lifting skywards as the spirit of those Mosquitoes with their aircrew leave Little Snoring perpetually for the last time ... stealing into the night sky:

An Airfield Remembered

We were hungry, tired and dirty,
From our shoulders rifles hung
Our clothes were torn, our faces bronzed
By long hours in the sun.
Here was to be our Station
For the war was not yet won,
When we came to Little Snoring
That fateful June had just begun.

Living here among you
We would join you at your play,
And in the quiet of your church
We knelt with you to pray.
We filled your lanes and byways
With laughter and with song,
We shared each other's sorrows
As through life we journeyed on.
Here both men and maidens tended
To the harsh and warlike needs,
Of men who through the dark hours
Flew their man-made steeds.
The sky at night their hunting ground
In which they sought their prey,
Returning only when the night
Gave way to breaking day.

At times when hope was fading
They would patient vigil keep,
Rejoicing if their crew returned
But often they would weep.
They wept for those who ere the sun
Had warmed the fresh-turned clod
Had fought in their last battle
And were at peace with God.

I returned to Snoring airfield,
The way was hard to find;
For over paths and taxiways
Nature had thrown a blind
Of grass and twisted bramble
Willow herb and clinging vine,
No longer there: the Nissen huts,
Where men slept and dined.

Forsaken then the hangars stood
Empty, broken, gaunt and grey,
Only wheeling birds were there
To welcome me that day.
And when some silent mystic hand
Rolled back the fleeting years
I saw this dead place filled with life
And my eyes were wet with tears.

For one vibrant fleeting moment
This vast airfield was reborn,
Through misty eyes I saw it rise
From amid the standing corn.
Men and buildings filled the skyline
At dispersals stood the planes,
Then like a wraith, all sank to rest
Beneath the quilt of grain.
I trod again the winding path,
Unlatched the old oak door,
And found there in the House of God
That men had kept the score
Of all the kills the Squadron made,
The Honours men had won
A humbled man, I closed the door,
My visit almost done.
I tried to find the work of him
Who, when released from duties,
Took paint and brush and from his hand
There grew a thing of beauty.

His gallery was the airmen's Mess
His canvas bare brick wall,
All we who served on Snoring
His picture can recall.

To plough-shares men shall beat their swords
To pruning hooks their spears
For us the artist there portrayed
Our hopes for future years.
I knew him well, the artist,
Who did those colours blend,
I knew what had inspired him
For you see, he was my friend.

From my full well of memories
I drew long and deep that day,
Recalled the bitterness of war
And the price we had to pay,
That we might live in freedom
To worship without fear
Is that not what we fought for?
And why we were stationed here?

Steve F. Ruffle, 23 Squadron, Little Snoring

CHAPTER 8
Blickling Hall

A Brief History

Blickling Hall estate covers 4,777 acres, with fifty-five acres of formal garden, 950 acres of woodland and parkland and 3,500 acres of farmland. It extends across the parish and into parts of Aylsham, Ingworth, Itteringham and Oulton.

It was originally owned from 1380 until 1459 by Sir John Fastolf of Caister who became a rich man following the Hundred Years' War. His Coat of Arms is displayed in the Hall. Blickling then became the property of the Boleyn family. Anne Boleyn, Henry VIII's wife remains the Hall's infamous ghost, despite arguments with historians as to whether or not Anne was actually born there or at Hever Castle. She is seen, some say, dressed in white, carrying her severed head each anniversary of her death, 19 May, gliding gracefully into the hall, through countless corridors and rooms until daybreak. The ghost of Anne's brother George (Lord Rochford) is said to visit also on that day, dragged by four headless horses around the countryside. Anne's father, Sir Thomas's penance for engineering his daughter's marriage to England's monarch and losing both son and daughter is to cross twelve bridges - from Blickling to Aylsham to Burg to Buxton to Coltishall to Meyton to Oxnead and Wroxham each 19 May before the cock crows, for one thousand years. Just like his daughter, he was beheaded, and carries his head under his arm.

Legend aside, the current Blickling Hall was built on the ruins of the property owned by the Boleyns. The structure was designed by Robert Lyminge in 1616, an architect of the Hatfield House. Sir Henry Hobart bought the Estate that year and built the current Hall from 1616 to 1624. It was Lady Caroline Suffield who built a mausoleum pyramid in the grounds in 1796-97. The remains of Sir Henry's son John and two wives remain buried there, while other members of the family remain in the church vault at St Andrews.

In 1932, the 11th Marquess of Lothian, Philip Kerr, made Blickling his principal English seat after inheriting the Hall in 1930. It was Lord Lothian in 1940, who passed the Hall to the National Trust under the terms of the Country Houses scheme. During the Second World War it was requisitioned and served as the Officers' Mess to RAF Oulton – home to RAF Officers and NCOs.

RAF Oulton was a Bomber Command satellite station of RAF Horsham St Faith, just north of Norwich, now home to Norwich International Airport and the City of Norwich Aviation Museum. It was a Base that played two very different war-time roles: first as home to 2 Group – the first Group of Squadrons to attack Europe – later becoming the centre for 100 Group, flying covert radio and radar counter-measure operations.

For the first part of the war, 2 Group suffered horrendous casualties, never finishing operations with the same crew. Blickling Hall and its acres of land offered respite: swimming in the lake, carving names in trees, spending evenings in the *Bucks Arms*.

However, such were the losses of Blenheim crews particularly during daylight operations, which reached catastrophic numbers, for some aircrew their stay at Blickling was short. For those who stayed longer, the grandeur of the building, the marvellous woods, park and lake are well remembered.

T. C. Long of 139 Squadron was Station Armourer in 1941:

> I have been nowhere that encapsulated the same degree of cama-raderie as at Blickling. I recall one Battle Order for 500-lb. semi-armour piercing, for an attack on shipping. It was a bad day. Of the six that went out, only three returned. Long before the Dambusters there were those on 139 practising skip-bombing, the pre-requisite of which was an attack on the beam at low level, infinitely more hazardous. With those three crews, the Squadron (139) lost a small amateur dance band!
>
> Often in the early morn of a warm summer's day, a placid quiet would drowse as the sun's shivering minions played over them. What deception! Re-armed, re-fuelled, bombed up and lethal. On one such occasion, 'Bunny', our one solitary WAAF armament assistant, floored us with her admiration of its sky-blue livery with the words: '*Isn't it pretty?*' Bless her, it was refreshing.

B. T. Roberts of 214 Squadron, 1944–1945, recalls the shop near the camp selling a cup of tea and a doughnut. While local girl, Eileen Cooper, whose parents kept 'The Bird in Hand' opposite the main entrance to the airfield, the Guard Rooms one side, a Shelter on the other; remembers they had no Shelter. When things got really bad, the man on Guard Duty during an air raid would arrive to take them to safety. A valuable service!

RAF 100 Group was very different to the Group which went before – much more secretive, serious and dark. There wasn't the same light-hearted banter, but on returning from a successful mission, there was still the *Bucks Arms* and *Black Boys Inn.*

Veteran Sidney Pike was a Navigator serving with 214 Squadron at RAF Oulton, stationed at the Hall from August 1944 to April 1945:

Ours was a much more secretive and deadly form of warfare. We were billeted in a Nissen Hut down by the lake. There was a music session in the Hall, about the only place we were allowed to inhabit because the Hall itself was definitely out of bounds! The Hall was for most senior Officers only. In a morning, you'd find out if you were on duty that night. If you were, you had to prepare for a Briefing later. They'd brief you on where you were going and what the Target for the night would be. Every one of us in aircrew experienced at least one hairy moment, some more hairy moments than others. But I believe for all of us who survived to tell the tale, it was down to sheer luck.

Blickling Hall continued to be used for Officers and NCO Quarters: the Sergeants' Mess near the Hall, with two WAAF Sites situated in the Park close-by, and the main NAAFI opposite Blickling Church. However, shades of the past emphasised by strange eerie happenings continued to intrude on wartime life, giving a very real sense they weren't the only residents ... doors opened at night, footsteps tread the corridor, drawers opened and closed. Ghostly tales of Anne Boleyn and her family still seemed to have a presence. But then, for a short while at least, came distraction. The 1945 film production of 'The Wicked Lady' was made on the premises, where stars stayed for the duration. Patricia Roc and Margaret Lockwood mingled freely amongst them *(and the ghosts!)*, with Margaret taking the title role as a nobleman's wife who secretly becomes a highwayman for excitement.

Today, we visit Blickling Hall during our annual RAF 100 Group Reunion each May, stepping through a portal to experience in a time out of Time how it was to live here during the war. It stands, a monument to the past in all its splendour, walls covered in a wonderful display of purple-flowered wisteria. RAF Oulton Museum is an integral part of Blickling, photographs stilled in time offer windows into the past, books covering its history, memorabilia including RAF uniforms and personal effects, together with a small collection of model aircraft. It is a place which is haunting, and yet vital in remembering men and women who served under Bomber Command Squadrons.

The Local

There's a little pub in Oulton Street
where Yanks and British often meet
and lads just coming off the 'drome
make it like their second home.

It owns the name of 'The Bird In Hand'
the landlord's great and the beer is grand.
all through the week it rings with song
and at 10pm they sound the gong.

The customers are a decent crew
and everyone enjoys their brew,
there's civvies playing darts all night
and AC2s getting tight.

Everyone is doing fine
while tipsy airmen 'shoot the line'.
but careless talk is never heard
under the wing of the dear old 'bird'.

Our stay at Oulton may soon end
and over the ocean our way we'll wend.
But wherever we are in any land
we'll always remember 'The Bird In Hand'.

LAC Johnnie Willis, 1944 [51]

The main House was de-requisitioned after the war and let to tenants until 1960. It opened to the public in 1962 renamed the *'Blickling Hall, Gardens and Park'*, under The National Trust.

Perhaps the words of veteran Peter Witts speak for all who shared the war years in Norfolk under RAF No. 100 (BS) Group. The only man to fly with three separate 100 Group Squadrons including No. 214 at RAF Oulton, each year he attended RAF 100 Group Reunions, re-visiting his old haunts, until his death:

… we were together as boys, now we are together as old men. There are no other people I would rather be with … we are like Family. We ARE Family. We shared so much, they and I, beginnings and endings; with a lifetime of experience between. Always, Norfolk is like Coming Home! [52]

CHAPTER 9
RAF Oulton: 1940–1947

A Brief History

At the beginning of summer 1940, farmland was cleared to create a dispersal area for aircraft at nearby Horsham St Faith where No. 2 Group Blenheim bombers were based, the prime concern being enemy air or ground hostilities. By the end of July, a grass landing strip was quickly established.

First airmen arrived to be billeted in old farm buildings, cattle sheds and barns at Green Farm where young Eric Dickens was growing up, intrigued by the sudden hive of activity. His father was Group Captain T. C. Dickens at RAF Oulton, well known and respected by Captains of crews flying under his command.

A number of Nissan huts were erected, with men arriving from St Faith to take up jobs of airfield defence, a vital role given the imminent threat of invasion. However, defence was minimal – a solitary Lewis gun mounted on a pole. Only later were gun-pits dug around the airfield perimeter. By the time first aircraft arrived, about seventy personnel were stationed here; the majority from the parent base. To local residents, the base was known as '*Bluestone* '*Drome*' – the name of the railway halt, level crossing and woodland adjoining the south side of the airfield.

All public roads around and inside the airfield boundary remained open to the public. Only with reconstruction work during 1943/44, were roads closed, making it impossible to reach the village from the south side. With no signposts, only those who knew the area well would find the village without difficulty. The highly secret nature of work under RAF 100 Group at the airfield meant activities were restricted, precautions taken. All members of crews were '*screened*' before operational flying and all personnel warned not to discuss operations.

The decision to move to Oulton had been a wise one. During late July/ early August 1940 air attacks on Norwich were made, including Mousehold aerodrome, Boulton & Pauls Works. On 9 August, enemy bombers raided Horsham St Faith, hitting hangars and aircraft. Next day, 114 Squadron moved its Blenheims over to Oulton. Further attacks came again on Horsham St Faith that evening. It was Blickling Hall that now became a haven to Officers and NCOs.

114 Squadron carried out a number of day operations from Oulton. But in March 1941, they moved north to assist Coastal Command. No. 18 Squadron's Blenheim IVs, another 2 Group Unit, arrived during April 1941 from Great Massingham, moving on to Horsham St Faith on 13 July. The same day, 139 Squadron moved in from Horsham St Faith, also with Blenheim IVs. 18 Squadron returned on 5 November to make way for the first Mosquito Squadron. Thankfully the end was in sight for Blenheim operations in Europe. Meanwhile, 139 Squadron returned to Horsham St Faith during October 1941, but was back at Oulton on 9 December.

139 Squadron and other Blenheim crews were assigned to the Middle East to operate aircraft such as the Hudson. For this purpose, a Hudson Conversion Flight, No. 1428, was formed at Oulton on 29 December 1941. The Flight was disbanded on 29 May 1942 with some Hudsons going to Horsham St Faith.

From 7 July 1942 until 19 September that year, Beaufighter 10s of 236 Squadron Coastal Command were based here and operated a variety of roles.

Things were moving at a rapid pace – putting the right people in the right place at the right time, with access and skills to the right kind of equipment. No-one knew how the enemy's mind worked. It was a game of cat and mouse, trying to cover all options. While Horsham St Faith was allocated to the USAAF 8th Air Force, control of RAF Oulton passed to 2 Group at Swanton Morley, while Boston 3s of 88 Squadron moved from Attlebridge to Oulton on 30 September 1942.

The Squadron then carried out a number of successful daylight operations, including 'Operation Oyster', a big daylight raid on the Philips Factory at Eindhoven led by Wing Commander Pelly-Fry, Commanding Officer of 88 Squadron. The target was heavily defended, situated near Dutch civilian residents. However, it was successfully hit, although fourteen bombers were lost and many others damaged. W/Cdr Pelly-Fry's Boston badly hit, managed to limp home to Oulton albeit in a crash-landing.

1943 was to prove a significant year for the RAF as a whole.

The 10th Anniversary of Hitler's rise to power came on 30 January. In Germany, commemorative rallies were organised. To coincide with these, first daylight raids over Berlin took place that day, with 3 Mosquito B Mk IVs from 105 Squadron carrying out low-level attacks on the main Berlin broadcasting station at 11 am, timed for Goering's address to an Anniversary parade commemorating Nazis being voted into power. Mosquitoes carried out two attacks, timed to disrupt speeches. The second was by three Mosquitoes from 139 Squadron, flying to Berlin at the exact time of Goebbel's speech. However, Berlin's anti-aircraft defences were on high alert. A Mosquito flown by Squadron Leader D. F. Darling was shot down, both Darling and Navigator killed. But the attacks had the desired effect, worrying the Germans, especially Hermann Goering:

> **In 1940, I could at least fly as far as Glasgow in most of my aircraft, but not now! It makes me furious when I see the Mosquito. I turn green and yellow with envy. The British, who can afford aluminium better than we can, knock together a beautiful wood aircraft that every piano factory over there is building, and they give it a speed which they have now increased yet again. What do you make of that? There is nothing the British do not have. They have the geniuses and we have the nincompoops. After the war is over I'm going to buy a British radio set – then at least I'll own something that has always worked. [53]**

On 31 March 1943, 88 Squadron moved to Swanton Morley, re-equipping to a later mark of Boston. A couple of days later, a new aircraft was seen at Oulton when 21 Squadron brought Venturas from Methwold. However, the Ventura medium day bomber was to prove the least popular!

During September 1943, 21 Squadron left Oulton to convert to Mosquitoes like other Ventura Squadrons. They looked forward to having the best having heard so much about the Mosquitoes. Meanwhile, Oulton was closed to all flying for reconstruction work.

During September 1943, the small grass landing field saw vast changes. Technical, Communal and other Sites were already established, but all were enlarged, while a Control Tower was built, with at least one blister hangar and bomb storage area.

Control of the Base was taken over by No. 3 Group Heavy Night Bombers, and became a satellite Base for RAF Foulsham. Oulton's future might have been a Lancaster Base like Foulsham, except for secret plans brewing at Bomber Command.

Reconstruction work complete, the new airfield layout comprised of three concrete runways, laid in the familiar wartime 'A' pattern. The main runway however, was not in the most common position, but the only available site in this instance. Two public roads going south from the village street were closed to enable this runway to be laid. It meant a long detour via Aylsham for many destinations. Len Bartram remembered:

My first personal memories of Oulton 'drome are of passing by in the train from Melton Constable to visit relations in North Walsham and seeing Blenheims parked on the grass near the railway line, and later Hudsons, some without their mid-upper turrets.

With the possession of a 'new' secondhand cycle, the 'drome came within range of a Sunday afternoon sortie. It would be first to Bluestone rail crossing. The road then continued along the edge of the airfield to the village street. Up to the crossroads and left down the back road towards the church and Corpusty. Here, I cycled past and around Bostons and Beaufighters parked close to the road. I presume this road had to remain open to allow villagers to get to church.

Even in wartime, refreshments were available on route from a house at Wood Dalling. Fruit and sweets could be purchased. On the main road near Bluestone, local mineral waters were sold from a cottage window. All of this if I had pennies to spare!

From my back yard at home on clear days I could see Blenheims, Bostons, etc take off or land at Oulton, also Horsa Gliders on nose-dive approach. One evening, tracer shells could be seen fired at and from the airfield, black smoke from a crashed aircraft on another occasion.

On our first visit after reconstruction work, it was a different welcome: 'Road Closed' and 'Keep Out' notices, barbed wire, RAF police vans and motorcycles. There was no road beyond the Bluestone gates. The next road was also blocked off with a new runway crossing over it. We sat on the gates and watched all-black Fortresses take off. They appeared to fill the complete length of the runway before lifting very slowly, pouring black smoke from all four engines. It was impossible to reach the other side of the airfield via the village, so we didn't go there anymore.

After the war, several Fortresses came to Foulsham for a few weeks. We often looked in one parked near the road.

A completely new bomb storage site was built on the north side of the airfield. Other sites after reconstruction included a Technical Site, with the airfield entrance west of the village street on the airfield proper. The Communal Site, including Airmen's Mess, was accessed by a track from the street and sites at the back. A Sick Quarters Site was located near Green Farm, with three Accommodation Sites on the back road to Abel Heath and Aylsham. However, Officers and WAAFs continued using Blickling Hall for accommodation, with the Sergeants' Mess and Quarters in the Park close-by.

By the time work at RAF Oulton was complete, control had passed to RAF No. 100 (Bomber Support) Group. The new Station Commander was Group Captain Thomas Charles Dickens.

On 16 May 1944, Oulton airfield was back in business.

RAF 214 Squadron and 803 Squadron USAAF arrived from Sculthorpe, both Units equipped with B-17 Fortresses. 214 Squadron had already commenced operations for 100 Group and 803 Squadron soon followed. The original role of 803 Squadron personnel at Sculthorpe had been to familiarise RAF crews with the Fortress. Colonel G. E. Paris was CO of 803 Squadron, later replaced at Oulton by Colonel C. A. Scott, when Liberators replaced Fortresses.

The Commanding Officer at 214 Squadron was W/Cdr D. J McGlinn DFC; who, on completion of his tour was replaced by W/Cdr D. D. Rodgers until March 1945 when W/Cdr R. L. Bowes DFC took over the post.

214 Squadron's role was Radio/Radar countermeasures. Fortresses carried special equipment in the bomb bay compartment and Special Operators as part of the crew to operate equipment for jamming and confusing enemy transmissions. Other duties included dropping 'WINDOW' and decoy ('Spoof') Operations.

During June 1944, 1699 Training Flight was formed to convert RAF crews onto Fortresses and Liberators, while in August, 803 Squadron USAAF left Oulton to become 36 Squadron, continuing Operations from Cheddington and Alconbury.

On 23 August 1944, a new RAF Liberator Squadron was formed, intended as a jamming Squadron. Special equipment it carried included the huge *Jostle* transmitter, sometimes described as a giant dustbin. It was said to have been installed in the aircraft by parking the Liberator over a hole in the ground. Some of its first Operations were against the V2 rockets but discontinued when it was realised the rocket was not radio-guided. Bomber support jamming, WINDOW and *Spoof* Ops continued until the end of the war.

The C.O of the new Squadron at RAF Oulton, No. 223 Squadron, was W/ Cdr H. H. Burnell.

Both 214 and 223 Squadrons were disbanded at Oulton during July 1945. From November 1945 until November 1947 the airfield became a sub-unit of 274 MU (Maintenance Unit) with hangars being used for storage and over-haul of Mosquito aircraft. Some of these aircraft were then supplied to Air Forces overseas. Later, Norfolk turkey sheds were erected on the concrete runways and most other land returned to agricultural use.

No. 214 (FMS) Squadron

Ultor in umbris – 'Avenging in the Shadows'
Reproduced with permission of the MOD

214 Squadron badge depicts a nightjar, a bird chosen because it is active at night, indicative of the Squadron's role; authorised by HM King George VI, March 1938.

Squadron codes: BU and PX

No. 214 Squadron was originally formed at Coudekerque, near Dunkirk, on 28 July 1917 as No. 7A Squadron, RNAS. Its role was heavy night bombing. On 9 December 1917, it reformed as No. 14 Squadron, RNAS; and on 1 April 1918 – the same day as the formation of the Royal Air Force – 200 was added to its number '14', hence No. 214.

214 Squadron was equipped with Handley Page twin-engined bombers flown from coastal airfields in France, engaged in night attacks against naval and army targets in Belgium and France. It operated under the Dunkirk Naval Command. But then from March to June in the 7th Brigade, it came under control of the Army, and from 4 June to the Armistice in the 82nd Wing, again under Naval Command.

In April and May 1918, the Squadron assisted in Naval blocking operations at Zeebrugge and Ostend. Worthy of note is that, during its wartime career, on the night of 24/25 July 1918, it dropped the RAF's first 1,650-lb bomb on the enemy. The Squadron was posted to Egypt in 1919 and on 1 February 1920, with crew and aircraft, merged into No. 216 Squadron.

On 16 September 1935, 'B' Flight of No. 9 Squadron was used to create a new 214 Squadron.

Again a Bomber Squadron, it had the Vickers Virginia X Night Bomber at RAF Boscombe Down. On 13 April 1937, it arrived at the newly-built Feltwell airbase from Scampton. From here it flew Harrows until July 1939, switching to Wellington Is during May that year.

The Squadron then moved to Feltwell satellite station, Methwold, in September 1939, until a move in February 1940 to Stradishall. Methwold had offered nothing but tents in a field, and they were grateful for something more substantial!

214 Squadron officially entered the war on 14/15 June 1940, its first raid being a fire-raising attack by 2 Wellingtons on German forests.

In September 1941, 214 Squadron was honoured in being adopted by the British Malayan Federation and given the fuller title: '*RAF No. 214 (Federated Malay States) Squadron*' with the FMS putting up funds to raise and equip the Squadron.

The Squadron then served in No. 3 Group for most of the Second World War, equipped with Vickers Wellingtons, replaced in 1942 with larger Short Stirlings after moving to RAF Stradishall. However, at a time when Stirling losses led to the aircraft being withdrawn from bombings on Germany, the Squadron transferred to Chedburgh and on to RAF Downham Market in

December 1943, continuing with Stirlings until January 1944 when its tour of duty with No. 3 Group ended.

It is worth noting that this Squadron had the highest percentage of losses of 3 Group, playing an active role in 'Gardening' or mine-laying operations.

RAF No. 100 (BS) Group

In January 1944, the Squadron joined 100 Group at Sculthorpe, re-equipping with American Flying Fortress aircraft, engaged in counter-measures (detection and jamming enemy radio and radar equipment) until May 1945.

After training, it commenced operations from Sculthorpe until moving to Oulton in May 1944 to fly Fortress Mk II and Mk III and Stirlings, using the jamming system code-named 'Airborne Cigar' (ABC) to block German Night Fighter communications. German-speaking radio operators identified and jammed Ground Controller' broadcasts, posing as Ground Controllers, steering enemy Night Fighters away from Allied bomber streams.

214 Squadron disbanded on 27 July 1945. However, later that same day, 614 Squadron, a Liberator Unit at Amendola, Italy; was re-numbered 214 Squadron, moving to Palestine in August to convert to Lancasters, re-numbered 37 Squadron on 15 April 1946.

Post-war, on 21 January 1956, No. 214 reformed at Marham as a Valiant Squadron of the V-Bomber Force. Leonard Trent VC was the first CO of the Valiant Squadron. In September 1956, the Squadron was detached to Malta for attacks on Egyptian airfields during the Suez campaign.

In April 1962, it became a tanker Squadron, but disbanded on 28 February 1965 with the grounding of the Valiant Force. The Squadron reformed at Marham the following year with Handley Page Victor tankers used for refuelling both fighters and bombers during long-range moves, maintaining beyond their normal range. It was finally disbanded on 28 January 1977.

On 4 November that same year, 214 was reformed at Upwood as part of post-war Bomber Command, re-equipped with Lincolns in February 1950. A detachment was based in Kenya during the Mau-Mau uprising and the Squadron disbanded again on 30 December 1954.

On 15 June 1955, it reformed at Laarbruch with Canberras for photographic reconnaissance duties, re-numbered 80 Squadron on 1 August 1955.

PERSONAL EXPERIENCES

Flt/Lt James W. Moore DFC
Blenheim Days

On 3 April 1941, No.18 Squadron, with new Commanding Officer: W/C C. G. Hill DFC; moved to Oulton. We found ourselves living in the beautiful Blickling Hall, house of landed gentry since the time of the Domesday Book. We occupied two-thirds of the house and most of the buildings, with access to acres of park, grounds and lake in which we were able to swim.

A decision was made by Bomber Command for 2 Group to adopt a more aggressive role. Instead of night ops, we would operate in daylight, concentrating on three tasks – attacks at low level on enemy shipping, with L/L attacks on industrial and military land targets. Later we were given one further task – to operate in formation at 10,000 feet with fighter escort. These ops knows as '*Circuses*' were flown with the primary object of persuading enemy fighters to attack us, becoming engaged, and destroyed by our fighters. Other ops known as '*Rhubarbs*' meant set targets becoming the prime objective.

Having been involved in night ops, we began a period of daytime low-flying exercises over East Anglia. Blenheims were fitted with twin .303 Browning machine guns in the upper turret, while black-painted undersides were replaced with light blue.

On 15 April, our CO was shot down attacking one of the first convoys sighted. W/C G. C. Key DFC took over command a few days later.

I joined 18 Squadron as a Sgt WOP/AG in August 1940 having flown twenty-eight night ops. But before the end of the year, I got pneumonia. On re-joining the Squadron, I crewed up with Sgts George Milsom (Pilot) and Ron Millar (Observer) RNZAF.

At the 25 April 1941 Briefing, we were told to patrol a shipping lane off the Dutch coast. If we failed to sight any ships, we could fly inland to search a suitable target. We carried four 250-lb bombs, flying at 0 feet to the search area. No ships to be found. We headed inland over flat countryside, not unlike Norfolk. On the outskirts of Flushing, we decided to drop our bombs on a railway line, finding no other suitable target. AA Defences immediately opened fire, pretty accurate as they knocked two large holes in our tail unit. Still at 0 feet, we dropped down over the sea wall into an estuary leading to the sea. I was looking up at enemy gun placements unable to depress their guns low enough to fire at us. However, I could fire at them! We landed back at Oulton two hours and twenty minutes after take-off feeling very pleased with ourselves!

From 3-12 May 1941, we were detached to RAF Portreath in the West Country for ops off the French coast. Then I was back at Oulton for more regular shipping patrols with the occasional 'Circus'.

On 25 May 1941, a long distance attack on a seaplane base in the Frisian Isles was planned, led by S/L Johnny Munro. Near the target, Me109s attacked the formation. One 18 Squadron Blenheim (F/S D. G. Keave) was shot down, several others damaged; the WOP/AG (Sgt E. A. Lloyd) in one aircraft being killed. Another 18 Squadron Blenheim was lost from a different operation. This was a bad day for the Squadron.

On 1 June, my brother Peter joined the Squadron as an AC2 Electrician.

On 6 June 1941, I was at West Raynham for a visit by Prime Minister Churchill. The 2 Group AOC was also present to hear first-hand from crews how Shipping Strike Operations were progressing. Several new types of aircraft not yet in service were on show, including a Blenheim replacement, the Douglas Boston.

On 16 June, there was another Shipping Patrol over two hours, ten minutes; where a Blenheim (P/O Aires) failed to return.

On 17 June, I was at Horsham St Faith for a 'Circus' Briefing, attacking a chemical works at Chocques in Northern France. Twenty-four Blenheims with fighter escort took part in a big air battle with enemy fighters. We were hit in both wings, putting the port engine out of commission. Despite this, we returned to Horsham St Faith, an example of marvellous flying by our Pilot George. The flight lasted three hours, ten minutes, but it seemed so much longer. I was credited with shooting down one enemy fighter, and the attack overall had been successful, with damage to the target and tempting the Luftwaffe to join in the battle.

On 25 June, Blenheim (Sgt W. H. Mounser) FTR (*Failed to Return*) from a convoy attack.

On 30 June, eighteen Blenheims on a '*Circus*' op to the Power Station at Pont-a-Vend had direct hits, flak, but no fighters. Our pilot George was promoted to P/O on 1 July, with the target for the day being the Chemical Works near Bethun, France. Again, we made two abandoned attempts due to bad weather.

On 5 July 1941, a Shipping Patrol took off at 6 pm, with two hours duration. This was also the end of the Tour for our crew. We'd taken part in twenty operations as a team, been hit three times, and flown a total of fifty-nine hours on operations.

During our stay at Oulton, forty-three of our Squadron aircrew were killed, others injured or PoWs. We'd intended to stay together as a crew, preparing for a posting on an O.T.U in the Middle East. However, on checking my Medical Records, the Powers-that-Be decided I couldn't go. Sadly we parted company. I was posted instead to the Gunnery Wing at 13 O.T.U Bicester as an Instructor.

Back to Blickling with the Bostons

From 13 O.T.U I was posted to 88 Squadron with F/L Johnny Reeves (Pilot), and P/O Freddy Deeks (Observer).

On 30 September 1941, we reported to the Squadron which had moved to Oulton. It was back to Blickling Hall and like return-ing home, although this time resident in the East Wing (Officers' Mess) instead of the West Wing (Sergeants' Mess). 88 was the first Squadron to receive Boston 3s during November 1941.

Ops commenced in February 1942. Over the next six months, 88 Squadron flew thirty-four '*Circus*' ops, the most demanding and memorable day being 19 August 1942. It was the Dieppe Raid. Three Boston Squadrons supplied close air support and laid smoke. Ten aircraft were lost, including seven from smoke-laying operations. The 88 CO was W/Cdr J. Pelly-Fry. My gun position had two .303 machine guns mounted on a scarf ring and behind me was the radio. An extra Gunner was sometimes carried on '*Circus*' Ops, lying on his stomach between my legs, a .303 machine gun mounted in the open escape hatch. Our extra A/G usually was a cheerful Newfoundlander, Johnny Legge.

It was at this time I met Norma my wife-to-be in Norwich. We were married in St Peter Mancrofts Church on 18 February 1943.

My first op with 88 Squadron was a recall after take-off on 13 October 1942. 16 October came a 'Circus' to Neumark-le Harve. November mainly low flying practice took place. 3 December was a Briefing for *Operation Oyster*, an attack on the Philips Works at Eindhoven – the most ambitious low-level raid of the war up to then. Eighty-four aircraft took part. We were to bomb the main factory. After Briefing, we were confined to Camp with all phone calls banned. However, the raid was not carried out until Sunday 6 December.

Operation Oyster

36 Bostons, 36 Venturas and 12 Mosquitoes were to be led by W/C Pelly-Fry, CO of 88 Squadron, Oulton. Cover was to be given by four Fighter Squadrons, while the USAAF 8th Air Force launched a high-level diversion raid on Lille. The operation was complicated by the different speeds of types of aircraft involved. It was vital each Squadron arrive over the target separately to avoid confusion, yet equally imperative for the whole attack to be completed in the shortest possible time.

Sunday, 6 December, 1942 dawned a suitable day. For a target in the centre of a Dutch town which required such precision bombing, I always felt Sunday should be the day planned. An 11.15 am take-off meant formatting at No. 3 with our W/C, with F/L Jock Campbell flying at No. 2, passing over the City of Norwich, then low level across the North Sea. Jock Caines, the Wing/Co, an excellent Navigator, guided us to our correct landfall.

It was a clear day. We skimmed over flat countryside seeing local people bedecked in Sunday best, many giving a cheery wave. Despite the occasion and obvious risks the sense of speed and being part of this large aerial Force was a thrilling experience. A lone enemy fighter was seen, who sheered off on seeing the approaching air armada. Finally, I heard Freddy say the target was dead ahead. Turning around, the factory towered over surrounding houses. The leading pair of Bostons with eleven-second D/A fused bombs, ploughed straight on at very low level. Johnny led the remainder of the formation up to 1,500 feet. Light flak opened up from batteries on top of the factory. We dropped our bombs, returning to 0 feet. Looking back, smoke rose from factory buildings, evidence our bombs had landed in the right place.

The AA gunfire hit the W/C and Sgt Tyler. Both lost contact to make their way home independently. The W/C was hit in the wing and later attacked by FW190s, but managed to survive and reach Oulton. Sgt Tyler was hit in the starboard engine and crash-landed near Lowestoft. Jock Campbell took over as Leader, bringing us home by an unplanned route. However, in doing so, he did us a favour. Apart from light flak, our departure was uneventful. We landed back at Oulton unscathed.

Other Squadrons weren't so lucky, hit by flak and fighters. Fourteen aircraft failed to return. Photographs showed both factory complexes badly damaged. It was later established there was little loss of life to local residents, justifying the decision for a low level raid in daylight. Press reports which followed raised the morale of the British people.

W/C Pelly-Fry was awarded the DSO for leading the Operation. Further Ops continued from Oulton by 88 Squadron throughout December 1942 and January 1943 into early February. After that, we didn't return to the fray, apart from some ASR missions until 28 June 1943. The reason two-fold. Blenheim 5s in service in North Africa proved less than satisfactory. It was decided to re-equip Squadrons quickly with our Boston 3s, meaning we had to wait for new ones to arrive. The other reason was we took part in numerous exercises with the Army in preparation for our role on D-Day, including operations from airstrips in Southern England (Exercise 'Spartan'). We returned to Oulton, but not for long because on 31 March 1943, the Squadron moved to Swanton Morley.

Above, left:. LACW Nina Chessall, WAAF (*author's collection*)
Above, right:. Flt/Lt Henry Victor '*Vic*' Alexander Vinnell (*author's collection*)

Above, left: Jack Fisher. (*Courtesy: Fisher Family, Canada*)
Above, right: RAFU 36th Bomb Squadron crest. (*Courtesy: Stephen Hutton*)

I

Above: 1st 803BS CO: Captain George Paris. (*Courtesy: Murray Peden*)

Below: ABL Div.15 at TRE. (*Courtesy: Shirley Merrill*)

Above: RAF Group Captain Thomas Charles Dickens, right. (*Courtesy: Eric Dickens*)

Below: Hutton & McCrory crew of The JIGS UP. (*Courtesy: Iredell Hutton*)

Overleaf, left:. WINDOW illustration. (*Courtesy: USAF Historical Research Agency*)

Overleaf, right: MANDREL illustration. (*Courtesy: USAF Historical Research Agency*)

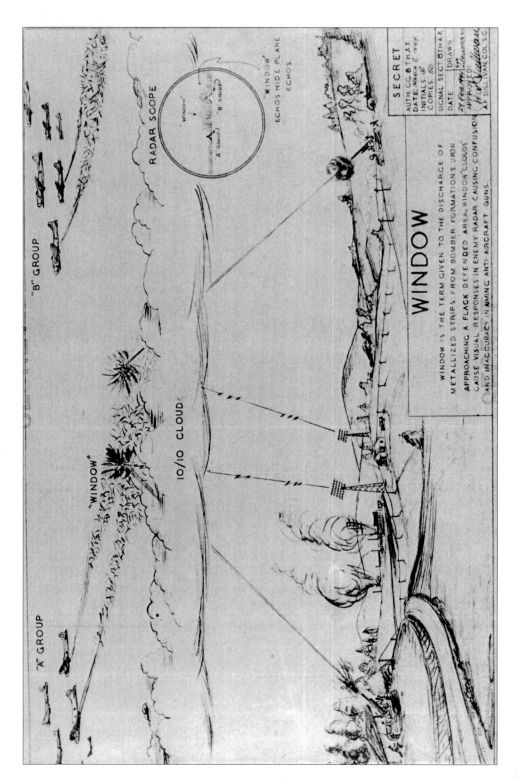

WINDOW

WINDOW IS THE TERM GIVEN TO THE DISCHARGE OF METALLIZED STRIPS FROM BOMBER FORMATIONS UPON APPROACHING A FLACK DEFENDED AREA. WINDOW "CLOUDS" CAUSE VISUAL RESPONSES IN ENEMY RADAR CAUSING CONFUSION AND INACCURACY IN AIMING ANTI-AIRCRAFT GUNS.

"A" GROUP

"B" GROUP

"WINDOW"

10/10 CLOUD

RADAR SCOPE

"A" GROUP

"B" GROUP

"WINDOW"

"WINDOW" ECHOS HIDE PLANE ECHOS

AUTH. C.G. 8 T.H.A.F.
DATE March 2, 1944
INITIALS DP
COPIES 60

SIGNAL SECT. 8TH A.F.
DATE 24 Feb 44 DRAWN
APPROVED
AT SULLIVAN, COL. S.C.

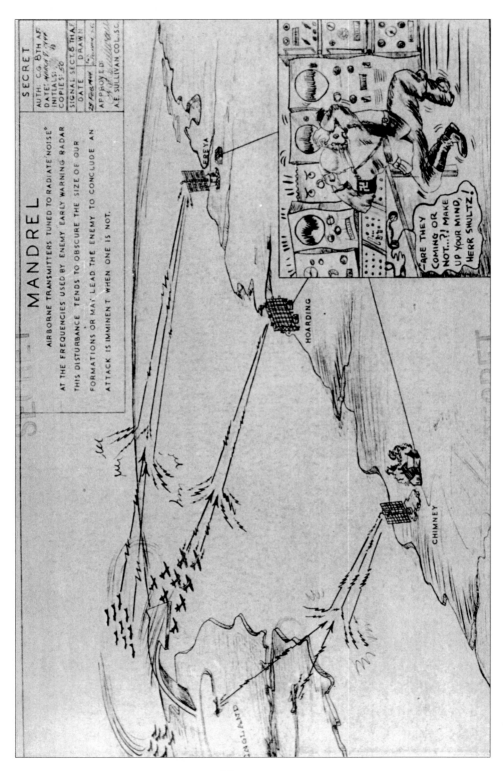

V

Above: Captain Sackett crew. (*Courtesy: USAF Historical Research Agency*)

Below: Lieutenant Hornsby crew. (*Courtesy: USAF Historical Research Agency*)

Above: Lieutenant Norman Landberg's crew.
(*Courtesy: USAF Historical Research Agency*)

Below: 36BS B24 #219 R4-I crash site. (*Courtesy: USAF Historical Research Agency*)

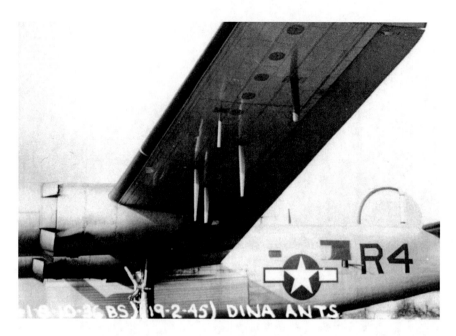

Above DINA antenna. (*Courtesy: USAF Historical Research Agency*)

Opposite: GEE illustration. (*Courtesy: USAF Historical Research Agency*)

Below: Lieutenant Boehm crew. (*Courtesy: USAF Historical Research Agency*)

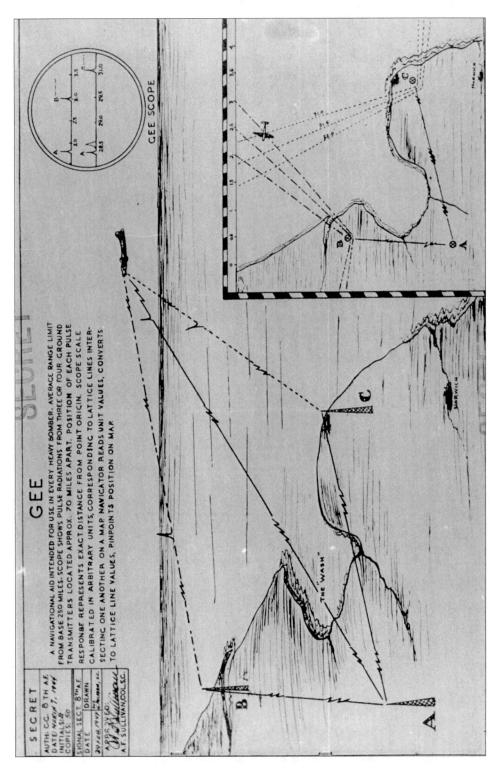

Above: Lieutenants Burch & Boehm. (*Courtesy: Donald Burch*)

Below: 36BS B24 The Uninvited. (*Courtesy: Charles M. Todaro*)

Above: Lieutenant McKibben crew. (*Courtesy: USAF Historical Research Agency*)

Below: MP Roy Tackett & The JIGS UP debris. (*Courtesy: Roy Tackett*)

Above: 7PRG F5 Droop Snoot. (*Courtesy:William B. Stallcup*)

Opposite: 36BS at Alconbury 23 May 1945. (*Courtesy: USAF Historical Research Agency*)

Below: Lt Col. Hambaugh presents S/Sgt Francis Preimesberger with Air Medal.
(*Courtesy: Roland A. Morin*)

36th BOMBARDMENT SQUADRON (H) - 4 -
8th AIR FORCE

ALCONBURY, ENGLAND   - o o o -   MAY 23, 1945

Above: Len Bartram receiving Gold Medal from Queen Elizabeth, Queen Mother.
(*Courtesy: Evelyn Bartram*)

Below: Bomber Command Theatre of Operations. (*Courtesy: Evelyn Bartram*)

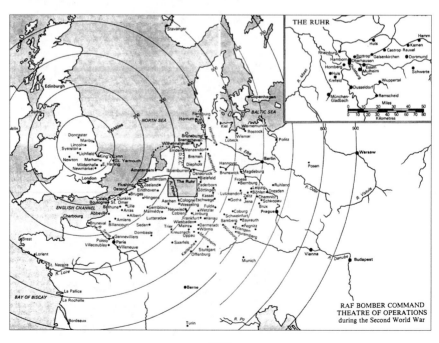

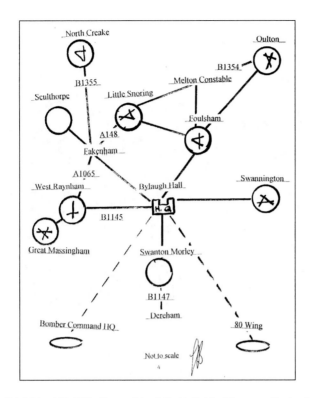

Above: RAF No. 100 (BS) Group Norfolk Airfields. (*Courtesy: Evelyn Bartram*)

Below: RAF Foulsham Airfield, drawn by Len Bartram. (*Courtesy: Evelyn Bartram*)

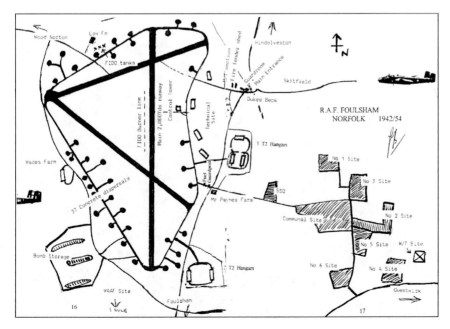

Above: C Flight, 192 Squadron, Foulsham - Far right: Ron Phillips, next right, Ted Gomershall. (*Courtesy: Ted Gomershall*)

Below: Jack Fisher, left front, in flying jacket, sitting capless 13 October 1944, before Tony Emett (with moustache) & Ted Gomersall (centre) – Acting, unpaid OC; skived off to Yorkshire in a Tiger Moth. (*Courtesy: Ted Gomersall*)

Above: Foulsham Mosquito pilots, 1944. Left to right: Sgt H. Crow, Jack Fisher, F/Lt C. 'Nobby' Clarke, F/O W. Crimmin, F/Lt M.W. O'Brien, F/Lt R. Burgess, F/Lt J. Cartwright (*Copyright: William Rees*)

Below: Left to right: W/O Gerry McEachern, RCAF Nav; W/O Bill Mitchell, RAF Air Gunner; W/O Reg Wilson, RAFVR Spec/Op; P/O Alan Thomsett, RAFVR Pilot; Flt/Sgt Ken Mainwaring, RAFVR W Op/Air Gunner; Flight/Sgt Cliff Lee, RAFVR Air Gunner. (*Courtesy: Anne Thomsett*)

Above: Blickling Hall air view, taken by Group Captain Thomas Charles Dickens, 1945. (*Courtesy: Eric Dickens*)

Opposite, top: Special Signals Section, 192 Squadron, Foulsham, 1944/45. (*Courtesy: Joe Sayer*)

Opposite, middle: Flight Engineers of 192 Squadron, Foulsham: F/Lt Howard DFC, Officer in charge 3rd from the right, front row. F/Sgt Eggert: extreme left in rear row. (*Courtesy: John Eggert*)

Opposite, bottom: 214 Squadron, MT Section, Blickling Hall, Oulton.
Back Row: ?, ?, ?, ?, ?, Walter (Curly) Houghton from Scunthorpe; ?, Corporal Barlow; 'Sparks' ?, ?, ?, ?, ?, Corporal Sidery; Doreen Roebotham.
Next Row of 2: ?; Corporal Scholes.
Middle Row: Corporal Dorothy (Dot) Butler; Hazel Robbins (m Southgate); Connie from Fakenham, Corporal Somerset; '*Paddy*' Stevenson from Ballymena (m Smith, London); Nan or Nen Mainwaring; Winifred Elizabeth Tomlinson (m Seeley); Olga Miller; Elsie Shultz; Janet Hodges (m Moyse); ?.
Front Row: Sergeant; Warrant Officer; Flying Officer Salew; Sergeant ('Snitch); Sergeant.
Not on photo: Nellie Dawson, always with Doreen Roebottom, they were very good pals. (*Courtesy: Win Seeley*)

XIX

Above RAF Little Snoring Control Tower. From left to right: F/Sgt Ikin, F/Sgt Hammond, F/L B. Hastings, Mary ? 'Ops' clerk. (*Courtesy: Tom Cushing*)

Below: F/O George Stewart DFC. (*Courtesy: George Stewart*)

Above: Little Snoring airfield: red dot marks George Stewart's parking spot, 001.
(*Courtesy: George Stewart*)

Below: 23 Squadron Mosquito: YPE PZ187 (Thursford in background behind tail)
RAF Little Snoring Autumn 1944. (*Courtesy: Tom Cushing*)

Above: Flying Officer Paul Beaudet and Flying Officer George Stewart, Hamilton 1945. (*Courtesy: George Stewart*)

Opposite: 23 Squadron, Little Snoring, 28 October 1944:
Left to Right: Wg/Cdr A.M. '*Sticky*' Murphy, Flt/Lt J. Curd, F/O J. L. Joynson, Flt/Lt D. J. Griffiths, Sqn/Ldr Phil Russell, F/O A. C. Cockayne, Flt/Lt T.A. '*Tommy*' Smith, F/O E. L Heath, W/O K.V. '*Scarper*' Rann, Flt/Lt R. J. Reid, Flt/Lt W. '*Bill*' Gregory, Lt J. H. Christie NAF, P/O G. S. '*George*' Sutcliffe, F/O D. J. Atherton, Flt/Sgt F. D. '*Freddie*' Howes, F/O J. R. '*Paul*' Beaudet RCAF, P/O R. Neil RNZAF, Flt/Sgt J. H. Chessel, F/O A.L. Berry RNZAF, Flt/Sgt Alex Wilson, Flt/Sgt Don Francis, Flt/Lt '*Buddy*' Badley, Flt/Sgt T '*Tommy*' Barr, F/O K. M. '*Kit*' Cotter RNZAF, Flt/Sgt J.W. Thompson, Flt/Sgt P. H. '*Jock*' Devlin, Flt/Sgt J. '*Jimmy*' Weston, Flt/Off. J. E. Spetch, Flt/Lt T. A. '*Tommy*' Ramsay RNZAF, Flt/Sgt E. C. '*Benny*' Goodman, Flt/Sgt J. '*Jimmy*' Gawthorne, Flt/Sgt S. F. '*Sid*' Smith.
On nose of aircraft: F/O G.E. '*George*' Stewart RCAF.
At the time of this photograph: F/O A. R. de C. Smith, F/Sgt C. Lewis on night vision course at RAF Great Massingham

Above: 23 Squadron aircrew, Little Snoring, June 1944. (*Courtesy: George Stewart*)

Below: *Drawing by Lionel Campbell of incident at West Raynham.*
(*Courtesy: Lionel Campbell*)

Above and Below: Drawings by Lionel Campbell of incident at West Raynham.
(Courtesy: Lionel Campbell)

Above: Pilot Officer William (Bill) Searle Vale. (*Courtesy: Helen Rankin*)

Opposite: 157 Squadron at RAF Swannington Mess. (*Courtesy: Helen Rankin*) Far back row: ?, ?, Gordon Lang, ?, John Collins, Bucky Cunningham, Lou Brandon, Oscar Wilde. Far right side: Les Scholefield, Chris Woodcock, Bryan Gale, Laurie Waters, Ken Pybus (Intelligence Officer). 2nd row from back: Les Butt, Satch Churches (RAAF), Jimmy Penrose, P/0 Vale (RAAF), ?, Ron Goss, Basher Broom. Far left, standing: Radar Officer. 3rd row from back: ?, ?, Dennis Crowther, Syd Astley, Geoff Edwards, R.N. Crew, R.N Crew, Alan Brookes, R.N. Crew, R.N. Crew. (Two slightly forward of last two persons unknown). 2nd row from front: F/O Balderstone, Frank Money, ?, F/Lt Sumner, F/Lt Tweedale, F/L Hanahan, Bill Tofts, Jimmy Matthews, ?, Brian Whitlock, F/O Gilbert Davidson. Front row: John Smythe, Steve Stephens, Sqn/Ldr Chisholm, W/Cdr Dennison, S/L Drummond, Flt/Lt Benson, Sqdn/Ldr Doleman (Doley) … not forgetting, Towser, Doley's Dog!

XXVII

Above: Flight Engineers of 192 Squadron, Foulsham. (*Courtesy: Anne Blair-Vincent*)

Below: Blickling Hall 2015 (*author's collection*)

Above: Ron Johnson (223 Squadron) holding piece of tail from his aircraft.
(*Courtesy: Betty Johnson*)

Above: Iredell Hutton at Memorial of *the Jigs Up*, Holyhead, Wales.
(*Courtesy: Stephen Hutton*)

Above: Sister Laurie with World War Two veteran John Beeching.
(*Courtesy: John Beeching*)

Above: RAF 100 Group Association at City of Norwich Aviation Museum
(*author's collection*)

Below: Sculpture at Southend Airport, London, shown at night.
(*Courtesy: John Atkin FRBS*)

Corporal Lawrence Round
2857 Squadron, RAF Regt
The Early Days

I was posted to Oulton during the summer of 1940. It was basic at that point, just a large grass field. Our billets were farm buildings at Green Farm with the farming family, the Drummonds, living in the farmhouse. At first, conditions were sparse with earth closet toilets. Later, buildings improved with cement floors and electricity. A number of Nissen huts were built nearby. Our duties were ground defence of the airfield. It was just after Dunkirk. We had few weapons, just one Lewis gun mounted on a metal pole and old American and Canadian rifles. Rations and other supplies came daily from Horsham St Faith, our parent station. We converted an old Fordson lorry into an armoured car with a cement body and Lewis gun on top. We called it '*The Armadillo*'. For night flying we had just one Chance floodlight on a tractor and a line of gooseneck flares, these being a sort of watering-can with a wick. There were a number of aircraft crashes in the area, and from the broken Perspex collected we made rings, bangles and model aircraft when off duty. The winter of 1940 was very bad. We all did much snow clearing to enable Blenheims to keep flying.

Four gun-pits were dug around the landing area containing two bunks and a stove, useful for a piece of toast at least. Coal was sometimes thrown to us from passing trains. By 1942, we had six Beaverette armoured cars made by the Standard Motor Company. By the end of that year, we had formed a Light AA Flight equipped with 3-ton trucks and new guns.

After that it was goodbye to Norfolk for me, and off to sunny Sicily ... but that's another story.

I do think that all wartime airfields need something like an obelisk or plaque to bring attention to the sacrifices of lives and service made by their forbearers. Let's not just remember these hallowed fields by the number of turkey sheds strewn across old runways!

Joyce Palmer
A WAAF at Oulton
1944 –1945

Being a 'townie' from the north, I was immediately struck by the beauty of Norfolk, hoping I would still be there when the following spring came. The WAAFry was in a clearing in a wood, part of Blickling Hall Estate, just up the road from the Hall, not far from the Buckinghamshire Arms Inn, 'The Bucks' as it was known. It became a regular meeting place for WAAFs, airmen and aircrew. As I played the piano fairly well, I was never short of a pint of wartime beer (*never touched a drop since!*)

Many girls didn't get up early enough for breakfast, but those who did had a cycle ride of one and a half miles to a site down a lane near Oulton village street. Having usually missed breakfast, sustenance would be obtained during a short break at 10 am at a little hut-type café opposite the main gates, run by a lady of about sixty years. She wore her hair in a bun at the back of her head and did a roaring trade with tea and wads. Her little hut was always full of airmen and women.

Part of my duties in Signals consisted of typing daily Code Sheets for aircrew. The codes were triple-checked for accuracy, being extremely important. They were changed on a daily basis and Top Secret. I was never told what they really meant. I heard the word 'WINDOW' mentioned many times at the Section, but didn't know what it was until I took the trouble to risk security and ask. They must have thought I was a good risk and told me about the thousands of strips of tin foil dropped over Germany to fool their radar systems.

After Christmas 1944, the snow came and one of the worst winters for many years descended on the country. Many operations were cancelled. When ops were off, there was a general flurry of preparation by WAAFs for unexpected dates with boyfriends. When ops were on, we girls listened for take-offs around 7 – 8 pm. The aircraft left at intervals every few minutes. We'd count them off. Then, during early morning, we'd count them returning, awakened by the roar of engines. Sometimes, aircraft were missing. But we always hoped they had engine trouble and diverted to other Bases.

There was one occasion when a WAAF, a lovely auburn-haired girl, refused to leave her bed for several days. We thought she was ill. But then we discovered her boyfriend had failed to return. That situation must have occurred many times over in the Air Force during the war, so we girls were always wary of falling for aircrew with the sadly, mostly inevitable consequences. At one stage in the war, the survival rate was less than one in five.

Spring arrived and my wish to still be at Oulton was granted. The lovely wild flowers in the woods and along the Saxthorpe to Aylsham roadsides where we often went rides on our RAF issue bikes brought colour and life. Other outings included Aylsham *The Black Boys* Pub, the cinema or chippy. Sometimes we went to a field near the church to watch football or cricket matches between various RAF station teams. Sometimes we were allowed to walk in the Park and Grounds at Blickling Hall. Occasionally, we went to Norwich full of GIs and jeeps, the former complete with the almost obligatory chewing gum. We also formed a musical concert party, performing shows on Camp, at Aylsham Town Hall and Saxthorpe village for local residents.

When it was all finally over, a grand party was held in the Airmen's Mess. What a day (*and night*) VE celebrations turned out to be! Shortly after the end of the war, Ground Crews and WAAFs were given the opportunity of a trip in a bomber aircraft over Germany to see the damage done by our air raids. I shall never forget as long as I live the complete and utter devastation seen from the air. Cities were literally flattened, reduced to heaps of rubble. I have wondered many times since how two of the most inventive countries in the world could have wasted their best brains in five years hammering away, destroying each other. Future generations will always ask the same question, and it was of course, all down to one mad man. May it never happen again!

Sgt Gerhard Heilig, Special Duty Operator
The only things I ever regret
are the things I have not done!

I was living in Vienna when, in March 1938, Austria became part of Nazi-Germany. Within forty-eight hours my father was arrested by the Gestapo and was to spend thirteen months in the concentration camps of Dachau and Buchenwald. He had been a prominent and well-known anti-Nazi journalist. Although just thirteen years of age, I was fully aware of the perils all Jews would face under this new regime and I did not expect to see my father again.

In December 1938, I was on the first of several children's transports, a trainload of some 600 Jewish children which would take most of them to the safe haven of England. There I had the good fortune to be taken in, along with three others, by a Quaker school in Yorkshire where, as day boys, we lived with families in the village. This experience turned out to be the foundation of my development which helped to make me the person I am today.

By the summer of 1940, having reached school-leaving age and funds for my maintenance run out, my formal education came to a sad and premature end. I was then offered a place at a Training Centre in Leeds where the likes of myself could learn a trade. I qualified as an electrician and in March 1942 joined my father in London. My mother had got his release from the concentration camp by subter-fuge, and I shudder to think what might have happened to her if she had been found out. My father had arrived in England two weeks before the outbreak of war, but before my mother was able to follow him hostilities put a stop to all civilian travel. She was en route in Italy and remained there for the duration, unable to re-join my father until 1947.

My father was living in a bedsitter in the basement of a large block of flats in Bayswater and similar accommodation was found for me there. I soon found a job with a small telephone company special-ising in office and factory intercom systems. I'd become very inter-ested in aircraft while still at school in Yorkshire, first on the design side. But by now I'd decided what I really wanted to do was to fly.

I, and others like me, were legally classed as enemy aliens. As such we could not be called up and any volunteers were limited to the Pioneer Corps, the so-called *Pick and Shovel Brigade*, a far cry indeed for a would-be bold aviator!

One day in January 1943 I noticed a recruiting office while passing along the Euston Road. On the principle of if you don't ask, you don't get, I marched boldly in where I was greeted by a very friendly Sergeant (*would they all be so nice?*) who asked what he could do for me.

'I want to volunteer for aircrew.'

'Oh, you've come to the right place, sign here.'

On explaining the problem, he said it had all changed, and there was no longer any limitation for the likes of me. However, each case was treated on an individual basis. I would have to write a letter to the Secretary of State for Air explaining who I was, and I would get a decision in about six weeks' time. I did just that, was accepted, and in mid-March presented myself at the Aircrew Selection Board. I wanted to be a Pilot of course, but in the end had to settle for Wireless Operator. This was very disappointing, but turned out to be a blessing in disguise. Pilot training was a lengthy business and, much of it being done in kinder climes such as America and Rhodesia involving extensive travel with its inevitable delays and bottle-necks, I may not have qualified before the end of the conflict brought it all to an end. As it turned out, I left the Service with useful experience for entering Civil Aviation.

Many well-wishers chided me for sticking my neck out instead of staying safe at home, to which I would reply – *where is safety? How many housewives lost their lives in their own kitchen?* There were still bombs dropping on London, I used to take my turn fire-watching on the roof of the block of flats and the buzz-bombs and V-2s were still to come. Years later someone said to me – *'If there's something you really want to do, go ahead and do it'* and *'the only things I have ever regretted are the things I have not done!'* I have always found these to be very good principles indeed.

The end of June 1943 found me at ACRC, the Aircrew Reception Centre at St. John's Wood. It was then on to Initial Training Wing at Bridgenorth, Shropshire and at the end of September at No. 4 Radio School, Madley, near Hereford. This was a dismal place, the usual widely dispersed camp where we seemed to spend as much time marching from one instructional site to another as actually being instructed in one of them. I found the technical part of our training interesting, but as for the practical – four hours a day, six days a week for six months getting Morse Code speed up to requirements, felt like being chained to an oar in a pirate's galley! When about mid-October a call went out for German speakers this seemed like a call for a more congenial existence. I lost no time putting my name down, but nothing more was heard of this and I continued minding my 'dits and dahs'.

My course should have finished at the end of March, but by the beginning of the month the previous intake were still struggling to complete their flying with no sign of us even starting. Then out of the blue, Johnnie Hereford and I were told to report to the Chief Instructor's office who informed us we had been posted with immediate effect to a Squadron. We were told to do our tests, then we would have priority to get our flying done. A couple of days later, it was Wednesday 15 March, six years to the day since my father had been arrested by the Gestapo; we received our Signaller's wings and Sergeant's stripes. Two days later we joined 214 Squadron at Sculthorpe, near Fakenham in Norfolk.

214 Squadron, having been transferred from 3 Group to 100 Group, was still converting from Stirlings to Flying Fortresses to operate in its new role of radio countermeasures. While the British bombers' under-floor bomb bays were ideal for carrying the largest bombs, the American mid-wing fuselage ones were better suited for the installation and maintenance of radio equipment we were to carry. Our tasks would be the disruption of enemy radar and radio transmissions, especially those used for the direction of night-fighters to our bomber stream. These would be operated by Special Duty Operators, of which Johnnie and I were among the first to arrive on the Squadron. It was all so secret even the Commanding Officer had not been informed what it was all about. So that call for German speakers had not been in vain and I was pleased at the prospect of

getting at least some of my own back on that Nasty Man Adolf. In fact, the Squadron's first operational flight was on 20 April – Hitler's birthday! I revelled at delivering my worst regards in person.

The equipment we carried was ABC, (*Airborne Cigar*), which consisted of a small cathode ray tube covering the German night-fighter frequency band. Any transmission would show as a blip, and we would tune one or more of our three transmitters to it to drown it in a horrible cacophony of sound. This had been pioneered by 101 Squadron in October 1943, hence that call for German speakers, and they continued this as a side-line to the end of the war. In time, more sophisticated and powerful equipment came into use, but that was after my time on the Squadron.

For some time there were not enough Specials to go round. We'd not yet received our full complement of aircraft and were flying with whoever happened to be on the battle order. Towards the end of July, we were at last able to continue with a crew of our own, I had become particularly friendly with Jackson's, when Johnnie and I were posted away to 101 Squadron in RAF Ludford Magna, Lincolnshire. We struggled and fought to remain with our friends, but to no avail; we had to go. Apparently 101's need was greater than 214's. We'd been picked to fill the gap. In fact, this probably saved my life, for Jackson's crew were shot down on their very last flight of their tour.

I'd flown ten operational flights with 214 and completed my tour of thirty with 101 towards the end of October. Though my Lancaster had suffered occasional damage by enemy flak, none was of a really serious nature and I came through it all unscathed. In fact, the nearest I ever came to losing my life was on my very own doorstep while on leave in London, when a V-2 exploded prematurely a few hundred feet directly above my head. Just goes to show – sticking out my neck by volunteering might have been the safest option after all!

Early in the New Year, I was posted to Transport Command, first to a Dakota Operational Training Unit near Carlisle, then in September to the Far East – first to a supply-dropping course in Baroda, then to 215 Squadron, soon to be renumbered 48, in Singapore. Here, fortune again favoured me, for our job was the carriage of Service personnel throughout the area as far as Rangoon and Hong Kong in the north, Java and Sumatra in the south. Here my work as Wireless Operator was the same, as I was to find later in Civil Aviation and the 800 hours I logged there the very experience I needed for my later career.

I left the Service in May 1947, flew as Radio Officer with several companies, qualified as a commercial pilot in 1954 and got my first command three years later. But that's another story.

However, I count amongst my most valued friendships those I served with on 214 Squadron, including John Gilpin, Peter Witts, and Jimmy Hollingworth (died serving his country). Jimmy's brother and niece continue to attend annual RAF 100 Group Association Reunions each May, as does John. It means so much, knowing that the true spirit of friendship I found in 214 is still a part of our today.

Gerhard's book: 'Circuits and Bumps' is available from Woodfield Publishing.

Gerhard Heilig also has a documentary sharing his early life as a Jewish Hungarian, filmed in Vienna where he lived before his death early this year, 2015: 'Into the Wind', produced by Steven Hatton of Electric Egg. A second film: 'Heilig', available through Amazon; has already won awards across the world, moving the story on to his mother Hilda's heart-breaking decision to send her youngest boy to safety in England as his father is imprisoned.

Flt/Sgt James 'Jimmy' Hollingworth
by niece Linda Fraser

I was very young when I first learned about my Uncle Jimmy and remember studying his log book, written in a very neat hand, but far too complex for a nine-year-old to decipher. He'd been a Wireless Operator in Bomber Command and lost his life after a terrible accident on a training flight, following many previous missions.

To me he was a Hero.

Soon after, I decided to go to his grave to pay my respects, so set off on my bicycle with two loyal friends in convoy. On arrival at the churchyard, we were searching for his grave but promptly told to go away by the Rector, no doubt thinking we were up to mischief. Undeterred, I have returned many times since with no further misunderstandings.

Over the years, I wondered about Uncle Jimmy and his life in the RAF. Unfortunately, my father cannot remember very much as he was quite young. All he knew was that his older brother was 'down south'. As everyone knows, to a Northerner, that means anywhere south of Birmingham!

The years went by and then it was December, my mother and father's Diamond Wedding Anniversary. I asked if I could have some photographs, the older the better, to frame and display at a Celebration Party. Mum produced an old-looking box and on sifting through the contents, I found pictures of Uncle Jimmy. Written on the back of one in that same handwriting I had last seen fifty years ago, were the names of the crew of Fortress BU-N of 214 Squadron:

Fg/Off 'Tommy' Thomas, Bomb Aimer
F/S 'Paddy' Gilpin, Mid Upper Gunner
Sgt Gerhard 'Harry' Heilig, 1892246, Special Operator, Royal Air Force, Nationality: Austrian
Plt/Off Ken Hovers, Navigator
Sgt Jackie Hewitt
Plt/Off Jake Walters, Pilot
Sgt Bill Howard, Flight Engineer
Sgt Jimmy Hollingworth
Sgt Alf Read, Rear Gunner

It was such an exciting moment! Maybe now I could begin to find out about Uncle Jimmy and hopefully contact someone who had known him. I presumed the gentlemen not named must be Ground Crew.

We were relative strangers to the internet, so I wrote a letter for publication in a favourite magazine: 'Best of British'; asking if anyone remembered my Uncle. A welcome response gave me contact details for Jock Whitehouse, Historian of 214 Squadron Association, who helped me enormously in my search. When I read out the names of the crew, he said he had known most of them and that two still came to their Reunions – John Gilpin and Gerhard Heilig. Jock kindly suggested that I attend the July Reunion in Derby where I could meet these two gentlemen. I had a further call from Peter Walker, Secretary of 214 Squadron Association, who was so informative and helpful.

The next day, I had a message on the answer phone from John Gilpin, Uncle Jimmy's old pal, and it was an emotional moment listening to his message. I nervously returned John's call and we were soon chatting away like old friends, and he cheerfully told me some of his memories of their time together. I was 'over the moon' and could never explain just how much this all meant to me.

I joined the 214 Squadron Association and Peter Walker helped me with my application for Uncle Jimmy's Service Record from RAF Cranwell. Our places were booked at the Reunion, but we were disappointed to hear that John and Gwen Gilpin were unable to attend. However, on hearing this, my husband Ian (luckily as keen as I) said 'We'll just have to go to Ireland to meet them!' I was so pleased, those were my thoughts also, and the trip was planned.

On arrival in Derby for the Reunion, we wandered into the bar and I spotted the first of my heroes – Gerhard Heilig, having seen his picture on the internet. I immediately rushed over to introduce myself, so eager to talk to him. Gerhard was charming and polite and all four of us had a great conversation over lunch together. We'd worried we were not really entitled to be there, never having served in the Squadron. But everyone was so warm and welcoming at the AGM and Dinner, we had a wonderful time. In his presentation, Gerhard kindly said that we were welcome as part of the Association.

Peter Witts then told us about the 100 Group Association Reunion and arranged for an application form to be sent to us. The following day, we attended a Memorial Service at the National Arboretum where I laid a wreath to honour the memory of Uncle Jimmy and all 214 Squadron. It had been a very memorable weekend.

Less than a week later, we flew to Belfast to meet John Gilpin and his wife Gwen. I was so excited to be meeting yet another hero, especially as John had been close friends with my Uncle. Any nervousness on our part was swept aside by the welcome we received. John told us that in recent years he had written to Uncle Jimmy's last known address, asking if anyone had any knowledge of his family, but never received a reply. Unfortunately, none of my relatives had lived there for over thirty years. Then, out of the blue, Peter Walker had called him to say I was trying to contact anyone who knew his old pal!

Our weekend with John and Gwen was wonderful. They took us to some beautiful places and showered us with kindness and hospitality. We found it very hard to tear ourselves away and they both remain very special and dear to me.

We have discovered so much about Uncle Jimmy and our thanks go to Jock Whitehouse (Historian of 214 Squadron Association), Peter Walker (Secretary), and especially dear John Gilpin for all the tales of their escapades when not flying! We were so glad that Uncle Jimmy's life was not just about fear and danger, but more importantly about friendship, loyalty and most of all fun. These fine gentlemen we met say they would not have missed those times for anything. They deny they were brave, saying that they were just *'doing a job'*. In our eyes, as in millions of others, they are the true heroes in this world.

It is a privilege now to be a part of RAF 100 Group Association. To meet all these wonderful heroes is truly an honour.

Linda's husband Ian sadly died before he could attend the RAF 100 Group Association Reunion with Linda, now Committee Secretary Support.

Flt/Sgt James Hollingworth
Known details of the accident:
Date: 14th January 1945 (Sunday)
Unit: No. 11 O.T.U.
Type: Wellington X
Serial: LN403 Code: OP-V
Base: R.A.F. Westcott, Buckinghamshire.
Location: Wotton

- Pilot: Fl/Lt Herbert Tricks DFM 169063 RAFVR. Age 32. Killed
- Pilot 2: Fl/Sgt Norman Steventon Shaw NZ4213940 RNZAF. Age 30. Killed
- Nav/W/Op: Sgt Leslie John Tarr 1605916 RAFVR. Age? Killed
- Air/Bmr: Fl/Sgt Harold Arthur Purvey 1578843 RAFVR Age 27. Killed

- (1) W/Op/Air/Gnr: Fl/Sgt Bertram Leslie Ireland NZ432207 RNZAF. Age 33. Killed
- **W/Op/Air Gnr: Flt/Sgt James Hollingworth 1132602 RAFVR. Age? Killed**
- Air/Gnr: Sgt Brown. No further details Survived, injured.
- Air/Gnr: Sgt Dickie. No further details Survived, injured.

Reason for Loss:

Took off from RAF Westcott at 13.35 hours on a simple flying practice operation. On approach to runway No. 7 the Wellington was seen to turn away and then crash at 16.44 hours near Wotton Underwood Railway Station, about eight miles north north west of Aylesbury. Amazing that two Air Gunners escaped from the inferno with only slight injuries. The pilot, Flight Lieutenant Tricks, gained his DFM in the Middle East serving with 148 Squadron. In a statement regarding the accident Sgt Dickie wrote he was of the opinion that the controls had jammed.

Uncle Jimmy didn't die at the site, he was taken to hospital at Aylesbury, my heart aches at the thought of his agony, being transported along those country lanes. My Grandma and Auntie Mary were notified of his condition and, on preparing to travel there, were visited by Auntie Mary's close friend (my Godmother, Auntie Alice) who emptied her purse on the table to help them pay to get there. Taken to his bedside, he was swathed in bandages and only able to acknowledge their presence with a murmur. I can only pray that adequate doses of Morphine were administered. Uncle Jimmy passed away two days after the accident, 16 January 1945.

My Dad recalls two young airmen attending the funeral, their hands shaking while smoking their cigarettes. The funeral procession walked the short distance from the house to the Church. I pass the house each time I visit his grave, remembering going there each Sunday as a child, looking at the framed picture of Uncle Jimmy on the wall, asking about him, but just being told his name and very little else.

Now in May each year at RAF 100 Group Association Reunions in Norfolk, many are the stories shared by John Gilpin and Gerhard as we sit around the Hotel dinner table on a Saturday evening. My father, Hugh, is firmly at John's side, still hardly able to believe that, after all these years, finally he is talking to someone who shared life with his brother Jimmy, and knew and loved him as a very dear friend.

Pilot Officer Peter Anthony Witts, Air Gunner

Peter Witts is believed to be the only veteran to serve in three separate Squadrons under RAF No. 100 Group – No. 214, No. 223 and No. 462 Squadron, RAAF; commissioned as a Pilot Officer after the war.

At the age of seventeen, my father volunteered and served in World War One – Royal Warwickshire Regiment. I was his firstborn on 4 July 1925 at Woolacombe, North Devon. In 1935, aged ten, I sat and passed my Scholarship. My parents couldn't afford to send me to Grammar School so aged eleven, I was sent to Ilfracombe Elementary School where I managed to attain 'top of the class' in 'A' Form for each year. I was still at school when World War Two was declared – hoping to take an exam for Boy Entrants into the RAF. However, the Boy Entrants Scheme was discontinued, so I left school at Christmas 1939 aged fourteen.

Some months later, the Air Training Corps was formed and I enrolled aged fifteen, in Ilfracombe Grammar School 722 Squadron. I sat for and passed the Aircrew Proficiency Exam aged sixteen for Pilot/Observer, and aged seventeen and three quarters was accepted by the RAF for Aircrew Training – the first cadet from 722 Squadron to wear 'white flash' which marked aircrew acceptance by the RAF. I had passed my Flying Medical and Educational Requirement Examinations – the RAF had automatically assumed I was Grammar School-educated, because my ATC Proficiency Certificate was date-stamped: '722 Ilfracombe Grammar School Squadron'. So now the RAF Aircrew Training School had an Elementary Schoolboy who left school at fourteen in their midst, and they didn't even know it!

I was posted to a Preliminary Air Crew Training Course in April 1943, then on to No. 6 I.T.W Aberystwyth and No. 29 E.F.T.S for flying on Tiger Moths and eventually to 'Aircrew Dispatch Centre' at Heaten Park-Manchester to be posted abroad to continue flying training.

The Training Scheme I had been selected for was P.N.B – Pilot, Navigator, Bomb Aimer. However, whilst at A.C.D.C, P.N.B Trainees were being approached by the RAF through the Commanding Officer to re-muster to 'Straight A.G' (Air-Gunner), having a desperate need for that category of Aircrew. Whilst most P.N.B chaps firmly resisted these approaches, a small number succumbed to cajoling and persuasion, and the offer of immediate Leave, eventually finding themselves posted to No. 10 Advanced Gunnery School – I was one of that small number, mainly because my best friend, a Scotsman, seemed fascinated by the idea ... or then again, was it the Leave? At the end of ten weeks at A.G.S we were awarded our Wings. I had achieved the top air-firing score at A.G.S. A number of us who had scored well in Air-Firing were then posted straight away to an Operational Squadron, in my case 223 Squadron, 100 Group; while the remainder went on Leave before being posted to an Operational Training Unit (O.T.U).

So, here we were, on Saturday, at RAF Oulton, 100 Group, as Air Gunners on 223 Bomber Command Special Duties, an Electronic Warfare Operations Squadron, having only the day before been awarded our Air Gunner's Wings at Air Gunners' School! The Squadron Gunnery Leader, being somewhat perplexed at learning that we had only been trained on Boulton-Paul, Bristol, Frazer-Nash gun turrets and .303 Browning Machine Guns, ordered an immediate crash course on Emerson-Electric and Consolidated (American) Turrets and .5 Browning Machine Guns with which those turrets were fitted and we would be operating on 223 Squadron's B-24 Liberators. The crash course consisted of only a couple of hours 'familiarisation' on the ground as we were to become operational immediately!

We were assigned to various crews and introduced to our Skippers. Les Matthews and I were to fly in Flight Lieutenant Stan Woodward's (DFM) crew. Les to fly Rear-Gunner while I was given the Nose Turret. My dear friend, Les Matthews, is the artist who went on to paint the '100 Group Set out to Confound' picture which hangs proud in the City of Norwich Aviation Museum, and who I would meet each year at our RAF 100 Group Association Reunions.

The Emerson Turret in the nose was very small, even for me, and I'm very small and slight! It was so small it meant I had to operate the '*clocking levers*' to cock the guns by leaning into the turret before clambering in, praying each time we didn't have a gun-stoppage! I couldn't even close and secure the turret doors after me – a courtesy supplied by the Navigator or Bomb Airmer once I was installed behind the guns in the turret and to whom I'd hand my parachute for safe keeping. No room for your parachute in the turret! (*More prayers*). Training was fun, but oh dear, what have I done? Please God keep me safe, were my prayers now.

In November 1944, it became operational policy to remove the guns from the front turret of the Liberators on 223 Squadron and black out the turret, while more new electronic equipment was installed in the nose of the Liberator, designed for operational jamming of the Luftwaffe Fighter Squadrons and German Anti-Aircraft Gun Batteries. On a personal level, this meant, along with all the other Front Gunners in 223 Squadron, we became redundant.

We were all transferred to 1699 Flight to await re-crewing. However, I was immediately assigned to Flight Lieutenant Allies' crew to fly as Mid-Upper Gunner on Flying Fortresses (B-17s) with 214 Squadron. Flight Lieutent Allies, who had been a Flying Instructor on a Training Station in Canada, had been posted back to England for reasons best known to the RAF Authorities and which he kept to himself. It meant he was yet un-bloodied in the heat of battle: ie he had never skippered a bomber crew, nor flown an operation over enemy territory. This became painfully apparent from the manner in which he spoke to and treated his crew. We were all, without exception, battle-hardened and operationally experienced. It was an unhappy crew – and that, for me, spelled disaster! After flying with Stan Woodward (DFC, DFM) and his crew I had experienced the tight bond of brotherhood that existed between all members of an operational bomber crew whose very survival depended on each man recognising his responsibility to every other man in his crew. We were a tightly-knit family.

After some weeks of flying with Flight Lieutenant Allies and, more specifically, after one particular flight; I determined to acquaint the Squadron Gunnery Leader with my apprehensions and asked to be removed from Flt/Lt Allies crew and posted to another Squadron ... *anywhere!* My request was immediately granted. (This was in accordance with aircrew's accepted rights.) Within a few days, I was asked if I would accept a posting to RAF Foulsham (also in Norfolk, about ten miles away, and under 100 Group) to fly as Rear Gunner on Halifax Bombers with 462 Royal Australian Air Force Squadron (the only Bomber Squadron in 100 Group to be granted special dispensation to carry a bomb-load and bomb as well as carry out the electonic nature of 100 Group's operations).

I remember, on arrival at the Guard Room gates at RAF Foulsham, enquiring of the Warrant Officer on duty: '*What's 462's Chop-Rate?*' knowing only too well many stories of the devil-may-care attitude and uninhibited derry-do of our ANZAC cousins. The reply to my '*by the way*' enquiry was a shrug of the shoulders and somewhat non-commital.

The next morning, I was introduced to my Australian Skipper (Flt Lt Bruce Drinkwater), now MBE; who may well have reflected that he would have a boy, a country yokel (Bruce was nine years older than me at twenty-seven, almost half as old again as me!) to represent the '*sting in the tail*'. However, he welcomed me warmly with: '*Peter, welcome aboard. You can call me Bruce. Let's meet the rest of the crew.*' We had a Canadian Bomb Aimer and a Southern Irish Mid-Upper Gunner and, as time would prove, what a family of big brothers to go to war with! They were all quite a bit older than me, so I was regarded as baby brother!

I was happy (*as happy as one can be under the circumstances, anyway*) to be flying again in a Gun Turret (a Boulton & Paul) with four .303 Browning Machine Guns to play with and in a British four-engined Bomber. After all, times change, circumstances change, but feelings, however whimsical, in pursuit of security and survival; remain tireless – a warrior, if called upon to do battle, would take comfort that he would ride to hell and hopefully back, on a faithful and trusted steed. Those were my feelings, engendered by tools with which I was familiar and workmates who could be relied upon.

I should admit that I felt a great sense of pride to be flying as a Rear Gunner in a Royal Australian Air Force Bomber Squadron. My Skipper, Flt Lt Bruce Drinkwater, was second to none and like a father to me. He had mastery of every situation and, for me at any rate, guaranteed our survival through thick and thin. Our crew were a wonderful family – a true band of brothers – and we flew together till and after the end of the war when, if the Japanese had not surrendered in August 1945, I would have volunteered to return to Australia with my Skipper and continued to fly as his *'sting in the tail'* in the Pacific war against the Japanese.

FOOTNOTE: On the night of 23 March 1945, Flt Lt Allies' crew, flying 'P' Peter B-17 (214 Squadron) were shot down over Germany – *all killed*! My premonitions of disaster were not without foundation. I lost many good friends with whom I had flown and four Air Gunner comrades with whom I had trained.

Of all the Air Gunners who originally flew with 223 Squadron and were transferred when the front turret was re-assigned, I was the only one to survive the war. The rest were all shot down and killed-in-action! This was a fact revealed to me by Squadron Leader Richard Forder, 100 Group and 223 Squadron Historian.

Per Ardua Ad Astra
'Through adversity to the stars'
The Skipper, My Skipper, Then and Now

Fly on Skipper – just keep flying
Banish any thoughts of dying.
With every tack I'm at your back
(and so's our crew).
Keep pressing on as we used to do.
We knew the score: *'been here before'*,
Time was when we danced to a war-time medley,
Flak was thicker then, so much more deadly.
Then tomorrow was a fifty-fifty bet,
Our chances, now, much better set.
Our Squadron's Motto: *'Brave and True'*,

So fly on Skipper – it's what men do!
Sixty-five years on, we still face the fray
And fight to live another day.
Through life's long struggle we've both been blessed
With family, friends – the very best!
Through conflict, hardship and disaster
We've triumphed – 'Per Ardua Ad Astra'!
So fly on, Skipper, brave and true,
And know, please God, I'm still with you.

By P/O Peter Witts

Peter died on 12 November 2011, but leaves a legacy of poetry and writings, together with an RAF 100 Group Standard which he designed and donated to the Association. He is remembered by all as a true gentleman, well known, well loved ... missed by his family and all who knew him ... in our hearts always, a Legend.

JOHN HEREFORD
Special Operator: 214, 101 and 219 Squadrons

John Hereford was a German brought up in the Jewish faith. During the Second World War he completed a full tour in bombers over Germany as a Wireless Operator, disrupting the Luftwaffe's night fighter operations by jamming their control frequencies.

Hereford was a member of a small group of aircrew known as 'Spec Ops' (Special Operators). Of this group, a number were Jews, some of them from Germany. They flew as the eighth member of a bomber crew occupying a screened-off, lonely and unheated position in the rear of the aircraft where they used specialised and highly secret radio equipment. Many of these Spec Ops never made it home.

Flying in the main bomber stream, Spec Ops tracked the Germans' VHF communications between the night fighter Controllers and their pilots. Using a three-stage jammer, code-named ABC (*Airborne Cigar*), the Operator tuned his own receiver over those most frequently used by German Controllers. As soon as one was identified, the Spec Op set his ABC to the same frequency, and emitted electronic '*noises*' to render the Controller's instructions unintelligible. The Spec Op then followed the Controller as he tried to communicate on another frequency and the jamming process would begin again. On a few occasions the Spec Op would broadcast false instructions to the enemy pilots.

ABC JAMMING
One Man's View

On arrival, the first thing was a few days introduction to the equipment we were to operate. It went under the codename 'ABC', ('*Airborne Cigar*'). I have no idea why they named it that. It consisted of three enormously powerful transmitters covering the radio voice bands used by the Luftwaffe.

To help identify the place to jam, there was a panoramic receiver covering the same bands. The receiver scanned up and down the bands at high speed, the result of its travel shown on a time-base calibrated across a cathode ray tube in front of the Operator. If there was any traffic on the band it showed as a '*blip*' at the appropriate frequency along the line of light that was the time-base. When a '*blip*' appeared, one could immediately spot-tune the receiver to it and listen to the transmission. If the language was German, then it only took a moment to swing the first of the transmitters to the same frequency, press a switch, and leave a powerful jamming warble to prevent the underlying voice being heard. The other two transmitters could then be brought in on other '*blips*'. If twenty-four aircraft were flying, spread through the Bomber stream, there were a potential seventy-two loud jamming transmissions blotting out the night fighters' directions.

The Germans tried all manner of devices to overcome the jamming, including having their instructions sung by Wagnerian sopranos! This was meant to fool our Operators into believing it was just a civilian channel and not worth jamming. I think ABC probably did a useful job, but who can say what difference it made in the long run?

In truth, the role of these specialists made a major contribution to defeating the formidable German night fighter organisation.

John Hereford first flew on Stirlings and Flying Fortresses with No. 214 Squadron in the bomber support role. In addition to jamming enemy radio frequencies, 'WINDOW' (small strips of metal foil) was dropped to jam the German early-warning radars.

After ten operations over Germany and in support of the Allied land-ings in Normandy, Hereford transferred to No. 101 Squadron operating the Lancaster. This Squadron specialised in the ABC role, and Hereford flew a further twenty-one operations during intense night bombing operations over Germany before he was rested early in 1945.

No. 101 suffered the highest casualties of any RAF Squadron, and it wasn't until the war was over that it was learned the Germans had perfected a tech-nique to home in on the Lancaster's transmissions. The Jewish Spec Ops flew in the full knowledge of the high casualty rate, and the fate of some who were shot down still, to this day, remains unknown.

The son of a lawyer, John Hereford was born Joachim Hayman Herzog at Wilmersdorf, Berlin, on 3 May 1925. His parents fled to England in 1933 and Joachim was educated at Sevenoaks School in Birmingham. In 1943, at the age of 17, he joined the RAF, volunteering for flying duties and changing his name to what he considered the nearest sounding English equivalent, John Hereford.

At the end of the war Hereford was sent to Germany with the Air Disarmament Wing and spent many months at the Hermann Goering Research Institute for Aeronautics at Volkenrode, near Braunschweig.

He acted as an Interpreter and Analyst for 'Operation Surgeon', the collec-tion of monographs and debriefings from German scientists about their research work. This was followed by the selection and removal to Britain of equipment thought to be most valuable. Hereford also monitored German telephone calls, and was intrigued by the number of messages that ended with 'acht und achtzig'. When he married up the numbers (88) to the letters of the alphabet, he realised the senders were actually signing off 'HH' – Heil Hitler. His discovery led to the arrest of a number of senior Nazis who might otherwise have escaped.

During his time at Volkenrode, Hereford fell in love with and married a leading ballerina; the blonde, blue-eyed Ursula Vaupel had danced for, and been introduced to Hitler in Berlin. At the end of the war, she had fled bare-foot as the Soviet Army advanced on her devastated city. Despite her ragged appearance, a fellow railway passenger recognised her and produced a photograph of her from his wallet.

Hereford left the RAF as a Warrant Officer in June 1947 to settle in London. He decided to make a career in the hotel business, learning his trade from the kitchens up. Starting at the Waldorf, he spent several weeks as the oyster-opener, becoming one of the youngest General Managers in London, taking over the running of the Southway Hotel in Victoria.

It was as Sales Director at Associated Hotels that Hereford became a pioneer of hotel sales and marketing in Britain. The now well-established mini, midi or maxi weekend breaks stemmed from his marketing initiatives. Following his success with Associated, Hereford never had to apply for a job; he was always being head-hunted. The Barclay brothers, Grand Metropolitan and Utel all made use of his marketing skills.

He became Chairman of the Hotel Industry Marketing Group, and in 1980 joined the Securicor Group as Sales Director, shortly afterwards becoming Managing Director of the Group's hotel business based at the Richmond Hill Hotel. With his protégé, Nigel Messenger, he expanded the Group with hotels in the Midlands and Scotland.

Hereford's colleagues put his success down to his fearlessness when dealing with the machinations of Senior Executives, as well as his skills as a Manager. He was greatly respected by his staff, whom he treated as equals whatever their positions.

In retirement, Hereford was Chairman of the Residents' Association at Sheldwich, Kent, and he remained a sought-after Consultant in the hotel business. A sociable man, he was always in demand at local parties. He played tennis into his sixties and continued to enjoy swimming. John Hereford's wife died in 2004, and he is survived by their three daughters.

George '*Ginger*' Fisher
We'll Meet Again

As I write this, it is thirty-six years since Joe, Mac, Frank, Lofty, Bill, Alan, Jim, Jock 'A', Jock 'B' and I climbed in a Boeing B-17G, HB795, to undertake our last flight together in a Flying Fortress. Since the beginning of May 1945 we had flown together in fifteen such aircraft totalling in time ninety-two hours. That last flight on 24 July 1945, was not a particularly spectacular one, just local flying. In no way could it compare with a flight undertaken ten years previously in the United States of America.

I was just a boy still at school while Seattle, the largest city of Washington State in the North Western corner of the United States, was home to Boeing – the aircraft people. It was here in July, 1935, that the Boeing design Model 299 flew. This all-metal four-engine mono-plane, designed specifically as a heavy bomber with its heavy gun emplacements and weighting up to fifteen tons was aptly called by the press: 'Flying Fortress'. A name that will long be remembered.

On 31 July 1940, the Royal Air Force opened a flying field at Oulton near Aylsham, Norfolk. From that day and throughout the war from this airfield many operations were mounted against the enemy.

In May 1944, after a period of major surgery to the runways, the building of extra hangers and expansion of living accommodation – 214 Squadron flying B-17s moved in. The Squadron undertook radar counter-measure operations until it disbanded on 29 July 1945.

A 214 Squadron pilot of that time, Murray Peden, wrote a book: 'A thousand Shall Fall' in which he describes life as it was then at Oulton. Today, little remains of the airfield where happiness, pathos and courage were inextricably mixed. Perhaps in years to come, people will visit such places. Maybe they will find an overgrown hardstand, a desolate shell of a flying Control Tower or part of a runway to remind them of its history. No way will it match the splendour of the nearby red rustic pinnacled Hall of Blickling – today maintained by the National Trust. Legend has it Anne Boleyn spent some time there. When I visited some summers ago, my memory could only recall days spent in the lake doing dinghy survival drill. One thing is certain, people today will never be able to appreciate the thrill of having been around when it all happened.

In 1968, there was a semi-reunion of our crew. Present were George, Mac, Joe, Frank and Jeff. In 1978, I started tracing the rest of the crew and by 1983 had managed to make contact with them all.

This is a story in itself!

In July 1945, Joe, Mac, Frank, Jock, Jeff, Lofty, Archie, Jim, Bill and I were ten little Fortress boys at RAF Oulton, Norfolk, but not for long because, by the end of the month, the Squadron disbanded and we were scattered on postings to RAF stations around the world.

It was while reading a book published earlier that year, I came upon a photograph of a Fortress aircraft. The book, by Martin Streetly, *Confound & Destroy – 100 Group the Bomber Support Campaign*, showed the aircraft, Fortress BIII KJ109-6G-F of 223 (RCM) Squadron. On 3 May 1945, it was in this aircraft, then BZ-C of No. 1699 BSTU, that Joe and his boys flew their first flight. Before service with 1699 BSTU, KJ109 was on the strength of 214 (RCM) Squadron, where it had been used on radar counter-measure operations over Germany. This unexpected discovery set the nostalgia adrenalin going, and awakened my urge to find the missing members of my crew.

The question uppermost was where to begin. Frank, in business trips around the country, had called at last known addresses to be told that the birds had flown. Mac's contacts had dried up years previous. Telephone directory enquiries could not help. *Where to start?* IBM inspired me with one word: '*Think*'.

Bill, I recalled, had told me his father was a policeman in the Liverpool Force. My letter to the Chief Constable of Liverpool was acknowledged. Shortly afterwards I heard from Bill. In his letter he informed me that my letter had been handed to him by his son, a Liverpool policeman.

Tracing Jock was reasonably easy when I remembered he graduated with an MA from Aberdeen University in 1944. The Uni confirmed this and also supplied his present address in Blairgowrie.

Despite further efforts during the next five years, the trail to Archie, Jim and Lofty went cold.

In the summer of 1963, I was fortunate to meet a reporter with the Reading Chronicle. By coincidence he also had undertaken a similar exercise and understood my difficulties. At his suggestion I wrote to the *Shrewsbury Chronicle* telling my story of the search for

Jim, also to the *Wallsend and South Shields Gazette* in regard to Lofty. Archie is another story.

Within two weeks, Jim wrote to say that, while away on holiday, an old neighbour from the area where he lived previously read my letter in the *Chronicle* and put a copy through his door. Delighted with my success, I wrote to the *Shrewsbury Chronicle* to thank them for their help. To my surprise, a *Chronicle* reporter telephoned to obtain a *'human story'*, and S – for Sugar Crew Reunion – thanks to the *Chronicle* were the front page headlines that greeted readers of the next edition, along with a photograph of Jim and a 1945 copy of the crew.

Jim's letter came in the morning post. Before the day was through, I knew I had found Lofty. In the afternoon post, a letter arrived from his cousin. She didn't know his address, but gave the address of another cousin who lived in a nearby town and thus I established that Lofty occupied a lighthouse off the coast of Queensland, Australia.

At the time I was making enquiries about him, Lofty had attended a very special Reunion. He informed me that, when he left the RAF, he joined the RAAF and enclosed with his letter was a cutting from the *Brisbane Sunday Mail* which reported his RAAF Crew Reunion.

Flushed with success, I was now determined to find Archie. Jim joined me and enlisted the aid of an advertising connection to run an enquiry in the Glasgow press. But … *no Archie!* So I put an entry in the Royal Air Force Association calling old colleagues. Two months passed – no response, so that was it. Call off the search, close the hangar doors, finish!

Then:

'Hello George, Ginger.'

What a wonderful surprise!

'Your advert reached me through the following sequence. Lady, not known, showed the magazine to a colleague at work who lived in Glasgow. She in turn showed it to her husband, an old school pal of mine. He didn't know my address, but was in touch with a mutual friend in Leeds who did …'

I had found Archie!

Fact is often better than fiction, especially since I left Glasgow thirty-three years ago to live in Yorkshire. Archie's letter came from Berwick-upon-Tweed. My case now rests. Bill is in the Philippines. Mac is in Windsor. Jeff is still in his home town of Rickmansworth; likewise Frank is in Stoke-on-Trent. Despite all my wanderings, by chance, I am still living in my home town of Reading. Perhaps one day we shall meet again, but sadly it will not be the ten of us as in May 1983 the reaper struck and Joe was taken from us.

December 1944, I believe, will best be remembered as the month in which the Germans flung all their might into the Ardennes offensive to be stopped by the heroic stand of the Americans at the Battle of the Bulge. That cold snow-ridden month I stood in a group of Navigators, along with Pilots, Wireless Operators and Air Gunners in a large drill hall. RAF Desborough, Northamptonshire, was a Wellington Operational Training Unit in Bomber Command. We were assembled that December morning to form crews among ourselves. Suddenly, before I had time to make a choice, a smiling Pilot Joe, with a Gunner Mac, stood before me with the question:
   'Will you be our Navigator?'
   This is when my story began.

Tales from George's Scrapbook/Box

In June 1942, my friend Geoffrey Danby and I had a conversation with a Clerk from Aircrew Records Office, RAF Reading. I enquired of the Clerk if I could join the RAF with Geoffrey in August 1942. 'Yes', he replied. 'But I can only mis-file your July 1942 Entry Card in Geoffrey's August 1942 box'. So Geoffrey and I went our separate ways into the RAF in 1942.

Herewith is my 'What If' and 'How One Thing Leads to Another', article:

What If?

On the night of 22 June 1944, Halifax LW656 MP-B of 76 Squadron, RAF Holme, crashed in France as a result of enemy action. All seven of the crew were killed and all are buried in France. A friend of mine, Geoffrey Danby, was the Navigator.

Two years earlier, in June 1942, Geoffrey and I were two trainee Observers waiting to report to Aircrew Receiving Centre, Lord's Cricket Ground. I was due to report in July and Geoffrey in August. Since joining the RAF, we had been sent to Ludlow, Aberystwyth and Brighton and the Observer trade had been reclassified as Navigator, Navigator Bomber, Navigator Wireless, etc. At ITW, Geoffrey opted for Navigator Wireless, and I for Navigator Bomber. Needless to say that, when our time to leave Brighton arrived, Geoffrey was posted a Navigator Bomber and I a Navigator Wireless. Somewhere along the line he became a Navigator.

On D-Day, I was on Leave in Reading, walking along the street. When I looked up I could see the armada of planes and gliders making their way to France. I said to myself: 'George, you have missed the war'. Little did I know then that within fourteen days, both my cousin and my good friend would be dead, killed on bomber operations.

After months of waiting in aircrew dispersal units and operational training in Bomber Command, on 6 June 1944 I was posted to 214 (RCM) Squadron, RAF Oulton as a Navigator on Flying Fortress aircraft. It was not until I left the RAF in 1946 that I learned of my friend's fate. What if I had gone to be a Navigator Bomber? What if I had joined up together with Geoffrey? Yes, what if?'

On the night of 24/25 May 1944, No. 214 Squadron suffered its first Fortress casualty when P/O Hockley RAAF was shot down on a patrol to Antwerp. It was on this flight that Special Duty Operator Lloyd Davis was a stand-in Operator. P/O Hockley stayed at the controls of the burning aircraft to give his crew the chance of baling out. In so doing, he forfeited his own life. All the crew, with the exception of the Pilot and Sgt Simpson; managed to parachute out and landed on one of the small Dutch islands in the North Sea. As the area was well guarded by Germans, they had no opportunity to evade capture and were quickly rounded up by the enemy. The aircraft was Fortress II SR384 BU-A.

Between November 1943 and April 1944 LAC George Fisher and LAC Alan Mercer were two Navigators, Wireless Operator Air Trainees Course No. 88A, No. 8 Air Observer School at L'Ancienne-Lorette, a city in central Quebec, Canada. Both graduated as Sergeant Navigator W/OPs in April 1944.

Posted back to the UK on 10 May 1944, we were together at No. 7 Receiving Centre, RAF Harrogate, until July 1944 when we were posted to other Units.

Between 10 August and 19 September 1944 I was stationed at No. 22 Aircrew Holding Unit RAF Kirkham.

Situated near Kirkham is the village of Freckleton. Not keen on drinking NAAFI tea, a few of us at morning tea-break would race down to the 'Sad Sack' Café in the village for our morning cuppa.

Freckletonians will never forget what happened on the morning of 23 August 1944.

It was a Wednesday. The bright morning sunshine suddenly vanished as the sky darkened and a ferocious thunderstorm struck the village. A four-engine Liberator bomber aircraft of the USA undergoing an air-test flight from nearby Warton airfield was immediately recalled. On its descent to the airfield, it was struck by lightning and crashed onto the 'Sad Sack' café. Some adjoining cottages and part of the wing and undercarriage continued across the road into the village school where morning classes were in session. In the school, thirty-eight school children and two teachers died. Two civilians and seven USA personnel were killed in the café, also two RAF Sergeants (Pilot & Navigator) were killed. Among my colleagues who were having morning tea, two RAF Sergeants (Navigators) died of wounds sustained and two other Sergeants (Navigators) survived having suffered serious wounds. In the village, seven civilians died. The Pilot and Engineer of the Liberator died. That night, two beds in my hut were empty.

Because I hate getting wet, that fateful morning I stayed on camp and had tea in the NAAFI!

On a Sunday afternoon years later, I had a telephone call from the Secretary of the then Thames Valley Branch of Aircrew Association. He'd had a request from a Bournmouth member who wanted my address. The person in question was none other than Alan Mercer who had seen my name on the article: 'I Hate Getting Wet!' published in the Aircrew Association's magazine 'Intercom'.

In conversation, he informed me he'd been posted to RAF Kirkham. On the day of the crash he was away on a Course. Also, I learnt that for about six weeks he was posted to 214 (RCM) Squadron where he undertook three operations RCM. Probably because of the bicycle accident, our paths did not cross. However, we did meet some years later when I called on him at his Dorset home. At this meeting we decided to search for the other trainees of Course 88A No. 8 Air Observer School, L'Ancienne-Lorette. As a result of this search, of thirty-seven successful graduates, we traced twelve alive; six had died, despite our efforts, nineteen gone away, not known, and no trace. Alan arranged a Reunion at his home at which seven of us turned up fifty years on.

I was saddened later to learn of Alan's death in the USA. To my knowledge, of the Magnificent 7, only three survive as I write this.

During the brief period of time I had at No. 1699 BSTU and No. 214 (RCM) Squadron, RAF Oulton, 3 May 1945 – 27 July 1945, I undertook several Ruhr Tour trips and two and a half Post-Mortem Operations. I shall never forget seeing the terrible destruction wrought upon Germany by Bomber Command. Cologne, towns and cities in the Ruhr Valley, Essen/Krupps and two trips to Hamburg. War no matter how GOOD the reason, has terrible terrible consequences.

Will they never learn!

On take-off, my position would be to stand behind the Pilot. However, there was the occasion when, on a circuit and landing trip, I sat in the Navigator's compartment.

At point of take-off, the port engine of the Fortress cut … instead of up, up and away it was walk about across the airfield, blood wagon to left and crash truck to right of us. As I watched with interest our predicament, I said to myself: '*I wonder what is going to happen next?*' Fortunately the aircraft stopped just over the perimeter fence, its nose overlooking the Norwich/Aylsham railway. If the aircraft had travelled further, it would not have been a case of '*Atlas carries the world on his shoulders*' but '*George carries a Fortress on his shoulders*'. As the old wag told me at O.T.U: '*you don't have to go on Operations, George, to get killed!*' How true!

No. 214 (RCM) Squadron disbanded on 27 July 1945. I spent three months in Aircrew Holding Units then on to Heavy Conversion Unit, Transport Command, where I had a choice of aircraft – Liberator or Avro York. Because of my Fortress experience I opted for Liberator.

Posted to No. 206 Squadron, RAF Oakington, I flew on the Curry Run India UK carrying goods and service personnel.

On 6 March, after a flight lasting nine and a half hours from Karachi to Aden, the Pilot had he landed according to the book, who knows if there could have been on the runway – five crew and thirty-two passengers, together with thirty-seven '*Walkers Crispy Potato Crisps*'?

My memory of seeing the Engineer's dip stick after dipping the four tanks means we had been flying on empty!

W/O Alan Mercer, Navigator
by Sgt Len White, Port Waist Gunner

Alan was born on 3 August 1924. He grew up in the Hammersmith area of London. On taking up employment, he worked for the then GPO telephones until 1942, when, as a volunteer, he enlisted in the RAF. He received training in this country and Canada, where he qualified as a Navigator in 1944. Returning to the UK, he was posted in November of that year to No. 11 Operational Training Unit at Westcott, Bucks. There he was crewed up with:

- F/O Ken Kennet (Pilot),
- F/O '*Lofty*' Baumfield (NZ) (Bomb Aimer),
- F/Sgt Steve Spregg (W/Op),
- Sgt '*Duke*' Maddox (NZ) (Rear Gunner),
- Sgt '*Curly*' Herlihy (NZ) (Mid Upper Gunner).

About three months later, after training, they qualified as a bomber crew.

At the end of the course at O.T.U. they were posted to a Special Duty Squadron, 214 (FMS) in 100 Group, based at RAF Oulton, Norfolk. On the journey by road transport from a nearby railway station to Oulton they saw the scattered remains of a BM Flying Fortress shot down a few nights earlier by a German fighter intruder aircraft. Eight of the crew had been killed in the incident. In 1994, Alan was to meet an Air Gunner, one of the survivors, at either a 214 Squadron or 100 Group Association Reunion.

On arrival at RAF Oulton, Alan and his O.T.U. crew were increased by:

- Sgt '*Smithy*' Smith (Flight Engineer),
- PO '*Olly*' Green (Special Radar Operator),
- Sgt Freddy Langhorn (Starboard Waist Gunner).

Steve Spregg, then about thirty years of age, was the oldest member of the crew and had previously completed a tour of operations in the Middle East. Ken Kennett, the Pilot, a former Flying Instructor, was about twenty-four, whilst the majority of the others were twenty to twenty-two, with the exception of the two Waist Gunners who were nineteen years of age.

The crew then spent four weeks at 1699 Heavy Conversion Unit, also at Oulton, getting accustomed to the B-17 Flying Fortress, doing such things as cross country exercises, bulls-eyes, air firing, fighter affiliation, etc. in readiness for operations with 214 Squadron.

In early April 1945, the crew became operational with 214 Squadron. While the European War was nearing its end, regretfully, Bomber Command aircraft were still being destroyed. Alan and the other NCOs in his crew shared a Nissen Hut with similar rank members of two other crews. One of these crews failed to return one night and their belongings were removed next day. This obviously brought home realisation of the dangers still involved, even at that late stage of the European War.

The first operation by the crew was a WINDOW dropping raid to Schleswig Holstein. The object was to jam and mislead German radar, and by using WINDOW, to spoof the Germans into believing a heavy force was making for a certain target, thus detracting their fighter defences away from the main bomber force who were en route elsewhere.

Flying at 22,000 feet on this particular night, vapour trails were observed and, as RAF aircraft were flying at staggered intervals about twenty miles or so behind each other, the trails appeared to indicate fighter activity. This was followed by searchlight activity involving the Fortress, causing the Pilot to corkscrew for quite a few minutes to evade searchlights and possible enemy fighters. Corkscrewing in a BM involved very severe movements with resulting 'G' effects and was not at all pleasant. In fact, so violent were the movements that, for the first and only time in his life, Alan was airsick. He was not alone! No doubt bacon and eggs before the flight had also helped unsettle their stomachs. Luckily, Alan was sick over a spare chart, so the operation was able to continue. It was later learned from Intelligence that fighters had taken off to attack the spoof raid.

The second op was a similar mission, disturbed in flight over Germany by a burst of gunfire from the mid-upper turret. The Pilot reduced height quickly, only to receive an apology over the intercom from *Curly*, the Mid-Upper Gunner, who stated he had caught his parachute harness in the gun triggers, which didn't have trigger guards. The operation was resumed and again carried out successfully. On this occasion, odd sights of flames were observed by the Gunners. These appeared to be connected with fighter aircraft and subsequently confirmed by Intelligence as being German jet aircraft.

The crew were ready at dispersal on another occasion for operations, but were not called on to fly.

The third and last operation for Alan was on 2 May 1945 (the last Bomber Command Raid over Europe). This was carried out without incident over Germany. But as the aircraft was about to land at Oulton, Alan, standing in his take-off and landing position behind the Pilot, saw exhaust flames of a plane crossing in front of the B-17 slightly above, some twenty to thirty feet away. Thoughts immediately went to the wreckage seen on arrival at the Station, shot down by an intruder hidden within returning aircraft. Ken Kennett, the Pilot, immediately reacted to it being an enemy aircraft, putting the nose down rather quicker than normal, to get on the runway and avoid a disaster.

Whilst waiting at dispersal for an hour before take-off on operations, there was obvious, though hidden tenseness. On one such occasion, a burst of gunfire came from the waist of one aircraft. It transpired that a Waist Gunner had left his gun strap on the gun trigger. The result was that, when the aircraft engines started, the vibrations which became considerable, caused the gun to swing round, tightening the strap on the trigger and firing it. This caused comments and laughter, thus relieving some of the tension build-up.

V.E Day Celebrations followed a few days after, resulting in a few sore heads, including Alan's next day.

Flying duties following this included taking members of ground staff on tours over Germany to see the effects of Bomber Command activities, being involved in two exercises to give experts and technicians opportunities to assess the quality and efficiency of German radar installations and equipment. Other duties consisted of air tests, fighter affiliation, and disposing of surplus ammunition and equipment over the North Sea and Wash.

On one of these air tests, *Curly*, the Mid-Upper Gunner, after firing a burst with his .5 Brownings, went against regulations and turned his guns towards the rear. Consequently, a round in one gun cooked in the hot breech, hitting his own aircraft about a foot above the Rear Gunner's head. Luckily no controls were damaged and the Pilot was able to land safely. Needless to say, feelings between the Mid-Upper and Rear-Gunner were very frosty for a few days.

Another incident involving Alan and the crew was on an air test when a lot of smoke came from one of the installations in the bomb bay, where radar jamming equipment was carried, indicating a fire of some sort. This was put out by extinguishers and the aircraft landed safely. This much to the joy of two crew members who, against all regulations, had gone on the test without their parachutes.

Much has been written about the merits of different aircraft. Alan and his fellow crew members had no experience of the Lancaster, but on one occasion when returning from a North Sea trip, a Lancaster came alongside the Fortress. After the exchange of 'V' signals, etc. the Lancaster shut off one engine and began to pull away. Ken Kennett pushed the Fortress throttles as far as possible, despite which the Lancaster, on three engines, continued to leave the Fortress behind. All were impressed by the Lancaster.

The Squadron was disbanded in mid-1945, the New Zealand crew members returning home and the remaining crew posted to various other duties. Alan was posted to 570 Squadron, Transport Command, flying in Stirling aircraft mainly carrying items to troops in Germany. He was demobbed in 1946 as a Warrant Officer.

Although Alan's crew served together for a relatively short period of time, companionships and friendships were established which have carried on ever since. Two of the New Zealanders have visited England with wives and families, when visits to, and get-togethers with other crew members have taken place. In 1985, Alan and his wife travelled to New Zealand and visited the three crew members there.

Unfortunately, Olly Green was killed in January 1947 whilst on a joy ride in an aircraft that crashed. Freddie Langhorn died in August 1981. Steve Spregg about a year later. *Curly* Herlihy in November 1992. Duke Maddox in April 1993. Ken Kennett in June 1993. *Smithy* in March 1995. *Lofty* Baumfield in August 2000. Alan in June 2009, leaving one, Chalky White still alive. Despite crew members passing, a number of their families are still in contact with each other. The connections forged in war continue on.

On retirement from the RAF, Alan returned to employment with the GPO telephones, rising to Managerial posts on contracts involving the construction of new exchanges, etc. He married Pam in 1948 and they resided in West London until Alan's retirement when they moved to Hampshire. They had two daughters, two sons-in-law, six grandchildren, two step-grandchildren, and Alan was very proud to become a great grandfather in March 2009. Unfortunately, Pam pre-deceased him in November 2001. Alan was visiting one of his daughters in America and been proud to attend the Graduation of one of his grandsons. He was later taken ill, hospitalised, and sadly passed away on 6 June 2009.

A man from humble beginnings, who worked tirelessly to improve himself and provide high levels of comfort and opportunity for his family. A true friend, trusty crew member, loyal to his country and who had great pride in his RAF Service.

Air Gunner Norman Storey
On a Wing and a Prayer

I was born in August 1924 and enlisted in February 1943. I volunteered for Air Crew and went before the Selection Board to be asked what I wanted to be. I, like ninety-nine percent of others, answered the same question: '*Pilot*'. I was informed that there were no Pilot courses available. As I was good at maths, they suggested I train as a Navigator. This I refused and said I would like to go as an Air Gunner. It was then suggested I train as a Wireless Operator Air Gunner. Again I refused saying: '*If I can't go on a Pilot's course, I want to be an Air Gunner*' and that is how I joined '*The Suicide Club*'.

On being posted to St John's Wood and billeted in a commandeered luxury flat, I was jabbed several times and given 'doctored' tea to drink. I was like so many others, still fresh from inoculations and told by sadistic Corporals to swing our painful arms. We were marched to London Zoo for meals. Being treated like animals, I presumed the Powers-that-Be thought this appropriate!

From here, I was posted to I.T.W in Bridlington, and instructed by an Officer to have two haircuts in one day – an experience to stay with me for the rest of my life and my excuse for not wanting to visit the barber too often! After three weeks, I was posted north of the town, to E.A.G.S. where I was taught to strip and assemble a V.G.O and Browning blindfolded, basic lessons on Morse Code, signalling and clay pigeon shooting; just managing to resist shooting one of our Instructors. From here I was posted to 7 A.G.S Stormy Down in South Wales.

Time for further classroom instruction and an initiation into flying Whitleys with Polish pilots. Our task was to fire one hundred rounds at a drogue being towed by a Lysander. As I managed not to shoot the Lysander down, I was awarded my brevet and promoted to Sergeant.

My next posting was 30 O.T.U. where a large number of aircrew of all trades were assembled and told to form a crew. I was very friendly with another Air Gunner and we approached a Pilot, asking if he wanted an Air Gunner. His reply was 'Yes', but only one was required. I magnanimously said to my friend: 'All right, you stay with this Pilot and I will crew up with somebody else'. This gesture probably saved my life! I approached another Pilot and on asking if he was looking for an Air Gunner replied: 'Can you swim?' I replied 'Yes, I quite often did half a mile and mile swims'. It was only later I found the reason for this question. The Rear Gunner was in charge of the dinghy in the event of a ditching.

We were now a complete crew. The Pilot, Len Young from Leeds, slightly older than most and a Flying Instructor for two years, obviously an experienced Pilot. Slightly younger than Len, our Navigator Alf Shields from London, also experienced with ten ops on Blenheims. Our Bomb Aimer: George Hathaway from Birmingham was slightly younger. Our Wop/Ag Ron Gardener from Croydon was also younger, and finally myself, Rear Gunner from Westcliffe-on-Sea, the '*baby*' of the crew at eighteen years old.

On 24 June 1943, we started flying training on Wellingtons, circuits and bumps, cross- countries, bombing practice, firing practice, night flying and fighter affiliation. This latter exercise consisted of a Spitfire loaded with a camera trying to get us in his sights. Len and I were very proficient with this procedure and the Spitfire Pilot was unable to get us at any time, an exercise that was to stand us in good stead.

We finally completed our training at O.T.U.

Our last exercise was on 12 August when we were sent on a *Nickel* to Versailles dropping propaganda leaflets. No doubt with a shortage of paper, Germans put them to good use! Whilst there, we saw one Wellington crash on landing and burst into flames.

We were now posted to 1662 Con. Unit where Len had to familiarise with conversion to the four-engine Halifax and Lancaster, and we had two extra members join the crew – a Flight Engineer from London and Mid-Upper Gunner from Harrow-on-the-Hill.

Between 19 September and 22 October 1943, we flew various exercises. The time had come for us to join a Squadron and march off to war. We were posted to 103 Squadron at Elsham Wolds in Lincolnshire.

The crew arrived at a very small country Railway Station to be met with a warm welcome from a friendly WAAF driver. We piled into the back of a 15-cwt and on the way to the camp, Ron asked the driver about the Squadron and its losses. She said it was a very good Squadron with hardly any losses at all. She was kind and caring ... *and a bloody liar!*

On arrival, we were allocated a Nissen hut to ourselves. Next morning, we reported to our various leaders. This was a Lancaster Squadron. From 10 – 17 November we did a Cross Country and a couple of other exercises. But then, on the morning of 18 November, '*Ops were on!*' Len was down to go as a second dickey. When he informed us we all joked, promising we would think of him whilst knocking back pints in the Mess. After a while, he came back to us to say we were going as a crew. We thought he was joking! But he soon convinced us this was fact and, discussing it amongst ourselves, came to the conclusion it must be an 'easy' target to initiate a sprog crew.

It was 18 November 1943 – the first raid in the Battle of Berlin and the heaviest defended target in Germany. We were to go again on 22 and 23 November.

Our baptism – three raids on Berlin in 6 nights!

We were to do a further seven ops to Berlin, bringing our total to ten. The crew was now visited by a reporter from a Lincolnshire newspaper asking questions with a photograph taken of us with our aircraft – D-Dog (*I will go on to mention the photograph later*). We were never told the reason for this visit, but can only imagine it was for propaganda purposes and a moral boost for their readers.

During the winter of 1943–1944, losses were horrendous. Bomber Command wiped itself out – '*The Lost Command*'. When we had completed eleven ops, we were the leading crew on the Squadron. We'd been on all the heavy loss raids including a Berlin and a Leipzig raid when the losses of each reached well into the seventies. The Nuremburg raid when Bomber Command received its highest losses was about ninety-five aircraft. I remember on our return the interro-gating officer asked the usual question: '*How many aircraft do you think we lost tonight?*' My reply was: '*A hundred*'. He refused to accept my estimate and said: '*I am not entering that on this report!*' I said: '*That is up to you, Sir. But I am not changing my estimate.*' I often wonder what he thought the next morning when the newspaper headlines were 96 – 97 – 98 aircraft lost.

Soon we were to switch to French Targets in a softening-up programme ready for the invasion. In its wisdom, 'The Powers that Be' decided French targets would count only as a third of an Op. That was until the Mailly-le-Camp raid on 3 May 1944. Pre-war, this had been a French Military Camp, but now being used by Germans for tank training.

We were circling over two German Fighter aerodromes, waiting for instructions to bomb on the flares. It was absolute chaos. Pilots on RT were asking when we could go in to bomb. The reply was always the same: '*Don't bomb ... wait!*' Aircraft were being shot down all around us and our Skipper decided to go in on a bombing run. On the way in, the order was received to '*bomb on the flares*'. We must have been the first to bomb. We had an aiming-point photograph, later informed we had probably killed 200 Germans much to the delight of our Bomb Aimer who had recently lost his brother in Italy.

Forty-nine aircraft were lost, over eleven percent – similar percentage losses to the Nuremburg Raid.

We were allocated a hut to a crew and when Len was commissioned there was just the six of us. On returning from the raid, we found a young Air Gunner had been billeted in our hut. I say young as by this time I was an old man of nineteen years old! He popped his head over the sheets: '*How was it tonight?*' Ron replied: '*Bloody terrible. We lost four on the other side and one back here*'. I can only imagine what the new boy must have thought: '*I wonder what I've let myself in for?*' I would wager he had no further sleep that night.

After two or three days, he came to me:

'*As Senior Air Gunner on the Squadron, I wonder if you can give me any advice?*'

My reply:

'*First of all, you need 95% luck. Then perfect your corkscrew evasive action, see the fighter first and immediately put into practice your evasive action. Finally, one tactic I use is, when over a target and it's near daylight, I close one eye, then when we leave the target area, I open it immediately. By doing this, I have night vision when we are most vulnerable instead of being temporarily blinded.*'

I could give no further advice and tragically he was lost on his first op.

On completing twenty-eight ops, we were informed we were being screened. We were never told the reason for our not having to complete the thirty ops required. I can only imagine the moral of the Squadron was so bad they were frightened we'd be lost on our last two ops. By screening us, it proved it was possible to complete a Tour. The next senior crew was captained by a Canadian, lost shortly afterwards on a French target.

Our last op was on Hasselt: 3 hours, 50 minutes. We were on the Aulnoye raid, 10 May 1944, when seven Lancasters were shot down by the same pilot, Hauptmann (Flight Lieutenant) Helmut Bergmann. He was awarded the Knights Cross in June 1944. After many more successful combats, he was finally shot down by a Mosquito and killed on 7 July 1944.

One unfortunate event was that, about the same time we arrived at Elsham, a new Squadron Commander was also posted to Elsham. He was a Wing Commander from Training Command with no operational experience. Hardly the sort of man to offer encouragement and help moral! One of his first ideas was to get all aircrew to change into gym kit and follow him for a run round the perimeter track. He pranced off with aircrew following. Soon after, we started to peel off back to our lockers, changed and went back to the Mess. I'd like to have seen his face when, at the end of the circuit, he looked behind to find only five or six runners still with him! The exercise was never repeated. He was posted after six months to the relief of those still serving on the Squadron.

A good well-run ship needs a good Captain, something lacking during our stay with 103 Squadron.

After our screening, we were all given Leave, and on return we were posted to various O.T.Us. I went as a Ground Instructor to Wymeswold where I spent the next five and a half months.

My next posting was to 214 Squadron, Oulton, Norfolk …

It was a bitterly cold December day when Jack Nash, fellow Air Gunner and myself arrived at Oulton. After all the necessary registration it was early evening when a WAAF driver of a 15-cwt delivered us to our billet. On entering, there were six members of a crew, both British and Canadians. Jack and I still in our great coats headed straight for the brightly burning stove to thaw out. Naturally, one of our first questions was: '*What aircraft are we flying?*' The reply, much to our amazement, was B-17s. Like so many at that time, we'd never heard of a Bomber Command Squadron equipped with Flying Fortresses. Our next question: '*Why?*' We were informed they couldn't tell us as operations were top secret. Rather a stupid reply as we'd be told everything on arriving at the camp next morning!

Determined to impress the '*sprogs*', they then began to tell us of their wonderful '*daring deeds*'. The final shoot line was when one of them said to the others:

'*Tell them how we looped the loop the other night in a B-17.*'

By now, Jack and I had thawed out, so removed our great coats. Under each of our Brevets was the ribbon of the 1939-43 Star. Immediately, they asked:

'*Have you been on ops before?*'

Jack's reply was:

'*Yes, we've both done a tour. I did nine on Berlin and my friend did ten*'.

There was a sudden hush and the conversation for the rest of the evening was remarkably subdued.

The next morning, we boarded a crew bus to take us to the Camp and called at the Officers' Mess to collect the Officers. I was sitting there as they climbed aboard, when suddenly I came face to face with Alfie Shields, my Navigator on 103 Squadron. I think we simultaneously said: '*What are you doing here?*' Apparently, like me, Alfie had arrived the previous day. On arriving at the Camp, we each went our separate ways. After reporting to register my arrival, I was summoned to the Adjutant's Office. When I was at Wymeswold, I was recommended for a Commission and to go on a Gunnery Leader's Course. I'd passed my four interviews for a Commission and only had to go before the Air Officer at HQ. I was informed this was more or less a formality as he was not known to turn anybody down. However, to go to this interview entailed going to HQ when transport was available. I'd been posted before this last interview had had the chance to take place.

When I reported to the Adjutant at 214 he had all my papers in front of him. He said I would only have to do two interviews and my Commission would come through quickly. However, I'd changed my mind, deciding not to progress further. The Adjutant was most friendly and spent time trying to talk me into taking a Commission, but I was adamant. The Adjutant was friendly, a far cry from the attitudes at 103 Squadron. I never regretted my decision for the rest of my stay in the RAF. However, on returning to Civvy Street, as an ex-Officer I would have been eligible to join the RAF Club, and living in the centre of London, I could have made good use of it for personal use and to entertain many of my foreign customers and colleagues.

When I was summoned to report to the Gunnery Leader, Flt/Lt Philips, with my Log Book, he looked through it and said:

'Why have you not got a DFM?'

I pointed out that Training Command were not very conversant with gongs, the attitude being if I haven't got a gong no-one else is going to have one! He immediately said:

'When you finish your tour here I promise you will be awarded one'.

I met Eric Philips after the war at Reunions. The first time I met him I said:

'I don't suppose you remember me?'

His immediate reply:

'Yes, I do and I will never forget your Log Book. I thought at the time: here am I, sitting here, having done only one op to Berlin with a DFC. It should be me standing!'

Eric Philips was a true Officer and a Gentleman. It was his kind and that of the Adjutant that made 214 such a friendly and efficient Squadron.

The morning came when all us new boys were standing around trying to form ourselves into crews. Jack and I went up to a Pilot: 'Are you looking for any Gunners?' His reply was: 'Yes', and then he said: 'I am looking for a Navigator'. I pointed to Alfie Shields: 'There is a Navigator I know'. He said: 'Is he any good?' My reply: 'If he was good enough to get me through my first tour, I have no doubt he will get me through my second tour'. Hence, by remarkable coincidence, Alfie and I were to do our second tour together.

Our first op with 214 was to Chemnitz on 14 February 1945 – the day after Dresden. I missed out not having been on that op as I was contacted by the Media: 'Were you on that Dresden raid?' Apparently I was to be invited to Dresden on an anniversary of the

raid and interviewed on radio or television. I missed out on a hospi-
table reception, rather different to the kind of 'hospitality' I was used
to on previous visits to Germany. We were attacked by a Ju88 on our
first op. Fortunately the Rear Gunner saw him before he opened fire
and, giving him a short burst, he broke away thankfully, not to be seen
again. We completed fourteen ops, the last on 2 May to Schleswig,
during 4.50 hours. This was the last day Bomber Command operated
against Germany.

After the war, we were sent on different postings. I took an M.T
Course and after several postings, finished up at Luneburg in
Germany, from where I was demobbed in February 1947.

During the war, men of Bomber Command were heroes. The day
war ended, they were mass murderers ... and murderers don't get
medals!

Top politicians who fully supported Arthur Harris during the
war now wanted to disown any connection with the bombing of
Germany. *Did they want to appease those nice Germans who bombed
London, Coventry and Plymouth?* Bomber Command was never repre-
sented in the Victory Parade. Their attitude: '*let Harris carry the can!*'
Members of Bomber Command and most of the general public
considered this an insult, especially as it is a known fact that Bomber
Command did more than any to bring about the defeat of Germany.

A small consolation was the decision of The Coin and Medal
News Magazine to arrange for the issue of a Bomber Command
Medal. The cost of this Medal was £15.95. This however, could not be
worn with official medals, but below them.

As President of the Air Gunners' Association, I annually laid a
wreath on behalf of the Association at the annual Memorial Service
at Runneymede. After the issue of the medal, I saw many ex-Bomber
Command veterans wearing the medal with pride, *and rightly so!*
Personally, I could never bring myself to wear a medal I could buy,
but I fully supported all who did. When I received an application for
the medal, I was surprised and proud of the fact that the illustration
of a crew on the front of the application was the photograph taken

by the Lincolnshire newspaper after our ten ops on Berlin with 103 Squadron.

I wish all members of RAF 100 Group Association 'Happy Landings' for many years to come!

Flying Officer Robert 'Bob' Moorby
Life with Stirlings on 214

I first realised I had a tenuous relationship with Norfolk when, in the mid-1930s, I found I had very distant relatives on my Dad's side, living in the county. As a result, my brother Robin and I cycled from our home in West London to Great Snoring for a week's holiday. We had some very enjoyable outings that week and found the surrounding countryside and lovely coastline attractive.

Almost immediately following this holiday came the 1938 Munich crisis and in September 1939, outbreak of war with Germany. About this time, I met up with Joan again and our relationship developed. She became very important to me. I first met her when we were both at school – me fifteen, Joan fourteen.

I was 18 the week after the declaration of war and, although I volunteered straight away for the RAF, I was told at the Recruiting Office that the Service was not accepting any more volunteers for the time being for Pilot or Navigator courses. The Sergeant suggested I came back in three months' time. So, early in 1940, I was back in his office, but the story was the same. He suggested I volunteer immediately for Air Crew duties and re-muster later for a Pilot's course. The immediate openings were for training as a Wireless Operator/Air Gunner. If I did, my records would still show my desire to become a Pilot and the opportunity to re-muster would come. I agreed to volunteer as a WOP/AG and left to wait for my Call Up.

Two months later I was called to RAF Uxbridge where I had a Selection Board and mental arithmetic test followed by a Medical. All who passed that day were sworn into the Service. Six weeks later,

I received my papers and was called up to Blackpool to start initial training.

However, between my Uxbridge visit and call up to Blackpool, we were bombed out of our house in Hammersmith. The bomb landed practically next door and all the top part of our house was blown away. Because we had a paved yard at the back, we had no Anderson shelter but a reinforced semi-basement room instead. This saved our lives – two of our neighbours were killed.

Life at Blackpool was pretty hectic – several weeks of square bashing on the front at North Shore mixed with Morse Code training (sending and receiving). There was also another Medical – the full Air Crew Medical this time, when it was decided whether you passed fit for pilot training or not. If you weren't passed you could continue as a WOP/AG. I passed the Medical okay and must say fully enjoyed my stay at Blackpool.

We left Blackpool in January 1941 to be posted to No 2 Signals School at Yatesbury, Wiltshire. Here, work was on the technical side of radio training and we experienced our first flights using wireless sets in the air. We were also issued with full flying gear. I passed out okay, ready for the next stage. This showed where the hold-ups in training occurred. We were obviously due for our Air Gunners Course next, but there was at least four to six months backlog. We were then dispersed around the country.

I was posted to HQ Flying Training Command at Shinfield, near Reading. The Signals Section here was kept very busy and we had several tele-printers and a number of telephone lines including a 'hotline'. It was here I encountered the other and darker side of Air Crew training. There were a number of crashes involving pupil pilots and details came through our Section. Quite often, both pupil and instructor were killed or seriously injured as well as the aircraft being written off. Part of my duties were 'listening out' during night duty, recording messages received. It helped keep my Morse Code training on top line because, at times, some pretty high speed stuff came through.

At last – the posting to No. 9 Gunnery School at Stormy Down near Bridgend in South Wales. Here, the course involved learning the parts, stripping them down and re-assembling the .303 Browning machine gun, aircraft recognition, machine gun firing on the range and best of all, air-to-air firing. Our flying and air firing was carried out in the Whitley bomber and Boulton Paul Defiant fighter. We all passed the course and received our brevets and Sergeants stripes.

We were then looking forward to postings to various Operational Training Units, but instead, we found ourselves outward bound to SS Strathaird in convoy to the Middle East via Durban. We changed ships at Durban and sailed on our own in the SS Mauretania to Port Tewfik in Egypt. It was early 1942. Our destination Egypt was the Middle East Air Crew Pool. We were at Abu Sueir (between Cairo and Ismailia) and it was obviously a pre-war RAF staging post for flights to the Middle East and India. It was well equipped and adjoining us was a Beaufighter Squadron under the command of Wing Commander Stainforth. He was one of the pre-war successful Schneider Trophy Pilots.

We marked time in Egypt, although one or two of our number went off for other duties. During our stay we were, in turn, given ten days leave and my close pal and I hitch-hiked to Palestine and spent time in Tel Aviv in a YMCA hostel. We visited all the well-known religious sites, including spending a lot of time in Jerusalem.

On our return to Base, we were on the move again following the good news of General Montgomery's chase of Rommel across North Africa. I think the powers-that-be at home realised, as things were getting worse for Bomber Command, we'd be better employed in the UK. Eventually, after a stay at Kasfareet, we embarked on what seemed like a small coaster and proceeded south. We sailed through a monsoon and, for this part of the journey, were escorted by the cruiser HMS Devonshire. We called in at Mombasa and spent a few weeks at Gil Gil transit camp.

Eventually we arrive at Cape Town and from there the majority of us embarked on SS Maloga for the trip home – an armed merchant cruiser, most passengers being families returning from India. As trained Air Gunners, we were earmarked to man some of the Oerlikon guns during periods of anti-submarine watches.

It was a marvellous sight to see Liverpool again and after a few days Leave, some of us found ourselves at an Advanced Flying Unit at

Penrhos in North Wales. During this Leave, Joan and I decided to get married. We'd got engaged on the Leave before I sailed for the Middle East. We eventually tied the knot on 17 January 1943 at our local home church.

Things now started to move and I was recalled from leave to O.T.U training at RAF North Luffenham. Here, all the training came to fruition and we 'crewed up' and started our serious work as an operation crew. Here is where the records of the RAF proved themselves. I was called to the Orderly Room one day and advised that my course for Pilot training had come through. As we were now an operation crew, I declined the opportunity to take the course. Everything went smoothly at O.T.U. and after three months training on Wellingtons, we moved to the Heavy Conversion Unit at Stradishall on four-engined Stirlings. Again things went well and at the beginning of June 1943 we were posted as a crew to 214 Squadron at Chedburgh. 214 shared RAF Chedburgh with another Stirling Squadron – No. 620.

However, we had an unfortunate welcome to 214. As we arrived on the lorry from Stradishall, we stopped at the Guard Room for clearance. Two Stirlings from 620 Squadron were flying overhead on an Air Test. It was usual on these occasions to take lads from Ground Crews if they fancied a flight. The two Stirlings were banking. As they did so, they touched wing tips. Immediately they were out of control, both plunging to the ground, wiping out the two crews and the lads from the Ground Crews. I believe they recovered sixteen bodies from the wreckage.

We settled in and the practice on 214 was for the new pilot to do a couple of 'affiliation' trips with an experienced operation crew before taking his own crew on ops. Our pilot, Henry Hall, (real name Harry, but we called him Henry after the band leader) did his two trips and then we were available. Again, procedure on 214 was to do two mine-laying ops to start your tour and these we did – one to the Frisian Islands (hit by flak) and the second to the South of France at the mouth of the Gironde River. Perfect trip – no problems.

We were now ready for the Big Time!

The next op was Hamburg – the operation when 'WINDOW' was used for the first time. A complete success – everything went to plan as far as we were concerned – bombing was good and losses low. The only downside when returning for de-briefing were comments from the Squadron Padre – he didn't appreciate the Squadron's success, his only thoughts with those *'poor people of Hamburg'*. We next went to Essen in the Ruhr and then back to Hamburg. We had to abort our next trip as the mid-upper turret was out of action due to hydraulic problems. We also had a bad oil leak on one of the engines. The next few ops went okay, however, and then we came to the trip to Nuremberg. This was a long flight – we were routed out over the South Coast and across France, before turning to approach the target from the south-west. As we approached the turning point, the starboard outer engine was overheating and causing concern had to be feathered. When we tried to restart it, the engine went on fire and had to be cut.

Almost immediately, we started to lose power on another engine. This loss of power has an immediate effect on a Stirling – with all engines functioning well it's usually difficult to maintain a height of 13 – 15,000 feet. We had problems and, although we went on to bomb the target, we knew it was going to be hard work getting home.

We gradually lost height all the way back across France. The crew were standing by to bale out if any further problems arose. As we approached the French coast our height was critical. We made a crew decision to try and make it back across the Channel. With 'ditch-ing' imminent, we immediately adopted the emergency procedure. While the crew took up their ditching positions, I proceeded with my duties – sending out SOS signals, switching the IFF to *'distress'* clamping the Morse key down so that a constant signal was being sent until we hit the water. This enabled any D/F Stations who picked up our distress calls to track our position. The last of my duties was to open the astrodome (one of the escape points) just above my wireless position. As I opened it and clamped it back, I thought how noisy the rush of the slip-stream was over the aircraft.

Next thing I remember is waking up soaking wet lying in a dinghy, spewing up sea water. Apparently, the plane had finally run out of petrol and plunged into the Channel. Two of the crew – Eric Smith our Navigator and Ken Buckle, Flight Engineer, were killed on impact (their bodies were washed ashore later). The rest of the crew got out okay and were in the dinghy. When Henry realised some of us were still in the aircraft, he got back in the fuselage to find me unconscious and floating face down. He'd dragged me out and put me in the dinghy with the other lads. Unfortunately, both Eric and Ken were dead, their bodies recovered later.

Eventually, the RAF Air/Sea Rescue launch arrived and took us back into Newhaven harbour. From there we were taken by ambulance to Naval Sick Quarters near Lewes. After a good sleep, Henry and the other lads went back to the Squadron next day, but I was knocked about quite a bit. I had badly gashed legs, severe bruising and a bad gash near my right eye. A Naval Surgeon came in next day to stitch up my legs and tend to my eye. At one stage I thought I might lose the sight in that eye, but thankfully everything healed.

This was the start of a three week stay at Sick Quarters. I was fortunate however in one respect – my wife Joan was living with her parents at Brighton at the time and when the Matron of Sick Quarters spoke to her on the phone, she was able to visit me regularly. Needless to say, when she first saw me she didn't recognise me. I was bandaged up and black and blue all over. When the Doctors considered me fit to move, I was sent to Brighton to get a new uniform and from there I was given three weeks 'Survivor's Leave'. (At that time the larger Brighton hotels were being used as Reception Centres for incoming Aussie and New Zealand air crews.)

After my Leave, I returned to the Squadron at Chedburgh, arriving back latish in the evening. I was told the Squadron was operating that night – the target was Hanover – and Henry had taken off with a made-up crew. When I woke the following morning, I realised something was wrong. Their beds hadn't been slept in. I learned later they had been shot down near the target and only the two Gunners were prisoners of war. The rest of the crew died in the crash.

It was about this time news came through that Henry had been awarded the British Empire Medal (Military Division) for saving my life when we ditched. How ironic he was not to know how his bravery, in returning to a sinking aircraft to rescue me, had been rewarded. I was now without a crew and still medically unfit to fly.

I was posted off to RAF Woolfax Lodge to get crewed up again, but nothing came of this and I was sent back to 214 as a supernumerary crew member. Once I was declared fit, I was ready to fly as a replacement for any Wireless Operator in another crew who may be sick.

My next op in early November 1943 was as a replacement for a pal of mine, Tommy Roberts, who was sent on a week's Compassionate Leave for family reasons. I knew his crew well and their pilot (F/O Bray) was very experienced. The target was Mannheim and this would be another very eventful trip.

After we crossed the enemy coast on course for the target, we were attacked by a Ju88 night fighter from almost dead astern. The Rear Gunner fired long bursts and strikes were seen on the enemy aircraft. F/O Bray was taking violent evasive action while the attack was underway and the Rear Gunner kept up a running commentary on the tactics of the German plane. Following long bursts of return fire from the Rear Gunner, the Ju88 broke away and was not seen again.

As we neared the target and started our bombing run, it was necessary to maintain a steady course with the bomb doors open. Just as we were settling on this 'run-in' to the aiming point, we were attacked again – this time by two enemy fighters believed to be FW190s. Both the rear and mid-upper turrets were put out of action and some of the electrics shot away. A total of nearly 3,000 rounds of ammunition were fired by Gunners during these three enemy attacks and before his turret was put out of action, the Mid-Upper Gunner scored direct hits on one of the FW190s. It was going down out of control and later claimed as 'destroyed' and confirmed. Fortunately during the attacks, none of our crew were injured. The bombing attack was made and we were finally on our way home. We did not return to base, but eventually landed at West Malling in Kent. We all went off to make-shift beds for the night and woke next morning to another tale of strife.

When Ground Crews at West Malling went out to the aircraft, they discovered damage to the electrics had prevented some bombs being released. It was apparently a very dodgy procedure – having to manually release each bomb left in the bomb-bay and gingerly lower it to the ground. We understood they used a lot of bedding mattresses under the bomb-bay to receive the bombs as they were lowered by hand. West Malling Flying Control advised us that, had they known about this when we called for landing instructions, they would have told us to set course for the North Sea and bale out so the Stirling met her fate in cold water. A Stirling arrived later in the day to fly us back to Chedburgh. Tommy Roberts came back off Compassionate Leave relieved his crew was still around.

Four days later I was on 'battle order' again. I was to fly with the Squadron C.O (W/Cdr McGlinn). The Wing CO only did occasional trips (by orders of Group HQ) and chose the next one because it was to be Berlin. I was stand-in Wireless Operator as the Squadron Signals Officer was on a week's Leave. When the Squadron CO went on an operation, he normally took all the heads of the various Sections to make up his crew. Most of these were experienced and had completed previous tours of operational duty. The trip to Berlin and back went okay, although the Wing CO did get tetchy once or twice. This was to be the last operation for our Squadron on Stirling aircraft. They were considered by Bomber Command to suffer too many heavy losses when statistics were analysed.

The Squadron was now at a standstill and we shortly had orders to move from Chedburgh to Downham Market. However, our stay at Downham Market was to be very short-lived and while there I only did three flights mainly of a routine nature.

Our next move was to be quite historical for the Squadron. We were being moved from 3 Group Bomber Command to 100 Group Bomber Command. 100 Group was a Special Duties Group and we were told we were transferring from Stirlings to the American B-17s. So our next move was from Downham Market to Sculthorpe. Here our conversion to B-17s was to take place. The aircraft arrived with American crews to give us instruction.

About this time, a replacement Pilot arrived on the Squadron to do his second tour of operations, having completed his first tour on Stirlings. This was W/O G. Mackie, a very brusque Scot but, as I was to discover, a very good Pilot. When 'Mac' arrived, he took over a full crew, but did very little flying before the move. The Wireless Operator in the crew was an Irishman and, one day, Mac collared me in the Sergeants Mess to ask if I would join the crew in place of the

Irishman as he was not satisfied with him. I jumped at the opportunity. It was a chance to complete my tour of ops.

Meanwhile, the conversion to B-17s continued and flying started early in 1944. I did as many trips as I could with any Pilot who wanted a Wireless Op. This included local flying for familarisation as well as trips to the big U.S Base at Burtonwood for spares for the B-17s. I did another couple of cross country exercises with the Wing Commander when he decided to 'have a go'. About this time 'Mac' obtained his Commission and moved from the Sergeants to the Officers Mess.

We were never fully briefed on the conversion programme, but understood the B-17 was chosen because of the shape of the bomb-bay. It was an entirely different layout to British Bombers. The bomb-bay was to house masses of special equipment – mainly electronic – for jamming purposes. A Special Operator would join each crew and operate this equipment. Our brief was to fly with the bomber stream and use the special equipment for picking up German RT broadcasts to their night fighters and to jam these broadcasts. We were told never to ask questions about the equipment.

The Squadron moved from Sculthorpe to Oulton where new B-17 aircraft arrived and soon the Squadron was up to full strength. I was enjoying my flying with Mac and his crew – his 'in flight' control was top-line and all the lads knew we had a very good Pilot.

Our operations started on 1 May 1944 and Mac completed his second tour and I my first tour in September that year. Most operations covered a wide area of France, Holland and Germany and I can only recall one trip when guns were fired in anger by the crew when an unidentified enemy aircraft approached. We were unlucky with a couple of ops when equipment failed to operate satisfactorily and we had a few flak holes after one trip.

The day after the first V-2 landed on West London, we were sent on an operation (just our crew) to orbit a point off the Dutch Coast to see if we could pick up any information on our special equipment on possible launch sites of these weapons. We were escorted and attended by four Spitfires of Fighter Command. Unfortunately, we were unable to obtain anything useful and returned to Base after a five-hour operation.

Having completed our joint tours of duty, we were posted away from the Squadron. In the meantime, I applied for my Commission and progressed from Warrant Officer to Pilot Officer – promotion to Flying Officer came six months later. For the remainder of my Service career, I was involved in several courses in Training Command and for the last six months I was posted to Transport Command, briefing crews on trips mainly out to the Middle and Far East to pick up personnel due for release.

I will always have a special feeling for East Anglia, both Suffolk and mainly Norfolk where I spent many months of Service life, including that special '*buzz*' being with an operational Squadron from June 1943 to September 1944. Mac got his DFC after completing his second tour – I don't know why they took so long!

I was de-mobbed in June 1946 and pursued a career in local Government, retiring in June 1979 as Assistant Town Clerk of the Royal Borough of Kensington and Chelsea. Incidentally, the Town Clerk and Chief Executive of the Borough also retired the same day as me. He was one of '*the few*' of Fighter Command in the Battle of Britain and awarded the DFC and DFM.

Joan and I had three sons. I have six grandchildren. Unfortunately, I lost my Joan after nearly fifty-two years of marriage when she died in 1994 after a short illness.

Bob continued to attend RAF 100 Group Association and 214 Squadron Reunions until his death in January 2008. It was always his joy to meet old colleagues and visit that particular part of Norfolk which held so many bitter-sweet memories and remained so special to him.

My Father: Bob Moorby
by eldest son, Michael Moorby

I feel my Dad was gifted. I know it's an unusual way to put it. But it's almost as if God had chosen his survivors.

Since Dad's death, I've been reading the book '*Bomber Command*', by Max Hastings, and it's opened my eyes to what they all went through and that anyone ever survived at all.

Dad was a lovely man and as they put it in Rowledge: 'The Gentleman'. He was the new man of his age. He helped our mother bring us up – washing us, feeding us, cooking and ironing, housework – they shared the work. They were in their forties before they could afford to buy a house, but the car came a little earlier.

I am the eldest of three sons. I was born in August 1944, my twin brothers coming four years later. But then, how do I start in terms of Dad?

I first remember Dad just before my brothers were born. He was pushing me in a swing in Ravenscourt Park, Hammersmith. That was the last time I had him to myself. It wasn't until after Mum died that that feeling returned.

Being the only unmarried son, I spent more time with him. I used to go down as often as possible. We had holidays together – Italy, Paris, Bournmouth, Sidmouth and Skegness. In Skegness we were looking for a village called Moorby. We also checked out airfields there.

His interest in the RAF came back to him after seeing a letter in *The Mail*. It was someone he flew with in the war. This gave him a sense of purpose again, especially after Mum's death. Now he could follow things up. On Reunions, he found new and old friends and I know he looked forward to going and being with them again. Now it became: 'sorry Mike, I can't see you, I'm away in Norwich!' Dad did however achieve a wartime ambition. He took flying lessons in his late seventies!!

As he was happy on his Reunions, it seemed to be the best place for his uniform and other memorabilia to be, donated to the City of Norwich Aviation Museum. Here he could continue to share his memories with friends old and new and I could still see him from time to time.

Remembering Bob Moorby
by friend, Shirley Whitlock

Many people will warmly remember Bob Moorby who became such a familiar and well-loved face at RAF 100 Group Association

Reunions in May each year. Sadly, he passed away in January 2008, and we met only a few short years before, in November 2005.

Reading the book: 'The Stirling Story', by Michael Bowyer; a crash of a Stirling in the sea off Bexhill is mentioned. Two crew members were killed, the date: 10 August 1943. I knew this must be the crash in which we lost my Uncle, Sgt Eric Smith, Navigator. The number of the plane and Squadron 214 was also given. I followed up this information and from various emails was put in touch with Peter Walker, Secretary of 214 Squadron Association, who put me in touch with Bob, the Wireless Operator who survived the crash and of course, the war. My family, had always believed all crew that survived was lost on their next mission. Not so as Bob, badly injured, was still in hospital recovering from the Bexhill crash.

We arranged to meet and it was wonderful just being able to talk about Eric's last mission and all the raids they'd been on together. He said Eric was his best friend. Probably a number of members read Bob's very interesting article in the October 2006 edition of 'Flypast' Magazine entitled: 'Forgotten Bombers'.

We became good friends and he meant a lot to my sons too. Going to Air Shows, etc. with my younger son and flying with my older son. With special permission, Ian flew him into Coltishall after it was closed and before it was sold. He was absolutely thrilled!

We also spent time with my brother and his wife, Ron and Jackie. Visiting Eric's grave, Bob's wish, and Ely Cathedral where there is a Memorial to the 100 Group depicted in the beautiful stained glass windows. The Verger opened the book in memory of those lost from 100 Group and left it open at Eric's name. She was most helpful.

Bob invited me to the 100 Group Reunion 2006 and I enjoyed each meeting since and met such wonderful people. His Reunions with both 100 Group and 214 Squadron meant so much to him.

I'm sure he would be happy to know his RAF belongings were donated into the care of the City of Norwich Aviation Museum, another of his special interests.

It was a pleasure and honour for me to have met Bob and to call him my friend, even for only a very few short years.

P/O Bill Foskett

In 2000, my youngest son (a Pharmacist in Chelmsford) was searching for news of my background in the Services. He eventually contacted a chap in Canada who was building a website, asking for information concerning 214. At that time I had no computer, but in rapid time I had, and made contact with Kevin Crawford. He was chuffed to be in contact with a *'live one'*. Over two or three years he became inundated with so many people giving or asking information, that literally it was driving him over the edge. He was offline for six months or so; I understand he tried to offload the site over a long period. Eventually Carol and John Edwards took over management of the website; and for those with computers and access to the internet, then it's become an informative site: www.214squadron.org.uk

The following is my own story which can be found there.

P/O **Bill Foskett, 151372**. RAF, Commissioned Officer. 10 January 1943 – 6 December 1944. Born: Great Yarmouth where the family had a small beach chalet in East Mersey. He lived most of his life in Hampstead. As a youngster, he spent time in the Sea Scouts on board the *'England'* every weekend; an old ferry boat permanently tied to one of two bridges over the Thames at Kew. He lived in Seaton, Cumbria, close to the shore overlooking the Solway Firth and Scotland.

I did my I.T.W in Newquay, stationed in one of the big Guest Houses on top of the cliff. That was in the first three or four months of 1942 (No. 11 Flight 'C' Squadron). It was all *'bags of swank and B.S. Stand by your beds, Officer on Parade'* stuff'. I loved it so much that I helped our Flight win the Drill Cup and the PS Cup. If I remember right, the latter was Rifle Drill without any verbal orders, just the whistle now and again. In later years, the Yanks did it almost like a Music Hall act. Anyway, we were the first and possibly only Flight to bring off the double.

As far as India was concerned, we were fully trained and operational on Wellingtons at 15 O.T.U Harwell. Our posting was to India and at that time we were with Squadron Leader Packe AFC as our pilot (he trained in Canada, and stayed on as an Instructor which earned him his 'gong'.) After receiving tropical inoculations I was informed I would not be going to the Middle East!

Our crew did a conversion course from Wimpies (Wellingtons) to Stirlings at Straddishal the back end of 1943. In fact, my first two ops were in them; one to the Fresians with six 1500-lb mines, the second to Biarritz with two 1500-lb mines. The difference in the load was due to the distance; a three-hour trip in the first instance against an eight hour on the second. In the Stirling, my position was in the second pilot's seat. Then after take-off, in the mid-upper turret, and approaching target, lying flat in the nose for bomb/mine release, then back to the turret; and finally back in the seat for landing. The crew's first operation was on 19 Nov 1943 piloted by F/Sgt Gilbert, the second operation followed on the twenty-fifth piloted by S/Ldr Jeffries. The crew make-up at this time was:

Flying Officer Bill Foskett (B/A),
Flight Sergeant Ted Bonner (WOP),
Flight Sergeant Fred Barber (ENG),
Flight Sergeant Jack Podger (NAV).

We were now fully trained, and waiting for our own skipper to complete his final trip as second pilot before being integrated as a fully operational crew. Around this time our Skipper literally disappeared. It was all very hush-hush. For full story on this you need to see the reference in Murray Peden's (RCAF) 'A Thousand Shall Fall' book; page 429, paragraph beginning 'Another chap ...'.) Although the crew was now operationally trained, having lost our Skipper, we had to re-train with a new Skipper, Flying Officer John Corke.

In January 1944, we converted to Fortresses and billeted at Blickling Hall, Oulton, Norfolk, together with the American Air Force who were flying daytime operations. In addition to our ex-Stirling crew, when we converted to Fortresses, there was Len Roose, Ray Delisle, WO Hepton, Sgt Stelling, Sgt Gregory and others.

In the Fortress, we carried no bombs, only a full load of jamming and electronic equipment which we took to the target and, of course, had to bring back. These operations required us to be between the Pathfinders and the mainstream, operating before, during and after the timed course of the raid. This meant the aircraft was at risk over or near the target for any great length of time. Sometimes a boffin was with us, but I have no record of the different toys we had to play with. I vaguely remember 'Gee', 'H2S', ABC', but I doubt if I could recognise them now. Note that the U.S Air Force flew Fortresses with a ten-man crew, as did others, but they were carrying bombs etc. I don't think there was a Norm for us involved in the countermeasures role. We were doing all sorts of other things. Jamming and scanning equipment was in its infancy, and sometimes we were accompanied by the boffin involved. To say exactly what everyone was doing is beyond me, but the point I make is that it would be difficult to pin down the crew at any given time, as the actual number varied. The only permanency would be the regular mainstay crew members.

Our third op, our first with Johnnie Corke as pilot; was on 24/25 April 1944, Karlsruhe. Note the amusing Intel Report that was issued following this operation on the 24th:

CORKSCREW WITH DEATH

KARLSRUHE   24/25 APRIL 1944
NO: 214 SQUADRON

One of our crews, Captain F/O Corke, had a shaky do over the target when his Gunner reported aircraft on their tail and the pilot went into combat manoeuvre, only to find himself on his back and spinning down towards the flak and flames. Everything spun, instruments, Corke's crew and the universe, but at 10,000 feet they managed to come out with fortunately the stars above them instead of the target ...

The de-briefing staff obviously found the incident hilarious. However, the boys didn't share the humour and made straight for the bar for a few stiff ones. All were well aware how lucky they were and that very, very few ever walk away from an INVERTED SPIN!

From that point on, we were humorously known as 'Corkescrew' after pilot F/O Corke and the incident described above.

Our sixth op was on Gelsenkirchen. On the night, we learned on our safe return that Murray Peden and Cassan had been lost. It later turned out that Peden crash-landed at Woodbridge, and again there is a special chapter on this in Peden's book. It makes grim reading. Just as a point of interest, on 11 September 1944, we were on an op to Darmstadt in our Fortress A (Able), not knowing then it was to be our last trip using that aircraft. It was lost next day on a raid on Frankfurt, piloted by Flt Lt Fillieul. This loss was taken very seriously by all crews as F/Lt Fillieul was a two-tour veteran of the Squadron.

On 9/10 November 1944, which was about my twenty-seventh, and I was reaching the end of my Tour, we carried out a spoof 'WINDOW' attack on Saarbruken, and for this we got a pat on the back from the AOC.

After numerous incidental experiences, we flew our last op on 6 December 1944 after completing thirty-two Sorties. The certification that the tour of duty had been completed was signed by B. D. Davies, Squadron Leader, A Flight and D. D. Rogers, W/Co. O/C 214 Squadron.

Bill recalled that F/T Sgt Fred Barber was an extremely efficient man who knew his job inside out, and expected everyone on Ground Crew to be likewise. 'They certainly 'popped to' when he was about, he was really meticulous.' One incident regarding Fred, he remembered, occurred on a Flight Test prior to the Gelsenkirchen Op on 21 June 1944:

As we got off the bus, the Ground Crew were hovering, and one of them was heard to say 'watch it lads; here comes Ali Barber and the 40 clangers'. I've not heard from him since we finished our tour, but the last thing he mentioned to me was that he was going to set up an Estate Agency in south London.

The summary in P/O Foskett's Log Book states that he completed thirty-two Sorties – twenty-seven Operations in total. However, it is important to note (this is not well known) that 'Ops' and 'Sorties' were two different things. As progress was made in ground fighting in Europe, the RAF began to specify that certain Ops only qualified as a half Op. (No doubt this was a way of stretching Tours!)

Air Vice-Marshal Jack Furner DFC, OBE, CBE
14 November 1921–1 January 2007

Air Vice-Marshal Jack Furner flew wartime operations with Bomber Command and took part in secret electronic counter-measure sorties on D-Day; in peacetime he made a major contribution to the development of the RAF's nuclear capability during the Cold War.

Derek Jack Furner was born at Southend on 14 November 1921, and educated at Westcliff High School where he excelled at mathematics. After a brief period working for the Imperial Bank of India he was *'called up'*, and volunteered for flying duties as a Navigator. He was sent to Canada under the British Commonwealth Air Training Plan.

In March 1943, Jack Furner joined No. 214 Squadron, flying the Stirling four-engine bomber. He flew twenty-five operations, including the major *'firestorm'* raids against Hamburg. On the night of 17 August, his Squadron was briefed to attack the scientific establishment at Peenemünde on the Baltic coast. Reconnaissance photographs had identified the site as the development centre for Hitler's terror weapons, the V-1 flying bomb and V-2 rocket. The raid successfully delayed their development, but forty bombers failed to return.

When Jack and his crew completed their tour a few weeks later, they were one of only two crews to survive the six-month period. He was awarded the DFC.

After a brief rest, Jack Furner volunteered to return to operations as Navigation Leader of his old Squadron, which was re-equipping with the U.S B-17 Flying Fortress to operate in the secret world of electronic countermeasures. The Squadron's role was to fly in support of the main bomber force and jam enemy radar and radio communications. On the night of the D-Day landings, Jack Furner was airborne, jamming the enemy's early warning radar sites by dropping strips of tin foil (*WINDOW*). His aircraft was attacked and damaged by a German night fighter.

In early 1945, he transferred to Transport Command and was sent to India, where he flew Dakotas on re-supply operations in support of the advance in Burma. As the war ended, he flew many sorties to Saigon and Bangkok to repatriate Allied PoWs, remaining in the Far East for a further two years flying VIPs and transport operations from Hong Kong and Singapore.

After a period as a Navigation Instructor, he attended the RAF's Specialist Navigation Course in 1950 before moving to Boscombe Down, where he was involved in the development of bombing and navigation aids, including the first *Doppler* equipment. These became the core of most of the RAF's operational aircraft systems for the next three decades.

He was awarded the DFC.

Jack spent two years on similar work with the USAF Weapons Guidance Laboratory, flying most of their strategic bombers before returning to complete the Flying College Course. As a specialist Navigator, in 1957 he was selected to command the Operations Wing at RAF Waddington, home of the first Vulcan V-bomber Squadrons. With his expert knowledge of the aircraft's navigation and bombing systems, he provided support for the training of new crews as well as the development of its operational capability; and in 1958 he was Navigator of the Vulcan that broke the Ottawa – London record (in 5 hours 45 minutes).

With the rapid expansion of the V-Force, Jack Furner was appointed to HQ Bomber Command to head the Operational Plans Division, where he had the task of planning action to be taken by Britain's 144 V-bombers and sixty Thor ballistic missiles in time of war. It was a job with 'a strange air of unreality', he recalled afterwards.

As the Cuban missile crisis developed, the atmosphere in the Bomber Command operational bunker became tense, and his immediate Superior described him as 'a tower of strength'.

After three years in charge of the Nuclear Activities Branch at HQ Shape in Paris, Jack spent two years in the Ministry of Defence before taking command in 1968 of RAF Scampton, home of three Vulcan Squadrons equipped with the Blue Steel stand-off weapon. He was the first Navigator to command an operational Flying Station in peacetime.

In 1969 he took command of the Central Reconnaissance Establishment, then had two years as Secretary to the Military Committee of NATO. At the end of this tour he was promoted to Air Vice-Marshal, one of the first two

Navigators to reach the rank. He spent the last two years of his service as the Assistant Air Secretary with responsibilities for the careers of the RAF's aircrew.

Jack joined his brother's firm, Harlequin Wall Coverings, as General Manager for five years before finally retiring. A man of great energy, commitment and service, he considered the last twenty years of his life as some of the busiest. He was Chairman of the Aries Association for Specialist Navigators, and administered the block of apartments in Eastbourne where he lived for many years. He was an active President of the Eastbourne Sinfonia and, with his wife, was a regular attender at Foyles' literary luncheons.

In 1987, the Furners moved to Cromer where they had met in 1944 when he was serving at nearby RAF Oulton. He became a stalwart of the Cromer Society and was in great demand to speak on a diverse range of subjects including space, computers, climate change and music.

In 1989, he was elected a member of Mensa and owned one of the first computers. He had been appointed an OBE in 1959 and a CBE in 1973. In its beginnings, he was also President of the newly formed RAF 100 Group Association, and present in 1994 at the dedication of its first Memorial Site at Oulton where he had served.

Just prior to his death, having almost completed his autobiography; he sent me the following letter:

Dear Janine,

Thank you for your very friendly letter of 5 July … I feel I'm getting lazy in my 85th year, but then I had a thought. I've made a little list and have this silly idea to create a challenge. I attach the list – a list of aircraft in which I have navigated. There are forty-two military aircraft in that list and as you see, I have navigated for 243 different pilots.

My challenge? Is there anybody out there who can better that?

With best wishes

List of Aircraft Navigated

Anson	Comet 2	Sunderland
Ashton	Dakota	Stirling
B17 Fortress	Dove	T29
B24 Liberator	Dragonfly	T33
B25	Halifax	Twin Pioneer
B26	Harvard	Valetta
B29 Superfortress	Hastings	Valiant
B36	Lancaster	Varsity
B47	Lincoln	Victor 2sr
B52	Meteor	Vulcan
Brigand	North Star DC4	Vulcan 2
Canberra B2	Oxford	Wayfarer
Canberra PR7	Prentiss	Wellington
Chipmunk	Princess Flying Boat	York

Jack Furner completed 1,200 flights with 243 different pilots, both RAF and USAF.

War Crime Survivor:
Flt/Lt Norman James Bradley DFM
by Grandson Matt Boucher

My Grandfather was Flight Sergeant Norman James Bradley DFM 1587915, a Waist Gunner on Flying Fortress HB779 BU-K. I am trying to find information on his time with 214 Squadron during the war. Thankfully some kind person pointed me in your direction.

I have so far gathered information from websites, books and online forums. However, most information is generic. What I am really looking for is detail, related directly to my Grandfather, his aircraft, his crew, sorties flown, etc.

I am aware they are quite a well-known aircrew, subject to a well-documented war crime. As you will appreciate, as a survivor, my Grandfather found it uncomfortable talking about his experience and because of this I never pressed him for details.

The war crime happened in Huchenfeld, Germany on 15 March 1945, when the crew bailed out and were captured. Thankfully, my Grandfather and another crewman managed to escape. However, five of the crew were murdered, four shot in the local graveyard, the other shot by a member of the Hitler youth. The bitter irony is that the aircraft which they thought was going down, managed to return to England and landed safely.

Towards the end of my Grandfather's life he was contacted by the other crewman who escaped that night and he journeyed with him to Huchenfeld. I think in the end he finally managed to come to terms with what had transpired. Unfortunately for me I did not see him much after his visit and never had the opportunity to question him before he died.

A resident of Huchenfeld is now investigating this war crime. He's doing an exhaustive and detailed investigation, with lots of photos, documents, videos, etc. coming to light. He has come up against the usual silence which surrounds these types of crimes and even been legally threatened, but this is not deterring him.

How sad it is that after so much time people are still trying to hide evidence and deny that a war crime ever took place, instead of acknowledging the sacrifices these and other brave men made. This is especially sad when those involved directly, be they aircrew or family, have returned to the scene of the crime and forgiven those involved.

I have a wealth of information including photos from his time with his previous 166 Squadron, but I assume that due to the secret nature of 214 Squadron's work, photos and diaries were frowned upon. I therefore have nothing from his time with 214 Squadron. I am also looking to find photos of him, his crew, aircraft, etc. I'd love to hear from anyone who knew my father and who served with him.

Murdered by the Mob
Crew of Flying Fortress Mark II HB779 BU-K

Wg/Cdr John Wynne DFC	Pilot	RAFVR	UK		
Flt/Lt Dudley Percy Heal DFM	Navigator	RAFVR	UK	PoW 15.3.45	
F/O Tom H. Tate	Special Wireless Operator	RAFVR	UK	PoW 15.3.45	
Flt/Lt G P 'Tubby' PoW DFC	Bomb Aimer	RAFVR	UK	PoW 15.3.45	
F/S Norman J. Bradley DFM	Waist Gunner	RAFVR	UK	PoW 15.3.45	
F/O Harold 'Jack' Frost DFM MiD	Non Com 1475544 Com 169864 Top Turret Gunner	RAFVR	UK	PoW 15.3.45	KIA 17.3.45 Age 24
F/O Gordon Albert Hall MiD	Non Com 1258412 Com 149916 Wireless Op	RAFVR	UK	PoW 15.3.45	KIA 17.3.45 Age 22
Flt/Lt Sidney Clayden Matthews DFC MiD	Non Com 1375209 Com 142217 Rear Gunner	RAFVR	UK	PoW 15.3.45	KIA 17.3.45 Age 25
F/S Edward Arthur Percival DFM MiD	1263001 Waist Gunner	RAFVR	UK	PoW 15.3.45	KIA 17.3.45 Age 30
F/O James William Vinall DFM MiD(twice)	Non Com 747157 Com 169518 Flight Engineer	RAFVR	UK	PoW 15.3.45	KIA 18.3.45 Age 40

B-17 Flying Fortress HB779 from 214 (Special Duties) Squadron, was returning from a *Jostle* patrol in support of an attack on Lutzkendorf on the night of 14/15 March 1945. Somewhere near Pforzheim it was hit by light flak. Fire took hold of No. 2 engine. Pilot Flt/Lt John Wynne, ordered the other nine of his crew to bale out. Intending to follow, he became so tangled up in his oxygen tubing that, by the time he had extricated himself, the fire was out.

Alone in the aircraft he flew back to RAF Bassingbourn. The rest of the crew, meanwhile, had baled out and been captured. The Navigator and Bomb Aimer were dispatched to a PoW camp. But the other seven were kept in Buhl prison before being transferred to Pforzheim, a few kilometres to the north-east. On 17 March they were being transferred on foot into Luftwaffe custody, but had only reached the village of Huchenfeld at around seven in the evening. On a cold day, none of the seven airmen minded being locked up in the warm boiler-room of the Neuen Schule (New School). With little sleep in the last three days, at least they had the chance to get comfortable. Some dozed in the warmth. Outside, a solitary Luftwaffe guard was on duty.

Earlier that afternoon, aware the airmen were on their way to Huchenfeld, the Kreisleiter of Pforzheim, Hans Christian Knab, got hold of his subordinate officers, including Hitler Youth Commander Max Kochlin: *'Now you must get hold of your Hitler Youth people and tonight we shall stage a demonstration.'* Knab also spoke to Standartenfuhrer Becker, in command of the SA at Dillweissenstein (locally known just as Dillstein): *'Becker, must get hold of as many men as you can and march to Huchenfeld from Dillstein. Your men will also take part in the demonstration. We shall all meet at the paper factory in Huchenfeld.'* Weapons were distributed to the Hitler Youth by Kochlin, whose fiery speech made their *'young blood boil'*, and the armed men and boys made their way to the rendezvous at Huchenfeld.

Half an hour after the Luftwaffe guard had taken up his post outside the boiler-room, a crowd of civilians, perhaps fifty in number, arrived, demanding access to the airmen: *'We want to revenge our women and children.'* The guard was powerless to stop the mob from bursting in and dragging the prisoners outside on to Forstrasse.

Flight Sergeant Norman Bradley DFM:

> **As soon as we got outside the building I realised in all probability we were going to be hung or shot. I decided to hang back with a view to escaping. There was a scuffle in front of me as though another member of the crew was trying to escape. It might have been more than one. I tried to hang back as did F/O Vinall with the two men holding him. There was another scuffle in front. It looked as if one of the members of the crew got away. The Germans holding us ran forward to give assistance and Vinall and I took the opportunity to hide between a wall and a car. I heard two screams of pain. Vinall**

moved forward in the shadow and I followed. He was shouting for me to follow. I shouted back that he was going the wrong way, in the direction of the shooting. I heard nothing more. I ran across some fences and wire netting and escaped across a field and on into the woods. I heard about six shots fired when Vinall shouted to me that final time. Later, while crossing the wire fence, I heard several bursts from automatic weapons. I was later captured about twenty-two miles the other side of Pforzheim. The day after I was captured, two of my guards told me that two members of my crew had been shot.

A third airman, F/O Tom H. Tate, also escaped but was recaptured. He and Bradley were not to know that the bursts of gunfire they heard signalled the end for four of their crew –

- Flying Officer G. A. Hall,
- Flight Lieutenant S. C. Matthews DFC,
- Flight Sergeant E. A. Percival DFM
- Flying Officer H. Frost DFM – who had been taken to the cemetery and was shot.

Flying Officer J. W. Vinall DFM MiD (twice), aged forty, was recaptured the next day and locked up in the police station at Dillstein, only a few yards from the Hitler Youth barracks. Ortsgruppenleiter Paul Ecker ensured that Kreisstabfuhrer Niklas, a Major in the Volkssturm, knew of Vinall's presence. Niklas prepared a warm reception for the prisoner before he went to the police station and ordered Vinall to be released into his custody. Vinall was taken outside where Wilhelm Maxeiner beat him about the head with a heavy stick until he was felled, probably unconscious. Hitler Youth, Gert Biedermann, then shot him in the back of the head. He was buried with the other four airmen.

At the Huchenfeld shootings on 17 March and at the Dillstein shooting on 18 March, neither Knab nor Kochlin was present. But the evidence was overwhelming that not only had these two men staged the murders to make them appear spontaneous outbursts of mob anger, but also none of those involved were dressed in uniform. It was not clear who fired the first shots at the cemetery at Huchenfeld, but two Hitler Youths, Gerhard Stahl and Rolf Heil, admitted they had fired some of the shots. Both were sentenced to fifteen years' imprisonment, as was Biedermann, whilst a dozen others received sentences ranging from two to twelve years. Knab, Kochlin and Niklas were sentenced to death by hanging.

The Murdered Airmen

F/O Gordon Albert Hall MiD

Flying Officer Gordon Albert Hall MiD, Non Com 1258412 Com 149916, Wireless Operator, RAFVR. Nationality: UK, KIA 17 March 1945, Aged 22. Date taken PoW: 15 March 1945, PoW number: None.

Flt/Lt Sidney Clayden Matthews DFC MiD

Flight Lieutenant Sidney Clayden Matthews DFC MiD, Non Com 1375209 Com 142217, Rear Gunner, RAFVR. Nationality: UK. KIA 17 March 1945, Aged 25, Date taken PoW: 15 March 1945.

Sidney was a former pupil of Wembley Hill School and assisted his father in business at Harlesden until 1940 when he joined the RAF. A Boy Scout and avid swimmer, he held several medals and certificates for swimming.

Sidney was made a Pilot Officer on Probation (Emergency) from 6 February 1943. He was promoted to Flying Officer on Probation from 6 August 1943.

He was awarded the Distinguished Flying Cross on 5 September 1944 while serving with 9 Squadron. By the time he won his DFC at the age of twenty-three, he had already flown an incredible fifty-seven operations, including several over the heaviest defended target: Berlin. Among others were attacks on two of Germany's greatest battleships: the *Scharnhorst* and the *Geneisenau at Brest*. (Note the *Scharnhorst* was sunk on 26 December 1943 in the Polar Sea in battle with British naval forces. Of more than 2,000 men aboard only thirty-six survived.) During the latter part of World War Two he was an Air Gunner in B-17 Flying Fortress HB779 BU-K as part of 214 Squadron based at RAF Oulton. On 6 February 1945 he was promoted to Flight Lieutenant.

Given the number of operations, of which many were essentially suicide missions from which most never returned, it is inconceivable how Flt/Lt Matthews could have survived as long as he did. It makes one wonder why the hand of fate kept him safe despite insurmountable odds, only to steal his life in 'the final months of war' in such a cruel and senseless manner.

F/S Edward Arthur Percival DFM MiD

Flight Sergeant Edward Arthur Percival DFM MiD, 1263001, Waist Gunner, RAFVR. Nationality: UK. KIA 17 March 1945. Aged 30. Date taken PoW: 15 March 1945

F/O James William Vinall DFM & MiD (twice)

James Vinall was a black man.

Flying Officer James William Vinall DFM & MiD (twice), 169518, Flight Engineer, RAFVR. Nationality: UK. KIA 18 March 1945. Aged 40. Date taken PoW: 15 March 1945.

Before serving with 214 Squadron, Flying Officer Vinall was with 9 Squadron in 1943. In September that year Vinall is mentioned when awarded his DFM in 9 Squadron, ORB.

F/O Harold 'Jack' Frost DFM MiD

Flying Officer Harold 'Jack' Frost DFM MiD, Non Com 1475544 Com 169864, Top Turret Gunner, RAFVR. Nationality: UK. KIA 17 March 1945. Aged 24. Date taken PoW: 15 March 1945.

Flying Fortress Mark II HB779 BU-K

From the cockpit of his B-17 Flying Fortress Flt/Lt Wynne could see through the clear night the oil tanks 22,000 feet below explode into flames.

At twenty-three, John Wynne was already a veteran bomber pilot. As he swung the nose of his aircraft towards home he was confident the mission had been a success. The Nazis had suffered another punishing blow. Now his task was to get his nine-man crew safely back to Britain in time for an early breakfast. Although German fighters and anti-aircraft fire would harass them much of the way, this was a gauntlet the cool-headed young RAF pilot had run many times before.

On this occasion, however, the return journey was to be brutally interrupted. For five of the men on board, it was not merely fear that loomed, but death – or more accurately, calculated murder of the most savage kind. Captured by German forces, they were to become the victims of one of World War Two's final atrocities whose grim details would remain hidden for many years to come, even from their own Skipper. Old hatreds and bitter shame conspired to conceal this ugly episode of war. Even in Britain, little was known of it. Only now, thanks to a sequence of coincidences and a remarkable escape has it become possible to piece together the full story of what happened to the crew of that B-17.

The target on the night of Wednesday March 14 1945 was the oil refinery at Lutzendorf, a few miles south of Leipzig. Although Germany was by now only months away from defeat, the Allied bombing campaign continued unabated in the hope of hastening the end. On this raid, however, Wynne's bomb-bay was empty. His task was not to drop high explosives on the oil refinery, but to fly above the main wave of 244 Lancasters, jamming enemy radar. The B-17 was specially equipped for the task, with two Wireless Officers (Gordon Hall and Tom Tate) trained to detect both ground-based and airborne radar transmissions, and to knock them out with signals powerful enough, it was said, to silence the BBC itself.

Tom Tate was the twenty-six-year-old survivor of a remarkable forty-four sorties, with his 45th almost completed. He settled at his post halfway down the fuselage for the four-hour journey home. The crew were at their stations around the very large plane: Rear-Gunner, Top-Gunner, two Waist-Gunners, Navigator, Flight Engineer, Wireless Operator, the Radar Jammer and the Pilot now bringing the aircraft down to a lower altitude.

Wynne was keenly aware that, after a raid like this, 100 or more enemy night-fighters would be directed towards the bomber stream seeking revenge. It was the reason the whole force, including the B-17, rapidly dropped to 3,000 feet. At such a low level, the echo from the ground would confuse German fighters' radar, even though it did make the lumbering bombers easier targets for the *ack-ack* batteries below. In two hours' time they should be across the Rhine and over territory held by the Allies. Ahead of him, Wynne saw two bombers hit by ground fire. He altered course, dodging the flak coming up at them. 'We were doing very nicely. Then suddenly a shell hit the port landing wheel, ricocheted and exploded. There was a bang and then a flash. Some of the hot fragments hit the inner port engine.' For a while it seemed the damage wasn't serious. Then the oil pressure plummeted in the stricken engine. Even so, they reckoned the aircraft could probably be nursed across the Rhine to the emergency Allied airfield at Rheims.

That hope was short-lived. Fire broke out in the engine. The pistons seized up. Soon the whole aircraft was shaking furiously, with gauges and light fittings breaking loose and flying about the plane. They were only 1,000 feet above ground.

Once they crossed the Rhine, he ordered the crew to put on parachutes and open escape hatches. When the vibration became so severe it seemed the whole plane would disintegrate, he told them to jump. *'Bale out! Bale out!'* The crew obeyed, hurling into the rushing darkness. The aircraft flew on. With remarkable bravery, Wynne decided to stay at the controls until the last possible moment, hoping the aircraft could be saved. At least his men were free and safe, landing in friendly territory. In truth, five of them would never be seen again.

Tom Tate drifted in the inky blackness. A strange sensation, until suddenly there came a mass of earth coming up to meet him. He landed safely to blunder about for half an hour before bumping into fellow crew-member, Norman Bradley. Together they set course west. It proved a short journey. At the first village they came to they were surrounded by local people and hauled off to a nearby interrogation centre. Clearly, there had been something dreadfully amiss with the B-17's navigation. They had not crossed the Rhine. They were east of Strasbourg rather than north-east, and dropped straight into enemy hands.

For all of Thursday and most of Friday, Tate was interrogated by German forces in a perfectly acceptable fashion. As well as Bradley, five other crew members had also been captured. Next day the seven men were transported under armed guard en route for a prison camp. The journey was to take them through a town called Pforzheim, which three weeks earlier had been the target of a devastating raid by Bomber Command.

The town lay in a valley. When the RAF men looked down on what had once been a thriving community of some 70,000 souls, all they could see was ruins. According to official records, a huge force of Lancasters and Mosquitoes had dropped 1,825 tons of bombs on Pforzheim in just twenty-two minutes, causing a firestorm that destroyed more than eighty percent of the town's built-up area, killing at least 17,000 people. Many died in their cellars, their lungs bursting with the intense heat. This crew had not taken part in the raid, but their shock at this ghastly evidence of the bombers' capacity for destruction was immense. Surviving townsfolk, catching sight of the prisoners' RAF uniforms, began stoning them furiously with rubble that lay at their feet. If it wasn't for armed guards defending them from the onslaught, all seven men might have been killed there and then. As it was, they reached the neighbouring village of Huchenfeld where they were billeted for the night in a boiler room filled with heaps of coal and given buckets of water. Exhausted, they lay back on the coal and were instantly asleep.

The next thing they knew, they were being violently dragged up the iron staircase out of the cellar, a gang of young men hauling them along the street. Their captors were dressed in ordinary civilian clothes, but they had a menacing air evidently in a state of high excitement. Someone hit Tom Tate on the head, while the mob turned right, taking their captives toward the church. Increasingly alarmed, they noticed a barn with a huge pair of doors. Inside was a small door which was open. An electric light burned. Tom Tate saw something that froze his heart: a stout beam from which hung several heavy ropes.

The sight made his survival instinct kick in, and he burst free from his captors, running in bare feet back up the road. It was a spontaneous action which saved his life. One shot was fired after him, but he ducked down past some houses, raced across a field and plunged into nearby woods. Most of the trees in the area were pines, difficult to hide among, but by chance he found a copse of oaks whose leaves lay thick on the ground. With the instinct of a wild animal he burrowed under the leaves until hidden from sight. For a while he lay awake, troubled by a sudden burst of gunfire coming from the village, wondering what had become of his comrades. Then he fell asleep. Tom Tate awoke in his leaf-mould bed at dawn on Sunday. By lunchtime he had been recaptured. But now, at least, he was in the hands of the German Army, not the dangerous youths of the night before.

He spent the remainder of the war as a PoW – much of it in horrendous conditions. For weeks he was on the road with thousands of near-starving men, mostly Russians, as Germans retreated from advancing Allied forces. But he survived as did four other members of the Flying Fortress crew. Norman Bradley had made a successful run for it at Huchenfeld, like himself, and then been recaptured and imprisoned. The Navigator, Dudley Heal, also survived a spell as a PoW. The Red Cross had already shipped another man, who had broken his leg when his parachute landed, home.

Meanwhile, their Skipper, John Wynne, managed to fly the crippled B-17 all the way back across the Channel single-handed. It was an astonishing feat. Trapped by the pipe supplying oxygen to his mask, he piloted the plane for much of the journey standing up, landing it safely at an unfamiliar aerodrome with his port landing wheel shot away.

It was the Air Ministry who asked Tom Tate to return to Pforzheim to help with a War Crimes Investigation following Germany's defeat. Only then did he learn the full, horrifying details of what happened to the other five men who had been marched towards the barn and its dangling ropes.

Four of his crew, he discovered, had been murdered soon after his own escape. They hadn't been hanged, as he feared when he'd glimpsed the dangling ropes. Instead, they had been shot in the churchyard in cold blood, at the very moment a little girl was preparing for her Confirmation Service. The fifth man, the Night Engineer, had made a run for it, but was caught later in a neighbouring village. A mob hauled him out of the police station, beat him half to death, and then shot him in the head.

When Tate walked into the churchyard at Huchenfeld with the Investigating Team, so very nearly the scene of his own death, he saw the five new graves. French soldiers who had been the first of General Patten's Army to enter the area, had inscribed each cross with simple but telling words: 'British airman, assassinated by the SA, 17/18 March 1945.'

A year later, in June 1946, Tom Tate and Norman Bradley returned to Germany as witnesses in the War Crimes trial against twenty-two men and youths who had taken part in the killings. They helped identify a few of them, some mere boys. In evidence at the trial, it became clear the murders were carried out as deliberate revenge for the Pforzheim bombing. Local Nazi leaders had ordered a lynch mob of Hitler Youth to dress in civilian clothes, posing as outraged villagers. They were to assault the schoolhouse where the RAF men were being held, and take them to their deaths. Seventeen were convicted. Three officials were hanged, others imprisoned. The youths were given lighter sentences. In years to come, the people of Huchenfeld hugged their shameful secret to themselves.

Then a remarkable thing happened. A retired Pastor from what was then East Germany came to live in the village. Dr Heinemann-Gruder, a former Army Officer, was a man of immense moral rectitude. On learning of the murder of the RAF men he resolved to put up a Memorial at the place where they died. Against strong local opposition he got his way, contacted relatives of some of the British airmen, and in November 1992 a simple plaque was erected on the wall of the church. It bore the names of the victims with the words: 'Father, forgive'.

From this brave act of expiation flowed an extraordinary series of events, beginning with the confession of one of the murderers at the Dedication Service itself. The by now elderly man broke into sobs. '*I was one of the boys who killed them'* he said. In response, the widow of one of the murdered men, Harold Frost, stepped forward unexpectedly to address them with great dignity, assuring them of her forgiveness. The reconciliation process was under way.

On hearing this story, a newspaper reporter tracked down John Wynne to tell him of the ceremony in Huchenfeld. For almost half a century on from that desperate night in March 1945, this was the first he had heard about the dreadful fate of his missing crewmen. Greatly moved, he commissioned an artist to make a wooden rocking horse that he and his wife donated to the kindergarten at Huchenfeld in 1994. The horse was called '*Hoffnung*', the German word for '*Hope*', and bore the inscription: '*To the children of Huchenfeld, from the mothers of 214 RAF Squadron.*' It was the start of a close relationship between the Wynnes and the villagers.

In turn, Tom Tate read this story in a magazine and made contact with his former crewmates. With understandable reluctance, encouraged by John Wynne, in 1995, he revisited the village where he almost lost his life.

Unbelievably, out of the horror of Pforzheim and the inhumanity of Huchenfeld has grown a very personal understanding between these former enemies. The bombs and the blood, the mayhem and murders are not forgotten. But for these people, in the words of the man who piloted the B-17 that fateful night, the future rides on the back of a rocking horse called Hope.

No. 223 Squadron

Alæ defendunt Africam – 'Wings defend Africa'
Reproduced with permission of the MOD

223 Squadron badge shows a lion statant, commemorating the Squadron's service in Kenya during the late 1930s. It was authorised by HM King George VI, August 1937.

Squadron Codes:

AO (Wellesley), 6G (Liberator and Fortress)

Duty
- 1936-1941: Wellesley Bomber Squadron, Middle East
- 1941: Operational Training Unit for medium bombers, Middle East
- 1941-1943: Bomber Squadron, Mediterranean and Italy
- 1944-1945: Electronic Counter Measures, Bomber Command

No. 223 Squadron was originally 'B' Flight, then 'B' Squadron under the Royal Naval Air Service (RNAS) – general duties units stationed on the island of Mitylene in the Ægean in 1917-1918. It was equipped with a mix of aircraft, including the Sopwith 1½ Strutter and Airco DH4.

On 1 April 1918, the RNAS merged with the Royal Flying Corps to produce the RAF, with B Squadron becoming No. 223 Squadron. It continued operations over the Ægean Sea, flying both reconnaissance and bombing missions from various bases until the end of World War One, disbanding at Mudros on the island of Lemnos on 16 May 1919.

No. 223 Squadron reformed at Nairobi in Kenya on 15 December 1936 as a day bomber Squadron when B Flight of 45 Squadron equipped with the Fairey Gordon was re-numbered. At first it only had a single Flight, using the two-seater day bomber Fairey Gordon aircraft until February 1937. It was then re-equipped with the Vickers Vincent until June 1938 when the Squadron received the Vickers Wellesley monoplanes – Barnes Wallis's first geodesic bomber.

After Italy entered the war in 1940, it was 223 Squadron which became one of the few to take the Wellesley (with a ceiling of 33,000 feet) into combat, and in June 1940, began carrying out bombing raids over Italian East Africa based at Summit in the Sudan.

In August, the Squadron moved to Perim Island, near Aden, at the start of the Italian invasion of British Somaliland from where, on 18 August, four of its Wellesleys bombed Italian airfields at Addis Ababa, destroying a number of aircraft, including the Duke of Aosta's private aircraft. It is worth noting that the conquest of the British Somaliland was the only campaign victory Italy achieved, without the support of German troops, during World War Two against the Allies.

In April 1941, the Squadron handed its Wellesleys to 47 Squadron, moving to Egypt to become an Operational Training Unit for Squadrons converting aircrews onto the Bristol Blenheim, Martin Maryland, Douglas Boston and later Martin Baltimore twin-engined bombers. In May, after training its own crews, it became an operational Baltimore Bomber Squadron with an active part in North African, Sicilian and Italian campaigns, flying more than 5,000 operational sorties and dropping more than 2,000 tons of bombs. Between October 1941 and January 1942 a detachment from the Squadron used the Maryland for strategic reconnaissance missions over the Western Desert.

It returned to the role of an operational light bomber Squadron equipped with Baltimores, and in May 1942 took part in the Battle of Gazala – Rommel's successful offensive. By the end of that year, the tables had turned, and the Squadron advanced through Libya in the aftermath of the British victory at El Alamein, reaching Tunisia in April 1943.

In July, the Squadron moved to Malta to attack tactical targets on Sicily during preparations for the invasion (aircraft moved first, joined by ground echelon in August). In September, the Squadron moved to Italy to attack enemy communications. Here, the Squadron was given 'Big Ben' equipment, mistakenly believed to be able to jam the guidance system of the V2 Rocket.

On 12 August 1944, still in Italy, it was disbanded and re-numbered No. 30 Squadron, SAAF (South African Air Force).

However, a couple of weeks later, 23 August 1944, the Squadron quickly reformed for a second time at Oulton, as the second 'Jostle' (radar jamming equipment) Unit in No. 100 Group, RAF Bomber Command. As a Bomber Support Squadron it was equipped with a mix of B-24Hs and B-24Js from the U.S 8th Air Force, using these aircraft effectively on radar countermeasures and electronic intelligence missions to support Bomber Command's main force. The B-24 could carry up to thirty radar jamming sets, carrying two Special Operators to work the equipment. Their role was so secret that even the rest of the crews didn't know what they were doing!

The first 'Big Ben' patrol came on 19 September (the Squadron's first countermeasures mission with the Liberator). The 'Big Ben' sorties involved four hour long daylight stints off the Dutch coast. However, this was having no effect, and equipment was removed in November, by which time the Squadron's last daylight patrol had already been flown on 25 October, after which it flew at night to support the Bomber stream.

The Squadron flew two main types of missions. The most common being *spoof* raids using 'WINDOW'. One line of aircraft would use 'WINDOW' to create a radar screen over the North Sea. Another flight of eight aircraft would then emerge from this screen and use 'WINDOW' to create the impression of a raid heading for a particular target. Once German fighters were heading for the wrong area, the main raid would emerge from the screen. However, as Germans grew familiar with this plan and ignored the feint, the order of events reversed, with the main raid leaving the radar screen first. The second type of mission saw two or three jamming aircraft accompany the main force, then circle above the target using jammers against German radar.

By December 1944 all Squadron aircraft carried *Jostle*, *Carpet* (designed to jam *Wurzburg* radar) and *Piperack* (used against SN-2 radar). The Squadron's jamming aircraft would remain over the target after the main force left to protect stragglers against German attack.

In March 1945, the Squadron began to convert to B-17s, although some B-24s were retained to the end of the war. The Squadron's last operational mission came on 2/3 May 1945 when it carried out a *spoof* 'WINDOW' raid over Kiel during the final Bomber Command raid of the war.

Post-war, the Squadron again reformed on 1 December 1959 as a Strategic Missile Squadron equipped with the Thor Intermediate range ballistic missile at RAF Folkingham in Lincolnshire. The Squadron was eventually disbanded on 23 August 1963, with the termination of the Thor Program in Britain.

PERSONAL EXPERIENCES

Flight Engineer Arthur Anthony
Author of: 'Lucky B-24'

Looking back all these years on, I don't really see this as a time for celebration but more of a time to remember what happened and of the role I together with thousands of others played in fighting for freedom. I lost a lot of friends and saw as many as five of our bombers shot down on a single night. We had to be a bit light-hearted about dying otherwise we couldn't have carried on. I remember it clearly and would never want to go through it again, or ever want anyone else to. We must remember what happened and the names of those who were there, those who survived and those who never returned … read their stories and remember … and never let it happen again!

Dr Peter Lovatt, Squadron Leader
September 1944

My first glimpse of the airfield at Oulton Street and of a few dispersed and darkened B-17 aircraft of No. 214 Squadron came just before eight one September morning in 1944 from the carriage of the Peterborough East train to Norwich, belonging to the long extinct M & GN railway.

I was one of thirty-eight reluctant Air Gunners, reluctant because all had been previously mustered under training as Pilots, Navigators and Air Bombers, who had to be persuaded to qualify at No. 10 Air Gunnery School, Walney Island, Barrow-in–Furness. Strictly speaking we should have gone to an Operational Training Unit, but these were full, so instead we were given indefinite Leave.

322

On our penultimate day, however, at Walney Island, a highly classified signal was received from the Air Ministry calling for thirty-eight
volunteers from among the sixty-strong course to help form a
special and secret unit in Bomber Command. No other information
was available, but the task turned out to be the reformation of No.
223 Squadron, recently disbanded in Italy. Unsurprisingly there were
no volunteers. The first thirty-eight names were simply taken from
the Passing-Out order of merit. As I came top of the course lasting
ten weeks, my name was placed first on the list of 'Volunteers'.

It was impressed on all concerned of the urgency of the situation
and that the detachment of 'Volunteers' should reach its destination as soon as possible. So we travelled through the night in order
to do so. It was after this first glimpse that I resolved to find out
why exactly Bomber Command in 1944 came to be equipped with
American aircraft – a subject which then was a closely guarded
secret, and remained so for many years long after the war was over.

It was to take me some time before I could find the answer as to
exactly why Oulton received American and not British aircraft and
involved me in the acquisition of a PhD.

Flt/Lt Robert Belton
How I Came to 100 Group... and Beyond

My arrival in 100 Group was as unexpected as it was a great
experience! It all started when in 1942 I was selected to join the
RAF-sponsored Short University Course entry system. This gave six
months at a University where you studied science-based subjects as
a student, with one and a half days a week on ITW subjects. At the
end, you joined the RAF full-time as an LAC. I was lucky enough to
go to King's College, Cambridge in October 1942.

After induction into the RAF at St John's Wood in 1943, I went to
Grading School, again in Cambridge, Marshall's, then via the Queen
Elizabeth to Halifax NS, and Muncton NB to the US Navy at Grosse
Ile near Detroit and on to Pensacola. Here, I graduated as a pilot
on Catalinas in May 1944. This course was meant to provide pilots
for Coastal Command, but by this time they already had enough!

So it was back to the UK and Oxfords. Then in January 1945 to Desborough for an Operational Training Unit on Wellingtons. This is where I 'acquired' my crew! This course finished in April 1945.

I was sent on Leave prior to a Heavy Conversion Unit on Lancasters, but a telegram diverted me to Oulton in Norfolk and the B-17 Flying Fortress Conversion Course prior to joining 223 Squadron. I think the Powers-That-Be felt my earlier U.S training would be an advantage. It was here that I got my Commission (which should have been awarded on graduation at Pensacola, because of my Short University Course, but they were unaware of the rules!)

I only went on one operation as an Observer as war was rapidly drawing to a close. We used to do 'Cooks Tours' to show the Ground Staff what happened to Germany in the bombing. A certain amount of low flying was permitted and I was able to take photographs. We also did dummy raids to see how effective 'Carpet', 'Jostle' and the rest had been in confusing the enemy.

While not flying, we watched the production of the film: 'The Wicked Lady' with Margaret Lockwood and Patricia Roc. We were living in the grounds of Blickling Hall where it was filmed on location. Other than a bit of sailing on Oulton Broad not far away there were few diversions available to us.

However, as aircrew we could get extra petrol coupons. I got my father's Prefect out of the garage and used it locally. The Flight Sergeant who looked after my a/c would always ensure the Prefect was suitably topped up while I was away flying! I was also engaged to marry at that time, so I would travel down to London where Betty worked for the BBC. All in all a very happy time.

My crew consisted of myself, Plt/Off R. O. Belton, plus:

Plt/O J B Mac McGarty	Manchester (I think)	Air Bomber
Flt/Sgt Cliff Cousins	Brixton?	Navigator
Flt/Sgt Dave Elbrow	Norfolk?	Radio Op 1
Sgt Butcher		Flt Engineer
Sgt Roy Leigh	Leeds?	M U Gunner
Sgt Stan Brough	Leeds?	Rear Gunner
Sgt Charlie Rimmer		Mid Gunner
Sgt Jack Ekers	?	Mid Gunner

I have no record of these chaps and regrettably lost contact with them all. They were a great bunch and we all got on pretty well and worked well together as a crew.

After the B-17s were disposed of, I was posted in September '45 to 512 Squadron on Dakotas and after a Conversion Course at Holme on Spalding Moor in Yorkshire we were sent to Qastina in Palestine in October, where we operated freight and Post Services in the Middle East, covering Naples to Aden and Jask. The airfield became too 'hot' due to the uprising in the area and in November we were moved to Gianaclis in Egypt, halfway between Alexandria and Cairo on the edge of the Delta. In mid-December we moved again to Bari in Italy.

Returning to the UK in March '46, I got married in April, just before joining 511 Squadron on Yorks where we operated as far as Calcutta.

On 1 January 1947, I went to the Central Flying School at Little Rissington on an Instructors' Course, but due to snow the twelve-week course was extended until June! I qualified as a QFI 'C' on Harvard a/c and posted to 7SFTS at Kirton-in-Lindsey, Lincs, on 1 July 1947. In June 1948, I was posted back to Central Flying School as a Staff Instructor where I stayed until May 1951, qualifying on all aircraft types – Tiger Moth, Mosquito T III, Spitfire 16, Lancaster VII, Auster 5, Balliol, Meteor 7, and became a QFI A1 with a Green Instrument Rating card.

I left the RAF in May 1951 to join No. 22 Reserve Flying School at Filton, Bristol, where reserve pilots came to keep their 'hands in'. Tiger Moths and Chipmunks were the aircraft, though one day I got the chance to fly and actually handle (*for 20 minutes!*) the Brabazon!

(*The Bristol Type 167 Brabazon was a large propeller-driven airliner, designed by Bristol Aeroplane Co. to fly transatlantic routes between the UK and U.S. Despite its size, roughly between an Airbus A300 and a Boeing 767; it was designed to carry only 100 passengers, each granted room about the size of the entire interior of a small car. A prototype was completed and flown in 1949, to prove a commercial failure when airlines felt the airliner was too large and expensive to be useful! In the end, only the single prototype was flown; broken up in 1953 for scrap, along with the uncompleted turboprop-powered Brabazon 1 Mk II.*)

I left Filton in February 1953 to join BOAC as a Flight Simulator Pilot Instructor on the Comet 1 Flight Simulator – the first jet simulator in the world, I believe. I later moved to Stratocruiser simulators and the Britannia 102 and 312, and then introduced the Comet 4 simulator into service for BOAC.

After nearly ten years of this work, I was appointed Flight Safety Officer under Sir Charles Guest, Air Safety Advisor to the Chairman. I was also Secretary to the Chairman's Air Safety Committee and edited the monthly Air Safety Review, detailing all incident and accident reports investigated by the BOAC Accidents Branch run by John Boulding. When the merger of BOAC and BEA took place, I became Assistant Air Safety Advisor, purely a change of title under a new Air Safety Advisor. I carried on with this aspect of Air Safety representing British Airways in various ways, both on the IATA Safety Advisory Committee (Chairman 1976-77), Flight Safety Foundation (USA) and the UK Flight Safety Committee (Chairman in 1974).

I finally left British Airways in 1982 hoping to take a post with IAM at Farnborough, but it seemed my face didn't fit! So I took retirement and enjoyed the period very much. I have much to be thankful for – the OC of the Training Flight at Oulton joined BOAC and I met him there – also an OC Flight on 223 Squadron turned up on Comets! These were all good contacts and I have to say my whole career in aviation has been enjoyable. My wife and I have been married for almost sixty-four years and my two children are well settled (pensioners too!) and a joy.

Sadly, Bob, a valued friend, who attended RAF 100 Group Reunions, died in January 2015. He is sadly missed by all.

Sgt Leonard Jack Vowler, Air Gunner

Leonard lived at Bickleigh in Devon working in a reserved occupation as Blacksmith and Farmer. His parents refused him permission to join up, so, to cover interviews for the RAF, he claimed the Leader of the ATC, of which he was a member, was leaving and he was attending Courses to take over his job. To meet requirements, the RAF thought him a year older than he was which meant on reaching twenty-one, he couldn't celebrate! He left to start in the RAF in 1942, arranging to be picked up in a lorry rather than use the train where his sister controlled the signal box.

He started as a Pilot Navigator Bomber, attending No. 7 Initial Training Wing at Newquay in Cornwall. Training continued until 1944. However, with too many RAF staff under training across the world, in June he went to a reclassification Wing in London providing Aptitude Tests, at the end of which they were all told they'd passed. Now came a stark choice – either join the Army or become Air Gunners!

He took the Air Gunners Course at Walney Island in Cumbria, No 10 AGS. Here he was in a group with the late Peter Witts and the late Harry Sykes. Leonard got a mark of 80.1%. This was calculated by shooting coloured bullets into a drogue and is a high mark. Thirty-nine from this Course went straight to 223 Squadron being reformed at RAF Oulton.

First crews were mixed, but then it was decided permanent crews worked well, and he joined Val Croft's crew. When, in December 1944, the front turret was removed from Liberator aircraft, improving their handling; Len was Front Gunner. His crew wouldn't let him go so they drew lots, but he still lost. He then went to 1699 HCU at RAF Oulton as they converted crews to B-24 Liberators, and while there he formed part of the crew with Norman Ayres.

Their final flight was on the night of 20/21 March 1945.

They were part of a 'WINDOW' Force, their mission to make it look as if Kassell was being attacked, and the Germans took the bait, sending fighters to this area. However, they were shot down by what is believed to be a Messershmitt Bf110 with upward-firing cannons called *Schrage Musik*.

Andrew Barron, a Navigator with Tony Morris' crew, believes he saw the aircraft go down. Ayres managed to gain control of the plane as they continued on, throwing out equipment to lighten their load. Len bailed out. He was later found dead in a tree still in his parachute. Probably there hadn't been enough height for the canopy to open properly. The aircraft crashed in a wood. Special Operator, Coles was the only survivor. He came to in the wreck and found the *Jostle* set on top of him. He was seriously injured and handed over to the Germans. One will never know how many other lives were saved by his crew giving the ultimate sacrifice.

The total night operations are depicted on the wall in the City of Norwich Aviation Museum in Norfolk. They also have on display Les Matthews painting of the B-24 aircraft in which he was shot down. This was 'T' Tommy, Arthur Anthony's lucky B-24. Arthur Anthony later had published a book: 'Lucky B-24'.

The crew were buried in Buhle. A picket fence and memorial cross was placed at the graves. But then sometime in 1948, the British Government decided that all outlying graves should be re-interred in Hanover. This is where Sgt Leonard Jack Vowler, RAFVR, of 223 Squadron now rests with his crew. Rod says: 'I have managed to visit his grave, and the cemetery is an excellent War Graves Commission site'.

However, the story doesn't end there.

While Rod Vowler, Leonard Vowler's nephew, continues to try to get re-published Arthur Anthony's book: 'Lucky B-24', there remained the question about the final resting place of the aircraft: 'T' Tommy'. Rod, a member of RAF 100 Group Association since its beginnings, relates what happened on discovering hidden truths, and how it feels visiting a crash site.

VISITING A CRASH SITE
TS526: B-24 Liberator of 223 Squadron, Oulton
by Nephew Rod Vowler

My uncle, Leonard Vowler, was in TS526, a B24 Liberator of 223 Squadron based at RAF Oulton. The aircraft was shot down on the night of the 20/21 March 1945.

It would appear it was shot down by a German Messersmitt 110 using upward firing cannons. All the German pilot had to do was to get under the aircraft of his enemy and shoot upwards. He would have had a good view looking up into what would have been a lighter area. The crew would not have the same clear view as they looked down into darkness.

The Air Gunners might see the aircraft beneath them, but would be unable to deflect and lower their guns far enough for any effect. Their aircraft went down. The pilot managed to gain enough control to level it out while the crew ejected spare equipment to lighten their load.

My uncle was seen to leave the plane via the escape hatch by Cole, their Special Radio Operator. However, the aircraft was too low. The parachute had no time to open effectively. He was found hanging in the trees. Meanwhile, the aircraft crashed into a wood on top of a hill and was immediately on fire. Cole came to and found the *Jostle* jamming equipment on top of him. Local people were attending. It was they who reached in to get him out and saved his life. He was then taken down the hill on a cart and placed in a building. Later, he was moved to a Convent where it was discovered he had broken his back and consequently handed over to the authorities. The rest of the crew were buried in a small cemetery at Buhla. It was the Germans who put a picket fence around the graves and a cross on the site.

Then around 1949 it was decided by the British Government the crew would be re-interred in Hanover.

I visited their graves in the well-kept War Graves Commission site. But my ambition was to visit the actual crash site. Having visited Hanover on an exchange visit several times, my hosts were never in a position to assist me. Then in October 2007, finally I made it as German police friends took me direct to the site where the aircraft had crashed.

On the way down to Wofhagen, near Kassell; it was foggy. I wondered if it might be clear on the hill I was to visit. In the centre of Wolfhagen, I met my helpers for the day. Hans Adler, Hans Hahn, Ingo Jung and Herr Klinkhart. In convoy, the vehicles set of to the site. We parked near the Schloss that Cole had been in all those years ago.

The sun came out, dispelling the fog. *What a brilliant day!* Then off along a lane into the wood, we started uphill. Herr Adler was using his metal detector, and unbelievably, after all these years, was finding parts of the plane. It was obvious the site had been visited on numerous occasions, but for me this was a personal mission and all the more emotive.

At the summit of the hill was a scene of devastation. There had been gale-force winds which had felled numerous trees. Some had been cut up and removed, leaving branches strewn around. I was looking for a tree with an engraving. The date 1948 was when all major parts of the aircraft were removed, but there should still be an engraving on the trunk of a tree with this date in memory of what had happened here. However, no trace of the tree was found. Damage to trees the aircraft had hit was pointed out to me, and there was a photograph as a point of reference taken some years previous. It showed a clearing with a patch of grass. In this area alone, no trees had grown since the crash. Then, while searching, we came across an area where there was plexi-glass, a positive indication we were in the correct place. Photographs were taken. I was holding a Union Jack flag and one of the others held the German flag. It was a proud moment to actually be at the site of the crash of the aircraft in which my uncle had flown sixty-two years ago.

I left a notice with a list of the crew pinned to a tree trunk, together with a solitary rose. It somehow felt appropriate. Another poignant moment was in the clearing during a spell of quiet reflection. Beech leaves were falling slowly down, reminding me of November, Remembrance Day, and poppies descending to the floor of the Royal Albert Hall in London. It was a moment to remember, not just my uncle, but all those many many others who made the ultimate sacrifice so that we could enjoy the kind of freedom we have today.

On arriving back at the cars, Hans Adler presented me with two carrier bags full of parts from the aircraft he had collected. I was deeply moved by this offer. However, I was not allowed to take them with me on my trip back to England and had to make do with small parts only as mementoes. Meanwhile, we went on to Buhla to visit the first burial site, a well-kept cemetery the other side of the hill where they crashed.

My grateful thanks to everyone who made this journey into the past possible. My everlasting gratitude to Richard Forder (a fellow Member of RAF 100 Group Association) for his research and introduction to the German Guides. Further information can be gleaned for those interested and with a computer by putting 'luftkrieg-ed-erbergland' into Google, then clicking on 'Translate'. When the web page comes up, click on 'News', and onto the date: '22.10.2007 Night Hunter'. From there you can easily see all the work this group performs.

WAAF Sgt Barbara Kerry

The other day I picked up an old newspaper to find an article about 223 Squadron ... and suddenly the memories came flooding back.

I had been a WAAF Sergeant in charge of the Officers' Mess at Oulton with an office in Blickling Hall where '*The Wicked Lady*' was filmed. Photographs were taken in the Sergeants' Mess where I moved in 1945 and became hostess to actress Pat Roc for the night.

We were at war ... all in the same boat, with cold Nissen Huts, huddling around a stove for comfort and warmth. It was always nice to know when crews got back, but very upsetting when we lost them.

I am ninety-one years old, but remember those years as being happy days most of the time! Strange to think that at Blickling Hall now there is only the echo of all those young voices, and a Museum dedicated to folk who served there.

I helped put the Museum together in its beginnings and would get requests for copy photos by some who visited. There was always a keen interest to know more about those days of war, what it was like to be there at the time.

F/O Mervyn Utah
Oct 1924 – Nov 2010
by Navigator Andrew Barron

Mervyn was co-pilot in Tony Morris' crew, in which I was Navigator (after their 4th Sortie). He joined the RCAF in October 1943 as soon as he was eighteen and gained his wings when he was just nineteen years old, after which he was posted to GR School on Prince Edward Island in the Gulf of St Lawrence. From there he went to 111 O.T.U in the Bahamas where, to his annoyance due to his age, he was not given a Command, but assigned as a co-pilot.

Posted to the UK, his crew was pitchforked into Bomber Command to crew Liberators of the newly re-formed 223 Squadron at Oulton. After a few minutes into their third '*Big Ben*' patrol off the Dutch Coast they found themselves in the centre of a salvo of flak.

Their Navigator, John Wallace, was wounded and they aborted the Operation. Mervyn wrote in his Memoirs:

... the trip changed my outlook on the war. Up to that time the war had been a bit of a game. You got to fly aircraft, had a nice uniform to wear, the pay was reasonable, people respected you. I now realised people on the ground were trying to kill us! I knew that they were shooting at us because there was no-one else there. We ran into a lot of flak on later trips. It was more impersonal as there were a lot of other bomber aircraft so you felt they were shooting in the hopes of hitting someone. The optimistic outlook of young people!

I was offered John Wallace's position. At the time, I was 2nd Navigator to Freddy Freake in Scotty Steele's crew and, effectively, 'redundant', flying as Front Gunner! Mervyn completed a further thirty-six sorties, culminating in the last Bomber Command sortie of the war on 2 May 1945. He left Oulton on 6 May to arrive back in Canada (via New York) on 24 May.

He was due to form part of Canada's *'Tiger Force'* (the British/ Commonwealth Bomber Force destined to attack Japan). When this was cancelled, in July he was offered the choice of staying in the Air Force or his Release, which he took to go to University. At the end of three years (of a four-year course) in Mining Engineering, he took a vacation job down a gold mine in Yellowknife (Northern Territories). Soon deciding that 5000 feet above ground was preferable to 5000 feet below, he quit University to seek a job in aviation. Unfortunately, airlines had all the pilots they needed. But then he was lucky to receive an invitation to rejoin the Air Force. However, attitudes don't change! The Senior Officer on the Interview Board refused to believe he'd completed a full Tour at the age of just nineteen! Someone should have told him the average age of Bomber Command crews was twenty-two!

After several years in Search and Rescue, in 1958 he was posted to pilot a ski-wheel DC3 on glacial research (Canada's contribution to the International Geophysical Year which involved landing on glaciers in Ellesmere Island (83 degrees North!) at 4000 and 6000 feet – the first time ever for such a large aircraft. He was sent to Europe in 1961 amongst Canada's NATO reinforcements, transferring in 1962 to Paris for the very pleasant job of flying Senior Officers etc. to northern destinations in summer and southern ones in winter! He had hardly returned to Canada when he was sent to Kashmir to fly a STOL aircraft for the UN for a year. He spent his final two years in the RCAF flying CL44s, retiring after twenty-five years in 1969.

He joined the Canadian Department of Transport that year flying as an Air Carrier Inspector, checking Airline Pilots for Type Endorsements and Annual and Route Checks.

Having lost his license for Medical reasons, he was made Project Manager for the introduction of the Micro-Wave Landing System and, later, Canadian Member on the ICAO All Weather Operations Panel, finally retiring in 1987 after forty-five years in Aviation.

Flt/Lt Ronald Walter Johnson RAFVR, Navigator
28 January 1922 – 28 August 2013
by Ron Johnson & Richard Forder (co-author: *Special Ops Liberators 223 (BS) Squadron, 100 Group & the Electronic War*)

Ron Johnson was employed in a Law firm in Grays Inn, London when war broke out. Like many of his contemporaries he was inspired to be a pilot and volunteered for aircrew. This was despite the advice of his elder brother, who urged him not to volunteer for aircrew. Already serving in the RAF, he had seen at first hand casualties amongst young fighter pilots flying from Kent airfields during the Battle of Britain.

His call-up papers duly arrived and he reported, as instructed, to the RAF Recruiting Office at Euston. After a very strenuous day of rigorous testing and examination he was pronounced A1 in all respects, and accepted for pilot training. At this early stage of the war, the training machine was swamped by an avalanche of recruits. Ron was placed on Reserve and returned home to await further instructions.

After a wait of seven to eight months, he received instructions to report to Aircrew Reception Centre at St Johns Wood where he was kitted out, jabbed and lectured. More waiting followed until he was called forward to 11 ITW at Scarborough to begin the first stage of aircrew training. Completing his ITW course it was on to No. 4 Elementary Flying Training School (EFTS) at Borough in East Yorkshire where initial assessment of his suitability for pilot training was carried out. This was his introduction to the De Havilland Tiger

Moth. Again he was successful and told that he would be going to Canada, taking part in the Empire Air Training Scheme.

He crossed the Atlantic in style, travelling in the *Queen Elizabeth* to Halifax, Nova Scotia. A long train journey followed across Canada to the Town of Virden in Manitoba, home of No. 19 EFTS. Ron enjoyed his flying training using the Tiger Moth and went solo after thirteen hours, twenty-five minutes in the air. Despite this success however, Ron was not convinced he wanted to be a pilot after all. Despite pressure to continue, he would not change his mind and reluctantly was posted away to a nearby Holding Depot. After a number of interviews he was offered an Observer's Course. This entailed an Air Gunner's course, a Bomb Aimer's course and full Navigator's course. This comprehensive series appealed to Ron and the die was cast.

His new direction commenced with his attendance at No. 31 Bombing & Gunnery School, Picton, Ontario flying in Blenheim and Bolingbroke aircraft. Completed in six weeks it was on to No. 9 Air Observers School (AOS) at St Jean, Quebec, near Montreal. The five month course was very intense, covering the theory and practice of air navigation. The practice took place in Avro Ansons involving flying some seventy-five hours by day and forty hours at night. Inevitably some of his colleagues fell by the way side, but Ron survived to finish a creditable 6th out of the twenty-four who finally emerged to earn their Observers' Flying 'O' badge and promotion to Sergeant.

There followed a brief interlude of an unforgettable week's leave spent in New York before it was off on the next element of the long training trail. He had been selected to join Coastal Command. This required another long rail journey, this time to Prince Edward Island in NE Canada, home of No. 1 General Reconnaissance School (GRS) at Summerside. The sun was certainly shining on him at this time as he was among a small number of his fellow AOS graduates to be granted a Commission. Ron spent his time polishing up navigational skills at Summerside, again flying in Avro Ansons.

Another surprise posting at the end of the course saw him on his way to No. 111 (Coastal) Operational Training Unit at Nassau in the Bahamas where he was to convert to one of Coastal Command's Very Long Range aircraft, the Consolidated B-24 Liberator. His move to Nassau had the bonus of extending his time away from the blackout, rationing and other miseries of wartime Britain. Here, Ron went through the crucial crewing up experience that was very much a lottery. However, he was lucky as he met an RCAF pilot, 'Tommy' Thompson, who after a chat, invited him to complete his crew. He was introduced to them, five more Canadians and an RAF Flight Engineer (F/E). Ron quickly gained a great respect for his new skipper, a big man in every way, quickly bonding with his crew mates.

Flying commenced on the twin engine B-25 Mitchell at Oakes Field. This was the first stint in their conversion training. It lasted five weeks, with training exercises day and night, including five hour anti-submarine patrols. It had the benefit of shaking them down as a crew in preparation for the second and most important phase which involved a move to the Island's other airfield at Windsor Field where their conversion to the Liberator would take place. This was successfully completed after three months.

At the end of the course it was back to Britain via Canada to await their posting to a Coastal Command Squadron. However, the war had moved on since their training began. The Allies had the upper hand in the U-Boat war, and the Command had started to disband some of its Squadrons creating an aircrew surplus. Fate decreed their return also coincided with a requirement to reform a Squadron in Bomber Command to be equipped with Liberators; given added priority to help deal with the then perceived threat of radio controlled V-2s.

What was the role of 100 Group and 223 (Bomber Support) Squadron, and where the hell was RAF Oulton?

They were soon to find out. Ron and his crew were entering the highly secretive world of Radio Counter Measures, and only the Squadron's Liberators would be initially familiar to them.

Arriving at Oulton in early September there was a hiatus whilst their aircraft were delivered and made ready for the new role. After a short work up they flew their first operation on 7 October 1944. Ron was ever present on their first nineteen missions.

On the night of 19/20 February 1945 the crew were on Battle Order for a *Window* Patrol. It was not a good night for them. They would be without their regular Wireless Operator, Flt/Sgt Rex Arnett RCAF who had reported sick and replaced by Flt/Sgt Des Bryant RAF.

For no apparent reason they felt apprehensive as they walked across the dispersal to their regular aircraft TS520, J-Johnnie. They were unsettled further by last minute minor faults, delaying take-off by eleven minutes, and finally airborne at 2236. More trouble developed in the climb when the turbo-supercharger on No. 4 engine was found to be u/s; this affected the aircraft's rate of climb and ability to maintain height and speed. The need to use higher boost and rpm settings resulted in a significant increase in fuel consumption. Notwithstanding these problems, F/O Thompson elected to continue, and surprisingly they were only one minute late at their first turning point.

The flight continued uneventfully until 0125 when they were approximately thirty miles SE of Dortmund at a height of 18,000 feet. Without warning they were attacked by two, possibly three, Ju88s. Thompson took immediate evasive action, corkscrewing to shake off the attackers. This appeared successful and they were left alone for a few minutes. Ron had just sorted out his plot and given Tommy a course correction to bring them back on track, when they were attacked both from ahead and rear. There was no escape this time and J-Johnnie was raked from end to end; there followed a violent rocking and the whole aircraft appeared to shudder before entering an uncontrolled dive.

The aircraft was now on fire. Smoke and flames reached Ron's position in the nose. Remarkably, Tommy and Jack Kendall briefly regained control. Over the intercom he heard Tommy say calmly: 'This is the end fellows, abandon aircraft'. Ron pulled the emergency handle to open the nose-wheel doors to provide his escape from the Navigator's position in the nose. He experienced a moment of panic as he could not move the handle. It took a kick from his boot before it operated to open the doors.

After the noise, smoke and flames all was peaceful as his chute opened and he descended to the snow-clad hills and forests of enemy territory below. He landed without injury, but had lost a flying boot during the descent. The snowbound conditions and his frozen foot eventually prompted him to seek help and he was taken prisoner. Four of the crew located in the rear of the aircraft also baled out successfully. They were the two Special Operators: W/Os Ron Palmer RAF and Bill Baker RAF, Rear Gunner Flt/Sgt George Graham RCAF and Waist Gunner Flt/Sgt Brian Maxwell RCAF. Those unable to escape from the doomed plane were:

- F/O 'Tommy' Thompson RCAF   Pilot
- Flt/Sgt Jack Kendall RAF   2nd Pilot
- Flt/Sgt Ron Woods RCAF   Mid Upper Gunner
- Flt/Sgt Ron Wynn RAF   Flight Engineer

- Sgt Ted Whittaker RAF   Waist Gunner
- Flt/Sgt Des Bryant RAF   Wireless Operator

Ron's period as a PoW was thankfully brief. After an initial period at the aircrew interrogation centre at Stalag Luft Oberusel near Frankfurt he was transported to Dulag Wetzlau, NW of Frankfurt. This was another temporary stop before he was moved on to Stalag Luft III in Nuremberg. From here in early April he was to join a march of fellow PoWs that ended on 20 April at Stalag VII AC located at Moosburg, near Munich. At the end of hostilities he was repatriated in a USAAF Dakota landing at RAF Westcott, near Aylesbury, on 10 May.

After a lengthy spell of Leave he attended a Medical Board where he was pronounced unfit for further flying duties. Whilst he waited for his release date he was posted to the RAF School of Administration at RAF Credenhill, Hereford, for a month's course to turn him into a Secretarial Officer. On course completion, he was posted to HQ 43 Group, Maintenance Command, at RAF Stanmore to be Camp Commandant. In July 1946, he married Betty and in September 1946, Flt/Lt Johnson returned to civilian life. He did not return to his pre-war Law occupation. In yet another change of direction, he attended Wandsworth College and trained as a teacher. A successful career in Education followed and he became a respected headmaster. He also lectured at the University of London.

I first encountered Ron at early RAF 100 Group Reunions in Norfolk, and always looked forward to meeting him and Betty through the years. Sadly, in later times, he did not enjoy good health and he and Betty had to give up attending this annual event. However, we kept in touch and it was always a particular pleasure to speak on the phone or see his familiar handwriting amongst my morning mail. He retained his interest in all things 223 Squadron. Fortunately, he placed all his wartime memories in his book: 'A Navigator's Tale', published in 2000. Particularly valuable, it was the second of only three personal accounts covering 223 Squadron's 100 Group activities. I have drawn on it for this account in addition to memories from conversations and correspondence over the years. He was a modest man, but always willing to discuss his experiences with me and interested to learn of my progress during my long period of research for my own book on 223 Squadron. Ron was a man of many parts. In addition to the varied aspects of his life already mentioned he was a talented writer of poetry. It was particularly poignant that he was able to read his poem: '*In Memoriam*' at the dedication of Oulton Memorial in May 1994; written in June 1945 in dedication to the six members of his crew in Liberator 'J' Johnny shot down over Germany on the night of 20/21 March 1945, who made the supreme sacrifice:-

In Memoriam – 'J Johnny'

Who loved life
Just as much as I
Nor wished to fight
Or fighting wished to die?
How shall I tell of you, my friends?
What songs shall satisfy

My heart? What verses
Penetrate the crowd
Of platitudes when crude
Pen-scribblings shroud
With drooping laurels your simple dignity?
The stars were lost in cloud

The night I left you
Four miles high
Above the German mountains
Falling from the sky,
Like flaming autumn leaves
There was no time to say goodbye.

Familiar voices heard
Above the engines' roar,
Our flying kit flung carelessly
Across the crew room floor
Are murals for my inner walls
Point, counterpoint of war.

And so for me
You did not die

Because the corn grew tall
Where you passed by
And you loved living
Every bit as much as I. [54]

Ron was a private man but warm-hearted to those who were lucky enough to come to know him. I count myself very fortunate to have been in the latter category. It was therefore with great sadness I received Betty's telephone call to break the news of his passing. I shall always remember him with respect and affection.

LACW Joan Stanfield, WAAF
Final Memories

I served with the WAAF at RAF Sculthorpe and moved over to RAF Oulton when 214 Squadron went in 1944. I am a member of the RAF 100 Group Association and attended the commemoriation in May 1994 at Blickling and Aylsham and the moving Service unveiling the stone near the airfield; known as Oulton Memorial. It was good to meet old comrades again and the people in the village were very kind.

I was an LACW in Accounts Officer Flight Lieutenant David Collins Section. He was a good Officer, a Christian man. I used to go to Sunday Church Parade with him on the Camp. We would all choose hymns in turn. As my husband was in the Royal Navy my choice was always '*Eternal Father*'. I have many happy memories of Hut 8 on the WAAF site under the trees near Blickling Lake where we would swim in summer.

There were Music Club nights in the Hall, wonderful records of classical and all kinds of music. I used to play the piano in the NAAFI – clouds of concrete dust rising from the dancers' feet, playing in the '*Buckinghamshire Arms*', also in a pub in Aylsham. My husband and I used to stay in when on Leave from the Royal Navy, I think it was called the '*Black (or White) Swan*'. The piano there was always in the parlour and kept locked, but I was allowed to play for sing-songs.

My wedding dress in August 1944 was made with me standing on my bed in the hut to have it pinned and fitted and sent home to be machined by my dear mother, then back for a fitting! There were happy times and sad when many gallant airmen were lost and faced death each operation they made.

In his writings (which follow), Flt/Lt Collins mentions briefly the Camp celebrations for 'V.E. Day' arranged with great thanksgiving and joy. We had a huge party, giant figures of Hitler and Mussolini were made and hung in the hangar. They were thrown on a huge bonfire on the airfield, a sheep was roasted and carved for sandwiches, a bit tough; barbeques became the norm years later. On the actual V.E. weekend my husband and I attended a service in the packed cathedral at Norwich. This was relayed to the many people outside in the grounds. There was a YMCA hostel during the war in the cathedral grounds.

In June, we WAAFs were allowed by the Air Ministry to fly over Germany in a B-17 to see the ruins of the cities and I clearly remember the devastation, many ships upside-down in Kiel Canal.

I was demobbed in September 1945 after three years service. It was a long time ago, but I am still in touch with dear friends from Hut 8.

Flt/Lt David Collins: Accounts Officer
Souvenir of Oulton

The hedges and trees which line the Aylsham road still wore the fresh green of summer when you left us. No doubt you still picture the tall chimneys of Blickling against the bright blue sky of early morning as you waited for the bus. The kites bask peacefully on the airfield in the warmth of the morning haze ... do those days seem far off now as you sit by the fire at your comfortable peacetime Station?

Since then the gales and fogs of winter have descended upon the wilds of Norfolk. The airfield is bare and desolate; the Control Tower is deserted. Not an echo of a clang disturbs the silence of the hangars. The Signals Block is locked and barred. The sites are swept and garnished. The Sick Quarters slumber quietly up the road, but the old Station dies very hard. An R.A.F uniform is still to be seen in the village shop. The sound of a scratching pen may still be heard at S.H.Q where an odd bod or two challenge the claims of rats and mice to undisputed occupation. Occasionally a Morris van limps by, and the hoot of the NAAFI wagon will evoke a surprising response at any hour of the day or night.

The Oldest Inhabitant staggers painfully around in his tattered uniform with the help of a crutch. Often his thoughts will turn to livelier and happier days of yore. Then, Oulton was a place of life, vigour and laughter; of coaches and vans and sports cars; of whirring aircrews, of taxying aircraft; of snappy salutes and bright-eyed Waffies. He has bidden farewell to many an airman and WAAF since those days, pressing a parting gift from the safe into their reluctant hands. He knows that almost without exception, they left full of pleasant memories of the weeks and months spent on the Unit. All have agreed that Oulton was an exceptionally 'happy' Station. Group Captain Dickens could not have failed to be gratified to hear the comments that were made.

Having an idle hour to spend whilst awaiting his own departure, the Oldest Inhabitant thought that an account of the gradual decline and final graceful expiry of Oulton might be of interest to some of her former inmates; while the setting down of the few memories which so often float through his mind might perhaps stir similar pleasurable recollections in those of his readers.

Big things happened at Oulton during 1944 and 1945. We knew little of what was going forward; each man did his job and asked no questions; each man and each woman had some share in those achievements. Big men lived among us, ate with us, played with us at Oulton. Some of them flew away into the night and never returned … They were gallant souls. We mourned their loss, but we didn't talk about it much. All that is another and a far greater story. The O.I is not the man to tell it. He was one of the 'chair-borne troops' whose task was glamourless and unspectacular. Still, maybe he experienced phases of Camp life which were missed by others. These too have interest. Anyway, here are some random memories – no attempt at a history, just a 'souvenir'.

On 1 January 1944 I set off for Sculthorpe, Oulton's forerunner. Late at night I arrived at Kings Lynn, and spent an hour in the crowded buffet waiting for the Peterborough train. What a line! Gosh, it was cold!! Eventually I reached Sculthorpe; even in the dark you could sense the flatness and bleakness of the place. Still, they were a jolly crowd that gathered in the Mess. Group Captain Dickens, Jean Woodman, Flt/Lt Martin, Sgt Wickenden and other pioneers had arrived from North Creake; Sigs Collins, the Adj. and F/Lt Brown had joined them. The next few days brought Squadron Leader Bradshaw, dear old 'Sado', the Catering Officer, Squadron Leader Howard, Doc Vyse, and sundry others and all set to with a will to get the place ready to receive the lads of 214 and the American Squadron. It wasn't exactly comfortable, but it was fun. The Officers Mess chiefly occupied themselves in the evenings with darts matches organised by the G/C; and troops settled as best they could with somewhat limited resources. There was plenty of wind and bags of rain; many an evening the Accounts Staff would foregather round the stove in the Section for warmth and dry off after the trek from office to site and site to Mess. There was much clamouring for coal, much searching for wood and the fires wouldn't light – ask the batman – but those were good days. As winter relented and the sun broke through and the evenings drew out, the bikes came out too and the troops began to explore the road to Fakenham (egg and chips!), to Wells and Hunstanton, and to Walsingham. ENSA (Entertainments National Service Association) came to visit us. We had working parades! The Accountants took to P.T. The kites were airborne; and rumours came of a move to the eastward.

Do you remember the long trek to Blickling in convoys from Sculthorpe? The '214' bods who couldn't be found when it was time to start – the D.Rs who trailed us, rounding us up like watch-dogs; and who turned up as if by magic at every signpost? The long wait up the lane on arrival while they manoeuvred the Queen Marys? I shall not forget in a hurry the first view of the Hall, flanked by creeper-covered 'almshouses' and great yew hedges; and the white 'Buck' with its red geraniums in window boxes, nestling amongst tall trees. Did you see the gardens about that time? What a show of rhododendrons and azalea, of lilac and laburnum, of bluebells in the woods, of prunus and cherry blossom, and at the end of a long walk, the Solarium shining in the sun. The swans had nine youngsters in 1944 and would sail up and down the lake in convoy. We watched them growing as summer lengthened, until in time they could all take off in formation and execute superb sweeps and dive-bombing operations.

The Lido at the head of the lake seemed more popular in those days. The rubber dinghies were very much in vogue until some silly fatheads got in them with spiked shoes. The WAAFs produced some very natty bathing ensembles and certainly appeared to enjoy them-selves, if one could judge by the amount of screaming and shieking heard in those regions. Remember the swimming sports and joust-ing? In 1945 fishing was popular. The more elderly gentlemen of the M.T. Section were usually to be found patiently waiting for pike in the evenings. I certainly saw a monster they caught one day. The batmen had their successes too; one sometimes wondered whether they had really come from the lake! The Met officers were often to be seen on a raft, but I never discovered what they were doing. The place was a real delight to lovers of nature. I wonder how many times some of us walked round in the course of the summer months.

The dwellers in the Hall in former centuries would have been sorely shaken had they beheld things which happened when the R.A.F. arrived. The ghost of Anne Boleyn must have been gravely disturbed. At first she mildly protested by such time-worn efforts as swinging open the great wardrobe in Lord Lothian's bedroom in the middle of the night when the G/C was sleeping there, but within a few days she grew more lively. At midnight in the 'Lothian' passage such phenom-ena occurred as the flinging open of bedroom doors with resound-ing crashes; bundles of stair rods were precipitated violently inside. On opening one's door in the morning fire buckets full of water would crash to the floor from the door handles. At all hours there were ghastly groans and shrieks – some of them strangely masculine. The inmates of the aforesaid passage celebrated their emancipation from the more restricted amenities of Nissen huts by some aston-ishly light-hearted exercises. I shall never forget the sight of Brad and Sammy tumbled in a struggling heap among the coats and Wellington boots in a cupboard linking my room with Brad's. Brad was an enter-taining neighbour. He had a most original vocabulary. The Padre used

343

to say he had never heard anyone swear so charmingly as Brad, and he was usually the first in the bathroom in the mornings, full of irrepressible high spirits whatever time he had gone to bed.

The part of the Hall which was usually locked up was extremely interesting, if you could gain entry. To do this you had to make friends with the custodian Miss O'Sullivan, the lady in slacks with the fierce hound, who was so often seen walking the grounds. She very kindly showed me round on one occasion. There was a magnificent library upstairs, with some fine old books. There were rooms where Royalty had been entertained in bygone centuries; and there was much fine old furniture and a number of interesting pictures and tapestries.

A noble feature of Blickling was the Concert Hall. It was only after the war began, of course, that the old barn was patched up and a stage added to produce the really excellent hall that we knew. Many were the pleasant evenings spent here. The distinctive atmosphere of these entertainments could hardly be reproduced outside the R.A.F. the notabilities with their wives in the front rows, the welcoming whistles of the troops and the pretty girls, and the precarious tiers of seats at the back, crowded to capacity. Perhaps the most dramatic episode was the noisy interruption of sirens and the doodle-bug at the curcial point of 'Gaslight'. Then there was the gruesome hanging scene from Maria Whatsit. Do you remember the Canadian Show – 'cakes wid-or-widout prunes'? and the ballet and 'Swinging on a Star' – and the Russian concert at Sculthorpe – and Ann Casson in the 'Taming of the Shrew'? The greatest success without a doubt were our own shows so excellently produced by Corporal Parish; and the dashing Ken May and dapper Cpl. Gratwick.

No reference of Blickling would be complete without reference to the famous Brains Trust. S/Ldr Foster, F/Lt James and Cpl Griffiths certainly established a reputation that night and compared very well with Professor Joad and Lord Winster. Leslie Mitchell as Question Master rounded off a tip-top performance, and if I remember rightly, Cpl Griffiths preceded the Trust with one of his famous quizzes.

One of the highlights, in the history of the Accounts Section at any rate, was 'Sports Day' in Farmer Mitchell's field. Let it be recorded for posterity that, fielding a team including four old men approaching forty, and two determined WAAFs, urged on by the enthusiastic Sandford and cheers of the crowd, they defeated a team of tough Armourers by two pulls to one and reached the final. Pretty good going! My word, I shan't forget pushing old Webby in the wheelbarrow race, we didn't get very far. What other memories are there of Blickling? The M.T. vehicles neatly stacked row on row, the rush for buses to Oulton, the trek of the officers back to lunch led by those absurd Aberdeens, the crowd in the *Buck* every evening and the inexhaustible energy of Mr. O'D in cutting sandwiches, the friendliness charm of little Susan Vyse and the cats!

The Music Circle must have a paragraph in itself. In the earliest days we had the privilege of some masterly programmes given by S/Ldr Sutton. Then we moved to Blickling and used the Solarium – a lovely setting for music, but also for midges. With the onset of winter, attendances of eighty and more were reached. These were the days of Jackie Furner's *'Bach to Baizy'* shows, and the operatic performance of F/O *'Your tiny hand is frozen'* Darracott. Then came the purchase of our own records and two programmes were given weekly for nine months. In the bitter cold of January we could sit in comfort by a roaring fire, the less highbrow members writing letters or knitting according to their sex; and when summer returned, Beethoven's 7th might be heard in the Tudor garden. A noble band of compares came into being, the soothing Goddes, the pugnacious Crowson, the voluble Cpl. Snell, the calm Harry Blyth, the witty Scott and very many others. First class pianists like F/O Heal and Weaver revealed themselves (almost too late) greatly added to the enjoyment. Nor must be forgotten the record short programme of LACW Haywood; the consistent production of *'wads'* by Keen; and the faithful distribution of the same with coffee by LACW Gamble, Newton, etc. There were more unorthodox meetings of the Music Circle such as the midnight performance in the water tower in the days of Uncle Jo. I think for Bach's *Toccata* and *Fugue,* the 'Pastoral' *Peter and the Wolf,* or the *Dance of the Hours* on the radio will awaken vivid memories; and that many will have a greatly increased appreciation of good music as a result of these evenings. I shall anyway.

The silence of the passages and the empty offices at S.H.Q are strange after all the activity and bustle of the old days, queues of airmen awaiting casual payments, or a less attractive interview with the S.W.O or C.O. They were a grand crowd at S.H.Q. S/Ldr Lowry, now in Civvy Street, had the most ferocious bark, but the gentlest and most benevolent bite that you ever met. S/Ldr Cox, ditto, ditto, was surely one of the world's hardest workers. Mr Norton, one of the most popular S.W.Os. There is no doubt we were exceptionally fortunate with our WAAF 'G' team – Flight/O Wareham and 'Little Betty'. Few would realise how many lame dogs were helped over the stiles by Padre Price. In P.2 we had the smiling and competent Gamble and the obliging Sgt Wickenden; in the Registry the glamorous 'Goo-Goo'. Corporate modesty forbids detailed reference to the efficiency of the Accounts Section – addressed so politely in public and referred to so scurrilously in private! Suffice it to say that it has been a great pleasure to work in their company for nearly two years. I shall miss them all.

Yes, I could go on for hours – could tell of the official V.E. Day celebrations, the unofficial V.J. Day celebrations in the Hall, the Savings efforts of the Signals Section, the gardening abilities of the Sick Quarters. I could say a lot about Pay Parades and the all-in salute-and-grab evolutions of the WAAFs, but you will want to hear of the last days of the Station.

It must have been about the end of August when most of the Aircrew Types left. Life seemed very quiet without them. F/Lt Wynne and others remained for a time to ferry the kites away. They occupied spare time in archery and other pursuits. A number of officers continued in the Mess for a while awaiting release. In fact, the Release Section was working at high pressure for several weeks and the golden voice of F/Sgt O'Connell could be heard on the Tannoy almost continuously, urging prospective civvies to step up and see him some time.

By the end of September about 400 bods were on the books, although we didn't see much of them. The dozen officers moved into the fragrant and hallowed precincts of Sick Quarters. Jack Clark still presided in the Little Bar there; *Crib* and *Patience* became in vogue about that time, but we did break out occasionally on more traditional lines, notably when the Sergeants visited us and the day when

S/Ldr Cox returned from hospital. Then came a Blitz from Command. Press gangs got to work. Troops were rounded up from local farms and the sites and real progress was made. Equipment fairly poured into the Stores, and overflowed all round. Bods were hounded off the Station, and on 29 October after many postponements the Station was officially handed over.

In October we fell below the 100 mark; all feeding together in the Airmens Mess. The cinema had closed of course, and liberty runs ceased. Even the NAAFI had shut up shop, but life was pleasantly informal, as it was no doubt in the earliest days of the Unit at North Creake in 1943. Six officers moved into the hut formerly used as the Padre's office, and thereafter the story of ten little nigger boys was enacted. The WAAFs had to be transported from Group H.Q. each day. Evenings were quiet; except on the famous occasion when my lonely slumber by the Mess fire was disturbed by the sound of female carollers about 9 pm and our six WAAFs appeared, having spent two hours losing themselves on the perimeter track, demanding accommodation for the night! However, we coped. Smithy has gone and the pheasants breathe more freely. Sgt Wickenden has left us. The last two Orderly Room staff, Newton and Mountain go in the morning. The remaining five Accounts leave at the weekend, and I go to Cheadle, Staffs on Wednesday. Only Sgt Wright and three Stores WAAFs Livingstone, Clark and Jones will be left of Bomber Command. Otherwise the C and M party will be in sole possession.

And that is the end of my story. Service life certainly has its bright side. Nothing has been said here of other aspects of war – the separation from home comforts, the monotony, the danger and the loss. The Oldest Inhabitant is an uncurable philosopher, and he asks will all this be allowed to happen again? If it does, the papers tell us the Atom Bomb will put paid to civilisation as we know it. Can this be prevented? He can see only one solution ultimately, and that is a return to a vital, genuine Christianity. We don't talk about this much in the Service, but we think quite a bit about it. Of course, there are plenty of objections – disunity, hypocrisy, fanaticism, and the rest, but the fact remains that if we were all Practical Christians any political system and International system would work 100%. H. G. Wells' latest pathetic book of despair is typical of the bankruptcy of the getting-better-every-day philosophy of the last 100 years – man has become very clever, but without God he is just a clever devil ...

Thank God the war is over!

Well, cheerio! All best wishes for 1946 – and Civvy Street. Thanks for all the memories.

The Summer of Forty-One

We were young, carefree and raring to go
Our fears we hid, not letting them show.
To Oulton they sent us to answer the call
'Sink German shipping' said Winston, 'give it your all'.
So into the daylight skies we flew, seeking their ships,
Bombing military targets inland on some of our trips.
We flew at nought feet on most of our 'Ops'
Skimming over trees, hedges, waves and crops.
At times we flew high with an escort nearby
Hurricanes tucked in close and Spits up on high.
They called this a 'Circus' which meant we were bait
Saying: 'Come on, Jerry, come and fight before it's too late!'
Their flak and their fighters accounted for many
Including John, Norman, George and dear old Lenny.
Their friends and relatives at home – oh they grieved
For the telegram saying 'Missing' they had received.
They gave their lives for us all here today,
We'll never forget them wherever they lay.

Flt/Lt James Moore DFC

CHAPTER 10
Use of Captured Aircraft by Germans

The Germans were short of long-range aircraft – aircraft such as the B-17 Fortress. As the war moved on and the need more critical, a plan began to form.

British aircraft crashed or were shot down all the time, especially in the early days of war. The more it happened, the more the Germans realised their potential, especially where components were salvageable. What they needed was a damaged aircraft to see if, with different markings, their plan might work.

Their chance came on 12 December 1942.

During a bombing raid, a B-17 Fortress was heavily damaged, its pilot, Lieutenant Flickinger, forced to land on Leeuwarden airfield in The Netherlands. The aircraft was repaired – with the addition of the German national insignia. Protected by two Bf 110s, it was then flown to Rechlin where it was thoroughly examined and tested. For German engineers it presented the chance of a lifetime to study at close quarters technical data and engineering their enemy was using. German pilots for the first time were also able to inspect an enemy aircraft, giving them a clearer understanding of the strengths and weaknesses of the Flying Fortress, giving them knowledge to fight them in the skies.

This became part of a much larger plan in the making.

Once this aircraft had been thoroughly tested and examined, it became the first of many captured and restored aircraft to be exhibited at Larz airfield on 12 June 1943, including an Avro Lancaster, a DH Mosquito, a Typhoon and a Spitfire. It must have served as a tremendous boost to morale in displaying these aircraft, before being transferred to a secret place known only by a select few as KG 200 in September that year.

It gave the Germans the advantage of being able to match aircraft for aircraft in the skies, with colours and markings designed to fool the enemy into believing it to be one of their own.

This was a project shrouded in mystery. Even as it became a special Luftwaffe Unit, most members maintained the secret after the war. KG 200, as it was named, was officially formed by order of the Air Force High Command on 20 February 1944. A celebrated Junkers Ju-88 bomber pilot, Colonel Werner Baumbach took command. However, his memoirs written later in a book entitled: 'Broken Swastika' omits any mention of the Unit, its work, and the part he played.

Nevertheless, KG 200 went on to become a unique Unit.

Alongside captured British and American aircraft, such as the Consilidated B-24 Liberator and Boeing B-17 Flying Fortress; it operated a variety of aircraft – from the Blohm und Voss Bv-222 Wiking (largest flying boat of the time) to the Junkers Ju-52, Ju-90, Ju-290 and Ju-188, and Heinkel He-111.

There were thirty-two types of aircraft ready for use together with seventeen fully trained crew. By the end of July 1944, special missions were being flown, with new crews entering a training programme.

KG 200 went on to expand its areas of work, dividing into several groups, each of which had subsidiaries across the German Empire responsible for a different aspect of work.

The first Group named I/KG 200 used heavier aircraft for dropping agents in the UK and France. Outstations were set up, the headquarters of each located in fairly innocuous places. Outstation Olga, for example, was located in a wooded area, with little more than a rough runway beside a forest, its command post consisting of two huts hidden deep in the woods. Operational aircraft included six Junkers Ju-188s and a pair of captured and renovated Boeing B-17s and Dornier Do-288s. Precautions were taken to make the airfield appear abandoned and avoid unwanted attention from the Allies. Personnel would dodge from tree to tree, never appearing in the open in daylight.

Outstation Olga covered Western Europe, England, Ireland and Iceland. But there were other Outstations, such as Outstation Carmen in Northern Italy covering the western and southern Mediterranean, North and West Africa. While Outstations Klara and Toska controlled the Eastern Front.

By 1944, with increased action on the Western Front, Outstation Olga was busy. Commanded by P. W. Stahl, an experienced pilot who had flown long distance supply missions; pilots were dropping agents in parts of France under Allied control by parachute, but also dropping a personnel drop device

– a metal and plywood container holding three agents and equipment. These secret operations were only flown at night, with runway lights turned off as soon as aircraft were airborne or had landed. Under cover of darkness, as they dropped passengers or acted as airborne listening posts, KG 200 pilots and planes were relatively safe from attack. However, in landing, the airfields were often attacked and extensively damaged even while pilots were still in the air making landings impossible, often leading to loss of aircraft and crew.

Agents were trained at the Reich Main Security Office's well-fortified luxury hotel, on a mountain in southwestern Poland, ringed by guards, reachable only by cable-car. When they graduated, agents would be sent to KG 200 for transport to various areas of operation.

1/KG 200 handled long distance operations, while 2/KG 200 covered short-range operations from various Outstations. 3/KG 200, based at the Baltic island of Ruegen, later Flensburg; was concerned with transport and training duties. 4/KG 200 handled technical matters.

The second Group under KG 200, II/KG 200; provided Pathfinders, radar-jamming aircraft, bombers and 'Mistel' composite aircraft – a smaller aircraft mounted on top of a larger unmanned aircraft, such as a medium-sized bomber, joined by a three-point strut apparatus, fitted with explosive bolts to sever the connection. While 7/KG 200 handled replacement and training for II/KG 200.

With smaller aircraft being used by other Units to train pilots against aircraft they would eventually fight, KG 200 was a well organised, committed German Group which maintained its secrecy throughout, each section focused on its own function, although it was only the first two Groups that were ever fully developed.

However, KG 200 also had a far more sinister role – in charge of German suicide pilots.

Using a theory developed by a veteran glider pilot of the famous 1940 assault on the Belgian fortress of Eben Emael, who believed that if glider pilots were sent to die then they should be armed with an appropriate weapon; the Germans mirrored Japanese kamikaze efforts with the Reichenberg IV suicide bomb. Thousands of men volunteered for operations vaguely described as 'Special Operations', with seventy being sent to KG 200.

Despite being trained on gliders, they were to fly a manned variant of the V-1 buzz bomb. The V-1, also known as the Fiesler Fi-103, was in mass production as a flying bomb. It was the German Research Institute for Gliding

Flight at Ainring that modified the V-1 to carry a pilot. However, by 1945, such were the feelings towards using the flying bomb that only criminals and pilots in a depressed state were allowed to fly Reichenbergs.

It is interesting to note that, what started out as a re-vamp of captured enemy aircraft to suit the purposes of fighting back with an unexpected 'new weapon' using its enemy's own materials, turned into a series of separate projects and plots that grew bigger and more bizarre with time.

The original intention had been to utilise materials which came into their hands, motivated by a shortage of long-range aircraft. It is therefore fascinating as well as sad to follow the journey of just a few of these fine aircraft:

- **Phyllis Marie, a Boeing B-17F**, was damaged on 8 March 1944 at Werben, Germany. The aircraft was captured and repaired from a large stock of B-17 parts the Germans had amassed during years of heavy daylight bombing attacks on U.S. aircraft. Maltese crosses were painted on its wings. A raked swastika decorated its rudder. Otherwise it remained unchanged and U.S. Forces re-captured it on a runway at Altenburg on 4 May 1945.

- **B-17F-85-BO 'Flak Dancer'** aircraft piloted by Lt Dalton Wheat became the second aircraft to land in the hands of the Germans when it force-landed at Laon airfield in France. After repairs, it was transferred to KG 200 in Spring 1944, coded A3+CE.

- **B-17F-90-BO 'Down and Go!'** Lt Ned Palmer had problems with this aircraft soon after take-off. Both inner engines failed and the pilot was forced to disable them. The crew wanted to drop bombs on Germany and they continued flying forward. However, shortly before the target, engine four overheated and the pilot was forced to disable this also. The Navigator set a course for Sweden, but they landed on a Wehrmacht exercise field in Avedore Holme, Denmark. Immediately, it was encircled by German soldiers, but not before the crew destroyed the secret Norden gunsight. The aircraft was then transported to Kastrup, Denmark, where it was repaired before a traditional period of trials and its transfer to KG 200 in Spring 1944, to be coded A3+EE (later re-coded A3+BB).

- **B-17F-100-BO 'Miss Nonalee II'** Piloted by Lt Glyndon G. Bell, the aircraft was damaged during a bombing raid on the Arado plant in Anklam (Eastern Prussia), on 9 October 1943. The crew decided to go to Sweden, but mistakenly flew to Denmark. All crew members excluding the pilot jumped and were caught by Danish police collaborating with the Germans. Lt Bell made a forced landing near Varde, Denmark and, after failing to set fire to the bomber, evaded Danish police and was transported to Sweden by the Danish Resistance. The aircraft meanwhile ended up with German technicians after which it is unknown what happened to it.

- **B-17G-25-DL** Piloted by Lt John G. Grossage, the aircraft was damaged on 3 March 1944. After the loss of one of its engines and heavy wounding to one of the crew, the pilot decided to fly to Sweden, but due to navigational error landed at Schlezwig-Jagel airfield in Northern Germany. After repairs and a period of trials at Rechlin, the aircraft was transferred to KG 200 in Spring 1944.

- **B-17G-10-VE** was the last airworthy B-17 to be captured on 9 April 1944 by the Germans.

Excluding 'Miss Nonalee II', all B-17s were transferred to KG 200. German aircraft did not have the range of a B-17 and they therefore remained in demand more than any other aircraft. They were applied German national insignia, code letters (beginning from A3 - the letters of KG 200) and special night camouflage. Germans also added equipment - barometrical altimeter ASI and radio altimeter FuG 101. All aircraft under KG 200 remained top secret, targets known only to Pilot and Navigator. Meanwhile service with KG 200 was hazardous - aircraft were lost during combat missions, heavily damaged, destroyed - such as 'Down and Go!' during a mission in the Spanish-French border area. Another with ten French collaborators on board which took off on 9 April 1945 before exploding with all on board killed.

All aircraft which survived were probably destroyed by their crews or captured by Soviets.

On a final note, it was the American advance into Germany that forced the relocation of Outstation Olga from Frankfurt am Main to Stuttgart, and on to the Munich area, where the Unit settled inside a Dornier aircraft factory. Stahl and his company continued their duties until their situation became untenable, whereby he issued discharge papers and final Service pay, before saying goodby to his men.

After the war, Allies sought out members of the *'ominous secret group'*, sure that they had been involved in spiriting Nazi officials out of Europe. However, the mysteries remain surrounding KG 200 and no single former member has ever been accused of any specific misdeed or been prosecuted.

CHAPTER 11
RAF West Raynham

Prohibitate et Labore – 'Honesty & Hard Work'
Reproduced with permission of the MOD

A Brief History

West Raynham airfield was built between 1938 and 1939 two miles west of the village as an expansion scheme airfield. A grass landing area was aligned roughly north-east to south-west, while immediately to the west was the main camp with housing, Headquarters, and hangars arranged in an arc fronting the bombing circle. Bomb stores were built to the south-east, with a Watch Office and fort-type Tower made from concrete, later replaced with a '*Control Tower for Very Heavy Bomber Stations*', one of only four such Towers to be built.

In May 1939, No. 2 Group moved No. 101 Squadron and its Blenheims from Bicester into RAF West Raynham which had the Station to itself as the Reserve Squadron of No. 2 Group through the remainder of 1939.

In February 1940, a target-towing Flight was formed at West Raynham. A Target Tug was an aircraft which towed an unmanned drone – a fabric drogue or other kind of target – for gun or missile target practice. They were often conversions of transport and utility aircraft, as well as obsolescent combat types. Some, such as the Miles Martinet, were specially designed for this role. The chief modifications for an aircraft taking on the role of a Target

Tug was a Station for the drogue operator and a winch (usually air-driven) to reel in the cable prior to landing. The drogue would often be jettisoned at some location convenient for recovery prior to the aircraft's landing.

In April, No. 76 Squadron was reformed with the prospect of becoming a second operational Blenheim Unit, but three weeks on, the crisis in France brought a hasty disbandment. With serious losses suffered in the Blitz, West Raynham became a temporary base for No. 18 and No. 139 Squadrons.

On 4 July 1940, individual aircraft from No. 101's Blenheims went into action for the first time, attacking German oil storage tanks and ports. Over the year, the Squadron lost fifteen Blenheims across 610 sorties. 101 Squadron then transferred from West Raynham to No. 3 Group, to be replaced by No. 114 Squadron, another detachment of Blenheims. They remained at West Raynham for over a year before being despatched to North Africa as part of 'Operation Torch'.

In August 1942, 101 Squadron converted to Blenheim Mk Vs in preparation for combat in Africa, while No. 18 Squadron went to RAF West Raynham to be refitted with Mk Vs.

In that same year at West Raynham, Squadron Nos. 180 and 342 were formed. 180 Squadron was equipped with North American B-25 Mitchells based at RAF Great Massingham – a Station founded as a satellite base to support West Raynham – while No. 342 was provided with Douglas Bostons crewed by Frenchmen in early 1943, later relocating to RAF Sculthorpe.

To manage the influx of aircraft, between May and November 1943, the grass landing area at West Raynham was replaced with two concrete runways. To build them, boundaries of the Station were extended and a country road closed. With the runways complete, additional accommodation was expanded to house 2,456 men and 658 women in total.

RAF No. 100 (Bomber Support) Group

RAF No. 100 (Bomber Support) Group took over West Raynham Station in December 1943 bringing two Mosquito-equipped Night Fighter Squadrons – Nos. 141 and 239. Their duties involved flying *Ranger Sorties* (seek and destroy enemy fighters in the air and on the ground) and *Serrate* Patrols. *Serrate* was an Allied radar detection and homing device used in Night Fighters to track German Night Fighters equipped with the early UHF-band *BC* and *C-1* versions of the *Lichtenstein* radar.

No. 141 Squadron, commanded by Wing Commander J. R. 'Bob' Braham flying a Bristol Beaufighter; had already commenced operations over Germany between 14 June and 7 September 1943 in support of Bomber Offensives. 179 operational sorties yielded fourteen claimed fighters shot down, for three losses.

The technique developed was for RAF Night Fighters to fly slowly off the bomber stream, mimicking characteristics of a heavy bomber, until the rearward-facing *Serrate* detector picked up emissions from a Luftwaffe Night Fighter approaching. The Radar Operator then passed directions to the pilot until the Fighter was 6,000 feet behind. At this point the Beaufighter would execute a swift turn onto the tail of the German Night Fighter, pick up the enemy aircraft on his forward radar, and attempt to shoot it down.

Serrate was subsequently fitted to de Havilland Mosquito Night Fighters.

141 Squadron

Caedimus Noctu – 'We slay by night'
Reproduced with permission of the MOD

141 Squadron badge shows a leopard's face on an ongress symbolising fighting in the dark.

Codes:
UD: allocated April – September 1939
TW: allocated April 1940 – September 1945/June 1946 – April 1951

No. 141 Squadron started as a Home Defence Unit for the London area, formed at Rochford on 1 January 1918. It operated a wide range of aircraft before moving to RAF Biggin Hill in February where it settled on Bristol F2B Fighters in March. The following year it moved to Ireland and disbanded on 1 February 1920.

The Bristol F2B Fighter favoured by 141 Squadron, was a British two-seater bi-plane fighter and reconnaissance aircraft of the First World War flown by the Royal Flying Corps. It was often known simply as the 'Bristol Fighter', the 'Brisfit' or 'Biff'. Despite being a two-seater, the F2B proved an agile aircraft, able to hold its own against opposing single-seat fighters.

141 Squadron reformed on 4 October 1939 at RAF Turnhouse. Equipped with Gloster Gladiators, replaced by Bristol Blenheims, both were used for training until April 1940 when new Boulton Paul Defiants arrived. The Squadron became operational on 3 June and flew its first operation on the 29th patrolling the English Channel, moving to RAF West Malling in July, with Squadron HQ at Biggin Hill.

On 19 July, the Squadron was scrambled to patrol over Folkstone. Nine aircraft took off in three rows of three. Soon after, the Defiants encountered a force of Bf109s which attacked, coming at them out of the sun. Only one Defiant reached base. Two days later, the Squadron withdrew to Prestwick to recover and re-equip. However, as a direct result of this disastrous encounter with the enemy, operations for the future changed for the Squadron – from fighting by day, they became a Night Fighter force – the Squadron motto: 'Caedimus noctu', derives from this period. The Squadron also received new Defiants, noting that lack of forward armament on the Defiant could be a serious disadvantage in daylight operations for the future.

In September, a detachment was sent back to southern England to shoot down its first enemy aircraft at night. The following month, the rest of the Squadron moved south, remaining until April 1941 when it moved to Ayr in Scotland, converting to Beaufighters, providing night defence to Scotland and Northern England.

Defence duties continued as the Squadron moved to Tangmere in June 1942, followed by Predannack in February 1943 from where it flew intruder missions over north-west France.

At the end of April 1943, 141 Squadron moved to Wittering and from June flew night intruder missions over German Night Fighter airfields in support of Bomber Command until the end of the war.

RAF No. 100 (Bomber Support) Group

In October 1943, Beaufighters of 141 Squadron were replaced with Mosquitoes, and in December that year, the Squadron transferred to No. 100 Group – the first Squadron to come under this secret Group. Squadron aircraft went on to join the main bomber stream, attacking enemy Night Fighters and airfields just as they had before, but working under this new Group, helped create what became known as 'Mosquito Panic', as Germans became threatened by this new, versatile and different kind of aircraft, so fast and lethal.

On the night of 16/17 December during the Battle of Berlin, a Mosquito crewed by Squadron Leader F. F. Lambert and Flying Officer K. Dear made Bomber Command's first successful Serrate-guided operational sortie, damaging a Bf110 with cannon fire. This Serrate Night Fighter offensive was followed by far greater and wide-ranging support operations by the specialist 100 Group during 1944 through to 1945.

Finally, in July 1945, 141 Squadron was transferred to Little Snoring where it was disbanded on 7 September 1945 at the end of the war.

On 17 June 1946, 141 Squadron was reformed to again take on the Night Fighter role, initially equipped with Mosquitoes and replaced by Meteor NF Mk 11s in October 1951. One further change was that, from 11 February 1949 to 27 June 1952, No. 42 was linked with 141 Squadron.

Venom NF Mk 3s arrived in June 1955, replaced by Javelins in February 1957 when the Squadron adopted a new role as an all-weather fighter unit. On 1 February 1958, the Squadron was disbanded at Coltishall.

Its final incarnation was as a Bloodhound surface-to-air missile unit at Dunholme Lodge, from 1 April 1959 until 31 March 1964.

PERSONAL EXPERIENCES

Flight Lieutenant L. D. Gregory DFC

Born 13 January 1923 in Southampton, 'Doug' Gregory left elementary school aged fourteen to work in a local solicitor's office. At eighteen, he volunteered for the RAF and joined at Uxbridge on 3 February 1941. Initial training completed at No. 8 L.T.W in Newquay, Cornwall, he sailed as an LAC in August 1941 for pilot training in Southern Rhodesia, now Zimbabwe.

Doug trained at No. 25 EFTS at Belvedere, Salisbury, Southern Rhodesia, flying Tiger Moths, moving on to No. 20 SFTS flying Harvards, followed by advanced SFTS at Cranborne, Salisbury, where he won his wings on 23 March 1942. Twin engine training on Oxfords followed at No. 23 SFTS at Heany, Bulawayo from May 1942, then, because of the forthcoming expansion of Bomber Command, he returned to the UK.

As a Sergeant Pilot, he flew at No. 6 Pilot Advanced Flying Unit at Little Rissington, Gloucester, where overseas-trained pilots were brought up to the standards required in a theatre of war. A posting to No. 54 O.T.U. at Charterhall, Scotland and its satellite at Winfield followed, where he trained as a Night Fighter pilot, flying Blenheims Mk 1, 4 and 5s and Beaufighters Mk II. Here he crewed up with Navigator/Radar Operator: Sergeant D. H. Stephens (Steve). They remained together until the end of the war.

In February 1943, they were both posted to 141 Squadron at Ford in Sussex. The Commanding Officer was W/Cdr J. R. D. Braham D.S.O**, D.F.C**, A.F.C., Croix de Guerre.

When the Squadron moved to Predannack in Cornwall, they began operations in Beaufighters Mk ls. Doug and Steve carried out 'Instep' operations over the Bay of Biscay and 'Ranger' operations over Brittany. 'Instep' operations were missions to restrict attacks on Coastal Command aircraft by maintaining a presence over the Western Approaches. 'Ranger' operations were freelance flights over enemy territory by units of any size, the intention being to occupy and tire enemy fighters. Doug and Steve also carried out several air/sea rescue searches, providing cover in case of E-boat attacks – the British used the term 'E' to indicate 'Enemy' fast attack craft.

In April 1943, as 141 Squadron moved to Wittering, Northamptonshire, and having been trained on 'Serrate' radar operations at Drem, in Scotland;

Doug and Steve started on a long, consecutive, double tour of operations with the Squadron on 'Serrate Bomber Support' over Germany and occupied Europe.

They began on Beaufighters Mk 1 and Mk 6. However, as 141 Squadron went on to change to Mosquitoes and moved to West Raynham in December 1943, they were amongst the first aircrew to join No. 100 Group, Bomber Command.

Doug was commissioned with Steve as a Pilot Officer in January 1944, and during this time did photographic research into radar jamming while on raids over Germany.

Later that year, they shot down a Ju88 in Northern France and another near Metz. On 4 August, both were awarded the DFC and promoted to Flying Officers in September. They completed their consecutive double tour of operations with 141 Squadron in October 1944, having operated continuously since March 1943, chalking up sixty-nine operational sorties. On the 13th, together they were posted as Instructors to 51 O.T.U – Night Fighter Training Unit at Cranfield and Twinwood Farm, Bedfordshire.

Five months later, in February 1945, they were posted overseas to the Royal Naval Air Station at Gibraltar, where, with their Mosquito, they carried out various forms of attack, high level bombing, dive bombing, torpedo and low level strafing, all simulated attacks on the new Battle Class destroyer HMS *Barfleur*. This was to test the destroyer's radar defences for its forthcoming part in the war against Japan.

While in Gibraltar, Doug had the opportunity to fly the Swordfish. This aircraft achieved spectacular successes, notably the sinking of one and damaging two battleships of the Regia Marina of the Italian Navy in the Battle of Taranto; and the famous crippling of the Bismarck.

Doug and Steve were finally parted in July 1945 when Doug was posted to No. 306 M.U. Allahabad in India to help sort out problems Mosquitoes were having with the tropical atmosphere. He tested a wide range of aircraft, including Beaufighters and Mosquitoes of different Mks, also Spitfires and Hurricanes.

In February 1946, Doug was promoted to Flight Lieutenant and posted to No. 307 M.U. at Lahore, in charge of the Test Flight. Here, he tested Mosquitoes, Beaufighters, Dakotas, Spitfires, Austers, Vengeances, Dominies, Expeditors and Arguses. He also flew with Professor P. S. Gill, who was researching into the behaviour of cosmic rays. This required flying to almost the maximum height of a Mosquito.

Doug returned to the UK in September 1946 in an unusual manner - delivered from Jodhpur, an Expeditor, to the American Air Force in Munich and released from the RAF that same month.

After Teacher Training College, he joined the teaching profession and for many years was Head of Faculty of Creative Arts in a comprehensive school. Doug returned to flying for pleasure in light aircraft and when he retired in 1983, at the age of sixty, he started to build a replica of an S.E.5a, World War One fighter biplane. It took four years to complete. He went on to fly with a group of World War One enthusiasts and performed at Air Shows around the South of England.

Anonymous
Just for the Sake of an Egg?

Does anyone ever think nostalgically about eggs? Well, I do - and the RAF is responsible.

They posted me to West Raynham in 1943 and there, in the Mess, I ate only powdered egg. It was the same in the restaurants of Kings Lynn, Fakenham, and even Norwich - only powdered egg.

But there was one glorious little village where things were different - Castle Acre, home of a ruined castle, a ruined Priory, a well-preserved church, and two hostelries. The *Albert Victor*, was a little old pub of two small main rooms, the first known as the '*Commercial*', the other being nameless. It had no Bar. Beer was served from a jug through a hole in the wall leading to a third room where barrels were stored. *You get the picture?*

However, there was one wonderful thing about this pub that made it my favourite forever. The landlord kept chickens and, in wartime England, he was allowed to sell eggs his hens produced as part of an afternoon tea, which was made available in the *Commercial Room*. This meal consisted of one fresh boiled egg (*scrumptious!*), two slices of buttered bread (*very tasty!*), two fairy cakes (*doubly delicious!*), and a pot of scalding hot tea (*greatly refreshing!*). My mouth still waters at the thought. It was, then, an incredible luxury.

Another incredible thing was that I was accompanied on my walk to the *Albert Victor* by a WAAF, Sgt Clerk SD, from Flying Control who was, in an entirely different way of course, even more wonderful, scrumptious and delicious than a fresh boiled egg. (*If you're still out there, gee, I'd love to hear from you, but come to think of it, having just been compared to an egg you're not likely to want to make the move. Why couldn't I 'compare thee to a summer's day?' Trust me to put my foot in it!*)

I've been back to look through the gates of RAF West Raynham now closed. I've driven along the road running parallel to part of the perimeter track, and continued to Castle Acre, clocking the mileage we covered. To my amazement (*not amusement!*) it was seven miles to the *Albert Victor* – and back would be the same.

Fourteen miles for a boiled egg. Ouch!

But it was well worth it. Mind, I'm not quite sure it was the wonderfully edible egg that created this impression or the even more wonderfully edible WAAF who accompanied me. There were a couple of haystacks on the way and I always recall the brown of her eyes far more easily than the brown of the hay, or even the yellow of the egg yolk. But, I must assure you, the haystack remained undisturbed. I just couldn't afford to mess up my uniform. I had the CO's parade to attend the following day. Besides, I'm a bit shy really. *Yes, really!* I always was a bit of a weakling, to be honest.

So there we have it: a fourteen mile walk just for the sake of an egg, and nothing else. Was it worth it?

Was it worth it?

What do you think?

239 Squadron

Exploramus – 'We seek out'
Reproduced with permission of the MOD

No. 239 Squadron badge is a winged spur representing this Squadron as the first to work with an armoured division, which included mechanised cavalry, during World War One.

Squadron Codes:
HB (Sept 1940 – Sept 1943 & Jan 1945 – July 1945)

The Squadron was formed at Torquay on 20 August 1918 from No. 418 (Coastal Reconnaissance) Flight. Equipped with the Short 184, it became an anti-submarine Squadron, flying anti-submarine patrols. It was disbanded on 15 May 1919.

The Squadron reformed at Hatfield on 18 September 1940 from Flights No. 16 and 225 Squadrons for Army Co-operation duties. They began with Westland Lysanders and later re-equipped with Curtiss Tomahawks and Hawker Hurricanes.

In May 1942, the Squadron converted to P-51 Mustangs for ground attack and reconnaissance operations over Northern France lasting until August 1943. During this time, the Squadron also took part in air cover during the Dieppe Raid.

In September 1943, the Squadron moved to RAF Ayr re-equipped with the de Havilland Mosquito to train as a Night Fighter Unit.

RAF No. 100 (Bomber Support) Group

No. 239 Squadron moved to RAF West Raynham to become part of the fledgling No. 100 Group, participating in night time operations against enemy fighters.

On 27 October 1944, during fighter affiliation training with 49 Squadron, a Mosquito piloted by F/Lt J. H. Roberts, accompanied by Flight Engineer Sgt A. M. Ashcroft, stalled and crashed in Stapleford Woods, Lincolnshire, with immediate death of both pilot and passenger.

For the rest of the war, the Squadron flew intruder missions over Germany, intercepting and destroying enemy fighters.

On 1 July 1945, 239 Squadron was disbanded.

During Bomber Command's time at RAF West Raynham and operations carried out at this Station during the Second World War, a total of eighty-six aircraft were claimed: fifty-six Blenheims, twenty-nine Mosquitoes and a Bristol Beaufighter.

Post-War

The airfield remained in RAF service use and post-war both the Hawker Hunter and Gloster Meteor saw operations from West Raynham. In the mid to late 1950s, RAF West Raynham took on the role of a Central Fighter Establishment of the Royal Air Force until 1962.

On the morning of Wednesday 8 February 1956, eight Hawker Hunter aircraft from the Central Fighter Establishment at West Raynham took off on an exercise. The weather closed in. They were diverted to RAF Marham. Two aircraft landed safely, but a third ran off the runway. A fourth crashed into a field killing the pilot. The remaining four pilots ejected, their aircraft crashing in open countryside. This was an incident of such significance it was raised at the House of Commons.

The airfield's main pilot training Squadrons in 1957 were Hawker Hunters comprising two wings – Red and Yellow. The latest arrival was a flight of Gloster Javelins, which appeared at Farnborough Air Show that year.

In 1964, a Tri-partite Evaluation Squadron made up of military pilots from Britain, the United States and West Germany formed at West Raynham to evaluate the Hawker P.1127 Vertical Take-Off and Landing (VTOL) strike fighter aircraft. The Hawker P.1127 and the Hawker Siddeley Kestrel FGA.1 were experimental and developmental aircraft that led to the Hawker Siddeley Harrier, the first vertical and/or short take-off and landing (V/STOL) jet fighter-bomber.

Kestrel development had begun in 1957, taking advantage of the Bristol Engine Company's choice to invest in the creation of the Pegasus vectored-thrust engine. Testing began in July 1960 and by the end of the year the aircraft achieved both vertical take-off and horizontal flight. The test programme also explored aircraft carriers landing on HMS Ark Royal. The first three aircraft crashed during testing, one at the 1963 Paris Air Show. Improvements to future development aircraft, such as swept wings and more powerful Pegasus engines led to the development of the Kestrel ... and hence to its evaluation by the Tri-partite Evaluation Squadron. Later flights were conducted by the U.S Military and NASA.

Related work on a supersonic aircraft, the Hawker Siddeley P.1154, was cancelled in 1965. As a result, the P.1127, a variant closely based on the Kestrel, came into production that year, named 'Harrier' in 1967. It was the *Harrier* that went on to serve with the UK together with several other nations often as a carrier-based aircraft.

In the mid-1960s, the east side of West Raynham airfield was developed as a SAM site, equipped with the Bristol Blood Hound Mk2 and its associated radars. The resident Unit at this time was 41 Squadron. Some of the radars, launch control units, and launchers were air portable for deployment else-where if required.

Between 28 and 31 March 1967, Hawker Hunters from West Raynham were involved in *Operation Mop Up*. This Operation saw repeated attacks by Hunters from Raynham and RAF Chivenor along with aircraft of the Fleet Air Arm, dropping aviation fuel and napalm on an oil slick being released from the wreck of the super-tanker '*Torrey Canyon*' which had run aground on Seven Stones reef near Land's End.

The following year, a Flight Commander and a Hunter from RAF West Raynham made headline news ... with far-reaching effects:

Hawker Hunter Tower Bridge Incident

It was April Fools' Day, 1968 – the 50th Anniversary of the forming of the Royal Air Force. At West Raynham, Senior Operational Flight Commander of the world's oldest Military No. 1 (Fighter) Squadron, Flt/Lt Alan Pollock, felt a particular responsibility to honour the occasion:

> For months I badgered my Station, Wing and Squadron Commanders to obtain permission for the Squadron to make an aerial contribution.

Nothing was planned, but Pollock eventually won approval for celebration Anniversary leaflet raids over Stations in the UK. His winning argument was that it raised morale and proved excellent training. Leaflets prepared, a Hunter F.G.A.9 was made ready to fly immediately after a Parade.

> We 'bombed up' the aircraft with leaflets in the flaps and fifty-seven special ceremonial leaflets (one for each full year of our own Squadron's service) ... My No.1 (F) Hunter was first up using a flapless take-off technique. Despite a strong gusty crosswind, by getting below the side of the hangar I was fortunate to have a good drop above 54 Squadron's pilots outside their crew room at West Raynham ... Apart from the Parade, there were no special celebrations for airmen, that vital body of skills, Service and sacrifice which had made the Air Force great ... no Anniversary Dance, no party, no half-day off ...

As with others in the RAF, he was frustrated, hungry to do something memorable. Leaflet drops were successful, despite some Station Commanders' complaints about bad flying, etc. Brighton put on an Air Display. Tangmere had a party. But the week was drawing to a close. Small celebrations were happening in different places yet still with no major recognition of a 50th Anniversary, something special, unique, a time to commemorate lives reaching down the years. To make matters worse, Pollock learned he was to lead the Squadron of Hunters out to El Adem in Labya later that month. Time was running out.

With a heavy cold and an important impending visit to Tangmere, he dosed himself with a strong quick-cure anti-histamine drug from the chemist before being prescribed stronger drugs by the Station doctor. Instead of making him sleepy, they actually kept him ultra-alert and sleepless!

> The Anniversary week was almost done. I could at least make one celebration flag wave across the Houses of Parliament, Downing Street, the Ministry of Defence and most of all the RAF Memorial. We'd been taught that an ounce of timely action and initiative was worth whole weighty volumes of passive, pompous pontification. When I was a youngster the solitary, camouflaged Spitfire had done just this to commemorate the Battle of Britain and so many unsung heroes in the Air Force's worldwide service.

The weather was ideal. Pollock was on his return route to West Raynham. All he need do was to lose contact with the other Hunter aircraft immediately he was airborne and slip north unobserved, without arousing suspicion. The other three pilots proved unenthusiastic regarding his venture. He was on his own.

His route over London had to be low level. He cut speed and dropped his flaps once over built-up areas to compensate for the noise. The Hunter was a quiet aircraft. The lower he was, the less likely to encounter other air traffic. He was breaking the odd regulation to carry out his protest celebratory flight, so needed it to be as safe, professional and perfect as he could make it. West Raynham had given the all clear about the weather. Everything seemed in his favour.

> I was taking off as Number Four in the lead section of four aircraft. A singleton Hunter with our Squadron Commander, Sqn/Ldr Spike Jones on board was taking off immediately behind me, making five in total, all FGA9 single-seat fighter ground attack aircraft. As we accelerated, rolling down Tangmere's runway in two pairs and a singleton, with a five-second stream spacing, I remained pre-occupied about breaking away from the rest of the section without attracting attention. Immediately after take-off, I watched the Hunter behind turn belly-on to beat up the airfield as a farewell fighter tribute to a legendary airfield, symbol of fighter excellence ... what a splendidly good and in-discretionary Boss! I knew I could not now be seen by him!

As they descended to low level, he told the formation leader, with speechless code on his R/T button, he had '*lost*' visual contact, pretending his radio had failed, using speechless transmissions to avoid further embarrassing conversations. Two minutes later he was over the lakes three miles south of London airport, with a stately Boeing 707 on its final approach onto Heathrow's westerly runway. He crossed Richmond Park, following the line of the Thames. Just seconds apart came the bridges. He swept over Wandsworth, Battersea and Chelsea bridges, keeping a special eye open for helicopters. Then came Vauxhall Bridge and a mile or so ahead, the Houses of Parliament. This was his main target area.

As I put the Rolls-Royce power on, I decided this was necessary to remind MPs and other august figures that we still had a fighting Air Force, one small Unit of which was celebrating its Anniversary, despite the dead hand of Government police and sickening cut-backs of previous years. Three times I circled, fascinated like any Gulliver at Lilliput looking down on the scene below. Big Ben struck twelve noon. With care, I kept well clear of Buckingham Palace, clearly visible outside my orbit, levelling out again over the Thames, dipping my wings past the RAF Memorial and statue of Viscount Trenchard who had helped form the RAF in 1918, fifty years earlier, despite tremendous opposition.

At one minute past noon Pollock turned happily down river, aware fuel was low, intending to head for home. But then, across the Thames was this famous structure blocking his low level path to the east. It wasn't until that moment he realised Tower Bridge would be there.

It would have been easy to fly over it, but the idea of flying through the spans suddenly struck me. I had ten seconds to grapple with the seductive proposition which few ground attack pilots of any nationality could have resisted. Years of fast low level strike flying made the decision simple.

From a trained low level pilot's point of view it presented an interesting penetration problem ... I jinked hastily to line up directionally and pre-position down low over the river, my eager fighter well beneath the tall cranes standing like silent, puzzled spectators on the

banks. This manoeuvre would give me a full extra three seconds of decision time to study defloration further.

There was considerable road traffic, including a red double decker bus, lumbering across the famous, double-basculed bridge from north to south. With less than half a mile to go, Pollock decided it was easy enough to fly through, but needed to consider the best and safest way.

At the last split second before he crossed underneath, the steel girders suddenly seemed to explode all about his cockpit, above, below and around his ears, totally engulfing him. For a micro-second he believed he'd over-cooked it and the top span would be certain to take his fin off. But then, something happened which had only occurred once before to him, when he had mushed after pull-out from an FAC attack with over-sufficient aircraft weight and 'g' and insufficient speed, power and thought!

Thinking I had hit the ground missing Cloud Ninety-Nine by a whisker, my heart actually missed a couple of beats with the shock of imminent disaster. After that there was the acute, physical reaction as the heart fires up to full stroke again, just like a fighter's fuel pump trying hard to catch up. My Hunter flew on, rather unexpectedly, still completely functional and not a finless wonder as I headed out over Greenwich and Hornchurch, heading towards Clacton.

With nothing to lose now, I opened up a separate Anniversary sortie call-sign on the R/T, Romeo Alfa Foxtrot 01 (*rather lost on the Controllers*). Then, with R/T permission from the ground, ceremonially I beat up RAF Wattisham – home to some of the Lightning Force and whose Station Commander was decidedly an accessory before this particular crime!

Lakenheath was next on his list and Mach .93 dive-brake sonic boom-letting where No.1's fellow Squadron with parked USAFF 100s were based.

Lastly, without really the fuel to do it justice and only very careful R/T checking on the position of a Victor on its extended final approach lane, he flew across RAF Marham. The flight had covered both halves of the former Bomber and Fighter elements which were just now combining as a new 'Strike Command'.

With less than 400 lbs of fuel remaining, he carried out a rather hurried, inadequate inverted run over the Squadron hangars at RAF West Raynham before breaking downwind, punching down the gear and landing, the brake parachute bobbing about behind his precious fin. He taxied slowly in, expecting a formal reception committee to be in readiness for his arrival.

His first priority was to casually walk in to Wing Ops, borrowing matches to burn the tatty quarter-million map on which he'd navigated up from Tangmere. Professionally, he was ashamed of the scribbled marks and state of disrepair, but more than anything else, he was getting rid of this dog-eared relic of evidence of his escapade. He fully expected to be Court Martialled!

His next port of call was the MT Section to chat up the switchboard girl and put in a private call to his wife, wife's mother and parents, telling them what had taken place, warning them to say nothing to any Press. He also took the opportunity to explain why he'd felt the need to break with protocol, telling them he would be under close arrest for at least a couple of days.

It was then back to the Squadron, climbing stairs to tell Boss Jones, OC Flying Wing Commander Ron Wood and later the Station Commander, Group Captain Basil Lock, what they already knew. By nature, used to fast moving situations, they took it in their stride. Spike Jones was relieved Whitehall wasn't littered with leaflets. Meanwhile, the Section Leader downstairs was in a panic – all five aircraft had taken off, verbally authorised, but certainly not signed up on any authorisation sheet. So 'cooking the books' and signing up belatedly was the next order of the day!

I went up to the Mess with Wing Commander Admin, an officer also called Wood, after the Station MO examined me, finding me absolutely normal. After such little sleep, I was restless, utterly exhausted, but unable to sleep. I asked the doctor for something to help, but my request was denied. Instead, I was forced to wait the obligatory seven hours to get hold of an RAF psychiatrist, who eventually arrived to pronounce me quite definitely of sure mind, but tired and with a cold-ridden body.

I was held under close arrest for obviously 'political' reasons, asking to be released to open arrest. My deaf AOC of last month grew even deafer. So, with spirits high, I started playing up, locking up my officer guard ...

The Press continued to make things uncomfortable and Pollock, under close arrest, was moved on to Nocton Hall where, always an athletic climber and in high spirits, he climbed out onto the roof unnoticed. He was moved on to

Wroughton where the terrible cold he had incubating finally broke out into pneumonia with a combination of drugs and disillusionment slowly sapped his spirit and strength.

Aftermath

Immediately after the incident, Pollock's Unit was posted to North Africa, leaving him behind still on a charge. It was to be a month later before a Summary of Evidence took place lasting five days. Despite recommendations from Wroughton that he was fit enough to stand Court Martial, he was instead invalided out of the RAF on medical grounds, thus avoiding a Court Martial and embarrassment to the Government if Pollock should offer a reason for his stunt, garnering public support.

> I was astounded, angry, repeatedly asking for what I believed was my statutory right to see my AOC-in-C. This was denied me. If I didn't accept my invaliding out, with the inducement of a small pension, my services could be dispensed with under a certain Queen's Regulation without any formal disciplinary action or come-back.

Following friendly counsel, Pollock realised he had to accept Hobson's choice, deciding he should receive his pension before making any further move against what he considered an unjust decision, taken to avoid a public enquiry into the Government's arbitrary decision to cancel any Anniversary Flypast.

Pollock received over 100 letters from the general public and more from present and former RAF personnel at all levels, as well as members of the Royal Navy and Special Air Service, both with which he had formerly operated. Other people were obviously not satisfied with the fact that the 50th Anniversary of the RAF had not been marked in the official manner it deserved, including the events which happened to Pollock as a result.

After a painful end to a career, Pollock's aggressive fighter training made way for success in the exporting industry for the future.

However, his story wasn't over.

The bizarre circumstances surrounding Flight Lieutenant Alan Pollock's unofficial marking of the 50th Anniversary of the Royal Air Force included a later arrest where a statement of his true position and the drug situation was given at a Summary of Evidence in front of four witnesses. In 1982, his case was finally vindicated.

The event became known as the '*Hawker Hunter Tower Bridge Incident*'. [55]

MEMORIES OF WEST RAYNHAM

… I was at RAF West Raynham from 1957 to 1958 and would love to contact Ted my Ambulance Driver mate at SSQ. I don't recall Ted's surname but he lived in Faversham, and he was a trained Plumber in 'Civvy Street'. Also Sgt Dave CUTTING, Radar and Wireless Techie at RAF HACK GREEN in the period 1958 to 1959. Many a happy hour spent at The Potting Shed in Nantwich with a couple of Boots the Chemist girls!

John

… *most nights we used to disconnect BBC Radio and broadcast our own Station programmes. These include such highlights as 'Anne's Half Hour' (family requests played by PIO Anne Hearn) and Keeper of the Flame (non-stop playing of a musical comedy LP). The studio was sound-proofed with old egg-boxes and faults with the broadcast equipment were solved by sliding out a valve rack and bashing it back in, hard!*

1956: *David Donald*

… I was posted to 751SU at Cape Greco in Cyprus (during the EOKA troubles). The Unit ceased operations in the summer of 1959 and I returned to the UK in June where I was misemployed for the last few months of my service in Air Traffic Control at RAF West Raynham, getting demobbed in January 1960. A group of us from 751SU have a Reunion each January in Huntingdon and a few of us take part in the Remembrance Ceremonies at the Cenotaph each November to remember those who did not return …

Unknown

Lest We Forget

One day a breed of men were born,
From every walk of life,
They came from near and far to fight,
For a certain way of life.

Some were tall and some were short,
And some were dark and lean,
And some spoke different languages,
But all were young and keen.

They all trained hard, and then one day,
A Wing Commander came
And pinned upon their breast, a badge,
Air-Gunners they became.

A Squadron was their final goal,
To join an aircraft crew,
On Wimpeys, Lancs and Stirlings,
And some on Blenheims too.

They fought at night and in the day,
Their Ops increased in number,
Some returned – and some did not,
For 'thirty' was the number.

Some survived to reach this mark,
And some continued flying,
Some spent years behind the bars,
With many of them dying.

At last the victory came in sight,
The runways now are silent,
The echoes of the past remain
A conflict, long and violent.

This breed of men are now but few
But they remember others,
Who flew with them so long ago:
Their Royal Air Force brothers.

Wing Commander Francis HP 'Bunny' Austin
RAF 36/214/419 Squadrons

CHAPTER 12
Why Norfolk?

It is in writing about how these pretty peaceful little country villages filled with so much history and legend came to unknowingly host wartime Squadrons under the very secret RAF No. 100 (Bomber Support) Group that I hear the echo of a question: 'Why Norfolk?'

The reason behind the secrecy has been developed through the words of veterans who have openly shared what it was like for them at the time. However, if this has whetted your appetite to know and understand more, I have a two-book series published under Fonthill Media which I suggest you read to feed your hunger for further knowledge and truths. The first book examines in detail specific operations undertaken by RAF 100 Group and the secret nature of their work, while the second explores reasons why this Group received neither recognition nor reward in the aftermath of war. Staring at pictures on a television screen we easily become detached, normalising the situation, viewing it as we would a film, with the ability to walk away or switch off when it suits us. Listening to news of a new crisis in a foreign country isn't the same as having the enemy on your own doorstep, realising with a sense of panic and dread that there isn't anywhere to run or hide.

If war happened in your country tomorrow, would you have the strength, the courage, to stand up and be counted, to do whatever it takes to make your country safe, pushing the enemy back where they belong?

Men and women who share their wartime experiences in this book were only teenagers. Could we as teenagers do the same? As parents or grandparents, can we imagine sending our children off to war, knowing we might never see or hear from them again?

Sometimes we don't have a choice.

Control is a terrible thing. I have a PhD in Life and know this to be true. Even when it is over, there are after-shocks, Post Traumatic Stress as it is called now. People going to war don't come back the same. Families never totally recover. But at least it's that much easier to cope with if we know our enemy, if we understand the truths of the situation and learn what happened to the people who never return.

I know how it shaped my mother's life when her wartime fiancé, just prior to their wedding, disappeared without trace. It has been spoken of in this book both by myself and others. It is what brought me to the start of this journey, and put me in touch with these wonderful brave souls, some of whom you have met here.

But let me answer the question: *why Norfolk?*

The county of Norfolk has a long and close association with aviation reaching back through time.

In 1915 during World War One, Boulton & Paul manufactured aircraft in Norwich, flying them from Mousehold Heath. Narborough became the biggest aerodrome in the country, while Pulham established a major airship base. The Royal Naval Air Service also had airfields around the Norfolk coast as a defence against Zeppelin raids.

Between the wars, Norfolk's permanent RAF stations continued to develop - Bircham Newton, Marham, Watton and West Raynham, while Mousehold Heath became Norwich Airport. Today, the City of Norwich Aviation Museum lies adjacent to this airport with rooms set aside for RAF No. 100 Group memorabilia. It also exhibits an impressive number of aircraft including a Handley Page Herald and Vulcan, together with a vast collection of historical mementoes from World War Two ... well worth a visit!

The Second World War saw the construction of around thirty new airfields in Norfolk for use by the USAAF 8th Air Force and RAF Bomber Command. During the latter part of the war, RAF No. 100 (BS) Group came to the the forefront of the development and use of electronic countermeasures, looking at Great Massingham to become an essential part of its growing network of secret airfields.

As with other small sleepy villages in and around Norfolk used to a slower gentler pace of life, it must have been a shock when the Royal Air Force stepped into Great Massingham's idyllic, peaceful vista of green to commandeer one of its largest farms. It wasn't until 1957 that the airfield could once more be restored to its former agricultural heritage, although it remains today still in use for private flying.

It was the second time in a generation that the RAF needed to meet the threat Germany presented. New aircraft were vital, airfields and personnel desperately important. It meant purchasing fresh plots of land. Most fighter airfields were in the south, with Yorkshire, Lincolnshire and East Anglia taking Bomber Stations. It was from these Bases, the newly-formed RAF Bomber Command began to operate a strategic bombing offensive against Germany.

From the RAF's point of view, 2 Group – the first Bomber Group formed in March 1936 – was expanding. Made up of light and medium bombers, originally it served as Army support rather than for strategic bombing. By 1939, 2 Group was located in the eastern counties, equipped with Fairey Battles and Bristol Blenheims, bombers which went on to become the spearhead for the RAF offensive against Germany from 1939 to 1941 when 'heavy' four-engined bombers came into service.

The RAF saw Norfolk as an ideal place to build new airfields having hosted airfields of World War One at Marham and Bircham Newton. Distance to the Low Countries, such as Holland and Belgium, measured 180 miles; to the borders of Germany approximately 300 miles.

The first task was to identify suitable land and liaise with local landowners to purchase large acres to concrete and build. The search led to Raynham Hall Estate, dating back to the 17th century. The Hall and Grounds had remained in the hands of the Townsend family from that time.

Raynham Hall is one of the most prolific and picturesque of the great houses of Norfolk, thought to be the first of its kind in England, according to genealogist G. E. Cockayne. It was certainly one of the most outstanding country houses of its period, giving its name to five Estate villages known as The Raynhams. The Hall's most famous resident was Charles Townsend, 2nd Viscount Townsend (1674-1738), leader in the House of Lords. For almost 400 years it has been the seat of the Townsend family, and one can only wonder at the feelings of the family in handing over even a portion of their estate to the RAF, breaking with tradition for the first time.

The Air Ministry also bought land from Raynham Hall's neighbours, the Coke's family Estate at Weasenham Hall where, since medieval times, the property and grounds belonged to John de Weasenham. John had been a notable and colourful character who held the important post of Butler to King Edward III (1327-1377). He and another wealthy merchant, Sir Robert Causton, were commissioned at the time to seize and fit out all ships between the Thames and The Wash and provide men-at-arms and archers to resist a threatened invasion by the French. In lieu of payment, he pawned the King's Crown!

The Hall was re-built in the early 1900s and in later years, used to accommodate evacuees and airmen from Raynham.

RAF Raynham was born as purchased land became Government property. Construction work was carried out by local labourers laid off during the agricultural depression of the 1930s. As with most other RAF airfields during this period, it remained a grass airfield until later in the war when concrete runways were laid.

Given the RAF's decision that each airfield should have a satellite field a few miles away from the main Station, in RAF West Raynham's case the site chosen was situated next to the village of Great Massingham ... and RAF Great Massingham airfield was born.

RAF Great Massingham: 1940–1957

Beginnings

By September 1940, Great Massingham airfield was fully operational. However, from the start, it was different to other older Norfolk airfields, including Marham, Bircham Newton and even West Raynham which by now was permanent and self-contained. People involved at the airfield became an integral part of the community surrounding them. Crews slept in the village of West Raynham and cycled over each morning, making the Station atmosphere unique, inextricably linked with the lives of local people. With close friendships forged, a more homely atmosphere was adopted than on other Bases.

Aircraftsman Leslie Soanes, arrived from Leuchars with 107 Squadron in May 1941:

> ... the informal atmosphere, no gates, no perimeter fence or restrictions, just a quiet Norfolk village.

As the airfield was extended and upgraded in 1944, the informality and almost gentle atmosphere remained:

> I had never been to Norfolk before the war. The only reason I am still here now is that all the local farmers and people were so good and kind and generous. They gave us lots of hospitality. I liked Norfolk,

thought it a marvellous place. I decided when I retired I'd go back and live there ... and I have done just that!

In April 1944, RAF Massingham was upgraded with concrete runways, and accommodation to house aircrew and up to 800 ground personnel.

First postings arrived during Autumn that year. After reporting to Station HQ close to the main entrance, each person was billeted with a family living in or close to the village. Some more lucky than most stayed in the grounds of the Birkbeck Estate, not far from Little Massingham Church. RAF personnel looked after by Lady Joan Birkbeck remember her generosity and kindness, befriending all who stayed at her home. Regardless of rank or status, she treated everyone as an equal. The house was requisitioned by the War Office and used by a Cipher Unit, who put up numerous huts in the Grounds. The Hall's Italianate water tower, which stood among outbuildings, is visible from roads around the Park. A Chapel also survives, equally derelict. The Birkbeck family owned the 9,000-acre Estate for more than a century, sold in 2012 to renowned artist Anthony Gormley.

Two miles separated West Raynham from farmland taken in 1940 for this satellite aerodrome. It was initially used to disperse West Raynham's Blenheims. But as sufficient facilities were constructed and requisitioned to maintain a Squadron, No. 18 was transferred to RAF Great Massingham from its parent Station.

No. 18 Squadron

Animo et fide – 'With courage and faith'
Reproduced with permission of the MOD

No. 18 Squadron was formed on 11 May 1915 as a Training Unit at Northolt, during the Great War, concentrating on bombing. After the Armistice, it moved to Germany as part of the Army of Occupation before returning to the UK in September 1919 when it was disbanded. The Squadron then remained dormant until reformed in October 1931 at Upper Heyford with Harts and then Hinds. As part of the Air Component of the BEF (British Expeditionary Force), equipped with Blenheims; the Squadron suffered heavy losses in attempting to stop the German advance before withdrawing to the UK in May 1940.

No. 18 Squadron stayed at RAF Great Massingham from September 1940 until mid-April 1941 when it moved a few miles away to RAF Oulton, another satellite airfield.

However, worthy of note is that a few months on, in August 1941, assigned to anti-shipping duties, during a raid over France one of their aircraft dropped a very special and much needed box over St Omer airfield. Inside its careful wrapping was an artificial leg, a spare for Wing Commander Douglas Bader who was, at that time, a PoW!

One month after their departure from RAF Great Massingham No. 107 arrived, another Blenheim Unit, and a few days following, the B-17 Fortress 1s of No. 90 Squadron. It was believed Great Massingham had more space for these giant aircraft with four engines, but better suited to hard runways moved on to Polebrook. However, No. 107 remained at Great Massingham until mid-August 1943 which was, up to this point, the longest resident Squadron this Station had seen. Late summer of 1941, aircraft from No. 107 Squadron were flown off to Malta and the detachment disbanded.

107 Squadron

Nous y serons – 'We shall be there'
Reproduced with permission of the MOD

The badge of No. 107 Squadron was a double-headed eagle, gorged with a collar of fleur-de-lys. The double-headed eagle is one of the supporters from the armorial bearings of Salisbury, in which district the Squadron was formed. The collar of fleur-de-lys represents their service in France during World War One, when the Unit was attached to the French Army. The motto is derived from the Squadron magazine produced in World War One: *The Objective 107th (Squadron Always Gets There)*. Its authority goes back to King George VI, April 1938.

The Squadron was formed at Lake Down, Salisbury, on 15 May 1918, and in early June went to the Western Front as a day-bomber Squadron equipped with DH9 aircraft. Its first raid was on 30 June and day bombing of enemy targets was maintained until the Armistice. On 21 July, the Squadron made its most successful raid on Saponay where large ammunition dumps were hit. From the Squadron's airfield twenty miles away, the reflection of explosions and fire could be seen going on all evening.

On 1 October, another notable raid took place on Aulnoye railway station and junction. This resulted in the destruction of several ammunition trains in the sidings and a Leave train carrying 900 troops. All were killed with the exception of one Officer and his batman.

The Squadron had been disbanded in 1919, but reformed at Upavon in 1936, again as a Bomber Unit flying Hawker Hinds, then Blenheims. The Squadron went on to take part in scores of raids flying Blenheims, then Bostons, finally Mosquitoes. Most noteable of these raids included mass low-level daylight raids on the Knapsack and Quadrath Power Stations near Cologne on 12 August 1941; the great combined raid on Dieppe on 19 August 1942 (bombing hostile shore batteries, reducing enemy opposition to the landing force); and the low-level daylight raid on the Philips radio and valve factory at Eindhoven on 6 December 1942.

During its stay at Great Massingham, No. 107 Squadron was re-equipped to fly the Douglas Boston which arrived soon after New Year's Day 1942.

The Bostons went into action on 8 March with a medium altitude attack on Abbeville rail yards. Raids at both medium and low-level were carried out during ensuing months from Great Massingham, the former eventually being the Norm. However, by the time No. 2 Group was transferred to the Second Tactical Air Force, No. 107 had suffered the highest loss rate of all its Squadrons, although it is said to have flown the highest number of sorties. In operations from Massingham, eleven Blenheims and twenty-six Bostons were lost in some 100 raids.

In July 1943, shortly before No. 2 Group vacated the airfield, No. 342 Squadron, a French-manned Boston Unit, moved in from Sculthorpe for a few weeks before moving to Hartford Bridge where No. 107 preceded them. Soon after, the Station was closed briefly for extension and upgrading work, relinquished by No. 2 Group to the Unit Construction Company Ltd. Hard runways were laid for the first time. The airfield was extended, with the distance from West Raynham reduced to 1.5 miles, resulting in an overlap when aircraft circled to land.

Four T2 hangars had been erected in previous years, two on the east side of the airfield north of the village, two on the north-east side. A single B1 hangar was located south-east. Bomb stores were to the north. The camp, north-west of the village, eventually consisted of dispersal Sites, two communal, two WAAF, five domestic and Sick Quarters.

Accommodation catered for 1,778 males and 431 females.

RAF No. 100 (Bomber Support) Group

On 22 February 1942, Air Chief Marshal Sir Arthur Harris took over his new appointment as Air Officer Commanding Bomber Command – one of the most controversial figures of World War Two. However, his success was that he went on to turn Bomber Command into the offensive force that for so long had been the dream of RAF Commanders.

As extension and upgrading work finished at RAF Great Massingham in February 1944, the Station re-opened in late April under RAF 100 Group.

No. 169 became the first operational Squadron to be based at the rejuvenated airfield, equipped with Mosquitoes from Little Snoring. Also present was No. 1692 Flight, a Bomber Support Training Unit with Beaufighters and Mosquitoes. No. 169's main task was *Night Ranger* and later *Serrate* sorties aimed at seeking out Night Fighters operating against Bomber Command main force operations.

169 Squadron

'Hunt and destroy'
Reproduced with permission of the MOD

No. 169 Squadron badge shows a bending hunting horn in front of a hurt. The '*hurt*' signifies the night, the horn the Intruder role, authorised by King George VI.

Squadron Codes: VI

DUTY
- June 1942 – September 1943: Tactical Reconnaissance

- October 1943–1945: Mosquito Intruder Squadron

No. 169 Squadron went through two incarnations during the Second World War.

Formed on 15 June 1942 at RAF Twinwood Farm as a tactical Reconnaissance Unit, part of Army Co-operation Command; it took over 'B' Flight 613 Squadron's North American Mustang Mk 1s. It was from Twinwood Farm that USAAF Major Glenn Miller's aircraft took off on 15 December 1944 for Paris. His aircraft disappeared over the English Channel and was never seen again. The story of what happened to both him and his aircraft remains a mystery.

After a training period which saw the Squadron move five times, operations began from Duxford in December 1942 during which the Squadron carried out a mix of maritime Reconnaissance and Ground Attack missions.

In July 1943, the Squadron was used against low-level German fighter-bombers making '*tip and run*' attacks on the south coast. The Mustang Mk 1, with its impressive low-level performance, was ideally suited for the role.

This first incarnation of the Squadron was disbanded at RAF Middle Wallop on 30 September 1943.

The following day, on 1 October, the second incarnation formed at RAF Ayr as a Night Intruder Squadron, this time flying the de Havilland Mosquito. The Squadron also now had a single Bristol Beaufighter, some Airspeed Oxfords for training and communication purposes, while the Mosquitoes and Beaufighter were fitted with *GEE* equipment.

In December 1943, No. 169 Squadron moved to RAF Little Snoring, and in January 1944 was re-equipped with Mosquito II Night Fighters to commence Night Intruder operations against German airfields and enemy Night Fighters. This field of work continued for the remainder of the war.

No. 169 Squadron finally disbanded on 10 August 1945 at RAF Great Massingham.

PERSONAL EXPERIENCES

F/O Keith Ross Miller AM, MBE

Keith Miller was a well known figure in civilian life. Sharing his story offers an insight into how war affected careers already in the making.

As an Australian Test cricketer, English journalist Ian Wooldridge called him *'the golden boy'* of cricket, leading to his nickname *'Nugget'*. Away from cricket, he was a successful Australian rules footballer. He played fifty games for St Kilda, kicking eight goals in one game against North Melbourne during 1941.

World War Two interrupted his sporting career.

On 20 August 1940, Keith joined the Militia (Army Reserve) to be assigned to the 4th Reserve Motor Transport Co. where clashes with authority became legendary and he was fined for *'using insulting language to a superior officer'*.

During the summer of 1940 – 41, he was granted Leave to play interstate cricket. In a war-shortened season, he scored 140 runs at 28.00 and took his maiden first-class wicket. The season ended early as he was recalled to duty.

He continued to have disciplinary problems, and he left the Militia on 8 November 1941, whereupon he and a friend attempted to join the Royal Australian Navy. When the Navy rejected his friend, Keith promptly tore up his own paperwork, left the Recruiting Office, and walked around the corner and on into the Royal Australian Air Force (RAAF).

Less than two months after the Japanese attack on Pearl Harbour in December 1941, Keith was called to active Service, training at No. 4 Initial Training School, Victor Harbour in South Australia to gain his wings in late 1942. He was promoted to the rank of Flight Sergeant in December 1942 after playing only one match during the year's football season while posted in South Australia. One month later, he sailed to Europe with a stopover at a training camp in Boston, United States, where he met future wife Peg Wagner. In March, he was deployed to Bournemouth, England, where he continued training.

Invited to join an RAAF team in London, officially formed in preparation for the 1943 season, it was Keith's selection which led to the first of his many brushes with death.

In April, while away with the team, some of his comrades were killed in a German air strike. Keith went on to play his first match at Lord's against Warner's XI, a team featuring past, current and future England players. The RAAF played eight matches that season with his top score: 141 against Public School Wanderers. However, it was playing for Dominions against Warner's XI in August, scoring 32 and two; that marked his first meeting with good friend, England batsman Denis Compton, drawing media attention. In the final match of the season between the RAAF and the RAF, he took 3/23 and scored 91. This success prompted Warner to plan a 'Test' series between respective armed Services of England and Australia.

By late 1943, Keith was based in Gloucestershire. One night, he threatened to punch his Commanding Officer. He was sentenced for insubordination to a three-week disciplinary course with hard labour. November brought a posting to Ouston, near Newcastle-upon-Tyne, where he trained in the use of radar, but during his stay, he sustained a back injury in a wrestling match which caused recurring and enduring problems, particularly diminishing his ability to bowl.

In 1944, Keith was again selected for the RAAF Team, and in a match against the British Civil Defence Services at Lord's in July, he reached his century just as a V-1 flying bomb landed nearby.

After ten months training, he was offered a Commission as a Pilot Officer and posted to 12 Advanced Flying Unit in Grantham, Lincolnshire, moving on to Cranfield, Bedfordshire. But on a trip back to Ouston to visit former comrades, his life began to unravel. A night of drunken revelry brought a charge of eight offences: the outcome a possible dishonourable discharge. Luckily, his new Commanding Officer was his old CO from Ouston and he escaped with a fine.

In training, Keith flew Beauforts, Beaufighters and Mosquitoes. Another near-death experience happened when mechanical problems forced an emergency landing of his Beaufighter. The aircraft was repaired for use by others, but on its next flight, the pilot was killed outright when the problem recurred. On another occasion, he avoided colliding with a hangar by centimetres. He also escaped death by skipping a social appointment where a V-1 bomb hit the venue and killed many of the patrons.

In October, he went AWOL to watch a concert and was summarily discharged. But the CO revoked his decision after Keith agreed to play for his cricket team. At the end of his Officer training, he was sent aboard a Royal Navy destroyer as part of an exchange programme between the Forces, and during a mission to Belgium, the vessel fought a German U-boat which was sunk. On his return to England, he was promoted to Flying Officer on 4 November 1944.

In March 1945, Keith was finally deployed to RAF Great Massingham, assigned to 169 Squadron flying Mosquito fighter-bombers.

The Squadron took part in missions against targets on mainland Europe in April and May 1945. They attacked V-1 and V-2 production and test launch sites on the island of Peenemunde in the North Sea. On 19 April, he took part in an attack on a German installation at Flensburg in Denmark. In May, his Squadron was deployed in *Operation Fire Bash* to attack Westerland Airfield on the Island of Sylt. One of his bombs failed to release and the load dangled precariously from a wing. He landed the aircraft with the bomb still attached, which fortunately failed to detonate.

Keith's wartime exploits were to give him a greater sense of perspective when he returned to the sports field. Asked years later by Michael Parkinson during a television interview about pressure in cricket, his response was: '*Pressure is a Messerschmitt up your arse, playing cricket is not!*'

In truth, Keith Miller was deeply affected by the war. It changed him.

In the first post-war Ashes Test, England were caught on a sticky and Bill Edrich came in, someone who shared war years with Keith as a friend at RAF Great Massingham. He was thinking: '*He's my old Service mate. The last thing he wants after five years' war is to be flattened by a cricket ball.* He eased up, and Bradman immediately came up to him: '*Don't slow down, Keith. Bowl quicker.*' Keith blamed that remark for putting him off Test cricket saying: '*I never felt the same way about it after!*'

Flight Sergeant John '*Curly*' Beeching

100 Group was a Special Duties section of Bomber Command and, although accompanying heavy bombers on operations over Germany, our fast Mosquitoes were never subjected to the frightful dangers of Lancasters. To some extent, our crews at Massingham never had the

same sort of stress as the heavies. In any event, Bomber Command crews were a pretty jovial lot. We were all twenty to twenty-three years old and full of the joys of life, notwithstanding they were often lives suddenly snuffed out.

I'm sure anyone there at the time would admit aircrew developed a pretty cavalier attitude towards death. Life was to be enjoyed as long as it lasted. This certainly applied to my associates on 169 Squadron and was the subject of quite a bit of black humour.

My Navigator/Radar Operator, Fred Herbert, was the only one who flew with me. He died in Canada a few years ago. Just fourteen days older than I, we crewed up at Cranfield Operation Training Unit and flew together until war's end, and one further year as Instructors on Blind Landing Systems, which required a two man crew, flying Airspeed Oxfords and Avro Ansons.

When 169 Squadron was disbanded, nearly all crews were posted to Woodhall Spa, Lincolnshire, flying Pathfinder Mosquitoes in preparation for going to Okinawa to bomb Japan. Fortunately, for us at least, the Americans dropped the 'big ones' and we became redundant overnight. I was released from the RAF aged twenty-three with just under 1,000 accident-free flying hours in my Log Book. I shifted back to Canada for seven years where I trained in 1942, before coming to New Zealand in 1953. Living in Nelson is as good as it gets and a far better place. Having lived here fifty-three years, I've never regretted one day. In the main, I have lived a long, happy and useful life and am happy to talk to anybody about it.

Flight Sergeant John 'Curly' Beeching, together with Navigator and good friend Flight Sergeant F. G. 'Fred' Herbert, were dragged off Christmas Leave 1944 to report to Great Massingham, initially to 1692 Bomber Support Development Unit (BSDU). The Unit was very short of crews. Suddenly, they were pitchforked onto Operations once Christmas was over. The Ardennes Battle was in full swing. Germans were going all out in what was to be a last major attempt:

There were about 2,000 people stationed there and naturally their presence brought quite a bit of prosperity to the village dwellers. I suppose our operational flying was somewhat different from the heavy bomber boys. Of a morning, air crews would gather in what was known as the Intelligence Library, in the Control Tower building. A lovely WAAF named Gwen would bring us all cups of tea and biscuits, and we'd discuss who would be flying, or available to fly, if there were operations that coming night. It was all very matey: '*I flew last night and want to see the picture in Kings Lynn,*' and '*Yes, Fred and I are available …*' We had only two-man crews and there were seldom more than a half dozen planes detailed for any particular operation, so there were never many people involved.

We'd then go out to the dispersals and take off, usually in pairs, on an air test to make sure everything was working okay, wartime radar being what it was. We would leave parachutes in the aircraft as it was virtually impossible to climb into a Mk XIX Mosquito wearing one. On top of the pilot chute, we had a one-man dinghy, a water-bag and a seat cushion. Sitting in one position for anything up to six hours plus could be very demanding. During nights of bad weather we often saw virtually nothing but an instrument panel, and the Navigator his radar screen. There was absolutely no relief from sitting in the one place, strapped in with a Sutton Harness, breathing oxygen continuously through a face-mask.

We normally flew at about 28,000 feet, a bit above the main bomber stream. Most 169 Squadron aircraft were fitted with 100-gallon drop tanks under each wing, giving us a total of 716 gallons of 100-octane petrol, or getting on for 3,000 litres. Each engine would burn about four litres every minute. Merlins were hungry beasts, but reliable. We had lovely, thoughtful ground crews and I often wonder what happened to them. As soon as war finished we never saw or heard from them again.

Taking off and flying in atrocious conditions was all part of the 23/6d a day we were paid, pretty poor compared with what airline pilots collect in pay packets today. In my time, I flew fifty-seven different Mosquitoes of many different types and never scratched one.

John's first operation was to North Germany. The Ijsselmeer (Zuider Zee) was flooded to become one giant frozen lake:

We were still over Holland when the Germans launched a V-2 rocket just underneath us — we were flying at about 26,000 feet, but knew nothing about these things, thinking it was aimed at John and Fred, not the UK. As it got closer I thought: 'Blimey, clobbered on our first operation!' But it went on, forever upward, about a mile away, leaving a jagged vapour trail.

We did another couple of ops during the next couple of days, soon learning what flak looked like at close quarters. Being young and stupid, it never really terrified us. We knew we were invincible and it was the other bloke who would cop it, which often turned out to be the case, otherwise I wouldn't be sitting here playing a tune on this keyboard! It was nearly all luck, although I pursued the heavy bomber boys practice and never flew in a straight line for long, which probably assisted slightly.

They were good times. There was a pub, *The Royal Oak*. It isn't there any more but was our focal drinking place, run by a Welsh couple from Mountain Ash, Jack and Doris Fraser. We would sing the filthiest of songs and pour beer into the innards of the old wooden framed piano in the tiny lounge *'to make it sound more mellow'*, but you can imagine what it did. It was invariably played by a Navigator, Frank Francis, who survived the war.

There were times when John and Navigator Fred would land at Foulsham to engage on bomber affiliation training exercises, rendezvousing with Halifaxes which they had on 192; in the middle of the night, doing training night-fighter runs on them.

It was pretty sad in a way, as the Gunners never seemed to spot us, even from almost touching distance behind – if we had been a German Night-Fighter they would have all been dead, and don't forget they were expecting us on these exercises! There were quite a few Australians stationed at Foulsham and by coincidence, Wendy and I met one of them, Llew Edwards and his wife at an Aircrew Reunion at Surfers Paradise some years ago. However, both Llew and his wife have now shifted to the big Married Quarters in the sky.

John's main drinking partner at Great Massingham was Albert Wigzell, known as *Wiggy*. He would drink copious amounts of beer, but had a very sober and stable pilot, Doug Waite. John remembers times spent with *Wiggy*, cycling down country lanes, in and around Norfolk villages, getting drunk, falling off their issue bikes, winding up sleeping in convenient ditches, damp and bramble scratched ... *'not the stuff of heroes!'* John says he happily lives with the memories of those beautiful times. *'Shakespeare's Salad Days: when I was green in judgement, cold in blood...' The enormity of what we were doing never reached us, nor what we were asked and expected to do. Lads of similar age today have barely stepped off their skate-boards!'* Their accommodation at Great Massingham left much to be desired. In the early days of the airfield, men and women arriving were billeted in the village. Later, until 'bunks' or rooms became available, they were quartered in Nissen huts; shared by about ten sufferers. In winter, the door would often blow open, or be left open by the last arrival, and in the morning snow would carpet about a quarter of the floor. They slept in their inner flying suits, borrowing extra blankets from beds of those on Leave,

Leave was generous. Operational aircrew got seven days Leave every six weeks, although Great Massingham's Flight Commander, Squadron Leader James A. Wright, a wonderful man and pilot according to John Beeching, stipulated they had to have flown at least twenty hours between Leave periods. Fred and he were reasonably keen – John had an *'Above Average'* Assessment by the time he left 169.

Our Squadron Commander was Wing Commander Neville Reeves, DSO, DFC and Bar, also a great Pilot sadly killed flying Meteor jets from Massingham just prior to the Berlin Air Lift. The full Report of this accident, makes it a very real and unexpected tragedy:

NEVILLE REEVES, EX C/O – 169 SQUADRON: GREAT MASSINGHAM, 1944/5
Andy Anderson re Neville Reeves

... many ex-Squadron members who were fortunate to know Neville Reeves probably remain unaware of the circumstances leading to his death. Someone stated that it happened during a C.F.E. trial and whilst this is not strictly accurate, some account of the trials will provide the background.

At the time of extreme East/West tension (the Berlin Airlift period) HQ Fighter Command envisaged a situation whereby Day Fighter Wings might have to be scrambled in marginal weather, with the consequent problem of getting them down safely at the end of

the sortie. C.F.E West Raynham was accordingly tasked with exam-
ining this aspect and devising a recovery system, hence The Rapid
Landing Trials of 1949. The Squadrons were equipped with Meteor
IVs which had neither navigation nor approach instruments, so the
automatic choice for the final approach element had to be Ground
Controlled Approach (G.C.A) which is where I became involved.

G.C.As were then mobile, self-contained units and No. 9 G.C.A
was sent to C.F.E. for the trials; the C/O was Squadron Leader Eddie
Le Conte, also ex-604. G.C.A comprises two quite separate radar
systems, one providing all-round coverage for locating, identifying
and marshalling aircraft to a position where the other, with precision
equipment but coverage limited to the runway approach, can take it
over for the final talkdown. The person doing the marshalling was
termed the 'Director', and the one doing the talkdown, the 'Controller'.
For the trials, F/Lt Jack Spruce was Controller. I was Director.

For trial purposes, the G.C.A. operational element was positioned
at Great Massingham, a disused wartime airfield some three miles
west of Raynham; mainly to keep trials aircraft clear of the very busy
Raynham circuit. Wing Commander Braham was in charge of the
trials as O.C Night/All Weather Wing; other pilots regularly involved
were Neville Reeves, Cas Castagnola, Red Armstrong, Duncan
McIver and Jimmy Thomas as distinguished and proficient bunch as
anyone could have wished for. The aircraft used were again Meteor
IVs which normally did touch and go landings at Massingham and
landed back at Raynham after each sortie.

The trial called for a landing rate of four aircraft a minute, which
was wildly optimistic; one aircraft every four minutes was fairly
normal for G.C.A. but obviously we would have to improve on
that or most of a Wing of short endurance jets would end up flying
gliders. Operating with the B29 (Superfortress Group) at Marham
we had achieved intervals of two minutes and I believe the Berlin
Airlift got it down to this figure too, but this was only possible with
crews arriving overhead beacons strictly to a pre-arranged schedule. Controlling Meteors for the Rapid Landing Trial proved to be an
altogether more exciting (stimulating!) experience.

When we thought we had a viable system, the Duxford or
Horsham Wing would be 'borrowed' to try it out on that strange
animal 'the average Squadron pilot', after which it was usually 'back

to the drawing board'. The best we achieved in the end was landing pairs of aircraft at around 1 min 20 sec intervals, and that involved a much modified system and a lot of fast talking. By this time N.A.W pilots and G.C.A crews were working as a highly efficient team with complete confidence in each other; sadly, events were to prove there was a degree of over-confidence.

That then was the position one autumn morning when Jack Spruce and I checked in at our Raynham Admin office, with radiation fog limiting visibility to around 200 yards; a call to the Met Office confirmed the obvious – no chance of improvement before early afternoon.

Definitely not flying weather, so we resigned ourselves to a morning in the rest caravan adjacent to the G.C.A. truck at Massingham, drinking tea, smoking and playing Bridge; life could be pretty tough on G.C.A. at times! First, however, a wander over to the N.A.W crew room for a natter and a coffee, where Bob Braham's cheerful greeting: *'What are you two buggers doing here? We're going flying'*, got the answer it deserved. 'No, seriously though ...' said Bob, *'Neville and I are going off shortly for a weather check followed by a Q.G.H. to be overhead Raynham at 2,000 feet, 20 minutes after take-off; you take over from there and talk us down to land at Massingham'*. The realisation that he really meant it had a sobering effect.

As the name implies, G.C.A is only an approach as distinct from a landing system, normally terminating with *'half a mile to touchdown, look ahead and land'*, the pilot having previously advised on over-shoot procedure should the runway not be in sight at this point. Our protest that conditions were way below our minimum were smilingly brushed aside with *'stop worrying, you'll get us down alright; and make sure the kettle's boiling when we land'*. Well, aircraft had been talked down in sub-minimum conditions before – I'd been involved in some myself – but these had been emergencies which had to be got down somehow.

Deliberately taking off in short range jets in fog to land at a dis-used airfield with no approach lighting, and no possible diversion if things went wrong, was something else again, and I didn't like it one bit. However, to work and in spite of our misgivings everything went exactly as planned. Neville landed first. Jack talking him down almost to touchdown and Bob followed again with no bother, calling, clear of the runway and shutting down. I was just beginning to relax and think how good that tea and cigarette would taste, when Neville called me to say he was taking off again on runway 10 (i.e. 'Downwind')for another G.C.A. The idea of taking off with at most fifteen minutes fuel remaining really startled me. I hadn't been outside for some time, so perhaps conditions were better than I thought, and anyway, Neville had just landed so knew exactly what they were like, so back to work.

Keeping the circuit as tight as possible I handed over to Jack for the talkdown and my part of the act was over, could lean over to watch proceedings. The approach was perfect, no wind so no drift or turbulence to worry about, and reached the point *'On the centre-line, on the glidepath, approaching to touchdown, look ahead and land'* when suddenly the aircraft response veered right and shot off the side of the radar display followed by Neville's call: *'Overshooting'*. We managed three more identical circuits, the tension mounting all the time, with identical results – a perfect approach, the sudden turn to the right at the last moment and the overshoot. Obviously Neville was seeing something he thought was the runway then realising his mistake. After the final call *'Overshooting'*, I went through the patter: *'Roger, pull up, turn port to 120 as soon as possible, level at 1,000 feet and call steady'*. I never received the call.

The Meteor crashed near Massingham village and Neville was killed instantly. I thought he must be out of fuel, but the crash investigators said not, the engines were on full power when he went in. Presumably, he stalled from a tight instrument turn at low level, trying to get another circuit before the fuel finally gave out.

The G.C.A. was completely exonerated at the subsequent enquiry, it had, after all, never been intended to cope with these conditions, but apart from the official verdict you always ask yourself if there was anything more that could have been done. In this case, I could sadly but truthfully answer: *'Not a thing'*. Could Neville have done more or differently under the circumstances? I leave that to the judgement of his peers, and there can't be many of those.

On reflection, John Beeching says the reason Neville Reeves crashed was because, during the steep turn over Little Massingham, near to the ground, of necessity, a collector ring on the port engine disintegrated and the Meteor went straight in.

L.A.C George Crudgington
by son Ted Crudgington

My father served in 15 O.T.U at Hampstead Norris from early 1941 to 1 October 1943. He was an Engine Fitter FIIE servicing Wellington bombers. In September 1943, he was posted to 169 Squadron to report on 1 October at Ayr. 169 Squadron had been a Recce Squadron equipped with Mustang MkI and been disbanded on 1 October at Middle Wallop, only to be reformed on the same day, to become the first Mosquito Squadron in 100 Group, Bomber Command. Personnel were hand picked. The aircrew comprised of two crews from all existing night fighter Squadrons and Squadron was urgently needed to become operational, initially with Beafighters, equipped with A1 Mk IV and Serrate.

169 Squadron moved to Little Snoring on 8 December 1943. Its Mosquitoes were very tardily delivered to them having been modified for Bomber Support operations with the installation of a *Serrate* homing device – giving the ability to home in on radar emissions of German Night Fighter radar. The Mosquitoes were NFI 1s, the .303 machine guns and magazines having been removed from the nose to provide space for the *Serrate* black boxes with *Gee* also installed. These aircraft were very old. W4076 was the 26th Mosquito to be built and also the first NFI 1, while WA085 was the 35th built and the 7th NFI 1. These aircraft needed new engines before they were ready to go.

The original crews of 169 Squadron were made up of the Commanding Officer: W/Cdr Gracie who had flown Hurricanes with 56 Squadron during the Battle of Britain, and Spitfires off aircraft carriers to Malta. He shot down many aircraft in Malta. B Flight was commanded by S/Ldr J. A. H. Cooper – a Cavalryman in the Army before joining the RAF and a keen huntsman. He used to blow his hunting horn before taking off on a sortie! He became a BEA pilot after the war. A Flight was commanded by S/Ldr E. Thorne, an ex-Halton apprentice. He flew Defiants with 264 Squadron in the Battle of Britain. I have been told he suffered from chronic insomnia. 'Handy' Millar, a northern Irishman, was the Squadron's highest scorer. Fred Bone was his Navigator who became a Merseyside policeman postwar. Tim Woodman, another high scorer, commanded Boscombe Down after the war. Pat Kemmis, his Navigator, went on to work for the Foreign Office. S/Ldr Fifield did the first live ejection at ground level. Jim Murphy, Navigator, became President of the National Union of Teachers after the war. Harry Reed went on to breed racehorses. Pete Dills, a Belgian, became an airline pilot, flying Boeing 707s with KLM. And Flt/Officer J. J. Southcott, USAF, was a Navigator.

1692 (BSTU) Flight moved into Little Snoring at the same time as 169 Squadron. It trained crews for 100 Group Squadrons, equipped with Beaufighters, Ansons and Wellingtons. One man who served on it told me there were many crashes.

Dad didn't talk about living conditions on the aerodromes where he was stationed, but Little Snoring must have been better than his previous two (Ayr and Hampstead Norris) having had 115 Squadron with Lancasters making it more permanent. Being there, meant Dad could easily get home. However, one thing he had to do was learn to ride a bike given the distance between living quarters, dispersals, cookhouse, etc. It gave him the freedom to explore the countryside in his time off duty, which he enjoyed immensely.

At this point, it's interesting to know the kind of rations civilians were allowed. Each person was allotted one fresh egg per week. Sweets were 10 oz per month. Dad soon found local farmers couldn't get cakes, so he would barter one NAFFI 1d cake for one egg. When he came home he would bring a few dozen eggs and mushrooms grown around the dispersals, also rabbits caught with snares around the airfield. Airmen who were country-born taught 'Townies' like Dad how to lay snares.

I am reminded of one thing I haven't said – Lord Mackie, the Liberal Peer, was an Observer with 115 Squadron.

On 20 January 1944, W/C Gracie and Flt/Lt Todd took off in HS707 to support a Bomber Command raid on Bremen. This was the first operation by 169 Squadron. On returning, 169 first reported to Coltishall and then to Little Snoring. I don't know the call sign for Little Snoring, but the call sign for 169 Squadron was 'Kaolin'. Each pilot had his own call sign. The CO was 'Kaolin 1', A Flight Commander was 'Kaolin 2', while B Flight Commander was 'Kaolin 3', and so on through the rest of the Squadron.

Sqdn/Ldr Cooper had a bet of 10/- with Sqdn/Ldr Thorne on which of them would shoot down the first enemy aircraft. On 27 January, Sqn/Ldr Cooper, returning over the North Sea, sent the following message to Little Snoring:

'Tell Kaolin 3 he owes me 10/-'

He was flying HJ711 and herein lies a mystery. On 15 March, Flt/Lt Foster and F/O Grantham were shot down and killed in HJ711 on a raid to Stuttgart. Today, a person in Yorkshire is rebuilding a Mosquito which he says is HJ711. Obviously one of these has the wrong serial number. But which one?

169 Squadron steadily increased its sorties from only five in January 1944 to forty-nine in January 1945. This effort was possible by the hard work of Ground Crews, despite the harsh winter of 1943-44, one of the coldest on record. Ground Crews had to maintain aircraft in the open on the Flights. Dad didn't say anything about crashes, but I know one was the aircraft he maintained, which overshot the runway, tipping it up on its nose in the overshoot area. Another was a Lancaster making an emergency landing with only two engines working, which also overshot the runway, again tipping it on its nose. Photos of these would have been taken at the time ... but where are they now?

During early May 1944, my dad was suffering from pleurisy and in Sick Bay. At this time, Mum was expecting my younger brother. Dad worked out if he signed himself off sick on 4 June he would be sent home on 'Convalesence Leave' and be home for the birth. He signed himself off to be immediately told all Leave was cancelled and there was to be a maximum effort. It was the eve of D-Day, which should have taken place on 5 June but postponed for twenty-four hours.

Dad had to go out on the Flights, although he wasn't fully fit. He did get home for the birth however, on 25 June.

169 Squadron, 1692 Flight and 1694 Flight moved from Little Snoring to Great Massingham on 9 June 1944.

23 Squadron, arriving from Malta, moved into Little Snoring. In the local church there is the Score Board of the Squadron stationed there, and also the poem written by Stephen Ruffle, a former member of 23 Squadron.

Great Massingham had just been rebuilt with concrete runways and wasn't fully functional when 169 Squadron moved in. The water supply was contaminated and all water had to be boiled. Great Massingham was not far from Little Snoring, so it became just as convenient for Dad. Great Massingham had been a satellite of West Raynham when it was just a grass airfield. In its early days, Ground Crews had lived in tents and Aircrews at West Raynham.

The first Squadron at Great Massingham was No. 18, one of its pilots was Bill Edrich, the England cricketer. No. 18 Squadron was replaced by 107 Squadron, both being equipped with Blenheims, and No. 107 with Bostons.

On 19 July 1943, 342 Squadron joined them. They also were equipped with Bostons. 342 was a Free French Squadron. One of its Navigators was Pierre Mendes-France, who later became Prime Minister of France. Both Squadrons moved to Hartford Bridge in September 1943.

In May 1941, No. 90 Squadron had been at Great Massingham with Flying Fortresses. West Raynham and Great Massingham were so close together aircraft had to fly round both in a combined circuit. The call sign for Great Massingham was 'Heyhoe'.

When Dad was home for the birth of my younger brother, the Doodle-Bugs were coming over thick and fast. Dad told Mum she couldn't stay in the south, promising to get lodging for them near Great Massingham. True to his word, Mum, myself and baby brother travelled to Norfolk, arriving at Great Massingham station where Dad met us. Obviously, he was delighted to see us. He was also amused because the engine that pulled our train in was the Sandringham

Class engine named 'West Ham United'. Dad had played for West Ham in his teens! We went by taxi to a village called East Lexham to stay with a farm tractor driver called 'Hunter' and his family. His daughter was Mabel. She worked as housemaid at a farm at West Lexham. It was rumoured the farmer came from Denmark with fourpence in his pocket, going on to buy and run the most modern farm in the area. It is this family that now own Great Massingham aerodrome.

The area around East Lexham at the time was infested with hornets, unpleasant insects. While there, I attended village school run by Miss Pogson. It was this one large room with rows of desks with gangways between. As a five year old, I sat at the left row of desks, then on my sixth birthday, moved across the gangway to the next row, and at seven moved to the next row, and so on until my eleventh birthday when I reached the far end of the room. There was only this one teacher. One of my tasks was to go to the farm with two one-pint enamel cans at milking time to get the milk (there were no fridges or freezers like we have now!). There was an Italian PoW Camp in the area and they used to work on the farms. I could tell them because they had yellow circular patches about the size of a football sewn to their uniform.

Getting back to Great Massingham, 169 re-equipped with Mk VI Mosquitoes. These were a special batch modified as the Mk IIs. These Mossies didn't have .303 machine guns. It was about this time that the original 169 Squadron crews were finishing their tours. Under Bomber Command, this meant a total of thirty ops. Among the replacement crews were Sgt John Ware, Sgt Brian Humphries (John called him Ben), Sgt Doug Waite, Sgt Albert Wigzell. There are stories I can tell about these later. But also joining was a Navigator called Sgt Frank Francis who was very popular in the Sgts Mess as he was a very good pianist, just the person to have in a party.

On D-Day, aircraft of 169 Squadron patrolled over Northern France individually to stop any German bombers getting to bomb the D-Day beaches. Doug Waite's call-sign was 'Kaolin 25' … this will be part of the story later. At this time, the Germans changed their radar, which meant Serrate equipment didn't home onto the new radar they installed and yet still the Squadron managed to shoot down the German night fighters.

The Squadron's top scorer, F/O W. H. Miller was brought down, however. At first, he was being passed along an escape chain until it was betrayed and he was taken prisoner. His Navigator, F/O F. Bone was captured straight away. Their aircraft had been brought down by debris from the Do217 they had shot down, damaging the Mosquito's radiators, causing the engines to fail.

Around the same time, there was also a crash of a Beaufighter belonging to 1692 Flight. Two young girls were near the crash-site and helped the Navigator drag the pilot out of the burning plane. Both were given a bravery award. The pilot went on to recover from his injuries and served in 169 Squadron. However, after the war, he committed suicide because of his disfiguring burns. We don't know what became of the Navigator.

There were also two special parades, the first being to receive the Squadron badge which had been approved by the *Chester Herald*. The second was when the Squadron was presented with a silver tankard in recognition of the shooting down of the 100th enemy aircraft by RAF 100 Group. I wonder where this tankard is today. Is a Squadron's silver collected by the RAF and placed in a depository until a Squadron is reformed?

As the bombing campaigns intensified, Squadron sorties also increased. After December, the Squadron's efforts however decreased. The V-2 rockets which started falling after the V-1 Doodlebugs did not worry us too much as they fell faster than the speed of sound. You heard the explosion and then the sound of it arriving, therefore you would not hear the one that dropped on you! The RAF thought they were radio controlled, and one 169 aircraft and crew flew sorties to try to find the radio signals. The V-2 rockets were not radio controlled and more like a giant motor bomb.

Towards the end of the year, the Squadron started to re-equip with Mk XIX Mossies. As 169 Squadron came under Bomber Command, it meant there was a steady changeover of crews when they finished their thirty ops and came to the end of their tour. Among them was Keith Miller, the Australian Test Cricketer, John Beeching, and

Squadron Leader Downing who shot down a large number of aircraft in North Africa. He later flew VC-10s with BOAC. Also at this time crews from 85 Squadron and 141 Squadron were attached to 169.

On 6 December, John Ware and Ben Humphries took off on their 29th sortie. When over enemy territory, their aircraft was hit in the port engine by flak. Unfortunately, John was unable to feather the propeller. The drag caused by this caused the aircraft to lose altitude. John set course for the nearest allied territory. However, on the way a night fighter attacked them which John managed to evade. As he approached Allied lines, he realised he was over high ground and they would have to abandon the aircraft. Ben obviously went first. John remembered taking off his helmet and putting it on top of the control column before leaving the aircraft. Ben landed on the German side of the line. He hid his chute and mae-west and blackened his face to set off to cross through the lines. Whenever he found an ammunition box, he looked at the writing to see if it was English or German trying to distinguish which side of the line he was on. Eventually, he came to an American Gun Battery. When he walked into the gun pit, the Americans were playing cards without posting sentries. Their reaction when he walked calmly in was: 'Where the hell have you come from?' Meanwhile, John had landed on the Allied side of the line and broken his leg. The aircraft crashed into a house in Malmedy, Belgium.

I visited John in the 1970s and during our chat, I told him he'd been flying the aircraft Dad maintained. That night Dad wasn't looking after it as he was Duty Crew – all Ground Crew had to take turns to look after all odd aircraft that landed at Great Massingham. It was as he was driving past the aircraft he had a premonition that it wouldn't be coming back. He couldn't say anything as he would be accused of not maintaining the aircraft properly. John said he wished he had said something as both he and Ben had the same feeling and if Dad had voiced his thoughts he would have turned back over the North Sea and said the engines were losing power. As it was on his 29th sortie he could have got away with it.

One odd thing about 169 Squadron was that some crews always flew the same aircraft, not always the senior crews; while others flew a variety of machines. Doug Waite, for example, flew thirteen different aircraft over his thirty sorties, the most flying in one aircraft being just five times.

The Squadron started flying ground attack sorties at night and also dropped T.1s away from the main force to entice German night fighters away. On two occasions, a few aircraft flew sorties from Juvaincourt, France, to extend their range over Germany.

In 1945, the number of sorties started to decrease. A few crews were attached from 85 and 141 Squadrons, and on 7 January 1945, F/Lt B. Bonakis and Sgt E. T. Garland of 85 Squadron failed to return from Munchen.

On 12 January 1945, NT06 VI-H flown by S/Ldr J. A. Wright with F/Lt H. B. Vine and NS 998 VI-S flown by F/O G. V. Hart together with F/Sgt G. Scott flew a fighter escort and air sea rescue for the Lancaster of 617 Squadron raiding Bergen. They were attacked by five Fw190s. The former circled a ditched Lancaster for 135 minutes. The Lancasters were from 9 and 617 Squadrons, tasked to drop tallboy bombs on submarine pens at Bergen, Norway. The ditched Lancaster appears to have been NF992 KC-B from 617 Squadron. Unfortunately, although a Warwick dropped an airborne lifeboat to them, all the crew drowned (Bomber Command Losses, 1945).

On 3 March 1945, S/Ldr V. J. Fenwick and F/O J. W. Pierce of 141 Squadron were shot down near Coltishall by German intruders.

From 19 April 1945, the Squadron started dropping napalm bombs on Fleasburg and Schleswig and Landburg aerodromes.

On 2 May 1945, twelve aircraft dropped napalm bombs on Westerland and Schelswig aerodromes. This was the last operation carried out by 169 Squadron. MM680 flown by F/O R. Caiterhall and F/Sgt D. J. Beadle were shot down and killed. F/O Caiterhall had flown bombers before he joined the Squadron. Doug Waite, one of the pilots on this raid, was very bitter because he believed it unnecessary. He said the German gunner who shot down F/O Caiterhall wrote to his mother and apologised for shooting him down. He said if he had known there were only seven days left he wouldn't have fired his gun. Len Turner, who was also a pilot on this raid, said he felt it was bullying, so he dropped his napalm in some woods away from the aerodrome.

On 6 May 1945, the Squadron flew a low level formation exercise (probably the only time the Squadron had ever flown together). Unfortunately, MME37 flown by F/Lt D. P. Williams and F/Sgt K. Phoden crashed near Hove. Their deaths were the last sustained by Bomber Command before the official surrender. Len Turner said they were flying alongside him. One moment they were there; the next ... gone!

169 Squadron converted to a peacetime existence. Dad had time to visit friends in other Sections of the Squadron and played in football matches. As he was in a reserved occupation, he was wanted back by London Transport so he was released by the RAF.

Unexpectedly, on 8 August he was mobilised again and when he got back to Great Massingham he found he'd been invited to the Squadron's Disbandment and Farewell Party. This was held in one of the hangars. Tables were set out with food and stocks of alcohol from the Officers and Sergeants Messes to be used up.

Dad finally left the RAF on 17 October 1945.

Last sorties from RAF Great Massingham were flown by No. 169 Squadron on the night of 2 May 1945. During hostilities a total of 52 Bomber Command aircraft were lost in operations from the Station: 11 Blenheims, 28 Bostons and 13 Mosquitoes. No. 1692 Flight was disbanded in June 1945 and No. 169 Squadron two months later.

Flt/Sgt Arthur Bradley
The Price Paid on Faulty Intelligence
by brother Cyril Bradley

Nearly six years of conflict was coming to an end, with Bomber Command having carried out its last attack on Germany on 25 April 1945.

It therefore came as a surprise on the morning of 2 May when the call came to 100 Group for a maximum effort on Kiel, using its countermeasures of *Mandrel* screen, jamming, feint attacks and *Window* and to follow in with bombing runs on the dockland area. Intelligence Reports gave details of ships assembling for the transporting of troops to Norway to carry on the war.

Some 293 aircraft took part in this last raid of the war drawn from 8 Group and 100 Group. 189 of these aircraft were from 100 Group and included Mosquitoes, Liberators, Fortresses and Halifaxes – twenty-two Halifaxes of 171 and 199 Squadrons from North Creake. They took off from their base at 20.31 hours, with the last leaving at 21.14 hours.

However, it was while on their bombing runs over the target area that two Halifaxes of 199 Squadron collided, scattering wreckage around the village of Meimersdorf. From the sixteen aircrew, thirteen perished.

It was to be many years later before it became known the Intelligence Report was false and the raid need never have taken place. The assembled ships in Kiel docks were, in truth, being boarded with prisoners from slave labour camps in the area with the intention of returning them to their original homeland. Instead, many thousands perished in this, the last air raid of the war.

My brother, F/Sgt Arthur Bradley, was Navigator of Halifax BIII RG375 EX-R, the last Bomber Command aircraft to be lost in World War Two. He lies at rest with his comrades in Kiel War Graves Cemetery; it was his 37th Operation.

Nearly six years of war was coming to an end on that night of 2/3 May 1945 as Bomber Command carried out its last devastating air attack on Kiel. Some 290 aircraft took part with three failing to return – two Halifax's of 199 Squadron and a Mosquito of 169 Squadron, all from RAF No. 100 Group. Their crews became the final victims of the RAF's offensive against the Third Reich.

Mosquito NFXIX MM680 from Great Massingham exploded at 2330 over the target. Two Halifaxes: RG373 and RG375 of 199 Squadron, North Creake, collided over the city, scattering wreckage around the village of Meimersdorf. Thirteen perished aircrew were buried in a field alongside the wall of the local cemetery. The bulk of RG373 EX-T finally came to rest in a field also next to the cemetery. Only three of the crew survived the ordeal.

Their graves were set alongside the cemetery wall by a large stone: a memorial stone within the cemetery. Many years ago the boundary wall was taken down and the cemetery grounds extended into the field, including the area where our thirteen airmen were laid to rest in 1945. That piece of hallowed ground, now lawned and planted with shrubs, reflects a lasting peace and tranquillity for our airmen following their tragic ordeal. In 1947, their remains were transferred to the Commonwealth War Graves Cemetery at Kiel.

The crew were –
- W/O W. F. Bolton,
- **F/Sgt A. Bradley,**
- F/Lt W. E. Brooks,
- Sgt F.T. Chambers,
- F/O K. N. J. Croft,
- W/O K.A. C. Gavin,
- F/Sgt D. Greenwood,
- F/O A. S. J. Holder DFC,
- F/Sgt J. R. Lewis,
- S/Sgt J. Loth,
- P/O W. H. C. Mackay,
- W/O R. H.A. Pool
- F/Sgt D. Wilson.

These men are all buried in the Kiel War Cemetery together with the crew of the 169 Squadron Mosquito killed earlier that night. We must remember them.

Post-War

More than 600 airmen from RAF Great Massingham lost their lives, seven are buried to the left of the east window in the graveyard. A pictorial and comprehensive history of RAF Massingham is now under the care of Massingham Historical Society.

Ant (Anthony) Robinson is a member of the Massingham Historical Society. Over many years he worked steadfastly alongside Sister Laurence, a lady he respects and admires, who sadly passed away towards the end of 2013. She founded a Museum, filled with threads of the past weaving the story of those who served at this wartime airfield. It is very much a story of the people and their experiences.

The Sister Laurence
RAF Massingham Museum
by Anthony Robinson, Curator

Sister Laurence, known as '*Laurie*', became '*a legend in her own lifetime*'. Ant knew her well as did others who served at RAF Great Massingham. For many she became a personal and valued friend. '*She was a person of many talents, involving many friends and contacts, who managed to combine the commitment of her Religious Life with her many outside interests and projects.*' To understand Laurie's passion means following her journey of life.

Ant Robinson writes this tribute to her:

Born 12 July 1933 in Brierfield, Lancashire as Rosemary Ashworth, she worked in the cotton mills. Her father was a lorry driver, and she learned to tie every knot in the book. A tomboy as a small child, during the early days of war, she preferred to kick a football in the street with the boys rather than play with dolls, which is probably why, at the age of eleven, her parents sent her to our Convent School in Colne, hoping nuns would make a lady of her – *without success*! She was popular in school mainly because she used to organise cricket in the Convent field at lunchtime recreation.

Laurie joined the Rangers/Guides and was a lifetime member till she died. She used her guiding skills in many ways: when she entered the Novitiate to train for life in the Convent, she was ever the Girl Guide, organising concerts, singing-games, exploring the countryside, etc. She was very good with children: she taught for a while at the little Parish School of St Monica's and loved organising football for the boys on the Green outside, where now stands the local school of Rickmansworth Park. She taught Catechetics to children at week-ends and later at an RAF Base in Buckinghamshire.

As her skills were more practical than academic, later she was engaged in pastoral activities, cooking, archives, gardening, domestic work, driving and general mechanical work. She was great at 'fixing' things: if you needed a shelf put up or a door fixed or a bolt put in she would do it – even if sometimes it might not be quite straight! On one occasion she was told she could **not** knock down a partition wall to access the attic from her bedroom, so she got a saw and cut a door-shaped hole in the wall instead!

She was a fund of knowledge and information, an avid reader of newspapers, journals, local affairs, Church affairs, world news; a fervent Royalist and football enthusiast; concerned about social and political matters. She had visited places up and down the British Isles, and could recall details of events, sights and sounds that others had long forgotten. She was also a keen photographer, recording everything, including stunning sunsets.

But then, there was one place she could not say she had visited – until now! Even there, she has beaten us to it!

It was in later years that Laurie developed a passionate interest in researching the lives and history of veterans of RAF Bomber Command, stationed during World War Two at Great Massingham airfield in Norfolk. Pilots were billeted at Little Massingham Manor, later bought by the Daughters of Jesus as their Provincial HQ and became a Retreat Centre. For over thirteen years it was here, in the one-time stable block, that Laurie started her work which developed into the Sister Laurence RAF Massingham Museum, responding to the many visits of former Officers billeted there throughout the war. She faithfully recorded everything, copying Flight Log Books, Operations and Raids on the enemy, and she kept in touch with all 'Her Lads' over many years. In 1988, her Roll of Honour (all hand-written by Laurie) was dedicated at St Andrews Church, Little Massingham.

Apart from these major passions in her life, she was given the task of Archivist for our Province, leading her to research the beginnings of our Congregation in England by the first Sisters from France who founded here. She researched the first foundations and went on to document the history of our house in Massingham and our present home in Rickmansworth – once Residence of an Ambassador – and the lives of our first Sisters. Coupled with this, she searched the Records of all Sisters buried in cemeteries around places where the Daughters of Jesus lived and worked. She also researched in great detail her own family history, about which she was equally passionate.

She was a trained and avid gardener, and the results can still be seen today in our lovely garden at Blakenhall. She insisted on having a section for wildlife with flowers for butterflies and bees. She kept a well-supplied bird table and spent time keeping away squirrels and magpies – 'the food is for the little birds', she would say! She spoilt the neighbour's cats with cuddles and titbits and they can't understand why she isn't around any more, visiting occasionally to see if she has returned!

Our Laurie was a remarkable person, unique in her brand of Christianity. She was deeply spiritual with a simple Celtic faith, sensitive, generous, brave and industrious, a prayerful and loyal Daughter of Jesus. She was active right to the end. In spite of lifelong poor health, up to the day before she died, she was working on a translation from French, of a document she was researching for a contact concerning information about an RAF Veteran … and finished it!

I was able to see the relative and hand over this last piece of documentation a few days after her death. Laurie would have been so pleased to see the delight and emotion of the recipient: her life's work thus complete.

> Today I sat on a bench
> At the bottom of Laurie's garden.
> A seed off a Lime tree floated down in a spiral.
> It landed at my feet … and I cried;
> I sobbed for that contact from her.
>
> Bless you Laurie, for all your Lads!
> There are few left to grieve.
> You will never be forgotten
> 'God Bless!'

Tribute to Laurie, by Anthony Robinson on a visit to Blakenhall

The Retreat was sold and in 1999 the entire Museum moved to the safe care of Massingham Historical Society.

In 2000, the entire Exhibition was displayed in St. Mary's Church, unveiled by Kenneth Wolstenholme DFC & Bar, officially naming it 'The Sister Laurence RAF Massingham Museum.' As Custodian of the Museum, Ant holds the key to a past which, like Laurie, he remains passionate should never be forgotten as the Museum continues to provide a fascinating insight of life in war, together with the people and their stories. Like Sister Laurence, Ant works tirelessly to continue what his close friend and mentor Laurie began. One instance of this is shown through Andre Duchossoy's experience:

In late July 2004 I had a knock on my door, not unusual as I get people all the time doing their Family History in Great Massingham. This time it was Andre tracking down the airfield where his father had flown from during World War Two. I had just packed away 'The Sister Laurence RAF Massingham Museum', on display every year in St. Mary's Church. But I found a photo of Jacques in the Free French Squadron. Andre drove around the airfield, continuously ringing with queries as to location of various buildings and sites as so few are left. Since that day, Andre has written to me:

I still remember knocking on your door that day Ant, as if it were yesterday. The way you just matter of factly went to retrieve photos of Dad and his mates just blew me away that day, leaving me with memories I will never forget – the kindness you and Jean showed to a complete stranger (and since) will always stay with me. My friend, thank you.

I told him the Museum would be on display the following year, but he said his father wasn't well. However, they did turn up in July 2005 and Laurie said we must make a fuss of Jacques as he was the only member of the Free French to return to Massingham (didn't like to ask where his plane was!) so we had a piece of glass engraved, saying, in French: 'Thank you for the Peace'. Alas, he died two weeks later.

Many stories have come out since. This was given to me by Andre Duchossoy:

Jacques Duchossoy
Free French Air Force (FAFL)

Jacques Duchossoy lived most of his life in Newhaven and for many years worked as a Marine Engineer on the cross channel ferries.

In 1942, at the age of seventeen, Jacques ran away from home and joined the Free French Air Force (FAFL). After initial Radio training at

Cranwell and Gunnery training at Morpeth on the Northumberland coast, he was posted to 342 (Lorraine) Squadron as an Air Gunner flying in Douglas Boston medium bomber aircraft, based firstly at West Raynham and then Great Massingham in Norfolk.

On his second operation he was wounded, a grim introduction to the reality of war!

From Great Massingham the Squadron moved to Hartford Bridge, (now renamed Blackbushe Airport), from where they continued operations until after D-day when they moved to Vitry-en-Artois, finally setting foot once more on liberated French soil.

Re-equipped with Mitchell bombers, their final move was to Gilz Reigen in Holland, where, having flown on sixty-four operations, his, and the Squadron's war, ended.

A postscript to my Dad's wartime experience is one story he related that never ceased to amaze me.

At the end of the war he returned to Dieppe to see his father whom he had not seen in over five years. During the course of their conversation, his father asked if by chance, at any time, his Squadron had attacked Abbeville. Rather baffled, my Dad replied 'Yes'. They had indeed attacked the railway marshalling yards at Abbeville. 'But how on earth did you know that'? His Dad replied: 'because I was waiting for a train on the platform at Abbeville Station when you attacked it!' He said that, as planes screamed into the attack, they were flying so low he could see the cross of Lorraine emblazoned on their 'noses'. As he ran for cover, with bombs starting to fall, he knew it was likely that his son was in one of them!

Ant Robinson adds one final note:

This was a remarkable wartime encounter between father and son. Andre and his Mum came to Laurie's funeral, so we had a chance to catch up.

The *Sister Laurence RAF Massingham Museum* is lovingly packed away after each display by Ant (Anthony) Robinson, each piece a reminder of his very special friend, a lady who cared passionately about people, and made it her life work to maintain the heritage of Great Massingham ... a Memorial to so many who did not return and gave their lives for the freedom we enjoy today.

The Massingham Historical Society was set up in 1997, concerned with creating a historical archive of life in the villages of Great and Little Massingham for future generations. The collection contains a wide variety of items from property deeds to videos to maps and welcomes donations. Research to supplement these items and the villages' history is carried out in local libraries.

An addition to the collection was the historical records from the RAF's wartime years. The '*Sister Laurence RAF Massingham Museum,*' contains photographs and memorabilia, including authentic RAF material, providing a comprehensive picture of the airfield's use during World War Two. The society is in the process of collecting oral recollections from current and former residents, and in talks with the City of Norwich Aviation Museum at Horsham St Faith with a view to moving the Sister Laurence collection for the future to become a permanent display.

CHAPTER 13
RAF Swannington: 1944–1947

A Brief History

The story of RAF Swannington begins in an area of outstanding beauty, and in order to understand its history and relevance to the Second World War we need to go back to its roots at Haveringland, described eloquently by John Marius Wilson in 1870-1872 in 'Imperial Gazetteer of England and Wales':

HAVERINGLAND or HAVERLAND, is a Parish in St Faith district, Norfolk, two and three quarter miles SE of Reepham, and 9 miles East of North Elmham railway station. Post town, Reepham, under Norwich. Acres: 2,062. Real property: £1,983. Population: 131. Houses: 29. The property is all one estate and belongs to E. Fellowes, Esq. Haveringland Hall, the seat of Mr Fellowes, is a recent edifice in the Corinthian style, and stands in a park finely ornamented with wood and water. A chapel, founded here in the time of King John, by William de Gisneto; was given by him to the Priory of Wymondham; and became a cell for a Prior and several black Canons. The living is a Vicarage in the diocese of Norwich. Value: £63. Patron: E. Fellowes Esquire. The church has a circular tower .... [56]

When the Second World War broke out, Haveringland Hall and its beautiful surrounding parkland was taken over by the Air Ministry. Outlying cottages and farms were offered for sale, first to tenants, then by public auction. Local people must have wondered what would become of this beautiful place. John Kett in his 'Haveringalanda Booklet' describes it well, with shocking revelations:

Looking at the Church today, sentinel-like in the bare landscape, it seems incredible that a few years ago it nestled in the shelter of a great forest of trees, oak, chestnut and beech, themselves the glory of a great park stretching through massive wrought iron gates on past the lodge which housed the village post office, through a majestic avenue of horse chestnut trees, beautiful in Spring with their pink candle-like blossoms. A wall some miles in length encompassed the whole. Further afield deep hollows by the wayside concealed a wealth of primroses ... while a group of pine and spreading woodland continued far outside the boundary walls.

All of this was levelled to the ground as the aerodrome took shape. A gap of a mile was torn in the wall, the lodge gates were removed and the lodge itself blown up without ceremony. As runways crossed and re-crossed the greenwood, each primrose hollow was obliterated with rubble brought by countless lorries from local gravel pits. The trees were carried off in mournful procession. The Hall survived for a time, useful for billeting the flying men, then that too was demolished. Gaping cellars and a few outbuildings are all that remains of the great mansion. The church however survived as it continues in its mission. The days are gone when its upkeep was attended by carpenters and builders, no more are its floral decorations supplied from hothouses in the Hall gardens, or the altar frontals and cloths stitched by the leisure ladies of the Hall. The dozen or so parishioners left somehow do cope with all the needs. The women by organising sewing parties and social events have paid for a modern heating system. The church is kept clean and the graveyard tidied. So, although the Squires have gone, the church continues to thrive ... [57]

Things had been set in motion for a Fighter Aerodrome to operate from Haveringland, with two Squadrons in residence: No. 85 and No. 157 under RAF 100 (Bomber Support) Group.

RAF No. 100 (Bomber Support) Group

The airfield was completed in early 1944. Haveringland Hall became the Officers' Mess with most of the remaining Station crew housed in huts on the Hall's parkland.

RAF Swannington as it became known, officially opened on 1 April 1944 as part of RAF 100 Group. It became home to 85 and 157 Squadrons, equipped with Mosquito aircraft. Their role was largely one of supporting Bomber missions over enemy occupied territory, and Mosquitoes provided 100 Group with long-range capabilities throughout 1943–1945.

Nos 85 and 157 Squadrons arrived with de Havilland Mosquito bomber support aircraft during the first week of May 1944. These two Units immediately transferred to the RAF's No. 100 Group intended to intercept Luftwaffe night fighters while accompanying the main RAF bomber force, and intruding over German night fighter airfields. They first went into action on the night of the D-Day invasion.

However, from late July 1944, 85 and 157 Squadrons dispatched large detachments to West Malling in Kent for over a month to combat the threat from German V-1 missiles at night, destroying seventy of them in the process.

Once back at Swannington and fully operational, both Units resumed their primary bomber support duty and by the end of World War Two had shot down seventy-one enemy aircraft. Luftwaffe intruders, in retaliation, bombed the airfield on the night of March 16/17 1945 in what proved to be one of the last attacks on a British airfield during the conflict.

85 Squadron moved to Castle Camps in June 1945, while 157 Squadron disbanded at Swannington the following August.

From October 1945, the airfield became home to No. 274 Maintenance Unit, many Mosquitoes either being stored or scrapped here until both this Unit and the airfield closed in November 1947. North Creake went on to serve as a Sub-Storage Site for the Unit, along with Little Snoring.

Tentative plans to retain and upgrade the airfield for post-war RAF operational fighter use came to nothing and the site was sold in 1957. The site is now used for agriculture. However, the village sign for Haveringland portrays a Mosquito, a lasting memorial perhaps to all who once served at RAF Swannington.

85 Squadron

Noctu diuque vanamur – 'We hunt by day and night'
Reproduced with permission of the MOD

No. 85 Squadron crest shows a hexagon voided on an ogress. The hexagon was No. 85's World War One identity insignia, with the ogress signifying the night.

Formed at Upavon on 1 August 1917, it briefly became home to the Royal Flying Corps Central Flying School until it moved to Mousehold Heath, near Norwich, under the command of Major R. A. Archer. During November 1917, the Squadron transferred to Hounslow Heath Aerodrome, and in March 1918, Major William Avery Bishop VC, DSO, MC, took command.

On 1 April, No. 85 Squadron transferred into the new Royal Air Force and deployed to France following a period of training. Equipped with Sopwith Dolphins and later the Royal Aircraft Factory S.E.5A, it flew fighter patrols and ground attack sorties over the Western Front until the Armistice was signed.

On 21 June, a new Commanding Officer arrived, Major Edward 'Mick' Mannock DSO, MC who immediately changed training methods. Rather than fighting as individuals, the Squadron was taught to act as one complete Unit when in combat. However, during a patrol on 26 July 1918, accompanying Lt D. C. Inglis over the Front Line, Major Mannock failed to return, depriving 85 Squadron of its leader. The Squadron returned to the UK in February 1919 and disbanded on 3 July 1919, while on 18 July, Major Mannock was awarded a posthumous VC.

85 Squadron amassed ninety-nine victories during its short involvement in the conflict.

On 1 June 1938, 85 Squadron was reformed from re-numbered elements of 'A' Flight No. 87 Squadron, and placed under the command of Flt/Lt D. E. Turner. The Squadron was based at RAF Debden in Essex, training with the Gloster: RAF's last biplane fighter until Hawker Hurricanes arrived in September.

At the outbreak of World War Two, the Squadron moved to Boos as part of the Air Component of the BEF 60th Fighter Wing, the role of their Hurricanes to support Squadrons of Bristol Blenheims and Fairey Battles.

By 1 November, 85 Squadron's Hurricanes had moved to Lille Seclin, and the Squadron scored its first victory of the war when Flt/Lt R. H. A. Lee attacked a He111 which crashed into the Channel, exploding on impact patrolling the Boulogne area. The Heinkel He 111 was a German aircraft designed by Siegfried and Walter Günter in the early 1930s in violation of the Treaty of Versailles.

December 1939 saw a Royal visit from his Majesty, the King, accompanied by the Duke of Gloucester and Viscount Lord Gort. However, the onset of winter proved challenging with bitterly cold weather preventing flying, causing damage to aircraft and taking its toll on the health of airmen living in primitive conditions.

As the German invasion (*Blitzkrieg*) commenced in May 1940, 85 Squadron was locked in bitter conflict with the Luftwaffe, and with attacks on its aerodromes commonplace, there was no respite from operations. In an eleven-day period, the Squadron had a confirmed total of ninety enemy aircraft alongside many more claims that remained unsubstantiated. The final sortie saw the Squadron giving fighter cover to Allied armies until its bases were finally over-run and three remaining aircraft retired to the UK.

During intense battles over France, the Squadron lost seventeen pilots – two were killed, six wounded, while nine were marked as '*Missing*'; this figure included their new CO: Squadron Leader Peacock. But it had served well in the face of many adversities. The Squadron then re-equipped to resume full operations early in June 1940.

After taking part in the first half of the Battle of Britain over southern England, the Squadron moved to Yorkshire in September, while in October there followed a change in role, commencing night fighter patrols before transferring to 100 Group on 1 May 1944. Now they flew bomber support missions, intruding over German night-fighter airfields and intercepting enemy fighters, accompanying the main bomber force.

Post-war, the Squadron continued to operate and in September 1951 converted to Meteor Night Fighters which it flew until disbanded on 31 October 1958.

PERSONAL EXPERIENCES

Wing Commander Branse Burbridge
DSO & Bar, DFC & Bar
Top Ace Pilot

Wing Commander Branse Burbridge DSO and Bar, DFC and Bar was an 85 Squadron pilot who gained his wings in 1941. Putting duty before personal feelings as a Conscientious Objector, Branse, together with his Navigator, Bill Skelton, became known as '*The Night Hawk Partners*'. Branse recalls:

I always tried to aim for the wings of enemy aircraft – not the cockpit. I never wanted to kill anyone.

Citations for their awards paid tribute to both men setting '*an unsurpassed example of outstanding keenness and devotion to duty*'.

Born in East Dulwich on 4 February 1921, Burbridge was living in Knebworth working as an insurance clerk when the Second World War broke out in September 1939. Initially he indicated that he would register as a Conscientious Objector, but came to the view that the war was a '*just cause*' and joined the Royal Air Force in February 1941, shortly after his 20th birthday, pre-empting his registration under the National Service (Armed Forces) Act 1939, due on 22 February 1941.

After training at No. 54 Operational Training Unit (O.T.U) Church Fenton, he was posted to No. 85 Squadron in October 1941, flying Douglas Havoc night fighters. Tour-expired, he was posted to 62 O.T.U and on to 141 and 157 Squadrons.

He returned to 85 Squadron in July 1943 as a Flight Lieutenant and with them, Burbridge had far more success flying Mosquitoes, initially on home defence duties prior to June 1944, than on Bomber Support operations with 100 Group against the Luftwaffe's *Nachtgeschwaders*.

Branse Burbridge with Navigator Bill Skelton, on 22 February 1944, destroyed a Messerschmitt Me 410. The pair then went on to shoot down a further twenty-one enemy aircraft in total together with three V-1 flying bombs, including a Bf 110 and three Ju 88Gs during the night of 4/5 November 1944. On this occasion, Burbridge fired only 200 rounds of ammunitions in downing four enemy aircraft.

In completing their tour of operations in early 1945, their number of enemy aircraft destroyed made them the top night-fighting crew in the RAF.

157 Squadron

'Our cannon speak our thoughts'
Reproduced with permission of the MOD

Squadron codes: RS (December 1941-August 1945)

The Squadron badge shows a lion rampant chequy: the lion denotes fighting power, while the black and white check the Squadron's day and night capability.

No. 157 Squadron was formed at Upper Heyford on 14 July 1918 to be a Ground Attack Unit equipped with Salamanders, but was not operational before the end of the war and disbanded on 1 February 1919.

The Salamander was a single-engined, single-seat bi-plane based on the Sopwith Snipe fighter, but with an armoured forward fuselage to protect the pilot and fuel system from ground fire during low level operations. It was ordered in large quantities for the RAF, with war ending before the type could enter Squadron service, although two were in France in October 1918.

The Squadron reformed on 13 December 1941 at RAF Debden as a Night Fighter Unit, equipped in January 1942 with the latest Mosquito Night Fighter aircraft at RAF Castle Camps, becoming the first Squadron to use the Mosquito as a Night Fighter.

The airfield at Castle Camps was built in September 1939 and opened as a Debden satellite in June 1940, with 85 and 111 Squadrons having already spent short periods there. 73 Squadron flew Hurricanes from Castle Camps in September, but with no permanent structures and only tents to live in, those Squadrons left in November 1940 to convert to night flying. Castle Camps was exposed and windy. Meanwhile, better facilities and operating runways were built, with original grass runways replaced by tarmac and hard-standing.

Mosquitoes assembled here in great secrecy in 1942, test flying with 157 Squadron. First patrols flew 27/28 April over East Anglia, but the first confirmed kill wasn't until 22/23 August that year. They were replaced in March 1943 by No. 605 Mosquito Squadron.

In July, Castle Camps became a satellite of North Weald for Mosquito intruder operations, and later Bomber Support. Mosquitoes left Castle Camps in October while 527 Radar Calibration Squadron replaced them until February 1944, when Spitfires arrived, then Typhoons, then 486 Squadron RNZAF of Tempests, all leaving quickly.

The Canadian 410 Squadron again flew Mosquitoes from Castle Camps until April 1944. While from July until October 1944, 68 Squadron's Mosquitoes arrived together with those of 151 and 25 Squadrons. In 1945, 307 and 85 Squadron flew from Castle Camps airfield also in Mosquitoes.

After moving to Hunsdon, patrols for No. 157 Squadron began on 27 April over East Anglia and in July 1943 some Mosquito VI fighter bombers were added to the Squadron strength taking part in intruder missions over France and the Netherlands.

In November 1943, the Squadron moved to RAF Predannack in Cornwall, closer to German bases, to perform similar duties. In 1944 it went north to RAF Valley for defensive patrols over the Irish Sea.

RAF No. 100 Group

In May 1944, 157 Squadron moved back to East Anglia, joining RAF 100 Group for the rest of the war based at RAF Swannington, receiving Mosquito Mk XIXs. Under RAF 100 Group, the Squadron was tasked with providing support for heavy bombers over Germany by flying sweeps in search of enemy Night Fighters.

SHARED EXPERIENCES

F/O Bryan Gale

I joined 157 Squadron when it was first formed in World War Two at Castle Camps in February 1943. I'd previously been with 534 Squadron at Tangmere – a turbinlite Squadron where my Navigator and I were one of the Havoc crews. We served at Camps for a month before the whole Squadron was relocated to Bradwell Bay. We were the first Mosquito-equipped Night Fighter Squadron in the RAF and AI equipment was MK4 and 5, severely limited by height above ground – the first thing radio waves struck, generating a carpet of ground returns which smothered anything at greater range.

When the Squadron moved to Hunsdon in defence of London, the Squadron formed a third Flight using straight MKVI fighter/bomber aircraft in an intruder role without any radar. At this time the battle of the Atlantic was hotting up. We were re-deployed to Predannack, on the tip of Cornwall close to Mullion Cove; employed in 'Operation Instep', which was us looking for Ju88s which were looking for Sunderlands, etc. which were looking for the U-boats.

We flew in 'Finger 4' formations at thirty feet above the Atlantic down as far as Cape Ortual on the north coast of Spain, which was Fascist-controlled and not friendly towards us. We were assured that any fishing vessels we saw would report our position to the Germans so were fair game for attack! We had a fair amount of success, getting several 88s and a 177 which my Flight Commander and I dispatched.

However, one of our formation, determined to get a shot in, struck the water and hit the sea, forcing him to ditch, which he did successfully. We returned, refuelled and re-armed at Predannack, before returning to the area to find our downed comrades. We returned to Base and returned yet again, in company with an airborne lifeboat successfully dropped. We saw two Mossie crews scramble into the lifeboat in which they sailed back to the Scilly Islands in four days, awarded the DFC and DFM for the Sergeant Nav.

In March 1944, the Squadron moved to Valley to re-equip with Mossie 18s with new centimetric radar not so badly affected by ground returns, with a much improved range reaching over ten miles at 20,000 feet. Eventually, we moved to Swannington, just outside Norwich, in May 44 in time for D-day, not allowed to take the new MKX radar out of the country until then.

My first raid as an Intruder with 100 Group was on 7 June, to the airfields of Lesquin-Chievres in France in support of the D-Day landings. We flew in this role until withdrawn to West Malling for operations against the Doodle-Bugs; we were the only thing anywhere near fast enough when refuelled with 150-grade petrol. These were called Anti-Diver Patrols and involved flying just about 10,000 feet to be above the target, parallel to the coast, watching for one flying out of France, turning towards it and well above, applying full throttle and rolling onto one's back, pulling through at speeds in excess of 400 mph to match them up and shoot them down. Of course, in those days, flight instruments were all air-powered Gyroscopes which didn't have full freedom of movement in all planes and were toppled by the aircraft's inversion, forcing us to fly on 'limited panel' for the recovery and subsequent kill, which, with four cannons, was inevitable

In September, we returned to Swannington and our role as Bomber Support acting as long range Night Fighters for the Bomber Stream, flying above and below and either side of them, looking for anything attempting to cross into the stream. This was good fun, if ever war can be; as with the superior speed of our aircraft we could watch the bomber stream set off and still arrive over the target simultaneously and patrol for about an hour, leaving with them.

I finished more than forty of these Sorties, completing my Tour just before VE day, prior to going to Bomber Support Training Unit at Great Massingham as an Instructor.

I was released in May 1946 to go to Edinburgh University (*paid for by the Service, on the understanding that if they wished I would return afterwards*); and in 1952, I was recalled, I thought for the Korean war with Meteor and Vampire Night Fighters, which is where all my experience had been. But, no, it was to Control Flying School, then at Little Rissington! For the next fourteen years, I was engaged in teaching people to fly, including the first All Through Jet FTS at Hullavington with the Jet Provost, which I was to meet again at The College of Air Warfare at Manby, before starting my last tour in the RAF with 99 Squadron at Lyneham.

I have worked for Airworks in Saudi Arabia at Rhyadh and for CAA, then the MOCA in London and BAA at Heathrow, before becoming Director of Operations at Birmingham Airport, from where I retired to live in Lincolnshire. It's been a bit of a mix up, but I've enjoyed it, except for getting older, which no-one can avoid.

A BOMBERS MOON?
LACW Dorothy Howard:
Reminiscences of a 'Met Girl'

I first took an interest in Meteorology when, as a youngster at the beginning of the war, I joined the Women's Junior Air Corp.

After surviving the heavy blitzes on Merseyside – at one stage I watched the famous Argyle Theatre burn down – and having passed exams; I decided at the age of sixteen to join the WAAF. In due course, I presented myself at Renshaw Hall in Liverpool, the local enlisting office. Naturally, I was asked for my birth certificate and convincingly I told the Recruiting Officer that we had been bombed out the night before and none was available. I cannot remember how I told my parents I had enlisted. My mother had no objection for she was an ambulance driver and did the same thing in World War

One. My father wasn't sure as my two brothers had been called up at the beginning of hostilities. However, I passed all the procedures and eventually landed at Innsworth to be kitted out, moving on to Morecombe where I did my square bashing. *What a rude awakening!*

My training was in a famous furniture store building in London where we learned to teleprint c/o GPO Hendon and how to read temperatures, do slide-rule calculations, recognise clouds etc. plot charts, read barometers, sort out the Stevenson Screen and code up Reports. At this time, Meteorologists were civilians.

Having passed the course exams, the time came for posting. I was asked where I would like to go. My posting was 250 miles from my choice to No. 9 Group, Royal Canadian Air Force – Middleton St George, Co Durham. They were flying Wellington Bombers on ops. My colleagues realised I was still only a youngster, took me under their wings and I had a good initiation into life in the Met Office. The weather wasn't always suitable for flying, but we still had to report it. There were nights when I went on duty in fog so dense that one time I was lost on a dispersal point and finished up on my hands and knees crawling around the edge until I got to the office! That was a time when I wished I hadn't joined.

From Durham I had three other short postings – Croft (now a car racing track), Liverpool Speke (now John Lennon Airport), and Sealand. At Speke we were contacted by N.W Army HQ nightly to give wind readings for the upper air, this apparently was to enable them to set their guns correctly – I was never quite sure how this worked, but often wondered if my slide-rule calculations would help them to sort out any German invasion of Liverpool! I had my uses there too – Irish planes would come in from Dublin and I looked forward to these for they brought gifts of sweets. Nevertheless, I still had to sit on the weather charts the forecasters didn't want pilots to see.

Life was different at the MU Unit at Sealand. Different aspects of Meteorology were used as there was no flying. One of these was to fill huge white balloons with hydrogen and tie a gondola underneath with a lighted candle, release and follow the light with a Theodolite to work out the upper winds. How I managed not to blow the office up never ceases to amaze me! Nevertheless, I was gaining experience all the time, particularly how to get home without a Pass.

From Sealand I was posted in 1943 to a new Station – RAF Swannington – where I stayed until 1946 with Mosquito Squadrons 157 and 85. There I met up with my WAAF colleagues by this time all RAF Meteorologist Officers: F/Os Ernie Dearing, Laurie Rendell, Corrigan and A.N. Other. The WAAF contingent was LACWs Joyce Dobb, Barbara Jeffries, Sylvia Cheeseman, Pam Watson and myself, Dorothy Howard.

As far as we Observers were concerned, we worked a three-shift system, 7 am – 3 pm, 3 pm – 11 pm and the night-shift: 11 pm – 7 am. The latter, unless there were ops, or circuits and bumps, I used to dread. *Why?* Well, having no running water we were supplied with a water bowser outside and filling a kettle meant running the risk of rats. There were also the odd occasions when we had tremendous thunder and electrical storms which lit up the whole countryside. Inside Flying Control they were snoring their heads off and I had to go outside to '*do*' the weather! I can be lyrical now when I say that I loved the starlit nights and, dare I say, the '*bomber moon*' nights. This wasn't a romantic streak in me – it was easier to calculate vision and report the weather, which had to be done every hour. Sometimes I might have nodded off if there was no flying, and if I had a phone call from Group quickly I repeated the last observation, with a slight variation, giving some excuse why I was late.

Plotting charts became skilful using two pens together, one black and one red, from the coded messages received from ETA via the teleprinter. They usually took a quarter of an hour as speed was often of the essence for the Forecaster. We also had to encode the weather report and send via teleprinter back to ETA for the next chart. It almost became an art form. I think we all took pride in producing neat and tidy charts every three hours.

The office was pretty hectic before ops, especially on the eve of D-Day when I was on night duty. We were always glad to hear the telling drone of the Mosquito engine and we knew they were safely back. There were sad times too, when any failed to return. They were brave men and my little bit was nothing compared to their efforts.

Times were helped when we played mixed hockey with the Air Crew. I remember playing a team with F/Lt Chisholm (Chris – his dog lay on the sideline) 'Get back Howard, I'll play forward' and they used to knock seven bells out of one another. Then off they'd go on ops. There were also trips into Norwich via the Liberty bus, one shilling (five-pence) return. It was good camaraderie and times on reflection I would not have missed.

I was often posted around the Group to stand in when they were short staffed – but always I managed to get back to Swannington. I'd made so many friends and I didn't want to miss the jollifications down at the *Ratcatcher*'s or the *Kings Head* in Cawston.

I still look at the sky and work out the clouds and amounts, often thinking of those days, some good, some bad and long gone, but am happy to recall and pleased that there is the RAF 100 Group Association to keep the memories alive.

If this epistle seems frivolous in any way with regard to my duties, please disregard it for they were taken very seriously which I was proud to do. It also meant that I grew up very very quickly. Eventually when the war was over, the time came to think about what I would do in Civvy Street. Because of my 'sporting' instincts and I mean that literally, I decided to re-muster as a Physical Training Instructor. Thereby hangs another tale and maybe I might write a bit more and head it 'Just before I go'.

Pilot Officer William Searle Vale, RAAF

As Secretary of the worldwide RAF 100 Group Association it is usual to receive letters and material from anxious relatives seeking truths about a loved one who died in recent years. These are, in part, my inspiration for writing this book. Often memoriabilia which families knew nothing about comes to light from a darkened attic. The work of 100 Group was so secret during the war, as with Bletchley Park, no-one spoke of the reality of their work, unable to share with sweethearts and wives, hence the reason my mother never knew the intense, dangerous and secret work her wartime fiancé Vic Vinnell was involved in serving under 192 Squadron at Foulsham. These were dedicated, committed, passionate men and women, fighting for the kind of freedom we enjoy today – sadly, forgotten heroes of our time. It is because they take their secrets to the grave, I remain passionate about preserving their names, their history and stories to take with us into the future, because they hold so much of value.

One such letter which came to me, opening a fresh avenue of friendship always welcome; shows in very real terms how these truths emerge and what it means to families concerned. It should also be said that, once one truth is unveiled, it can become addictive in trying to track remaining pieces of the puzzle to make up the whole!

Dear Janine

I am doing research on my late uncle, Pilot Officer William Searle Vale (RAAF), 401553, who flew for the RAF and was killed, along with his Navigator F/L A. E. Ashcroft (RAF) DFC, when their Mosquito aircraft MM678 crashed at Drieslinter, Belgium on 6 October 1944.

William, known as Bill, was in Squadrons 456 and 600 prior to joining 157 Squadron at Predannack in December 1943. Based at Swannington, under RAF 100 Group in support of Bomber Command as an intruder night fighter, all we know is that, on the night of the tragedy, he failed to return and nothing was heard from the aircraft after take-off. William's Log Book states in the final entry: 'High Level Intruder Ruhr area'. Both men are buried in Brussels, Belgium.

I found your details on the City of Norwich Aviation Museum website and to my disappointment, discovered at the end of your quarterly Association magazine that a person I wanted to contact regarding 157 Squadron is listed amongst names of people who have died since the war. His name was Bryan Gale and I was saddened to find this.

I am keen to find a photo and information about his navigator F/L A. E. Ashcroft (RAF) DFC. A photo of him would be wonderful as the family has never known anything about him. I would be grateful of any help you can offer.

Helen Rankin (Australia)

With the help of Richard Forder, (author and Association member), we now know that Mosquito MM678 took off from RAF Swannington at 1807 hours on 6 October 1944, detailed to carry out an intruder support sortie of targets: Bremen and Dortmund. Nothing was heard from the aircraft after take-off which failed to return to base.

I have since learned the aircraft crashed five miles north-east of Tirlemont, east of Brussels, Belgium. Both crew members were killed and they are buried in the Brussels Town Cemetery, Belgium, in the district of Evere:

- RAAF 401553 P/O Vale, W. S. Captain (Pilot)
- RAF Flt Lt Ashcroft, A. E. DFC (Navigator/Radio)

Some people we are able to support in their research and happily find answers. It is the reason it remains vital to gather as much material from the war years while we still can, before all its secrets die forever, together with those who served under this very special Group. We owe it to them and to the work in which they were involved to honour their memory ... always.

But then again, sometimes, the past has a strange way of unexpectedly offering up secrets as if with a life of their own! Read on to discover a fascinating story washed up by the tides of Time:

100 Group Mosquito Found off Norfolk Coast

A de Havilland Mosquito, operated by 85 Squadron, RAF 100 Group flying from Swannington, was recovered from the Wash, west of King's Lynn, by the Royal Air Force in late summer 2004.

The Mosquito: FB.MkVI, NS998 crashed into the sea during an air-to-air gunnery training flight on 20 March 1945. The crew were Flight Lt Gabriel Hitch Ellis from Norwich, and Sgt William Reidy from Bournemouth. They had lain in the wreckage of their aircraft for almost sixty years until strong tides shifted sand in the Wash. The deputy Harbour Master of Kings Lynn port noticed a propeller standing clear of the mud at low tide which began the process of identification and recovery.

It was to be the Royal Air Force who undertook to rescue the wreckage, thankfully left undisturbed despite Norfolk press revealing its location. Meanwhile, the Royal Navy bomb disposal team arrived to recover the Mosquito's cannons from the silt and make them safe. The RAF could then recover the Mosquito's engines propellers, landing gear and parts of the fuselage and wings, transporting them to RAF Marham in Norfolk.

The Central Casualty Section of the RAF then tried to trace families of the crew. As the salvage operation was being completed, the son and daughter of Flight Lt Ellis travelled to King's Lynn to see the wreckage of their father's aircraft. Aged just one and four when their father died, their emotions can only be imagined. Their mother remarried, giving them another father figure. But as they grew older, they must have wondered about their natural father. The discovery of Mosquito NS998 and its crew, distressing as it must have been, could at least bring closure, and answers to questions about what happened. There is comfort in knowing. It is the unknowing which continues on the pain. The Royal Air Force arranged private funerals with the families giving loved ones finally the dignity and peace they deserved.

But then, in the work in which I remain passionately involved, there is always another story, giving yet more reason to remember the past, the war, the courage of airmen, those left behind and the many who did not return home.

Wartime Crash Tribute

The following article and letter was sent to Martin Staunton (Co-Founder, with sister Eileen Bowman, of RAF 100 Group Association) by Philip Brazier, a teacher at Scarning Primary School, near East Dereham, Norfolk:

> Villagers gathered on Saturday 28 May 2005 to commemorate a wartime plane crash with the presentation of a painting. The event, attended by about 150 people, was part of Scarning church flower festival and arranged in memory of the incident in January 1945 in which Flight Lt Michael Allen brought down his Mosquito in a field near the village. The two-man crew survived, but had to be rescued by Herbert Farrow, Jimmy Andrews and Walter Ward. Specially commissioned paintings by aviation artist John Stevens were presented to the Parish Hall and Doris Farrow, Herbert Farrow's widow.
>
> The event came after pupils at Scarning Primary School learned about the crash from teacher Philip Brazier who, along with local historian Denis Duffielt, had studied the accident. Mr Brazier said: '*I thought it would help bring history home to children if they could study*

something which had some relevance to their lives. It's got people from all different generations talking and the whole village seems fascinated by this'. [58]

Martin Staunton and his sister Eileen cared deeply about people, and were always delighted to receive letters and news, just as I am today as daily they come from around the world. Philip Brazier wrote to them later:

The presentation of the print of the crash at Scarning went very well. I have recently been down to Cornwall to visit Pam Allen, the Navigator's widow to give her a print of the painting. She was really impressed and gave me a kneeler that Mike Allen had stitched just before his death. The kneeler features the RAF emblem and I will present it to Scarning Church soon.

I also visited Doris Farrow at her retirement home last week and gave her a print. She showed me the tankard her husband Herbert received from Mike Allen and Harry White shortly after the rescue.

I have really enjoyed researching and meeting the different people involved with this story. The children learnt a great deal from it.

Nothing Happened

Could you tell us, Flight Lieutenant
Of your battles in the skies?
We see scenes of burning aircraft
And it's hard to realize
How the air crews stayed undaunted
Hour on hour up there so high.

Well, nothing really happened –
There's not that much to tell,
You just did what you had to
And you tried to do it well.
If fires broke out we dealt with them
As anyone would do.

The injured men were cared for
In the usual sort of way.
But when the flak was heavy
And the opposition strong
You hadn't time to notice
If little things went wrong.

It was pretty noisy up there
But you had your job to do,
The boys were counting on you –
This applied to all the crew.

For many years the battle raged
And many friends were lost,
Which made us more determined
To succeed at any cost.

What stories can I tell you
That would stand the test of time?
We did succeed, that's very true,
With humour masking fear –
Don't think ahead – count yourself dead.
Pray God to stay with you.

Hazel Southgate, January 1997

This poem depicts the frustrations of a wife wanting to know of her husband's wartime experiences about which he refuses to share.

CHAPTER 14
RAF Swanton Morley: 1940–1996

'Steadfast to Serve'
Reproduced with permission of the MOD

Swanton Morley is named after Lord Morley who held the Lordship of the Manor. The village was home to Richard Lincoln (1550–1620), local Church Warden who built the mansion which is today *The Angel Free House* pub. Lincoln was the wealthy grandfather of Samuel Lincoln and Richard's coat-of-arms is shown in the east window of All Saints Church in Swanton Morley.

However, when Richard Lincoln disinherited Samuel's father Edward from his will in favour of his fourth wife, it threw the Lincoln family into penury, forcing young Samuel to flee to Hingham, Massachusetts. His great-great-great-great-grandson was Abraham Lincoln, 16th President of the United States.

Richard Lincoln was interred under the centre aisle of St Andrew's Church in Hingham, Norfolk, a privilege reserved for gentry.

Swanton Morley started RAF life as a Bomber Station on 17 September 1940 within No. 2 Group Bomber Command. 2 Group was allocated mostly light Bomber Squadrons, retaining Bristol Blenheim aircraft. In time, it operated de Havilland Mosquitoes, Douglas Bostons and North American B25 Mitchells, with the Group's Communication Flight also based here.

Two things are noteworthy. The first is that the airfield was a notorious dome shape. Standing on the concrete perimeter track at ground level, it was impossible to see from one side of the airfield to the other. The second is that RAF Swanton Morley was acclaimed by pilots throughout Britain as the finest grass airfield in the country, and the largest grass airfield in Europe with 334 acres. The total construction of the airfield cost £490,000.

An advance opening-up party from RAF Watton was first to arrive under the command of Flight Lieutenant J. L. Newton:

- 1 NC Clerk,
- 1 NCO WOM,
- 1 NCO cook,
- 2 AC cooks,
- 2 AC equipment assistants.

Main work areas were still incomplete. Airmen had to be billeted in the village. However, main office accommodation was available by the time Wing Commander L. B. Duggan took command on 28 September.

On 31 October, while the Battle of Britain raged over south-east England, 105 Squadron moved in from nearby RAF Watton with Bristol Blenheim Mk IV aircraft, immediately ready to undertake operations, despite accommodation remaining a problem.

105 SQUADRON

Fortis in Proeliis – 'Valiant in battles'
Reproduced with permission of the MOD

Nickname: '*Hereford's own Squadron*'

Squadron Codes
MT (Oct 1938)
GB (Sep 1939 – Jan 1946)

The Squadron badge shows a battle-axe commemorating that at one time it was equipped with Battle aircraft.

The emerald green handle of the axe signifies the Squadron's service in Ireland.

Formed on 23 September 1917 at RAF Waddington, 105 Squadron moved with a variety of aircraft to RAF Andover, Hampshire, to train as a Bomber Squadron. However, before becoming operational, they were sent to Omagh, County Tyrone, with RE8 bi-planes on anti-submarine and reconnaissance duties. Within the year, it re-equipped with Bristol F2B Fighters. While other Squadrons were disbanded after Armistice, 105 Squadron continued duties in Ireland until February 1920 when the Squadron was disbanded, to be re-numbered 2 Squadron at Oranmore.

The Squadron reformed on 12 April 1937 at RAF Harwell from B Flight, 18 Squadron; as a day Bomber Squadron. Its first aircraft was the bi-plane Hawker Audax, until the more modern monoplane Fairey Battle arrived in August 1937, making 105 Squadron one of the first operational on this type of aircraft.

In September 1939, as part of the Advanced Air Striking Force, the Squadron moved to France on reconnaissance operations along the France-German border. By May 1940, with the invasion of France, the Squadron was busy attacking advancing German troops. One of the most important targets was the bombing of bridges over the River Meuse to slow the German advance. It suffered heavy casualties and was forced to retire to England the following month.

At RAF Honington, the Squadron was re-equipped with Bristol Blenheims to join 2 Group's offensive against the invasion ports and German shipping. The Squadron had many losses, particularly from German *Flak* ships.

In October 1940, part of the Squadron was detached to Malta to attack Axis shipping in the Mediterranean Sea, while the remainder moved to RAF Swanton Morley.

The enemy had a keen interest in the new Norfolk airfields, aircraft and Squadrons, picked up by German Intelligence sources. This became obvious at 0745 hours on 5 November 1940. Ten bombs dropped directly onto Swanton Morley airfield. Luckily, only eight exploded causing little damage. It was to be another three months before further attacks took place.

Meanwhile, 15 November brought Swanton Morley's first casualty amongst its own aircraft against enemy aerodromes.

The previous afternoon, 105 Squadron with Blenheim Squadrons 101 from RAF West Raynham and 110 from RAF Horsham St Faith, were briefed for the coming night's attacks on enemy aerodromes. The enemy too was briefed – not for the favoured attack on London – but the now infamous raid on Coventry with twenty Blenheim crews involved.

The first took off from Wattisham at 1800 hours. Minutes later, the lead enemy aircraft bound for the Midlands crossed the Dorset coast. While German bombers set Coventry ablaze, Blenheims attacked enemy airfields – Amiens, Etaples, Knocke and Rennes. None had anything to do with the Coventry raid. Instead, they attacked three airfields, engaging a Heinkel He 111. There was little achievement compared with what the enemy accomplished that night.

The following day, Intelligence Reports indicated that enemy operations would be from airfields in the area of Antwerp and Brussels. There was no surprise at intended targets.

Nine 105 Squadron crews were briefed, with bad weather preventing all but five departing. A number of airfields were hit before Pilot Officer Murray and three other crews turned in to strafe Dieghem, a forward airfield used by the Luftwaffe in the Battle of Britain. He was met by intensive ground fire, his Blenheim disintegrating into a fireball.

Within a fortnight, two more Blenheims were lost.

On 27 November 1940, 105 Squadron Blenheims attacked targets in Boulogne and Cologne. A total of eight crews were involved. But the weather deteriorated before all crews could bomb and they were forced to return.

Sgt Costello-Brown and his crew were flying above dense cloud, unable to find their Base, seeking a gap in the cloud, ending up near Liverpool, 200 miles away. They flew around desperately calling for help, then ran out of fuel. Pilot and crew finally bailed out as their aircraft crashed near Manchester. Another crew returning early, discovered ten/tenths cloud over the airfield. Receiving clearance at 2325 hours to land, they flew towards the airfield beacon at Foxley Wood some three and a half miles away, readying for approach. With poor vision due to intense fog, the Blenheim crashed into the wood, bursting into flames. None of the three crew members survived.

During the winter of 1940-41, 105 crews carried out night bombing of enemy coastal defences and installations in addition to shipping strikes, notwithstanding very bad weather and crude accommodation pending the completion of the hangar at Swanton Morley.

As with most Blenheim Squadrons, No. 105 at Swanton Morley was taking heavy losses.

The first aircraft to be completely written-off was not an aircraft from the Base, but a Blenheim Mk IV from 139 Squadron, another No. 2 Group Unit at Horsham St Faith. On 28 February 1941, the first three crews, two from 'B' Flight and one from 'A' Flight, were briefed and sent to attack a submarine crew's rest hotel on the Normandy coast at Quisberom, in the Brest area. The target was subsequently covered with light flak, and crews and aircraft returned safely. But four remaining crews, said to be envious of this plum operation, hoped they too would attack another such target.

Flt/Lt Hughie Edwards (the VC to-be) and crew including Sgt Bennett with crew from 'A' Flight, were allocated a target at dusk in the Den Helder area. Sgt McPhee with crew of 'A' Flight and Sgt Vivian of 'B' Flight drew the short straw: Flushing Dock area – a heavily defended and dangerous target in daylight, even using cloud cover. McPhee and his crew were to attack first, leaving Vivian to patrol out of range of the flak, attacking once McPhee had bombed and escaped.

The element of surprise would be lost for the second aircraft!

McPhee and his crew in R3907, on their 25th operation, took off at 1755 to circuit Horsham St Faith airfield, waiting for Vivian to join the formation. However, Sgt Vivian, wheels up, headed straight for the coast. He had no intention of waiting for his briefed leader. Hence, the attacking roles were reversed!

When Sgt Vivian arrived over the dock area 'all hell was let loose', the element of surprise gone. Defences were alerted. Flak quietened as Vivian bombed. But searchlights probed the skies, reflecting off the 4,000 feet cloud base. Blenheim R3907 was coned. Drastic evasive action was required. The Blenheim's nose went down into a diving turn. Sgt McPhee up front, shouted: 'Searchlight. Port beam. Get it, Ken!' Sgt Ken Whittle, W/Op/AG, shot out two searchlights. The holocaust faded from view. R3907 was performing well, if damaged, with no crew injuries. They were over the sea, heading home.

However, the night was not over for the three crews of 139!

Nearing Horsham St Faith, Sgt Bennett's operator pipped Ken Whittle to the post, requesting landing permission after Sgt Vivian landed. Sgt Bennett was given permission, while R3907 was told to continue a circuit, awaiting instructions. Sgt Bennett's red and green wing formation-keeping lights were visible on final approach. Suddenly, a red cartridge flare was fired representing the signal: '*Do not land*'. An explosion of fire broke out towards the end of the grassed runway. With horror, McPhee and his crew knew it to be Bennett's aircraft.

Flt/Lt Edwards, on landing with a damaged under-carriage, had blocked the runway, so the runway was changed. Sgt Vivian landed alright. But at the end of the grassed runway, his Blenheim was bogged down. Sgt Bennett's Blenheim, flak damaged, could not go round again. He landed safely, but over-shot the runway, colliding at speed with Vivian's bogged-down Blenheim and crew. On impact, both Blenheims caught fire.

Ground crews were superb, all injured crews evacuated safely. Bennett was hospitalised, re-joining 139 Squadron in April 1941 and lost within the month – '*missing on Ops: Ijmuiden Steel Works, 7 April 1941*'. His Navigator, Sgt Severn, fractured his skull and died before dawn. Sgt Vivian and Navigator, Sgt Mills, both badly injured, did not return to 139 Squadron. The W/Op/AG, with slight injuries, lived to fight another day.

Sgt McPhee and crew, battle-weary and depressed from the view seen below of the tragedy, were instructed to divert to Swanton Morley. McPhee turned onto the course given by Geoff Atkins. Swanton Morley was alerted, the flare path a welcome sight. Radio contact was established and permission to land given. With relief, wheels and flaps responded on final approach.

Then... sudden darkness below!

McPhee cursed at having to go round again when, just as suddenly, the flare path lighting was restored. A second final approach followed. Again, a repeat performance – blackout at the critical point. Third attempt, same action ... same result. Tired bodies and minds were at screaming point! On the fourth attempt, McPhee shouted over the radio: '*For Christ's sake, let us in!*' They were allowed to land and the lights stayed on.

There was a natural tiredness in this final approach given what had gone before. But at 2155 hours, wheels made contact with grassed field. Flak damaged, the port oleo leg collapsed, the port wing dug firm in the ground, breaking off at the engine. Half the wing and engine parted company with the aircraft. Sgt McPhee calmly stated: '*Okay chaps, I've got her!*' The Blenheim slewed around to a shuddering stop. A tinkling metallic sound of the starboard engine cooling down galvanised tired limbs and minds into action evacuating the stricken Blenheim.

It was an agitated Duty Pilot who arrived, relieved to see the battered and buckled remains of R3907 slewed clear of the landing area and crew tired, but alive and well. 105 Squadron Blenheims were about to take off on a night op when, with an intruder aircraft in the area, the flare path was extinguished. In the circuit, they'd had their formation lights on. An intruder could have picked them off any time. The crew were transported back to Horsham St Faith to learn the sad fate of Sgt Bennett's and Sgt Vivian's burnt-out Blenheims and injured crews. Three out of four Blenheims were written off.

At the end of June 1941, Germany invaded Russia. Bomber Command was ordered to increase attacks on Germany day and night. Winston Churchill visited Swanton Morley to address crews from 2 Group. Standing on a fitter's servicing platform, he praised the crews' anti-shipping performances which he called: 'the charge of the Light Brigade' in view of heavy losses. He said 2 Group was to lead aid to the Russians with daylight attacks, forcing Germans to pull back fighter defences from the Russian Front. His rousing speech had the same invigorating effect as ever.

In May, Hughie Edwards had been made Commanding Officer of No. 105 Squadron, replacing their Squadron Commander killed in an anti-shipping raid on Stavanger. Less than two months on, he led one of Swanton Morley's most famous raids – 'Operation Wreckage'. To understand the enormity of what Hughie Edwards achieved it is important to understand the life of this incredible man awarded the Victoria Cross for his actions.

PERSONAL EXPERIENCES

Wing Commander 'Hughie' Idwal Edwards VC, DSO, DFC

Hughie Idwal Edwards was born on 1 August 1914 in Fremantle, Western Australia, the third of five children, to Welsh parents Hugh, a blacksmith and farrier, and wife Jane. Named after his father, he was referred to by his middle name *Idwal* within the family.

Initial education was at White Gum Valley School, before attending Fremantle Boys School, achieving well academically. However, Edwards was forced to leave school at the age of fourteen as family finances could no longer support him. Described as a *'shy, under-confident, introspective and imaginative lad'*, he gained employment as a shipping office clerk.

With the onset of the Great Depression he was unemployed, before working with a horse racing stable in Fremantle, giving him a lifelong interest in horse racing.

Working later in a factory, he enlisted in the Australian Army in March 1933 and was posted to the 6th Heavy Battery, Royal Australian Artillery, as a Private. He became an active sportsman, excelling in Australian Rules Football – playing six matches with leading Western Australian Football League (WAFL) Club, South Fremantle – and cricket with the Fremantle Garrison Team.

In 1935, he was selected for flying training with the Royal Australian Air Force at RAAF Point Cook after which he transferred to the RAF, being granted a short service commission as a Pilot Officer on 21 August 1936. Posted to No. 15 Bomber Squadron, he was appointed Adjutant of No. 90 Squadron in March 1937 flying Blenheim bombers. He received a promotion to Flying Officer on 21 May 1938.

In August 1938, Hugh was piloting a Blenheim near the Scottish border when he flew into a storm at 2,300 metres. When the ailerons froze, the aircraft was forced down to 1,600 metres whereupon he ordered the Navigator and Rear Gunner to bail out. Down to 230 metres, he made an effort to jump clear, but his parachute became entangled with the bomber's radio mast pylon. In the ensuing crash, he sustained head injuries and badly broken leg only saved after extensive surgery, leaving one leg shorter than the other. After the accident, he was declared unfit for flying duties ... until April 1940, when he was posted to No. 139 Squadron for wartime active service.

He was promoted to Flight Lieutenant on 21 May 1940.

In truth, he was so disabled a wire was attached between his right hip and foot to assist walking. He fractured both feet badly when forced to parachute from an iced-up aircraft – his parachute caught with the tail-plane, dragging him down with the aircraft, hitting the ground close to the crashed aircraft. He was determined to get back to flying, even more determined to lead attacks on the enemy.

His chance came unexpectedly in May 1941 when Hugh was made Commanding Officer of No. 105 Squadron, after their Squadron Commander was killed. On 15 June, as Acting Wing Commander, he led six Blenheim bombers in a search for enemy shipping, sighting a convoy of eight merchant-men anchored near The Hague. Launching an attack at low level, his bombs struck a 4,000-ton ship, and he was awarded the Distinguished Flying Cross (DFC).

The port of Bremen was one of the most heavily-defended towns in Germany. Several operations towards the end of June were abandoned due to lack of cloud cover vital to protect poorly armed Blenheims, including two attempted raids on Bremen on the north German coast. 'Operation Wreckage' on 4 July represented third time lucky. Nine crews from 105 Squadron and six of 107 Squadron from Great Massingham took part, although one sub-flight of three from 107 were forced to abort. The recommendation for the Victoria Cross which he was awarded after, details the raid:

The raid comprised nine aircraft from 105 Squadron and six from 107 Squadron. For various reasons, three aircraft of 107 Squadron failed to cross the German coast and returned to home base. Undeterred, Wing Commander Edwards flying at sea level entered the Heligoland Bight and flying a south-easterly course, crossed the German coast in the vicinity of Cuxhaven. Several ships had been seen and therefore the leader knew his approach into Germany would be reported.

Flying close to the ground, with a compact formation of bombers, he continued his overland leg to Bremen. During the approach, he flew so low that he had to fly underneath high tension cables to avoid collision, while one of his other aircraft in the formation collided with, and brought back on the tail wheel, telegraph wires.

Bremen was reached in fairly clear conditions with slight river mist and the sun breaking through an early morning haze. The formidable balloon barrage at Bremen was a risk he decided to ignore and he first saw these when leading his Squadron in at chimney height. Flying in between the cables, he carried out a most determined attack in which some six tons of bombs were dropped on the city.

Direct hits were scored on a large factory resulting in explosions, debris and masonry being thrown to a height of over 800 feet. Direct hits were also obtained on a timber yard, and derricks on the inland dockside were seen to be hit and crash into a nearby factory. At the moment when the formation crossed the perimeter of Bremen, a barrage of flak was opened up on the Squadron described by crews as being terrific.

In view of serious losses encountered by flak by the night bomber phase of this operation, there is no doubt that the anti-aircraft defence was one of considerable magnitude. Two aircraft of No. 107 Squadron were immediately shot down, while two aircraft of No. 105 Squadron were also destroyed by flak fire. One of these crashed in flames on a factory, its bombs detonating on impact. All eight aircraft remaining in the force were heavily hit by anti-aircraft fire and three members of crews in these aircraft wounded.

Wing Commander Edwards with, in his mind, a clear well-made plan of attack and withdrawal from the objective, flying low, turned away for the valley of the Weser River and later, having made good tactical use of a cloud bank north-west of Bremen, withdrew his Squadron and avoided being brought to action by enemy fighters. The aircraft returned to home base flying low over the sea.

Successful attacks had been made on the docks, factories, a timber yard and railways. There was no cloud cover, so the element of surprise was lost from the outset when seen by a coastal convoy near Nordeney. As they penetrated the defences at rooftop height, the utmost bravery was shown by all, none more so than by their leader, Hughie Edwards. [59]

Sgt Jackson had been forced to belly-land with his Observer and Gunner wounded, while the CO's Gunner, Sgt Quinn, also badly wounded; had to be lifted out of the aircraft with a Coles crane. However, Hughie Edwards brought his remaining aircraft safely back, despite all having been hit including his own Blenheim (serial V6028) over twenty times.

The attack on Bremen resulted in immediate awards of four DFMs, a Bar to a DFM, and a DFC. For the courage and leadership he displayed throughout, Wing Commander Edwards was subsequently awarded the VC. The full citation for this Victoria Cross appeared in the *London Gazette* on 22 July 1941:

ROYAL AIR FORCE

The KING has been graciously pleased to confer the Victoria Cross on the undermentioned officer in recognition of most conspicuous bravery –

Acting Wing Commander Hughie Idwal Edwards, D.F.C. (39005), No. 105 Squadron.

Wing Commander Edwards, although handicapped by physical disability resulting from a flying accident, has repeatedly displayed gallantry of the highest order in pressing home bombing attacks from very low heights against strongly defended objects.

On 4th July, 1941, he led an important attack on the Port of Bremen, one of the most heavily defended towns in Germany. This attack had to be made in daylight and there were no clouds to afford concealment. During the approach to the German coast, several enemy ships were sighted and Wing Commander Edwards knew that his aircraft would be reported and that the defences would be in a state of readiness. Undaunted by this misfortune, he brought his formation 50 miles overland to the target, flying at a height of little more than 50 feet, passing under high-tension cables, carrying away telegraph wires and finally passing through a formidable balloon barrage. On reaching Bremen he was met with a hail of fire, all his aircraft being hit and four of them being destroyed. Nevertheless, he made a most successful attack, and then with the greatest skill and coolness, withdrew the surviving aircraft without further loss.

Throughout the execution of this operation which he had planned personally with the full knowledge of the risks entailed, Wing Commander Edwards displayed the highest possible standard of gallantry and determination. [60]

The CO had landed without most of his port wingtip, the port aileron, a cannon shell in the radio shack and telephone wires round the tail wheel. Congratulations came from the C-in-C Bomber Command and Chief of Air Staff, Sir Charles Portal. The operation received much publicity with one

Sergeant having to broadcast his impressions of the raid on the *BBC Home Service*. However, some aircraft survived the Bremen battle only to return and crash-land on the airfield.

Before the end of the month, a batch of tropicalised Blenheims arrived. Painted brown on top and bright blue underneath, these new aircraft had crews and Intelligence Officers worried. Meanwhile, on 25 July, Wing Commander Edwards took the Squadron to Malta. Twelve aircraft departed with him for the journey to conduct operations against Axis shipping.

Despite heavy losses, great damage was caused to tankers and transports loaded with vital stores. The detachment was not expected to exceed three weeks; in fact 105 Squadron stayed until the end of September. At the end of August, Wing Commander Edwards was posted to AHQ Malta, replaced by Wing Commander Scivier from 110 Squadron. He was in action on his first day, yet on 22 September collided with another Blenheim and crashed. Five days later, the last sortie was flown. Next day, the whole Squadron sailed home in a cruiser. After three weeks, the elation of arriving home safe was removed at Greenock during a dock strike!

Participating in a goodwill mission to the United States, Hughie Edwards was appointed Chief Flying Instructor at an operational Training Unit in January 1942, before re-assuming command of No. 105 Squadron on 3 August. During this time, he married Cherry Kyrle '*Pat*' Beresford; the pair later had a son, Anthony, and daughter, Sarah. He was promoted to Temporary Wing Commander on 1 September.

On 6 December, Hughie Edwards participated in the daylight bombing raid on Philips Factory at Eindhoven in the Netherlands. Despite heavy opposition, the bombers successfully damaged or destroyed many targets, with two gun posts being silenced. Several members of the raid were decorated, again including Hughie, awarded the Distinguished Service Order (DSO) and becoming the first airman to receive the Victoria Cross, Distinguished Service Order and Distinguished Flying Cross in World War Two.

Promoted to Acting Group Captain, he went on to assume command of the Bomber Station at Binbrook in February 1943, where, despite his senior position, he continued to participate in operations. On 18 August, he was promoted to War Substantive Wing Commander.

With the end of the European campaigns in sight, Hughie was transferred to the Pacific theatre, first to Ceylon as Group Captain, Bomber Operations.

In January 1945, he was 'Mentioned in Despatches' and appointed Senior Administrative Staff Officer at Headquarters, South East Asia Command, serving in this position until the conclusion of the war.

Wing Commander Edwards and Flight Lieutenant Charlton both survived the war, with Edwards becoming Governor of Western Australia in 1974.

88 SQUADRON

En garde –'Be on your guard'
Reproduced with permission of the MOD

Shortly before 105 Squadron departed for Malta, No. 88 Squadron arrived from Sydenham, Belfast; their motto: '*En garde*', meaning '*Be on your guard*'. Their badge depicted a gliding serpent based on the 1914–1918 War Badge of the French Air Service (Escadrille SPA 88) with which this Squadron was associated. The compliment of adopting this badge was warmly welcomed by the French Air Service at that time, authorised in November 1939 by King George VI.

Like 105 Squadron, they operated Blenheim Mk IVs. However, by the end of the month, a new machine arrived at the airfield for 88 Squadron – a Douglas DB-7B Boston III. Earlier versions, including some originally destined for the French Air Force, had been converted into intruders and night fighters for Fighter Command. These were the first for Bomber Command.

No. 88 Squadron's move to RAF Swanton Morley using the new Douglas DB-7B Boston III, with the prospect of a new, fully grassed airfield; brought a tremendous buzz of excitement, and also rumours. High landing speed, high-speed stall, no gun turret, unsuitable for bombing, poor endurance – stories were rife, spreading quickly around the Station.

When the first new aircraft arrived, crews gathered to watch. The sleek new aeroplane broke into the circuit at an alarming speed, roared round the airfield, then touched down and taxied in. The real surprise came when a shapely young blonde jumped from the ATA. Someone from the assembled mass shouted: *'how many hours have you been flying this amazing machine?'* She calmly replied: *'It's the first time I've ever flown one!'* All worries about the new aircraft evaporated immediately.

While more Bostons arrived in August, 88 Squadron and crews moved to the satellite airfield of Attlebridge, remaining under the operational control of Swanton Morley.

At the end of August, Swanton Morley received its first Fighter Unit with 152 Squadron arriving from Snailwell, bringing seventeen long-range Supermarine Spitfire Mk IIAs and a personnel strength of eleven Officers and fifteen Sergeants. One week on, 152 Squadron were in action, escorting Blenheims of 110 and 226 Squadrons from Wattisham on a daylight raid on the Dutch coast. They continued this type of operation and convoy patrols before departing for Coltishall three months later, the beginning of December 1941.

Meanwhile, September 1941 had seen the formation of a new Flying Unit at Swanton Morley.

No. 15 Blind Approach Training Flight (BAFT) used 6 Airspeed Oxford aircraft to train pilots in Blind Approach Techniques (BAT), with radio beams for directing the aircraft – later re-designated 1515 BAFT Flight. The Flight came under the command of Flt/Lt R. J. Raphael, based at RAF Swanton Morley from October 1941 – November 1943.

Beam Approach (sometimes known as Blind Approach) was essential training for bomber pilots returning to Bases in the dark where visibility was marginal.

No. 1515 Beam Approach Training Flight were equipped with Airspeed Oxford aircraft, and on 24 March 1942, it was two of these Oxford aircraft that collided over Foxley Wood, near Bawdeswell, on a training flight, killing all four aircrew.

105 Squadron arrived back from Malta mid-October and, over following weeks, rumours spread of another new aircraft: an incredibly fast top-secret bomber made of wood! Meanwhile, Squadron Observers began conversion

training on a new W/T (Wireless Telegraphy - Morse transmissions between aircraft and ground stations) and Gunners took a Navigation Course.

On 15 November 1941, Squadron Leader A. R. James describes what happened when, without warning: 'a grey and green shape streaked across the airfield, pulled into a steep climb, then joined the circuit and made a sedate landing - the Mosquito had arrived!'

The Mosquito Mk IV was the first to be delivered to an operational Squadron, flown in by the Company Chief Test Pilot in person, Geoffrey de Havilland. After lunch, the CO was treated to a demonstration trip and, after an exhilarating display of aerobatics, was reported to be 'looking a bit green on landing'. It gave No. 105 Squadron the opportunity to convert from Wellingtons to this new bomber aircraft before a reorganisation within the Squadron. Just over a fortnight later, they moved to Horsham St Faith. The vacancy was filled by 226 Squadron, arriving from Watisham on 9 December.

1941-1942 was the busiest period of the war for Swanton Morley airfield, with established personnel growing in numbers, and visits by VIPs a regular occurrence.

Lord Trenchard: 'father of the RAF', and Air Marshall 'Bomber' Harris: C-in-C Bomber Command made several visits to the Station and to Headquarters of 2 Group at nearby Bylaugh Hall. The Duke of Kent also visited a week before he was killed. On 22 December 1941, Captain Garcia, the Chilean Air Attache, and Captain Peluffo, the Argentine Air Attache, visited Swanton Morley to view an operational Bomber Station.

In February 1942, the first contingent of WAAFs arrived. Due to delays with a new WAAF accommodation block half a mile south of the airfield, the girls were temporarily billeted in the White House in Swanton Morley village, also the residence of the Station Commander!

Between 1941 and 1943, four T2 Hangars and four Blister Hangars were erected. Also thirty-one loop hard standings and a perimeter track laid. Other work involved utility buildings for Barracks with the Station's total accommodation rising to 1,968 males and 390 females.

RAF No. 100 GROUP

No. 100 Group was looking at Swanton Morley to become a part of its growing network of secret airfields because it was close to its HQ: Bylaugh Hall.

In February 1944, 226 Squadron ended its long association with Swanton Morley, moving to Hartfordbridge, leaving the Station committed to training aircrew for the major offensive against Europe. The time seemed right for 2 Group to respond to the need of 100 Group and relinquish Swanton Morley to them, moving their Support Unit to Fersfield, an airfield in south Norfolk just vacated by the USAAF.

RAF Swanton Morley was the only Norfolk airfield to have been retained by 2 Group which, at the beginning of April 1944, formed No. 2 Group Support Unit at the Station. This body was primarily a holding Unit for aircrew and other personnel to make good losses in 2 Group Squadrons during the forthcoming cross-Channel invasion.

Once the invasion of France began, No. 100 Group focused on Bomber Support duties with sorties involving a number of electronic countermeasure devices:

- *Serrate*
- *Mandrel*
- *Jostle*
- *Monica*
- *Airborne Grocer*

The BSDU (Bomber Support Development Unit) had been instrumental in developing these special installations, undertaking operational trials with new equipment whenever possible, using a fleet of nine Mosquitoes of various Mks.

- **SERRATE:** British radar device designed to detect German night fighter radar transmissions from their Lichtenstein aircraft interception radar (A1). Luftwaffe fighters were causing increasing losses amongst RAF bombers attacking targets in Germany and occupied Europe.

- **MANDREL:** device designed to jam enemy Electronic Warfare radar.

- *JOSTLE:* device designed to provide high-power jamming of enemy radio transmissions between aircraft and ground Stations.

- *MONICA:* active tail-warning device designed for use against enemy interceptors.

- *AIRBORNE GROCER* (ABC): device designed to jam enemy A1 (airborne interception) radar.

100 Group's first task at Swanton Morley was to establish its Bomber Support Development Unit (BDSU) on the airfield, equipping with Bristol Beaufighter, Avro Lancaster, Supermarine Spitfire and de Havilland Mosquito aircraft, carrying out experimental operational flights.

The BDSU was joined, shortly after arrival, by workshop facilities from Radlett, to become the Radio Engineering Section. The Mosquito major servicing section also moved in from West Raynham – fifty-four Maintenance Unit Salvage Squad were based as a lodger Unit and 100 Group Communications Flight was established at Swanton Morley Station.

1945 was only two days old when the BDSU lost its first aircraft from Swanton Morley –MM797, a Canadian-built Mosquito Mk30.

Flt/Lt Harry White, with Navigator of many missions: Flt/Lt Mike Allen (both DFCs) took off in early evening darkness. As the aircraft climbed away to the south-west, fully fuelled and armed, the port engine cut out. The propeller would not '*feather*', ensuing drag prevented Harry White from keeping the Mosquito airborne.

He responded to the problem by jettisoning the wing fuel tanks before crash-landing in a field near Scarning. Miraculously, the crew were virtually unharmed, but still trapped in the cockpit, Mike Allen's leg punctured the fuselage side and wedged in tight. With full fuel tanks, the aircraft was enveloped in flames.

Three men from a farm several hundred yards away ran to the wreck as ammunition started to explode. Mike Allen heard a shout: '*She's going up!*' and resigned himself to his fate. However, ignoring bullets whizzing past their ears, all three raced up to the now fiercely burning fuselage to pull Mike Allen to safety.

Only then did they see Harry White lying beneath him. With a supreme combined effort, he too was pulled free. They ran into a ditch at the edge of the field as the Mosquito disappeared in a ball of fire. The three farm hands were each later awarded the BEM for their bravery in rescuing the trapped crew under such impossible circumstances.

In June 1945, the BSDU acquired the Window Research Section – an organisation formed in February 1945 to regularise the development of automatic WINDOW dispensers. The dispensers contained small strips of metal foil cut to precise lengths, dropped by bombers to jam enemy radar, creating a false impression of the size or location of the bomber force. This work originally started in 199 (Special Duties) Squadron under the direction of Flight Lieutenant Merryful, now commanding the Section. Tragically, he was killed, along with passenger, LAC Grady, when his Mosquito crashed at Docking in July. The BSDU also took part in *Operation Post Mortem*, an assessment of the wartime campaign. However, with the intention to form the Radar Warfare Establishment at Watton (RWE) the order was given to disband the BSDU on 21 July 1945.

During these final months of war, flying activity at Swanton Morley slowed considerably, mostly affecting 100 Group Communications Flight and the occasional Mosquito flying in for major servicing. The only urgent call-outs on the Station involved aircraft crashes in the vicinity of which Swanton Morley had certainly had its share.

Flying accidents attended included a 608 Squadron Mosquito from Downham Market which crashed on Bawdeswell Church in November 1944. There were also two USAAF Liberators from Attlebridge which crashed on take-off at Hoe and Gressenhall within minutes of each other. On the same day, a 49 Squadron Lancaster was abandoned over the airfield and survivors who bailed out were cared for by the Station Medical Centre.

The Station Operational Record Book for 1945 showed a complete change of character. It was the first time in five years that any Station social activities were listed – ENSA and Gang Show visits, with references to extra-mural activities like the Woodwork Club. Local meetings between USAAF personnel and villagers discussing a range of topics centred on differences in British and American ways of life. The USAAF were not always popular. Complaints relating to American aircraft buzzing the airfield were sent to USAAF Bases at Attlebridge and Wendling. After months of relative inactivity, it must have been with some relief that, following the cessation of hostilities in May 1945, Bomber Command ultimately relinquished control of Swanton Morley Station.

Operations launched from Swanton Morley under Bomber Command incurred a total loss of thirty-nine aircraft – twenty-one Blenheims and eighteen Bostons together with the inevitable training flight accidents from the airfield. Some of these crews remain buried in the churchyard of Swanton Morley village.

Post-war, little use was being made of Swanton Morley Station until Flying Training Command took control in November 1945. Many wartime aircrew returned for refresher courses and No. 4 Radio School moved there in December 1946, changing its name to No. 1 Air Signallers, then to Air Electronic School, in residence for the next ten years.

In 1947, the Station was officially transferred to No. 27 Group, Technical Training Command hosting a range of training and summer camps including Air Experience flights.

In 1957, the Station transferred to Command Support, main departments being Central Servicing Development and Maintenance Data Centre.

Finally, the Government programme of 'Options for Change' was announced in 1995 resulting in RAF Swanton Morley being selected for closure.

Swanton Morley was taken over by the Army in 1996. The Government's review of Army Bases – in the regular Army Basing Plan – identified Swanton Morley as one of seven 'core Bases' in which it would invest, with the RAF relinquishing the site to the Army after a Closing Ceremony including the only example of a Blenheim Flypast as the Last Post was played.

RAF Swanton Morley Station became Robertson Barracks, and remains so to this day; re-named in honour of Field Marshal Sir William Robertson, the first Field Marshal to rise from the rank of Private to Chief of the Imperial General Staff 1916–1918.

Looking back over the history of RAF Swanton Morley/Robertson Barracks, I am reminded of many Squadrons, and one worthy of note, although its time at the Station wasn't a happy one. No. 305 (Polish) Squadron's motto was: 'Ziemia Wielkopolska', meaning 'Land of Greater Poland'. It was part of RAF Bomber Command Second Tactical Air Force, and one of the last Polish Bomber Squadrons.

305 Squadron's stay at Swanton Morley and use of the Mitchell aircraft was short. They remained unpopular and were never truly accepted. The animosity towards them wasn't helped when a woman and child were killed by a 305 Squadron vehicle close to the airfield. It was a tragic accident. However, the Squadron was considered '*jinxed*', perhaps a contributing factor for its early departure at the end of November to Lasham, re-equipped within a month with the Mosquito Mk VI. Yet nothing can take away the impressive span of operations and creditable record the Squadron left under Bomber Command. Over a span of twenty-seven months, it logged 1,117 sorties, dropping/laying 1,555 tons of bombs and mines. On the debit side, 136 airmen were killed, ten missing, and thirty-three taken prisoner.

Two notable '*Firsts*' claimed by this Station – the delivery by Geoffrey de Havilland of the first Mosquito into RAF service, and on 4 July 1942, the 15th Bomb Squadron (Light), flying from Swanton Morley airfield as part of the first official combined British and American bombing raid over Europe. Both Churchill and Eisenhower were present to mark this auspicious occasion.

PERSONAL EXPERIENCES

W/O F. L. '*Richie*' Richards, DFM

'*Richie*' Richards joined the RAF in 1941 in Plymouth and was posted to Gunnery Training at Blackpool where he became a Rear Air Gunner and posted to 192 Squadron.

Initially based at Foulsham, Richie began operations over Germany mainly flying Wellingtons from Bases including Swanton Morley. He was tasked with discovering the German radar frequency, using adapted aircraft with Special Operators. For this he was awarded the DFM, presented by King George VI at Holyrood Palace, Edinburgh.

He was transferred to the Desert Air Force serving in Egypt, where he completed sixty operations before transferring to Coastal Command (Lossiemouth) eventually completing his RAF career training new Air Gunners. He rose to the rank of Warrant Officer and married a lady he met at RAF Lossiemouth. Often he talked about his RAF Service to his family and regularly corresponded with old comrades in Canada, New Zealand and Australia.

Post-war, he trained as a bricklayer, working on several sites including the restoration of Smithfield Hall. After a particularly bad winter, he found employment working as a Press Operator at Lorival Ltd, progressing to Senior Supervisor in the Battery Container Division. Before retirement, he worked for a short period as Caretaker to a local shopping precinct. However, the love of his life was always the RAF and in particular, RAF No. 100 Group, 192 Squadron.

WHO ARE THESE MEN?

Who are these men who march so proud,
Who quietly weep, eyes closed, heads bowed?
These are the men who once were boys,
Who missed out on youth and all its joys.
Who are these men with aged faces
Who silently count the empty spaces?
These are the men who gave their all,
Who fought for their country for freedom for all.
Who are these men with sorrowful look
Who can still remember the lives that were took?
These are the men who saw young men die,
The price of peace is always high.
Who are these men who in the midst of pain,
Whispered comfort to those they would not see again?
These are the men whose hands held tomorrow,
Who brought back our future with blood, tears and sorrow.
Who are these men who promise to keep
Alive in their hearts the ones God holds asleep?
These are the men to whom I promise again:
'Veterans, my friends – I will remember them!'

Unknown

CHAPTER 15
RAF North Creake

A Brief History

When Len Bartram procured a bicycle, it enabled him to travel further distances, filling notebooks with observations along the way. The curious schoolboy was on a mission. Something was driving him ever forward, needing to understand what was happening to his home area and beyond, within the boundaries of Norfolk. Everything was so secret, which made a young boy yearn to discover more.

Egmere Drome

It was Len Bartram who noted that it was the Air Ministry who gave RAF North Creake its official name. Those living near the site tended to consider it an insult. To them it was Egmere Drome.

> Well, blast me! North Creake is a village which lay over there out west, miles away! Just yew ask them Becks, Carvers, Dewings and Beaumonts ... they'll tell y, cos it wer in their back gardens.

The medieval village of Egmere today has long gone. The church is in ruins, made into a barn during the 1600s. Close by was the village. The 1,200 acres which made up the total land area of the Parish equals that of many established Norfolk villages. The reason for its demise along with others in the neighbourhoods of Waterden, Quarles, etc, remains open to debate. Changes in farming practices is one theory.

The first Military presence came in 1940 when the 57th Heavy Newfoundland Regiment of the Royal Artillery moved from Sussex to Norfolk for coastal defence duties against the expected enemy invasion. Part of 'D' Battery, with two giant 9.2" Howitzers of World War One vintage, were set in position close to Egmere Farm. The target area for these guns covered sea approaches to Wells and Holkham. They stayed in Norfolk sixteen months.

A British Army Regiment occupied the Egmere site for a time after the Newfoundlanders left for overseas. A number of Land Army girls lived for a while in the farmhouse during the war. While through 1941–1942 there was a Dummy (Decoy) airfield site for Docking Airfield off the Burnham Road.

The Airfield: Description and Construction

Construction of the airfield was by Taylor Woodrow in October 1942. The site was on an area of farmland known as Bunker's Hill with the camp on the east side. The land was owned by nearby Holkham Estate. Two old cottages near Egmere Farm earlier damaged by blasts from big guns were demolished, while hedges, banks and trees within the site were removed.

The road from Burnham Thorpe to Little Walsingham running across the airfield site was closed. Technical and administrative sites bordered unclassified country roads between Wells and Fakenham, with domestic sites for 2,951 males and 411 females dispersed in farmland to the east. Construction plans changed twice during the time of building. One rumour was that the Base was intended for a new RAF super-heavy bomber being built, with runways lengthened accordingly. Len Bartram posed the question: *Could this be for the top secret Vickers Windsor, four engine high altitude bomber designed to replace the Wellington?*

After further survey work, however, the airfield fell from favour and Sculthorpe took its place. The need for Bases in the area for the new RAF No. 100 (Bomber Support) Group changed all other plans. In December 1943, it passed to them.

Station workshop buildings, Admin Block, Communal, Messes and Billet sites were all to the right of the road. At one point, aircraft crossed the road to a maintenance area. The road remained open to the public, but as it became part of the airfield, farm and Estate workers were issued with a Pass to access certain areas.

Sick Quarters were along the Great Walsingham road. Two WAAF sites and others were in the area behind Crabb Castle Farm. For a time, the Station was held for '*Care and Maintenance*' until required by 100 Group.

On 1 April 1944, F/Lt J. I. Harris MC arrived to assume command with other personnel arriving daily. On 16 April, the Base was officially declared open and on 25 April, S/Ldr N. C. Hewnham promoted from F/Lt, took over command.

On 28 April, the AOC: Air Commodore E. B. Addison CBE commanding 100 Group, visited to inspect both airfield and personnel. The first No. 199 Squadron had arrived, also fifty RAF Regiment men for airfield defence together with seven WAAFs and Section Leaders including:

- F/Lt I. D. Foley (Flying Control),
- F/O Beaumont (Intelligence),
- F/O Playfoot (Catering),
- F/O Clark (PT),
- F/O Faulkner (i/c Flying),
- F/L W. R. Dyke (MO from Wyton),
- F/O Harrison (Signals),
- F/L P. M. Cox (CTD Duties),
- J. W. Curtis (Armourer from Foulsham),
- F/O S. W. Blackford (Accountant Officer from Downham Market),
- F/Lt Boby (from Foulsham),
- F/Lt Bullock (Equipment Officer)

199 SQUADRON

'Let Tyrants Tremble'
Reproduced with permission of the MOD

The Squadron Badge depicts two swords, one pointing up, the other down, in front of a fountain. The swords symbolise the Unit's function of mine-laying and bombing.

It was authorised by King George VI in July 1944.

Squadron Code Letters on aircraft: EX
   Letter as a designator – for example EX-N (under RAF 100 Group)

The Squadron had a short existence during World War One as a night flying Training Unit. Formed during November 1917 at East Retford, it disbanded at Harpswell in June 1918.

Reformed on 7 November 1942 at Blyton, Lincolnshire, it became a heavy bomber Squadron in No. 1 Group, Bomber Command, equipped with Wellington Mk 3s. During February 1943, the Squadron moved to Ingham, Lincolnshire and received Mk 10 Wellingtons.

In June 1943, the Squadron again moved, this time to Lakenheath, Suffolk to join No. 3 Bomber Group where, by the end of July, Short Stirlings replaced Wellingtons. The Squadron carried out regular night bombing and mine-laying operations. In addition, from February 1944, they were chosen to carry out special secret supply-dropping operations to French Maquis Resistance Fighters and other underground Resistance Forces in occupied Europe. These were dangerous and hazardous operations, vital to make a drop on the correct spot often by torchlight. A number of aircraft were lost in these operations and from mine-laying, raids on Berlin and other targets.

On 1 May 1944, the main party of 199 Squadron including the servicing echelon No. 9199, travelled by road from Lakenheath to North Creake airfield. Taking the main road, they inquired of residents about the location of the airfield, and politely told: 'There's no Drome around here'. Not a word was said about Egmere up the road. One resident said later: 'Well, you never know, they might have bin them there Garmens dressed up as ours!' It's said some vehicles actually returned to Lakenheath for directions!

On arrival at the airfield, Group Captain N.A.N. Bray DFC assumed position as Station Commander, having previously commanded the Squadron at Lakenheath. Known as *Little Nan Bray* because of his size and initials, he was well-liked by all ranks and local residents. He once put himself on *Fatigues* because he was late for P.E! He lived in a cottage on the Holkham Estate, next to Estate workers, but sadly was killed in a flying accident while serving in Denmark after the end of the war.

Meanwhile, Wing Commander Bevington became Squadron Commander – unusual as he was a Navigator not a Pilot which most Squadron Commanders were. Squadron 'B' Flight Commander was S/Ldr Lumsdaine.

By 31 May, several new aircrew and other personnel had arrived, bringing the Squadron up to full strength in time for Air Commodore Milne visiting the Station. On 3 and 4 June, RAF and WAAF personnel from the Squadron took part in the *Salute the Soldier Week* parades in Walsingham where Lord Leicester from Holkham took the salute.

A new Mess Bar opened on 18 June, presumably in the Officers' Mess with room also for dances. Civilian guests were invited to attend Opening Night with over 250 people present. A well equipped Station Library and Reading Room was opened the same day.

There were facilities on the Camp for regular cricket, tennis and swimming. Local men from Egmere played the Squadron at cricket on 8 July 1944, unfortunately, rain stopped play. The Squadron team played the 100 Group team at Little Snoring on 12 July. One airman wrote in the Squadron History:

They were the happiest days of my life, even though there was a war on. Comradeship was terrific!

On 30 June, there had been a torrential thunderstorm. The WAAF and Accounts Sites were flooded out. Books and ledgers hung out to dry after the storm passed, while the WAAFs requested permission to evacuate their Quarters because of an invasion of thousands of earwigs, beetles and other insects after the rain had stopped. Permission was denied.

However, it wasn't all fun and frolicks.

RAF No. 100 Group

Squadrons 199 and 171 were both based at North Creake, working together on Special Duties under 100 Group.

171 SQUADRON

Per dolum defendimus – 'Confound the enemy'
Reproduced with permission of the MOD

Squadron code letters on aircraft: 6Y.

Its badge showed a portcullis in front of a displayed eagle. Formed 15 June 1942 at Gatwick, equipped with Tomahawk and then Mustang aircraft, it was disbanded in December that same year, before being reformed on 8 September 1944 at North Creake.

199 SQUADRON

'Let Tyrants Tremble'
Reproduced with permission of the MOD

Badge:
   In front of a fountain, two swords, one pointing upwards and one pointing down.
   The swords symbolise the Unit's function of mine-laying and bombing.

Authority:
   King George VI, July 1944

Squadron Code Letters on aircraft:
   EX

Both 171 and 199 Squadrons used electronic warfare, each playing a separate but vital role with specific tasks:

Mandrel

The main role of aircraft based at North Creake was to provide a radar (*Mandrel*) screen to protect main RAF heavy night bomber forces from being detected by enemy early warning radar stations such as '*Freya*' devices.

   For these operations, *Mandrel*-equipped aircraft carried up to eight special radio transmitters tuned to different wave-bands inside the aircraft. Eight extra sword aerials of different lengths were fitted below the fuselage of the aircraft. To operate this special equipment an extra crew member: the '*Special Wireless Operator*' or S.O was on board.

The aircraft used a variety of tactics – flying with or ahead of the bomber stream to create a side screen; or flying circular and creeping patterns. Great skill was required by Pilot and Navigator to maintain accurate speed, height and position to achieve the task successfully.

WINDOW was also dropped to assist the jamming task.

WINDOW

Strips of silver metallic paper of various lengths and widths packed in brown paper bundles or cardboard boxes with a string pull on each to rip them open when dispensed. Special chutes were fitted to the underside of the aircraft down which bundles were dropped through at specified rates.

Aircraft from both Squadrons were out on operations most nights, sadly not without loss, using aircraft fitted with special secret wireless equipment. *Spoof* (Diversion) operations were also flown, sometimes a combination of all.

Training commenced immediately on arrival at North Creake using this new equipment, with *Mandrel* jamming operations first taking place on the eve of D-Day. Many personnel were in the cinema at Wells. Suddenly, the main film was interrupted by a large message on the screen requesting all North Creake personnel to return to Base immediately. All available 199 Squadron aircraft took part in providing a *Mandrel* (Radar) screen in front of the allied invasion D-Day air armada. Squadron operations then continued regularly from D-Day.

Final sorties from North Creake were flown on the night of 2 May 1945. The two Squadrons, 199 and 171, had lost a total of seventeen aircraft during operations from the airfield – eight Stirling, nine Halifaxes. Three months later, both Squadrons were disbanded and the airfield pressed into use for aircraft storage, mainly Mosquitoes. The RAF finally relinquished North Creake in the Autumn of 1947, whereupon the flying field was returned to agriculture and runways removed apart from narrow strips used as farm roads and the Control Tower which took on a new lease of life (*see Update Section at the back of this book*). Yet memories remain, together with the echo of ditties airmen would sing:

Goodbye Nineteen Forty Four
We don't want you any more;
But we'll work like bees inside a hive

To end this war in Forty-Five.

There are many who still remember the end of January 1945 when blizzards left snowdrifts up to seven feet high making the airfield impossible to use. The Water Tower froze. Water was rationed until it thawed ... and operations commenced:

Fourteen aircraft took off this e'ven
To carry out a Mandrel Screen,
They filled the sky so full of jam
Hun controls were not worth a dam!
Then three more dropped their WINDOW bright
To further fox Hun fighters' night,
Who cursed and swore from beacon to beacon
Mein Gott in Himmel sie haben North Creake!'

PERSONAL EXPERIENCES: 199 & 171 Squadrons

Flt/Sgt John Rees, Medical NCO
Aircraft Crashes & Other Memories

After returning from serving in the Middle East, I was posted to North Creake when the airfield opened just before 199 Squadron arrived from Lakenheath. The Squadron had Stirlings and later a flight of Halifaxes. 171 Squadron was also later formed here. The servicing echelons for these Squadrons were known as Nos 9199 and 9171. I was Flight Sergeant in charge of Station Sick Quarters. S/Ldr Peter Gorrie was Chief MO (Medical Officer) and F/Lt Bob Dyke his second-in-command.

The Station had a short life. 199 became operational just before D-Day, closing in August 1945. By then, I had been posted again and was well on my way to Burma.

As NCO i/c Sick Quarters, I was always involved in the unpleasant side of any crashes or accidents on and off the Station. I vividly remember the following incidents, but actual dates and crew names escape me:-

1. A Stirling taking off at night on ops failed to get airborne. It swung off the side, off the runway, causing its undercarriage to collapse and burst into flames. It was heading straight for the Control Tower near where I was sitting in an ambulance. Luckily it came to rest and all crew got out safely.

2. A Stirling failed to get airborne while taking off at night, ploughed into the Station potato field and, although there was no fire, the Navigator had one of his legs amputated except for the popliteal artery. F/Lt Dyke decided to try and save the limb. I gave anaesthetic gas and air having been taught in the Western Desert during emergencies. The bones of the leg were lined up, the leg put in plaster. He was then taken to the RAF Hospital at Ely. Luckily, the RAF Chief Consultant in Orthopaedics was there when he arrived and his expert help saved the leg.

3. A Stirling's undercarriage collapsed on take-off. The aircraft came to rest in what locals called 'the sunken' or 'low road' which crossed the middle of the airfield. It burst into flames, shedding a propeller just before stopping. It was a messy job. I remember it well, so much mud and foam.

4. On a lovely afternoon shortly before the end of war, a Halifax going up on an Air Test swung on take-off, leaving the runway. It continued on and crossed the main Fakenham to Wells road where it headed straight for a number of buildings, but struck a large old oak tree and caught fire. The Pilot was badly injured, the rest of the crew suffering minor injuries. On a visit during the 1970s, I noticed the tree was now dead but still there.

5. On the night of 3/4 March 1945, German Night Fighter Forces mounted a large Intruder attack (*Operation Gisela*) on our

returning heavy Night Bomber Force. One of our Halifaxes was attacked by a Ju88 while preparing to land at North Creake. The crew of eight were able to parachute out before the aircraft crashed at Walnut Tree Farm, South Lopham. One of the crew actually landed in the local churchyard where an angle structure broke his fall, causing slight injury. The Pilot was S/Ldr Procter from 171 Squadron.

6. A low flying Halifax crashed head-on into the cliffs at Cromer on 25 June 1945. The aircraft was completely wrecked, all on board killed. Some wreckage fell onto the beach below injuring an American serviceman. Records stated there were five crew members on board, but we only recovered four. It later transpired the missing crewman was at the dentist and missed the flight. It's said the aircraft made a low flypast along the beach, then turned back heading towards town.

7. When a 100 Group Mosquito crashed in a village close to our airfield we were first on the scene. It had spun in from 16,000 feet.

8. We went out to the village of Edgefield near Melton Constable where one of our Stirlings crashed returning from ops, killing the crew. One crew member, F/O L. Barham, lived in Cawston not far from the crash-site, where he was buried with a Squadron Guard of Honour.

I wonder if there is any record of an incident concerning 199 Squadron Gunnery Leader Flt/Lt Frank Fenning. His aircraft was hit over France and he made his exit by parachute which failed to open completely. Luckily, he landed on a large haystack and returned to the Squadron with nothing worse than a sprained ankle. He was a particularly close chum of mine – older than most other aircrew on the Squadron.

I saw several bad cases of frostbite during the winter of 1944/45 when faulty gloves or no gloves at all were the cause. Some were from American shot-up bombers which landed at our Base.

I was surprised to find there was a salt-water breeding and malaria-carrying mosquito (insect) living in an area near Wells. 100 Group established a sort of Rest Camp in the pine woods down at the end of the road running from Wells lifeboat station. No airman with a record of having malaria was allowed to attend this Camp. The Camp was not a success and most who attended were glad to get back to Base away from the gnats, flies and mosquitoes.

I also remember some V-1 Doodle Bugs going over, but none came down near here. There was enemy air activity, but we were not bombed.

Station Sick Quarters

The Station Sick Quarters (SSQ) was the first Site down the Walsingham Road on the right. We could drive to the Control Tower and runways in less than five minutes if need be. The SSQ Site was in its own compound and the number and type of buildings were of standard World War Two Bomber Command layout. The Staff here were:

Senior Medical Officer – S/Ldr Peter Gorrie
Deputy/2nd in Command – F/Lt Robert Dyke
(Any time the S/Ldr was away or off duty F/Lt Dyke was in charge)
Dental Officer – F/Lt Ralph Syder
Dental Nurse – Cpl Gertrude Cross
Senior NCO – Myself: F/Sgt John Rees
Corporal NCOs – Fred Chalkely, Alex Gavard, Jock Sinclair
LAC/AC Medical Orderlies – Alf Clague (a World War One veteran), Tich Wightman, A. C. Robinson, plus two others
WAAF Medical Orderlies – Corporal Catherine Murray, ACWs – Anne Bland, Zietta Boultan, Barbara Barret-Cox (who married F/Lt Paddon, 199 Squadron)
Ambulance Drivers – Jock Gillies, Roy Copus, WAAF ACW Holland

We also had our own SSQ Cook who was a WAAF on a weekly rota from the Sergeant's Mess. The Medical Staff had their own Billet in the SSQ Compound.

Sick Quarters contained twelve beds for RAF personnel and separate section with six beds for WAAF personnel, also two separate isolation rooms with one bed in each. There was a fully-equipped Crash Room always ready for any emergencies, where nearly any operation could be carried out. But our work was mainly daily routine such as morning sick parades, inoculations, vaccinations and various medical examinations.

At night, there were two RAF and one WAAF personnel on duty with an ambulance at the Control Tower at all times while any of our aircraft were airborne. It was a very cold and boring job during winter nights. We were not issued with any extra cold-weather clothing, but sometimes we got the odd tot of rum if any was left over after de-briefing. It has long been proven that rum does not actually warm you up, but is a potent allayer of nerves, especially after a dodgy experience in the air.

Aircraft weren't flying every night, but we only had about three nights off in any fortnight. Often Training Flights took place when there were no ops. Bad weather was our main chance of a night off. Our staff had rota weekends off, but it was not until VE Day we had any week days to ourselves.

When able to get away, the SSQ Local was *The Half Moon* in Great Walsingham. It was small and scruffy, but the landlord, Eddie Rivett and locals were a great friendly bunch.

Jim Feasey, Gunner
171 Squadron

No. 171 Squadron was formed at North Creake on 8 September 1944 from a nucleus of aircraft and crews of 'C' Flight, 199 Squadron.

Other crews were posted in to complete the complement of the new Squadron. The Squadron number existed for a short time during 1942, but was disbanded. The new 171 Squadron was intended as an extra Halifax (*Mandrel*) Squadron. Halifaxes were in short supply so Stirlings from 199 Squadron were used for a while.

The Commanding Officer appointed to command the new Squadron was Wing Commander Michael Renaut DFC., personally picked by the AOC of the Group. He had already completed a

Tour on heavy bombers in the Middle East and was serving as an Instructor on a Halifax O.T.U from where he joined 171 Squadron.

The first batch of new crews posted in for the Squadron were not quite what the W/Cdr had requested. Instead of a special hand-picked bunch came a number of crews which other Units needed to shed for one reason or another. These he quickly returned until he got what he wanted.

Listed as Flight Commanders were – S/Ldr K. Eddy (RAAF), S/Ldr Robertson, F/Lt Dickenson and F/Lt R.W. Baker.

I crewed up as a Gunner with F/Sgt J. Philipson (RAAF), Pilot at Wellington O.T.U at Desborough. We then went to a Stirling HCU at Chedburg where we made up our crew with:

Sgt N. Harington (Bomb Aimer),

Sgt P. Curran (Navigator),

Sgt J. Cowell (RAAF) W/Operator,

Sgt L. Evans (Mid Upper-Gunner),

Sgt D. Johnson (F/Engineer).

I was just nineteen years old. We'd hoped to get on a Lancaster Squadron, but hearing crews were still urgently needed for Stirlings, we went for that; we were just raring to go! It was the policy of Bomber Command to keep crews together once formed if possible.

With 171 Squadron, we did five ops as WINDOW spoofs on Stirlings:

Loovain on 25 September 1944 in LJ611.

26 September – Frankfurt, 4 hrs 40 mins, in LJ651.

29 September – LJ567 to Mainz.

5 October in aircraft LJ568 to Mannheim where we were attacked by a Me210 Night Fighter. Jack did a terrific corkscrew to get us clear. Both Les and I got a good long burst at it, but then my four guns jammed due to the ammo belt twisting. Luckily, the Fighter lost us and we saw no more of it.

7 October – Hamburg in LJ559.

Halifaxes finally arrived on the Squadron, so later, during October, our complete crew went up to 1659 HCU at Topcliffe to covert to Halifaxes as did other Stirling crews. On return to North Creake, we were soon on our first Halifax operation, a WINDOW spoof to Mannheim on 21 November 1944 in NA112. On 2 December we flew our first *Mandrel*-jamming op. On 4 December we took a brand new Halifax to Kassel, returning on one engine, making a belly-landing and writing off the aircraft. It proved an expensive trip!

Life at North Creake was very spartan. We lived in Nissen huts which, during the winter of 1944/45 were freezing. Fuel rations for the stove were soon used up and we had to scrounge what we could. No-one bathed until they went home on Leave. I remember the awful cold while in the rear gun turret, ice forming on my oxygen mask and tube which had to be broken away every few minutes when at our operating height. Thankfully, we had super electric-heated suits and gloves which helped. An orange could freeze solid in a very short time. It was like a deep freeze.

During December, the Armourers removed the cushions from the Gunner's seat to enable the Rear Gunner to wear and sit on his parachute rather than having to climb back into the fuselage to put it on if required, which all took time. Now once in the turret, we had to remain until back at Base.

It would be impossible to detail all the hair-raising incidents which occurred during our eight months based at North Creake. We operated mainly through the bad winter period of 44/45 which was extra bad; the weather alone was one of the major dangers.

One night, we took off and climbed through solid cloud all the way to 20,000 feet, icing up all the time. At one stage, Jack thought he was going to lose control. We got all ready to bail out, but broke into the clear and went on.

Another occasion, we ran into dreadful turbulence and 'St Elmos' fire and static lightning covered the aircraft. It saw off several aircraft of the main force that night.

I flew an op as replacement Mid-Upper Gunner with our CO Mike Renaut to Berlin during April 1945. Despite the war being in its last month and contrary to popular belief that Jerry had no more opposition; it was one of my worst nights. We were coned by groups of searchlights all the way across the city and for fifteen minutes took continuous heavy *Ack-Ack* fire before getting three attacks by Night Fighters. That night, we dropped a load of heavy bombs and incendiaries, not our usual duty. Because of corkscrewing and weaving around for such a long time, we ran very short of fuel and just made Manston in Kent with a few minutes of flying time left. We had been airborne nearly eight hours.

We had some great parties at the Mess and sometimes the Earl and Countess Leicester were guests at the Dinners. They came over to the airfield to watch the evening take off with their two daughters. We all remember the time as mentioned in Mike Renaut's book: '*Terror by Night*' when the Leicester party came in at the far end of the airfield and proceeded down the active runway to where a line of aircraft was ready to take off!

After VE Day, North Creake was quickly run down. I was posted to the new RWE based at Watton in Norfolk, serving on the GCA Flight until demob in 1947. Then I joined the Police Force, eventually retiring to Suffolk.

Group Captain George Cubby MBE, FRMets

Born in December 1920, George was a native of Whitehaven in Cumberland. He joined the RAF in 1940.

In December 1942, George was commissioned in the Royal Air Force Volunteer Reserve and served throughout the war in Bomber Command. He completed two operational tours with No. 199 Squadron and No. 171 Squadron at RAF Lakenheath and RAF North Creake.

Immediately after the war, George was seconded for duty with the British Military Administration of Malaya and during 1945 and 1946 served as District Officer in the State of Kelantan, Malaya. In 1947, he returned to normal RAF duties to serve in Java and after, on flying boats with No. 88 Squadron based in Hong Kong.

After serving for two and a half years as ADC to the AOC-in-C Maintenance Command, George was posted to Germany for administrative duties at RAF Butsweilerhof. He returned to the United Kingdom in 1956, serving at the RAF Record Office as Personal Staff Officer to the ACC until posted to the Air Secretary's Department of the Air Ministry in 1959.

In January 1961, George was promoted to the rank of Wing Commander and posted to the Headquarters of the United States 3rd Air Force at Ruislip as Senior Liaison Officer. From 1963-1965 he then served on the staff of the Headquarters of the Far East Air Force in Singapore. He returned home in April 1965 and appointed to command the RAF Youth Selection Centre at RAF Stafford.

On 28 December 1966, George was promoted to the rank of Group Captain, assuming command of RAF Upwood with responsibility for the professional training of Equipment and Secretarial Officers and for Specialist Management and Work Study Training.

Then, in February 1969, he was posted to Germany as Assistant Chief of Staff (Personnel and Administration) at the Headquarters of the Second Allied Tactical Air Force.

George's chief interests were Mountaineering and sailing. He climbed extensively in the Alps, Great Britain and in the Far East where a 'First Ascent' was made with members of an RAF Expedition. He was a member of the RAF Mountaineering Association as well as other climbing clubs, and elected to Membership of the Alpine Club in 1967.

Since 1947, George was also a Fellow of the Royal Meteorological Society.

George Cubby died in 2005. His widow, Betty, would value hearing from anyone who knew her husband, and knows why he was 'Mentioned in Dispatches'. She has donated various memorabilia to the City of Norwich Aviation Museum.

Roy Smith was in the same crew as George and believes he is today the only survivor:

George and I were in the same crew for a considerable time. Our pilot was an Australian named Alex Noble.

We did our first tour from Lakenheath over the last four months of 1943. If you survived this, you were granted six months non-operational flying – instructing, admin, or something equally boring.

However, in our case, we were offered a chance to go direct to 100 Group, as a reward we only had to do fifteen ops to complete our second tour. At the time, this seemed a good bargain – we unanimously accepted. I have often wondered if this was wise and we were pushing our luck. The war would have been over by the time our six months expired. It was sad when we all had to split up. I met up with each member of my crew over the years … In fact George and I were members of the RAF Club, Piccadilly.

Pilot Officer Gordon Joshua Dennison 199 Squadron

P/O Gordon Joshua Dennison, better known as *Billy*, served two years in Canada as an Air Engine Mechanic at one of the Bomb and Gunnery Schools, near the town of Dafoe Saskatchewan. He re-mustered and tried for Pilot, but was recommended for Air Gunner instead. He left Canada after completing Gunnery School in January 1944, arriving in Liverpool at the end of January and moved to four different Bases to be crewed and trained for active duty in 199 Squadron at North Creake.

On 15/16 September 1944, Gordon (*Billy*) Dennison took off at 2131 hours from North Creake as part of a crew tasked to provide a *Mandrel* Screen for a bombing run on the Kiel Canal with about 490 bombers. (*Mandrel* Screen was an airborne radar jamming device to counter the *Freya* Early Warning System.)

Stirling III LJ536 EX-P
Crew
- F/S A. D. Heggison
- Sgt S. C. Rennie
- F/S M. Kesselman RCAF
- F/S L. G. Langley RCAF
- Sgt J. B. Sowden
- W/O D. T. Hughes
- Sgt J. D. Campbell RCAF
- **Sgt G. J. Dennison RCAF**

199 Squadron allocated seventeen aircraft for RCM support that night, eleven flew *Mandrel* and six were to drop *WINDOW*.

The course for EX-P was to fly from Base (North Creake) to point A for 10.40 pm. They were then to fly to point B, arriving at 11 pm. This back and forth between point A and point B was to be repeated until the last time at point B at 2.35 am. They were then to fly to Base (North Creake). This set up a sort of race-course pattern, flown in partnership with plane EX-E (Pilot F/O Lampkin). *Mandrel* was to be turned on from 10.15 pm until 2.35 am. This operation would have put EX-P close to the Holland coast and over the North Sea. The 'Market Garden' campaign was taking place in Holland, so a lot of activity going on.

However, Stirling III LJ536 EX-P was lost without trace. There is no indication as to whether the aircraft was outward or inward bound.

Jerry Dennison and his family still mourn the loss of a dearly-loved brother with no known resting place. Their search for answers continues. However, with the British Government honouring those who served in Bomber Command with a wonderful bronze statue unveiled on 28 June 2012 in Green Park, London; an additional medal became available through the Canadian Government – a Bar to go on the ribbon of the Canadian Volunteer Service Medal. Jerry's application on behalf of his brother was successful, and he is able to display proudly this new award.

P/O Gordon Joshua Dennison, Rear Gunner, RCAF, aged 22, from Assiniboia, Saskatchewan, Canada, is remembered on the Runnymede Memorial, London; Panel 249.

Unexplained Mysteries of War

Another Stirling – LJ531 EX-N – was lost without trace on the night of 16 June 1944. Its crew were:
- Pilot Officer T. W. Dale – Pilot RNZAF
- Pilot Officer R. J. Whittleston – Navigator RNZAF
- Warrant Officer F. C. Brittain – Wireless Operator
- Warrant Officer F. Lofthouse – Special Wireless Operator
- Flight Sergeant K. K. Swadling – B/A
- Sergeant J. Higginbottom – Mid Upper Gunner
- Sergeant W. Lattimer (Jock) – Rear Gunner
- Sergeant J. Watts (Flap) – Flight Engineer

A mural of their aircraft was found after North Creake closed as an airfield and taken over by Seamans, the animal feedstuff company. It was discovered on the internal brick wall of the original Flight Office being used as a store-house. John Reid, today a member of the RAF 100 Group Association, was instrumental in managing the removal of the wall to keep the mural intact. It is now displayed at the Royal Air Force Museum in Hendon, London. Removal of the mural was a project never attempted before, and the true story behind the painting remains a mystery to this day, as written under the painting someone had written 16-6-44 R.I.P.

On 17 June 1984, an Unveiling of the Stirling Mural Ceremony took place at Bomber Command Museum, RAF Hendon, London. Mrs Allan, wife of the artist: Flight Sergeant Ted Allan of 199 Squadron, unveiled the Mural now in a place where it could be preserved and seen for the first time by the public

A dedication of the Mural by Padre Schofield to the memory of the crew of EX-N followed, honouring the sacrifice of all men of 199 Squadron and 100 Group who gave their lives during World War Two. An Address was given by Lance Smith, ex-Squadron Adjutant of 199 Squadron.

F/E Ernie Hughes
Under the Spreading Chestnut Tree

How did it come about that in Spring 1945 I was serving as a Flight Engineer on No. 171 (SD) Squadron based at RAF North Creake in Norfolk?

I go back to December 1943 when our crew were screened after completing a tour of operations with No. 76 (Bomber) Squadron in Yorkshire. Then I was posted to No. 1663 HCU (Heavy Conversion Unit) at RAF Station Rufforth, near York. My duties were instruct-ing F/Es into new crews converting to four engined Halifax heavy bombers.

In October 1944, I carried out similar duties at 1669 HCU, at RAF Station Langar, near Nottingham. Here, I met another F/E, Bob Ledicott. Bob came from the Isle of Wight. We chummed up and often would go to the nearest pub for a few beers. The end of the war in Europe was getting near and there was much speculation on what would happen to us aircrew. We were both fed-up with life on these Training Stations.

Usually when we were downing the odd pint, Bob and I came to agree we'd be safer from being grounded and suffering routine jobs if we were back on ops. It was when Bob was on Leave that a notice came out asking for volunteers to serve in a new Squadron being formed for special duties. *This is our chance,* I thought, and went to the CO's office. He was pleased at my offer to go, but couldn't tell me anything about the new Squadron.

'*I'm sure that Flight Sergeant Ledicott would also wish to go, Sir, but he is on Leave at the moment.*'

'*Fine, I'll put him down.*' I saluted and retreated.

A few days later, Bob returned.

'*Good news ... we're back on ops!*'

Bob nearly exploded.

'*You idiot!*' he shouted among a torrent of unkind words. '*I've just got engaged.*'

Once at the Mess bar he calmed down and became resigned to his fate. In December we found ourselves in Norfolk on No. 171 (SD) Squadron, North Creake.

Bob had a motorbike and we'd tour the nearby Norfolk countryside, calling in at the occasional village Inn for a re-fuel. It must have been about March 1945 when I became the owner of a small sports car and so, often, we went our separate ways.

Then tragedy for me when a rear drive half-shaft sheared and my little car became immobile. As a trained car mechanic, I soon had the hub in my hand, the small part of the shaft tuck in it. How to get this broken piece out? Someone suggested going to the blacksmith whose Smithy was in a nearby village. On Bob's bike we followed instructions and arrived at the Smithy. Inside was the Smith, a medium-sized man and strangely, dressed in a suit wearing a countryman's cap.

I explained my problem and he looked at me, then at Bob.

'*Are you chaps married?*' he asked.

'No', we replied.

Bob looked across at me and I guessed he was thinking: *'Thanks to you, I probably never will be!'* I looked away. The Smith continued:

'This is my advice, when you go looking for a wife, forget the pretty faces and figures; look for a girl who can cook and keep a clean house; one not afraid to work. Too many young fellows are led astray by a pretty face and live to regret it. Now I have to go. There's the anvil, sledgehammers and tools, help yourselves.'

'What about paying you?' I asked.

'When you've finished, go to my house over there,' was his reply; and off he went.

I placed the car hub on the jaws of a large vice; Bob picked up a sledge and gave the end of the broken shaft a mighty thump. Out it shot. We went over to the house and I banged the knocker. Footsteps – door opened – I was looking at one of the loveliest women I'd ever seen. Her smile radiated serenity.

'Yes?'

I blurted out that the Smith had told us to call when we'd finished and, how much did I owe?

'Oh, nothing,' she replied. *'He said you boys were welcome.'*

I asked her to thank her husband for his kindness. Again came that enchanting smile.

'I will', she said.

Stepping back, she closed the door. I looked at Bob who stared at me. We'd both been expecting a very plain-looking lady, at best.

'What was all that lecture about?' I asked.

'Search me', said Bob.

Only later did I discover his wife was a lovely lady ... but couldn't cook! The blacksmith had been dressed to go for dinner at the nearby pub.

F/E Ernie Hughes
Reminiscence

I was watching a TV programme in which a few World War Two veterans were being interviewed, connected to Remembrance Sunday. The interviewer asked one lively-looking gentleman, who'd said he was a Flight Engineer in RAF Bomber Command; what his duties had been? His somewhat inane reply: '*Looking after the engines, I suppose.*' Obviously, caught off balance, this was the best he could come out with. It brought home to me that I should try and fill this gap in general knowledge, before it's too late.

There isn't a need for me to write of Briefings; egg and chips; the bumpy ride out to the aircraft; for you will read of such by different aircrew. So, we have arrived at our Kite and been greeted by our ground crew with a grin and the words: *All's well*'. With one hour before take-off, as the F/E, my first action is to carry out an external inspection of the aircraft.

Starting at the nose, I check for damage and note the pilot head cover has been removed (otherwise – no airspeed indication in the cockpit). Then, I inspect the port (left), wheel, tyre, and undercarriage bay for leaks or damage; move on to the propellers, engines (all cowlings secure and no leaks), no damage to the leading edge of the wing. Check no visible damage to the trailing edge of the wing, aileron and flap (the first controls us in roll; the second, when partially down, gives more lift; fully down, acts as an airbrake).

Probably, the bomb-doors will be open, I carry on around the tail gun-turret to follow the same procedures on the starboard (right), side of the aircraft. I would check the tailplanes, elevators, rudder and fin for damage, on passing.

Then I and the pilot (Captain/Skipper) enter the aircraft. He takes his seat; checks his harness, instruments, and controls for full and free movement. At the same time, he engages the auto-pilot clutches. On my way up to my position, just behind him, I select four fuel tanks by pushing levers forward, located at the front of the rest position – a separate tank for each engine.

Note. This text is mainly based on the time I flew with the Main Bomber force, in Merlin-engined Halifax MkII and MkV aircraft.

I check fuel gauges for contents and all panel readings, correct. The pilot and I then start each engine in turn. From the starboard u/c bay, the ground crew prime engines with fuel so they fire and pick up smoothly. All engines are warmed to a minimum temperature, then the pilot starts his checks by switching off each magneto in turn, to ensure all are working. He then increases power and checks each propeller for constant speeding (the speed of the propellers remains constant, regardless of the aircraft's altitude). He opens the throttles and checks take-off RPM and boost; throttles back and checks each magneto for RPM drops then fully closes throttles and checks each engine's slow-running speed. The engines will be kept running a short time to cool down; then switched off. All this time, I'm checking and recording engine pressures and temperatures, noting down readings from the pilot's checks, which he tells me over the intercom. The pilot finally checks the pneumatic brakes and brake pressure.

That's about it and some of you will know that this procedure was very similar to any pre-flight inspection of a piston-engined aircraft.

So, all checks by the aircrew completed satisfactorily, we leave the aircraft, have a last smoke and chat until about fifteen minutes before take-off; then back inside. I am last; stamping my foot on the door to ensure it's safely locked, then I go forward to my position, passing the mid-upper 'Gunner, Wireless/Op, Navigator, all seated in the rest position until after T/O. Engines are started, at the set time we taxi out to join a queue to the runway. The bomb-aimer sits alongside the pilot to assist in the T/O, adjusting the throttles and RPM levers at the pilot's request. He also monitors the instrument readings. At T/O I would have closed the radiator shutters to reduce drag, and sit on my small, folding seat, watching my instruments. Once airborne, the pilot raises the undercarriage, then flaps and selects climbing power, the rest of the crew move to their own positions. Nearly forgot, as soon as I can I open the radiator shutters just enough to bring engine temperatures down to normal.

I make entries on my log-sheet; check with the Navigator the German colours of the day and load the Very pistol, located in the roof, with one of these cartridges. There were times when it seemed we were in trouble and I fired the pistol and we were left in peace. We are now on a steady climb to operational height, heading for the enemy coast. Usually, 19,500 feet is the best we can do.

So far, all I have written is, more or less, universal and routine. My official duties from now on are to enter on my log-sheet, instrument readings and the fuel state; this, every twenty minutes; to follow the selection plan schedule of fuel tank changes (the Halifax has twelve fuel tanks), and compute the fuel consumption. *'Computers in those days?''Yes – why not!'* My computer consisted of two cardboard discs, one smaller than the other, with holes through the middle of each. A rivet held them together, the small one on top of the larger one.

On one disc was graduated the engine RPM, and opposite, the altitude we're flying at. On the other the engine boost pressure and opposite, fuel consumptions for one engine. From memory, I might have got this all wrong, but you get the idea. Turn the small disc until the RPM and boost, which the engines are running at, are in line. On the opposite side, read off the fuel consumption in gallons per hour, against the altitude. Eg: turn the inner disc to line up the RPM with the boost pressure on the outer disc. Say – 2650 + 4-lb boost. On the other side, read off the fuel consumption against the altitude we're flying at. Say – 10,000 feet = 48 galls per hour. So, for twenty minutes we have used sixteen galls per engine. Multiply by 4 = 64 galls total used. Simple, isn't it and so accurate. *Why all this?* Because one could not rely on fuel gauges.

When I calculated a fuel tank was nearly empty, I would tell the skipper and go back to where the fuel cocks were. Soon, a red light would show and I'd turn off the empty tank and turn on a fresh one.

During F/E training, we went through a short Airgunners' Course. On this, we were instructed about evasive action against enemy aircraft; searchlights, and anti-aircraft fire (this was against ordinary Flak – *'Try to avoid it'*). Very early in our tour, I came to realise that I could do more to ensure our, hoped for, survival than filling in a log sheet and checking my panel. Above me was a large, clear Astro-dome of Perspex in which my shoulders fitted and I could brace myself against my instrument panel. I had a 360 degree view; in fact, I was in a similar position to that of a Tank Commander in battle. However, as the Mid-Upper in his turret was not far from me down the fuselage, we teamed up. He kept a backward and upper search pattern; I took the forward and upper search. Here, I could watch for searchlights swinging onto us and for radar, predicted flak.

Against searchlights, I would try to pick the right time to tell the pilot when to turn and cut through the beam. Carried out correctly the searchlight would continue swinging away. Not so, against the blue-beamed radar controlled searchlights. Then we would call on the W/Op (Wireless Operator), to switch on the IFF (Identification – friend or foe). More often than not, it worked – the beam would go out or move away.

Doing this was strictly against rules and, today, we're told this practice did not have any effect on these Master searchlights. All I can say is that, for us, quite a few times, it seemed to – except one. Then, we never had a chance to see it. The beam swung and locked onto us. Immediately, about thirty or so normal white beams had us in the dreaded position of being coned. What happened next I hardly knew, for I was stuck on the aircraft's roof, but I take it that the Skipper slammed the control column right forward and we went straight down and away, thankfully into the darkness. We were lucky or blessed for I have watched aircraft, like a moth, coned in sixty to a hundred beams, with flak bursting all around them. A hopeless situation!

Then there was the predicted flak; radar-controlled AA fire. I can't remember having any instructions regarding this, except by an Army Officer who told us of how little the chance of being hit was. One had to learn to recognise it – three shell bursts close together and very close. I was best positioned to recognise this and say – *Port*, or *Starboard, Go! Skipper*. Our aircraft would peel off one way or another. The rapid, next burst of flak was, probably, where we would have been.

Lastly, there were the enemy night fighters; heavily armed with machine guns and cannons. Some of these had upward firing cannons and so would stalk you, getting into position underneath and – *Bang!*

One instance of this happened came just when I was filling my log sheet. Over the intercom I heard Slim, our American Rear 'Gunners voice: '*Say, skipper, I think we've got company*'. I leapt up into the astro-dome as he said: '*It's OK, it's another Halifax*.' Now, I could see where he couldn't, the full shape of the aircraft. '*Halifax be damned, it's a 110. Port go, Skipper!*' The night fighter was below us and very close so all the Rear Gunner saw were the twin tail fins; so like the twin fins of a Halifax. We straightened out and the Messerschmitt was now below, to our starboard (right) side. Our Skipper tilted the aircraft so the Mid Upper 'Gunner could bring his guns to bear and *Ginger* blazed away, but he still couldn't depress his guns far enough down. He must have given the enemy a fright, though, for he dived away into the night. So, only I was in a position to safely identify this aircraft, but it was thanks to Slim for the initial warning. From the mid-upper turret, *Ginger* wasn't able to look down to where the enemy was first seen. Thus, the value of another pair of eyes in the astro-dome.

Many Messerschmitts were fitted with upward-firing cannon, so we were, probably, within seconds of having a ticket to Eternity. I suspect I spent at least seventy percent of my time in the astro-dome and it paid off. One good reason to be thankful was that I could continue to keep a lookout until we were back on the ground.

One night, with the second crew I flew with, we were orbiting the airfield, waiting our turn to land, when I noticed lights some way off our port wingtip. I told the Skipper who immediately recognised these were lights of another aircraft on a collision course; he went into a steep, diving turn and the other aircraft passed overhead.

There! I've gone way beyond the laid down duties of a wartime, Halifax, F/E. But now you know why I (and so many other aircrew), loved our Halifax aircraft – *Halibags* we called them. *F/Es – looking after the engines?* Well, many of us did a little more than that! [61]

SQUADRON MEMORIES
The Mess

I wonder if anyone else recalls
That wartime Sergeants Mess,
And the feeling of doom in the ante-room
Which grew as the time grew less.

Perhaps it was only I who saw
The weary and hunted look
On an airman's face which he tried to erase
With the wit in a crumpled book.

At a corner table tension eased
As a game of chess was won,
'*Check*', said a Gunner – '*That waitress's a stunner!*'
'*Checkmate – my word, she can run!*'
The black piano tinkled a tune
Then mood of the player changed
To classical theme – as heard in a dream –
Of a drama that Mozart arranged.

And last to my memory comes pencil and pad
Of a pilot sketching a face;
Intent, as he captured the features enraptured
By melody, none could debase.

Now chatter was muted and words unsaid
Were the ones that told me most;
The air now taut with a thousand thoughts
Was home to the Squadron's ghosts.

And their ranks were joined, that Summer Eve,
By the airmen now I recall
When the dice were played, on that final raid,
The '*Reaper*' – he beat them all! [62]

By Ernie Hughes
'The Welsh Poet'
'Theirs was the light in the encroaching darkness'

****

Per Ardua Ad Astra

When I was young, my uncle gave his life for me
He and others like him died to keep our country free
They were young and full of life
We much younger still
Not knowing above us in the strife

They had enemies to kill.
Whilst we ate, and played, and slept,
They a grim assignment kept
Into the skies on wings of hope
Day and night villainy to stop
Tyrants trembled to their shame
When he and all the others came
Home on Leave, they'd sweeties bring
And laugh and joke and dance and sing
We children at bedtime would say
Such fun with Uncle Len today!
They were our heroes, brave and strong,
Until the day would come along
No blue uniform at kitchen door,
A certain voice was heard no more.
Adult tears and adults sigh
Puzzled, we knew not why
Planes no longer drone all day
Time has gone and we are grey
The 'dromes have all returned to leas
The graveyard's full of buzz of bees.
Above your resting place of sod
The buttercups and daisies nod
Sleep on in peace dear Uncle Len,
For that is what you brought us then

Rosemary Bower, May 1994

The above poem was written and dedicated to Rosemary's Uncle: F/O L. A. Barham of 199 Squadron, killed when his Stirling crashed at Edgefield Street, Norfolk, returning from ops on 25 September 1944 (a few miles from his home).

CHAPTER 16
Arthur Pigott, FRTS:
One Final Story

This final story offers a different perspective to those which have gone before, with a unique insight into the world of subterfuge. It begins with a letter:

Dear Janine,

... I am certain I do not qualify for a mention in the proposed publication and I seek no glorification from my Service in World War Two.

I was Ground Crew, having been rejected for Air Crew on the grounds of ENT (Ear, Nose, Throat), but trained as a Wireless Operator Mechanic. By some fluke I became a 'specialist' in radio and radar equipment and, being young at the time, volunteered for anything just for the excitement. My civilian occupation was that of a Compositer (type-setter in hot metal printing, no longer used).

Whenever a RAF bomber was shot down but remained intact, the Germans would thoroughly inspect all its equipment and, if need be, devise an 'Anti-Device'. We would devise improved versions. These were originally tested on Operations by the designer Boffin; if that aircraft was shot down, we lost a Boffin too. Hence, Operational Testing was passed onto 'Other Ranks', we were more dispensable.

I was overseas at the time. There were very few Wireless Mechanics in the RAF who could receive and send Morse Code. On five occasions I was sent for by my Signals Officer and told that a volunteer was required by Bomber Command for a Special Operator; since I was qualified for that task, would I volunteer? It was an urgent matter. Being fearless, I could only say: 'Yes'. I was flown to RAF Northolt, taken to a Manufacturer for familiarisation and Briefing; then flown to a Bomber Squadron for the Special Operation.

Plessey and Boffin Bob Roberts can easily be recalled. From memory, the aircraft was always a modified Halifax which comfortably took *'aircrew member No. 8'* on board. The Operation was more difficult because *'results'* were written in a form of code in case of capture, but I doubt if I would have withstood any torture without spilling the beans.

On return, after de-briefing and a sleep, I was whisked back overseas to await the next *'Special Operation'*.

Since I was only an LAC (Leading Aircraftsman) and the minimum aircrew rank was Sergeant, I *'borrowed'* a Sergeant's jacket for the flight out and back and actually received that rank's pay (just the two days involved). What generosity!

On the very first Special Operation, I was sworn to secrecy even hearing the words *'under sentence of death'* for any disclosure of operations, place names, equipment used, people involved, dates, etc. This put great fear in me and I can remember hiding my personal camera and never using it again out of sheer fear.

Whenever I arrived on a Norfolk RAF Station, I was always *'Confined to Barracks'* with visits so brief I never even knew the Station's name or even the Squadron No. of the aircraft I was flying in; with one exception – *'Little Snoring'*. It is from where we flew and came back to on my last trip. There were no 'signposts' around to give me a clue as to where I was anyway.

At that time, if it was ever mentioned, 100 Group meant nothing to me.

Although being Ground Crew, I did do an awful lot of flying: testing equipment, especially on Air Tests whilst on RAF Transport Command.

On Repatriation, I was posted to RAF Uxbridge where I was *'attached'* to many operations:

- High Speed Flight at RAF Tangmere where Group Captain Donaldson and Squadron Leader Townsend reached the fastest speed of 470 mph in the jet-engined Meteor,

- Air Ministry, London, to install the *'Direction Finding Beam'* from Air Ministry roof for the very first Flypast, which was a long one,
- Ending up at RAF Duxford on No. 91 Squadron, equipped with Meteor aircraft.

I was de-mobbed in January 1947 only to find myself still an Apprenticed Compositor and having to serve out my time, aged twenty-four.

All this sounds like a Fairy Tale, but the memories are still as vivid now as the events some seventy odd years ago. Having survived whilst some of my school mates did not, I still think it was the best time of my life. I still attend Whitehall on *'Remembrance Sunday'* to lay crosses in memory of my mates who did not return.

The following extracts are from Arthur's autobiographical writings which he shares on the understanding that they do not in any way contravene the Official Secrets Act he signed. He gives nothing away of exactly what he was expected to do, and yet, his writings show immense courage and fortitude ... and a gentle humble manner. It is as if he is saying: *'I was just doing my job!'* Yet at the same time, they illustrate he had exceptional skills and was very experienced and knowledgeable, despite his young age.

LAC Arthur W Pigott 1397335, Wireless Operator Mechanic Transport Command, Fighter Command, Bomber Command, Special Operations

At the age of seventeen, way back in 1939, I joined No. 41 (Deptford) Squadron of the Air Training Corps. The ATC did have its own monthly magazine, the *'ATC Gazette'*. World War Two started and I received my 'Call-Up' and 'Medical Papers' prior to joining the Royal Air Force hopefully to become aircrew.

I remember the day of my Medical very clearly. I made my way to Euston House (then War Department) in London by tran-car, travelling via the 'Kingsway' (under-tunnel) from the Thames Embankment to Holborn. The train halted almost outside the Medical Centre.

Why do I remember this so clearly?

On the tram journey, I read an article in the '*ATC Gazette*' on '*Radio*', in which it gave several definitions of wireless components. One of these was for a condenser: '*Condenser – consists of two parallel plates, separated by a dielectric, used for the storage of electricity*'.

As any ex-Service person will recall, a Service Medical is thorough: heart, lungs, feet, *cough!* eyes and ears. It was during my hearing examination that it was discovered I suffered from perforated ear-drums – hence I would not be selected for aircrew. The letters E.N.T. (Ear, Nose and Throat) were stamped over all my documentation – it meant I was destined for ground staff duties only.

During subsequent interviews, to decide which ground staff trade I was to be employed whilst in the RAF, the questioning went something like this:

RAF	'*What is your employment?*'
AP	'*An apprenticed compositor.*'
RAF	'*There's no print-shop in the RAF. Can you drive?*'
AP	'*No.*'
RAF	'*What do you know about radio?*'
AP	'*Nothing much.*'
RAF	'*What is a Condenser?*'

AP   '*A Condenser consists of two parallel plates, separated by a dielectric, and used for the storage of electricity.*'

RAF   '*That's right. Good – I'll put you down for the Group I Trade of Wireless Mechanic.*'

I was disappointed at not being fit enough for aircrew although most of my colleagues and friends who did become pilot, navigators or air-gunners did not survive the war, so I was really fortunate in that respect. But reading that definition and being able to quote it word for word changed my whole life!

I spent a year training to become a Wireless Mechanic, first at Glasgow Technical College (Fundamentals), then at Glasgow University (Radio Theory); I was then posted to the Technical College, Bolton, for familiarisation of RAF ground and aircraft wireless equipment. We had tough examinations every six weeks; the mark of my first exam was 37% with the letters C.T on top of my paper meaning: 'Cease Training'. My tutor, a Dr Jameson, asked if I wanted another chance, so I continued. Subsequent results: 53%, 75%, and in the final exam: 97% with the option of becoming either a Radar or Wireless Mechanic. I felt Radar was rather specialist and thought Wireless more useful if I ever made 'Civvy Street'. Gaining my 'Sparks' I still consider my greatest achievement!

So I'm glad that a condenser consists of two parallel plates, separated by a dielectric, used for the storage of electricity!

Special Operations Duties, S.O.Ds

During World War Two, in order to gain first-hand information, it was vital for the British to have 'Intelligence Agents' on German territory. Immense help was given by the few brave 'Resistance' fighters, who in turn had to be supplied with weapons, equipment and money to maintain their activities.

Britain had its network of Intelligence and a team of spies. This branch of Intelligence was co-ordinated by MI5 and the War Department with its own Section called the 'Special Operations Executive' (SOE) which meticulously vetted and picked personnel for this vital and dangerous intelligence work.

Agents were infiltrated into Germany by all three Services: the Royal Navy, Royal Air Force, and British Army. Routes chosen were varied – by sea, including the use of submarines; by air, either landing or dropping by parachute; or travelling by overland using some form of transport, or on foot with false documents.

Radio played an important part of Intelligence operations. Codes were used; radio transmissions could be intercepted, but also traced with pin-point accuracy. Many agents were caught by the Germans, interrogated usually by torture, and hence some SOE activities became known by the Germans. Confiscated equipment and its codes, etc were then used to carry on the subterfuge by Germans themselves and we were never 100% certain of such deception.

From time to time, the British were compelled to check up on its SOE operations by sending out additional Intelligence personnel. Equipment-wise throughout the war, new devices were continually developed which needed testing under operational conditions. Even these new devices found themselves in German hands who then developed 'counter-devices' to render ours inoperative in the field. Once this was known, we would develop 'counter-counter measure' devices and so it went on until completely new techniques had to be sought.

This account is about one particular operation in which I participated, with none of the technicalities involved being disclosed.

It was in the early Spring of 1945. The Allied invasion of Europe was well underway and being stubbornly resisted by the Germans all along the Front. The Americans, from time to time, requested assistance from the British, especially when they discovered British equipment in German hands and difficulty was encountered in its operation. The American advance, near Frankfurt (USA 9th Army) was such an occasion, but before continuing, I must offer the reader my background to this episode.

I was one of only seven Wireless Operator Mechanics (WOMs) in the Royal Air Force at this time; our training lasting far longer than that of aircrew. We were specialists in the operation and maintenance of all RAF radio equipment, except RADAR which was an RAF Trade in itself. Radio equipment consisted of a variety of transmitters, aerial arrays, receivers, power-supplies, etc, and included equipment used in both aircraft and ground Stations. Concerning aircraft equipment, there was constant development of new devices, mainly in the area of accurate direction and location-finding. Initially, War Office Boffins flew when testing out their designs and modifications, but alas some Boffins were lost and killed when aircraft were shot down; one of our great Boffins, Bleufield, was one of them. Then it became War Department Policy to employ RAF ground personnel to test under operational conditions. Again, Germans would discover such equipment in crashed shot-down aircraft, and produce 'counter-measures', hence any advances made were soon counter-manded and made redundant.

Very early one morning, on an RAF No. 101 Staging Post in Lydda, Palestine, I was awakened and instructed to report to the Orderly Room immediately, to be greeted by the Signals Officer who informed me that a WOM was urgently required to volunteer for an SOD (Special Operations Duty) somewhere in Germany. Being the only WOM on the Station, I was expected to 'volunteer', which I did as on many other occasions before. Within the hour, I was receiving VIP treatment, on my way flying to Cairo West for another aircraft to whisk me off to Rome, then to Germany. Before the second take-up, being an LAC, I was kitted out with a Flight Sergeant Air Gunner's uniform (which seemed to fit). This procedure was to confuse the enemy in the event of capture and ease conditions in the case of captivity. A holster, a revolver and ten rounds of ammunition were handed to me ... on my remark that I'd never used one before, I was given a very brief run-through on how to load the barrel, the impor-tance of the 'safety-catch', and how to aim and fire with the trigger; never thinking I would ever have to use the weapon.

Before take-off, a sealed packet was handed to me and I was asked to study it carefully and remember its contents as it was unlikely I would receive another Briefing on landing. As usual, on SOD Briefings, there was no note-taking; all instructions and details had to be committed to memory. The information given was rarely complete, always there was some other instruction to be given by an unknown person later. Handing back my 'Brief', I eventually made my way to a twin-engine aircraft, I believe a Lockheed Hudson. The flight over the 'Med' was pleasant, like going on holiday. I was advised to load my issued revolver, just in case! We finally lobbed down on a grass strip, somewhere in Germany, in the American zone of opera-tions somewhere near Frankfurt. As soon as I was out of the aircraft, it revved up and took off, leaving me alone, expecting to be met by some welcoming Yanks and given further instructions and some 'comforts'.

But there was not a soul in sight.

I heard gun fire in the distance, presumably the 'Front'. It occurred to me to make for nearby hedgerow and, as it turned out, I had arrived in the middle of a small German counter-attack.

Not long after I arrived at the hedgerow I was suddenly physically assaulted by a young German soldier, possibly sixteen years old. He charged, holding a fixed-bayonet, and at close quarters, thrust it towards my stomach. The whole incident happened incredibly quickly and unexpectedly. Instinctively, I went for the loaded revolver, automatically releasing the 'catch', aimed it at my attacker and fired once, but not before the blade of the bayonet thrust right through the twin bones of my left arm. Although the bayonet had been destined for my guts, it had gone through my left arm, probably saving my life. I fell to the ground with my assailant, killed with the one-shot. I cannot remember much pain, just a shocked numbness, of being deafened, bewilderment, being in a helpless motionless heap with another person, not knowing what was happening ... I seemed unable to move and must have remained on the ground bleeding for some time for there was plenty of blood on the pair of us. I never did discover whether or not the German rifle was loaded (*perhaps there was a shortage of bullets, hence the bayonet attack*). Then I heard American voices ... '*the Yanks were here!*' I remember the utter relief at seeing my rescuers, who disentangled me from the dead companion beside me.

'*Hang on, buddy, I'll pull it out for you.*'

I remember the strong tug, but must have passed out ... I came round looking into the eyes of who then was the most beautiful female nurse in the whole wide world. There was pain, or a rather big hurt; I was lying in an American field hospital; had been attended to, cleaned up and bandaged without knowing anything about it. Next day, I got a glimpse of the hole right through my left arm. It looked a mess! But I was assured, luck was on my side and I would make a full recovery. My left hand showed no signs of movement though, but again was assured that, after therapy, I would gain full use again. Being a compositor, the left hand holds the '*composing stick*'; this would be the end of my career. After a few days, I was posted and flown back to Egypt to recover; the healing process was swift, too swift, therapy seemed more painful than the wounding; but the long rest was enjoyable and I considered myself very lucky indeed.

However, I didn't complete my Special Operations Duty, so will never know what resulted in it not being carried through. I wonder how important these escapades were and if the risks were warranted. Servicemen were expendable. There were always others to carry on. There was no 'counselling' in those days; if aircrew refused to continue to fly on missions because of genuine trauma, fright and mental fatigue, they were considered cowards. I remember full parades being called, in which these brave sick men, who would now be considered 'sick', were on the parade ground, humiliated in front of comrades ... being 'de-ranked', having aircraft flying badges and tunic buttons torn from their uniforms.

Within just five weeks, I was posted back to my Staging Post Unit serving in Paiforce, RAF Transport Command, Palestine, where Britain was preparing to transfer troops to the Far East to assist the Americans. After the European ceasefire was declared in 1945, Palestine was a bloodier place to be than some war postings in Germany. This time, we British servicemen were confronting the Jewish nation, especially the Stern Gang in their endeavour to illegally take over that country for themselves. It was to become my most dangerous assignment.

I am now an ex-airman (an ex-serviceman) with a war wound and two large nasty scars, one on each side of my left forearm to prove it. An airman who was bayoneted in World War Two, and survived. There cannot be many RAF personnel in this category. On being de-mobbed and having been engaged in Special Operations Duties, I had to sign a 'Secrecies' document that I would not disclose or communicate in any form, any information concerning SOE activities, purposes, give names of other personnel, equipment, documents seen, instructions given ... and so it went on ... until thirty years after my de-mobilisation. The penalty was either death or long-term prison sentences, so I never did. Then, to the very day, thirty years later, I received a letter from the Ministry of Defence stating that from then on, I could, if I wished, speak or write about my experiences. This is my first attempt in so doing. But why all the fuss?

A footnote on pay.

My rank was that of Leading Aircraftsman, Grade One (LAC) – badges were: 'props' and 'sparks', but whenever being detailed (volunteering) for SODs, especially if it involved operational flying missions; I was always temporarily promoted to Sergeant (lowest rank for aircrew) and received that pay for the period I donned the stripes, then reverted back to normal LAC pay ... mean, I call it! For instance, testing radio equipment on a flying mission, I'd receive a Sergeant's pay for day/night of the outward journey and for the next morning/ day when the return journey was made, normal LAC's pay would resume immediately the day after the operation. This arrangement was not a permanent promotion, but considered necessary in the event of capture. Although my injury was sustained on European soil, I was transferred to Egypt to make a full recovery, and 'Accounts' should have been informed of such a transfer, but were not, so on 'sick' Pay Parades I received the higher amount. What a lucky bastard, I then thought! But alas, the War Office had other ideas and, realising their mistake, I had future pay 'docked' until the excess had been repaid ... unlucky bastard!

I was not considered 'fit' for Aircrew because of bad hearing at the time of my Medical when joining the Royal Air Force. Yet, when it was considered that work carried out by 'Boffins' and their loss on operations could not be justified, 'operational testing' was assigned to 'other ranks', suitably qualified, since we were expendable. Which is the reason I experienced so much operational flying over Germany (called 'Special Operations Duties') ... and survived. 'Lucky Piggy' became my nickname amongst aircrews with whom I flew. But they were the real heroes. Nowadays they would be referred to as 'volunteer suicide bombers'; their survival chances: 3:1).

'Lucky Piggy'

The purpose of one particular mission was the setting up of and the transmitting and receiving of ground equipment of the improved Mark IV 'Oboe' (known as by code name) target plotting system that was useful but not necessarily a successful system when used over Germany, although we were not informed of this at the time. This target location system was to be extended to Burma eventually. To give purpose to the dangers that might be encountered, the dropping of leaflets was given. Originally four aircraft were assigned, but only three serviceable aircraft were able to take off. Crews were not acquainted with the area to be flown and only limited practice runs were undertaken, although ground stations and aircraft systems were extensively tested in operations Lydda and Haifa Med. sea areas.

Before take off, all aircraft were prepared, including guns loaded and leaflets loaded in specially designed containers to assist in the coverage of large ground areas when they were released from bomb-bay, in separated batches.

Crew consisted of Skipper (pilot), Co-Pilot, Flight Engineer, Navigator (and RADAR), Wireless Operator (Gunner), Observer-Bomb Aimer, Rear-Gunner, and myself who was assisting the W/Op and Navigator and recording the detailed performance of 'Oboe'.

After take off, it was an uneventful flight over a semi-moonlit sea up to Greece, without any problems and with equipment behaving perfectly. We were using a system of three co-ordinates, which proved extremely accurate. There was no opposition and the limited targets were located and leaflets dropped. After which we turned for base, slightly surprised and relieved, thus far, but inwardly, perhaps, a little disappointed (with nothing to report).

However, about forty-five minutes into the return journey, the Engineer reported one engine was showing signs of problems. The starboard outer engine eventually caught fire but was extinguished; much relief; but the fire re-started. By this time we were approaching the 'Haifa' zone and Skipper announced over the intercom that we might have to abandon aircraft and should put on and fasten our chute belts and prepare ourselves accordingly. There was no panic but the engine was still on fire and we were losing height slightly. Then over the intercom came 'Piggy, you are number one out'. Since the rear underbelly door was already open, I naturally assumed it was a command and grabbed the dinghy 'tether' and jumped out with the dinghy following after me. You count six, pull your ripcord and wait anxiously until you feel the parachute opening, then begin to 'enjoy' the trip down!

It didn't seem long after that I hit the water, without injury. I cannot remember hearing the dinghy strike water, but it did, and on doing so automatically inflated and was upright when I eventually pulled on the tether either floating towards it or pulling it towards me (which I doubt). After struggling into the dinghy feeling very wet and uncomfortable, at least I was floating and not immersed in the sea. Looking around for my companions I saw nobody, but heard the aircraft fading away into the distance. Hoping my colleagues would still be okay, I settled down to drift, who knows where, in the Mediterranean somewhere off the coast of Palestine knowing full well that assistance in the form of a motor launch would eventually be sent to rescue me. (When falling from a height, even if you failed to pull the rip cord, the parachute will automatically open at 2,000 feet.)

A high-speed launch was sent from Haifa, in Palestine, to search for me after the dinghy beacon had been switched on by me soon after entering, which was also reassuring. It felt safe, since these dinghies held four people, there was plenty of room; but being wet was very uncomfortable, my legs stretched out and in sea water. I tried to enjoy the experience, but remember being very annoyed at the situation that had developed; it was just a question of being patient and waiting for assistance, by this time dawn had broken and it was getting light.

After being picked up, I was landed at Port Haifa, then taken by road to RAF Haifa where I was 'debriefed' and two days later returned to RAF Lydda by a Dakota where I joined my unit. Shortly after this incident, I was told to report to HQ to see the CO. Thinking a Court Martial was upon me, I was surprised to get the sympathy of Groupie and to my amazement, he handed me a silk parachute panel as a souvenir of my 'adventure' as he put it.

(Information concerning 'Gee' and 'Oboe': the Ground Stations involved were El Hag (Cairo West); Ramleh (Palestine) and Nicosia (Cyprus) we were later to learn. They had obviously been effectively sited.)

As a footnote to this little episode, on entering the dinghy I had the presence of mind to use the paddle to reach the parachute still float-ing in the sea nearby, picking it up and pulling it in with me. I'm glad I did. It is tradition that a parachute is only used once in saving a life; it was made of silk; and one of the panels is cut out and presented to the survivor. I still possess this panel of silk which I come across in the house from time to time; it should be preserved as a permanent souvenir. I must try and find it again.

Needless to say, shamefully for me, the Liberator was not abandoned, but got back to base unharmed, with just an unserviceable engine and one member of crew missing. I remain uncertain whether the Skipper was playing a joke on me, because, having such a large number of operational flying hours to my credit, all crews I flew with on SODs always considered me as and called me 'Lucky Piggy'.

THE DRESDEN RAID
Air Ministry Briefing

Request by the Russians to seriously dislocate German transport communications, especially marshalling yards near the Eastern Front.

Special Operations Mission

Independent of the main scheduled bombing raid on Dresden by Bomber Command, another operation was initiated to test, operationally, **Impact Point (IP)** equipment being developed for the war in the Far East. Such equipment were designed to re-transmit directional location signal beams from directions received from ground stations in the UK, thus vastly extending its range. Extreme accuracy was the criteria.

A minimum of two aircraft were required, to be converted with the necessary equipment to receive and then re-transmit radar/radio signals to their cross-over points. To test this over Germany was a high-risk strategy and very dangerous operation, especially at a height of 20,000+ feet. German radar detection could be anticipated both in the reception and transmission modes, but it was considered a reasonable hazard for the experience and verification to be gained from it.

Requirement demands of the RAF were to provide aircraft for the installation of this new array of equipment and to familiarise and train

RAF personnel to operate, evaluate and assess effectiveness and efficiency under operational conditions. In addition to any recommendation for modification and improvements if found necessary.

Aircraft used: two modified and super-powered HALIFAX bomber aircraft.

Personnel used:

RAF *'volunteered'* specially-trained Wireless Operator Mechanics, possibly there were Radar Mechanics among them too. The Boffins couldn't be risked in such an operation; if they were shot down, a boffin was lost too. (*Ref:* A. L. BLUMLEIN who was shot down (*classified as an accident*) and killed in 1942 in such an operation, being a great loss to the nation's counter-operations. Note: The Germans possessed a superior skill in RADAR beam operations to the Allies.)

Date: 13–14 February 1945

Operation: Codename *'Thunderclap'* but a Special Operation Duty (SOD).

Station: RAF Little Snoring, Norfolk; ETD 21.15 hours; IP midnight+; ETA 07.20 hours (nine hours).

Halifax crew:

Pilot, second Pilot, Flight-Engineer, Wireless Operator, Front Gunner, Rear-Gunner, Mid-Gunner, no Bomb-Aimer, but a *'number eight'* Operator ... *me!* (The Air Ministry had suggested all armoury be stripped (ie no Gunners required) and the weight saved be utilised for additional equipment. But the Pilot and other crew objected to this and Gunners were retained, mainly for psychological reasons, I guess).

Height: zig-zag 20,000 feet. The flying flight pattern was no concern of mine.

??? 100 Group: No. 138 Squadron; modified Halifax bomber, AWP a number 'eight' crew member, but could have been No. 161 Squadron. (Note: probably not 138 or 161 Squadrons as it was an SOD mission.)

Other aircraft were used, but what and from which bases is not known to me.

Some background:

Heavy and clumsy valve equipment; R.F. carriers; analogue, pulse-modulated; experimental loop and rotating aerials, some fixed, some hand controlled. Plus Radar equipment.

Familiarisation and operational instruction:

Took place in an undisclosed venue near Hatfield, although I did hear the name PLESSEY mentioned, but cannot fit into what context. Modifications were being carried out even at this stage.

The Mission:

I flew up from RAF Northolt to RAF Little Snoring where I met the aircrew and saw the installed aircraft equipment, spending one day on further familiarisation with only one short Air-Test a day before the operation. It was here that I was fitted with a temporary Sergeant's uniform to conform with flying rank conditions. Meals were good, but on advice, laid off the drinking fluid.

Boarding and take-off seemed routine and for me the outward flight was uneventful; we were not in the mainstream. Dresden was well alight on arrival, which was seven minutes later than ETA, still at 20,000 feet. All the prescribed operational procedures were carried out and diagnostic results recorded, using pre-arranged coded language in case of falling into the hands of the enemy. Instructions were to destroy such in the event of a forced landing (I was later informed by other crew members they had instructions to shoot me in such circumstances!). We wore 'Mae West' life jackets, although no-one thought we would endure the cold North Sea very long at that time of year should we have to ditch.

Crew safety was paramount, but since there were no barrage balloons over the city, Skipper decided to stay and circle over the venue, going down to 5,000 – 6,000 feet. We seemed to stay for a very long time to the extent of feeling the heat from the blazing city.

Much apprehension was apparent on the return flight at 20,000 feet (which is bloody cold at that height!); further beams had been planned south of the Frankfurt area and the crew anticipated German fighter problems during such trials. Alertness was the keyword by all members aboard. Some evasive actions and the skill and alertness of all crew members allowed us to survive the incidents.

For me as a 'number eight', I thought the return trip uneventful in spite of the many dangers of being easily located due to tell-tale Radar pick-up of our several beam receptions. It was still dark when we flew over the Wash, landing unharmed back at Little Snoring. On reflection, I cannot remember any fear whilst flying over Germany … there were many other things on my mind. But I was not doing this sort of activity regularly. However, we all felt tired and slept well after a lengthy de-briefing. Having to make out a thorough report of the equipment in action came several hours later … two tots of rum made all the difference to my sleep pattern!

Footnote:

This was considered the most infamous bombing raid by most post-war commentators. Bomber Command sent two waves of bombers three hours apart to attack Dresden on the night of 13/14 February 1945. The first wave consisted of 244 Lancasters from No. 5 Group; this raid was hampered by cloud but considered a success. The second wave comprised 500 plus of bombers that dropped a further 1,800 tons of bombs in clear weather. There were six Lancaster losses which was light for such a long-distance raid. Dresden was devastated and as the city's population had been increased by an influx of refugees, there was a heavy loss of life mainly women and children. On 14 February it was again blasted by the 311 USAAF B-17s which added to the devastation and confusion.

The RAF and Bomber Command and UK Boffins were extremely active in their efforts to originate accurate bomb-aiming impact positioning; much time, energy and expense went into the work. The higher the dropping point the less dangerous it was and it certainly helped in cloudy weather experienced over the Continent. To accurately hit the target blind was the real goal. To my knowledge and understanding, the Allies never successfully achieved this goal and it seemed the Germans were always a little ahead of us.

It is a great pity that Bomber Command was never considered worthy by any British Government of being awarded its own medal like many other spheres of War Service organisations; Bomber Command only carried out the wishes and aims of its Government.

Biographical

From his writings, it is obvious that Arthur Pigott was no ordinary man and from humble beginnings achieved great things. One man *can* and *did* make a difference!

I was born Arthur William Pigott on 25 June 1922 in Deptford, South East London. An Elementary schoolboy, I was voluntarily coached Algebra by one of the teachers. Leaving school at fourteen, I became a seven-year Apprentice in hot-metal printing as a Compositor. This was interrupted by World War Two, with four and a half years Service in the Royal Air Force as a Wireless Operator Mechanic (*one of only seven in the RAF*) with three years Service overseas. (Whenever an aircraft was shot down intact, the Germans would clamber all over it to find its secrets and then design '*anti-devices*'; we would improve our devices which had to be operationally tested; originally this was done by a '*Boffin*', but if he was shot down we lost him too. So all operational testing was transferred to Ground Crew.) Since I was a Specialist, I was asked to '*volunteer*' five times for Special Operations. Comment: German '*flak*' was extremely powerful and accurate. I made two parachute jumps, one into the sea!

Just two weeks before being de-mobilised, I was called into the CO's Office at RAF Duxford with the express purpose of the RAF getting me to sign on for another nine years. I was even given the bribe of being promoted to Sergeant, almost with immediate effect. Alas, I was unable to accept because, in Civvy Street, I was still an Apprentice (at the age of twenty-four) and had to return to complete it.

At that age, I had become a man with the strength and realisation that a promised 'promotion' was an attempt for me to say: 'Yes please!' Instead, I remarked: 'Thanks for the opportunity. I have spent over four and a half years in the Royal Air Force, perhaps the offer could have been made sooner. Now, because of my Apprenticeship commitment, I have to refuse' ... to their amazement! I often had thoughts of how wonderful it would be to work up from the Ranks to become a Signal's Master Warrant Officer in a RAF Group, with a trade too. But the epilogue to this is that, on my ninetieth birthday, my eldest daughter acquired a recent over-sized RAF great coat with a 'Master Warrant Officer' badge sewn on each sleeve. Not that I will ever be able to wear it, but what a lovely gift which is much appreciated, and is often touched! It possesses shiney brass buttons ...

After I was de-mobbed in 1947, I discovered that I was still an Apprentice and had to complete my time, earning little money. All my girlfriends had to treat me, which to my surprise, they did!

I've had a varied career: Compositor, Proof Reader, Typographer; was Composing Manager for 'Picture Post'. I became a printing teacher, then switched to film and television teaching at 'Degree Level' (not bad for an Elementary schoolboy!). By joining the Royal Television Society it found me at 'Mecca' (BBC Television Centre, alas no more). I retired in 1986, having left school at fourteen (fifty-one years working), so have been retired for some twenty-seven years. Thatcher prevented me from continuing teaching! I have kept abreast of the industry, although I consider myself an 'Analogue' person, I have little respect for 'digital' techniques but have never allowed myself to be exploited and become a 'DPI' (Digital Product Idiot; the idiot part is allowing oneself to be exploited) hence I do not possess any gadgets ... I would dispose of the telephone, but my family implore me to retain it. In 2000 I was awarded a 'Television BAFTA' for twenty-five years in television...

CHAPTER 17
Updates:
How to claim and get involved

Bomber Command Memorial
Green Park, London, UK

With no national Memorial in existence anywhere to those who served on Bomber Command, particularly those who lost their lives on operations or as ground crew, from the outset this Memorial in a London Park attracted enormous interest amongst veterans worldwide. Finally, tens of years after the war, there would be a permanent reminder of lives lost, somewhere for families to lay a wreath on Remembrance Day, to commemorate those with no known grave.

The Monument was promoted by the Bomber Command Association with assistance from the Royal Air Force and the Heritage Foundation. Singer Robin Gibb spearheaded the campaign to raise funds, and in April 2011 it was announced the £5.6 million needed had been raised and the foundation stone laid on 4 May 2011.

Westminster Council gave permission for an open style pavilion at the Picadilly entrance to Green Park to house the Memorial, commemorating 55,573 crew of Bomber Command, with an average age of twenty-two, killed in World War Two.

The Memorial was designed by architect Liam O'Connor, also responsible for the design and construction of the Commonwealth Memorial Gates on Constitution Hill near Buckingham Palace.

While the roof of the 8.5 metres-tall pavilion was made from Portland Stone, open to the sky, the open entrance came from melted down aluminium sections of a Halifax bomber shot down during the war in which all seven of the crew died. The Memorial contains inscriptions, carvings and a dedication.

Sculptor Philip Jackson, best known for his statues of Queen Elizabeth, the Queen Mother in The Mall and Bobby Moore at Wembley Stadium; was commissioned to produce a large bronze structure standing within the Memorial. It consists of seven figures nine-feet tall, representing the aircrew of a Bomber Command heavy bomber.

The grand unveiling took place at a Ceremony including Royalty, Government representatives, dignatories and Armed Forces together with veterans from home and abroad. They gathered at Green Park on 28 June 2012 to see it dedicated and unveiled by Queen Elizabeth II; truly proud to be part of something they waited for so long.

For The Fallen

Sightless now, once watchful eyes,
Blank or shuttered to stormy skies;
Through shattered glass and twisted frames
The keening winds proclaim the names
Of those – or so they said,
Were members of the living dead.
For many, true, their time short leased
Death prevailed and living ceased.

Some still come, we that remain,
To pause, and live those times again.
To linger and to wonder why,
We should live whilst others died.
A lot of luck, no doubt of that,
Your number taken from a hat?
A raffle for the Devil's hod,
Or was it by the Grace of God? [63]

****

Canadian Bomber Command Clasp

Canada many years ago, decided to commemorate their veterans with no known grave by giving their names to previously un-named Canadian creeks. There is today *'Fisher Creek'* named after Jack Fisher, the Canadian pilot who flew his final fateful operation with my mother's fiancé Navigator/Special Operator Vic Vinnell in Mosquito DK292. Both were lost on 26/27 November 1944.

A special Bar has also now been created for Canadian Bomber Command veterans to wear on the ribbon of the Canadian Volunteer Service Medal (CVSM). It follows the unveiling of the Bomber Command Memorial in Green Park, London, on 28 June 2012.

Jim Fawcett, was one of forty-two Canadian veterans of Bomber Command who attended the London ceremony. *'A little late, but better than never!'* Nearly 50,000 members of the Royal Canadian Air Force served in Bomber Command operations, many in the only non-British group in Bomber Command – the RCAF Squadrons of No. 6 Bomber Group. At the end of the war, medals and honours were awarded to veterans, but no special recognition was ever given to those involved in the perilous operations of the many Squadrons which served under Bomber Command, including those of RAF No. 100 (BS) Group.

Jerry Dennison in Canada is delighted to finally have something which personally recognises the sacrifice made by his brother Billy and so many others who paid the ultimate price. The Bar is burnished silver with the dorsal view of a four-engine bomber.

Bomber Command veterans or their families may contact Veterans Affairs, Canada, online for further information about the Bar and how to apply at www.veterans.gc.ca or by calling the *'Honours and Awards Department'* on 1-877 995 5003.

****

Bomber Command Clasp

In 2012, British Prime Minister asked Sir John Holmes (former senior diplomat) to undertake a review into several medal controversies which had been allowed to run on for many years. He concluded that airmen of Bomber

Command had been treated inconsistently with pilots of Fighter Command who had been awarded the Battle of Britain clasp. A clasp was deemed appropriate as aircrew had already been awarded the Aircrew Europe Star or the France and Germany Star. A Bomber Command medal would have meant *'double medalling'* for the same service.

There was much grumbling amongst those who flew operationally after D-Day, denied the Aircrew Europe Star, which many regarded as the only Bomber Command medal but was actually awarded to all aircrew who flew operationally from British bases – Fighter, Coastal, Bomber regardless of whether they were under RAF No. 100 (Bomber Support) Group; and to those who fought in France before its fall in 1940.

The requirement for the Bomber Command Clasp is one operation, the same as for the Battle of Britain clasp. It is available by sending an SAE for an application form to: Vivienne Hammer, Registrar, Bomber Command Association, RAF Museum, Grahame Parkway, Hendon, London NW9 5LL, 020 8358 4841.

In response to an enquiry, a form is sent out asking for supporting documents e.g. copy of a Log Book, preferably identifying the Unit with which you flew. Anyone wishing to gain the clasp on behalf of a relative who served in RAF 100 Group under Bomber Command through the war should make this plain from the outset to the Bomber Command Association when applying for the form.

****

Ely Cathedral Dedication Window

On Sunday 6 November 1955, Memorial Books Nos. 2, 3, 8 and 100 Groups were laid in Ely Cathedral below a stained glass dedicated to the memory of those who served in those Groups during the years 1939-1945. It is here that RAF No. 100 (BS) Group are actually mentioned.

There was already a Memorial Window and Books of 1 and 5 Groups in Lincoln Cathedral, while Memorial Books and Astronomical Clock in York Minster commemorate those who gave their lives flying in Nos. 4, 6 and 7 Groups from that area. All were to serve as a reminder of our great heritage and become an inspiration for the future.

The ceremony at Ely Cathedral was held with all the pageantry of Church and State, with the Memorial Books – made of exquisite craftsmanship, bound in Morocco leather of Air Force Blue containing 19,000 aircrew lost in operational missions during the war – laid in a special cabinet. At the same time, a Memorial Window was unveiled by Air Vice Marshall A. Mckee CB, CBE, DSO, DFC, AFC.

The stained-glass window of four panels installed in the North Choir Aisle, shows an aircrew member in flying clothes above the Badge of No. 2 Group. To the left is the Archangel Michael above the badge of No. 3 Group. The centre light portrays St George and the Dragon above the badge of No. 8 Group, incorporating the Lion of St Marks, Patron Saint of the Royal New Zealand Air Force. Finally, the right-hand light shows an airman above the badge of No. 100 Group. At the bottom of each light are scenes of Wellington Bombers during different phases of an operational bombing sortie and the wording:

In honour and memory of the members of Nos. 2, 3, 8 and 100 Groups who served in the Ely district during the Second World War, 1939-1945.

The choice of Ely was because it was from Stations around Ely that Squadrons of these Groups flew out against the enemy. To them, the towers of the beautiful Cathedral Church became a familiar and homely landmark, as if welcoming them 'Home'.

****

North Creake Control Tower

Nigel Morter and Claire Nugent moved into North Creake Control Tower in October 2011 – as passionate about its history as they were about its architecture. Their aim was to restore the exterior with its bold modernist lines to become an authentic Control Tower again, while renovating the interior into a comfortable 1940s home and bed and breakfast.

Over time, they stripped away clutter around the Tower – cedar shingles on the upper half; a shallow pitch roof addition; outbuildings and structures that surrounded it, taking great pains to preserve its heritage. It now stands proud against the landscape with its commanding position overlooking the remains of the airfield.

Guests can now stay in one of their two B&B rooms the former Signal Room or Controllers Rest room both with art deco en suites or enjoy an evening sitting by the fire in the old Meteorological Office soaking up the atmosphere of days gone by.

They are piecing together history of the Tower and airfield from its construction to present day and will, for the future, house a small permanent exhibition about North Creake airfield in the old Speech Broadcast Building at the bottom of their garden so that visitors can discover just how important this site was and understand what happened in this sleepy corner of North Norfolk.

We've already had some wonderful events and discoveries regarding the history of North Creake Airfield, not least meeting several veterans who have shared their experiences with us. One in particular, Bernie How, served at North Creake as a Flight Engineer. He told us many tales of his time here, including showing us a picture of his wrecked Stirling after it crashed on take-off as a result of a burst tyre.

We have been delighted to receive original wartime photographs of the Tower. These were taken by Sgt Norman Turnball who served here as Caravan Controller and was also, luckily for us, a keen photographer. We have been given his aircraft spotter book and exercise book from his training by his great niece – both fascinating documents. A more sobering discovery, by a metal detecting friend, was that of a fuse for a 500-lb bomb.

We love to open the Tower and share it with others and now take part in the English 'Heritage Open Days' annually. At these we've had Tony Nelson's fantastic 1/6th scale Stirling with its 199 Squadron identification marks and insignia – 'The Jolly Roger' who flew from North Creake – a real thrill for us and our hundreds of visitors.

Nigel Morter & Claire Nugent, The Control Tower – Bunkers Hill, Egmere,
Walsingham, NR22 6AZ
01328 821574
mail@controltowerstays.com | www.controltowerstays.com

****

London Southend Airport Sculpture

During the week of Armed Forces Day, to reflect the wartime and commercial history of London Southend Airport, Mark Francois, Minister of State for Defence Personnel, Welfare and Veterans, joined local World War Two veterans and airport MD, Alastair Welch, to open a new sculpture installation created by John Atkin FRBS. The airport worked with Commissions East and Rochford and Southend Councils to commission John, a world renowned sculptor, to create public art for the new terminal and hotel. However, behind the work, which depicts the beacons of light, commonly known as 'cones' during the war; which came together from the ground to highlight aircraft flying overhead; lies a rich tapestry of inspiration and a very personal interest.

> My interest in human innovation and industry stems from my upbringing in North East England, where from an early age I was exposed to the visual plethora of engineering forms from a variety of industries, including the railways: heavy engineering: shipbuilding: steelworks, etc. This framed the way I looked at the world and consolidated my interest in engineering. My wife's father was Duty Officer at Teesside Airport for many years, so aircraft became part of this rich visual culture.
>
> When I moved to London, where I was personally funded for three years of Postgraduate study at the Royal College of Art by Henry Moore, (who I'd met at his studios in Much Hadham earlier in 1982); I became more aware of the rich variety of Museum collections at my disposal in the Capital. The Imperial War Museum was a key focus of interest, partly motivated by my interest in poetry of Wilfred Owen, Siegfried Sassoon and Robert Graves. The archive collection of World War One and World War Two artefacts was particularly stimulating and I began to make innumerable sketchbook studies of a variety of forms, some based on aircraft. This was doubly compelling because the studio I took over in Kingston-upon-Thames (as part of the Stanley Picker Fellowship in Sculpture at Kingston University) was the site of the Sopwith Aviation Company, which later became part of Hawker, etc. I could not escape aircraft, not that I wanted to!

Searchlight Beacons & Pod Seating

My research involved exploring the history of the airport through-out the 20th Century and its strategic importance in two World Wars, as well as its peacetime role in the present day. I examined how this untold history could be deployed within the framework of the sculpture, as well as have a seating design to link the terminal building to other areas of the airport site.

Early research identified wartime criss-crossing searchlight beams as an idea for the sculpture, simultaneously interpreted through the use of stainless steel as (celebratory) 'beacons', heralding a new enterprise era for LSA. Three different types of aircraft that helped define the role of LSA in wartime as well as peacetime populate the surfaces of the light beams stainless steel surfaces. These silhouettes of aircraft are laser cut from the stainless steel and illuminated inter-nally with LED lighting.

The development of the sculpture is characterised by traditional and digital methods of manufacture. The positioning of the crosso-ver intersection points of light beams was established using MAYA 3D modelling software, enabling the laser-cutting of cone forms to precisely locate on three separate points of intersection. The fusion of digital and traditional methods of design and making was central to my successful Bridging the Gaps Plug-In EPSRC Project, which explored cross-departmental approaches to design and build cultures within Loughborough University.

Evenly populating the surface of the sculpture with aircraft that met seamlessly at the folded seam of each cone was part of 3D opti-mized topography-modelling research that facilitated the placement and scale of each aircraft onto three separate cone forms.

How to shape the cones without the steel buckling was also a problem eventually solved using brake press technology, since the airplane perforations punctuating the steel surfaces meant that folding the cones on rollers was not possible.

Pod-Seats are derived from studies I made from early 20th Century airplane tail fins, which I was attracted to initially because they bore distinct similarities to contour forms I had earlier experimented with, based on garment template patterns. The Pod Seats are made from granite and reflect the surface texture and colour of surrounding architecture. The sculpture and seating designs act as landmark and way-finding devices, as well as a statement that reflects on the history of Southend, linking the 20th Century to present day.

http://aajpress.wordpress.com/2011/09/20/john-atkin-12th-chang-chun-sculpture-symposium-china-september-2011
John Atkin Website: www.johnatkin.net

****

THE PEOPLE'S MOSQUITO
To Fly * To Educate * To Remember
Introduction to de Havilland DH.98 Mosquito
Restoration Project
by Nick Horrox

It may be presumptuous, but I'd like to introduce you to possibly the best aircraft of the Second World War.

The de Havilland Mosquito was very nearly a footnote in the history books. Indeed, the motto of the Royal Air Force – *Per Ardua Ad Astra* – might well be said to apply to the Mosquito. If it were not for the struggles of Air Chief Marshal Sir Wilfred Rhodes Freeman, Air Member for Research and Development, and Geoffrey de Havilland Snr, the aircraft might never have been.

The prototype of this wooden-built, twin Merlin-engined light bomber and fighter first flew on 25 November 1940, and in subsequent trials out-flew a Spitfire, proving it was going to be something very special. Indeed, when it entered service it became known as one of the fastest operational aircraft in the world. Within eleven months, the Mosquito had entered production and in late 1941, RAF Squadrons started taking delivery of their new steeds. The first operational mission was a photo-reconnaissance sortie over France, on 19 September that year.

The Mosquito was one of the only Allied aircraft of the war to serve in all major roles: bomber, fighter, night-fighter, anti-shipping/anti-submarine, photo-reconnaissance, Pathfinding and transport. It was also used to test a variation of Barnes Wallis' bouncing bomb – the Highball. Post-war, it went on to serve in many diverse overseas Air Forces, including Turkish, Chinese Nationalist, Israeli, Dominican, Czech and Yugoslavian among many others, and in some areas was used in civilian roles. Its last operational mission with the Royal Air Force was in Malaya in 1954 – rather congruously, another photo-reconnaissance sortie. Several remained in service as target tugs until 1963.

Around 7,800 Mosquitos were built between 1941 and 1950: mostly in the UK, but also at de Havilland works in Australia and Canada. Of those, only around thirty survive. At my time of writing there is only one flying example in the world – Mosquito FB.26 KA114, restored in New Zealand for American collector Jerry Yagen. There is also a second machine, VR796, a B.35 bomber variant, being restored to flight in Victoria, Canada.

If you are a regular UK Air Show attendee or familiar with the British 'Warbirds' scene, Spitfires, Hurricanes, Mustangs and even the Lancaster are familiar sights. So, the inevitable questions hang in the air:

If the Mosquito is such an important part of our aviation history, and played a major role in defending our freedom, why do we not have a flying example in Britain? And when will we have a flying Mosquito in the UK?

These were questions troubling the mind of warbird enthusiast and part-time aircraft restorer, John Lilley in late December 2011. John was mulling over these questions when he had a sudden flash of inspiration and answered them himself. Firstly: *Why?* Because there is no one out there building one. Secondly: *When?* The sooner we start the sooner we *will* have a flying Mosquito.

The idea was born.

The plan to bring a Mosquito back to British skies was hatched. Against all odds, Britain would have its own flying Mosquito as soon as feasibly possible. An avid social media user, John put this wild and audacious suggestion out to the world on social media network *Twitter*. There was a good deal of support for the idea, and, it must be said, a good deal of negativity and naysaying from people who saw the idea as an impossible fantasy. But John's *tweet* ended up with a core group coming together to take this vision and turn it into a project.

To go back a moment to John's original questions: there are very good reasons why Britain does not have a flying example of a Mosquito. The aircraft was in large part built of wood, much of which was held in place by Casein-based glue. Both these materials are prone to the effects of ageing and atmospheric conditions. After seventy years it would be surprising if an aircraft built of such materials would be in sufficiently good condition to fly. One only has to visit the fascinating de Havilland Aircraft Museum near Hatfield to view the prototype Mosquito, W4050, for evidence to support this assumption. Another reason so few of the type exist today is that after the war, the majority of Mosquitoes were literally chopped up and burned. Their engines and guns were recovered for spares, and burnt remains buried in big holes on airfields around the world. This seems shocking and incomprehensible to younger readers and aviation enthusiasts, but times were very different.

An acquaintance of John Lilley's was involved in 2006 with the recovery of the remains of Mosquito RL249, a post-war NF.36 Night Fighter serving with 23 Sqn at RAF Coltishall. The aircraft crashed shortly after take-off on 14 February 1949, when launching for an air-to-ground night-firing exercise at Holbeach Gunnery Range. Eventually, 'The People's Mosquito' managed to secure those crash and fire-damaged remains – along with the aircraft's all-important identity to be used as a basis identity for the project. Although the project owns the identity of an NF.36, 'The People's Mosquito' itself will be built to represent a more widely used variant of the Mosquito – the FB Mk.VI – a fighter bomber whose production numbers far outstripped any other version, accounting for close to a third of all Mosquito production.

The idea behind 'The People's Mosquito', as it came to be known, is a simple one. Using the wartime concept of the people's aircraft, where communities or companies funded the building of a Spitfire, for example, the project will be funded by the public – individuals, organisations and sponsors. It is a non-profit organisation set up as a charity, under the name 'The People's Mosquito Ltd', whose main aim is to inform and educate the public and future generations about the Mosquito and its place in history by returning this important aircraft to the sky, in conjunction with building a valuable web-based Mosquito resource.

From monies raised, the airframe will be built in New Zealand with recently resurrected technology for producing the aircraft's main parts using complex concrete moulds, jigs and templates. The original moulds were destroyed in 1950, so they have had to be re-engineered and built from scratch, making these New Zealand moulds unique. Using these newly- manufactured main wooden parts and other modern technologies such as resins and other new materials, the aircraft will hopefully be fit for a fifty-year life.

Once built and tested in New Zealand, the aircraft will be dismantled and put in a specially- made container. It will then start its long journey north by ship to the United Kingdom. On arrival, it will be transported to its new home at a base in either Lincolnshire or Cambridgeshire, generally accepted as home of the UK warbirds scene. Once reassembled, re-fitted and flying, the aircraft will be operated and maintained by the charity for educational and display purposes, keeping the history of the Mosquito alive for future generations for many years to come.

'The People's Mosquito' project is being run along very different lines to the usual aircraft restoration project, with heavy reliance on online social networking. This has had the benefit of bringing the project team and its supporters together quickly, and given both parties access to feedback and discussion, more than if we'd gone a more traditional route. In that time-honoured British fashion, we are together attempting to achieve something from nothing. It is not an easy journey. The project will need a large amount of funding, and several years of hard work, but we are heartened by support already received and we now need to grow that support base to achieve our goal.

Find out more about The People's Mosquito and how you can support the project: www.peoplesmosquito.org.uk

RAF 100 Group Association

In December 1944, Eileen Boorman married Stafford Sinclair, a Pilot Officer. His loss three months later over Hamburg on 21 March 1945 affected her deeply. Her father died in the same period and her caring nature became apparent as, in later years, she nursed her mother.

In 1991, she and her brother Martin Staunton visited Norfolk and the site from which her husband had flown all those years ago. It was a shell of its former self ... derelict, lifeless, abandoned. The once proud RAF Oulton Station filled with the chatter and laughter of young airmen was no more. It was such a desperate sight that they decided to form an Associaton and erect a Memorial as well as a Book of Remembrance at the local church so that these brave men would never be forgotten, and their memory live on.

RAF 100 Group Association was in the making!

Eileen's pride in making this dream a reality was exceeded only by the pleasure of being able to meet and spend time with those who knew and flew alongside her husband. On the first Reunion of the newly-formed RAF 100 Group Association as veterans with family and friends converged on Norfolk again after so many years, many for the first time since the war; Eileen asked ex-Squadron members to sign paintings according to which Squadron they had served. Peter Witts, the only person to serve in three separate Squadrons under RAF 100 Group, explained this to her. It was agreed he sign all, and they began to talk together:

'What Skipper were you with on 214 Squadron?'
　'F/Lt Allies.'

Eileen paled at Peter's response.

'You knew my husband, Peter, then.'
　'He was in F/Lt Allies Crew? I left in December '44.'
　'But he was still there!'
　'I didn't know a 'Boorman'.'
　'My married name was Stafford-Sinclair.'

Then it dawned on Peter:

'You mean Vic! I flew mid-upper Gunner. It was he who would hook me into my seat!'

Eileen was ecstatic!

'Peter, I had begun to believe I married a ghost – until meeting you. Thank you.'

Eileen went on to explain that her husband had wanted a posting away from 214 Squadron. Stafford had written to her about it in letters. He was so unhappy. It was an unhappy crew. Peter lost a lot of friends in that crew. They were happy together, but weren't happy with the Skipper (see Peter Witts' writings in earlier pages).

On 22 March 1945, the crew had been tired. Despite this, F/Lt Allies knowingly volunteered the crew for further missions. The crew were all killed. But then, as Peter would say: *'there had to be one person left to survive, to put that lady's mind at rest ... and so I survived!'*

Until his dying day, Peter was to remember that moment, and spoke of it often. When Eileen died, Martin her brother told Peter: *'Eileen died happy because of what you were able to tell her.'*

Every year since, (other than in 1998) veterans with family and friends and anyone wishing to understand the secret world of RAF No.100 Group, come together in Norfolk during a long May weekend to take part in a series of programmed events. Villagers at Foulsham welcome us with a tea each year, with a brief remembrance ceremony at the Memorial. Saturday afternoon we enjoy a wonderful spread of tasty delights under a Marquee Tent in the garden of a farmhouse at Oulton where Chris Lambert, our Oulton Representative, puts on a programme of readings and poetry read by villagers as we come together at the Oulton Memorial which Martin and sister Eileen placed there all those years ago.

Last year we marked the 20th Anniversary of the dedication of Oulton Memorial with a tsunami of red-poppy crosses each showing the name of someone who never returned home. This year, 2015, is the Anniversary of the end of World War Two ... and again, we will remember.

It is so easy, while slipping through a portal into times past, to feel the spirits of those departed welcoming us, surrounding us with their love, guiding us back through the annuls of history and the paths they trod, the airfields where they flew, reminding us of the sacrifice paid to give us the freedom we enjoy today.

We will remember them!

There have been changes in the Committee since Martin and Eileen first formed the RAF 100 Group Association, or the RAF 100 (Memorial Museum) Group Association as it was then known. Eric Phillips, Gunnery Leader on No. 214 Squadron at Oulton was first Chairman, with Eileen Boorman and brother, Martin Staunton, Arthur Anthony and Hazel Southgate, an MT Driver who married Jimmy Southgate, Rear Gunner on No. 214 Squadron, and Len Bartram (*the once curious schoolboy*) Historian; with Air Vice Marshall Jack Furner as President.

One of the most important changes has come this year, 2015, as Stephen Hutton (*his writings appear earlier in this book*) joins the Committee to represent the USAAF. He is as passionate as I about preserving both the history and stories of both RAF 100 Group, the USAAF's 803rd & 36th Bomb Squadron Radar Countermeasure Units, and all who flew in partnership with them on secret airfields in Norfolk during World War Two.

Membership has risen to over 200 people worldwide, including both RAF 100 Group and USAAF veterans. As Secretary, I hear from members daily, as well as families where a loved one has died leaving writings and Log Books they know nothing about. To understand the lost years of the lives of loved ones they start researching, and somehow discover the path leading to our Association.

RAF 100 Group remains under layers of secrecy. Still too few know about it, even in the main RAF. A Book of Remembrance rests at Blickling Church, testimony to the many young lives snuffed out before their time. While we will continue to remember, gathering in Norfolk in May each year for Reunions, reaching out to families to widen understanding, bringing RAF 100 Group out of the shadows and finally into the light.

One vital ingredient which hasn't changed in over twenty years of the RAF 100 Group Association is the comaraderie, respect, honour, pride, and more than anything, the tremendous spirit of warmth, friendship, strength, support, commitment and love. These qualities were present, binding crews together in wartime. Today, these same qualities connect us now, like a tangible thread of gold reaching right around the world. It is a wonderful Family to be a part of. I feel very privileged and proud to be among this wonderful group of people, and count my blessings my mother and I read the advertisement Len Bartram put into '*Yours Magazine*' all those years ago, trying to attract members.

Phil James, MBE, our **Lifetime President**, served with 192 Squadron, stationed at Foulsham. He remains connected in a number of ways to the RAF.

For me, coming to Reunions is about honour and remembering. I have been part of RAFA since 1946 and continue to be a part of it now. My uncle flew Lancasters with Australians out of Binbrook. My other uncle was an Engine Fitter who spent most of his time in North Africa. He also had a pilot licence. My brother-in-law was an electronic expert on Lincolns. My nephew was a technician on Vulcans, Red Arrows, the Vulcan Display Team and Boing Sentries. He is now Crew Chief on a restored Vulcan. My daughter and grand-daughter were officers in the Air Cadets. My grand-daughter is now married to a Wing Commander. My son-in-law is a Warrant Officer in the ATC. That is why I have always been and will get involved in the RAF. It is a part of my life.

Peter Witts served in 223/214/462 as an Air Gunner in 100 Group, and was a familiar face at Reunions until he died. His feelings about attending Reunions were very much to the fore ...

There is not a prouder man, especially surrounded by my family at Reunions. They share the occasion, and it's truly wonderful! It means so much to me in so many different ways it's hard to put into words. I will continue to come back again and again each and every year even if I have to crawl on my hands and knees it means that much ... the Association *is* my Family, and that's just the way it is.

It is thanks to Peter that RAF 100 Group can now present its own Standard. He designed and donated it to the Association. Rod Vowler is our proud official Standard Bearer, chosen by Peter because Rod's uncle Leonard served with him in 223 Squadron, Oulton.

To become an RAF 100 Group Association Member

Membership of the RAF 100 Group Association is open to all – veterans who served in any Squadron under 100 Group during World War Two; relatives and friends, researchers and historians, people of all ages wanting to learn about the work undertaken by this secret Group, and to share experiences of the life and work of people who served. We have members around the world.

Membership is £15 per year. It entitles you to a membership card, with free admission to the City of Norwich Aviation Museum; four quarterly magazines crammed with stories, information and advice and so much more; plus an invitation to join us at our annual May Reunion in Norfolk with a full programme of events and very special Saturday evening dinner with Guest Speaker.

Association Website: www.raf100groupassociation.org.uk

Further information and to contact me direct: Janine Harrington, Secretary, 7 Ashley Court, Filey, North Yorkshire YO14 9LS; Email: raf100groupassociation@gmail.com

****

City of Norwich Aviation Museum

While in 1994 Martin Staunton and sister Eileen Boorman gained expertise in establishing the Memorial at Oulton and founding the RAF 100 Group Association, forming a committee for support; they tried to find a place to display and store veterans memorabilia. Finding a suitable venue proved difficult until a letter arrived from the City of Norwich Aviation Museum offering a newly-built room at no cost. The rest, as they say, is history.

In 1997, we shared an Opening Ceremony attended by many veterans who served under RAF 100 Group with family and friends. In the evening, we shared a dinner at the Wroxham Hotel. It was a thoroughly enjoyable day which set the tone of our Association with the Museum ever since. But the climax of that day was the expression on Eileen Boorman's face at finally seeing her husband's uniform proudly displayed in a showcase at the Museum.

Located within the City of Norwich Aviation Museum today, on the northern edge of Norwich International Airport is a wealth of material with an impressive display of aircraft outside. It also has a special section dedicated to the top secret electronic countermeasures, deception and night intruder operations of 100 Group:

City of Norwich Aviation Museum, Old Norwich Rd, Horsham St Faith, Norwich NR10 3JF. Telephone: 01603 893080. www.cnam.co.uk

****

Obtaining a Copy of an RAF Service Record

You can obtain a copy of a parent's RAF Service Record if they are no longer alive, or indeed your own Service Record if you have left the RAF. Only certain people can obtain these copies, so even if you don't want the copy, other family members may like it, either now or in the future. More details are on this website, and be aware that a cheque for £30 is required: www.veterans-uk.info/service_records/raf.html

> Service Records for Officers and Airmen that served after these dates are retained by the Royal Air Force. RAF Service Records are retained by Service Number, Rank and Full Name, and will also contain the Date of Birth. It is important that as much of this information as possible is provided to assist in locating the correct Record.

Enquiries about RAF-held Records should be made as follows:

From Current/Former RAF Personnel

A **Subject Access Request** (SAR) Form needs to be completed and sent to:

RAF DPA SAR Section, Room 220, Trenchard Hall, RAF Cranwell, Sleaford, Lincs NG34 8HB. 01400 261201, Ext 8175/8172/8173

From Family Members and Other Authorised Individuals

A **Certificate of Kinship Form** needs to be completed and sent to:

RAF Disclosures Section, Room 221b, Trenchard Hall, RAF Cranwell, Sleaford, Lincs NG34 8HB. 01400 261201, Ext 6711; Ext 8161/8159 (Officers); Ext 8163/8168/8170 (Other ranks)

POSTSCRIPT: Kindred Spirits

This book has led me on a remarkable journey. It has proved an incredible experience, stepping through the portal of Time each day, learning through the eyes of different people what it meant to serve during the Second World War under the very secret RAF 100 Group.

Even as a Wordsmith, I cannot find the words to say how much this book means to me ... and to veterans around the world who have shared experiences, wanting to become a part of this Magnus Opus.

There were times I could have given up. I could so easily have simply switched off and walked away because this book became the most demanding challenge of my entire writing career ... if not my life! I didn't believe I could ever see this published. Yet, just when I needed it most, the phone would ring, the voice of a veteran thanking me for giving them a purpose in life, sharing how much it means to them and their family ... a family who doesn't yet know what their wartime work entailed because they couldn't speak of it at the time.

One airman said this Group was so secret it produced awkward questions. Like when he couldn't be with his girlfriend one evening. She thought he was two-timing. Meeting up the following evening, she asked where he'd been:

'I was flying ... I would have been there if I could.'

'You're lying!'

'But why would you say that when it's true?'

'Because I asked. Bomber Command weren't flying ops last night!'

He had been flying. He was telling the truth. But his operation was classified, under the Official Secrets Act. He couldn't explain. There must have been many such occasions for those serving under 100 Group. Another veteran shares:

'The main bombers we were flying over didn't even know we were there ... what we were doing ... our work was so secret it just had to be that way!'

It is veterans who inspire and energise me into wanting to record every word they share, so that future generations might listen and learn ... following the footsteps of those who served in this very secret wartime Group, using covert counter-measures, at constant risk to themselves, to give us the kind of freedom we enjoy today.

In a time out of Time I have spent months writing and recording experiences shared through the post, by email attachment, through tapes and phone calls, each a treasure from the past.

All I can offer is a deep-rooted passion for preserving this history, their stories. I can't bear the thought of these words ending on a bonfire somewhere on their death, without people having the chance to read them and know. I can't bear the thought of writings lost and neglected, forgotten in some attic, mice nibbling away memories that mean so much more than paper hidden in the shadows.

There are no words to describe the gamut of emotions driving me on this quest, urging me to seek out truths, bridging the gap between past and present.

There are days when I have driven myself to write at twelve hour stretches because I couldn't leave a story alone, then having to spend the next few days getting over the madness. Disabled from birth, I have the most horrendous attacks, especially under stress, which disable me as a person, making me feel as if my body doesn't belong to me any more. My head explodes into a zillion stars, the pain riding down my back and spine into my legs. Yet, as soon as I am able, I'm back at the desk, letters arriving in every post, consuming words written with a passion that cannot and will not be ignored.

Thank you everyone who has shared this journey with me!

It has truly been a privilege, an honour, a joy, and a deeply humbling experience. I have shed lakes of tears. I have ridden rainbows up and over the clouds and on into the heavens. These experiences which shaped people into who they are today deserve to be shared. My hope is that, through this book, the name of RAF No. 100 (BS) Group will be spoken for the future ... and veterans who served under its many Squadrons, *never* forgotten.

Their names are right here. So many more have passed away before I had the chance to grab hold and preserve what they had to offer.

For many years I have taken great joy in creating our quarterly RAF 100 Group Association magazine which goes out to members each year around the world. It is this magazine that provides a bridge between us, connecting, bringing us together into one united worldwide Family today. It's a truly wonderful thing to feel that spirit of friendship and love, the same kind of comradeship forged through war - one of the positives that came from the hell and fury of those years.

Despite the pain, the suffering, the loss, the sadness, veterans often say they would go back to those years in a heartbeat. They were young and carefree, part of something almost hallowed. At first they didn't realise. How could they know where their journey might lead? For some, there was PTSD (Post Traumatic Stress Disorder) as we know it today. Others walked away to join with loved ones, moving on into another life. There were also those who continued with the RAF and flying. I've spoken with veterans who remain passionate about their aircraft, particularly the Mosquito, battling the enemy in the skies, drifting through clouds, reaching for distant horizons ... and reluctantly ... home ... at least the Base where they were stationed.

Reading their experiences makes you want to join them. To feel that same thrill, to know and experience as they did living on the edge of life, the kind of love my mother Nina shared with her fiancé Navigator/Spec Op. Vic Vinnell, serving in the lead Squadron, 192, with Canadian Pilot Jack Fisher, knowing each time they met might be their last. Being in contact with Jack Fisher's family in Canada means we never lose that connection. These lifetime connections forged through war provide this spirit of eternal love. I feel it in what people share. It's that kind of connection we are missing today.

In books I write to honour these people, I wish there was a way to preserve this precious gift that was theirs. I know it because I felt it through my mother, seeing the fire in her eyes when she spoke of Vic. It took nothing away from the love she went on to share with my father who also served in the RAF. But it's the feeling I get during Reunions, as we meet in Norfolk and come together to talk about the past, to remember those who did not return.

Previous pages offer ways you can discover your own family member's wartime past, and access their RAF records. I also invite you to join our RAF 100 Group Association if you have a yearning to learn more. The Association brings you in direct contact with veterans and secret places in Norfolk which became their wartime Home. Use the information provided in *Updates* about people and places to visit, places where we can continue to honour and remember, letting them leave an imprint on our own lives today.

To veterans, I would hope this book has done you justice. I pray I have done right by you. More than anything else, I want to thank you for every blessing you have given to me, simply in being there, sharing with me your lives, words of support spoken when I felt like giving up, offering inspiration and truths to spur me on ... and that never-ending connection which transcends time.

Thank you Readers, whoever you are, wherever you may be, for joining me on this journey which remains incomplete, because still there are so many more people to meet and so much still to learn.

THANK YOU xxx

APPENDICES
Anniversaries of RAF 100 Group
&
American Eighth Air Force (8AF) Squadron

- **8 November 2013**: 70th Anniversary of authorisation for creation of RAF No. 100 (BS) Group
- **28 March 1944**: 8th Air Force 803rd Bomb Squadron Heavy (Provisional) formed
- **6 June 1944**: 70th Anniversary of D-Day
- **13 August 1944**: 8th Air Force 36th Bomb Squadron Radar Counter-Measure Unit established.
- **23 September 2014**: 70th Anniversary of crash of Mosquito DZ 535 which crash-landed at Craymere Beck, Briston, piloted by F/Lt Clark, with Navigator/Special Operator F/O Richard *'Dobbie'* Dobson, 192 Squadron (father of Roger Dobson, Chairman of RAF 100 Group Association).
- **26/27 November 2014**: 70th Anniversary of crash of Mosquito DK292 and death of Canadian Pilot Jack Fisher with Navigator/Special Operator Vic Vinnell (author's mother's wartime fiancé) 192 Squadron.
- **December 2014:** 70th Anniversary – crash of USAAF 36th Bomb Squadron *'The Jigs Up'* with death of crew at Holyhead, Wales
- **5 February 2015:** 70th Anniversary – crash of USAAF 36th Bomb Squadron's B24 R-4C *'The Uninvited'*
- **19 February 2015:** 70th Anniversary – crash of USAAF 36th Bomb Squadron's B24 R-4H *'The Beast of Bourbon'*
- **2015:** 70th Anniversary of the end of World War Two.

ENDNOTES

Introduction
1 Nina and Vic's belief
2 Gloria, Jack Fisher's sister
3 Mary Cassidy, cousin to Nina
4 Nina's final words to Vic Vinnell
5 Map Clerk unknown

RAF No. 100 (Bomber Support) Group
6 *Operation Bodyguard* – several separate operations aimed at delaying Germans reaching Normandy
7 After the fall of France, Churchill wrote to Lord Beaverbrook, Minister of Air Production.
8 Courtesy: Stephen Hutton
9 International review of the Red Cross No. 323, pages 347 – 363, The Law of Air Warfare, 1998.
10 *General der Jagdflieger*, Adolf Galland, Lancaster – the Biography, Iveson and Milton, 2009, page 122.
11 Announced 26 February 2013: Minister of State for Defence Personnel, Welfare and Veterans, Mark Francois
12 Veteran Norman Storey
13 Sir Arthur Harris, letter to Churchill, 3 November 1943

The Mighty Eighty Air Force's Squadron of Deception
14 Dr Reginald V. Jones: '*Most Secret War*'

Jack Hope, USAAF
15 Courtesy: Lt Brookshire, via Jack Hope
16 Farewell letter to 36BS from Colonel Sullivan
17 Lt Brookshire's writings

Len Bartram

18 Courtesy: Evelyn Bartram

19 Courtesy: Rev. Robert Marsden, Briningham Association of Churches (April 2002)

20 Courtesy: Evelyn Bartram

Bylaugh Hall: Update

21 Courtesy: Rev. Beane, ex-Vicar at Horsham St Faith

22 Courtesy: Eastern Daily Press

RAF Foulsham

23 Courtesy: Evelyn Bartram

24 Courtesy: Evelyn Bartram

25 Author's collection

26 Courtesy: Roger Dobson

27 Courtesy: Vic Willis

28 Courtesy: Vic Parker

29 Courtesy: David Donaldson

30 Courtesy: Eric Clarkson

31 Wing Commander Donaldson

32 Courtesy: Diane Cooper

33 Compiled by the Forsyth Family, 214

34 Courtesy: David Hales

35 Courtesy: John Eggert

36 Courtesy: Les Pedley

37 Courtesy: Arthur Newstead

38 Written & researched by Richard Forder (RAF 100 Group Association), with permission from Ken Spriggs' daughter, Wendy

39 Paragraph 1, SO 228, HQ, 1st Bomb Division

40 Thanks to Bill & John Rees (authors of: *Espionage in the Ether*), the Kunze family and Ian White, U.K. & European representative and Historian for U.S 305th Bomb Group Memorial Association. In memory of Captain Fred B. Brink Jr, Air Medal with four Oak Leaf Clusters, Purple Heart, 13th Photographic Squadron, 7th Photographic Reconnaissance Group, & Lieutenant Francis I. Kunze, Air Medal, Purple Heart, Special Wireless Operator, 364th

Bombardment Squadron, who flew in 1944 under RAF 100 Group control on RCM Operations.

RAF Little Snoring

[41] Libby, Frederick (2000). '*Horses Don't Fly*'. Arcade Publishing.

[42] *Mosquito Fighter/Fighter-Bomber Units of World War 2*, by Martin W. Bowman: pges 1 and 2.

[43] '*Mosquito Fighter Bomber Units of World War 2*', by Martin Bowman

[44] *Belfast Telegraph* 25 April 1944 and 605 Squadron

[45] Courtesy: 23 Squadron

[46] David Oliver's '*Airborne Espionage: International Special Duties Operations in the World Wars*' The History Press

[47] Courtesy: Pilot Officer Henry Cossar

[48] With thanks to *Sticky*' Murphy's daughter Gail Hanekom for information received

[49] Courtesy: Gail Hanekom

[50] Accredited: Anne Morrow Lindbergh

Blickling Hall

[51] Written 9 July 1944 by LAC J. C. Willis: '*Johnnie*', donated by Eileen whose family owned *The Bird in Hand*.

RAF Oulton

[52] Peter Witts, RAF 100 Group Association Reunion 2007

[53] Allan Williams: *Operation Crossbow: The Untold Story of the Search for Hitler's Secret Weapons*

[54] Copyright: Ron Johnson

[55] *Flypast Magazine*, September 1981/82

RAF Swannington

[56] Courtesy: David Kett

[57] Courtesy: David Kett

[58] '*Dereham & Fakenham Times*', 2 June 2005

RAF Swanton Morley

[59] '*Fifty Australians: Sir Hughie Edwards*', Australian War Memorial

[60] *London Gazette*, 35225, pp 4213 - 4214, 22 July 1941

RAF North Creake

[61] Originally published in 76 Squadron Newsletter

[62] Taken from his book: 'The Silver Thread', dedicated to all who served in RAF Bomber Command 1939-1945

UPDATE

Bomber Command Memorial

[63] Words by Rex Polendine

BIBLIOGRAPHY
Relating to RAF 100 Group

Anthony, Arthur: 'Lucky B-24' (Janus Publishing Co. 1993)

Baldwin, Jim: *RAF Sculthorpe – 50 Years of Watching & Waiting* (Jim Baldwin Publishing)

Bond, Steve; & Forder, Richard: *Special Ops Liberators 223 (Bomber Support) Squadron, 100 Group and the Electronic War* (Grub Street, 2011. ISBN: 978-1-908-11714-4)

Bowman, Martin: *We were Eagles: The Eighth Air Force at War: Volume 1: July 1942-November 1943* (Amberley Publishing, 2014)

Bowman, Martin: *The Men Who Flew the Mosquito,*

Bowman, Martin: *100 Group (Bomber Support): RAF Bomber Command in World War II* (Pen & Sword/Leo Cooper, 2006. ISBN 1-84415-418-1)

Bowman, Martin: *Mosquito Fighter/Fighter-Bomber Units of World War 2*

Bowman, Martin; & Cushing, Tom: *Confounding the Reich* (Pen & Sword/Leo Cooper, 2004. ISBN 1-84415-124-7)

Bowman, W. Martin: *Mosquito Fighter/Fighter-Bomber Units of World War 2*

Bowyer, Michael: *The Stirling Story*

Bowyer, Michael: *Action Stations*

Brettingham, Laurie: *Even When the Sparrows are Walking: The Origin & Effect of No.100 (Bomber Support) Group RAF, 1943-1945*

Chisholm: *Cover of Darkness*

Cordingly, N. W/Cdr: *The Era of the Nocturnal Blip*

Gunn, Peter B.: *Sculthorpe, Secrecy and Stealth: A Norfolk Airfield in the Cold War* (History Press Ltd (2014) ISBN-10: 0752476831; ISBN-13: 978-0752476834)

Gunn, Peter: *RAF Great Massingham, a Norfolk Airfield at War, 1940-1945*

Hambling, M: *Airfields of Norfolk*

Hambling, M: *Norfolk Crash Diaries*

Hampton, James: *Selected for Aircrew: Bomber Command in the Second World War'* (Red Arrow)

Harrington, Janine: *Nina & Vic: A World War II Love Story,* (direct from author)

Harrington, Janine: *Sealed with a Kiss: Post-War Love Story* (FeedARead)

Harrington, Janine: *Series of 12 booklets each on a Norfolk airfield,* direct from author (all profits to RAF 100 Group Association)

Harrington, Janine: *RAF 100 Group 1942-1944: The Birth of Electronic Warfare* (Fonthill Media, 2015, 1st in a 2-book series)

Hastings, Max: *Bomber Command*

Heilig, Gerhard: *Circuits and Bumps* (Woodfield Publishing)

Hutton, Stephen: *Squadron of Deception, the 36th Bomb Squadron in WWII* (Schiffer Military History ISBN: 0-7643-0796-7)

Iveson, Tony DFC & Milton, Brian: *Lancaster – the Biography* (Andre Deutsch, 2009, ISBN: 978-0-233-00270-5)

James, S/Ldr: *Swanton Morley History*

Johnson, Ron: *A Navigator's Tale* (Irregular Records, 2000)

Middlebrook, M.: *The Bomber Command War Diaries*

Moyes, Philip J. R.: *Bomber Squadrons of the RAF and their Aircraft* (Macdonald and Jane's (Publishers) Ltd, 1964. (New revised edition, 1976) ISBN: 0-354-01027-1)

Neillands, Robin: *The Bomber War – Arthur Harris and the Allied Bomber Offensive 1939-1945* (John Murray)

Oliver, David: *Airborne Espionage: International Special Duties Operations in the World Wars* (The History Press)

Overy, Richard Professor: *Bomber Command: Reaping the Whirlwind* (Harper Collins)

Parry: *Intruders over Britain*

Peden, Murray: *A Thousand Shall Fall: the True Story of a Canadian Bomber Pilot in World War Two,* (Stoddart Publishing Co Ltd, ISBN: 0-7737-5967-0)

Probert, Henry, Air Commodore: *Bomber Harris – His Life and Times* (Greenhill Books Lionel Leventhal Ltd)

Rees, William & John; *Espionage in the Ether* (Compaid Graphics)

Rees, William J., *The Final Fling, Bomber Command's Last Operation*

Renaut, Michael: *Terror by Night*

Richards, Denis: *The Hardest Victory* (John Curtis / Hodder & Stoughton)

Russell, Ronald Cohn: *No. 199 Squadron RAF*

Streetly, Martin: *Confound & Destroy* (Macdonald & Jane's (Publishing) Company Ltd, 1978. ISBN 0-354-01180-4)

Streetly, Martin: *The Aircraft of 100 Group*

Taylor, W.: *West Raynham History*

Taylor, Bill; Group Captain: *Raynham Reflections* (self-published, 1990s)

Thomas, Andrew & Davey, Chris: 'Mosquito Aces of World War 2'

Williams Allan: *Operation Crossbow: The Untold Story of the Search for Hitler's Secret Weapons*

Wilson, Kevin: *Bomber Boys, the RAF Offensive of 1943*

Young, Scotty: *Descent into Danger* (Allan Wingate Publishers Ltd.)